A

HISTORY

OF THE

TOWN OF CONCORD;

MIDDLESEX COUNTY, MASSACHUSETTS,

FROM ITS EARLIEST SETTLEMENT TO 1832;

AND OF THE ADJOINING TOWNS,

BEDFORD, ACTON, LINCOLN, AND CARLISLE;

CONTAINING

VARIOUS NOTICES OF COUNTY AND STATE HISTORY
NOT BEFORE PUBLISHED.

BY LEMUEL SHATTUCK,
MEMBER OF THE MASSACHUSETTS HISTORICAL SOCIETY.

Nobler records of patriotism exist nowhere. — Nowhere can there be found higher proofs of a spirit that was ready to hazard all, to pledge all, to sacrifice all, in the cause of their country, than in the New England towns. WEBSTER.

The local historian is sure of obtaining the gratitude of posterity, if he perform his task with faithful diligence. — His work would have a great and increasing value within the narrow sphere of its subject, even if confined to that sphere ; but must be very imperfectly executed, if it does not contain some matter of illustration for the national annals, for the history of manners, for literature, philology, natural history, and various other departments of knowledge.
QUARTERLY REVIEW.

CLEARFIELD

Originally published
Boston, Massachusetts, 1835

Reprinted for
Clearfield Company, Inc. by
Genealogical Publishing Co., Inc.
Baltimore, Maryland
2002

International Standard Book Number: 0-8063-5140-3

Made in the United States of America

PREFACE.

The author of the following History, having had occasion several years since to consult some of the earlier town records in Concord, discovered many important facts and documents which were wholly unknown to the public, and very imperfectly to the inhabitants of the town itself; and it occurred to him that a series of communications in a periodical work, embracing them, would be interesting and valuable, and he immediately began to collect materials for this purpose. But, in the progress of his investigation, the quantity of interesting matter increased so much, that it was thought best it should be published in some other form than that originally intended. The result of his inquiries appears in the following volume. It has been compiled at such intervals of time as could be conveniently abstracted from the almost constant engagements of business.

Those only, who have been engaged in similar works, can be aware of the great labor required to collect the materials for a volume like this, and arrange them for the press. And the difficulty and labor have been much increased in this instance by the imperfections of the town and church records. The first volume of the records of the town, containing its proceedings prior to 1696, about sixty years after its first settlement, is lost; and likewise the proceedings of the church prior to 1738, more than one hundred years after its organization. There is however in the clerk's office an old volume, containing an imperfect record of several grants of land, and a few unconnected proceedings of the town; with an incomplete list of marriages, births, and deaths, prior to 1696. This renders the early history of the town, less perfect than it would have been, had the records been preserved, though from other sources much important information has been obtained. The early records and documents in the offices of the Secretary of the Commonwealth and of the county of Middlesex, and the private papers of individuals, and various other scattered fragments of traditionary, manuscript, and printed history have, with great labor and no little expense, been consulted, which, though they do not furnish a complete history, have been found interesting and important, and in some respects supply the place of town records. Traditions, however, are often contradictory, tending to embarrass rather than to elucidate. They should be depended upon only as leading the investigator *towards* the truth, which, on further inquiry and comparison of different traditions with records, may be discovered. I have seldom been willing to state a fact positively, unless verified in this way. A tradition has prevailed in Concord, that the early records of the town were burnt; and this is said to have taken place when part of the first settlers removed to Connecticut. If this were true, it could not apply to the town records from 1650 to 1696, nor to any part of the church records prior to 1738. This tradition is undoubtedly incorrect. The town records were destroyed in some other way, and, if burnt, it must have occurred subsequently to 1696. The loss of the church records was probably occasioned by the difficulty in the church detailed in the following History.

Few places have so many interesting incidents associated with their history as Concord. From its local situation, it has been the centre of many of the important operations in the county of Middlesex, and of some of the most interesting in the Commonwealth. Being the first inland town settled above tide waters, it endured great hardships in the commencement of its history. The progress of the settlement, the exertions to civilize the Indians, the warlike operations in the town as a military post during Philip's war, the distinguished part it took in the Revolution and in other peculiar eras in the history of Massachusetts, are but imperfectly, if at all, known; but fortunately many important facts have been preserved in manuscript. — The ecclesiastical history also has been considered of unusual importance, and especially during Whitfield's time. This work, besides the minute details of civil and ecclesiastical history, interesting to readers generally, as well as to the citizens of this town in particular, contains the Natural History, Topography, Statistics, Notices of Early Families and Distinguished Men, and other subjects of general or local interest, which may be appropriately embraced in such a history.—The towns of Bedford, Acton, Lincoln, and Carlisle were incorporated principally within the original limits of Concord; and, as their history is intimately blended with that of Concord, it was thought expedient to embrace within the work the history of each of those towns since its separate incorporation.

In arranging facts on such a great variety of subjects as are embraced in a town history, it is difficult to present them in such a manner as will be entirely satisfactory. I have adopted that mode which appeared most intelligible and interesting to my own mind. To present a work like this free from errors cannot be expected. Some may appear in this History; yet the author is conscious of having taken unusual care to avoid them. Those who are competent to detect them will, it is hoped, make all due allowance, should they be found.

The volume is submitted to the public with diffidence. The author lays no claim to the qualifications, which such an undertaking would seem to require. His object has not been to make an attempt at fine writing, (had it been possible for him to have succeeded, or had he deemed it proper in a town history,) but to relate, in as plain, simple, and intelligible a manner as was within his power, such facts as he deemed most worthy of preservation. The object of local history is to furnish the first elements of general history, to record facts rather than deductions from facts. In these municipalities,—these separate incorporations,—are to be found many of the first moving causes which operate on, and revolutionize public opinion. Many facts, minute in themselves, are in this view important. The details, which it is the appropriate province of the local historian to spread before the public, are not so much history itself as materials for history. It is the work of the general historian, who has before him all the particulars of each portion of the great natural and political landscape, to exhibit the connexion of the several parts, and to show how they depend, one upon another, in bringing about the great changes, which have been taking place and affecting the condition of society. Strong inducements to take such an enlarged and philosophical view of the facts which have been detailed, and to submit the ideas that arose in my own mind from such a view, have been often presented. But it would increase the size of a volume already enlarged far, very far, beyond its original design.

To trace the history of our ancestors, and transmit a record of their deeds to posterity, is a duty we owe to the past and the future. Such a record must be preserved as invaluable by the immediate descendants and kindred of those, who once lived and acted where they now do, and whose ashes repose beneath their soil. And it cannot be without interest to those who have gone out from their kindred to dwell in other parts of the country, nor to those who have come to dwell in the habitations made vacant by the removal or death of the original occupants. What this town once was, who originally occupied it, and by what means and by whom it has become what it now is, are questions which can be answered only by minute topographical history. If the work shall satisfy the public, and contribute to the gratification of those for whom it is more particularly designed, the author will feel himself compensated for the labor and expense, in preparing and publishing it.

To the Hon. Abiel Heywood, town clerk of Concord, to the town clerks of the several surrounding towns, to the Secretary of the Commonwealth, to John Farmer, Esq. of Concord, N. H., and to various others, who have aided by the use of manuscripts, by the communication of facts, and by various services rendered him, the author feels under special obligations.

L. S.

Boston, August, 1835.

CONTENTS.

Page.

CHAPTER I. — Indian Tribes. — Musketaquid Indians. — Local Situation. — Settlement projected. — Act of Incorporation. — Purchase from the Indians. — Depositions. — First Settlers. — Johnson's Account. — Additional Grants. — Sufferings of the Inhabitants. — Wet Meadows. — Petition to the General Court. — Condition of the Town. — Chronological Items.

CHAPTER II. — Efforts to civilize the Indians. — Eliot begins the Work. — Effects at Nonantum and at Concord. — Laws for the Indians. — Opposition. — Eliot's Labors and Petition. — Nashobah. — Notices of several Indians. — Account of the Praying Indians. — Nashobah sold. - - - - 19

CHAPTER III. — Division of the Town. — Records. — Additional Grants. — Indian Deeds. — Iron Works built. — Town Farm. — Town of Stow granted. — Chronological Items. - - - - - - - - - - 33

CHAPTER IV. — PHILIP'S WAR. — State of the Country. — Garrison Houses. — Expedition to Brookfield. — Proceedings of Government; and of the Town. — Lancaster burnt. — Christian Indians in Concord. — Feelings towards the Indians. — Abraham and Isaac Shepherd killed. — Groton burnt. — People remove to Concord. — Proceedings of Government. — Sudbury Fight. — Henchman's Letters. — Soldiers at Concord. — Christian Indian Soldiers. — War Taxes. - - - - - - - - - 46

CHAPTER V. — Year 1684 important. — Blood's farms annexed to Concord. — The Fifty subsequent Years. — Lovewell's fight. — Cuba Expedition. — French War. — Notices of various Services in the War. — Divisions in the Town and Incorporation of new Towns. — Emigration to other places. - 64

CHAPTER VI. — American Revolution. — Proceedings of the Town. — Act respecting Tea. — Non-consumption Covenant. — Sentiments of the People. — County Convention. — People march to Cambridge. — Courts stopped. — Treatment of the Tories. — Proceedings of the Town. — Provincial Congress meets. — Public Stores. — New Town Covenant. — Minute Companies formed. — Mr. Emerson preaches. — Expedition of the British Spies. — Provincial Congress. — Public Stores. — Excitement. - - - - 76

CHAPTER VII. — BATTLE OF CONCORD, April 19th, 1775. - - - 100

CHAPTER VIII. — State of feeling on the 20th of April. — Tories. — College removed to Concord. — Committees of Correspondence. — Proceedings in Relation to the Monopoly Acts. — Revolutionary Soldiers. — Table of Different Campaigns. — Public pecuniary Sacrifices. — Taxes. — Constitution adopted. - - - - - - - - - - - - 118

CONTENTS.

Chapter IX. — State of Feeling subsequent to the Revolution. — Proceedings of the County and of the Town. — Mr. Avery's Letter. — Armed Men assemble at Concord. — Courts stopped. — Notice of the Insurgents. — Proceedings of the Town. — The War of 1812. — County Courts and Shire Towns regulated. — Proceedings of the Town on this Subject. - - - 129

Chapter X. — Ecclesiastical History. — Organization of the Church. — Installation of the Rev. Mr. Bulkeley and Mr. Jones. — Church Covenant. — Proceedings of the Church. — Notice of the Rev. Mr. Jones. — Letters of the Rev. Mr. Bulkeley, and Notice of his life and Writings. — Rev. Edward Bulkeley. — Rev. Joseph Estabrook. — Rev. John Whiting. - - 148

Chapter XI. — Ordination of Mr. Bliss. — State of the Church. — Revivals. Proceedings of different Ecclesiastical Councils and of the Church. — Divisions in the Parish and Church. — Death of Mr. Bliss. — Ordination of Mr. Emerson. — Proceedings of the Church. — Notice of the Rev. Mr. Emerson. Ordination of Mr. Ripley. — Proceedings of the Church. — Covenants. — Funds. — Ordination of Mr. Goodwin. — Succession of Deacons. — Trinitarian Church. - - - - - - - - - - - 166

Chapter XII. — Natural History. — Climate. — Geology. — Botany. — Ponds. — Rivers. — Brooks. — Fish. — Quadrupeds. — Birds. - - 196

Chapter XIII. — Topographical History. — Boundaries. — Roads. — Bridges. — Stages. — Post-Office. — Public Buildings. — Printing Office. — Burying-grounds. - - - - - - - - - - - 204

Chapter XIV. — Statistical History. — Population. — Valuation. — Finances. — Employment. — Maintenance of the Poor. — Education. — Bill of Mortality. - - - - - - - - - - - 210

Chapter XV. — Social and Official History. — Military Companies. — Various Associations. — Concord Bank. — Agricultural Society. — Insurance Company. — Official History. — Town-Officers. — Representatives. — Senators. — County Officers. — Attorneys and Counsellors at Law. — Physicians. 227

Chapter XVI. — Biographical Notices of College Graduates and other Individuals belonging to Concord. - - - - - - - - 240

Chapter XVII. — History of Bedford. — General History. — Ecclesiastical History. — Description. — Miscellaneous Notices. - - - 255

Chapter XVIII. — History of Acton. — General History. — Ecclesiastical History. — Description. — Miscellaneous Notices. - - - - 274

Chapter XIX. — History of Lincoln. — General History. — Ecclesiastical History. — Description. — Statistics. — Biographical Notices. - - 294

Chapter XX. — History of Carlisle. — General History. — Miscellaneous Notices. — Ecclesiastical History. - - - - - - 320

Appendix. — No. I. Historical View of the Evidence relating to the Events of the 19th April, 1775. - - - - - 333
    No. II. Notices of Military Services performed by the People of Concord in the Revolution. - - - - 352
    No. III. Notices of Early Families and Distinguished Men. - 360
    No. IV. Old and New Style. - - - - - - 390
    No. V. Notice of the Rev. Samuel Stearns. - - - 391
    No. VI. Votes for Governor. - - - - - - 392

HISTORY OF CONCORD.

CHAPTER I.

Indian Tribes. — Musketaquid. Indians. — Local Situation. — Settlement projected. — Act of Incorporation. — Purchase from the Indians. — Depositions. — First Settlers. — Johnson's Account. — Additional Grants. — Sufferings of the Inhabitants. — Wet Meadows. — Petition to the General Court. — Condition of the Town. — Chronological Items.

WHEN the English settlements first commenced in New England, that part of its territory, which lies south of New Hampshire, was inhabited by five principal nations of Indians: — the Pequots, who lived in Connecticut; the Narragansets, in Rhode Island; the Pawkunnawkuts, or Womponoags, east of the Narragansets and to the north as far as Charles river;[1] the Massachusetts, north of Charles river and west of Massachusetts Bay; and the Pawtuckets, north of the Massachusetts. The boundaries and rights of these nations appear not to have been sufficiently definite to be now clearly known. They had within their jurisdiction many subordinate tribes, governed by sachems, or saga-

---

[1] I have supposed that the Indians living south of Charles river did not belong to the Massachusetts tribe. Chickatabot, sachem of Neponset, and Obatinuat acknowledged submission to Massasoit in 1621, and were at enmity with Squaw Sachem. No instance within my knowledge is recorded of a petty sachem going to war with his own tribe. It is also worthy of remark, that these sachems and their descendants executed deeds of lands within Massasoit's territories, but never in the Massachusetts territories. As the country became settled by the English, and the jealousies between different tribes were forgotten, all the Indians living within the Massachusetts patent were rather erroneously classed among the Massachusetts Indians. Hence the statements of Winthrop, Gookin, and other historians, See Prince, Annals, 1621.

1

mores, subject, in some respects, to the principal sachem. At the commencement of the seventeenth century, they were able to bring into the field more than 18,000 warriors; but about the year 1612, they were visited with a pestilential disease, whose horrible ravages reduced their number to about 1800.[1] Some of their villages were entirely depopulated. This great mortality was viewed by the first Pilgrims, as the accomplishment of one of the purposes of Divine Providence, by making room for the settlement of civilized man, and by preparing a peaceful asylum for the persecuted Christians of the old world. In what light soever the event may be viewed, it no doubt greatly facilitated the settlements, and rendered them less hazardous.

Musketaquid, the original Indian name of Concord and Concord River, for a long time before it was settled by our fathers, had been one of the principal villages of the Massachusetts tribe. Nanepashemet was the great king or sachem of these Indians. His principal place of residence was in Medford, near Mystic pond. " His house was built on a large scaffold six feet high, and on the top of a hill. Not far off, he built a fort with palisadoes 30 or 40 feet high, having but one entrance, over a bridge. This also served as the place of his burial, he having been killed about the year 1619, by the Tarrantines, a warlike tribe of eastern Indians, at another fort which he had built about a mile off." He left a widow — Squaw Sachem, and five children. Squaw Sachem succeeded to all the power and influence of her husband, as the great queen of the tribe. Her power was so much dreaded, when she was first visited by the Plymouth people in 1621, that her enemies, the sachems of Boston and Neponset, desired protection against her, as one condition of submission to the English. She married Wibbacowitts, " the powwaw, priest, witch, sorcerer, or chirurgeon " of the tribe. This officer was highest in esteem next to the sachem; and he claimed as a right the hand of a widowed sachem in marriage; and by this connexion became a king in the right of his wife, clothed with such authority as was possessed by her squawship.[2] Both assented to the sale of Musketaquid, though Tahattawan, hereafter to be noticed, was the principal sachem of the place. This tribe was once powerful. Before the great sickness already mentioned, it could number

---

[1] Mass. Hist. Coll. vol. i.   [2] Letchford.

3,000 warriors. That calamity, and the small-pox, which prevailed among them with great mortality in 1633, reduced it to nearly one tenth of that number. The Musketaquid Indians suffered in common with the brethren of their tribe elsewhere. When first visited by the English, their number was comparatively very small. Their manners, customs, and character form a subject for general rather than town history. Such notices, as are particularly applicable to this place or vicinity, will be given in a separate chapter. The place where the principal sachem lived was near Nahshawtuck (Lee's) hill. Other lodges were south of the Great Meadows, above the South Bridge, and in various places along the borders of the rivers, where planting, hunting, or fishing ground was most easily obtained. From these sources the Indians derived their subsistence; and few places produced a supply more easily than Musketaquid. South of Mr. Samuel Dennis's are now seen large quantities of clamshells, which are supposed to have been collected by the Indians,' as they feasted on that then much frequented spot. Across the vale, south of Capt. Anthony Wright's, a long mound, or breast-work, is now visible, which might have been built to aid the hunter, though its object is unknown. Many hatchets, pipes, chisels, arrow-heads, and other rude specimens of their art, curiously wrought from stone, are still frequently discovered near these spots, an evidence of the existence and skill of the original inhabitants.

The situation of the place, though then considered far in the interior and accessible only with great difficulty, held out strong inducements to form an English settlement, and early attracted the attention of the adventurous Pilgrims. Extensive meadows, bordering on rivers and lying adjacent to upland plains, have ever been favorite spots to new settlers; and this was peculiarly the character of Musketaquid. The Great Fields, extending from the Great Meadows on the north to the Boston road south, and down the river considerably into the present limits of Bedford, and up the river beyond Deacon Hubbard's, and the extensive tract between the two rivers, contained large quantities of open land, which bore some resemblance to the prairies of the western country. These plains were annually burned or dug over, for the purposes of hunting or the rude culture of corn. Forest trees or small shrubbery rarely opposed the immediate and easy culture of the soil. And the open meadows, scattered along the borders of the small streams, as well as the great rivers, and in the solitary glens, then producing, it is said, even larger crops and of better quality, than they now do, promised abundant support for all the necessary stock of the farm-yard. These advantages were early made known to the English emigrants.

Traditionary authority asserts that the settlement was first projected in England. It is not improbable that this may have been partially true, and that William Wood, the author of "New England's Prospect," and the first who mentions the original name of the river or place, might have come here in 1633, and promoted its settlement by his representations after his return to England. It must have been effected, however, in conjunction with others who were residents in the colony. The plan of the settlement was formed on a large scale, and under the most sanguine anticipations of success. Nearly all the first settlers were emigrants directly from England; and a greater number of original inhabitants removed, during the first fifteen years after the settlement, to other towns in the colony, than permanently remained here. This sufficiently characterizes it as one of the "mother towns." It was the first town settled in New England above tide waters; and was in fact, as it was then represented to be, "away up in the woods," being bounded on all sides by Indian lands, and having the then remote towns of Cambridge and Watertown for its nearest neighbours.

The uniform custom of the early settlers of the Massachusetts colony was first to obtain liberty of the government to commence a new settlement, and afterwards to acquire a full title to the soil by purchase of the Indians. This title was never obtained by conquest. The first undertakers, as a preliminary step towards the settlement, had this town granted to them by the General Court, at its session at New-Town (Cambridge) Sept. 2, 1635, under the following Act of Incorporation:

"It is ordered that there shall be a plantation att Musketaquid, and that there shall be 6 myles of land square to belonge to it; and that the inhabitants thereof shall have three yeares imunities from all public charges except trainings. Further that, when any that shall plant there, shall have occasion of carrying of goods thither, they shall repair to two of the nexte majistrates, where the teams are, whoe shall have power for a yeare to press draughts att reasonable rates, to be paid by the owners of the goods, to transport their goods thither at seasonable tymes; and the name of the place is changed and here after to be called Concord." [1]

Governor Winthrop[2] says this grant was made " to Mr. Buckly and ——— merchant, and about twelve more families, to begin a town." This was undoubtedly the Rev. Peter Bulkeley; and the merchant intended, Maj. Simon Willard, two distinguished individuals, who will be more particularly noticed in the sequel. The loss of early records renders it impossible to ascertain who the twelve other families were. Their names may, however, be inferred from an account of early families, to be given in this history. Others were soon after added; and on the 6th of October, the Rev. John Jones, and a large number of settlers, destined for the plantation, arrived in Boston.

The time from which the town should be free from immunities or public charges, mentioned in the act of incorporation, was calculated from the October following. In 1636 the order to press carts was renewed for three years more. These peculiar privileges were probably granted to the first settlers, as an encouragement in their hazardous enterprise. That legal authority should be given to compel any person, at any time, to carry goods through a wilderness untrodden by civilized man, appears singular to us, but was probably necessary then, as it would have

---

[1] The late Samuel Davis, Esq., of Plymouth, supposed (MS. letter), that the original name was "formed of two Indian words, *moskeht*, signifying 'grass,' and *ohkeit*, signifying 'ground'; and unitedly 'grass-ground.' Musketaquid, as nearly resembling this word as the Indian dialect would permit, was probably applied to the land near the river, as indicating its character, or to the river itself, in which case it would mean 'grassy brook' or 'meadow brook.'" *Concord*, the present name, is said by tradition to have been given on account of the peaceable manner in which it was obtained from the Indians. This opinion, however, is not supported. Johnson, (2. Hist. Coll. vol. iii. p. 155.) says, it was named Concord " from the occasion of the present time, as you shall after hear," but does not tell us any thing further about it. It probably received its name from the Christian union and *concord*, subsisting among the first company, at the commencement of the settlement.

[2] Journal, vol. i. 2.

been difficult, if not impossible, to *hire* them "at reasonable rates." Though some privileges were granted to Concord, from its peculiarly remote situation, which were withheld from other towns, it did not entirely escape censure. Being required to perform military duty, it was, in 1638, fined 5s. for want of a pair of stocks, and a watch-house. In June, 1639, it had a similar fine imposed, and another for "not giving in a transcrip of their lands." In 1641 it was again fined " 10s. for neglecting a watch and for non-appearance."[1] Such fines were imposed on several towns by the General Court, pursuant to an act, passed June 7, 1636, providing that every town should keep a military watch and be well supplied with ammunition, as a guard against the incursions of unfriendly Indians.

It does not appear from any sources of information extant, that all the land, included in the incorporated limits, was purchased of the Indians till some time after the settlement had begun, though a part of it might have been. Till May, 1637, no order on the subject appears. The court at that time gave "Concord liberty to purchase lande within their Limits of the Indians; to wit: Attawan and Squaw Sachem." The land was accordingly fairly purchased, and satisfactory compensation made; and Aug. 5, 1637, the Indian deed was deposited in the Secretary's office in Boston. The Colony Records give the following account of this transaction. " 5th. 6mo. 1637. Wibbacowett; Squaw Sachem; Tahattawants; Natanquatick, alias Old man; Carte, alias Goodmand; did express their consent to the sale of the Weire at Concord over against the town: and all the planting-ground which hath been formerly planted by the Indians, to the inhabitants of Concord; of which there was a writing, with their marks subscribed given into court, expressing the price."[2] Whether this transaction related to the whole town is uncertain.

A tradition has been handed down that the purchase took place under a large oak, which was standing in front of the Middlesex Hotel within the memory of our oldest inhabitants, and called, after one of the original settlers, "Jethro's tree"; and which is said to have been used in early times as a belfry on which the town bell was hung.

---

[1] Colony Records. [2] Ibid.

I have sought in vain for the Indian deed. It was probably lost very early, since measures were taken in 1684, when the colony charter was declared to be void, and the claims of Robert Mason to large portions of the country were asserted, to establish the lawful title, which the inhabitants of Concord had in their soil. The original petition was also lost. The following depositions, relating to the subject, were taken, and are inserted in the Middlesex Records, and in the Town Records, to answer the purpose of the original deed.

"The Testimony of William Buttrick, aged sixty-eight years, or thereabouts, sheweth; — That about the year one thousand six hundred and thirty-six, there was an agreement made by some undertakers for the town since called Concord, with some Indians, that had right unto the land then purchased of them for the township. The Indians' names were Squaw Sachem, Tahattawan, sagamore, Nuttunkurta, and some other Indians that lived and were then present at that place, and at that time; the tract of land being six miles square, the centre being about the place where the meeting-house now standeth. The bargain was made and confirmed between the English undertakers and the Indians then present and concerned, to their good satisfaction on all hands." — "7: 8: 84 [7th. Oct. 1684]. Sworn in court, Thomas Danforth. Entered in Register at Cambridge, Liber 9. page 105, by Thomas Danforth."

"The testimony of Richard Rice, aged 74 years," like William Buttrick's, is recorded in full immediately after it, and attested in the same manner.

"The Deposition of Jehojakin, *alias* Mantatukwet, a Christian Indian of Natick, aged 70 years or thereabouts.

"This Deponent testifieth and saith, that about 50 years since he lived within the bounds of that place which is now called Concord, at the foot of an hill, named Nahshawtuck [Lee's], now in the possession of Mr. Henry Woodis, and that he was present at a bargain made at the house of Mr. Peter Bulkeley (now Capt. Timothy Wheeler's)[1] between Mr. Simon Willard, Mr. John Jones, Mr. Spencer, and several others, in behalfe of the Englishmen who were settling upon the said town of

---

[1] This was between the houses of Daniel Shattuck, Esq. and Capt. John Stacy.

Concord, and Squaw Sachem, Tahattawan, and Nimrod, Indians, which said Indians (according to their particular rights and interest) then sold a tract of land containing six miles square (the said house being accounted about the centre) to the said English for a place to settle a town in; and he the said deponent saw said Willard and Spencer pay a parcel of Wampumpeage,[1] hatchets, hoes, knives, cotton cloth, and shirts, to the said Indians for the said tract of land. And in particular perfectly remembers that Wibbacowet, husband to Squaw Sachem, received a suit of cotton cloth, an hat, a white linen band, shoes, stockings, and a great coat, upon account of said bargain. And in the conclusion, the said Indians declared themselves satisfied, and told the Englishmen, they were welcome. There were present also at the said bargain Waban, Merchant; Thomas, his brother-in-law; Notawquatuchquaw; Tantumous, now called Jethro. — Taken upon oath the 20th of October 1684, before Daniel Gookin, sen. Assistant, Thomas Danforth, Dep. Gov. Entered in the Register at Cambridge, Lib. 9. page 100, 101; 20: 8: 84 [20th Oct. 1684] by Thomas Danforth, Rec'r."

"The Deposition of Jethro, a Christian Indian of Natick, aged 70 years or thereabouts:

"This Deponent testifieth and saith, that about 50 years since, he dwelt at Nashobah, near unto the place now called by the English Concord; and that coming to said Concord was present at the making a bargain (which was done at the house of Mr. Peter Bulkeley, which now Capt. Timothy Wheeler liveth in) between several Englishmen (in behalfe of such as were settling said place) viz. Mr. Simon Willard, Mr. John Jones, Mr. Spencer, and others, on the one party; and Squaw Sachem, Tahattawan, and Nimrod, Indians, on the other party; and that the said Indians (according to their several rights) did then sell to the said English a certain tract of land containing six miles square (the said house being accounted about the centre) to plant a town in; and that the said deponent did see the said Willard and Spencer pay to the said Indians for the said tract of land a parcel of Wampumpeage, [like Jehojakin's testimony as far as "said bar-

---

[1] Indian money curiously made of shells strung on strings and valued by the fathom at 5s.

gain "]; and that after the bargain was concluded, Mr. Simon Willard, pointing to the four quarters of the world, declared that they had bought three miles from that place, east, west, north, and south; and the said Indians manifested their free consent thereunto. There were present at the making of the said bargain, amongst other Indians, Waban, merchant; Thomas, his brother-in-law; Natawquatuckquaw; Jehojakin, who is yet living and deposeth in like manner as above." [1]

This was sworn to, attested, and recorded, like the preceding.

The first settlement commenced in the fall of 1635, fifteen years after the Pilgrims landed at Plymouth, and five after the settlement of Boston. The first houses were built on the south side of the hill from the public square to Merriam's corner; and the farm lots laid out, extending back from the road across the Great Fields and Great Meadows, and in front across the meadows on Mill Brook. This spot was probably selected because it contained land of easy tillage, and because it afforded the greatest facilities in constructing such temporary dwellings, as would shelter the inhabitants from the inclemency of storms and winter. These huts were built by digging into the bank, driving posts into the ground, and placing on them a covering of bark, brush-wood, or earth. The second year, houses were erected as far as where the south and north bridges now stand. This plantation, however, like others in the colony, was limited in its extent. In 1635, the General Court ordered that "no new building should be built more than half a mile from the meeting-house in any new plantation." This order was probably passed for greater safety against the Indians, and appears to have been enforced in Concord about eight years, after which the settlement began to be much more extended.

Many of the first settlers were men of acknowledged wealth, enterprise, talents, and education, in their native country. Several were of noble families. The Rev. Peter Bulkeley brought more than 6,000 pounds sterling, the Hon. Thomas Flint 4,000, and

---

[1] The town received its name in 1635, and not, as here stated, "since" 1636. If the purchase took place before the act of incorporation, Mr. Jones could not have been present; if in 1636, he was. These errors in the depositions, not materially affecting their importance. probably arose from their being given from memory.

others had very respectable estates. Many of them were men of literary attainments. Mr. Bulkeley became an author of distinguished celebrity. William Wood, if, as is probable, he was the author of "New England's Prospect," was a man of considerable intelligence and sagacity. But they were eminently a religious people partaking largely of the spirit which governed the companies that first landed at Plymouth, Salem, and Boston. Having been persecuted in their native country, and deprived of the liberty of worshipping God, and enjoying His ordinances, agreeably to their views of Scripture and duty, they accounted no temporary suffering or sacrifices too great to be endured, in order to be restored to their natural rights, and to freedom from religious oppression. Though some were men of fortune and eminence, and from their infancy had been unaccustomed to hardship, they cheerfully gave up all their personal comforts, crossed the ocean, and planted themselves in this lonely wilderness to endure suffering, for which no pecuniary compensation would have been adequate. No purpose of worldly gain could have prompted so hazardous and expensive an enterprise. It was emphatically a religious community seeking a quiet resting-place for their religious enjoyments and religious hopes. The remark, in reference to the whole colony, that " God sifted a whole nation that he might send choice grain over into this wilderness,"[1] might, with propriety, be applied to the resolute and pious fathers of this town. Though they came from various parts of England, they were united, and had high hopes of happiness and religious prosperity, and emphatically lived in *Concord*. Nothing but the unexpected hardships, peculiar to their situation, could have produced contrary, but almost necessary results.

The following extract is from Johnson's "Wonder-working Providence."[2] Being an inhabitant of Woburn, and often associated with the citizens of Concord in public business, the author had good opportunity to become familiarly acquainted with its early history. This account may, therefore, be received with more implicit faith, than some of that author's statements of facts; and, for its curiosity and information, is worthy of insertion in this connexion.

---

[1] Lt. Governor Stoughton's Election Sermon.
[2] 2 Mass. Hist. Coll. vol. iii. pp. 156 – 159. Written about 1650.

"Upon some inquiry of the Indians, who lived to the North West of the Bay, one Captaine Simon Willard, being acquainted with them, by reason of his trade, became a chiefe instrument in erecting this towne. The land they purchase of the Indians, and with much difficulties travelling through unknowne woods, and through watery swamps, they discover the fitnesse of the place; sometimes passing through the thickets, where their hands are forced to make way for their bodies passage, and their feete clambering over the crossed trees, which when they missed they sunke into an uncertaine bottome in water, and wade up to their knees, tumbling sometimes higher and sometimes lower. Wearied with this toile, they at end of this meete with a scorching plaine, yet not so plaine, but that the ragged bushes scratch their legs fouly, even to wearing their stockings to their bare skin in two or three hours. If they be not otherwise well defended with bootes or buskings, their flesh will be torne. Some of them being forced to passe on without further provision, have had the bloud trickle downe at every step. And in time of summer, the sun casts such a reflecting heate from the sweet ferne, whose scent is very strong, that some herewith have beene very nere fainting, although very able bodies to undergoe much travel. And this not to be indured for one day, but for many; and verily did not the Lord incourage their natural parts (with hopes of a new and strange discovery, expecting every houre to see some rare sight never seen before), they were never able to hold out and breake through." * * *
"After some dayes spent in search, toyling in the day time as formerly said, like true Jacob, they rest them on the rocks where the night takes them. Their short repast is some small pittance of bread, if it hold out; but as for drinke they have plenty, the countrey being well watered in all places that are yet found out. Their further hardship is to travell sometimes they know not whither, bewildred indeed without sight of snn, their compasse miscarrying in crouding through the bushes. They sadly search up and down for a known way, the Indian paths being not above one foot broad, so that a man may travell many dayes and never find one." * * * "This intricate worke no whit daunted these resolved servants of Christ to go on with the worke in hand; but lying in the open aire, while the watery clouds poure down all the night season, and sometimes the driving snow dissolving on

their backs, they keep their wet cloathes warme with a continued fire, till the renewed morning give fresh opportunity of further travell. After they have thus found out a place of aboad, they burrow themselves in the earth for their first shelter under some hill-side, casting the earth aloft upon timber, they make a smoaky fire against the earth at the highest side. And thus these poore servants of Christ provide shelter for themselves, their wives and little ones, keeping off the short showers from their lodgings, but the long raines penetrate through to their great disturbance in the night season. Yet in these poor wigwams they sing psalmes, pray and praise their God, till they can provide them houses, which ordinarily was not wont to be with many till the earth, by the Lord's blessing, brought forth bread to feed them, their wives and little ones, which with sore labours they attain; every one that can lift a hoe to strike it into the earth, standing stoutly to their labours, and tear up the rootes and bushes, which the first yeare bears them a very thin crop, till the soard of the earth be rotten, and therefore they have been forced to cut their bread very thin for a long season. But the Lord is pleased to provide for them great store of fish in the spring time, and especially Ale-wives about the bignesse of a Herring. Many thousands of these they used to put under their Indian corne, which they plant in hills five foote asunder, and assuredly when the Lord created this corn, he had a speciall eye to supply these his people's wants with it, for ordinarily five or six grains doth produce six hundred. As for flesh they looked not for any in those times (although now they have plenty) unlesse they could barter with the Indians for venison or rockoons, whose flesh is not much inferiour unto lambe. The toil of a new plantation being like the labours of Hercules never at an end, yet are none so barbarously bent (under the Mattacusets especially) but with a new plantation they ordinarily gather into church fellowship, so that pastors and people suffer the inconveniences together, which is a great means to season the sore labours they undergoe. And verily the edge of their appetite was greater to spirituall duties at their first coming in time of wants, than afterward. Many in new plantations have been forced to go barefoot, and bareleg, till these latter dayes, and some in time of frost and snow; yet were they then very healthy more than now they are. In this wildernesse worke men of estates speed no better than others, and some much worse for want of being inured to such hard labour, having laid out their estate upon cattell at five and twenty pound a cow, when they came to winter them with in-land hay, and feed upon such wild fother as was never cut before, they could not hold out the winter, but ordinarily the first or second yeare after their coming up to a new plantation, many of their cattell died, especially if they wanted salt-marshes. And also those, who supposed they should feed upon swines flesh were cut short, the wolves commonly feasting themselves before them, who never leave neither flesh nor bones, if they be not scared away before they have made an end of their meale. As for those who laid out their estate upon sheepe, they speed worst of any at the beginning (although some have sped the best of any now) for untill the land be often fed by other cattell, sheepe cannot live, and therefore they never thrived till these latter days. Horse had then no better successe, which made many an honest gentleman travell a foot for a long time, and some have even perished with extreme heate in their travells. As also the want of English graine, wheate, barley, and rie, proved a sore affliction to some stomacks, who could not live upon Indian bread and water, yet were they compelled to it till cattell increased, and the plowes could but goe. Instead of apples and pears, they had pomkins and squashes of divers kinds. Their lonesome condition was very grievous to some, which was much aggravated by continuall feare of the Indians approach, whose cruelties were much spoken of, and more especially during the time of the Pequot wars. Thus this poore people populate this howling desert, marching manfully on (the Lord assisting) through the greatest difficulties, and sorest labours that ever any with such weak means have done."

Additional grants of land were occasionally made, adjoining Concord, after the first purchase. On the 2nd of May, 1638, Governor Winthrop had 1,200, and Thomas Dudley 1,000 acres granted them below Concord. When they came up to view it, " going down the river about four miles, they made choice of a place for one thousand acres for each of them. They offered each other the first choice, but because the deputy's was first granted, and himself had store of land already, the governor yielded him the choice. So, at the place where the deputy's land was to begin, there were two great stones, which they called the Two Brothers, in remembrance that they were brothers by their children's marriage, and did so brotherly agree, and for that a little creek near those stones was to part their lands. At the court, in the 4th month after, two hundred acres were added to the governor's part."[1] The governor's lot lay southerly, and the deputy governor's northerly of those rocks, and they were divided by a little brook, which may now be seen a short distance below Carlisle bridge. Governor Winthrop selected (judiciously, I think) a lot in Concord, which "he intended to build upon," near where Captain Humphrey Hunt now lives. The changes, which took place in his property and family, probably prevented him from putting his plan into execution.

In Nov. 1639, 500 acres of land were granted to Increase Nowell Esq. " on the north side of the bounds of Concord beyond the river against the governor's 1200;" and 500 acres to the Rev. Thomas Allen of Charlestown, on the north side of Mr. Nowell's; and, Oct. 7. 1640, to the Rev. Thomas Weld of Roxbury 533 acres, next to Mr. Allen's.[2] Another tract of 400 acres was also granted to Mr. Atherton Hough. All these lands were sold about 1650 to John and Robert Blood, and comprised what was afterwards known as the *Bloods' Farms*, which became a part of Concord, and which will be hereafter noticed.

About this time the Rev. Peter Bulkeley had 300 acres granted him towards Cambridge; and Mr. William Spencer 300 acres, "beyond Concord by the Alwife River."

It appears that the inhabitants were not well satisfied with their situation; and that other places, either adjoining the town or at a distance from it, were sought, to which they might remove. In a petition on this subject to the General Court, it is said: — "Whereas your humble petitioners came into this country about 4 years agoe, and have since then lived at Concord, where we were forced to buy what now we have, or the most of it, the convenience of the town being before given out: your petitioners having been brought up in husbandry, of children, finding the lands about the town very barren, and the meadows very wet

---

[1] Winthrop's Journal, vol. i. p. 264. The Colony Records give a more particular description of this and the subsequent grants.
[2] Col. Rec.

and unuseful, especially those we now have interest in; and knowing it is your desire the lands might be subdued, have taken pains to search out a place on the north west of our town, where we do desire some reasonable quantitie of land may be granted unto us, which we hope may in time be joined to the farms already laid out there to make a village. And so desiring God to guide you in this and all other your weighty occasions, we rest your humble petitioners." This petition is signed by Thomas Wheeler, Timothy Wheeler, Ephraim Wheeler, Thomas Wheeler, Jr., Roger Draper, and Richard Lettin; is dated Sept. 7. 1643; and endorsed by the court — " We think some quantitie of land may be granted them provided that within two years they make some good improvement of it."

The uplands, which the first planters selected for cultivation, proved to be of a poor quality; and the meadows were unexpectedly much overflowed with water. All the fish and other manure which were applied to enrich the sand hills east of the village were useless. These were causes of great disappointment and suffering. Among other projects to make the meadows dry, one was formed and then considered practicable, to deepen the channel of Concord river at the falls " to drain the water off." A petition was presented to the court, the first year after the incorporation of the town, which produced the following order, dated Sept. 8, 1636. " Whereas the inhabitants of Concord are purposed to abate the Falls in the river upon which their towne standeth, whereby such townes as shall hereafter be planted above them upon the said River shall receive benefit by reason of their charge and labour: It is therefore ordered that such towns or farms as shall be planted above them shall contribute to the inhabitants of Concord proportional both to their charge and advantage."

This subject continued to be agitated for several years. Nov. 13, 1644, Herbert Pelham, Esq., of Cambridge, Mr. Thomas Flint and Lt. Simon Willard of Concord, and Mr. Peter Noyes of Sudbury, were appointed commissioners " to set some order which may conduce to the better surveying, improving, and draining of the meadows, and saving and preserving of the hay there gotten, either by draining the same, or otherwise, and to proportion the charges layed out about it as equally and justly (only upon them that own land) as they in their wisdom shall see meete." All their efforts, however, were unavailing. Johnson says "the rocky falles causeth their meadowes to be much covered with water, the which these people, together with their neighbour towne [Sudbury] here several times essayed to cut through but cannot, yet it may be turned another way with an hundred pound charge." A canal across to Watertown or Cambridge was then considered practicable at a "hundred pound charge!"

In addition to these difficulties, it is intimated by Mather, author of the Magnalia, that others arose between the ministers and the people, which were settled by calling a council after the abdication of one of them. Some refused to bear their proportion of the public charges; and the town continued to decrease in population. Some families returned to England, others removed to older, and others to newer settlements. In 1644, a large number went to Connecticut with the Rev. John Jones. The grievances of the people were set forth in a petition to the General Court.

"To the Wor:ll Governor, Deputy Governor, with the rest of the Assistants and Deputies of the Court now assembled. The humble petition of the Inhabitants of Concord sheweth:

"That whereas we have lived most of us at Concord since our coming over into these parts, and are not conscious unto ourselves that we have been grosly negligent to imploy that talent God hath put into our hands to our best understanding; Neither have wee found any special hand of God gone out against us, only the povertie and meannesse of the place we live in not answering the labour bestowed on it, together with the badness and weetnes of the meadowes, hath consumed most of the estates of those who have hitherto borne the burden of charges amongst us, and therewith the bodily abilities of maney. This being soe eminent above what hath befallen other plantations, hath occasioned many at severall times to depart from us, and this last summer, in the end of it, a 7th or 8th part of the Towne went to the southward with Mr. Jones [the Rev. John Jones] and many more resolved to goe after them, so that maney houses in the Towne stand voyde of Inhabitants, and more are likely to be; and we are confident that if conscience had not restrained, fearing the dissolution of the Towne by their removeall, very many had departed to one place or other where Providence should have hopefully promised a livelihood.

"This our condition we thought it our duty to informe you of. fearing least if more go from us we shall neither remayne as a congregation nor a towne, and then such as are most unwilling to depart, whiles there remayne any hopes of ordinance amongst us, will be enforced to leave the place, which if it should come to pass, wee desire this may testify on the behalf of such, it was not a mynd unsatisfyed with what was convenient, which occasioned them to depart, but meerly to attaine a subsistence for themselves and such as depend on them, and to enjoy ordinances. If it be sayd, wee may go to other places and meete with as many difficulties as here, experience herein satisfies us against many reasons. Such as hardly subsisted with us, and were none of the ablest amongst us, either for labour or ordering their occasions, have much thriven in other places they have removed unto. Our humble request is you would be pleased to consider how unable we are to beare with our brethren the common charges, the premises considered.

<pre>
        Richard Griffin   Robert Fletcher
        Joseph Wheeler   Walter Edmonds
        Timothy Wheeler   William Hunt
        George Wheeler   William Wood
        John Smedley   James Blood
        Thomas Bateman   Joseph Middlebrooke
</pre>
These in the name of the rest."

This petition was presented 14 May, 1645, and is attested by the proper authorities. It is endorsed;—"We conceive the petitioners of Concord should (in consideration of the reasons alledged in this petition) be considered in their rates; but how much, wee leave to those that are appoynted to assess the several towns when any levie is to be made."[1]

---

[1] A colony tax of £1,200 was assessed in 1640, £800 in 1642, £616 in 1645, and another tax in 1676. The following table shows the relative proportions which a few of the towns paid.

Towns.	1640	'42	'45	'76.	Towns.	1640	'42	'45	'76.
Boston,	£179	120	100	300	Watertown,	£90	55	41	45
Cambridge,	100	67	45	42	Concord,	50	25	15	34
Charlestown,	90	60	55	180	Sudbury,	—	15	11	20

These difficulties hastened the settlement of other towns. About half of the original petitioners of Chelmsford were citizens of Concord. All of them, however, did not remove thither. Groton, Lancaster, and other towns, received some of the early inhabitants when they were settled. To restrain this spirit of emigration, the General Court passed the following order in 1645:

"In regard of the great danger that Concord, Sudbury, and Dedham will be exposed unto, being inland Townes and but thinly peopled, it is ordered that no man now inhabiting & settled in any of the s'd Townes (whether married or single) shall remove to any other Towne without the allowance of the majistrates or the select men of the towns, untill they shall obtain leave to settle again, or such other way of safety to the s'd townes whereupon this Court or the Council of this Commonwealth shall sett the Inhabitants of such s'd towns at their former liberty." [1]

Concord was probably less populous from 1645 to 1650 than at any other period. Johnson had that time in view, when speaking of the statistics of this town. "This Towne," says he, "was more populated once than now it is. Some faint-hearted souldiers among them, fearing the Land would prove barren, sold their possessions for little, and removed to a new plantation, which have most commonly a great prize set on them. The number of families at present are about 50. Their buildings are conveniently placed, chiefly in one straite street under a sunny-banke in a low levell. Their herd of great cattell are about 300; the church of Christ here consists of about 70 soules; their teaching elders were Mr. Buckly, and Mr. Jones, who removed from them with that part of the people, who went away, so that onely the reverend grave and godly Mr. Buckly remaines." [2]

The following chronological items, collected from the colony records and other sources, are given as matters worthy of preservation here, and as showing the care exercised by the General Court over the towns. November 2, 1637, Robert Fletcher was chosen constable of Concord. Thomas Brooks was in the same office the next year. March 12, 1638, Lt. Willard was allowed "to sell wine and strong water"; and at the same Court an order

---

[1] Colony Files.   [2] 2 Mass. Hist. Coll. vol. III. p. 154.

passed, that "the freemen of Concord, and those that were not free, which had hand in the undue election of Mr. Flint, should be fined 6s. 8d. a piece." In 1639, Mr. Flint, Lt. Willard, and Richard Griffin, were appointed "to have the ending of small matters this year." They were reappointed the two next years. June 4, 1639, William Fuller, "who kept the mill built by Mr. Bulkeley by the 'Mill-dam' was fined three pounds for gross abuse in over-tolling." In 1640, Lt. Willard, Thomas Brooks, and William Wood, were appointed, under a law, "for valuing horses, mares, cows, oxen, goats, and hoggs," in Concord. The town paid its taxes this year in such property. The same year, Thomas Flint was allowed to marry in Concord and Sudbury. In 1641, George Fowle was appointed "for the breading of Salt-petre in some out-houses used for poultry and the like," under penalty of 12s. A company was incorporated this year "to carry on the beaver trade," of which Simon Willard was appointed superintendent. Mr. John Bulkeley was paid 40s. for services as a soldier.[1]

"At Concord a bullock was killed, which had in his maw a ten shilling piece of English gold, and yet it could not be known that any had lost it."[2] In April, 1641, a house and child were burnt in Concord; fire having been put into a stack of hay standing near, by another child, while the people were at meeting on the Sabbath.[3]

Cattle then ran at large on "commons," as they were called; and each town was required, by an act of the General Court, to have a mark placed upon its respective cattle.

CHAPTER II.

Efforts to civilize the Indians. — Eliot begins the Work. — Effects at Nonantum and at Concord. — Laws for the Indians. — Opposition. — Eliot's Labors and Petition. — Nashobah — Notices of several Indians. — Account of the Praying Indians — Nashobah sold.

IT would be inconsistent with my design to portray at length the general character of the Indians, or give a full view of the

---

[1] Colony Records. [2] Winthrop, vol. II. p. 310. [3] 2 Hist. Coll.

early efforts to civilize and Christianize them. This is properly the province of the historian of the State or Country. So far, however, as they were made within our own territory, or in connexion with the native inhabitants, it will be proper that the local historian should describe them; and, more especially, since erroneous statements have been promulgated by writers whose authority is received with implicit faith.

One of the objects of the original settlers of the colony, as expressed in their charter, was to "win the Indians, natives of the country, to the knowledge and obedience of the only true God and Saviour of mankind, and the Christian faith." When they were actually surrounded by the natives, this object was not forgotten, though nothing effectual was done till nearly sixteen years after their arrival.

Squaw Sachem, at Concord, Kutshamikin, sachem at Dorchester, Musconomok, sachem at Ipswich, and Nashacowin and Wassamug,[1] two sachems near Wachusett, made a formal submission to the English government on the 8th of March, 1644, and put themselves and their subjects under its protection. In their examination, as to their moral and religious views, they express their desire, "as opportunity will serve and English live among them," to learn "to read God's word, to know God aright, and to worship him in his own way." Two sachems (Pumham and Socononocho), near Providence, the preceding June, and Passaconaway, sachem at Merrimack, and his sons, on the 20th of the succeeding June, submitted in like manner. Though the motives of these Indians might have been selfish, these were considered encouraging circumstances by the friends of their civilization. And the government, 13 Nov., 1644, ordered the county courts "to take care of the Indians residing within their several shires, to have them civilized, and to take order from time to time to have them instructed in the knowledge of God."[2]

These movements, and the disposition shown by particular Indians,[3] led some individuals specially to prepare themselves to instruct them. The Rev. John Eliot of Roxbury was the first

---

[1] The Rev. Samuel Danforth, in his Almanack for 1647, spells these names as follows: Cutchamakin, Mascanomet, Wassamegen, Nathawanon.
[2] Col. Rec.   [3] See "New England's First Fruits."

and most distinguished in these Christian labors. He has justly been styled the "Apostle, not a whit behind the chiefest Apostles." He preached his first sermon Oct. 28, 1646, on the high grounds east of Newton corner, afterwards called Nonantum,— "a place of rejoicing," where he was joyfully received by Waban and several other Indians, who assembled to hear him. Four other meetings took place there, the 11th and 26th of November, and the 4th and 9th of December.

The Rev. Thomas Shepard of Cambridge, in his "Clear Sunshine of the Gospel," informs us, that "the awakening of these Indians raised a great noyse amongst all the rest round about us, especially about Concord[1] side, where the Sachem [Tahattawan], as I remember, and one or two more of his men, hearing of these things, and of the preaching of the Word, and how it wrought among them here, came therefore hither to Noonanetum to the Indian Lecture; and what the Lord spake to his heart wee know not, only it seems he was so farre affected, as that he desired to become more like to the English, and to cast off those Indian, wild, and sinfull courses they formerly lived in; but when divers of his men perceived their sachem's mind, they secretly opposed him herein: which opposition being known, he therefore called together his chiefe men about him, and made a speech to this effect unto them, viz. 'That they had no reason at all to oppose those courses the English were now taking for their good, for (saith he) all the time you have lived after the Indian fashion under the power and protection of higher Indian sachems, what did they care for you? They only sought their owne ends out of you, and therefore would exact upon you, and take away your skins and your kettles, and your wampum from you at their own pleasure, and this was all that they regarded: but you may evidently see that the English mind no such things, care for none of your goods, but only seeke your good and welfare, and instead of taking away, are ready to give to you:' with many other things I now forget,

---

[1] The Rev. Dr. Holmes, in his valuable "Annals," Vol. I. p 284, errs in saying "the Indians at the place *afterwards* called Concord," &c. Concord was incorported and named *eleven years before*. Another expression "near to the place where Concord now stands" is equally erroneous. It was then in Concord.

which were related to me by an eminent man [Rev. P. Bulkeley?] of that town. What the effect of this speech was, we can tell no otherwise than as the effects shewed it: the first thing was, the making of certain laws for their more religious and civill government and behaviour, to the making of which they craved the assistance of one of the chief Indians in Noonanetum [Waban?], a very active Indian, to bring in others to the knowledge of God; desiring withall an able and faithful man in Concord [Simon Willard] to record and keep in writing what they had generally agreed upon. Another effect was, their desire of Mr. Eliot's coming up to them to preach, as he could find time, among them: and the last effect was, their desire of having a town given them within the bounds of Concord near unto the English. This latter, when it was propounded by the sachem of the place [Tahattawan], he was demanded why he desired a towne so neare, whereas there was more roome for them up in the country. To which the sachem replyed, that he therefore desired it because he knew that if the Indians dwelt far from the English, that they would not so much care to pray, nor could they be so ready to heare the word of God, but they would be all one Indians still; but, dwelling neare the English, he hoped it might be otherwise with them then. The towne therefore was granted them."

The following are the orders agreed on at Concord, which Mr. Shepard assures us were drawn up by "two faithful witnesses," and "their own copy with their own hands to it."

"Conclusions and orders made and agreed upon by divers Sachems and other principal men amongst the Indians at Concord in the end of the eleventh Month (called January) An. 1646.

"1. That every one that shall abuse themselves with wine or strong liquors, shall pay, for every time so abusing themselves, twenty shillings.

"2. That there shall be no more Powwawing amongst the Indians. And if any shall hereafter powwaw, both he that shall powwaw, and he that shall procure him to powwaw, shall pay twenty shillings a piece.

"3. They do desire that they may be stirred up to seek after God.

"4. They desire they may understand the wiles of Satan, and grow out of love with his suggestions and temtations.

" 5. That they may fall upon some better course to improve their time than formerly.

" 6. That they may be brought to the sight of the sinne of lying, and whosoever shall be found faulty herein, shall pay for the first offence five shillings, and the second ten shillings, and the third twenty shillings.

" 7. Whosoever shall steal any thing from another shall return fourfold.

" 8. They desire that no Indian hereafter shall have any more but one wife.

" 9. They desire to prevent falling out of Indians one with another, and that they may live quietly by one another.

" 10. That they may labour after humilitie and not be proud.

" 11. That when Indians doe wrong one to another, they may be lyable to censure, or fine, or the like, as the English are.

" 12. That they pay their debts to the English.

" 13. That they do observe the Lord's day, and whosoever shall prophane it shall pay twenty shillings.

" 14. That there shall not be allowance to pick lice as formerly, and eat them, and whosoever shall offend in this case shall pay for every louse a penny.

" 15. They will weare their haire comely as the English do, and whosoever shall offend herein shall pay four shillings.

" 16. They intend to reform themselves in their former greasing themselves, under the penalty of five shillings for every default.

" 17. They do resolve to set up praying in their wigwams, and to seek to God both before and after meate.

" 18. If any commit the sinne of fornication, being single persons, the man shall pay twenty shillings, and the woman ten shillings.

" 19. * * * *

" 20. Whosoever shall play at their former games shall pay ten shillings.

" 21. Whosoever shall commit adultery shall be put to death.

" 22. Wilful murder shall be punished with death.

" 23. They shall not disguise themselves in their mournings as formerly, nor shall they keep a great noyse by howling.

" 24. The old ceremony of the maide walking alone and living apart so many days twenty shillings.

"25. No Indian shall take an English man's canooe without leave under penaltie of five shillings.

"26. No Indian shall come into an English man's house except he first knock : and this they may expect from the English.

"27. Whosoever beats his wife shall pay twenty shillings.

"28. If any Indian shall fall out with and beat another Indian, he shall pay twenty shillings.

"29. They desire they may be a towne, and either dwell on this side of Beaver Swamp,[1] or at the East side of Mr. Flint's Pond.

"Immediately after these things were agreed upon, most of the Indians of these parts set up prayer morning and evening in their families, and before and after meate. They also generally cut their haire short, and were more civil in their carriage to the English than formerly. And they do manifest a great willingness to conforme themselves to the civil fashions of the English. The Lord's day they keepe a day of rest, and minister what edification they can to one another. These former orders were put into this forme by Captaine Simon Willard of Concord, whom the Indians, with unanimous consent, intreated to bee their Recorder, being very solicitous that what they did agree upon myght be faithfully preserved without alteration.

  "THOMAS FLINT.   SIMON WILLARD."

I have not been able to find, after a careful examination of the Colony Records, that land was then definitely granted, either to the Concord Indians or to those at Newton ; and I have been led to doubt whether any grants were made, as has been mentioned by many writers. The first order was passed 26 May, 1647, four months after the Concord Indians had adopted their code of laws, and seven months after Eliot first preached to Waban ; and this did not relate to grants of land, but to the civil regulations of the Indians generally, " where they assembled to hear the word of God." It is probable they lived by sufferance on lands claimed by the English, prior to their gathering at Natick.[2]

---

[1] This was in the Southerly part of Lincoln.

[2] Historians speak rather indefinitely, as appears to me, on this subject. Mention is frequently made of the Natick Indians as a distinct tribe, whereas none were known by that name till a place was settled in 1650, and then named Natick, granted like other tracts of land in which to form

As has been already intimated, these benevolent efforts were opposed by some of the natives. This opposition arose principally from the powwaws or priests. The Indians universally believed in " the existence and agency " of invisible spirits. " They worshipped Kitan, their good God, or Hobbamocco, their evil god." Johnson speaks of them generally, as being " in very great subjection to the Divel," and of the powwaws, as " more conversant with him than any other." As his agents they pretended to perform cures by enchantment and witchcraft. So long as the peculiar sanctity of their office was recognised by their brethren, their influence was very great; and, to say the least, they were " back friends to religion." Whenever civilization and Christianity were introduced, these erroneous notions were corrected, and their power ceased. Of this they seemed to be aware.

In the discussions produced by the occurrences that have been described, Wibbacowitts, already mentioned, took an active part. He asked the English, why some of them had been twenty-seven years in the land, and never taught them to know God till then. " Had you done it sooner," said he, " wee might have known much of God by this time, and much sin might have been prevented; but now some of us are grown old in sin, &c." To whom the English answered, " We doe repent that we did not long agoe, as now we doe. Yet withal," they added, " we told them that they were never willing to hear till now, and that seeing God hath turned their hearts to be willing to hear, we are desirous to take all pains we can to teach them."

This opposition prevented their immediate settlement in civil order, and was considered, says Shepard, " a special finger of Satan resisting these budding beginnings;" though it did not prevent the gradual progress of Christianity. The influence of the Rev. Mr. Bulkeley and other citizens of Concord, as well as of the native

---

a civil community. The Christian Indians, gathered there from various tribes, were *afterwards* called Natick Indians, as the inhabitants of a town are called by the name of the town. And in regard to Indian titles, when the claims of Mason were asserted, and the charter forfeited in 1684, the settlers in various places endeavoured to get confirmatory deeds and titles to their land; and obtained such deeds from the Christian Indians, not because they were in all cases legal heirs, but probably because they could give as good titles as any in their power to obtain.

Indians, hereafter to be noticed, was great in this Christian enterprise.

Eliot preached about three years at Nonantum and Neponset; and also occasionally at Concord and other places. About the beginning of the year 1648, he "went with Mr. Flint, and Capt. Willard of Concord, and sundry others, towards Merimack river unto the Indian sachem Passaconaway, that old witch and powwaw, who, together with both his sons, fled the presence of the light for fear of being killed." In 1651, he made another visit there with considerable success. In 1650, a township was granted to the Indians, and called Natick, to which those in the vicinity were gathered, and denominated *Praying Indians*. Many of these were originally inhabitants of Concord, and had taken up a temporary residence at Nonantum and other places.

Those who had endeavoured to unite in civil order at Concord had been frequently disturbed in the places where they settled, as will appear from the following petition to the General Court.

"The humble petition of John Eliot of Roxbury, in behalfe of some Indians, sheweth, — That whereas the Praying Indians have their dwellings in sundry places, and in many respects cannot be all brought to any one place, and, in particular, not to that of Natik; it seemeth therefore very necessary to further theire civile cohabitation, in sundry fitting places, that so the Saboths may be sanctified by them, and other poynts of religion and civility may be promoted among them. And wheras there hath bene and is much trouble by some of theire sittings downe upon such lands as are, some way or other, taken into the bounds of grants made to the English by the honord Gen: Court: These desire as much as may bee, to fix themselves in such places, as (so far as we know) are free from any just challenge of any English interest.

"First, therefore, the inhabitants of Nashoba, living 7 or 8 miles west of Concord, desire to have liberty to make a towne in y[t] place, with due accommodations thereunto. And though Concord have some conditional grant of lands y[t] way, yet I understand, that we shall have a loving and Christian agreement betwixt them and the Indians.

"Secondly, the inhabitants of Ogkauhquoukanus [Marlborough], living about 7 or 8 miles west of Sudbury, where no English have yet desired any land, desire to have liberty to make a towne in y[t] place, with due accommodations thereunto.

"Thirdly, the inhabitants of Hasnemesuhkoh [Grafton], living about 16 miles west of Sudbury, desire the like liberty.

"And, they comiting this honord Court, and all the weighty affaires thereof unto the mercy and goodnesse of the Ld., I rest your unworthy petitioner

Boston this 4th of the 3d : 54.   JOHN ELIOT."

This petition was granted, " provided it doe not prejudice any former grant; nor that they shall dispose of it without leave first had and obtayned from this Court." Nashobah, lying near Nagog Pond, partly in Littleton and partly in Acton, as now bounded, accordingly became an Indian town; and here a part of the Praying Indians in Concord, with others in the vicinity, gathered, and adopted civil and religious order, and had a *Ruler* and other municipal officers, though no church was formed. Such as were entitled to Christian ordinances probably went to Natick to celebrate the communion, after a church was organized there in 1660.

Nashobah, however, was not a very prosperous community. Certain rights of its inhabitants to lands granted to Concord in 1655, were sold to Concord in 1660; but in 1665, the Court granted them 2,000 acres more. In consequence of the war, which was carried on between the Maquas or "Inland Indians," and the neighbouring tribes, from 1665 to 1670, this town suffered severely, and was entirely deserted. Some of the principal men were killed. After the peace in 1670 it was repeopled, and was thus described by Gookin in 1674. " The inhabitants are about ten families, and consequently about fifty souls. The dimensions of this village is four miles square. The land is fertile, and well stored with meadows and woods. It hath good ponds for fish adjoining it. The people live here, as in other Indian villages, upon planting corn, fishing, hunting, and sometimes labouring with the English. Their ruler of late years was John Ahattawance [Tahattawan], a pious man. Since his disease, Pennakennit is the chief. Their teacher is named John Thomas, a sober and pious man. His father was murthered by the Maquas in a secret manner, as he was fishing for eels at his wear, some years since during the war. He was a pious and useful person; and that place sustained a great loss in him. In this village as well as in other old

Indian plantations, they have orchards of apples, whereof they make cider; which some of them have not the wisdom and grace to use for their comfort, but are prone to abuse unto drunkenness. And although the laws be strict to suppress this sin, and some of their own rulers are very careful and zealous in the execution of them; yet such is the madness and folly of man naturally, that he doth eagerly pursue after that which tendeth to his own destruction."[1]

This gives but a sorry picture of a civilized community; but it is far from being applicable generally to this, or the other Indian towns. There were in them some examples of the Christian character, which would have been honorable in any community. Some of the most distinguished were of the Musketaquid Indians.

TAHATTAWAN (sometimes written Tahattawants, Attawan, Attawance, and Ahatawance) was a sagamore, or "sachem of the blood, or chief of the royal line," of Musketaquid; and appears to have possessed rights in the soil equal if not superior to Squaw Sachem; and like her to have consented to its sale. What the connexion between him and Squaw Sachem was, does not fully appear. He had a powerful influence over his subjects; and was one of those who early attended the preaching of Eliot at Newton, and spoke, as already mentioned, in favor of forming a civil community in this town. He was a worthy, upright Indian. The following members of his family embraced Christianity; and they and their descendants were always among the most persevering, influential, and exemplary persons at Natick and Nashobah, — the places to which the different individuals removed after they left Concord.

1. *Waban* married Tasunsquaw, eldest daughter of Tahattawan, sachem of Concord. From documents given in this history, and others in my possession, it appears that he originally lived in Concord, where he was probably born. He is called "merchant" in the records, probably on account of his occupation. He was not a sachem by birth, as some have asserted, but acquired rights in the soil and assented to its sale, by virtue of his marriage into the "royal family." After the English settled

---

[1] 1 Hist. Coll. vol. i. p. 188.

Concord, he removed to Newton, where, in 1646, as already mentioned, he became the first convert to Christianity under the instruction of Eliot. It is said by Shepard that Indians gave "names to their children, usually according to appearances of providences; and the most active Indian for stirring up other Indians to seek after the knowledge of God in these parts is Waban, which signifies *wind;* although they never dremt of this, that this their Waban should breath such spirit of life and incouragement into the rest of the Indians, as he hath endeavoured in all parts of the country both at *Concord,* Merrimack, and elsewhere." He assisted in gathering the society and church at Natick, of which he was chosen chief ruler during his life. He is represented as a man of great prudence, piety, and usefulness. His confession, or account of his religious exercises of mind, was published in 1653, and also an exhortation, made in 1658.[1] He died in the full exercise of the Christian faith in 1674, aged 70. "His last words immediately before he expired were, I give my soul to thee, O my Redeemer, Jesus Christ. Pardon all my sins, and deliver me from hell. Help me against death, and then I am willing to die ; and when I die, O help me and relieve me." [2]

His widow was living at Natick in 1684. His son Weegrammomenet, *alias* Thomas Waban, received a tolerable education, and was many years town clerk of Natick.[3] His name frequently appears in Indian deeds, granting rights to the English, which he acquired rather indefinitely from his father, and like many others as an associate of the Praying Indians.

2. *John Tahattawan*, son of Tahattawan, removed to Nashobah. He was chief ruler of the Praying Indians gathered there, and is said to have been a pious, good man. He died about 1670. He married Sarah, daughter of John, Sagamore of Patucket, who after her husband's death married again Onamog, one of the rulers of the Praying Indians at Marlborough, with whom she lived a short time only. She was living at Patucket, as a widow, in Nov. 1675, when she was wounded by some unfriendly whites, and her only son by Tahattawan was slain.[4]

---

[1] Tears of Repentance, p. 8.
[2] 1 Hist. Coll. vol. v. p. 264.
[3] Biglow's Hist. Natick.
[4] Gookin's MS.

Tahattawan's sole heir was Kehonowsqua, *alias* Sarah ; and is first mentioned in the deed of Nashobah given to the Hon. Peter Bulkeley in 1686, hereafter to be noticed.

3. *Naanishcow*, *alias* John Thomas, married Naanashquaw, *alias* Rebeckah, another daughter of Tahattawan. His father had been a leading man at Nashobah, but was murdered by the Maquas Indians, as has been mentioned. He was teacher at that place till it was abandoned, when he removed to Natick, where he died, Jan. 17, 1727, at the great age of 110 years. He was exemplary through life, and had his reason and speech till within a few hours of his death. His eldest son was Solomon Thomas, *alias* Naashiomenett, who became influential at Natick.

Pennahannit, *alias* Captain Josiah, who was marshal-general or high-sheriff to all the Praying-Indian towns, and attended the chief courts held at Natick and elsewhere, dwelt at Nashobah, and was chief ruler of that place after the death of John Tahattawan.

Jethro, *alias* Tantamous, was present at the first purchase of Concord. He embraced Christianity and removed to Natick. In 1674, he was appointed missionary to the Indians at Weshakim [Sterling], but continued there only a short time.

Notices of other Indians, whose names occasionally occur in connexion with the affairs of Concord, might be given ; but these are the most prominent.

The missionary labors of Eliot and his associates were attended with considerable success. At Natick was a kind of theological seminary, where the natives were educated and sent forth to be rulers and teachers in other places. The Bible and several other books were translated and printed in their language, which requires the word, *Kummogkodonattoottummooootiteaongannunnonash*, to express in English " our question." This was indeed a Herculean task. In 1674, Eliot had organized two churches and fourteen towns, containing 1100 inhabitants [1] who had ostensibly embraced Christianity. A part of them only, however, appear to have been influenced by Christian principles. During Philip's war, this number was very much reduced. Many of them became treacherous, and were among the worst enemies of the En-

---

[1] 1 Hist. Coll. vol. i. p. 195.

glish. Some of them suffered death for their defection.[1] The remainder were gathered in English towns, behaved like exemplary Christians, and were of essential service to the English in Philip's war. The whole number, on the 10th Nov. 1676, was 567 only, of which 117 were men and 450 women and children. The Nashobah or Concord Praying Indians, who remained friendly to the English, were 10 men and 50 women and children; and they then lived in Concord under the inspection of the committee of militia, and the selectmen of the town. The other places where the Praying Indians met on the Sabbath for religious worship at this time, were Medfield, Andrew Devens's Garrison (near Natick), Lower Falls, Nonantum, and Dunstable.[2]

Some other notices of the Nashobah Indians, while resident in Concord, will be given when the events of Philip's war are treated of. After this time, they appear to have nearly abandoned their plantation, and to have removed to Natick. May 19, 1680, twenty-three inhabitants of Concord petitioned the General Court that the lands, belonging to those Indians, might be granted to them, but it was refused; because there were "debts due from the country which might be provided for by the sale of the land, if the Indians have no right or have deserted the place." In reply the petitioners say, "There never were any lands purchased of the country for townships." The petition was ineffectually renewed in 1691. It appears, however, that the Hon. Peter Bulkeley of Concord, and Maj. Thomas Henchman of Chelmsford, on the 15th of June, 1686, bought the easterly half of the Nashobah plantation for £70 sterling. The Indian grantors were as follows, " Kehonowsquaw, *alias* Sarah, the daughter and sole heiress of John Tahattawan, sachem, and late of Nashobah, diseased; Naanishcow, *alias* John Thomas; Naanasquaw, *alias* Rebeckah, wife to the said Naanishcow; Naashkinomenet, *alias* Solomon, eldest son of said Naanishcow, and Naanasquaw, sister to the aforesaid Tahattawan; Weegrammominet, *alias* Thomas Waban; Nackcominewock, relict of Crooked Rob-

---

[1] Mattoonus, constable at Pakachoog, was executed.

[2] I have communicated to the American Antiquarian Society for publication, among other papers, a document in the hand writing of Major Gookin, giving a particular account of the disposition of all the Praying Indians at this time, from which the above facts are taken.

in; and Wunnuhhew, *alias* Sarah, wife to Neepanum, *alias* Tom Doublet." This tract of land was bounded " by Chelmsford plantation (about three miles nd three quarters) on the easterly side, by Concord Village land southward about two miles and three quarters; northward it is bounded by land sold by the aforesaid Indians to Robert Robbins and Peleg Lawrence, both of Groton towne, which land is part of the aforesaid Nashobah plantation, and this line is exactly two miles in length and runs east three degrees northerly, or west three degrees southerly, and the south end runs parallel with this line; on the westerly side it is bounded by the remainder of said Nashobah plantation, and that west line runs south seven degrees and thirty minutes east, four miles and one quarter. The northeast corner is about four or five poles southward of a very great rock that lieth in the line between the said Nashobah and Chelmsford plantation."[1] The remaining history of Nashobah properly belongs to Littleton. It may be well, however, to remark, that in 1714, when that town was incorporated, 500 acres of land were reserved for the Indian proprietors. Sarah Doublet, an Indian, was the only heir to it in 1734, being then old and blind, and committed to the care of Samuel Jones of Concord. She then petitioned for liberty to sell it to pay her maintenance; and it was granted for that purpose to Elnathan Jones, and Mr. Tenney. One corner was near the southeast part of Nagog Pond; and the south line ran 279 rods to a point 90 rods south of Fort Pond, then across t' e pond, north ten degrees west, 133 rods north of said pond to a point, and then making a right angle, it ran 286 rods, and then across Nagog Pond to the first place mentioned.

---

[1] Reg. of Deeds, vol. x. p. 117.

CHAPTER III.

Division of the Town. — Records. — Additional Grants. — Indian Deeds. — Iron Works built. — Town Farm. — Town of Stow granted. — Chronological Items.

We shall now recur to the civil history of the town from the time to which it was brought up in the first chapter. As the lands became more cleared, the meadows were somewhat dryer, and ceased to be a subject of frequent complaint. The inhabitants sought other spots for cultivation, more productive than the sandy ones on which they first settled; and those that remained became more contented with their situation. Their numbers soon after began to increase. Some additional land was granted to the town; and parts of the old settlement had become vacant by the removal of the original inhabitants. A second division of lands now took place.

The town met several times to consider in what manner this division should be made. On the 2d of Jan. 1654, it was voted to divide the town into three parts or *quarters*, and to have the lands first divided in the quarters; but this was not entirely satisfactory to the inhabitants. " Much weariness about these things," say the Records, took place before the system was matured. On the 8th of March, 1654, " at a publique training," nine men were chosen, " three out of each quarter, empowered by the town to hear and end former debat, according to their best light, and discresion, and conscience; only eight of the nine must agree to what is determined, or else nothing to be of force; and none voted to the contrarie, but Georg Wheeler, Henry Woodies, Joshua Edmands, William Buttrick, and Thomas Stow." The labors of this committee resulted in the following agreement : —

" We whose names are under written conclude that 20 acres of meadow shall be resarved for a minister in the Hogepen-walke about Annursnake, and 20 acres of plowland out of the south quarter, and 20 acres of woodland in the east quarter. We agree also that 20 acres of woodland shall be resarved for the public good of the towne, lying neer the old hogepen, at each sid of the townes bounds line. — That some particular persons shall have some inlargement, whoe are short in lands, paying 12*d*. per acre, as others have don, and 6*d*. per acre, if the towne consent thereto : — the persons are as follow ; Georg Wheeler 20 acres ; Obadiah Wheeler 20 acres ; Michel Wood 12 acres ; Thomas Daken 10 acres ; Thomas Batman 15 acres; Bapties Smedly 14 acres. These to have second divition as others have had. That all pooremen in the towne that have not commons to the number of four, shall be allowed so many as amounts to foure with what they have already, till they be able to purchase for themselves, or untill the townsmen shall see cause to take it from them, and bestow it on others that want : and we mean those poore men, that at the present are householders. And upon these conditions and those that folow, the Hogepen-walke is resigned up to the north quarter.

"The divitions of the heighwaies are as foloweth ; The north quarter are to keepe and maintaine all there heighwaies, and bridges, over the great river in there quarter ; and in respect of their greatness of charg thareabout, and in regard of the ease of the east quarter above the rest in there highwayes, they are to alow the north quarter three pounds. — The east quarter are to keepe and maintain all there heighwayes, and the bridge over the north river [Darby's bridge] and the heighway there to the heighland, by estimation 3 or 4 rods, where the commissioners of Concord and Lanchaster being chosen by there townes to lay out there heighwayes did appoint it. — The south quarter are to keepe and maintaine all there heighwayes and bridges over the south river, except that at the north river before expressed that is laid on the east quarter ; the south river bridge being to be set where the aforesaid comisoners appointed it, as there agreement declares : and all these heighwayes and bridges are to be maintained for ever by the quarters on whom they are now cast. — And it is further concluded that if any damiag shall com to the towne by the neglect of any part of the towne in any part of there wayes, that part of the towne so neglecting either bridges or wayes, shall beare the damage and secure the rest of the towne.

"The limits of ech quarter as foloweth ; — The north quarter by there familyes are from the north part of the training place to the great river and all on to the north sid thereof. — The east quarter by there familyes, are from Henry Farweles all eastwards with Thomas Brooke, Ensign Wheeler, Robert Meriam, Georg Meriam, John Adames, Richard Rice. — The south quarter by there familyes are all on the south and southwest side of the mill brooke except those before acsprest, with Luke Potter Georg Heaward, Mihel Wood, and Thomas Dane.

"We doe choose overseeres in ech quarter for the faithful performance of there duty in that case in all particulers, so far as may conduce for the profit and good of there quarters, as to make rates to pay workmen and to see that all persons come in seasonable time and keepe them to there bisiness faithfully, and keep accounts and so see the worke suffisiently done; and they are impoured to call fitt men and cattle in there quarter to the worke and pay them there wages; and if any shall refeuse to attend these nesery workes there names shall be returned to the selectmen of the towne, who shall impose findes according to law upon all such ofenders in that case. Also the overseeres as aforesaid shall keep an exact account of there owne time expended, and shall have suffisient satisfaction for the same. The names of the overseeres as follow; — for the east quarter, Ensign Wheeler, and William Hartwell; for the north quarter, John Smedly, and Thomas Batman; for the south quarter Georg Wheeler, James Hosmer, Georg Heaward, and sargent Buss.

"This company doe for the present joyne to make rats in way as foloweth; — the east end 2*d*. parts for all menes estates according as Mr. Bulkeley last rate was mad; the north quarter 2*d*. parts; and the south quarter 4*d*. parts.

Witness our hands this 7th of the 1st mo. 1654.

'It is further agreed by the nine men aforesaid, that there shall be a parcell of wood lying on the north of the way that goeth to Lancaster to the number of 5 acres, the most whereof is pines to be set out to Ensigne Wheeler, John Smedly and Georg Heaward for the use of the north bridge.'

SIMON WILLARD
ROBERT MERIAM
THOMAS BROOKS
JOSEPH WHELER
JAMES BLOOD
GEORG WHELER
GEORG HEAWARD
THOMAS BATMAN
JOHN SMEDLY."

Regulations were established in each quarter, similar to those in wards of a city. Each chose its own officers, kept its own records, made its taxes, &c. The records of the south quarter (first commencing in 1654, in the hand-writing of Simon Willard, first quarter-clerk) are the only ones now extant. The second division of lands was made in the quarters, and afterwards recorded in the town book, in which the first and second divisions are particularly described. These municipal regulations were continued in force about 50 years; and the distinction which was then given to the different parts of the town, is still preserved.

To the oldest book of records in the clerk's office in Concord is prefixed an account of the proceedings of the town in relation to recording the individual titles to lands, from which it appears, that "the latter grants of land to particular persons were only written on paper books [?] as granted, and not in a register booke." The selectmen were desired to consider the expediency of obtaining "a new booke to record them and all other land that men now doe hold;" and "the thing tending to pece and preventing of strife," they desired "the help herein" of their "Reverend pastor Mr. Edward Bulkeley, Thomas Brooks, and liff. Joseph Wheeler, which company sett about it the 25th of Jan. 1663, and at the end of the day, concluded to call a meeting on the 29th of the aforesaid month, to come to a conclusion about transcribing every man's land in a new booke so that it might be for the comfort and peace of ourselves, and posterity after us." When the town was assembled, it was agreed, that a new book should be procured, — that "what is in the old booke that is useful shall be transcribed into the new, with all lands which men now hold;" — "that every man that hath not his proportion of lands laid out too him, that is due to him, shall gitt it laid out by an artis" before 1665; — and that each one should give to the town clerk a description of their lands, approvd at a meeting of the inhabitants of the quarter in which he lives, and certified by the quarter-clerk.[1]

From these Records I have compiled the following table, which gives the greater part, though not all of the names of the proprietors of the town, at that time. The places of their residence, when known, are indicated by the names under which they now pass.

---

[1] For all the facts thus far in this chapter I am indebted to the the Town Records. The committee to divide the S. Quarter were William Wood, George Hayward, George Wheeler, William Buss, and John Miles. E, stands for east quarter; N, for north quarter; and S, for south quarter in the table on the opposite page.

GENERAL HISTORY.

Proprietors.	No. lots.	Acres.	Residence.	Tax in 1666.
Grace Bulkeley,	1	750		
Thomas Wheeler, sen.	16	373	E. Jotham Wheeler's,	———
Francis Fletcher,	17	437	E.	———
Richard Rice,	3	189	E.	———
Widow Heald,	6	161	N. Joshua Buttrick's,	———
John Heald,	4	86	N. north of the above,	———
William Buttrick,	12	215	N. Jonas Buttrick's,	———
John Flint,	9	534	N. John Flint's,	———
James Blood, sen. } James Blood, jun. }	12	660	N. Rev. Dr. Ripley's,	———
John Smedly,	17	668	N. south of J. Jones's,	———
Thomas Bateman,	7	246	N. near R. French's,	———
Baptise Smedley,	10	186	N. Ephraim Brown's,	———
Humphrey Barret,	11	316	N. Abel B. Heywood's,	———
Richard Temple,	5	291	N. Barrett's Mills,	———
George Meriam,	16	259	E. near Alms-house,	———
John Blood,	1	61	N. near T. Blood's,	———
Robert Blood,	4	169	N. do.	———
John Jones,	9	351	N. James Jones's,	———
Joshua Brooks,	11	195	E. Isaac Brooks's,	———
Caleb Brooks,	12	150	E.	———
Eliphalet Fox,	14	106	E. Bedford Road,	———
Thomas Pellet,	1	14		———
Joseph Dean,	1	22	S. William Heyden's, .	———
Thomas Pellet, } Joseph Dean, }	7	244		———
John Meriam,	8	262	E. Virginia road,	———
William Hartwell,	20	241	E. Bedford road,	———
John Hartwell,	3	17	E. do.	———
Nathaniel Ball,	11	137	E. do.	———
William Taylor,	14	117	E. do.	———
John Farwell,	18	280	E.	———
Joseph Wheeler,	29	357		———
William Baker,	5	43	E.	———
William Buss,	19	319	S. Elijah Wood's,	£ 5 18 2
Moses Wheat,	22	339	E. Bedford road,	———
Luke Potter,	22	249	S.	2 10 0
Robert Meriam,	16	595	E. Eb. Hubbard's,	———

John Heywood,	13	285 S.		1 15 0
George Hayward,	10	505 S.		3 6 10
Daniel Dean, ⎫				1 10 18
Thomas Gobble, ⎭	1	600 S.	Jones's tavern	2 2 0
Henry Woodhouse,	1	360 S.	Joseph Barrett's,	5 1 6
Joshua Wheeler,	11	77 S.	John Vose's,	1 19 9
Boaz Brown,	6	86 N.	The Dakin house,	—
Thomas Brown,	14	186 N.	Reuben French's	—
Nathaniel Billings, sen.	4	51 S.	Amos Baker's,	1 6 8
Nathl. Billings, jun.	7	196 S.	" "	1 13 6
John Billings,	6	185 S.	" "	1 1 1
John Wheeler,	1	67 S.		—
George Wheeler,	24	434 S.	near James Adams's	—
Edward Bulkeley,	11	183 S.	new Meeting-house,	—
Samuel Stratten,	6	254 S.	Alms-house,	—
Edmund Wigley,	4	31 S.		1 19 1
John Miles,	23	459 S.	Josiah Davis's,	3 17 2
Thomas Dakin,	4	87 S.		1 12 10
James Hosmer,	4	164 S.		1 8 7
Samuel Wheeler,	5	21 S.		—
James Smedley,	9	287 S.		—
John Scotchford,	10	120 S.	near Cyrus Stow's,	1 14 2
Michael Wood,	13	230 S.	Samuel Dennis's,	4 3 4
Samuel Hunt,	13	277 N.		—
Ephraim Flint,		750 E.	in Lincoln.	—

It has already been intimated that additional grants of land were made to Concord about 1652. The following details relate to these and other grants.

"To the Honored Generall Court assembled at Boston. The returne of the nommber of acres of land granted as an addition to the Towne of Concord according to the order of the General Court in 1654.

"Whereas the Court was pleased to grannt to our Towne a village some fouer years since upon condition they should improve it before others, but neglecting theire opportunity, the plantation of Chelmsford have taken a good parte of the same, also Nattatawants [Tahattawan] having a plantation granted him which takes up a good some also, we whose names are subscribed have taken a survey of the rest remayning, and wee finde about seven thousand acres left out, of which Major Willard hath two thousand acres, except a little part of one end of his farme which lyes in the place or parcell of vacant land, that was since given to Shawshine, this tract of land being by the last Court granted to our Towne on this condition that at this Court we should acquaint the Court of the quantitye of what wee have.

" This is a true copie compared with original on file, as it was exhibited to the Generall Court may 1655 as attest.

Tho. Brooks
Timothy Wheeler
Joseph Wheeler
George Wheeler
George Heaward
John Jones."

Edward Rawson, *Secretary.*

At the same Court, on the 23d, May 1655 " Five thousand acres of Land were granted to the Inhabitants of Concord for feeding, according to their petition, provided it hinder not any former grants." This was all the tract of land described in the above return, excepting the farms belonging to Major Willard. When his farms were granted I have not been able to find out. One of them lay in the southeast part of the tract, and the other at the northeast. This distinguished individual had several subsequent grants. On the 6th of May, 1657, he had, " for services to the colony, 500 acres of land in any place where he can find it according to law ; " and 21st May, 1658, he had 500 acres more " on the south side of a river that runneth from Nashua to Merimack, between Lancaster and Groton, and is in satisfaction of a debt of £44 " due from John, sagamore of Patucket. His execution to be given up. This farm was laid out in May, 1659, by Thomas Noyes.

The Praying Indians claimed some right to the land granted to Concord "for an enlargement to the towne;" in consideration of which, " the town of Concord doth give to them, the planters of Nashoba, fifteen pounds at six a penny, which giveth them full satisfaction. In witness whereof they doe set to their hands this 20 of the 10 mo. 1660." This agreement was signed by " Nassquaw, marchant Thomas [Thomas Waban], Wabatut, great James Natototos — a blind man, Pompant, and Gomgos," by their marks ; and John Thomas, and John Tahattawan, by their names ; and witnessed by Joseph Wheeler, John Shepard, and John Jones.[1]

---

[1] Town Records. The compensation, mentioned in this agreement,

"At a Generall Court held at Boston the 11th of October, 1665. In answer to the peticion of Concord for an enlargement of their bounds, this court doe grant them a tract of land conteyned in a plott returned to this court under the hand of Ensigne Noyes, by estimation the whole being about five thousand acres, whereof the court reserveth two thousaad acres to be layd out to either Indians or English, as this court shall see meete hereafter to dispose and grant, and the remaynder, being about three thousand acres, this court grant to Concord so as the same doe not abridge any former grant made by this court; and doe order Leift. Beers and Leift. Thomas Noyes to lay out the same and to make returne thereof to the next Court of Election. A true copie. Attest, EDW. RAWSON. *Secr.*"

The following is a copy of the return made 25 May, 1667, and approved by the proper authorities. "We, Richard Beers of Watertown and Thomas Noyes of Sudbury, being appointed to lay out and measure to the inhabitants of Concord a tract or tracts of land next adjoining to their first grant; in order to which, we the above said, did lay out and measure unto the inhabitants of Concord their second grant, being five thousand acres of land granted in the year 1655, as also their grant of three thousand acres granted in the year 1665, next adjoining to their first grant, beginning at the southwest angle of their old bounds [near Maj. Hayward's], extending their said southerly line upon a norwest point, four degrees northerly (according to the Meridian compas) two miles and 280 rods; there making a right angle on a bare hill, and from thence a line upon a northeast point 4 degrees easterly, two miles one half and fifty rods, there meeting with Nashoba plantation line, running the line of the said plantation to their angle one mile one quarter and 60 rods, nearest hand upon an easterly point, there making a right angle, running a line, being the line of the Indian plantation, two miles one quarter and 60 rods, there being bounded by Chelmsford line and Bilrica line as is more plainly described by a plott; in which plott is contained nine thousand and eight hundred acres of land,

---

was paid by Lt. Joseph Wheeler, for which the town granted him in 1660 a tract of land "lying between Chelmsford line and the line of Nashoba township, and joining to the further corner of the great pond." Nagog Pond appears to have been the southeast corner bound of this township.

one thousand and eight hundred acres being formerly granted to Major Williard, the other eight thousand being granted to the inhabitants of Concord, and laid out the 5th May, 1666. Given under our hands.

Richard Beers,
Thomas Noyes, } *Surveyors.*"

The town agreed 20th Jan. 1668, that these additional grants of land " shall lay for a free comon to the present householders of Concord, and such as shall hereafter be approved and allowed to be inhabitants ; except such parts of it as shall be thought mete to make farmes for the use and benefit of the towne." A full title was then acquired from the Indians, though it was thought proper in 1684, for reasons already mentioned, to obtain the following confirmatory deeds.

"To all people to whom these presents may come, greeting; Know ye that we, Mary Neepanaum, John Speen and Sarah Speen, Dorothy Winnetow, Peter Muckquamuck, of Natick, and James Speen, and Elizabeth Speen, his wife of Waymeset, Indians, for and in consideration of a valuable sum of money to us in hand payd by Capt. Timothy Wheeler, Henry Wooddis, James Blood, and John Flint, the receipt whereof we do by these presents acknowledge, and therewith to be fully satisfied and contented, have sold and by these presents do sell, alien, enfeofe, and confirm unto the said Capt. Timothy Wheeler, &c.[1] of Concord in the county of Middlesex in ye Massachusetts Colony, in New England, for the use and behoof of themselves and the rest of the proprietors of the s'd town of Concord a certain tract or parcell of land conteyning by estimation a thousand acres, be the same more or less, and is situate, lying, and being within the last grant of land by the Generall Court to ye s'd town of Concord, and is bounded south-east by Sudbury, and the land of Stow *alias* Pompasitticutt, and norwest by the s'd Stow, running by them upon that line about a mile and a quarter, near to the hill by the Indians called Naauuhpavil ; and from thence by a streight line to the North River at the old bounds of ye s'd town of Concord, unto them the said Timothy Wheeler, &c. &c. to

---

[1] Where " &c." occurs the parties and expressions are repeated.

them, their heirs and successors for ever. And we the said Mary Neepanaum, &c. do hereby covenant and promise to and with the foresaid Timothy Wheeler, &c. &c. that we are the true proprietors of, and have good right and full power to grant, bargain, and sell, the above granted and bargained premises unto the said Timothy, &c. &c. and that the said Timothy, &c. &c. shall and may at all times and from time to time for ever hereafter have, hold, occupy, possess, and enjoy the above granted premises in full, be the same more or less, without any let, denial, or contradiction of us the said Mary Neepanaum, &c. or any of us or any of our heirs, or any other person or persons whatever, lawfully claiming or having any right, title, or interest therein, or to or in any part or parcell thereof. In acknowledgement of this our act and deed, we have hereto put our hands and seals this fifth day of May in the year of our Lord one thousand six hundred eighty and four."

All the abovenamed Indians signed this deed — James Speen by writing his name, and the others by their marks, in presence of Moses Parker, Noah Brooks, Samuel Wheeler jr., Benjamin Bohow and Sarah Bohow (the two last of whom were Indians), and acknowledged " before Pet: Bulkeley, Assistant."

The foregoing deed applied to the south part of the tract. The same individuals, in behalf of Concord, bought of " John Thomas, and Naanoushqua, his wife; Tasunsquaw, the relict of Waban, diseased, and eldest daughter to Tahattawan, Sagamore, diseased; Thomas Waban, her son; Solomon Thomas; John Nasqua; James Casumpal, sen., and Sarah, his wife; and Sarah, the relict widow of Peter Conaway, Indians," for £21; by estimation, 8000 acres, lying in " the last grants of land by the General Court to the town of Concord, and is bounded southeast by the old bounds of the said town of Concord, easterly partly by Bilrerca, partly by a farm formerly layd out by Major Willard for himself, and partly by Chelmsford, till it meet with Nashoba line, and then westerly by the said Nashoba to the southeast corner of the said Nashoba, then northerly by the said Nashoba till it meets with Stow, and so bounded norwest by the said Stow, till it comes near to a hill by the Indians called Naaccuhpavil, and then running upon a straight line to the North River, at the old bounds of the said town of Concord." This deed was executed and acknowledged in the same form as the preceding, on the 13th of Aug. 1684; and witnessed by Ebenezer Engoldsbey, Joseph Wooley, Joseph Shambery, and Andrew Pittemey.

These several grants were afterwards known as the "Town's New Grant," — the " Enlargement of the Town by the General Court," — and generally " Concord Village "; till after about seventy-five years they were in great part separated from Concord and incorporated as the town of Acton.

A company was incorporated, on the 5th March, 1658, " to erect one or more iron-works in Concord." These were built near the present Cotton Factory; and operations were commenced in 1660. The " zinder holes and plates " were cast at Oliver Purchis's iron-works at Lynn, and put in by Joseph Jenks.

The company had permission, 30th May, 1660, " to digg iron ore without molestation in any land now in the Court's possession." The southern grant to Major Willard, above mentioned, was subsequently sold to this company, and became known as the " Iron-work Farm." It lay partly in Concord, in Acton, and in Sudbury, as they are now bounded. Nathaniel Oliver, John Eyre, and Joseph Parsons, of Boston, sold one half of the whole property of this company, on the 23d May, 1684, then consisting of the iron-works and 1668 acres of land, to the Hon. Peter Bulkeley of Concord, and James Russell of Charlestown, for £300.

In 1668 the town leased to Capt. Thomas Wheeler, for 20 years, 200 acres of upland near Mr. Silas Holden's present residence, and 60 acres of meadow lying in several parcels on Nashobah brook, on condition that he should keep, " except 12 Sabbath days yearly," a herd of 50 cattle for 1s. per head for the inhabitants, to be paid " one third part in wheat, one third part in rie or pease, and the other third part in Indian corn." They were to be constantly watched by a " herdsman," and kept in a yard at night to protect them from the wild beasts. Capt. Wheeler agreed to build a house " 40 feet by 18, and 12 stud," covered with shingles, and to have a " pair of chimneys "; and a barn 40 by 24, and 12 high, to be left for the use of the town after the ex-piration of the lease.

Lieutenant Joseph Wheeler, by trading with the Nashobah Indians, became their creditor, aud petitioned the General Court, in 1662, for a grant of 200 acres of land at the southerly part of their plantation as payment for his debt; but it was refused. In 1669, he, with several inhabitants of Concord, petitioned for a tract of land at Pompasitticutt; and the Court appointed him, with John Haynes of Sudbury, William Kerley of Marlborough, James Parker of Groton, and John Moore of Lancaster, a committee to view it and report at their next session. This report was made May 11, 1670; and it was found "to contain 10,000 acres of country land, whereof about 500 is meadow. The greater part of it is very mean land, but we judge there will be planting ground enough to accommodate 20 families. Also there is about 4000 acres more of land that is taken up in farmes, whereof about 500 acres is meadow. There is also the Indian plantation of Nashobah, that doth border on one side of this tract of land, that is exceedingly well meadowed, and they do make but little or no use of it." George Hayward, Joseph Wheeler, Thomas Wheeler, John Hayward, William Buttrick, Sydrach Hapgood, Stephen Hall, Edmund Wigley of Concord, and Joseph Newton and Richard Holdridge, petitioned for this tract of land; and it was granted to them " to make a village, provided the place be setteled with not less than ten famyles within three years, and that a pious, an able, and orthodox minister be maintained there." Daniel Gookin, Thomas Danforth, and Joseph Cook, were appointed " to order the settlement of the village in all respects; " and the various proceedings in relation to it resulted in the incorporation of the town of Stow, May 16, 1683;[1] which has since been found able to accommodate *more* than twenty families!

---

[1] Twelve " foundation lots," containing 50 acres of upland and 15 of meadow, were at first granted in the following order: — to the Minister, *Boaz Brown, Gershom Heald, John Buttrick, Ephraim Hildreth,* Thomas Stevens, *Stephen Hall, Samuel Buttrick,* Joseph Freeman, *Joseph Darby,* Thomas Gates, and *Shadrach Hapgood*. Others were afterwards granted.

John Wetherby, Dec. 18, 1679.	Richard Whitney, jr. do.
Richard Whitney, sen. June 3, 1680.	Jabez Rutter, do.
James Wheeler, April 8, 1681.	Thomas Steevens, jr. June 17, 1684.
Moses Whitney, do.	Boaz Brown, jr. do.
Henry Rand, Jan. 13, 1682.	Samuel Hall, do.
Isaac Heald, Jan. do.	*Thomas Darby,* June 17, 1684.
Israel Heald, March 13, 1682.	Mark Perkins, Jan. 1, 1685.
Benj. Bosworth, Aug. 7, 1682.	Richard Burke, sen. March 1, 1686.
Thomas Ward, Oct. 24, 1682.	Roger Willis, do.

In 1653, Concord subscribed £5 a year for 7 years, for Harvard College. — Thomas Brooks was appointed in 1654, to carry the law to prevent drunkenness among the Indians into effect. — The selectmen petitioned to the County Court, in 1660, that sargeant Buss might keep an " ordinary " or tavern in Concord, they having " found much difficulty in procuring such an one as we could rest well satisfied in." — The town agreed in 1668, " that all the waste land should pay 2s 6d for every 100 acres for public charges." In 1672, seventeen articles of instruction were given to the selectmen by a committee, consisting of Nehemiah Hunt, John Flint, John Miles, William Hartwell, Thomas Wheeler, Joshua Brooks, Joseph Haywood, Gershom Brooks, Humphrey Barret, and John Billings; from which the following items are extracted: — " 3. That care be taken of the Books of Marters and other bookes, that belong to the Towne, that they be kept from abusive usage, and not be lent to persons more than one month at one time." — " 7. To take order that all corne fields be sufficiently fenced in season, the crane field and brickil field especially. — 8. That incorignment be given for the destroying of blackbirds and jaies." — " 11. To make a record of all the habitations that are priviledged with liberty at commons." — " 14. To take care that undesirable persons be not entertained ; so as to become inhabitants. — 15. To take care that persons do not overcharge their commons with cattle. — 16. That all persons that have taken the oath of fidelity be recorded."

Concord was presented in 1660 for not having a common house of entertainment, and ordered to get one before next Court under penalty of 2s 6d. Richard Temple recovered 20s damage of John Gobble for calling him a " Lying rascal."

Benj. Crane, Dec. 23, 1682.   Thomas Williams, do.
Joseph Wheeler, April 19, 1683.   Stephen Handell, March 10, 1686.
Jabez Brown, June 15, 1683.   Benj. Crane.

These were the original inhabitants of Stow. Those in Italics went from Concord.

CHAPTER IV.

PHILIP's WAR. — State of the Country. — Garrison Houses. — Expedition to Brookfield. — Proceedings of Government; and of the Town. — Lancaster burnt. — Christian Indians in Concord. - Feelings towards the Indians. — Abraham and Isaac Shepherd killed. — Groton burnt. — People remove to Concord. — Proceedings of Government. — Sudbury Fight. — Henchman's Letters. — Soldiers at Concord. — Christian Indian Soldiers. — War Taxes.

WE are now to record the events of a most interesting period in the history of New England, remarkable for the occurrence of the most distressing Indian war that ever desolated the country. Though Concord suffered little in comparison with many other towns, yet the part her citizens took in this war is deserving of particular notice.

At this time the number of warriors in the five nations of Indians in the immediate vicinity of the English settlements, as has been noticed in the commencement of this history, was estimated at about 1800; the whole number of English inhabitants in New England at 120,000; and the effective military force of the four United Colonies at 16,000; of which Massachusetts had nearly three fourths. She had twelve troops of cavalry of 60 men each. The county of Middlesex then contained 17 incorporated towns,[1] and its militia was embraced in one regiment. A majority of these towns were but recently settled by inhabitants living remote from each other, without even tolerably good roads to facilitate their intercourse.

Concord then contained a foot, and part of a horse company.[2] In 1654, an expedition had been undertaken by the United Colo-

---

[1] Charlestown, Watertown, Medford, Cambridge, Concord, Sudbury, Woburn, Reading, Malden, Lancaster, Chelmsford, Billerica, Groton, Marlborough, Dunstable, Mendon, and Sherburne. Worcester County was not incorporated till 1731.

[2] The former was organized in 1636, when Sergeant Willard was appointed to exercise it. He was appointed Captain in 1646, and promoted to be Major in 1654. In 1662, the County Court made the following appointments in this company. Timothy Wheeler, Captain; Joseph Wheeler, Lieut.; William Buss, Ensign; Richard Rice, Thomas Bateman, and Thomas Wheeler, sen. Sergeants; William Buttrick, Samuel Stratten, and John Scotchford, Corporals. The Horse Company was organized Oct. 13, 1669, embracing some soldiers in the adjoining towns. Thomas Wheeler

nies against Ninigret, principal Sachem of the Naraganset Indians, when 250 foot and 40 horsemen were raised and "sent fourth under the Christian and courageous Major Willard of Concord as commander in chief."[1] Several of the Concord troops accompanied him; and this was the first time that our early settlers were engaged in war.

At Wamesit (Lowell), Nashobah (easterly part of Littleton), Okommokamesit (Marlborough), and several other places near the frontier English settlements were incorporated Indian towns, containing in 1676 about 500 inhabitants, including women and children, who had ostensibly embraced Christianity, and were friendly to the whites. At length jealousies arose among the unfriendly Indians against these and against the English; and Philip, the bold chief of the Wampanoags at Mount Hope, determined to destroy their infant settlements, and exterminate the inhabitants. To aid him in this barbarous conspiracy, he endeavoured to obtain the alliance of all the neighbouring tribes; and in most instances he effected his designs.

The government ordered that garrison-houses should be erected in the several towns, or that dwelling-houses already built should be fortified, which were to serve as a kind of fortress into which the inhabitants, by districts or companies, might collect at night, or in case of an attack. Houses were also erected for the accommodation of military watches, which were maintained in each town to perform patrol duty, and forewarn the inhabitants of danger.

We have no other means than tradition to ascertain the number or situation of the garrison-houses in Concord. The house now occupied by Dr. Hurd was originally one; another stood near John Flint's; another near Meriam's corner; two others within the present limits of Bedford; another near John Hosmer's; and another near Silas Holden's. An Indian fort was built near Nashobah Hill in Littleton, then in Concord. These were not all. The number and situation varied, at different times, for the subsequent twenty years.

---

was appointed first Captain; Thomas Henchman, Lieut.; and Henry Woodhouse, Quarter Master. This was the second and western horse company in the county, and from it the present Concord Light Infantry descended.

[1] Mather's Relation, p. 69. See Hoyt, Antiquarian Researches, p. 70.

Though several acts of hostility had been committed in Plymouth Colony, the Nipmuck Indians, residing near the centre of the present limits of Worcester county, had not fully united with Philip in his blood-thirsty designs of extermination. And since some of these were Praying Indians, the government flattered themselves that they might be reclaimed and enlisted permanently on their side. Having professed friendship and promised fidelity to the English, a mission was sent forth to meet these Indians at Quabaug (Brookfield). Capt. Edward Hutchinson was commissioned to negotiate a treaty; and Capt. Thomas Wheeler of Concord, with 20 or 25 of his company, was ordered to go with him, as a guard, and to assist in the objects of the expedition. Two sons of old Robin Petuhanit of Grafton, Sampson and Joseph,[1] and George Memecho, three Christian Indians, accompanied them as guides and interpreters. They marched from Cambridge to Sudbury, 28th July, 1675; and arrived at Brookfield 1st August, when they found the Indians were assembled about 10 miles distant. Four messengers were sent to acquaint them with the intentions of the English, but an alarm was raised, and the Indians assumed a warlike attitude. The messengers endeavoured to convince the Sachems of their peaceful intentions; and they promised to meet the English the next morning a short distance from Brookfield. They doubted whether to proceed; yet, being urged to go by the inhabitants of Brookfield, they marched to the place assigned for holding the treaty. Finding no Indians there, the company continued their march, contrary to the advice of their guides, four or five miles further near to a swamp, when they were suddenly attacked by 200 or 300 Indians. Eight were killed by the first fire, and three wounded, among whom were Capt. Hutchinson and Capt. Wheeler. Capt. Wheeler had two horses shot under him, and received a ball through his body. Seeing this, his son, whose arm was then fractured by a ball, dismounted, and placed his wounded father upon his own horse; and himself mounting another whose rider had been killed, they both escaped. The surviving

---

[1] Sampson was afterwards killed near Wachusett. Joseph was taken and sold as a slave to go to the West Indies. His wife and two children, taken captive with him, were redeemed by the Rev. Mr. Eliot; and she was employed two years after to teach a school among the Indians at Concord. She is represented as being a very sober, Christian woman. Gookin's MS.

English retreated to Brookfield, and had scarcely entered the town, before it was set on fire in various places by the pursuing enemy. All the houses (20) were consumed excepting one, in which the inhabitants and the company were gathered. In this distressing situation, Capt. Wheeler appointed Lt. Simon Davis of Concord and two others to take the command, being disabled himself; and gave orders to Ephraim Curtis of Sudbury, and Henry Young of Concord, to proceed to Boston to give information of these lamentable occurrences to the Council. After two unsuccessful attempts to proceed, in which they were driven back by the Indians and Young was killed, Curtis escaped. On his arrival at Marlborough, he met Major Simon Willard and Capt. James Parker of Groton with 46 men, who had been despatched to scout between Marlborough, Lancaster, and Groton. On hearing of the sufferings of the people at Brookfield, he altered his course, and rushed on immediately to their relief. He arrived late in the evening of the 4th of August, just in time to save the lives of a few of the English, who still survived; when the engagement was renewed with vigor, and continued most of the night. Towards the morning of the 5th, the Indians were compelled to retreat. They lost 80 men killed and wounded. The inhabitants of Brookfield suffered the total loss of their houses and property. Twelve or fifteen of the English fell in this hard-fought battle, of whom Samuel Smeadly, Henry Young, and some others, belonged to Concord.[1]

A part of the company remained there on account of their wounds nearly a month; the remainder came away about a fortnight after the battle. "The 21st of October, 1675, was kept in Concord, by Capt. Wheeler and those who returned with him, as a day of praise and thanksgiving to God for their remarkable and safe re-

---

[1] The assertion first published by Rev. Mr. Fiske, and by many writers since, and recently with additions by the author of the History of Plymouth Colony, in relation to the conduct of Major Willard at Brookfield, in Aug. 1675, is entirely destitute of truth. He was in commission, in February and March, 1676, and in a letter from the secretary of the colony now before me, dated Feb. 11, 1676, he was requested "to be in a readiness if he should have a full command over the forces to be sent forth from this colony." He also received, just before his death in April, the highest number of votes but two in the choice of eighteen gentlemen for magistrates. These honors would not have been conferred, had the other assertion, resting *entirely* on tradition, been true.

turn, when the Rev. Edward Bulkeley preached a sermon to them from Psalm cxvi. 12: 'What shall I render to the Lord for all his benefits towards me?'"[1]

Though important services had been rendered to the country by the Praying Indians, yet such a great and indiscriminate prejudice had arisen among the common people against all natives, that the very name of Indian had become hateful. Under these circumstances the government passed an order, 30th August, 1675, to confine all the Praying Indians to five towns; and none were allowed to go a mile from any town under forfeiture of their lives. The same day, 15 of the Christian Indians were unjustly seized at Marlborough, and carried to Boston, bound neck to neck. They were confined in prison nearly a month before their trial, which resulted in their honorable acquittal. This was done by a captain without authority, but was a most unfortunate occurrence for the country, and the cause of much of the subsequent trouble.[2]

In October, 1675, the government ordered that the militia of Suffolk and Middlesex be "put in a posture of war; and be ready to march at a minute's warning to prevent danger;" and at the same time authority was given to Capt. Timothy Wheeler "to impress an able gunsmith to repair to Concord to be resident there for the fixing up of arms from time to time during the war for this and the towns adjacent." "Committees of militia," somewhat resembling the committees of safety in the revolution of 1775, were appointed in the several towns. The Hon. Peter Bulkeley was chairman of that committee in Concord. He and Joseph Dudley were appointed in November to "attend the forces that are now to go forth against the enemy, and to be ministers unto them."

About the last of November, the Nashobah Indians removed to Concord; and December 13th, Major Willard, the Rev. Mr. Eliot, and Major Gookin, were appointed to order their settlement. They

---

[1] A narrative of this expedition, written by Capt. Wheeler, was published, from which the foregoing facts are principally taken. It was reprinted, with notes, by John Farmer, Esq. in Vol. II. of the N. Hamp. Hist. Coll. from the original edition in the library of the Essex Historical Society, where may also be found a copy of Mr. Bulkeley's Sermon above alluded to.

[2] The assertion of many writers, that these Indians were suspected of treachery, does not appear true after reading Gookin's MS. account of this affair.

were placed under the care and superintendence of Mr. John Hoar, "the only man in Concord," says Gookin, "who was willing to do it. He was compensated by being exempted from impressment and taxation. They had pitched their wigwams on his ground near his house. This man was very loving to them, and very diligent and careful to promote their good, and to secure the English from any fear or danger by them."[1] The excitement generally was so great, that the Natick Indians had been previously carried to Deer Island for fear of being attacked by the English.

From this time depredations continued to be frequently committed by the unfriendly Indians on the frontier settlements; and notwithstanding the precautions of the government, the friendly Indians occasionally suffered unjustly from the enmity of the whites. Companies of soldiers were often sent for the relief of these suffering towns, in which Concord was usually represented.[2]

On the first of February, 1676, the Indians burnt the house of Thomas Eames of Framingham, and £330 12s. worth of property, and either killed or carried into captivity his wife and nine children. The next day orders were given to Major Willard to raise a party of troops to scour the country between Groton, Lancaster, and Marlborough. Similar orders were given to Major Gookin in relation to the country between Marlborough and Medfield. Intelligence was brought to Major Gookin, Feb. 9th, at 10 o'clock (evening), by Job Kettenanet, one of the Christian Indians who had been sent out as spies, that 400 of the enemy were at Menemese, and had already marched forth intending to burn Lancaster the next day. He immediately sent orders to Marlborough, Concord, and Lancaster, mustering forces for the defence of Lancaster forth-

---

[1] Gookin's MS.

[2] Soldiers often volunteered on these occasions. When they could not be obtained in this manner, they were impressed into the service. Precepts were issued by the committees of militia in the several towns to the constable; and none were freed from his arbitrary will, except by a special act of the government. Nathaniel Pierce, with several others, of Concord, were pressed in September, 1675, went to Springfield, and continued in the service nearly a year, till they were thus liberated. Daniel Adams belonged to a party which went from Concord to Groton when that town was destroyed. He fired from Willard's garrison and killed an Indian. It is impossible, however, to ascertain the names of all those who were engaged in this bloody war; but it is said that nearly all the able-bodied men bore arms in defence of their homes, at some time during this conflict.

with; and 40 soldiers were collected and marched from Marlborough under Capt. Wadsworth by break of day. But notwithstanding they succeeded in getting possession of one of the garrisons, they could not prevent the Indians from carrying their threats into execution. Lancaster then contained about 50 families, out of which the Indians killed and captured forty persons. Among the latter were Mrs. Rowlandson and her children, the family of the minister. By the bold and successful exertions of Mr. John Hoar of Concord, in connexion with Tom Doublet, and Peter Conaway, Christian Indians of Concord, they were subsequently redeemed from captivity. Hubbard says the Indians burnt a house and murdered three persons in Concord, on the 19th of February, but who they were I know not.

About the 21st of Feb., says Gookin in the manuscript before quoted, "there befel another great trouble to the Christian Indians of Nashobah, who sojourned in Concord. The Council had by several orders empowered a committee, who, with consent of the selectmen of Concord, settled those Indians at that town, under the government and tuition of Mr. John Hoar. The number of those Indians was about 58 of all sorts, whereof were not above 12 able men, the rest were women and children. These Indians lived very soberly and quietly and industriously, and were all unarmed, neither could any of them be charged with any unfaithfulness to the English interest. In pursuance of this settlement, Mr. Hoar had begun to build a large and convenient work-house for the Indians, near his own dwelling, which stood about the midst of the town, and very nigh the town watch-house. This house was made, not only to secure those Indians under lock and key by night, but to imploy them and set them to work by day, whereby they earned their own bread; and in an ordinary way (with God's blessing) would have lived well in a short time. But some of the inhabitants of the town, being influenced with a spirit of animosity and distaste against all Indians, disrelished this settlement, and therefore privately sent to a captain of the army [probably Capt. Mosely], that quartered his company not far off at that time, of whom they had experience that he would not be backward to put in execution any thing that tended to distress the Praying Indians. For this was the same man that had formerly without order seized upon divers of the Praying Indians at Marlborough, which brought much trouble, and disquiet to the country of the Indians, and was a great occasion of their defection. This captain accordingly came to Concord with a party of his men upon the Sabbath day into the meeting-house, where the people were convened in the worship of God. And after the exercise was ended, he spake openly to the congregation to this effect, " that he understood, there were some heathen in the town committed to one Hoar, which, he was informed, were a trouble and disquiet to them; therefore if they desired it he would remove them to Boston." To which speech of his, most of the people being silent, except two or three that encouraged him, he took, as it seems, the silence of the rest for consent, and immediately after the assembly were dismissed, he went with three or four files of men, and a hundred or two of the people, men, women, and children at their heals, and marched away to Mr. Hoar's house; and there demanded of him to see the Indians under his care. Hoar opened the door and showed them to him, and they were all numbered and found there. The captain then said to Mr. Hoar, that he would have a corporal and soldiers to secure them; but Mr. Hoar answered there was no need of that for they were already secured, and were committed to him by order of the Council, and he would keep and secure them. But yet the captain left his corporal and soldiers there, who were abusive enough to the poor Indians by ill language. The next morning the captain came again to take the Indians, and send them to Boston. But Mr. Hoar refused to deliver them unless he showed an order of the Council; but the captain could show him no other but his commission to kill and destroy the enemy. Mr. Hoar said these were friends and under order; but the captain would not be satisfied with his answer, but commanded his corporal forthwith to break open the door, and take the Indians all away, which was done accordingly; and some of the soldiers plundered the poor creatures of their shirts, shoes, dishes, and such other things as they could lay their hands upon, though the captain commanded the contrary. They were all brought to Charlestown with a guard of twenty men. And the captain wrote a letter to the General Court, then sitting, giving them an account of his action. This thing was very offensive to the Council, that a private captain should (without commission or some express order) do an act so contradictory to their former orders, and the governor and several others spake of it at a conference with the deputies at the General Court, manifesting their dissatisfaction at this great irregularity in setting up a military power in opposition to the chief authority of the country, declaring of what evil consequence such a precedent was, instancing the evil effects of like practices in England in later times, urging that due testimony might be borne against the same, by the whole court. The deputies seemed generally to agree to the reason of the magistrates in this matter, yet, notwithstanding, the captain (who appeared in the Court shortly after upon another occasion) met with no rebuke for this high irregularity and arbitrary action. To conclude this matter, those poor Indians, about 58 of them of all sorts, were sent down to Deer Island, there to pass into the furnace of affliction with their brethren and countrymen. But all their corn and other provision, sufficient to maintain them for 6 months, was lost at Concord, and all their other necessaries except what the soldiers had plundered. And the poor Indians got very little or nothing of what they lost, but it was squandered away, lost by the removal of Mr. Hoar, and other means, so that they were necessitated to live upon clams as the others did, with some little corn provided at the charge of the Honorable Corporation for the Indians, residing in London. Besides, Mr. Hoar lost all his building and other cost, which he had provided for the entertainment and employment of those Indians, which was considerable."

It appears from a manuscript letter of Mr. Hoar in my possession, that the English were very insolent to the Indians, and threatened to destroy them. One of the Lancaster soldiers, stationed at Concord, snapped his gun three times at one of them while standing at Mr. Hoar's door. It is believed, however, that this prejudice existed rather among the soldiers, who had witnessed the horrid barbarities of the Indians in other places, and who did not distinguish justly between the friends and enemies of the English, than among the citizens generally. By the influence of this class of men, the unfortunate occurrences detailed above were brought about.

About the middle of February, Abraham and Isaac Shepherd were killed near Nashobah in Concord village, while threshing grain in their barn. Apprehensive of danger, says tradition, they placed their sister Mary, a girl about fifteen years old, on a hill a little distance off to watch and forewarn them of the approach of an enemy. She was, however, suddenly surprised and captured, and her brothers were slain. She was carried captive into the Indian settlements, but with great heroism made her escape. While the Indians were asleep in the night, probably under the influence of spirituous liquors, she seized a horse, which they had a few days before stolen at Lancaster, took a saddle from under the head of her Indian keeper, mounted, swam across the Nashua river, and rode through the forest to her home.[1]

On the 15th of February, a party attacked Joseph Parker of Chelmsford with his friends, who had been to visit Major Willard. The latter part of this month they burnt Medfield, and killed 20 of the inhabitants; and on the 13th of March nearly all of Groton was reduced to ashes. Major Willard was engaged in this battle.[2] A company from Concord, and another from Watertown were also there. March 10th, says Hubbard, a man going after hay was killed in Concord.

March 14th, the Council ordered " that the committees of militia of Concord and Sudbury, doe forthwith impress so many carts as may bee sufficient to bring off the goods and provisions belonging to the people left at Lancaster, unto Concord or any other towne, they desire to come unto; and for guarding the said carts it is ordered that Sargant Lamson, commander of the garrison soldiers at Lancaster, do send two files of soldiers, to guard the said carts up and down." Besides the inhabitants of Lancaster, several of Groton and other frontier towns resided in Concord till after the peace. The proprietors of Groton held a meeting here, Dec. 12, 1677, when many of them bound themselves to rebuild the town. They commenced the next year.

The government of the colony, justly apprehensive of the dangerous condition of the frontier towns, appointed a committee on

---

[1] Hubbard. Foster's Century Sermon, p. 25.

[2] Major Willard and his company remained there several days. They were ordered, on the 16th, if they had " issued that business of Groaten, at least done what you can, and no likelihood of your reaching or engageing the enemy, that you with your forces thereabout keep so scouting or ranging towards Marlborough, as may seasonably give present relief and further prevent what increase may be." Colony Files.

the 15th of March, consisting of Capt. Hugh Mason of Watertown, Jonathan Danforth of Cambridge, and Richard Lowdon, to consider the best means to be provided for their safety. After consulting " the several towns in the county of Middlesex with reference to the best means for the preservation of our out-towns, remote houses, and farms," they submitted the following propositions, March 28th, which were approved.

"1. That the towns of Sudbury, Concord, and Chelmsford be strengthened with forty men a piece, which said men are to be improved in scouting between town and town, who are to be commanded by men of prudence, courage, and interest in the said townes: and the parties in each towne are to be ordered to keep together in some place comodious in the said towns, and not in garison houses: and these men to bee upon the charge of the country.

"2. That for the security of Billerica there be a garrison of a number competent at Waymesett [Lowell], who may raise a thousand bushels of corn upon the land of the Indians in that place; and may be improved daily in scouting and ranging the woods between Waymesett and Andover, and on the west of Concord river on the east and north of Chelmsford, which will discover the enemy before he comes to the towns, and prevent lurking Indians about our towns. Also they shall be in readiness to the sucor of any of the three towns at any time when in distress; also shall be ready to joine with others to follow the enemie upon a sudden after their appearing.

"3. That such towns as Lancaster, Groton, and Marlborough, that are forced to remove; and have not some advantage of settlement (peculiar) in the Bay, be ordered to settle at the frontier towns that remain for their strengthening: and the people of the said towns to which they are appointed are to see to their accomodations in the said towns.

"4. That the said towns have their own men returned, that are abroad, and their men freed from impress during their present state.

"5. That there be appointed a select number of persons in each town of Middlesex, who are, upon any information of the distress of any town, forthwith to repair to the relief thereof; and that such information may be seasonable, the towns are to dispatch posts, each town to the next, till notice be conveyed over the whole country, if need be."

Another subject is embraced in the report from which the above is extracted. The committee were instructed to consider the propriety of erecting a "line of stockadoes or stone worke" across the county, to include Chelmsford, Concord, Sudbury, and the other most populous places; but they deemed this inexpedient, on account of the length of way to be fortified, the difficulty of crossing ponds and rivers, the peculiar season of the year, and the scarcity of laborers. For these and several other reasons the project was abandoned. It would indeed have been a work of no small magnitude to erect such a barrier as would have been effectual against the incursion of savages. A line of garrison-houses was, however, erected on the frontiers of all these towns; and it is probable that in fixing upon the location of the Christian Indian towns before the war, reference might have been had to the safety of the English in case of danger. They served, says Gookin, as a "wall of defence."

The month of April witnessed other horrible events to this county. Having destroyed most of the remote towns, the Indians looked to those remaining, and formed a determination to destroy them also. At this time they collected in great numbers, and approached nearest to Boston; and the colonists were called upon to make the most vigorous defence. On the 21st of April an alarm was spread abroad that a large number of Indians, said to be 1500, were about to attack Sudbury. They had already burned several houses,[1] and the day before killed Thomas Plympton, and a Mr. Boon and his son, returning from the west part of the town, where the former had been to bring the two latter to a garrison-house.[2] A company from Watertown, aided by several of the citizens, had attacked them on the east side of Concord river; where a severe battle was fought, and they were compelled to retreat across it. At this time several of the citizens of Concord immediately went to their relief. Arriving near the garrison-house of Walter Haynes,[3] they observed several squaws, who, as they drew near, danced, shouted, powwawed, and used every method to amuse and decoy them. Eleven of the English pursued and attacked them, but

---

[1] Gookin's MS.   [2] Tradition.   [3] Ibid.

found themselves, too late, in an ambuscade, from which a large number of Indians rushed upon and attacked them with great fury. Notwithstanding they made a bold resistance, it was desperate, and ten of them were slain. The other escaped to the garrison, where the neighbouring inhabitants had fled for security, which was bravely defended.[1] Of those who were killed at this time belonging to Concord, I have been able to ascertain the names of five only, — James Hosmer, Samuel Potter, John Barnes, Daniel Comy, and Joseph Buttrick.

Capt. Samuel Wadsworth of Milton was then at Marlborough, having been left there to strengthen the frontiers on the return of the army from the interior. Understanding the situation of Sudbury, he marched with 32 soldiers to its relief. Capt. Broclebank, whose quarters had been at Marlborough, also accompanied him as a convoy to Boston, where he was intending to go to communicate with the Council. They marched in the night, and fell into an ambuscade early in the morning, when all but a few, who escaped to a mill, were slain. These unfortunate soldiers were buried the next day, principally by a company of Christian Indians, who had been organized and sent out the day before by direction of the English under Capt. Hunting from Charlestown. Four dead Indians only were found.[2]

---

[1] Tradition.

[2] It will be perceived that these statements differ somewhat from Hubbard, and particularly in the date. He places it on the 18th, while Gookin in the MS. from which I have extracted, says it was the 21st. I had been led to adopt the same date previous to seeing that MS. Judge Sewall's MS. Journal says: "Friday about 3 o'clock in the afternoon, April 21, 1676, Capt. Wadsworth, and Capt. Broclebank fall — about 50 men slain 3 miles off Sudbury — the said town burnt — except garrison-houses." The Middlesex Records, in speaking of the settlement of James Hosmer's estate, have this expression: "Being slayene in the engagement with the Indians at Sudbury on the 21st of the second month [April] in the year 1676." The order of the Council on the 22d of April affords presumptive evidence that the unfortunate loss of the Concord party was on the same day, though Hubbard does not positively assert it. The Roxbury Records say: "Samuel Gardner, John Roberts, Nathaniel Seaver, Thomas Hawley, sen., Wm. Cheaver, Joseph Pepper, John Sharp, Thomas Hopkins, Lieut. Samuel Gardner, slain by the Indians at Sudbury under command of Samuel Wadsworth, April 27, 1676. This was probably the day of entry, or a mistake for 21st.

From this time, which was more propitious to the Indians than any other, their success gradually diminished. This battle was the turning point. The principal body of the Indians, however, tarried in the vicinity of Groton, Lancaster, and Marlborough, whence they could easily make incursions to annoy the English.

On the 22d of April, the Council ordered 40 troopers out of Suffolk, under command of Cornet Jacob Eliot; and the same number from Middlesex under Major Gookin, to march forthwith to Sudbury to make discovery, whether "the motion of the enemy be either toward Concord or Medfield," by visiting the bounds of those towns, and scouting through the woods. An attack on Concord had been expected,[1] and this was one of the effectual means which were promptly taken to prevent it.

On the 26th, six cart-loads of provisions were sent by the government to Concord, and John Flint was appointed commissary to take charge of them. The commander-in-chief engaged to be there the next day, making that his place of rendezvous. The following original letter addressed to Gov. Leverett is deemed worthy of publication.

"*Concord, April* 29, 1676.

"Hon'd Sir. — By reason that I had not a guide to go with me, it was yesterday in the forenoon ere I reached this place, where I found a few men; but ere night, all the commanders, and most of the soldiers that yet appeare, were come up with the provision. This day we rendezvoused and find a great defect, an account of which is here inclosed. Upon receipt of the Hon. Major Gen.'l's letter, I have by advice of the commanders, as well for the ease of this town as the securing of as many as we can at present, ordered Capt. Sill to Chelmsford, Capt. Haughthorn to Bilrica, and Capt. Holbrook to abide here,

---

[1] Tradition has handed down the following anecdote. A consultation among the Indian chiefs took place about this time on the high lands in Stow, and, as they cast their eyes toward Sudbury and Concord, a question arose which they should attack first. The decision was made to attack the former. One of the principal chiefs said — "We no prosper, if we go to Concord — the Great Spirit love that people — the evil spirit tell us not to go — they have a great man there — he *great pray!*" The Rev. Edward Bulkeley was then minister of the town, and his name and distinguished character were known even to the red men of the forest.

and proportioned the horse accordingly; and am going myself to Chelmsford about some Indians to be ready in order to what is in my instructions, and shall wait for further orders as commander. I have not yet taken any of our provision, supposing it to be for us when in motion; but it is expected by the inhabitants that we should spend thereof. I crave directions herein. Some things is much wanting and desired by the captains to be sent for, viz. flynts, tobacco, liquor, pipes. There is but 29 that appeareth of my troop, and not above 7 carbines among them. I desire there may be a supply thereof; as also a saddle and case of pistols for myself; having here borrowed a saddle and left the tree and skinn that was pressed for me. Colours wanting also for the troop and one company, and a trumpeter. Not any appearance of the 30 Norfolkmen. It is desired that some more of the Indians may be sent to us, hearing them at Chemsford are fortifying about a fishing-place there. A chyrurgeon with medicaments is much expected also a minister; the which I hope may be procured here. All the commanders, officers, and souldiers, express much cheerfullness, and have hopes that the defects will be made up; that we may be in a better capacity to serve the country. I shall not further inlarge, but to begg your honors prayers for us. Remaining, Hon. S'r. your. humble servant.

D. Henchman."

May 5th, the court addressed a letter to the Indians, requesting them to meet the English at Concord or Boston, to find out their wishes, and try to effect a peace. Concord was now a distinguished military post, and the centre of many of the operations against the enemy.[1]

The detachments of soldiers for the relief of the frontier towns were frequent and heavy in May. Early in that month 80 from the troops of Essex, Suffolk, and Middlesex, were ordered to repair to Concord for the country service. On the 20th, 270 garrison soldiers from the same counties, were ordered to be stationed at the following " frontier towns for the better secu-

---

[1] "May 12th, goodwife Devens, and goodwife Kether, upon ransom being paid, came into Concord; and upon like ransom presented, John Morse of Groton, and Left. Carter of Lancaster were set at liberty; and more without ransom, as goodman Emery, and his little boy."

Rev. Mr. Cobbet's letter in the Mather papers.

rity of them from the incursions of the enemy." Concord 20, Sudbury 30, Chelmsford 20, Billerica 20, Andover 20, Haverhill 20, Bradford 10, Exeter 20, Medfield 30, Dedham 20, Milton 10, Braintree 15, Weymouth 15, Hingham 20. These soldiers were to be maintained at the cost of the several towns, and to be under the direction of the committees of militia.

Maj. Daniel Gookin succeeded Major Willard after his death in April, in command of the military forces in Middlesex; Thomas Clark was commander in Suffolk, and Daniel Denison in Essex; all of whom were in Concord, May 30th. The following letter was addressed to Gov. Leverett.

"*Concord, June* 2, 1676.

"Hon. Sir, — I did hope with this to send up all the returns but have yet received only Capt. Pools here enclosed. The Major Gen'l was even wearied out about them; and two Capts. beside myself still labouring under the toile. My Lt. gave his, as he tells me, to the Maj : Gen : the rest I shall dispatch. The reason of our stay here for two days Mr. Clark who is now going to Boston will make known, and what is now in hand, being by the unanimous advice of a council of war, and hopefull. Capt. Holbrook's return, received while writing, is also inclosed by

S'r Y'r Hon.'s humble servant,

D. HENCHMAN."

Capt. Joseph Sill [1] commanded one of the companies which were at Concord several months, and was frequently sent out on scouts. His list was returned with those stated in the above letter.

Letter from the Council to Capt. Henchman, dated June 10, 1676.

"Capt. Henchman, — The bearer, John Hunter, with ten Indians was intended a scout for Concord, but, through his much importunity and our persuasion of his capacity and intention upon the service, he is dispatched to the enemy, and in lieu of him and his party we send ten Indians to Concord, for the scout service, and if possible to attempt something upon Philip. In marching upward with him are several sachems, but few fighting men, and having

---

[1] This officer was afterwards sent to the Eastward against the Indians. See Belknap, Hist. N. H. vol. i. p. 75.

planted at Pacacheog and Quabadge, they will scarce depart thence. Deal kindly with Hunter, and as much as may be satisfy him. His spleen seems to be such against Philip, that we are persuaded of his resolution against him."

About this time Capt. Henchman and his company left Concord. In a letter to the Council, dated Marlborough, 11th June, he says, "Some Indian scouts sent out this day have brought in Capt. Thom, his daughter, and two children, being found about ten miles to the soudest of this place. There was more of them, viz: two that were gone a fishing, so not lighted of. This company with some others at other places, of which James Prenter [1] is one, did as they say leave the enemy by times in the spring with an intent to come in to the English, but dare not for fear of our scouts. These prisoners say that many of the enemy hereing that there was like to be a treaty with Samuel did intend to go in to him. Mr. Scott also coming from Concord yesterday informs me, that one of the old squaws there doth not question but that if shee may have liberty to go to Samuel, he and his company will come in to the English."

There had been a company of 80 Christian Indians, friends to the English, who had acted as spies, messengers, scouts, and soldiers during the war, whose officers were Capt. Andrew Pittimee, one of the owners of Concord Village; Quanahpohkit, *alias* James Rumney Marsh; John Magus; and James Speen. On the 1st of June, they petitioned for the release of "Capt Thom, his son Nehemiah, his wife and two children, John Uktuck, his wife and children, Waanum and her child," who were prisoners of war. The women and children were released, but the others were executed. "Capt. Thom," say the minutes of their trial, "was not only an instigator to others, over whom he was made a captain, but also was actually present and an actor in the devastations of some of our plantations." [2] Companies were sent

---

[1] Is he not the same who is mentioned by Thomas, in his History of Printing?

[2] Strict regard was paid to the rights of friendly Indians by the government. On the 6th of August, 3 squaws, and 3 children, were killed while picking whortleberries on a hill in Watertown, now in Lincoln. Two persons were executed for this murder.

"Sept. 21, 1671, Stephen Gobble of Concord was executed for the murder of Indians. Three Indians for firing Eame's house and murder. The

from this town towards Connecticut river in pursuit of Philip; and after traversing the country in various directions for nearly two months without finding him, they proceeded towards Rhode Island, where, with the assistance of some other troops who joined them, they killed and captured 150 Indians.[1] These and other instances of success encourged the English, and calmed the fury of the savages. After a year's absence Philip, reduced to a miserable condition, returned to his native place, near which he was killed, Aug. 12, 1676. One of his own men, whom he had offended, and who had deserted to the English, shot him through the heart. His death put an end to this most horrid and distressing war.

About 3000 warriors were combined for the destruction of New England, and the war terminated with their entire defeat, and almost total extinction. About 600 of the English inhabitants, the greatest part of whom were the flower and strength of the country, either fell in battle or were murdered by the enemy. Twelve or thirteen towns were destroyed and about 600 houses burned.[2]

A tax was made this year for the support of the war from which the following items are extracted.[3] In consequence of the losses sustained by Concord and Sudbury, their taxes were abated, Concord having £50 abated in May, 1676, and Sudbury £40.

Boston	£ 300 0 0	Lancaster	£11 16 0
Charlestown	180 0 0	Woburn	25 18 1
Watertown	45 0 0	Marlborough	17 13 0
Cambridge	42 2 0	Chelmsford	14 18 0
Concord	33 19 1	Billerica	14 7 0
Sudbury	20 0 0	Groton	11 10 0

---

weather was cloudy and rawly cold, though little or no rain. Mr. Mighil prayed. 4 others set on the the gallows — two men and 2 impudent women; one of which laughed on the gallows, as many testified."

"Sept. 26, 1676, Sagamore Sam goes, and Daniel Gobble is drawn in a cart upon bed-clothes to execution. One-ey'd John, Maliompe, Sagamore of Quaboag, gen'l at Lancaster &c. Jethro (the father) walked to the gallows. One-ey'd John accuses Sag. John to have fired the first gun at Quaboag and killed Capt. Hutchinson." Sewall's MS. Journal.

[1] Hubbard. [2] Trumbull, vol. i. p. 350; Holmes's, Annals of America, i. 384. [3] Colony Records.

On the 22d of Jan. 1677, the government made allowance to the people distressed by the war in Massachusetts; and allotted to the selectmen of the several towns in proportion to their losses, out of the "Irish Charity," in "meal, oatmeal, wheat, malt at 18s. per ball, butter 6d. and cheese 4d. per pound." In the list accompanying this order the following towns appear.[1]

Towns.	Families.	Persons.	Amount.	Towns.	Families.	Persons.	Amount.
Charlestown	29	102	£15 6	Sudbury	12	48	£7 8
Watertown	19	76	11 8	Woburn	8	43	6 9
Cambridge	14	61	9 3	Billerica	1	4	0 12
Concord	18	72	10 16	Boston	125	432	66 6

CHAPTER V.

Year 1684 important. — Bloods' Farms annexed to Concord. — The Ffty subsequent Years. — Lovewell's Fight. — Cuba Expedition. — French War. — Notices of various Services in the War. — Divisions in the Town and Incorporation of new Towns. — Emigration to other Places.

THE events just detailed reduced the number of the Indians, and prepared the way for the more safe and peaceable settlement of remote towns. Most of the temporary residents in Concord removed to other places, but some became permanent settlers here; and the population had increased. The Prescots, Lees, Minots, Whittemores, Wilsons, &c. who settled here between 1675 and 1700, were subsequently distinguished in the town.

The year 1684 was a time of great distress in the colony. The people were told that the titles to their lands were forfeited with their charter, and now belonged to the king. Under this pretence they were called upon to take out new patents for their lands, subject to such fines as should be imposed; and writs of ejectment were brought against such as refused to put them out of their possession. This was tyranny with a witness![2] — Under these circumstances the depositions and deeds from the Indians already given, were obtained.[3]

---

[1] The whole list is published in the N. H. Hist. Coll. vol. iii. pp. 102, 103.
[2] Murray vol. i. p. 144.   [3] See page. 7, 8, 41, 42.

Some difficulties having arisen between the town of Concord and Robert Blood, sen. respecting the payment of civil and ecclesiastical dues, an agreement was made, on the 17th of March, 1685, between him and the Hon. Peter Bulkeley, Henry Woodhouse, and John Smeadly, sen. in behalf of the town, by which Bloods' Farms, now comprising a large part of the present town of Carlisle, were annexed to Concord. This agreement, an extract of which is given below, was assented to by Robert Blood, jun. and Simon Blood, sons of Robert Blood. It specifies:—

"1. That the said Robert, his heirs and assignes, living within any peculiar, shall be from time to time freed and exempted from all town offices, and also from town rates (except what concerns the repairing of the meeting-house or building upon that account) provided the said Robert, his heirs and assignes, have no benefit or profit accruing to them from the said town rates.

"2. That in rates for the ministry the said Robert, his heirs and assignes, living within any peculiar (as aforesaid) shall bee exempted from the duty laid on waste land, and that in other respects the said Robert, his heirs and assignes, shall pay to the ministry according to the rule and custom of the said town.

"3. That the said Robert, his heirs and assignes, shall (at the charge of the said town) as occasion doth require, have highways according to law laid out for them in order to their convenient passing to and from the said town.

"4. That the said Robert, his heirs and assignes, shall have meet places assigned to them in the meeting-house of the said town."

These proceedings distinguish the period from 1684 to 1686 as very important in the history of the town. From this time its jurisdiction extended over a large territory, including the original purchase, the "Village, or New Grant," part of Littleton, and Bloods' and Willard's farms; which was continued till the incorporation of other towns in which parts of this territory were included.

During the fifty subsequent years few important events mark the history of the town. The generation who first emigrated from England had nearly all departed, and others taken their places; but with habits and education somewhat different from their fathers and peculiar to their own period. Compelled to labor hard to supply their own necessities, parents had little time or ability to educate their children, and the people generally were, in consequence, less enlightened than the first settlers. More signed legal instruments by their *marks* at this than at any other period. Their history (and such is the history of the country generally) exhibits this as the *dark age* of New England. Superstition and supposed witchcraft now prevailed. Concord, however, was not a bewitched town; it never took a part in that horrible delusion. The increase in numbers, wealth, and intellectual improvement of the people, was subsequently slow, but progressive.

The government was under the direction of the arbitrary Sir Edmund Andros from 1687 to 1689. He became so unpopular, however, that the people, assembling in Boston in April, 1689, seized and confined him. A company went from Concord under Lieut. John Heald. In this state of affairs the wishes of the people, in relation to the government, were solicited, and Concord voted, May 22, " for the old authority chosen and sworn in the year 1686, with the deputies then chosen and sent to the Court to resume their places." The new province charter was soon after obtained.

A large number of men from Concord took a part in the wars of William and Mary and of Queen Anne, and in the various expeditions against the Indians from 1688 to 1740; and many died. But our printed and manuscript histories of those times are so imperfect, that I am unable to state the extent of the services they rendered, or the names of many of the sufferers.

Capt. Joseph Bulkeley with a company of 51 soldiers, chiefly from Concord, was engaged at Groton, Lancaster, and other frontier towns in 1704. Penhallow remarks that " Capt. Prescott, Bulkeley, and Willard, with their companies, were so vigorous in pursuing the enemy that they put them all to flight." The account of provisions furnished to this company mentions among others the names of " Mr. Choat, Dr. Simon Davis," and several Indians.

Dunstable, Groton, Lancaster, and other frontier towns, were often attacked by the Indians from 1694 to 1712, and many of the inhabitants were killed or carried into captivity. Sometimes they extended their incursions to Chelmsford and Sudbury. Maj. Tyng was wounded by them in 1711 between Groton and Concord, and came to the latter town, where he died. It was necessary at all times to maintain scouts, garrison-houses, and forts to protect the inhabitants. Some of the citizens of Concord were constantly employed in this manner. Nothing, however, is known to have occurred of much interest to the inhabitants till 1725.

One of the most fierce and obstinate battles in the annals of Indian warfare was fought May 8, 1725, at Pigwacket, near Fryeburg, on Saco river. The Indians in that vicinity had become troublesome; and rewards were offered for their scalps. Capt. Lovewell with a company of men had killed 10 of them, and received at Boston £100 each for their scalps. Encouraged by this success, he organized another company of 47 men to attack the villages of Pigwacket. They marched from Dunstable, April 16th. After proceeding to Ossipee pond, they built a fort. Benjamin Kidder, being taken sick, was left there, and also William Ayer, surgeon of the company, Nathaniel Woods, Zachariah Parker, John Goffe, Isaac Whitney, Obadiah Asten, and some others; and were not in the battle. Thirty-three proceeded on; and when they arrived near a point of land extending into Saco pond, they were attacked; and during a most desperate battle 15 of them were killed, or mortally wounded; 9 others were wounded, but were able to march. Paugus, the bold Indian chief, was killed by John Chamberlain under circumstances of bravery, which have consigned their names, to the lasting rememberance of posterity.

The following are the names of this company.[1] From *Dunstable*, Capt. *John Lovewell; Lieutenants, † Josiah Farwell and * Jonathan Robbins; Ensign, * John Harwood; Sergeants, ‡ Noah Johnson, * Robert Usher, and ‡ Samuel Whiting. — From *Andover*, † Jonathan Frye, Chaplain. — From *Weston*, Sergeant * Jacob Fullam. — From *Nutfield*, Corporal Edward Lynnfield. — From *Woburn*, Ensign Seth Wyman, Thomas Richardson, ‡ Timothy Richardson, * Ichabod Johnson, ‡ Josiah Johnson. — From Concord, ‡ Eleazer Davis, * Josiah Davis, ‡ Josiah Jones, David Melvin, Eleazer Melvin, * Jacob Farrar, and Joseph Farrar. — From *Billerica*, * Jonathan Kittridge and ‡ Solomon Kies. — From *Groton*, * John Jefts, * Daniel Woods, * Thomas Woods, ‡ John Chamberlain, † Elias Barron, ‡ Isaac Lakin, and Joseph Gilsom. — And from *Haverhill*, Ebenezer Ayer and Abiel Asten.

---

[1] I have prefixed an * to those who were killed on the spot; a † to the wounded and lost on the way; and a ‡ to the other wounded.

A remnant of the company returned by the fort and arrived in Dunstable, May 15th. Four others, Davis, Jones, Fry, and Farwell, were left behind to endure the most excruciating suffering. After waiting several days, expecting that some one would return to their assistance, they proceeded on, though their wounds had become putrid and offensive, and they themselves nearly exhausted by hunger. After travelling several miles Fry was left and lost. Farwell was also lost a few miles from the fort. Eleazer Davis, after being out 14 days, came in to Berwick. He was wounded in the abdomen, and the ball lodged in his body. He also had his right hand shot off. A tradition says, that arriving at a pond with Lieut. Farwell, Davis pulled off one of his moccasins, cut it in strings on which he fastened a hook, caught some fish, fried, and ate them. They refreshed him, but were injurious to Farwell, who died soon after. Josiah Jones, another of the four, was wounded with a ball, which lodged in his body. After being out 14 days, in hourly expectation of perishing, he arrived at Saco, "emaciated and almost dead from the loss of blood, the putrefaction of his wounds, and the want of food. He had subsisted on the spontaneous vegetables of the forest; and cranberries, which he had eaten, came out of wounds he had received in his body."[1] This is said to have been the case with Davis. He recovered, but became a cripple. Davis, Jones, Johnson, and several others of the unfortunate sufferers in this company, and their widows, were pensioners on the Province many years; and the Journals of the General Court show that they were treated with liberality. The township of Pembroke, N. H., originally Suncook, was granted them for their services, on the petition of David Melvin and 30 others, in 1729.[2]

War was declared by Great Britain against Spain in Oct. 23, 1739, and the next year the expedition against Cuba was undertaken. The inhabitants of the colonies were invited to embark in it. In presenting the subject to the General Court, and urging preparations to be made for 1000 men, Gov. Belcher said, "it would open

---

[1] Smith's Journal. pp. 141, 142.

[2] Some of these facts, beautifully dressed up in fiction, in which Chamberlain is erroneously said to be from New Hampshire, were published in the Philadelphia "Album," in 1828. Another paper, describing the enmity of young Paugus towards Chamberlain, was published in "The Atlantic

a more extensive, rich, and beneficial trade for ourselves in the West Indies than we have yet enjoyed." This, and the promise of booty, and lands in Cuba, as bounties to individual soldiers, and expectations of being settled there, were the most plausible reasons for engaging in this most unfortunate enterprise. Though the General Court treated the wishes of the governor rather coolly, yet five companies of 100 men each were raised, and put under the command of Captains John Prescott of Concord, David Goffe, Thomas Phillips, George Stuart, and John Winslow. The governor himself paid the expenses of one company, and Winslow paid that of his own. They embarked Sept. 23, 1740. Hon. Wm. Gouch of Virginia was Colonel of the regiment; Hon. Henry Cope, Lt. Colonel; Wm. Blakeley, Adj. General. Gen. Thomas Wentworth commanded the land forces at Cuba; and Admiral Edward Vernon,[1] the fleet. The whole expedition was under Lord Cathcart.

After arriving at Cuba, several unsuccessful attempts to accomplish the objects of the expedition were made. Many of the Americans were taken sick and died. They were placed on board

---

Souvenir," in 1829. From the former I extract an account of the interview between Chamberlain and Paugus, which is substantially confirmed by tradition. In the engagement their guns had become foul. While washing his out, Chamberlain discovered Paugus, whom he personally knew, engaged in the same act.

"They slowly and with equal movements cleansed their guns, and took their stations on the outer border of the beach. 'Now Paugus,' said Chamberlain, 'I'll have you;' and with the quickness and steadiness of an old hunter sprung to loading his rifle. 'Na—na—me have you,' replied Paugus, and he handled his gun with a dexterity, that made the bold heart of Chamberlain beat quick, and he almost raised his eye to take his last look upon the sun. They rammed their cartridges, and each at the same instant cast his ramrod upon the sand. 'I'll have you, Paugus,' shouted Chamberlain, as in his desperation he almost resolved to rush upon the savage, with the breech of his rifle, lest he should receive his bullets before he could load. The woods across the pond echoed back the shout. Paugus trembled as he applied his powder-horn to the priming; Chamberlain heard the grains of his powder rattle lightly upon the leaves beneath his feet. Chamberlain struck his gun breech violently upon the ground — the rifle *primed herself;* he aimed, and his bullets whistled through the heart of Paugus. He fell, and as he went down, the bullet from the mouth of his ascending rifle touched the hair upon the crown of Chamberlain, and passed off without avenging the death of its dreadful master."

[1] Mount Vernon, Washington's residence, was named for him.

Vernon's fleet, and received such treatment as called forth frequent complaints. They were separated into different vessels and compelled to sail among the West India islands; 468 were on board July 6, 1742. It was not long before the remnant, who had not fallen a sacrifice to the climate and other hardships, returned to this country, without accomplishing any of their original intentions. They were paid off and dismissed, Oct. 24, 1742. The expedition cost the province £37,500 currency, equal to £7,000 sterling.[1] Of the 500 men from Massachusetts, 50 only returned. Fifteen, beside Capt. Prescott, went from Concord; three only returned, — Jonathan Heywood, Eben. Lampson, and Henry Yours. Tradition says that Thomas Barnes, Zachariah Blood, Nathaniel Monroe, Sergeant Benjamin Pollard, Aaron Lyon, and Darius Wheeler, were among those who died there.

The period from 1744 to 1760, was remarkable for the large drafts of men and money from the town to carry on that series of wars, which then took place between the Indians and French on one part, and the English and Americans on the other. Col. John Flint had commanded the regiment of militia in which Concord was included; and was succeeded by Col. Buckminster of Framingham about 1735. The Hon. James Minott was Lieut. Colonel, and succeeded to the command in 1756. Most of the orders for men passed through his hands. There were three foot companies and a troop in Concord; and all the able-bodied men from 16 to 60 years of age were enrolled. They, as well as their arms, were pressed into the service when required. Sometimes whole companies were called upon to perform actual service at once; and few escaped the call at some time, either to go themselves, or furnish a substitute, in those troublesome wars. What precise amount of service was rendered by Concord, it is impossible now to ascertain; and the insulated facts about to be given present a very imperfect view of the subject.

Massachusetts furnished 3,250 men in 1745 for the reduction of Louisburg. David Melvin of Concord commanded a company

---

[1] Vernon's Letters. Holmes's Annals. The other members of Capt. Prescott's company were enlisted from the neighbouring towns. Twelve went from Hopkinton; 1 Mass. Hist. Coll. vol. iv. p. 16, where the year is erroneously stated to be 1746. See a further notice of Prescott under the head of College Graduates.

there, and received a wound, of which he died Nov. 18, 1745, in his 57th year, after his return home. Benjamin Prescott, son of Dr. Jonathan Prescott, was killed there in the May previous. Amos Row was also killed, and Samuel Wood was sick, and became disabled. Eleazer Melvin, a brother of the above, was a lieutenant there, and engaged as captain in several subsequent campaigns. During a year from Oct. 1746, he was out, and marched on an "intended expedition to Canada" with a considerable number of soldiers from Concord. Joseph Buttrick was clerk of the company. After one of their marches, called *the long march*, in which he went to Canada, he returned, and with 25 men went to Lunenburg for the protection of that town; some persons having been taken by the Indians there a short time before. From March to September, 1747, he was stationed at Northfield. Humphrey Hobbs was his lieutenant, and Thomas Fletcher of Concord, ensign; Benjamin Hoar, Benjamin Kidder, and Alexander Heald, sergeants. Capt. Melvin, with a party of 26 men, went out through the woods in May as far as Crown Point, where he killed several Indians; and on his return home, at the head of West river, about 35 miles from Northfield, he was surprised and attacked by a party of Indians, who killed six of his men (John Hayward, John Dodd, Daniel Mann, Isaac Taylor, Joseph Petty, and Samuel Severance.) The others escaped.[1] John Hoar was captured in an engagement at Fort Dummer July 14, 1748, and remained with the Indians three months. Mark Perkins was also carried into captivity. Mr. Melvin died October 18, 1754, aged 52. He was son of John Melvin, who died 1724, aged 74. Grandchildren of his are now living.

On the 23d of September, 1746, a company of 50 men were detached and marched to Boston on an alarm, on account of an expected attack from the French fleet under the Duke D'Anville. They returned in ten days. Joseph Hubbard was captain; Joshua Brooks, lieutenant; Jonathan Billings, ensign; Stephen Wesson, Amos Heald, Hezekiah Stratten, and Stephen Hosmer, sergeants; John Miles and Ebenezer Meriam, clerks; Nathaniel Colburn, Jonas Heywood, Henry Gould, and Nathan Miles, corporals.

The following names of individuals from Concord, in the expedition to Nova Scotia in May, 1755, appear in Winslow's Army Rec-

---

[1] Doolittle's Narrative, p. 17. Journal of the General Court.

ords. Charles Bulkeley and Timothy Wheeler, 1st and 2d lieutenants in Capt. Osgood's company; and James Fletcher, Samuel Brown, Thomas Brown, Wm. Wilson, Wm. Stephens, Joseph Blanchard, John Knowlton, Nathaniel Carter, Wm. Barker, Jonathan Conant, Nicholas Brown, and William Corey, privates.

Ephraim Jones then commanded a company of 92 men. Jacob Melvin, Nathan Melvin, and Ezekiel Brown were sergeants; Samuel Chandler, corporal; and Deliverance Davis, drummer. Nine privates besides in this company were from Concord. Peter Prescott also commanded a company there. Daniel Brooks was taken captive near the Bay of Fundy, April 26, 1756.

Capt. Stephen Hosmer commanded a company at Fort Edward. He left Concord in September, and returned in December, 1755. Jonathan Hoar, one of the native graduates, was a major in this expedition. Col. James Minott was also there. The Rev. Mr. Bowes, who had been minister of Bedford, was chaplain of the regiment. The journal of Capt. Hosmer is before me. While at Fort Edward, he says: " Nov. 1st. — Sat in a court of enquiry on the complaint of Maj. Hoar against Col. Gilbert." " Nov. 9. — Sabbath ; Rev. Mr. Bowes preached." " Nov. 23d. — Col. Minott and the rest of the commissioners arrived." " Nov. 27th. — Maj. Richardson died at evening." A company from Acton, under Capt. Gershom Davis, was mustered with one of the Concord companies in this town, September, 1755, and soon after marched for Fort Edward.

Jonathan Hoar was lieutenant-colonel in the expedition to Crown Point in 1756, and aid to Maj. Gen. Winslow. Capt. Peter Prescott was there, and was left at Lake George to take care of the sick.

Capt. Jonathan Brooks, with 30 men from this town, marched on alarm for the relief of Fort William Henry, Aug. 17, 1757. They went only to Palmer, and returned in ten days. Oliver Miles was out there three months, being wounded, taken prisoner, stripped naked, and treated in a very cruel manner. Robert Eastabrook, Jonathan Harris, jr., Joseph Wheeler, and several others were taken at Fort Edward. The Journal of the General Court gives the following names of " sick and wounded soldiers" in the Crown Point expedition from this town, who received aid from government: Amos Parlin, Daniel Brown, drummer, Stephen Hosmer, Wm. Richardson, John Barker, Samuel Brewer, Samuel Wheeler, Samuel Buttrick, Jonathan Buttrick, Amos Hosmer, Thomas Billings, Ephraim Brooks, Ephraim Stow, Samuel Eastabrook, John Robbins, Boaz Brown, Daniel Brewer, Solomon Whitney, Peter Prescott, Timothy Barrett, Consider Soper, Wm. Pool, John Savage.

Dr. John Cuming, a Lieut. Colonel in the northern expedition, in 1758, was wounded, and taken prisoner. Daniel Fletcher, a captain from Acton, was also treated in like manner. Capt. Samuel Dakin, grandfather to Dea. Dakin of Sudbury, was killed near Halfway Brook, July 20, 1758. James Hosmer, brother to the late Elijah Hosmer, was killed at Fort Miller. Phineas Wheeler of Acton, son of Samuel Wheeler, Boaz Brown, and Timothy Heald of Concord were killed in Major Rogers's fight, 1758. Abel Farrar died, Nov. 4. 1758, at Lake George. He had been taken prisoner at Fort Miller, April 9th. Abel Marshal died at Albany, Sept. 20, 1758.

The following "sick and wounded soldiers," says the Journal of the General Court, received aid from the government. Danforth Howard, John Barker, James Dudley, Zachariah Davis, Reuben Hosmer, Francis Wheeler, John Barnes, John Darby, John Cragin, and Wm. Eaton. Jonathan Harris died at Crown Point, Nov. 8, 1761. Thomas Brown and John Flagg died in the public service, in 1762; and John Savage died abroad of the small-pox.

Jonathan Hoar was Lieut. Colonel in the expedition to Nova Scotia, in 1760. He sailed for that place from Boston, May 10, 1762, as Colonel, with 500 men, 16 of whom were from Concord.

During the period under review in this chapter several divisions were made in the town. Littleton, Bedford, Acton, and Lincoln were incorporated. The proceedings in relation to several of these towns will be given in their respective histories. Some facts, however, may be properly stated here.

Littleton, about half of which had belonged to Concord, was incorporated, Dec. 3, 1715, sixty years after it was first granted to the Indians and to the English. The first minister was ordained, Dec. 25, 1717, when it is probable the church was organized. March 4, 1717, "four families living on the farms called Nashobah, namely, Walter Powers, John Powers, David Russell, and John Meriam, were dismissed from the minister's rates in Concord for three years ensuing." In May, 1720, they were freed seven years longer.

Twenty-two of the inhabitants of Concord and Chelmsford petitioned the General Court, May, 1721, to be annexed to Littleton. A similar petition was made, in 1725, and granted, so far as relates to Concord; the six families belonging to Chelmsford to continue in the west parish of that town.

When a new town was proposed to be erected, it was customary first to obtain liberty of the town from which it was to be taken, and afterwards of the General Court. When leave could not be thus obtained, a petition was presented directly to the Court. Bedford was incorporated, Sept. 23, 1729, and Acton, July 3, 1735, after having belonged to Concord about 100 years, without opposition from the mother town. Thirty-one persons petitioned, Feb. 6, 1738, to have all the land lying northwesterly of the North river set off as a separate township. Fifteen remonstrated, and the petition was not granted. It was renewed in March, "there being 80 families north of the river, and able to build a meeting-house;" but it again met with a like fate.

After repeatedly petitioning the town and the General Court, the southeasterly part became a precinct, in 1746, and a town, called Lincoln, April 19, 1754. The north part of the town was incorporated, in 1754, as the District of Carlisle; but, the inhabitants not being able to agree where to place the meeting-house, it was set back again after three years. Several of the opposers of the Rev. Mr. Bliss lived in the southwest part of the town, and a petition was presented, Jan. 4, 1750, for liberty to set up public worship among themselves, but it was not granted.

The ostensible reason of those, who had endeavoured to be separated from the main society, was their remoteness from public worship. This was true in some cases, but not always. The cause is rather to be found in the internal divisions, which will be more particularly described in the Ecclesiastical History.

Another peculiar feature of the period under review is seen in the spirit of emigration which was excited. The discoveries made by those, who had been engaged in the public military service, as was the case in the revolutionary and in the last war, induced many to seek other places, than their native soil, to obtain subsistence and wealth. Hence we find that an unusual number of new towns were settled about that time. Many of the worthy sons of Concord left their native homes; and many towns in Worcester County and other places westerly in Massachusetts, in New Hampshire, in Vermont, and in Maine, now give evidence that they and their descendants were a hardy and industrious race of men.

June, 1723, Thomas Howe and 64 others of Marlborough, Stow, and Concord, petitioned for a township of land west of Rutland. The August succeeding, Gershom Rice and 65 others, part of whom were from Concord, petitioned for land between "Turkey Hills and Rutland, including Wachusett." In the same year James Watson, Samuel Hill, Zerubabel Eager, and 32 others, inhabitants of Concord, Sudbury, Marlborough, and Stow, petitioned for liberty to purchase land of the Indians at Hassanamisco (Grafton).[1] Samuel Chandler of Concord renewed the petition, June 3, 1726. Turkey Hills, now comprising part of Townsend, Ashby, Fitchburg, and Lunenburg, were granted principally to the Concord petitioners. Narraganset township, No. 6, lying west of Pembroke, N. H., was granted in 1733 to Concord and 13 other towns, for services rendered in Philip's war, in 1676. Dec. 3, 1735, a township of land "on the east side of Connecticut river below the great falls," was granted to John Flint and others of Concord, Groton, and Littleton. This might have been Keene, since the proprietors of that town held several early meetings in Concord, and Samuel Heywood of Concord was proprietor's clerk. Ephraim Jones and Daniel Adams of Concord, in 1737, cut out a road from Townsend to Ashuelot river, and asked the General Court to pay for it. Refused. Dec. 6, 1737, a township, "eastward of Monadnock hills on the southern branch of Contoocook river," was granted to Samuel Heywood, Joseph Wheeler, Joseph Barrett, and sundry other inhabitants of Concord. Jonathan Prescott, one of the grantees, called the first meeting. This township might have been Peterborough, which was afterwards principally owned, and was named, by Peter Prescott of Concord. Dr. John Cuming, Charles Prescott, and Joseph Hayward had township No. 5, now including Cummington and Plainfield, granted them in 1762.

These are a few of many instances in which the enterprising citizens of Concord were interested in the grants and settlements of new townships in the then remote wilderness.

---

[1] Christopher C. Baldwin, Esq. has kindly furnished me with a list of the proprietors of Grafton in 1728; of whom the following were from Concord: John Flint, Benjamin Barrett, Ebenezer Wheeler, Joseph Barrett, Eleazer Flagg, Joseph Meriam, Jacob Taylor, Samuel Chandler, John Hunt, and Joseph Taylor.

CHAPTER VI.

American Revolution. — Proceedings of the Town. — Act respecting Tea. — Non-consumption Covenant. — Sentiments of the People. — County Convention. — People march to Cambridge. — Courts stopped. — Treatment of the Tories. — Proceedings of the Town. — Provincial Congress meets — Public Stores. — New Town Covenant. — Minute Companies formed. — Mr. Emerson preaches. — Expedition of the British Spies. — Provincial Congress. — Public Stores. — Excitement.

The most interesting period in the history of the United States is undoubtedly that in which they shook off their allegiance to Great Britain, and assumed the right of governing themselves. Much of the spirit of those times may be known from a general survey of the country, and especially the state of Massachusetts; but the main springs of that great revolution, the feelings and acts of the people, are best understood from the minute histories of the towns. All, however, are not equally interesting. Some from their locality, accidental occurrences, or peculiar patriotism, were more distinguished than others; and such, from some of these circumstances, is Concord. The events of the 19th of April, 1775, the proceedings of various state and county conventions held here, and especially the proceedings of the town, would afford matter for an interesting volume; and give to the history of Concord more than ordinary value. Though I shall draw liberally from all my sources of information, this history can contain a small part only of the important productions of those eventful times.

From the commencement of the controversy between England and the colonies, the citizens of Concord took a rational but decided stand in favor of liberty. They watched with interest the progress of this controversy, and did not fail to express their disapprobation of the obnoxious acts of the British Parliament. As early as October, 1767, the town instructed their representative to oppose the operation of the stamp act, and to unite in all constitutional measures, that might be taken to obtain its repeal. In Dec. 1767, the selectmen were chosen a committee to consider and report on those measures, " which threaten the country with poverty and ruin." After accepting their report, the town voted, " to encourage industry, economy, frugality, and manufactures, at home and abroad, and to prevent purchasing so much as we have done of foreign commodities." Capt. James Barrett was chosen a delegate to the convention held in Boston, Sept. 22, 1768, "to consult on the best measures for the good of the province in this critical day." The spirit of liberty was thus early and effectually kindled in Concord.

The address of the citizens of Boston, of the 20th of Nov. 1772, relating to the distressed state of the Province, was laid before this town, Dec. 20th following; and a committee, consisting of Mr. Joseph Lee, Charles Prescott Esq., John Cuming, Esq., Daniel Bliss Esq., Mr. John Flint, Dea. Thomas Barrett, Capt. Stephen Hosmer, Capt. James Barrett, and Mr. Ephraim Wood, jr., was chosen to prepare an answer, and instructions to the representative of the town. Their reports, made at an adjourned meeting, Jan. 11, 1773, "after being several times read, and very coolly and deliberately debated upon," were unanimously accepted in full town-meeting. They appear at length on the town records, and express "firm attachment and ardent love to our Most Gracious Sovereign, King George, in defence of whose person and dignity we are always ready, not only to spend our fortunes but our lives, while we are in the enjoyment of our inestimable privileges, granted to us by royal charter:" but specify at the same time several ways in which these privileges have been curtailed and the charter violated. "As men," they said, "we have a right to life, liberty, and property; as Christians, we, in this land, (blessed be God for it) have a right to worship God according to the dictates of our own consciences; and as subjects, we have a right to personal security, personal liberty, and private property. These principal rights we have as subjects of Great Britain; and no power on earth can, agreeably to our constitution, take them from us, or any part of them without our consent." They denied the power of Parliament to tax them without their consent, and expressed their firm determination, "never tamely to submit" to any infringement of their liberties. Several other meetings were held during this year.

The act of Parliament in relation to exporting tea into the colonies, was laid before the town, 20th of Jan. 1774, and referred to a committee. Their report, made at an adjourned meeting, held four days afterwards, was, after full discussion, unanimously accepted. It breathes a tone of ardent patriotism and fearless independence, worthy of the age in which it was produced.

"This town, at this and a former meeting, taking into serious consideration the present alarming situation of our public affairs, in consequence of the advice received from the united committees of correspondence in the vicinity of Boston, communicated to us, do, expressive of our gratitude to them, freely and cheerfully give our sentiments thereon.

"We cannot possibly view with indifference the past and present obstinate and unwearied endeavours of the enemies of this, as well as the mother country, to rob us of our inestimable rights, that are the distinguishing glory and felicity of this land; — RIGHTS that we are obliged to no power under heaven for the enjoyment of, as they are primarily the sole purchase, and glorious product of the heroic enterprises of the first settlers of these American colonies, under the smiles of Heaven. And though we cannot but be alarmed at the great majority in the British Parliament, for the imposition of unconstitutional taxes upon the colonies, yet it gives life and strength to every attempt in opposing such despotic measures, that not only the people of this but the neighbouring provinces (a few only excepted) are remarkably united in the important and interesting opposition, which, as it succeeded before in some measure, by the blessing of Heaven, so we cannot but hope will be attended with still greater success for the future. Animated with such a prospect, we cheerfully come into the following resolves.

"Resolved, 1. That these colonies have been, and are still, illegally and unconstitutionally taxed by the British Parliament, as they are not really or virtually represented therein.

"2. That purchasing commodities subject to such illegal taxation is an implicit, though an impious and sordid, resignation of the liberties and privileges of this free and happy people.

"3. That as the British Parliament, in addition to repeated incroachments on our liberties, have empowered the East India Company to export their tea into America, subject to a duty for the sole purpose of raising a revenue, which we view as a new invention, inadvertently to catch us in those chains of slavery, that have long been forged for that purpose, therefore, — We, to render such vile designs abortive, absolutely and determinately resolve,

"4. That we will not, either by ourselves or any from or under us, buy, sell, or use any of the East India Company's tea, imported from Great Britain; or any other tea, while there is a duty thereon, affixed by act of Parliament for raising a revenue in America; neither will we suffer any such tea to be made use of in any of our families. Also resolved, that all such persons as shall purchase, or sell, or use any such tea, shall be for the future deemed unfriendly, and inimical to the happy constitution of this country.

"5. That we will, in conjunction with our brethren in America, risk our fortunes, and even our lives, in defence of his Majesty, King George the Third, his person, crown, and dignity; and will also, with the same resolution, as his free-born subjects in this country, to the utmost of our power and ability, defend all our charter rights, that they may be transmitted inviolate to the latest posterity.

"6. That if any person or persons whatsoever, inhabitants of this province, shall for the future, so long as there is a duty on tea, import any from the India House in England, or shall be factors for the East India Company, we will treat them as enemies to their country, and with contempt and detestation.

"7. That we think it our duty, at this critical time of our public affairs, to return our hearty thanks to the town of Boston, for every rational measure they have taken for the preservation or recovery of our invaluable rights and liberties. And, should the state of our public affairs require it, we hope they will still remain watchful, vigilant, and persevering, with a steady zeal, to espy out every thing that shall have a tendency to subvert our happy constitution.

          Ephraim Wood, Jr. ⎫
          John Flint   ⎬ *Committee.*
          Timothy Wheeler, Jr. ⎭
Concord, Jan, 24, 1774."

Another similar document, showing the peculiar feelings of those times, was the non-consumption covenant. This was considered and adopted at a town-meeting, June 27, 1774; and was signed by more than 300 voters.

"We the subscribers, inhabitants of the town of Concord, having taken into our serious consideration the precarious state of the liberties of North America, and more especially the present distressed condition of this insulted province, embarrassed as it is by several acts of the British Parliament, tending to the entire subversion of our natural and charter rights; among which is the act for blocking up the harbour of Boston: And fully sensible of our indispensable duty to lay hold on every means in our power, to preserve and recover the much injured constitution of our country; and conscious at the same time of no alternative between the horrors of slavery, and the carnage and desolation of a civil war, but a suspension of all commercial intercourse with the Island of Great Britain: do in the presence of God, solemnly, and in good faith, covenant and engage with each other: —

"1. That from henceforth we will suspend all commercial intercourse with the Island of Great Britain, until the said act for blocking up the said harbour be repealed, and a restoration of our charter rights be obtained.

"2. That there may be the less temptation to others to continue in the said now dangerous commerce, we do in like manner, solemnly covenant that we will not buy, purchase, or consume, or suffer any person by, for, or under us to buy, purchase, or consume, in any manner whatsoever, any goods, wares, or merchandise, which shall arrive in America from Great Britain from and after the last day of August next ensuing. And in order, as much as in us lies, to prevent our being interrupted and defeated in this only peaceable measure, entered into for the recovery and preservation of our rights, we agree to break off all trade, commerce, and dealings whatsoever with all persons, who, preferring their own private interest to the salvation of their now perishing country, shall still continue to import goods from Great Britain, or shall purchase of those who shall import: arms, ammunition, and medicines for the sick only excepted.

"3. That such persons may not have it in their power to impose upon us by any pretence whatever, we further agree to purchase no article of merchandise from them, or any of them, who shall not have signed this, or a similar covenant, or will not produce an oath, certified by a magistrate, to be by them taken to the following purport; viz. 'I, —— of ——, in the county of ——, do solemnly swear, that the goods I have now on hand and propose for sale, have not, to the best of my knowledge, been imported from Great Britain into any part of America since the last of August, 1774 ; and that I will not, contrary to the spirit of an agreement entered into through this province, import, or purchase of any person so importing, any goods as aforesaid, until the port or harbour of Boston shall be opened, and we are restored to the freedom of our constitution and charter rights.'

"4. We agree that after this or a similar covenant has been offered to any persons, and they refuse to sign it or produce the oath aforesaid, we will consider them as contumacious importers, and withdraw all commercial connexion with them, so far as not to purchase any article whatever of merchandise imported from Great Britain.

"*Provided nevertheless;* notwithstanding the obligations which we have laid ourselves under by the above instrument, should there be a congress of the provinces on the continent, or the major part of them, to consult and advise suitable measures to be taken in this difficult and alarming day, which is already begun by the late House of Representatives, and the example is likely to be followed by the neighbouring governments : — should said body, when convened, adopt measures, after deliberation, which they shall judge more salutary and safe for the whole community ; then what has been signed above we hereby reserve liberty to disannul, and make void this present covenant upon our acceptance thereof. As witness our hands this 24th of June 1774."

This covenant, copied partly from one sent from Boston, was scrupulously regarded. It may well be supposed, that where proceedings like these were had, the attention of the people would be greatly awakened. If there were any "enemies of liberty," they might be easily detected. In a careful review of that period, however, I am astonished that so few arrayed themselves on the side of England in opposition to the wishes of the colonies. The whole town, excepting two or three individuals, was a united family of " sons of liberty." The excitement, or rather the opposition to British oppression, gradually increased ; and its progress from the year 1773 was uncommonly rapid. Petitions having been presented in vain for a redress of their grievances, the people began seriously to think of asserting their rights by an appeal to arms, should other means to accomplish their object fail. Such a crisis seemed then to be approaching : for England had already assumed a hostile attitude ; large numbers of soldiers and munitions of war had arrived in Boston ; and the people had every indication that they were to be compelled into submission by military force.

In July the " Act for the better regulation of the government of Massachusetts Bay " was received in Boston ; in conformity to which the Mandamus Council and many other officers were appointed. This produced great excitement in the community, and evil consequences were anticipated. The people seemed determined not to submit to an act so unconstitutional and oppressive. During this commotion an individual went secretly to Cambridge, on the 1st of August, contrary to the unanimous wish of his fellow citizens, to inform some of the members of the Council of the state of public feeling, and to put them on their guard against an attack from the people, which he thought likely to take place.

In August frequent meetings were held in Concord to consult on the proper measures to be pursued in those gloomy times. A county convention was also recommended, and it was invited to meet here on the last of the month. This convention, consisting of 150 delegates, from every town in the county, held a session in Concord on the 30th and 31st of August. Messrs. Ephraim Wood, jr., John Flint, and Nathan Meriam were delegates from Concord; Mr. Samuel Farrar, Capt. Abijah Pierce, and Capt. Eleazer Brooks, from Lincoln ; Messrs. Francis Faulkner, John Hayward, and Ephraim Hapgood, from Acton ; Messrs. Stephen Davis, John Reed, John Moore, and John Webber, from Bedford ; and from other towns an able delegation. The Hon. James Prescott of Groton was chairman, and Mr. Ebenezer Bridge, clerk. The objects of the convention were brought forward, and discussed with great energy, talent, and most ardent patriotism ; and a committee of nine were chosen to take them into consideration. They reported as follows :

" It is evident to every attentive mind, that this Province is in a very dangerous and alarming situation. We are obliged to say, however painful it may be to us, that the question now is, whether, by a submission to some late Acts of the Parliament of Great Britain, we are contented to be the most abject slaves, and entail that slavery on posterity after us, or, by a manly, joint, and virtuous opposition, assert and support our freedom. There is a mode of conduct, which, in our very critical circumstances, we would wish to adopt, — a conduct, on the one hand, never tamely submissive to tyranny and oppression, on the other, never degenerating into rage, passion, and confusion. This is a spirit which we revere, as we find it exhibited in former ages, and which will command applause to the latest posterity. The late Acts of Parliament pervade the whole system of jurisprudence, by which means we think the fountains of justice are fatally corrupted. Our defence must therefore be *immediate* in proportion to the suddenness of the attack, and *vigorous* in proportion to the danger. We must NOW exert ourselves, or all those efforts, which for ten years past have brightened the annals of this country, will be totally frustrated. LIFE and DEATH, or what is more, FREEDOM and SLAVERY, are in a peculiar sense now before us; and the choice and success, under God, depend greatly on ourselves. We are therefore bound, as struggling not only for ourselves, but for future generations, to express our sentiments in the following resolves; — sentiments, which we think are founded in truth and justice, and therefore sentiments we are determined to abide by.

"*Resolved,* 1. That as true and loyal subjects of our gracious Sovereign, George the Third, King of Great Britain, &c. we by no means intend to withdraw our allegiance from him; but, while permitted the free exercise of our natural and charter rights, are resolved to expend life and treasure in his service.

" 2. That when our ancestors emigrated from Great Britain, charters and solemn stipulations expressed the conditions, and what particular rights they yielded; what each party had to do and perform; and what each of the contracting parties were equally bound by.

" 3. That we know of no instance in which this province has transgressed the rules on their part, or any ways forfeited their natural and charter rights to any power on earth.

" 4. That the Parliament of Great Britain has exercised a power contrary to the abovementioned charter by passing acts, which hold up their absolute supremacy over the colonists; by another act blocking up the harbour of Boston, and by two late acts, the one entitled, "an Act for the better regulating the government of the province of Massachusetts Bay;" the other entitled "an Act for the more impartial administration of justice in said province;" and by enforcing all these iniquitous acts with a large armed force to dragoon and enslave us.

"5. That the late act of Parliament, entitled "an Act for the better regulating the government of the province of Massachusetts Bay," expressly acknowledges the authority of the charter granted by their Majesties, King William and Queen Mary, to said province; and that the only reasons, suggested in the preamble to said act, which is intended to deprive us of the privileges confirmed to us by said charter, are the inexpediency of continuing those privileges, and a charge of their having been forfeited, to which charge the province has had no opportunity of answering.

"6. That a debtor may as justly refuse to pay his debts, because it is inexpedient for him, as the Parliament of Great Britain deprive us of our charter privileges, because it is inexpedient to a corrupt administration for us to enjoy them.

"7. That in all free states there must be an equilibrium in the legislative body, without which constitutional check they cannot be said to be a free people.

"8. That the late act, which ordains a council to be appointed by his Majesty, his heirs and successors from time to time, by warrant under his or their signet or sign manual, and which ordains that the said counsellors shall hold their offices respectively during the pleasure of his Majesty, effectually alters the constitutional equilibrium, renders the council absolute tools and creatures, and entirely destroys the importance of the representative body.

"9. That no state can long exist free and happy, where the course of justice is obstructed; and that when trials by juries, which are the grand bulwarks of life and property, are destroyed or weakened, a people fall immediately under arbitrary power.

"10. That the late act, which gives the governor of this province a power of appointing judges of the superior and inferior courts, commissioners of oyer and terminer, the attorney general, provosts, marshalls, and justices of the peace, and to remove all of them (the judges of the superior court excepted) without consent of the council, entirely subverts a free administration of justice;. as the fatal experience of mankind in all ages has testified, that there is no greater species of corruption, than when judicial and executive officers depend for their existence and support on a power independent of the people.

" 11. That by ordaining jurors to be summoned by the sheriff only, which sheriff is to be appointed by the governor without consent of council, that security which results from a trial by our peers is rendered altogether precarious; and is not only an evident infraction upon our charter, but a subversion of our common rights as Englishmen.

" 12. That every people have an absolute right of meeting together to consult upon common grievances, and to petition, remonstrate, and use every legal method for their removal.

" 13. That the act which prohibits these constitutional meetings cuts away the scaffolding of English freedom, and reduces us to a most abject state of vassalage and slavery.

" 14. That it is our opinion these late acts, if quietly submitted to, will annihilate the last vestiges of liberty in this province, and, therefore, we must be justified by God and the world in never submitting to them.

" 15. That it is the opinion of this body, that the present act, respecting the government of the province, is an *artful, deep-laid* plan of oppression and despotism, that it requires great skill and wisdom to counteract it. This wisdom we have endeavoured to collect from the united sentiments of the county. And although we are grieved that we are obliged to mention any thing, that may be attended with such very important consequences as may now ensue, yet a sense of our duty as men, as freemen, as Christian freemen, united in the firmest bonds, obliges us to resolve, that every civil officer now in commission in this province, and acting in conformity to the late act of Parliament, is not an officer agreeable to our charter, therefore unconstitutional, and ought to be opposed in the manner hereafter recommended.

" 16. That we will obey all such civil officers now in commission, whose commissions were issued before the first day of July, 1774, and support them in the execution of their offices according to the manner usual before the late attempt to alter the constitution of this province: nay, even although the Governor should attempt to revoke their commissions. But that if any of said officers shall accept a commisssion under the present plan of arbitrary government, or, in any way or manner whatever, assist the Governor or administration in the assault now making on our rights and liberties, we will consider them as having forfeited their commissions, and yield them no obedience.

"17. That whereas the Hon. Samuel Danforth and Joseph Lee, Esqrs, two of the judges of the Inferior Court of Common Pleas for this county, have accepted commissions under the new act by being sworn members of his Majesty's Council, appointed by said act: we therefore look upon them utterly incapable of holding any office whatever. And whereas a *venire* on the late act of Parliament has issued from the Court of Sessions, signed by the clerk, we think they come under a preceding resolve of acting in conformity to the new act: we therefore resolve that a submission to courts thus acting and under these disqualifications, is a submission to the act itself, and of consequence, as we are resolved never to submit one iota to the act, we will not submit to courts thus constituted, and thus acting in conformity to said act.

"18. That as, in consequence of the former resolve, all business at the Inferior Court of Common Pleas and Court of General Sessions of the Peace next to be holden at Concord must cease, to prevent the many inconveniences that may arise therefrom: we resolve that all actions, writs, suits, &c. brought to said court, ought to remain in the same condition as at present (unless settled by consent of parties), till we know the result of a provincial and continental congress. And we resolve that no plaintiff, in any case, action, or writ aforesaid, ought to enter said action in said court thus declared to be unconstitutional. And we resolve, if the court shall sit in defiance to the voice of the county, and default actions, and issue executions accordingly, no officer ought to serve such process. And we are also determined to support all constables, jurors, and other officers, who from these constitutional principles shall refuse obedience to courts which we have resolved are founded on the destruction of our charter.

"19. That it is the opinion of this body of delegates, that a provincial congress is absolutely necessary in our present unhappy situation.

"These are sentiments which we are obliged to express, as these acts are intended *immediately* to take place. We must *now* either oppose them, or tamely give up all we have been struggling for. It is this that has forced us so soon on these very important resolves. However, we do it with humble deference to the provincial and continental congress, by whose resolutions we are determined to abide; and to whom, and the world, we cheerfully appeal for the uprightness of our conduct. On the whole, these are 'great and profound questions.' We are grieved to find ourselves reduced to the necessity of entering into the discussion of them. But we deprecate a state of slavery. Our fathers left a fair inheritance to us, purchased by a waste of blood and treasure. This we are resolved to transmit equally fair to our children after us. No danger shall affright, no difficulties intimidate us. And if in support of our rights we are called to encounter even death, we are yet undaunted, sensible that he can never die too soon, who lays down his life in support of the laws and liberties of his country."

The causes of the oppostion to the mother country, and the then state of the controversy, are clearly brought to view in these important proceedings. They were not mere paper resolves, to remain a dead letter, but were to be rules of *action:* and they were executed! The question on their acceptance, after being " maturely deliberated," was taken by yeas and nays; 146 were in favor, and 4 in opposition. An additional vote, recommending a " provincial meeting " to assemble in Concord, on the first Tuesday of October, was passed; and another, to transmit these proceedings to the several towns and to the Continental Congress. On the same day, a county convention was held in Worcester, and, nine days after, one in Suffolk, for similar objects.[1]

On the last week in August, some of the British troops had taken from Cambridge two brass field-pieces, and from Charlestown several barrels of powder. These hostile proceedings alarmed the

---

[1] Some historians have asserted that the *Suffolk* convention was the *first* one held; but this is undoubtedly erroneous. Middlesex took the lead in those important proceedings.

people, and some hundreds from this and the neighbouring towns, met here, on the 2d. of Sept. and proceeded to Cambridge, a part of whom were under arms. Their object appeared to be to learn the cause of those unfriendly movements of the British soldiers, and to demand the resignation of those officers who had accepted commissions under the new law. No violence was committed, nor was any intended, unless they were violently opposed. "Finding no armed force to combat, they laid aside their muskets, and went to the houses of several individuals, who had taken part on the side of government, and compelled them to recant, and forswear all concern in any offices under the law for altering the charter." Ephraim Wood was one of the committee chosen to wait upon them. They afterwards returned peaceably to their homes.

September was fruitful in interesting events. Informal voluntary meetings of the people were frequent. The Court of Sessions and Court of Common Pleas for the county were to hold their sessions in Concord, on the 13th of September. On that day, great numbers of the inhabitants of this and the neighbouring towns assembled on the public common. They expressed their willingness that the court should sit, if it proceeded on in the old way; but if under the new organization, they were determined to prevent it, agreeably to the recommendation of the late convention. A committee from each town then represented was chosen to take such measures as would prevent the opening of the courts, who voted it "as their opinion, that the Court of General Sessions of the Peace ought not to be opened or sit at this time," and chose a sub-committee of five to wait on the justices of the court, and inform them of the wishes of the assembly. After some little time the court produced a written declaration, which was read before the multitude, by whom it was pronounced satisfactory, and afterwards published, declaring it inexpedient to open the court, "lest it should be construed that we act in consequence of the late unconstitutional act of parliament"; and publicly promising, that they would "not open nor in any way proceed to the business of said court." This declaration was signed by Thaddeus Mason, Joseph Haven, Josiah Johnson, William Stickney, Henry Gardner, Abraham Fuller, Jonathan Dix, Daniel Bliss, and Samuel Bancroft, — all the justices then present.

In consequence of these occurrences, and the determined disposition of the people, the Court of Common Pleas was adjourned to the 3d Tuesday of October. Public notice of this was drawn up by David Phipps, sheriff of the county, by order of the unpopular judges, and given to the criers, Antill Gallap, and William How, who made proclamation of the same at the court-house door. This was so displeasing that they were taken before the people, and obliged to make public confession that they were "heartily sorry for what they had done"; and to promise "not to make any return on said proclamation, nor in any way be aiding or assisting in bringing on the unconstitutional plan of government." A similar confession was published by Charles Prescott, Esq. "for signing in favor of the late governor, Hutchinson." Another was made by Daniel Heald, a deputy sheriff, for posting the notice of the adjournment of the court on the court-house door. These declarations were signed by the respective individuals, read to the multitude, and published in the newspapers of those times. The people voted that such declarations were satisfactory; and then adjourned to the 3d Tuesday of October, agreeably to the adjournment of the court.

.The people did not long remain quiet. Another large meeting took place on the Common the next week. A committee was chosen, of which Robert Chafin of Acton was chairman, and William Burrows[1] clerk, before whom every person suspected of being a *tory* was compelled to pass the ordeal of a trial. If found guilty, he was compelled to endure such punishment as an excited multitude might inflict, which they called "humbling the tories." Several suffered in this manner. Dr. Joseph Lee was most scrupulously examined and severely treated. To satisfy their minds, he subscribed the following declaration, which was read and published.

"Whereas I, Joseph Lee of Concord, physician, on the evening of the first ultimo, did rashly and without consideration make a private and precipitate journey from Concord to Cambridge, to inform Judge Lee, that the country was assembling to come down,

---

[1] Mr. Burrows died a few years since in New Ipswich, N. H., over 100 years of age.

(and on no other business,) that he and others concerned might prepare themselves for the event, and with an avowed intention to deceive the people; by which the parties assembling might have been exposed to the brutal rage of the soldiery, who had timely notice to have waylaid the roads, and fired on them while unarmed and defenceless in the dark: by which imprudent conduct I might have prevented the salutary designs of my countrymen, whose innocent intentions were only to request certain gentlemen, sworn into office on the new system of government, to resign their offices, in order to prevent the operation of that (so much detested) act of the British Parliament for regulating the government of the Massachusetts Bay: by all which I have justly drawn upon me the displeasure of my countrymen:

"When I coolly reflect on my own imprudence, it fills my mind with the deepest anxiety. I deprecate the resentment of my injured country, humbly confess my errors, and implore the forgiveness of a generous and free people, solemnly declaring that for the future I will never convey any intelligence to any of the court party, neither directly nor indirectly, by which the designs of the people may be frustrated, in opposing the barbarous policy of an arbitrary, wicked, and corrupt administration.

"*Concord, Sept.* 19, 1774.   JOSEPH LEE."

This is selected from many similar facts to show the highly excited state of public feeling; and this excitement continued to increase. The covenant of the town, already given, was scrupulously regarded, and all those who refused obedience to it were in reality " treated as enemies." The meetings hitherto this month took place without much formal invitation. They were the " sudden assembly of the day." The people felt that they had evils heaped upon them, and they feared others. They were determined resolutely, but rationally, to have them removed. Though their object appeared as yet to be to obtain a peaceable redress of their grievances, yet evil consequences were anticipated from the frequency of the meetings, unless placed under proper legal restraint. To effect this, a special *town* meeting was called, Sept. 26th, when the " whole town resolved itself into a committee of safety to suppress all riots, tumults, and disorders in the town; and to aid all untainted magistrates, who had not been aiding and assisting in bringing on a new mode of government in this province, in the execution of the laws against all offenders."[1] At the same time it was also voted to raise one or more companies to march at a minute's warning in case of alarm, to pay them reasonable wages when called for out of town, and to allow them to choose their own officers; to buy 420 pounds of powder and 500 pounds of ball in addition to the town stock of ammunition, and a chest of good fire-arms, " that those who are unable to purchase them themselves may have the advantage of them if necessity calls for it." At this meeting also Mr. Samuel Whitney, Capt. Jonas Heywood, Mr. Ephraim Wood, jr., Mr. Joseph Hosmer, Ensign James Chandler, and Mr. James Barrett, were chosen a committee of correspondence to hold intercourse with similar committees in other towns. The selectmen had hitherto acted in that capacity. Delegates were also chosen to the proposed Provincial Congress.

The Provincial Congress met here, Oct. 11th, which was an important event. The delegates from Concord were Capt. James Barrett, Mr. Samuel Whitney, and Mr. Ephraim Wood, jr.; from Bedford, Mr. Joseph Ballard, and John Reed, Esq.; from Acton, Messrs. Josiah Hayward, Francis Faulkner, and Ephraim Hapgood; and from Lincoln, Capt. Eleazer Brooks, Mr. Samuel Farrar, and Capt. Abijah Pierce. The whole number of members was 288; and it was in all respects a most important assembly. The Hon. John Hancock of Boston was chosen president, and Mr. Benjamin Lincoln, Secretary. The meeting was first held in the old court-house, but that being too small to convene so large an assembly, it was adjourned to the meeting-house. The Rev. William Emerson, by invitation of the Congress, officiated as chaplain. Two sessions, one at nine, and the other at three o'clock, were held each day. The state of public affairs was taken into consideration, and an address to Gov. Gage agreed upon; but it was unavailing, and did not accomplish its intended object. After remaining in session till the 15th, the Congress adjourned

---

[1] It is said to be characteristic of the people of Concord to act with great deliberation, but when they do act, to act effectually. This may be seen in the proceedings just described. From the beginning of the controversy, they were opposed to taking any *unconstitutional* measures to recover their lost privileges.

to Cambridge, probably for a more easy communication with the capital.[1]

The presence of the Provincial Congress tended to animate the citizens of Concord, and inspire them with increasing confidence in the cause of liberty and patriotic action. They approved the recommendations of that body. Several cannon were purchased and brought here, Oct. 13th. On the 24th, the town directed the selectmen to mount them, and to purchase 100 pounds of four-pound cannon ball, 200 pounds of grape-shot, and 392 pounds of powder; and raised £120 to pay the expense.

About this time a liberty-pole was erected, on which the people's flag was first hoisted here. The occasion brought together a large concourse of people, and was hailed as an auspicious event.

November 21st, the town authorized the constables to pay the money in their hands, belonging to the province, to Henry Gardner, Esq. of Stow, who had been appointed by Congress "Receiver General"; and at the same time voted to annul the non-consumption covenant, which, as already noticed, was entered into on the 27th of June. The articles of association, as agreed upon by the Continental Congress, were adopted in its stead. A committee of inspection, composed of Col. James Barrett, Mr. Joseph Hosmer, Capt. Jonas Heywood, Mr. Abijah Bond, and Capt. David Brown, was chosen "to see to the punctual and particular observance of the said association agreement." A preamble — "we, whose names are underwritten, promise for ourselves and

---

[1] The records in the Secretary's office give the following account of the different Congresses: —

First Congress.

Convened at Salem, Oct. 7, 1774; adjourned the same day.
Convened at *Concord*, Tues. Oct. 11; adjourned Sat. 15th, same month.
Convened at Cambridge, Mond. Oct. 17; adjourned Sat. 29th do.
Convened at do. Wed. Nov. 23; dissolved Sat. Dec. 10th.

Second Congress.

Convened at Cambridge, Wed. Feb. 1, 1775; adjourned Thursd. 16th do.
Convened at Concord, Tues. March 22; adjourned Sat. 15th April.
Convened at do. Sat. April 22; adjourned same day.
Convened at Watertown, Mond. April 24; dissolved May 29th.

Third Congress.

Convened at Watertown, May 31, 1775; dissolved July 19th.

those under us, that we will strictly adhere to the Continental Congress Association, which is hereunto annexed, in all its parts and clauses;"—was adopted Jan. 25, 1775; and a copy furnished to each inhabitant for his signature, by a committee chosen for the purpose, consisting of Ensign James Barrett, Mr. Ephraim Wood, jr., Mr. Samuel Whitne , and M:. Jchn Green. One of these original papers I find to be signed by seventy-two men and two single women. Stephen Hosmer excepted "tea for his wife only,"— all the others were unconditional.

The organization and compensation of the minute companies was brought before the town in December, and referred to a committee, who reported, Jan. 9, 1775, the following regulations:

"1. We, whose names are hereunto subscribed, will, to the utmost of our power, defend his Majesty, King George the Third, his person, crown, and dignity.

"2. We will at the same time, to the utmost of our power and abilities, defend all and every of our charter rights, liberties, and privileges; and will hold ourselves in readiness at a minute's warning with arms and ammunition thus to do.

"3. We will at all times and in all places obey our officers chosen by us, and our superior officers, in ordering and disciplining us, when and where said officers shall think proper."

The town agreed to pay each minute man for three hours on two half days in each week, 1s. 8d. for each half day, and a "cartouch-box";[1] for ten months, unless otherwise ordered by the town. On the Thursday following a meeting was held to enlist the men, when the Rev. William Emerson preached from Psalm lxiii. 2. About sixty enlisted, including many who were either too young or too old to be required by law to do military duty. The number was subsequently increased to 100, and divided into two companies. Mr. Samuel Whitney was muster-master. On the 27th, a committee, chosen to examine them then exercising, reported that fifteen in the company were unable to furnish themselves with guns. These were supplied by the town. One of the companies was called the *Alarm Company*, and directed to take

---

[1] The pay was increased in February as follows: To each captain, 2s. 4d.; 1st lieutenant, 1s. 8d.; 2d lieutenant, 1s. 4d.; sergeant, 10d.; corporal, 8d.; and private, 4d.

care and learn the exercise of the cannon. Much military enthusiasm prevailed.

During the month of February the town used the greatest caution to have the articles of association observed. Several meetings were held; and such measures, as the state of the times required, adopted. Capt. Timothy Wheeler, Mr. Andrew Conant, Mr. Samuel Whitney, Capt. John Greene, Mr. Josiah Merriam, Mr. Ephraim Wood, jr., Mr. William Parkman, and Capt. Thomas Davis, were added to the committee of inspection, and directed to return the names of those who declined signing the articles of association. Such were to be treated with neglect and detestation.[1] Three only were returned.

On Monday, 13th of March, 1775, there was a review of all the military companies in the town. They went into the meeting house, accompanied by a large concourse of spectators, and the Rev. Mr. Emerson preached from 2 Chronicles, xiii. 12; "*Behold God himself is with us for our captain, and his priests with sounding trumpets, to cry alarm against you. O children of Israel, fight ye not against the Lord God of your fathers; for ye shall not prosper.*" These religious services were a powerful appeal to the feelings and understanding of his audience, and to Heaven for the justness of their cause. They were repeated before the companies in Acton the week after. The Thursday following was kept as a solemn fast, on account of the gloomy state of public affairs, when the Rev. Mr. Emerson again preached. His text was Micah, vii. 1 — 7.

The Provincial Congress, in February, ordered, that large quantities of provisions and military stores, sufficient to furnish 15,000 men, should be collected and deposited in Concord and Worcester, principally at the former place.[2] In the October preceding, Messrs. Hancock, Orne, Heath, White, Palmer, Watson, Devens, and Pigeon had been chosen by Congress a committee of safety; and Messrs. Cheever, Lincoln, Lee, Gerry, and Gill, a committee of

---

[1] This vote remained in force till May 14, 1778, when the town annulled it, " so far as respects any persons who reside among us, and no farther."

[2] William Lincoln, Esq., to whose kindness the author is indebted for many favors, says, that 20 barrels of pork were all the public stores deposited at Worcester.

supplies. These committees usually met together. November 2d, they voted to procure and deposit at Concord 200 barrels of pork, 400 barrels of flour, 50 tierces of rice, and 150 bushels of pease. February 13th, they requested Col. Robinson to send four brass field-pieces and two mortars to Concord, and voted to procure 15,000 canteens; February 21st, 100 bell-tents for arms, 1000 field-tents, 10 tons of lead balls, cartridges for 15,000 men, 30 rounds each; 300 bushels of pease and beans, 20 hogsheads of molasses, 150 quintals of fish, and two chests of carpenter's tools. February 23d, they ordered 20 hogsheads of rum to be sent here; and the next day 1000 pounds of candles, 100 hogsheads of salt, wooden spoons, two barrels of oil, six casks of Malaga wine, nine casks of Lisbon wine, 20 casks of raisins, 20 bushels of oatmeal, 1500 yards of Russia linen, and 15 chests of medicine.

Col. James Barrett, who had been appointed by Congress to have the care of all the military stores, was directed on the 15th of March by John Pigeon, " clerk of the committee of safety," to get a sufficient number of faithful men, " to act constantly as a guard every night over the magazines of stores"; and " to engage a number of teams to be in readiness on the shortest notice, by day or night, sufficient to carry off the stores, on a courier's informing him of attempts being ready to be made on the magazine; and on a courier's informing him of danger, he was to alarm the neighbouring towns." On the 17th, Mr. Cheever sent from Charlestown John Austin and several other men, to be constantly employed in carrying on the military preparations. He directed Col. Barrett to provide them all necessary provisions, and a house to work in retired from company, " as our operations depend upon secrecy." Guards were stationed at the old south and north bridges, on the Boston road, and in the middle of the town, for the safe keeping of the stores, and to alarm the surrounding country, should occasion require. Every teamster, suspected of carrying any article to the British, was carefully examined. Concord now became, as it had been a hundred years before, a distinguished military post.

British spies were often sent in disguise into the country, to learn its geography, the state of public feeling, the quantity and condition of the provincial stores, &c. Two of these, Capt.

Brown and Ensign D'Bernicre, of the British army, went to Worcester in February; and on the 20th of March visited Concord. They went up through Weston and Sudbury, and entered the town over the south bridge. In a narrative of this expedition D'Bernicre says, "The town of Concord lies between two hills that command it entirely. There is a river runs through it with two bridges over it. In summer it is pretty dry. The town is large, and contains a church, gaol, and court-house, but the houses are not close together, but in little groups. We were informed that they had fourteen pieces of cannon (ten iron and four brass), and two cohorns. They were mounted, but in so bad a manner that they could not elevate them more than they were, that is, they were fixed to one elevation; their iron cannon they kept in a house in town; their brass they had concealed in some place behind the town in a wood. They had also a store of flour, fish, salt, and rice; and a magazine of powder and cartridges. They fired their morning gun, and mounted a guard of ten men at night. We dined at the house of Mr. Bliss [Daniel Bliss, Esq.], a friend of government; they had sent him word they should not let him go out of town alive that morning; however, we told him if he would come with us, we would take care of him, as we were three, and all well armed. He consented, and told us he would show us another road, called the Lexington road. We set out, and of consequence left the town on the contrary side of the river to what we entered it." * * * "In the town of Concord a woman directed us to the house of Mr. Bliss; a little after she came in crying, and told us, they swore if she did' not leave the town, they would tar and feather her for directing tories on their road."[1] The British officers remarked to Mr. Bliss, that the people would not fight. He urged a different opinion, and pointing to his brother, Thomas Theodore, just then passing in sight, said, "There goes a man who will fight you in blood up to his knees!" This brother was opposed to him in politics; and was subsequently a brave, though unfortunate officer in the American army.[2]

On the 22d of March the Provincial Congress met again in Concord. There was reason to expect, from intelligence received from Boston, that attempts would be made to take away the stores

---

[1] 2 Mass. Hist. Coll. vol. iv. pp. 214, 215.   [2] Willard's Address, p. 66.

here collected; and to prevent, as far as possible, the militia arming in self-defence. "It was the great object of Congress at this meeting to support the committee of safety in the measures they had adopted for protection; and to urge the people to prepare for a firm and united resistance, should the crisis require it. They particularly recommended to the companies of minute-men to improve themselves in military discipline; and ordered several companies of artillery to be immediately organized. A system of rules and regulations for a constitutional army was adopted, should one be raised. And they earnestly solicited the selectmen of the several towns to provide for the speedy collection of all public taxes; and to raise, money by loans of any individuals able and disposed to furnish it." * * * "On the 8th of April it was voted to raise an army with all possible despatch, for the defence of the province against any attack which should be made by the British troops, which had a short time before been much increased."[1] When Congress adjourned, on the 15th of April, it agreed to meet again on the 10th of May; but gave authority to the committee of safety, and the members in this neighbourhood, to call an earlier meeting, if necessary.

Meantime the committees of correspondence, in conjunction with the citizens, were actively making the military preparations necessary for defence. From a manuscript "account of the provincial stores sent to Colonel Barrett of Concord, partly in his own custody, and partly elsewhere, all under his care," found among his papers, the following facts are obtained. These stores were principally brought here in March by the citizens of the town.

There were received from Mr. David Cheever of Charlestown, one of the committee of supplies, 20 loads of stores, containing about 20,000 pounds of musket-balls and cartridges, 50 reams of cartridge-paper, 206 tents, 113 iron spades, 51 wood axes, 201 billhooks, 19 sets of harness, 24 boxes of candles, 14 chests of medicine, 27 hogsheads of wooden ware, 1 hogshead of matches, cords, irons, and balls, 20 bushels of oatmeal, 5 iron worms for cannon, rammers, &c. These were stored at Captain Elnathan Jones's, Joshua Bond's, Willoughby Prescott's, Jonas Heywood's, Colonel Barrett's, and the town-house.

---

[1] Bradford, vol. i. pp. 367 — 369.

From Moses Gill of Boston, 11 loads, containing 150 tents, axes, pickaxes, hatchets, spades, wooden spoons and dishes, and canteens, stored at Captain Thomas Hubbard's, Ephraim Wheeler's, Willoughby Prescott's, and Ephraim Potter's. Also received from R. Pierpont 47 firkins and 2 barrels of butter, stored at Colonel James and Mr. Humphrey Barrett's; and 55 barrels of beef, stored at Thomas and Elisha Jones's, and 25 barrels at Daniel Cray's.

From Colonel Jeremiah Lee of Marblehead, 6 hogsheads, containing 35 half-barrels of powder, 6 of which were stored at Colonel Barrett's, 5 at James Chandler's, 6 at James Barrett's, jun., 6 at Ephraim Wood's, 6 at Joseph Hosmer's, and 6 at Jonas Heywood's. This was received in December, and in the accompanying letter, Colonel Lee writes, "Don't so much as mention the name of powder, lest our enemies should take advantage of it." Eight hogsheads more were soon received from Colonel Lee, 6 of which were sent the last of March to Leicester. He also sent to Concord another load, containing tents, poles, axes, and hatchets, stored at Abishai Brown's; and also 318 barrels of flour, 68 of which were stored at Ebenezer Hubbard's (which was partly destroyed on the 19th of April), 66 at Captain Timothy Wheeler's, 56 at Samuel Jones's, 23 at Isaac Hubbard's, 16 at Jonas Heywood's, 82 at Samuel Whitney's, and 7 at Jonathan Heywood's.

From Elbridge Gerry of Marblehead, 7 loads of salt fish, containing about 17,000 pounds, stored at Elisha Jones's; 18 casks of wine, 20 casks of raisins, and a quantity of oil, (which were carried to Stow;) and 47 hogsheads and 50 barrels of salt, which were stored in 15 different places in town; 4 loads of tents, tow-cloth, and canteens, stored at Ephraim Potter's; 1 bundle of sheet-lead, several hogsheads of molasses, and a quantity of linen.

From Salem 46 and from Boston 12 tierces of rice, estimated to contain about 35,000 pounds; 20 stored at Ebenezer Hubbard's, 6 at Thomas Hosmer's, 3 at Thomas Davis's, 7 at Stephen Blood's, 7 at Edward Richardson's, 5 at Deacon George Minott's, and the remainder in the town-house.

All the stores brought to the town are not mentioned in the above account. Many articles were afterwards brought, and many were prepared here. Firearms, gun-carriages, &c. were manufactured at Barrett's mills; cartouch-boxes, holsters, belts, and other articles of sadlery, by Mr. Reuben Brown; saltpetre, by Josiah Melvin; oatmeal, by Captain Timothy Wheeler; wooden plates, spoons, and various other articles used in the camp and the field, by other individuals. Large quantities of beef and pork were put up here for the public service. These military operations continued more than a year afterwards. A part of the building owned by Daniel Shattuck, Esq. was erected at this time for a public store-house.

On the 29th of March a report was circulated that the British troops were coming to Concord, which produced considerable alarm. The Provincial Committee of Safety met here on the 1st, 5th, 14th, and 17th of April. At the last date they directed Colonel Barrett to mount two cannon, and raise an artillery company, and to send four cannon to Groton and two to Acton. They met at Mr. Wetherbee's in West Cambridge the next day, and gave orders for the removal of some of the stores from Concord. These were ordered to be deposited in 9 different towns; 50 barrels of beef, 100 of flour, 20 casks of rice, 15 hogsheads of molasses, 10 hogsheads of rum, and 500 pounds of candles were ordered to Sudbury; 15,000 canteens, 1500 iron pots, the spades, pickaxes, bill-hooks, axes, hatchets, crows, wheelbarrows, and several other articles, were to be divided, — one third to remain in Concord, one-third to be sent to Sudbury, and one third to Stow; 1000 iron pots to be sent to Worcester.

Meantime the minute companies were often out for military exercise. The excitement was so great that some carried their guns with them at all times, even while attending public worship on the Sabbath. The committee of correspondence met daily with other distinguished citizens in town. Though very indefinite ideas prevailed, respecting the objects of the enemy, yet all the people were daily discussing in groups the great crisis, which seemed near at hand. What that crisis might be was yet doubtful.

CHAPTER VII.

BATTLE OF CONCORD.

"Some future historian will relate with pleasure, and the latest posterity will read with wonder and admiration, how three hundred intrepid rural sons of freedom drove before them more than five times their number of regular, well-appointed troops, and forced them to take shelter behind their own bulwarks."— *Article entitled " The Rural Heroes; or the Battle of Concord,"* Boston Newpaper for May, 1775.

At length came the 19th of April, a day destined to live in the annals of Concord and of the world, as long as freemen exist. The preceding winter had been one of great mildness.[1] The spring vegetation was uncommonly forward. Fruit trees were in blossom, winter grain had grown several inches out of the ground, and other indications equally propitious were observed on that memorable day. And on the morning of the 19th the weather was as delightful, as if Providence intended thus to mark with peculiar favor the commencement of a series of glorious events, which happily resulted in the establishment of an independent republic. The exclamation of Adams on that morning, "O what an ever glorious morning is this!" was doubtless true, whether applied to the weather or the occasion.

At this time there were stationed in Boston ten large regiments of British troops, of seven companies each, the 4th or King's own regiment, 5th, 10th, 23d, or Royal Welch Fusileers, 38th, 43d, 47th, 57th, and 59th, and a battalion of marines of six companies. A detachment of 800 of these troops, consisting of grenadiers, light infantry, and marines, had been taken off duty on Saturday the 15th, under pretence of learning a new exercise; and about

---

[1] In a journal kept by the Rev. Thomas Smith at Falmouth, Maine, where the weather is colder than here, are the following entries; "January 23, 1775, very moderate weather; 27th, a summer day; 28th, wonderful weather. February 7th, there has been no snow and but little rain since the 29th of December; wonderful weather, we saw two robins; 11th, warm day; 18th, cold; 20th snow, incomparable sledding; 21st, a summer day; 23d, a great snow-storm. March 7th, the frost seems out of the ground in the streets; 15th, we have wonderful moderate weather; 28th, it has been a wonder of a winter; so moderate and unfreezing."

10 o'clock on Tuesday evening, the 18th, embarked from Boston, under command of Lieutenant-Colonel Francis Smith, of the 10th regiment, and Major John Pitcairn, commander of the marines; and landed at Lechmere Point. After having received a day's provisions and thirty-six rounds of cartridges; they began their march about 12 o'clock, in silence and under cover of night, towards Concord. The object of this expedition was to destroy the military stores deposited here, and to apprehend Messrs. Hancock, Adams, Barrett, and other distinguished patriots, who had become obnoxious to the British government. To facilitate the accomplishment of their object, officers were despatched during the day and evening of the 18th, to intercept any messengers who might be sent by the friends of liberty, and thus to prevent the discovery of their approach. Happily for the provincials it could not be concealed. The first movement of the British troops in Boston was known; and no sooner known, than messengers were immediately despatched towards their intended destination. Paul Revere left Charlestown about 11 o'clock, passed through Medford, awoke the captain of the minute company there, and alarmed almost every family on his way to Lexington. Nearly at the same time William Dawes set out for the same destination and passed through Roxbury. Having arrived at the Rev. Mr. Clark's in Lexington, Revere found Hancock and Adams, who had tarried there on their way from Concord, after the adjournment of the Provincial Congress, to whom he related what he knew of the intended expedition. They also received similar intelligence from the committee of safety then in session at West Cambridge. After he had stayed there a short time, Dawes arrived, and both proceeded together towards Concord. They had not travelled far before they were overtaken by Dr. Samuel Prescott of Concord, who had spent the evening at Lexington, at the house of Mr. Mulliken, to whose daughter he was paying his addresses; and having been alarmed, was hastening his return home. All rode on together, spreading the alarm at every house. When they arrived near Mr. Hartwell's tavern in the lower bounds of Lincoln, they were attacked by four British officers, who belonged to the scouting party sent out the preceding evening, and Revere and Dawes were taken. Prescott was also attacked, and had the reins of his bridle cut; but fortunately succeeded in making his escape by jumping his horse

over the wall; and, taking a circuitous route through Lincoln, he proceeded with all possible expedition to Concord. Elijah Saunderson, Solomon Brown, and Jonathan Loring of Lexington, who had been sent out to watch the movement of the British officers, and several others passing on the road, were taken prisoners a short time before 10 o'clock by another party. After detaining them till 2 o'clock, and asking many questions about the magazines at Concord, whether any guards were posted there, and whether the bridges were up, they conducted them back to Lexington, where they were released. Hancock and Adams, having remained at the Rev. Mr. Clark's, around whose house a guard had been placed, after consultation now proceeded towards Woburn.

Between 12 and 1 o'clock the same night, information was brought from the Hon. Joseph Warren, that the king's troops were marching to Lexington, and soon after the militia were alarmed and ordered to assemble. An express was sent to Cambridge, and returned between three and four o'clock, without obtaining any intelligence of the movements of the enemy, upon which the militia were dismissed for a short time. The commanding officer, however, thought best soon to call them together again, " not," says the Rev. Mr. Clark, " with the design of opposing so superior a force, much less commencing hostilities; but only with a view to determine what to do, when and where to meet, and to dismiss and disperse."

" Accordingly, about half an hour after four o'clock, alarm guns were fired, and the drums beat to arms; and the militia were collecting together. — Some, to the number of fifty or sixty, or possibly more, were on the parade, others were coming towards it. — In the mean time the troops, having thus stolen a march upon us, and to prevent any intelligence of their approach, having seized and held prisoners several persons, whom they met unarmed upon the road, seemed to come determined for murder and bloodshed; and that whether provoked to it or not! When within about half a quarter of a mile of the meeting-house, they halted, and command was given to prime and load; which being done, they marched on till they came up to the east end of said meeting-house, in sight of our militia (collecting as aforesaid) who were about twelve or thirteen rods distant. Immediately on their appearing so suddenly, and so nigh, Captain Parker, who commanded the militia company, ordered the men to disperse and take care of themselves and not to fire. Upon this our men dispersed; but many of them not so speedily, as they might have done, not having the most distant idea of such brutal barbarity and more than savage cruelty, from the troops of a British king, as they immediately experienced. For no sooner did they come in sight of our company, but one of them, supposed to be an officer of rank, was heard to say to the troops, 'Damn them; we will have them!' Upon which the troops shouted aloud, huzza'd, and rushed furiously towards our men. About the same time, three officers (supposed to be Colonel Smith, Major Pitcairn, and another officer) advanced on horseback to the front of the body, and coming within five or six rods of the militia, one of them cried out, 'Ye villains, ye rebels, disperse; damn you, disperse!' or words to this effect. One of them said, 'Lay down your arms; damn you, why don't you lay down your arms!' The second of these officers, about this time fired a pistol towards the militia as they were dispersing. The foremost, who was within a few yards of our men, brandishing his sword, and then pointing towards them, with a loud voice, said to the troops, 'Fire! by God, fire!' which was instantly followed by a discharge of arms from the said troops, succeeded by a very heavy and close fire upon our party dispersing, so long as any of them were within reach. Eight were left dead upon the ground; ten were wounded." [1]

The British troops then passed on without molestation to Concord, six miles further. In the mean time Prescott had arrived there; and the guard, the committee of safety, the military officers, and principal citizens, had been alarmed. The church bell rung a little before three o'clock. Major John Buttrick requested Mr. Reuben Brown to proceed towards Lexington, obtain what information he could, and return. Another messenger was sent to Watertown on the same errand. Mr. Brown arrived at Lexington just before the British troops fired on the devoted Lexington militia, and immediately returned to Concord, without waiting to ascertain what effect their firing had produced. On his arrival Major Buttrick inquired if they fired bullets. "I do not know, but think

---

[1] "Plain and faithful Narrative of Facts," by the Rev. Jonas Clark, minister of Lexington, published as an appendix to his Sermon, preached at the anniversary of these events in 1776. — See APPENDIX.

it probable," was the answer. It was supposed at that time, that they fired nothing but powder, merely to intimidate the people, though various reports were circulated of a different character. The provincials were unwilling to be the aggressors, and could not then believe the mother country was in earnest, and intended to murder the inhabitants of her colonies. The object was conceived to be, to destroy the public stores. The people, however, wished to be prepared for any event. Mr. Brown proceeded by the direction of Colonel Barrett to Hopkinton to alarm the people in that direction. Other messengers were sent at the same time to other towns with the intelligence; and the alarm spread like electric fire from a thousand sources, and produced a shock that roused all to action.

The committee of safety in Concord had been engaged the preceding day, according to the direction of the provincial committee, in removing some of the military stores to the adjoining towns, and immediately gave directions for removing and securing such as yet remained. This occupied the attention of Colonel Barrett and a large number of citizens a considerable portion of the morning. Four cannon were carried to Stow, six to the outer parts of the town, and some others covered with hay, straw, manure, &c. Loads of stores of various kinds were carried to Acton, and other towns, and many others were concealed in private buildings and in the woods. The utmost activity prevailed in preparing for the approaching crisis.

The road from Lexington to Concord enters the town from the southeast along the side of a hill, which commences on the right about a mile below the village, rising abruptly from thirty to fifty feet above the road, and terminating at the northeasterly part of the public square. The top is plain land, commanding a pleasant view of the village and vicinity. Here, in the rear of Reuben Brown's, stood the pole on which the flag of liberty was first unfurled. The meeting-house stood in its present situation; the court-house was near the county-house, now occupied by the jailer; Captain Timothy Wheeler's store-house was near Mr. Stow's. There was no house between Elisha Tolman's and Abel B. Heywood's. The main branch of Concord river flows sluggishly in a serpentine direction on the westerly and northerly side of the village about half a mile from the principal houses. This river was then passed by two bridges, one by Deacon Cyrus Hosmer's, called the " old South Bridge," the other near the Rev. Dr. Ripley's, called the North Bridge, about half a mile from the meeting-house. The river, which before ran easterly, turns at this place and runs northerly. The road, just beyond Dr. Ripley's, turned nearly at right angles, and passing over the bridge went parallel with the river over wet ground below the house then owned by Captain David Brown, and by Humphrey Hunt's, to Colonel Barrett's, who lived about two miles from town. This road was entered by another, about thirty rods above the bridge nearly at right angles, leading from the high lands at Colonel Jonas Buttrick's, also about fifty rods direct from the bridge, on which the main body of the provincial militia paraded. This bridge was taken up in 1793, and two others, one above and the other below the old site, were erected.

Guards were stationed at the north and south bridges, below Dr. Heywood's, and in the centre of the village. Jonathan Farrar was then commander of the guard. In case of an alarm, it was agreed to meet at Wright's tavern, now Deacon Jarvis's. A part of the company under Captain Brown paraded about break of day; and being uncertain whether the enemy was coming, they were dismissed, to be called together by the beat of drum. Soon afterward the minute-men and militia, who had assembled, paraded on the common; and after furnishing themselves with ammunition at the court-house, marched down below the village in view of the Lexington road. About the same time a part of the minute company from Lincoln, who had been alarmed by Dr. Prescott, came into town, and paraded in like manner. The number of armed men, who had now assembled, was about one hundred. The morning had advanced to about seven o'clock; and the British army were soon seen approaching the town on the Lexington road. The sun shone with peculiar splendor. The glittering arms of eight hundred soldiers, " the flower of the British army," were full in view. It was a novel, imposing, alarming sight. What was to be done? At first it was thought best that they should face the enemy, as few as they were, and abide the consequences. Of this opinion, among others, was the Rev. William Emerson, the clergyman of the town, who had turned out amongst the first in the morning to animate and encourage his people by his counsel and patriotic example. "Let us stand our ground," said he; "if we die, let us die here!" Eleazer Brooks of Lincoln was then on the hill. "Let us go and meet them," said one to him. "No," he answered, "it will not do for *us* to begin the war." They did not then know what had happened at Lexington. Their number was, however, very small in comparison with the enemy, and it was concluded best to retire a short distance, and wait for reinforcements. They consequently marched to the northern declivity of the burying-ground hill, near the present site of the court-house. They did not, however, leave their station till the British light infantry had arrived within a few rods' distance.

Major Buttrick went to one of the companies then under command of Lieutenant Joseph Hosmer, the other officers not then being at their posts, and requested him to act as adjutant. He remonstrated by telling him "his company would be left alone if he did." "It must be so then," said Buttrick; "you must go." He accordingly left his company, and officiated as adjutant the remaining part of the morning. About the same time Colonel James Barrett, who was commander of the regiment of militia, and who had been almost incessantly engaged that morning in securing the stores, rode up. Individuals were frequently arriving, bringing different reports. Some exaggerated the number of British troops; some said that they had, and others that they had not killed some Lexington militia men. It was difficult to obtain correct information. Under these circumstances he ordered the men there paraded, being about one hundred and fifty, to march over the north bridge, near the present residence of Colonel Jonas Buttrick, and there wait for reinforcements. "This shows," says Murray, "that they did not intend to begin hostilities at this time, otherwise they would have disputed the ground with the light infantry."

In the mean time the British troops entered the town. The six companies of light infantry were ordered to enter on the hill, and disperse the minute men whom they had seen paraded there. The grenadiers came up the main road, and halted on the common. Unfortunately for the people's cause, the British officers had already been made somewhat acquainted, through their spies, and the tories, with the topography of the town, and the situation of many of the military stores. On their arrival they examined as well as they could, by the help of spyglasses from a post of observation on the burying-ground hill, the appearance of the town, condition of the provincials, &c. It was found that the provincials were assembling, and that no time was to be lost. The first object of the British was to gain possession of the north and south bridges to prevent any militia from entering over them. Accordingly, while Colonel Smith remained in the centre of the town, he detached six companies of light infantry, under command of Capt. Lawrence Parsons of his own regiment, to take possession of the north bridge, and proceed thence to places where stores were deposited. Ensign D'Bernicre, already mentioned, was ordered to direct his way. It is also intimated that tories were active in guiding the regulars. Captain Beeman of Petersham was one. On their arrival there, three companies under command of Captain Lawrie of the 43d regiment were left to protect the bridge; one of those, commanded by Lieutenant Edward Thornton Gould, paraded at the bridge, the other, of the 4th and 10th regiments, fell back in the rear towards the hill. Captain Parsons with three companies proceeded to Colonel Barrett's to destroy the stores there deposited. At the same time Captain Mundey Pole of the 10th regiment was ordered to take possession of the south bridge, and destroy such public property as he could find in that direction. The grenadiers and marines, under Smith and Pitcairn, remained in the centre of the town, where all means in their power were used to accomplish the destruction of military stores.

By the great exertions of the provincials the principal part of the public stores had been secreted, and many others were protected by the innocent artifice of individuals. In the centre of the town the grenadiers broke open about sixty barrels of flour, nearly one half of which was afterwards saved; knocked off the trunnions of three iron twenty-four pound cannon, and burnt sixteen new carriage-wheels, and a few barrels of wooden trenchers and spoons. The liberty-pole on the hill was cut down, and suffered the same fate. About five hundred pounds of balls were thrown into the mill-pond and into wells. "The shrewd and successful address of Captain Timothy Wheeler on this occasion deserves notice. He had the charge of a large quantity of provincial flour, which, together with some casks of his own, was stored in his barn. A British officer demanding entrance, he readily took his key and gave him admission. The officer expressed his pleasure at the discovery; but Captain Wheeler with much affected simplicity, said to him, putting his hand on a barrel ; ' This is my flour. I am a miller, Sir. Yonder stands my mill. I get my living by it. In the winter I grind a great deal of grain, and get it ready for market in the spring. This,' pointing to one barrel, ' is the flour of wheat ; this,' pointing to another, ' is the flour of corn ; this is the flour of rye ; this,' putting his hand on his own casks, ' is *my* flour ; this is *my* wheat ; this is *my* rye ; this is mine.' ' Well,' said the officer, ' we do not injure private property ' ; and withdrew leaving this important depository untouched."[1]

Captain Ephraim Jones kept the tavern now owned by Hartwell Bigelow, and had the care of the jail near by. Henry Gardner, Esq., the province treasurer, had boarded with him during the session of the Congress, and had left in his custody a chest containing some money and other important articles. Captain Jones was taken by the British, and placed under a guard of five men with their bayonets fixed and pointing towards him. After being thus detained a short time he was released to furnish refreshment at his bar. In the mean time they entered his house in search of public stores, and went to the chamber where Mr. Gardner's chest was deposited. Being about to enter, Hannah Barns, who lived in the family, remonstrated, telling them it was her apartment, and contained her property. After considerable parleying, they left her and the chamber unmolested.

The court-house was set on fire, but was extinguished by Mrs. Martha Moulton, a near resident, assisted by a servant of Dr. Minott. They remonstrated, saying to the British, " The top of the house is filled with powder, and if you do not put the fire out, you will all be killed." On this they lent their aid. They seized and abused several unarmed inhabitants who remained in the village.

The party at the south bridge entered several adjacent houses, where at their request milk, potatoes, meat, and other refreshments, as a breakfast, were provided. They entered the house of Ephraim Wood, Esq. and endeavoured to take him prisoner. He was town clerk and a distinguished patriot. Being actively engaged in directing the important events of the day, and assisting in removing the stores, he was not at home and escaped detec-

---

[1] Holmes's Annals, vol. ii. p. 326.

tion. At Mr. Amos Wood's they paid a guinea apiece to each of the female attendants to compensate them for their trouble. They searched the house; and an officer observing one room fastened, significantly inquired of Mrs. Wood, " whether there were not some females locked up there ? " By her evasive answer he was led to believe it was so, and immediately said, " I forbid any one entering this room ! " — and a room filled with military stores was thus fortunately preserved. This party remained here till they heard the firing at the north bridge, when they recrossed the river, took up the planks of the bridge to render it impassable, and hastened to join the main body in the middle of the town.

After Colonel Barrett had ordered the militia to march over the bridge, he rode home to give some directions respecting the stores at his house. He set out on his return to the militia companies just before the party of British troops arrived. They said to Mrs. Barrett, " Our orders are to search your house and your brother's from top to bottom." · Leave was granted. The soldiers here, as at other places in town, requested and were provided with refreshments. One of the sergeants asked for spirit, but it was refused; and the commanding officer forbid it, as it might render him unfit for duty, saying, " We shall have bloody work to day, — we have killed men at Lexington." The officers offered to pay Mrs. Barrett, but she refused, saying, " We are commanded to feed our enemies." They then threw some money into her lap. Hesitating some time, she accepted it with the remark, — " This is the price of blood." They assured her of good treatment, but said they must execute their orders. Mrs. Barrett had concealed some musket-balls, cartridges, flints, &c., in casks in the garret, and had put over them a quantity of feathers, which prevented discovery. They however took fifty dollars in money from one of the rooms. On seeing Stephen, a son of Colonel Barrett, the officer demanded his name. Being answered " Barrett," they called him a rebel, and taking hold of him said, " You must go to Boston with us, and be sent to England for your trial." Upon Mrs. Barret saying, " He is my son, and not the master of the house," they released him. They collected some gun-carriages in order to burn them; but before they executed their intention the firing at the bridge was heard, and they immediately retreated.

While the British were thus engaged, our citizens and part of our military men, having secured what articles of public property they could, were assembling under arms. Beside the minute-men and militia of Concord, the military companies from the adjoining towns began to assemble; and the number had increased to about two hundred and fifty or three hundred.

There were at this time in this vicinity, under rather imperfect organization, a regiment of militia, and a regiment of minute-men. The officers of the militia were James Barrett, colonel; Ezekiel How of Sudbury, lieutenant-colonel; Nathan Barrett and George Minott of Concord, Joseph Robbins of Acton, John Moore of Bedford, Samuel Farrar of Lincoln, and Moses Stone and Aaron Haynes of Sudbury, captains. The officers of the minute-men were Abijah Pierce of Lincoln, colonel; Thomas Nixon of Framingham, lieutenant-colonel; John Buttrick of Concord, major; Jacob Miller of Holliston, 2d major; Thomas Hurd of East Sudbury, adjutant; David Brown, and Charles Miles of Concord, Isaac Davis of Acton, William Smith of Lincoln, Jonathan Wilson of Bedford, John Nixon of Sudbury, captains. There were also two small companies of horse, one in Concord, and one in Sudbury; but they were out among the foot companies at this time. Joseph Hosmer, David Wheeler, Francis Wheeler, and James Russell of Concord; John Hayward, Simon Hunt, and John Heald of Acton; Samuel Hoar of Lincoln; Moses Abbott of Bedford; and Jonathan Rice, David Moore, Asahel Wheeler, and Jabez Puffer of Sudbury, were lieutenants. All these, however, were not present at the engagement at the North Bridge.[1]

---

[1] It has been customary in giving notice of deceased revolutionary soldiers, who met the British at any time on that day, or marched to meet them, to say they were present at the North Bridge. This in many instances is doubtless incorrect. Scarcely any, except those from Concord and the towns immediately adjoining, were or *could be* present, though troops came with celerity and bravery from a greater distance, and were in the engagement on the retreat. Two companies from Sudbury, under How, Nixon, and Haynes, came to Concord; and having received orders from a person stationed at the entrance of the town for the purpose of a guide, to proceed to the north instead of the south bridge, arrived near Colonel Barrett's just before the British soldiers retreated. They halted in sight, and Colonel How observed, "If any blood has been shed, not one of the rascals shall escape;" and disguising himself rode on to ascertain the truth. Before proceeding far, the firing began at the bridge, and the Sudbury companies pursued the retreating British.

The officers of the minute companies had no commissions. Their authority was derived solely from the suffrages of their companies. Nor were any of the companies formed in regular order. John Robinson of Westford, a Lieutenant-Colonel in a regiment of minute-men under Colonel William Prescott, and other men of distinction had already assembled. The hostile acts and formidable array of the enemy, and the burning of the articles they had collected in the village, led them to anticipate a general destruction.

Joseph Hosmer, acting as adjutant, formed the soldiers as they arrived singly or in squads, on the field westerly of Colonel Jonas Buttrick's present residence; the minute companies on the right and the militia on the left, facing the town. He then, observing an unusual smoke arising from the centre of the town, went to the officers and citizens in consultation on the high ground near by, and inquired earnestly, "Will you let them burn the town down?" They then, with those exciting scenes before them deliberately with noble patriotism and firmness "resolved to march into the middle of the town to defend their homes, or die in the attempt;" and at the same time they resolved not to fire unless first fired upon. "They acted upon principle and in the fear of God."[1]

Colonel Barrett immediately gave orders to march by wheeling from the right. Major Buttrick requested Lieutenant-Colonel Robinson to accompany him, and led them in double file to the scene of action. When they came to the road leading from Captain Brown's to the bridge, a part of the Acton minute company under Captain Davis passed by in front, marched towards the bridge a short distance, and halted. Being in files of two abreast, the Concord minute company, under Captain Brown, being before at the head, marched up the north side, till they came equally in front. The precise position, however, of each company cannot now be fully ascertained. This road was subject to inundations, and a wall was built with large stones on the upper side, in which posts were placed, connected together at their tops with poles to aid foot-passengers in passing over in times of high water.

The British, observing their motions, immediately formed on the east side of the river, and soon began to take up the planks of the

---

[1] "History of the Fight at Concord," by the Rev. Dr. Ripley.

bridge. Against this Major Buttrick remonstrated in an elevated tone, and ordered a quicker step of his soldiers. The British desisted. At that moment two or three guns were fired in quick succession into the river, which the provincials considered as alarm-guns and not aimed at them. They had arrived within ten or fifteen rods of the bridge, when a single gun was fired by a British soldier, the ball from which passing under Colonel Robinson's arm slightly wounded the side of Luther Blanchard, a fifer in the Acton company, and Jonas Brown, one of the Concord minute men. This gun was instantly followed by a volley by which Captain Isaac Davis and Abner Hosmer, both belonging to Acton, were killed, a ball passing through the body of the former, and another through the head of the latter. On seeing this, Major Buttrick instantly leaped from the ground, and partly turning to his men, exclaimed, " Fire, fellow-soldiers, for God's sake, fire "; discharging his own gun almost in the same instant. His order was instantly obeyed; and a general discharge from the whole line of the provincial ranks took place. Firing on both sides continued a few minutes. Three British soldiers were killed; and Lieutenants Sunderland, Kelley, and Gould, a sergeant, and four privates were wounded. The British immediately retreated about half way to the meeting-house, and were met by two companies of grenadiers, who had been drawn thither by " the noise of battle."

Two of the soldiers killed at the bridge were left on the ground, where they were afterwards buried by Zachariah Brown and Thomas Davis, Jun., and the spot deserves to be marked by an ever-enduring monument, as the place where the first British blood was spilt, — where the life of the first British soldier was taken, in a contest which resulted in a revolution the most mighty in its consequences in the annals of mankind.

Most of the provincials pursued them across the bridge, though a few returned to Buttrick's with their dead.[1] About one hundred and fifty went immediately across the Great Field to intercept the enemy on their retreat at Merriam's corner. From this time

---

[1] Luther Blanchard went to Mrs. Barrett's, who, after examining his wound, mournfully remarked, " A little more and you'd been killed." " Yes," said Blanchard, " and a little more and 't wouldn't have touched me;" — and immediately joined the pursuers.

BATTLE OF CONCORD.

through the day, little or no military order was preserved. Every man chose his own time and mode of attack.

It was between 10 and 11 o'clock when the firing at the bridge took place; and a short time after Captain Parsons and his party returned unmolested from Colonel Barrett's. They might have been attacked and taken, had the party that went across the Great Fields remained, and had strict military order been preserved; but it was probably feared, that, if this had been done, the grenadiers would have burnt the village, or committed some other act of retaliation, which it would have been impossible for the number of Americans then assembled to prevent. War, too, at this time was not declared. Though some may suppose the provincials here made a mistake, and neglected the advantages they possessed, yet no one who views all the circumstances correctly, will hesitate to consider this, as one of the most fortunate events, or be dissatisfied with what the provincials did on that memorable day.

By this time the provincials had considerably increased, and were constantly arriving from the neighbouring towns. The British had but partially accomplished the objects of their expedition; the quantity of public stores destroyed being very small in comparison with what remained untouched. They observed, however, with no little anxiety and astonishment, the celerity with which the provincials were assembling, and the determined resolution with which they were opposed. Hitherto their superior numbers had given them an advantage over such companies as had assembled; but they now began to feel that they were in danger, and resolved, from necessity, on an immediate retreat. They collected together their scattered parties, and made some hasty provision for the wounded.

Several were taken into Dr. Minott's (now the Middlesex Hotel), where their wounds were dressed. One of the officers left his gold watch, which was discovered after he had gone out, by an old black servant. She, with honest simplicity, called out "Hollo, sir, you have left your watch," and restored it without fee or reward. At Wright's tavern, Pitcairn called for a glass of brandy, and stirred it up with his bloody finger, remarking, "He hoped he should stir the damned yankee blood so before night."[1] One of

---

[1] Major Pitcairn was killed at the battle of Bunker Hill, June 17th.

the wounded died and was buried where Mr. Keyes' house stands. A chaise was taken from Reuben Brown,[1] and another from John Beaton, which were furnished with bedding, pillaged as were many other articles from the neighbouring houses, in which they placed some of their wounded; and began a hasty retreat a little before 12 o'clock. Several were left behind. About the same time they fired at Mr. Abel Prescott,[2] whom they saw returning from an excursion to alarm the neighbouring towns; but, though slightly wounded in his side, he secreted himself in Mrs. Heywood's house and escaped.

The designs of the enemy were now fully developed; and the indignation of the provincials was highly excited. Many of them were determined to be revenged for the wanton cruelties which had been committed. They had followed the retreating party between the bridge and the village, and fired single-handed from the high ground, or from behind such shelter as came in their way; and thus began a mode of warfare which cost many a one his life.

The king's troops retreated in the same order as they entered town, the infantry on the hill and the grenadiers in the road, but with flanking parties more numerous and farther from the main body. On arriving at Merriam's Corner they were attacked by the provincials who had proceeded across the Great Fields, in conjunction with a company from Reading, under command of the late Governor Brooks. Several of the British were killed, and several wounded; among the latter was Ensign Lester. None of the provincials were injured. From this time the road was literally lined with provincials, whose accurate aim generally produced the desired effect. Guns were fired from every house, barn, wall, or covert.

---

[1] Lieutenant Joseph Hayward, who had been in the French war, took these two chaises in Cambridge, and brought them to Concord, having killed a man in each. A little before, observing a gun pointed out of the window of a house by a British soldier, he seized it, and in attempting to enter the house found it fastened. He burst open the door, attacked and killed by himself two of the enemy in the room, and took a third prisoner. One of their guns is still owned by his son, from whom I received this anecdote.

[2] He was brother of Samuel Prescott, who brought the intelligence from Lexington in the morning. Samuel was taken prisoner on board a privateer afterwards, and carried to Halifax, where he died in jail. Abel died of the dysentery in Concord, September 3, 1775, aged 25.

After they had waylaid the enemy and fired upon them from one position, they fell back from the road, ran forward, and came up again to perform a similar manœuvre. The Sudbury company attacked them near Hardy's hill on the south; and below the Brooks tavern, on the old road north of the school-house, a severe battle was fought. Some were killed in the woods, and others in or near Mr. Hartwell's barn, close by. It was here that Captain Jonathan Wilson of Bedford, Nathaniel Wyman of Billerica, and Daniel Thompson of Woburn were killed. Eight of the British, who fell here and were left on the ground, were buried in the Lincoln burying-ground the next day, one of whom, from his dress, was supposed to have been an officer. Several were killed near where Viles's tavern now is; and at Fisk's hill, a little below, Lieutenant Colonel Smith was wounded in his leg, in a severe engagement. At the house at the bottom of this hill a rencontre between James Hayward of Acton and a British soldier took place. Hayward, on going round the house for a draught of water, perceived his antagonist coming through the house on the same errand. The Briton drew up his gun, remarking, it is said, "You are a dead man"; "And so are you," answered Hayward. Both fired and both fell; the former dead, and the latter mortally wounded. He died the next day. All the way the enemy were compelled to pass through ranks of men they had injured, and who were armed and eager to avenge the blood of their slaughtered fellow citizens.

An express was sent from Lexington in the morning to General Gage to inform him of what had happened there; and about 9 o'clock a brigade of about 1100 men marched out under the command of the Right Honorable Hugh Earl Percy,[1] a brigadier-general; consisting of the marines, the Welch Fusiliers, the 4th, 47th, and 38th regiments, and two field-pieces. This reinforcement arrived at Lexington about 2 o'clock, placed the field-pieces on the high ground below Monroe's tavern, and checked for about half an hour the eager pursuit of the provincials. During this time they burnt the house, barn, and other out-buildings of Deacon

---

[1] "Providence, May 10, 1777. On Monday General Percy, the hero of Lexington (weary of the American war, *though covered with laurels*), sailed from Newport for England in a ship mounting 14 *guns only*. The command has devolved on General Prescott." — *Boston Gazette.*

Joseph Loring, the house, barn, and shop of Mrs. Lydia Mulliken, and the house and shop of Mr. Joshua Bond. By the aid of this reinforcement they were able to effect their retreat to Charlestown, though not without sustaining continual losses on the way. They arrived about 7 o'clock, having, during a day unusually hot for the season, marched upwards of 36 miles, and endured almost incredible suffering. All the provisions they had had were obtained by purchase or plunder from the people; their provision-wagons having been taken by the Americans. Some of them "were so much exhausted with fatigue, that they were obliged to lie down on the ground, their tongues hanging out of their mouths like dogs after the chase." [1] Our militia and minute-men pursued them to Charlestown Neck, many of whom remained there during the night; others returned home. The damage to private property by fire, robbery, and destruction, was estimated at £274 16s. 7d. in Concord; £1761 1s. 5d. in Lexington; and £1202 8s. 7d. in Cambridge.[2]

Of the provincials 49 were killed, 36 wounded, and 5 missing. Captain Charles Miles, Captain Nathan Barrett, Jonas Brown, and Abel Prescott, jr., of Concord, were wounded. Captain Isaac Davis, Abner Hosmer, and James Hayward, of Acton, were killed, and Luther Blanchard, wounded. Captain Jonathan Wilson, of Bedford, was killed, and Job Lane wounded.

Of the British, 73 were killed, 172 wounded, and 26 missing; among whom were 18 officers, 10 sergeants, 2 drummers, and 240 rank and file. Among the wounded were Lieutenant Colonels Francis Smith and Benjamin Bernard. Lieutenant Edward Hall was wounded at the north bridge, and taken prisoner on the retreat. He died the next day, and his remains were delivered up to General Gage. Lieutenant Edward Thornton Gould was also wounded at the bridge, and taken prisoner on the retreat. He was confined and treated with kindness at Medford till May 28th, when he was exchanged for Josiah Breed, of Lynn. He had a

---

[1] Holmes's Annals, vol. ii. p. 206.

[2] Files of the Provincial Congress. Another paper in the Secretary's office, dated 1782, gives the amount of loss to Lexington £2576 2s. 1d., currency; — real estate £615 10s., and personal £1960 12s. 1d. And the Selectmen say in this paper, "As it is almost eight years since the 19th of April, 1775, some considerable part of the loss and damage sustained by the town cannot be ascertained at this time."

fortune of £1900 per annum, and is said to have offered £2000 for his ransom. Lieutenant Isaac Potter, of the marines, was taken prisoner, and confined some time at Reuben Brown's. Colonel Barrett was directed, April 22d, to give him liberty to walk round the house, but to keep a constant guard of three men, day and night, to prevent his being insulted or making his escape. Eight of the wounded received medical attendance from Dr. Cuming, at the house then standing near Captain Stacy's. One of them, John Bateman, died and was buried on the hill; and none of them were known to return to the British. Samuel Lee was taken prisoner early in the morning, between Lexington and Concord, and afterwards lived in Concord till his death. He always stated that he was the first prisoner taken on that day. Fourteen prisoners were confined in the jail in Concord during the year, and a number of others were permitted to go out to work. Fifteen were ordered to Worcester, April 26th. Sergeant Cooper, one of the party who went to Colonel Barrett's, married a woman who lived with Dr. Cuming.

Such is an imperfect sketch of the occurrences of the 19th of April, 1775, " the greatest of that age." " Concord," says the late President Dwight, " will be long remembered as having been, partially, the scene of the first military action in the revolutionary war, and the object of an expedition, the first in that chain of events, which terminated in the separation of the British colonies from their mother country. A traveller on this spot, particularly an American traveller, will insensibly call to his mind an event of this magnitude, and cannot fail of being deeply affected by a comparison of so small a beginning with so mighty an issue. In other circumstances, the expedition to Concord, and the interest which ensued, would have been merely little tales of wonder and of woe, chiefly recited by the parents of the neighbourhood to their circles at the fireside; commanding a momentary attention of childhood; and calling forth the tear of sorrow from the eyes of those who were intimately connected with the sufferers. Now the same events preface the history of a nation and the beginning of an empire, and are themes of disquisition and astonishment to the civilized world. From the plains of Concord will henceforth be dated a change in human affairs, an alteration in the balance of human power, and a new direction to the course of human improvement. Man, from the events which have occurred here, will, in some respects, assume a new character, and experience, in some respects, a new destiny."

CHAPTER VIII.

State of Feeling on the 20th of April. — Tories. — College removed to Concord. Committees of Correspondence. — Proceedings in Relation to the Monopoly Acts. — Revolutionary Soldiers. — Table of Different Campaigns. — Public pecuniary Sacrifices. — Taxes. — Constitution adopted.

THE events just described spread terror over the minds of some, indignation over others, and gloom over all; and predisposed them to new alarms. The death of several fellow citizens, in defence of their rights against British soldiers, was indeed a novel sight of fearful interest. The next day, April 20th, a messenger brought a report into town by way of Lincoln, that the regulars were again on their march to Concord. For a while this was believed, and the most active preparations were made for their reception, by removing the women and children from the village, and concealing them in the remote parts of the town, and in the woods, the men parading under arms, determined to defend themselves or perish. After a few hours the report was contradicted, and the inhabitants returned to their homes.

Meantime the patriot-soldiers were continually marching to Concord from remote towns. On the 21st, 700 of them went into the meeting-house, where prayers were offered up by the Rev. Mr. Emerson, and an address made by the Rev. Mr. Webster of Salem. In the afternoon Mr. Emerson and several others went to Cambridge. Great commotion prevailed. The next day the town was again alarmed. The minute companies paraded and marched to Cambridge; but, finding no enemy, they returned. The Provincial Congress met here on the 22d, and orders were given to raise an army forthwith.

These occurrences brought out the friends and opposers of liberty. Two or three individuals in town were yet inclined to toryism. It was not strange it should be so. It was a tremendous step to take up arms against the mother country; and, to say the least, the issue of the contest was doubtful. Men honestly differed in opinion as to the propriety of the measures of England, and others as to the proper course to be taken to obtain redress. Some had sworn allegiance to the king, and were afraid they should break their oath. While entertaining such opinions they did not enter warmly into the popular cause. They were, however, sure to receive the unwelcome notice of the people. One individual, who had been a selectman, was heard to say, " For myself I think I shall be neutral in these times;" and his name was immediately taken from the jury-box. The government was dictated by the force of public opinion. The town assumed, in some respects, the authority of an individual community, — an independent republic. Its committee of correspondence met daily, and acted in a legislative, executive, and judicial capacity. All suspicious persons were brought before it for trial, and, if found guilty, were condemned. The people supported them in their decisions. The following is a copy of one of these sentences, and most remarkably shows the peculiar spirit of those times.

" We the subscribers, committee of correspondence for the town of Concord, having taken into consideration the conduct of Dr. Lee of said town of late, are fully of the opinion, that he be confined to the farm his family now lives upon; and that, if he should presume to go beyond the bounds and should be killed, his blood be upon his own head. And we recommend to the inhabitants of the town, that, upon his conducting well for the future, and keeping his bounds, they by no means molest, insult, or disturb him, in carrying on his common affairs on said farm.

    JONAS HEYWOOD,
    EPHRAIM WOOD, JR. *Committee*
    JAMES BARRETT, JR.   *of*
    JOSEPH HOSMER, *Correspondence.*
    SAMUEL WHITNEY.

" Concord, April 26, 1775."

Dr. Lee was not set at liberty till June 4, 1776. His house was fired at several times by soldiers who passed through town; and so strong was the feeling against all called tories, that he would probably have been killed, had he gone beyond his bounds. All his privileges were, however, restored to him.[1] The estate of one individual only in Concord, that of Daniel Bliss, Esq., was confiscated and sold by government.

The citizens of Boston, called by a notice published in the newspapers, held their town meeting in Concord, July 18, 1775, when they elected a representative, and transacted other town business. At this time that town was occupied by the British troops, and many of its inhabitants removed to Concord.

The Provincial Congress ordered that the probate records, " supposed to be at Mr. Danforth's and Dr. Kneeland's houses, and the other records of the county at Mr. Foxcroft's, should be removed to Dr. Minott's in Concord."

The buildings of Harvard College were occupied as barracks for the American army, while stationed at Cambridge, and the students were dispersed. The college was removed to Concord, and commenced its operations on the first of October, 1775. President Langdon lived at Dr. Minott's (now the Middlesex Hotel); Professor Sewall lived at James Jones's; Professor Wigglesworth at the Bates place on the Bedford road; and Professor Winthrop at Darius Merriam's, near which was the library and philosophical apparatus; and other officers in different parts of the town. Twelve of the students boarded in the house now owned by Joseph Barrett, Esq., and others in many different places. The recitations were at the court-house and meeting-house. Prayers were attended at the latter place. The following proceedings of the government of the college were communicated to the town when it was about to be removed to Cambridge.

" Concord, June 12, 1776. At a meeting of the President, Professors, and Tutors of Harvard College, voted, that the following address of thanks be presented by the president to the selectmen, the gentlemen of the committee, and other gentlemen and inhabitants of the town of Concord, who have favored the college with their encouragement and assistance, in its removal to this town, by providing accommodations.

" GENTLEMEN, — The assistance you have afforded us in obtaining accommodations for this society here, when Cambridge was filled with the glorious army of freemen, which was assem-

---

[1] Dr. Lee's son, Jonas, was a warm friend of liberty, and for his son's sake many were restrained from committing outrages upon him.

bled to hazard their lives in their country's cause, and our removal from thence became necessary, demands our grateful acknowledgments.

"We have observed with pleasure the many tokens of your friendship to the college; and particularly thank you for the use of your public buildings. We hope the scholars while here have not dishonored themselves and the society by any incivilities or indecencies of behaviour, or that you will readily forgive any errors which may be attributed to the inadvertence of youth.

"May God reward you with all his blessings, grant us a quiet re-settlement in our ancient seat to which we are now returning, preserve America from slavery, and establish and continue religion, learning, liberty, peace, and the happiest government in these American colonies to the end of the world.

SAMUEL LANGDON, President.
Per order."

The committee of correspondence, &c., chosen March, 1776, were John Cuming, Esq., Ephraim Wood, Jr., Esq., Captain Jonas Heywood, Captain Joseph Hosmer, James Barrett, Esq., Captain David Brown, and Captain George Minott. In 1777, Colonel John Buttrick, Josiah Merriam, Isaac Hubbard, Captain Abishai Brown, Captain David Wheeler, Mr. Ephraim Potter, and Lieutenant Nathan Stow. In 1778, John Cuming, Esq., Colonel John Buttrick, Ephraim Wood, Jr., Esq., Jonas Heywood, Esq., James Barrett, Esq., Captain David Brown, and Mr. Josiah Merriam. These were reëlected in '79, '80, '81, and '82. In 1783, James Barrett, Esq. Jonas Heywood, Esq., Ephraim Wood, Jr., Esq., Captain David Brown, and Lieutenant Joseph Hayward. This committee was not chosen afterwards.

A convention of about 100 members of committees of correspondence from 32 towns in the county, called by the members in Concord, was held here August 20, 1776, and passed some spirited resolutions in relation to the duties of committees, and guarding against any efforts of the enemies of liberty. Ephraim Wood, Jonas Heywood, and James Barrett, Esquires, were chosen a county committee to call other meetings.

Efforts were often made during the revolution to regulate the prices of labor and merchandise. In 1777, a committee, chosen by the town for the purpose, reported the prices of various kinds of "common labor, carpenters', cordwainers', blacksmiths', women's labor, firewood, charcoal, live swine, horse-hire, chaise-hire, upper leather, saddlery, entertainment at public houses, flax, spirits, milk, clothiers' work," &c. &c. All who varied from the established prices were prosecuted and treated as enemies. Colonel John Buttrick was chosen to collect evidence against such as might be brought to trial. It does not appear, however, that any prosecutions took place in Concord.

A state convention met in Concord, July 14, 1779. The delegates from this town were John Cuming, Esq., Jonas Heywood, Esq., James Barrett, Esq., Colonel John Buttrick, Ephraim Wood, Jr., Esq., Captain David Brown, and Mr. Josiah Merriam; from Bedford, Mr. John Merriam; from Acton, Captain Joseph Robbins, Mr. Seth Brooks, and Mr. Thomas Noyes; and from Lincoln, Capt. Samuel Farrar and Abijah Pierce, Esq. The whole nnmber was 174. The object of this convention was to establish a state price-current, and to adopt other means to prevent monopoly, extortion, and unfair dealing. The meeting was opened and closed with prayer by the Rev. Mr. Ripley. The Hon. Azor Orne, of Marblehead, was Chairman, and Samuel Ruggles, Secretary. After passing some very spirited resolutions, fixing the prices of several articles of merchandise, and agreeing upon an address to the people, the convention adjourned on the 17th, recommending another similar one to meet again in October.

Their proceedings were laid before the town, July 30th, when they were approved, and a committee of thirteen chosen, " more fully to regulate the prices of articles of produce among us." Thi. committee reported, August 9th, when another, of six, was chosen, in conjunction with the committee of correspondence, "to keep a watchful eye over the people, and proceed against any who should *dare transgress* the regulated prices of articles enumerated, either in or out of town, by taking more than they are set in the report; and to treat them as enemies to their country." The town voted also " to support their committee in every regular method they shall take to punish those that violate them."

Another convention, having similar objects in view, of delegates from Concord, Billerica, Lexington, Westford, Stow, Bedford, Acton, and Lincoln, was held here, August 5th, which revised previous price-currents, and endeavoured to make one which should be uniform through the towns represented. John Cuming, Esq. was Chairman, and Ephraim Wood, Jr., Secretary.

A state convention met in Concord again, October 6th, and continued in session seven days. Colonel Cuming and Captain David Brown were delegates from Concord. A revised edition of the state price-current, several new spirited resolutions, relating to trade, currency, &c., and an address to the people, were adopted and published. County, town, and district meetings were recommended to carry these resolutions into effect. They were laid before this town, November 1st, and a committee of fourteen chosen, to fix the prices of such articles as were not therein enumerated. They reported, the next week, " that, as the regulations agreed upon by the late convention had been broken over by the inhabitants of Boston and many other places, they thought it not proper to proceed in the business assigned them, but to postpone the matter." Thus ended the proceedings relating to this difficult subject. It was indeed a fruitless attempt to enforce a system of uniform prices of merchandise, while the currency was constantly depreciating in value. And it is believed, that the attempts just noticed were means to increase private property, more than to promote the public good. The value of money was regulated monthly. January 1st, 1777, $100 in silver was worth $105 currency; in 1778, $328; in 1779, $742; in 1780, $2934; and in February, 1781, $7500. Such a rapid depreciation introduced great embarrassment and distress into all commercial transactions, which no body of men could remove by resolutions, addresses, price-currents, or prosecutions.

The number of men furnished by Concord for actual service in the war of the revolution was very great in proportion to her population; but how great cannot now be fully estimated. From the commencement of the war till May, 1778, unless voluntary enlistments could be procured, the militia officers were called upon to make drafts. These drafts were often made on the property, and sometimes included females and persons ordinarily exempted from military duty, who were obliged to hire a man. These were hired in or out of town, as was most convenient. From that time the town by its committees, or in classes, procured men. On the 10th of May, 1777, the 9th of December, 1778, and the 4th of April, 1780, estimates were made by the town of the "several services done in the war, 3 years' men excepted, by the town, classes, or individuals," and an average of the same made and assessed upon the inhabitants, and called average or war taxes. The amount of the first average was £2161 0s. 3d.; the 2d, £5192; and the 3d, (in silver), £1295 4s. 11d. The following table, compiled with labor and care from these estimates and other authentic sources of information, exhibits, though imperfectly, the number of men from Concord, the date of the resolve of the Council, or General Court, when they were required, at what place they were employed, and the bounties paid by the town. In this abstract are not included many who enlisted voluntarily, or marched on a sudden alarm for a short period, or were procured in classes, or where it is doubtful to what campaign they belonged. This would swell the list very much. In some instances they were not exclusively stationed as mentioned in the table, but marched to other places.

	When required.	Men.	Time.	Where employed.	Bounty.	Amount.
1	Jan. 1, 1775	100		Minute Men.		£ 58
2	April 20, 1775	56	8 mo.	Cambridge.	£ 5¼	308
3	Dec. 1, 1775	18	2 —	Cambridge.	1¼	27
4	Jan. 20, 1776	36	2 —	Cambridge.	1⅘	63¼
5	March 1, 1776	145	10 dys.	Dorchester Heights.		
6	April 9, 1776	31	9 mo.	Near Boston.		55⅘
7	June, 1776	19	12 —	New York.	10	190
8	June 25, 1776	48	6 —	Ticonderoga.	9	432
9	Sept. 12, 1776	23	3 —	White Plains.	8	184
10	1776	7		Dorchester.		
11	Nov. 21, 1776	34	3 mo.	New York.	10	340
12	Dec. 1, 1776	8		Boston.		
13	Dec. 1776	6		Rhode Island.		
14	Jan. 26, 1777	44	3 yrs.	Continental Army.	20	880
15	April 12, 1777	11		Rhode Island.	6	66
16	— 30, 1777	5	6 mo.	Continental Army.	8	40
17	July, 1777	29		Rhode Island.	10	290
18	Aug. 9, 1777	16	5 mo.	Northward.	35	560
19	Sept. 22, 1777	46	41 dys.	Taking of Burgoyne.	16	640
20	Nov. 28, 1777	23	5 mo.	Guard at Cambridge.	9	207
21	March 3, 1778	22	3 —	Do.	10	220
22	April 12, 1778	11		Rhode Island.	18	198
23	— 20, 1778	10	9 —	Continental Army.	130	1300

GENERAL HISTORY.

	When required.	Men.	Time.	Where employed.	Bounty.	Amount.
24	April 20, 1778	9	8 mo.	Guard at North River.	100	900
25	June 23, 1778	8	6 —	Guard at Cambridge.	15	120
26	—— 27, 1778	26	6 wks.	Rhode Island.	30	780
27	Sept. 6, 1778	7	4 mo.	Do.	73¼	514¼
28	—— 19, 1778	46	— —	To march to Boston.	$ 3	$ 138
29	April 27, 1779	5	6 wks.	Rhode Island.	——	——
30	June 8, 1779	8	9 mo.	Continental Army. }		3248
31	—— —, 1779	4	6 —	Rhode Island. }		
32	Aug. 9, 1779	9		Rhode Island.	——	——
33	Sept., 1779	4		Works at Boston.	12	48
34	—— 1, 1779	20	2 mo.	Rhode Island.	——	——
35	June 5, 1780	19	6 —	Continental Army.	1000	16000
36	—— 22, 1780	19	3 —	Rhode Island.		17090
37	Dec. 2, 1780	16	3 yrs.	Continental Army.	Hired in Classes.	
38	Dec. 28, 1780	10	9 mo.	Do. at Fishkill.	——	
39	June 15, 1781	3	5 —	Rhode Island.		——
40	—— 30, 1781	14	4 —	Continental Army.		——
41	March 1, 1782	——	3 yrs.	Continental Army.	Hired in Classes.	

Some particulars respecting each of these campaigns will be given in the Appendix.

The pecuniary sacrifices made by Concord on account of the revolution were also very great; but how great, it is impossible fully to estimate. I have gathered the following facts on the subject.

Whilst Boston was occupied with the British troops, in 1775, the poor endured great sufferings. In January and February £70 in money, 225 bushels of grain, and a quantity of meat and wood were, at different times, contributed by Concord for their relief. May 1st, the provincial Congress ordered that they should be supported by the country towns; 66 were assigned to Concord, 32 to Acton, 29 to Bedford, and 29 to Lincoln. It appears, however, that 21 families, containing 82 persons, were supported here. £80 was paid for them between May 13th and October. In the winter of 1775 and 1776, the town carried to Cambridge, for the use of the army, 210 cords of wood, 5 tons of hay, and some other articles, for which it paid £150. In July, 1775, the town was required to furnish "37 pairs of shirts, breeches, and stockings, and 75 coats." In January, 1776, Concord provided 20 blankets, Bedford 12, Acton 10, and Lincoln 14. In November, 1777, and at several other times, the town voted to provide for the families of those engaged in the continental army. £1214 was paid for this purpose before September, 1779. The town voted, in March, 1778, to procure, at an expense of £285, "shirts, shoes, and stockings, equal to the number of soldiers in the continental army, or the seventh part of the male inhabitants of the town over 16 years of age:" 60 were assigned to Concord, 19 to Bedford, 28 to Acton, and 28 to Lincoln. Captain Joseph Hosmer was the receiver for the whole county. From October, 1780, to the July following, 42,779 lbs. of beef were furnished by the town for the army. Every aid, whether in men, money, clothing, or provisions, required for the public service during the war, was readily furnished.

As a specimen of the enormous expenses of the town at this period, I select, from its records, the taxes actually assessed and collected during 1780 and 1781. In 1779 the taxes amounted, in silver, to $6,281·88, in 1782 to $9,544·98, and in 1783 to $5,208·69. When it is recollected that the town then contained about 1300 inhabitants only, their sacrifices will appear still greater. The annual taxes, principally for the public benefit, were then double what they have been for some time past with a population more than one third greater. The currency having been fluctuating, I have reduced the several sums to their real value in silver at the time they were assessed, according to the authorized tables of depreciation.

When assessed.		For what object.	Currency.			In Silver.	
Feb. 2,	1780	Continental tax.	£12,433	4s.0d.=		$1,412	54
April 4,	—	3d town "average or war tax."	1,295	4	11	115	56
— 22,	—	Half of the minister's salary.	3,438	15	0	286	56
— —,	—	Highway tax.	1,800	0	0	150	00
June 14,	—	To hire continental soldiers.	16,921	12	6	818	92
— 30,	—	To pay drafted militia.	17,090	5	6	837	75
July 14,	—	State tax to call in bills of credit.	26,852	18	0	1,297	24
Sept. 2,	—	do. do. in silver.	346	18	0	1,156	33
Oct. 25,	—	To purchase 11,520 lbs. of beef.	18,731	2	0	879	39
— —,	—	County tax.	1,158	10	0	54	39
— —,	—	Town charges.	15,495	11	0	727	49
Dec. 21,	—	To hire soldiers for 6 and 3 months.	40,801	3	0	1,837	89
— —,	—	Half of the minister's salary.	7,101	3	0	319	81
— 28,	—	State tax to call in bills of credit.	26,880	0	0	1,210	81
		Total amount of the assessments in 1780				$11,104	68

When assessed.	For what object.	Currency.			In Silver.	
March 1, 1781	To purchase 22,125 lbs. of beef.	33,259	8	0	1,478	19
July	State tax to be paid in silver.	692	2	9	2,307	12
	To pay town debts.	229	10	8	765	12
Sept. 15,	Half of the minister's salary.	85	9	2	268	20
—— 18,	To purchase clothing for soldiers.	57	10	9	191	79
Nov.	To purchase beef.	216	0	1	720	01
Dec. 30,	Continental tax.	1,369	9	9	4,564	96
	Total amount of the assessments in 1781				$10,295	39

In addition to these oppressive taxes, large sums were raised in classes to hire soldiers, and by individuals who were drafted and compelled to go into actual service, or hire a substitute. It is as impossible to estimate the exact amount paid by the citizens of Concord to purchase our independence, as it is too much to admire their exalted patriotism.

On the first of October, 1776, the town was called upon to act on the question, "whether it would give its consent that the House of Representatives with the Council should enact a constitution or form of government for this state." The subject was referred to a committee, consisting of Ephraim Wood, Jr., Nathan Bond, Colonel James Barrett, Colonel John Buttrick, and James Barrett, Esq., who reported the following resolves, which were unanimously accepted by the town.

"*Resolved*, 1. That this state being at present destitute of a properly established form of government, it is absolutely necessary that one should be immediately formed and established.

"2. That the supreme legislature, in their proper capacity, are by no means a body proper to form and establish a constitution or form of government, for reasons following, viz. 1. Because we conceive that a constitution, in its proper sense, intends a system of principles established to secure the subject in the possession and enjoyment of the rights and privileges against any encroachments of the governing party. 2. Because the same body that forms a constitution have of consequence a power to alter it. 3. Because a constitution alterable by the supreme legislature is no security at all to the subject against the encroachments of the governing party on any or all their rights and privileges.

"3. That it appears to this town highly expedient, that a convention or congress be immediately chosen to form and establish a constitution, by the inhabitants of the respective towns in the state, being free and twenty-one years of age and upwards, in proportion as the representatives of the state were formerly chosen: the convention or congress not to consist of a greater number, than the House of Assembly in this state heretofore might consist of, except that each town and district shall have liberty to send one representative or otherwise, as shall appear meet to the inhabitants of this state in general.

"4. That when the convention or congress have formed a constitution, they adjourn for a short time, and publish their proposed constitution for the inspection and remarks of the people of the state.

"5. That the House of Assembly of this state be desired to recommend to the inhabitants to proceed to choose a convention or congress, for the purpose above mentioned, as soon as possible."

Notwithstanding these wholesome instructions, a constitution was made by the General Court and sent to this town; but it refused, June 15, 1778, unanimously, by 111 votes, to accept it, for reasons above mentioned.

A convention, to which John Cuming and Ephraim Wood, Jr., Esqrs., were delegates from Concord, met in Cambridge in the fall of 1779, and formed a constitution, which was submitted to the town, May 27, 1780. The bill of rights was approved with the following exceptions. The 2d article had 2 votes against it; the 3d, 8; the 9th, 3; and to the 29th, one desired to add the words "no longer." The 1st, 2d, 4th, 5th, and 6th chapters were unanimously adopted with the following exceptions. The 1st and 2d article of the 2d section, 1st chapter, had 3 votes against it; the 8th article in the same section, 8; the 3d and 6th articles of the 3d section, in the same chapter, had 1 vote each against them. The 2d article, 1st section, 2d chapter, was proposed to be amended by inserting the word "Protestant"; and the 13th of the same section, by having the "salary of the governor," &c. stated yearly. The word "Protestant" was also proposed to be inserted in the 1st article in the 6th chapter.* The first town

---

* The votes on the constitution, as revised, in 1820, were as follows. The first article 46 yeas and 77 nays; the 2d, 46 yeas, 81 nays; the 3d,

meeting under the new constitution was held, August 23, 1780, when 121 votes were given for governor, all for John Hancock.

CHAPTER IX.

State of Feeling subsequent to the Revolution. — Proceedings of the County and of the Town. — Mr. Avery's Letter. — Armed Men assemble at Concord. — Courts stopped. — Notice of the Insurgents. — Proceedings of the Town. — The War of 1812. — County Courts and Shire Towns regulated. — Proceedings of the Town on this Subject.

CONCORD, from its central situation and importance in the county, was also the theatre of many interesting events during the insurrection of 1786, known as " Shays's Insurrection." In common with other towns, it felt, with great severity, the pressure of the times immediately succeeding the revolutionary war. The large drafts on the town for men and money to carry on that war, the scarcity of money, and the depreciation in value of that received for public service, the decay of business, the increase of public and private debts, and the numerous law-suits arising therefrom, the introduction of profligate manners, and the want of confidence in government, with other existing evils, were *grievances* (as they were then generally called), which produced great public and private embarrassment. There were a few persons in this, and many in other towns in the county, who were inclined to join in such an appeal to arms as would, in their opinion, compel the government to grant relief. A great majority of the inhabitants of Concord lamented the existing evils, but their proceedings were constitutional, conciliatory, and highly commendable. Interesting and able instructions, given to the representatives in 1782, 1784, and 1786, express the sentiments of

---

76 yeas, 49 nays; the 4th, 59 yeas, 68 nays; the 5th, 55 yeas, 72 nays; the 6th, 78 yeas, 50 nays; the 7th, 69 yeas, 58 nays; the 8th, 67 yeas, 60 nays; the 9th, 62 yeas, 65 nays; the 10th, 58 yeas, 68 nays; the 11th, 78 yeas, 48 nays; the 12th, 68 yeas, 58 nays; the 13th, 81 yeas, 44 nays; and the 14th, 49 yeas, 69 nays.

the town on the subjects which then agitated the community, and are found in the town records.

A convention of delegates from a majority of the towns in the county of Middlesex was held in Concord, August 23, 1786, " to consult on matters of public grievance under which the people labor." This convention was called by Captain John Nutting, of Pepperell, chairman of a convention of committees from Groton, Pepperell, Shirley, Townsend, and Ashby, which had met at Groton the 29th of the previous June. Concord was represented in the convention by Messrs. Isaac Hubbard, David Brown, Jonas Lee, Joseph Chandler, and Samuel Bartlett; and, to guard them against any rash proceedings, the town instructed them " to oppose every unconstitutional measure that may be proposed by said convention, strictly to adhere to the rules prescribed by the constitution of this commonwealth; in particular, to oppose any instructions in favor of paper money being emitted; and that they endeavour to take every measure to encourage industry, frugality, and good economy through the country." John Merriam and Timothy Jones were delegates from Bedford; Simon Tuttle and Thomas Noyes, from Acton; Samuel Farrar and Samuel Hoar, from Lincoln; and Thomas Hutchins and Asa Parlin, from Carlisle. After the objects of the meeting had been considered, ten articles of grievance voted, and an address to the public adopted and ordered to be published, the convention adjourned to meet again on the first Tuesday in October. There were several in this convention who took an active part in the subsequent opposition to government.

These proceedings did not meet the entire approbation of the people of Concord. They were aware that some of these sentiments were highly improper, and, if carried into effect, would lead to open rebellion. On the 22d of August, conventions had been held in the counties of Hampshire and Berkshire, whose proceedings were similar to those in Middlesex; and about 1500 men had actually assembled under arms at Northampton, and prevented the sitting of the court there. The Court of Common Pleas, which was to sit in Concord on the 12th of September following, had been mentioned, by the Middlesex convention, as one of the public grievances. And though there was good ground to believe the people of this county were more averse to rebellion than some others, yet disturbance was anticipated.

September 8th, the Governor ordered that the artillery companies of Roxbury and Dorchester be called upon to march to Concord " to support the court on Tuesday next, to be under the command of General Brooks." Such other companies as the exigencies might require were to be ordered from the county of Suffolk.

At this critical period, a special town meeting was called on Saturday the 9th, when the riotous measures, which had taken place in other counties to suppress courts of justice, were " seriously and deliberately " discussed. The town voted that they were " alarming," and " declared their utter abhorrence of such riotous conduct." A committee, consisting of the Hon. Joseph Hosmer, Rev. Ezra Ripley, Mr. Samuel Bartlett, Jonas Heywood, Esq., and Captain David Brown, was chosen to prepare a circular letter to other towns in the county, " inviting their coöperation in acting as mediators between the government and the opposition, and in using their utmost endeavours to calm the people's minds," should they meet the next week to prevent the session of the court. After an adjournment of half an hour, the committee reported the following address, which was several times read, and unanimously adopted.

" *To the Town of* ─────────

" Gentlemen, ─ Alarmed at the threatening aspect of our public affairs, this town has this day held a meeting, and declared, unanimously, their utter disapprobation of the disorderly proceedings of a number of persons in the counties of Hampshire and Worcester, in preventing the sitting of the courts there. And apprehending the like may be attempted in this county, and probably attended with very dangerous consequences, we have thought it advisable to endeavour, in conjunction with as many of the neighbouring towns, as we can give seasonable information to, by lenient measures, to dissuade from such rash conduct as may involve the state in anarchy and confusion, and the deprecated horrors of civil war. We conceive the present uneasiness of the people to be not altogether groundless; and although many designing men, enemies to the present government, may wish and actually are fomenting uneasiness among the people, yet we are fully persuaded, that the views of by far the greater part are to obtain redress of what they conceive to be real grievances. And since the method they have taken cannot fail of meeting the hearty disapprobation of every friend of peace and good order, we cannot but hope, from what we know of the strenuous exertions which have been made by the towns around us, and in which those disorders above mentioned now exist, to purchase at the expense of blood our independence, and the great unanimity with which they have established our present government; and from what we know of the real grounds of their complaints; were lenient measures used, and a number of towns united to endeavour, by every rational argument, to dissuade those who may seem refractory from measures which tend immediately to destroy the fair fabric of our government, and to join in legal and constitutional measures to obtain redress of what may be found to be real grievances; they would be attended with happy effects. We have therefore chosen a committee to act in concert with the neighbouring towns, for the purpose of mediating between opposing parties, should they meet. And we cannot but hope, our united endeavours to support the dignity of government and prevent the effusion of blood, will meet with general approbation, and be attended with happy consequences.

"If the above should meet with your approbation, we request you to choose some persons to meet a committee of this town, chosen for that purpose, at the house of Captain Oliver Brown, innholder in Concord, on Monday evening or Tuesday morning next, that we may confer together, and adopt measures which may be thought best calculated for the attainment of the ends above proposed. We are, gentlemen, with great esteem and friendship, your humble servants.

JOSEPH HOSMER, *Chairman*,
in behalf of the Town's Committee.

"Concord, September 9, 1786."

Copies of this address were immediately sent to the several towns in the county, and, notwithstanding the short notice, *twenty-four* were represented in the convention. Captain Duncan Ingraham, of Concord, was chosen to present the address to the Governor for his approbation. This was done the next day (Sunday), when, on account of the critical state of public affairs, a special session of the council was convened in Boston. The proceedings of Concord were highly approved, and the address was copied, by order of the Executive, and sent to Bristol county, with an urgent request that similar measures might be adopted there. In consequence of these timely proceedings, the orders to General Brooks for calling out the militia were countermanded; and much good was anticipated from the proposed mediation.

The following letter to the Honorable Joseph Hosmer from the Secretary of the State, in relation to the proceedings of Concord, is deemed worthy of preservation.

"*Boston, September* 10, 1786.

"Dear Sir, — The address of the town of Concord, to the several towns in the county of Middlesex, does the town great honor; and I cannot but think, that the measures you have adopted will have a happy tendency to conciliate the minds of the people, and be productive of great good. Your address came in a critical moment, which his Excellency communicated to the judges of the Supreme Judicial Court, and several gentlemen of the Senate and of the House of Representatives, who were assembled, by the desire of the Governor, to consult on measures necessary to be adopted at this very alarming crisis of our affairs, who expressed their approbation, in the warmest terms, respecting the proceedings of your town. And be assured, that the measures that were taken in consequence thereof gave me the highest satisfaction; and as a convincing proof, I have set myself down this evening to express it to my good friend Major Hosmer, whose goodness of heart I have long been acquainted with through very perilous times."

[Here follows a copy of the counter order to General Brooks above noticed.]

"It is the greatest grief to me to see people, who might be the happiest in the world, adopt measures to sap the very foundation of our excellent constitution. I am sensible that we are under great embarrassments and there are grievances, but in my humble opinion they are most of them really imaginary. If a little more industry and economy were practised by the community at large, they would be very happy; but there are some idle people going from county to county, inflaming the minds of many, filling their heads with stories of the most improbable nature, sowing sedition, and making every attempt to overthrow our excellent constitution. The stopping of the Courts of Common Pleas, in the several counties, is but a small part of their infernal plan, which many worthy good people, who join these persons, are little aware of, but sooner or later they will be acquainted with it.

"I have not time to add further, except wishing that the gentlemen, who shall meet at Concord on Tuesday next, upon the subject matter of your address, may have divine direction in their deliberations.

"I am, Sir, with respect, your friend and humble servant.

JOHN AVERY.

"Hon. JOSEPH HOSMER, Esq."

Notwithstanding these precautionary measures, about 100 men under arms from Groton and its neighbourhood, commanded by Captains Job Shattuck, of Groton, and Nathan Smith and Sylvanus Smith, of Shirley, assembled at Concord, about 5 o'clock on Monday afternoon, September 12. They lodged that night in the court-house, barns, and such temporary shelter as they could obtain, and on Tuesday took possession of the ground in front of the court-house, marked out their lines, and formed in columns around it, to prevent any but their own party from entering. About 2 o'clock, P. M. one of the party, acting as a sergeant, with two drums and fifes, went some distance, and in about half an hour returned at the head of about 90 men, armed and on horseback, from the counties of Hampshire and Worcester, led by one Wheeler of Hubbardstown, and Converse of Hardwick, and joined the other party, which had increased to about 200.

The convention, invited by Concord, convened at the meeting-house on Tuesday morning, and was organized by choosing Isaac Stearns, of Billerica, chairman, and Samuel Bartlett, of Concord, secretary. It was opened with prayer by the Reverend Ezra Ripley. A committee was appointed to confer with the people under arms, to know the purpose of their assembling; and another to wait on the justices of the courts to inform them of the objects of the convention and of the insurgents. In this manner, commucation was opened between the different parties. The committee to confer with the armed men were unsuccessful in convincing them of the impropriety of their conduct. About one o'clock they received the following note.

"To the Honorable Justices of the Court of General Sessions of the Peace and Court of Common Pleas for the county of Middlesex, &c.

"The voice of the people of this county is, that the Court of General Sessions of the Peace and Court of Common Pleas *shall not* enter this court-house until such time as the people shall have a redress of a number of grievances they labor under at present, which will be set forth in a petition, or remonstrance, to the next General Court. JOB SHATTUCK.

"*Concord, September* 12, 1786."

After the reception of this paper the committee used further arguments to dissuade from violence, and to be contented with the opening and adjournment of the courts, which finally produced the following endorsement.

"*Half past* 3 *o'clock.*

"Since writing the within, it is agreed that the Court of Sessions *may* open and adjourn to the last Tuesday of November next without going into the court-house.

JOB SHATTUCK."

The committee laid these communications before the justices of the courts, and stated the particulars of their conference with the insurgents; and it was recommended that they should suspend their session. While this subject was under consideration, the insurgents became impatient. Smith beat round for volunteers, and addressed the people, declaring that "any person who did not follow his drum and join his standard, should be drove out of town at the point of the bayonet, let them be court, town committee, or what else." "I am going," said he, "to give the court four hours to agree to our terms, and if they do not, I and my party will compel them to it. I will lay down my life to *suppress* the government from all *triannical oppression*, and you, who are willing to join us in *this here affair*, may fall into our ranks." Few, however, joined his standard. His language was offensive even to his own party.

Two companies, one on horseback, and another on foot, marched to Jones's tavern, where the court was assembled, and halted and faced about towards the house in a menacing manner. They were informed that neither court would be opened; and the party marched off to the main body. The court soon after left town; and the convention separated, after choosing a committee to lay their proceedings before the Governor, and adopting the following expression of their sentiments.

"This body cannot forbear to express their disagreeable and painful sensations, that their endeavours to dissuade from rash and unlawful measures have proved so ineffectual. They declare their utter abhorrence of the measures adopted by the body in arms, and are fully sensible of the high criminality of such opposition to established authority, which, if not speedily prevented, must unavoidably involve the commonwealth in calamities innumerable and inexpressible."

The insurgents increased during the day to about 300, nearly 200 of whom were armed with guns, and the remainder with swords, clubs, &c. They generally looked wretchedly. "Almost all the muskets," says a cotemporary writer, "were rendered useless by the rain, and the men by New-England rum, so that probably, if occasion required, not above 30 or 40 men would have been procured capable of opposing any governmental measures." They dispersed late on Tuesday night; and it was several weeks from that time before any new exertions were made in Concord in opposition to government. The discontented turned their attention to other counties. These events, however, produced great excitement among the people. All classes arranged themselves with, or in opposition to the government. Even the boys in the streets were seen with their hats labelled with "government," or "opposition." It was indeed a day of great anxiety.

The county convention, which met here, as already noticed, on the 23d of August, met again by adjournment on the 3d of October. Eighteen towns were represented. The following petition to the general court was drawn up, and signed by Samuel Reed, chairman, praying relief for seventeen specified articles of grievance. The first ten were the same as voted at the first meeting of the convention, on the 23d of August. It specifies,

"That your petitioners, being chosen by their respective towns for the purpose of collecting the sentiments of those towns which they represent respecting their present grievances, and to seek relief in a peaceable, orderly, and constitutional way; viewing, with the greatest abhorrence and detestation, the late riotous proceedings of a rash and inconsiderate body of people, in opposing the sitting of the courts of justice, notwithstanding their leaders did falsely pretend to signify the ' voice of the people' in this county in so doing; and, having collected the sentiments of the several towns, which we here represent, do point out the following particulars as grievances, and pray the honorable court for redress, viz.

" 1st. The sitting of the General Court in the town of Boston, which, for reasons we trust obvious to the honorable Court, is by no means adapted to expedite public business.[1]

" 2d. That the Court of Common Pleas is so burthensome by reason of the extraordinary expense arising therefrom, without any considerable advantage to the people.

" 3d. That lawyers are permitted to exact such exorbitant fees, to the great injury of many in the community.

" 4th. That the salaries of several public officers are greater than the abilities of the people will admit of.

" 5th. The want of a circulating medium has so stagnated business, that, unless speedily remedied, it will involve the greater part of the community in a state of bankruptcy.

" 6th. The taking of men's bodies, and confining them in jail for debt, when they have property sufficient to answer the demands of their creditors.

" 7th. That the accounts of the United States are not settled, by which means we apprehend ourselves disproportionably burthened.

" 8th. That greater duties, or imposts, are not laid on superfluities, imported from foreign nations.

" 9th. The manner of electing jurors, as to their qualifications and pay. Serving as jurors has been esteemed as a burthen on the subject, which has been the means of filling our boxes with many men entirely unqualified for that business.

" 10th. That such heavy taxes are laid on lands, and no encouragements given to agriculture and our own manufactures.

" 11th. That our unappropriated lands are not disposed of towards the discharge of our domestic debt.

---

[1] The people wished the General Court should sit in the country; and Concord was, for several years about this time, talked of as the place of meeting.

"12th. That the moneys arising from the imposts and excise are not appropriated towards the discharge of our foreign debt.

"13th. That the registering of deeds, under the present establishment, is far more expensive than is necessary, as the same might be done in the several towns.

"14th. That the duties on writs and executions should be exacted of the debtors.

"15th. The present fee table, as it now stands, being higher, in some instances, than is necessary.

"16th. The present method of collecting excise, as the same might be collected in the several towns at much less expense to government.

"17th. That the thirtieth article in the bill of rights in the Constitution is not more strictly attended to, — in admitting persons to hold seats in our legislature to enact laws, and at the same time hold and exercise the judicial powers of government, as thereby our government becomes a government of men and not of laws.

"Your petitioners humbly beg your honors' attention to these our grievances, and pray for a speedy redress, and, as in duty bound, will ever pray.

By order of the committee,

SAMUEL REED, *Chairman.*"

The proceedings of this convention were taken into consideration by the town of Concord at a meeting held October 9th, when, after long deliberation, it was voted not to approve of them. A committee was chosen to draw up instructions to their representative, who reported, at great length and with great ability, the reasons which governed them.

On the 31st of October the Supreme Court met at Cambridge, and it was anticipated that efforts would be made to oppose its proceedings; and about 3000 of the militia marched thither for its protection. They were shortly dismissed. The chief justice, in his charge to the grand jury, spoke of the riotous proceedings of the insurgents in strong terms of disapprobation.

On the 28th of November the Court of Common Pleas was to sit in Cambridge; and though the leading insurgent of the 12th of September had been persuaded not to take any measure in opposition to government, his agreement was overruled in secret council with the leaders in Worcester county. On the 27th a party, headed by Oliver Parker, marched into Concord, intending to proceed to Cambridge. Job Shattuck came in a secret manner; and, after his arrival, went under cover of night " to Weston to get intelligence of the Worcester forces; but though they had begun their march, they did not appear; and from want of coöperation the whole plan fell through. The insurgents at Concord, growing disheartened, scattered before any force could reach them."

Warrants were issued for apprehending the leading insurgents in Middlesex, and were committed to the sheriff. A military force volunteered to assist him, leaving Boston the 29th of November, and proceeding immediately to Concord. The militia of this town stood ready to afford any assistance. A party of horse was despatched to secure the subjects of the warrants, and returned at night with Page and Parker prisoners. Not having succeeded in apprehending Shattuck, the principal leader, they proceeded to his house in Groton, and on their arrival found he had taken the alarm and fled to the woods. A search was made, and after considerable exertion he was taken, about 10 o'clock, A. M. November 30th. He received several wounds from his pursuers during his arrest, some of which were very dangerous, — a treatment which was generally censured. He was taken to Boston the next day and confined in prison, where he received medical aid, but never entirely recovered the use of his limbs. In the following May he was tried at Concord, and condemned to be hanged. But the government treated him with lenity, as they did all those who unfortunately acted, as he did, from mistaken views, and gave him a full pardon, September 20, 1787.[1] Ephraim Wood, Esq. obtained this pardon from government.

---

[1] Captain Job Shattuck died in Groton, January 13, 1819, aged 84. He had been a brave and successful officer in the French and revolutionary wars, and often affirmed, that he looked on no act of his life with more satisfaction than that to which I have adverted; though he is said to have felt grateful for the pardon at the time, and remarked, he "would always be a good subject afterwards." Whatever the object of those acts might originally have been, the ultimate results were undoubtedly good. The people were thereby taught the necessity of a general union of the states, and of the speedy adoption of the federal constitution. They were induced to take such measures as gave the people confidence in the government, and promoted the general prosperity.

After the apprehension of the opposing leaders in Middlesex, the insurrection was confined to other counties. Detachments of soldiers were made in January to suppress it. One from Concord marched to Worcester, Springfield, Hadley, Amherst, Petersham, back to Amherst, Hadley, Northampton, Westhampton, Pittsfield, Farmington, Loudon, Sandersfield, Southwick, West-Springfield, back to Worcester and home. The officers of this company were Roger Brown, Captain; Amos Barrett, Lieutenant; and Jonas Heald, of Acton, Ensign; and were attached to the regiment commanded by Colonel Henry Woods, of Pepperell, and Lieutenant Colonel William Monroe, of Lexington. They left Concord, January 19th, and returned February 26th. On the 27th of January the town voted "to provide the families of those soldiers, that were gone, with the necessaries of life, while absent, if asked for." A bounty was paid by subscription. All the militia marched as far as Marlborough; but, before they had been long absent, they were ordered back again. The people of this town took no further part in the insurrection.[1]

From the following instructions, given to the representative in May, 1787, it will be perceived that the town had not forgotten the critical state of the times. As it was the last time the town instructed its representative, it is thought proper to present them entire.

"To Mr. ISAAC HUBBARD,

"SIR, — The critical period, in which you are appointed to represent this town in the General Court, points out to us the importance of a strict adherence to the principles of our constitution, while we express our sentiments on those measures we suppose necessary to be adopted. With real sorrow we have seen, in the course of the year past, an attempt made by wicked and unreasonable men to destroy that constitution we have so lately established, and to interrupt the execution of those laws, without which our lives, property, and every thing dear and sacred, would be insecure. We should be wanting in gratitude should we neglect, on this occasion, to express our hearty approbation of the

---

[1] General Daniel Shays, the leader in this insurrection, died at Sparta, New York, September 29, 1825, aged 84. Notwithstanding his conduct in this affair, he was pardoned, and was afterwards a pensioner on government.

wise and spirited measures, adopted by the legislature, for preventing the calamities which of late threatened this commonwealth, and for supporting the dignity and authority of our government, and for the effects which have happily followed those measures. We conceive it to be highly expedient, that a similar line of conduct should still be preserved in order to perfect peace and tranquillity among us.

" The happy privilege enjoyed by us of choosing annually our rulers, men from among ourselves, who must share equally with their brethren the weight and burthen which may be necessarily laid, and who are responsible to their constituents for the faithful discharge of their duty, must greatly aggravate the folly and madness of those, who, under pretence of procuring a redress of grievances, have drawn the sword against their own government and laws; especially as our representatives, if they are men of ability and integrity, may remove every real grievance complained of. Many causes concur to render our present situation critical and distressing. The debts contracted in the late war, public and private; the decay of public faith and credit; the want of public and private virtue; the shameful neglect of economy, frugality, and industry; an unbounded fondness for foreign luxuries, fashions, and manners, with a restless, impatient, and unreasonable jealousy of our rulers, are the causes of our present unhappiness; to remove which we conceive no effectual remedy can be applied, unless as a people we tread back the steps that have led us to our present unhappy situation.

" The want of confidence in public promises requires, that every exertion should be made, when promises are made by public bodies, that they should be held sacred and inviolable. To restore public and private virtue, those in higher stations (whose manners are readily copied by the lower classes of men) should set the example; and all orders endeavour to revive and practise that honesty and simplicity of manners, that have hitherto been the characteristic of the inhabitants of this state.

" There is certainly need of economy and prudence in the expense of government, as far as it consists with the preservation of the same; that *every encouragement be given to our own manufactures, and that such further duties be laid on foreign luxuries as shall tend to stop their importation.* And that our government may be preserved and respected, it is necessary that the laws should be punctually executed. To provide some way for raising some supplies for the public expenses, which shall be less burdensome on the landed interest, is an object we particularly recommend to you. And we especially instruct you to oppose the emission of paper money. When any matter of importance is to be transacted, respecting which the mind of your constituents is not known, you will have recourse to them for direction. And at the close of the session, or at the end of the year, in order that your constituents may have the fullest information of the doings of the legislature, as well as the reasons therefor, that you be ready to satisfy them. And in every respect, that you make the constitution of this commonwealth your rule, and the happiness and prosperity of this and the United States the end, in all measures adopted. By order of the committee,

" *Concord, May* 28, 1787. EPHRAIM WOOD, *Chairman.*"

These instructions were drawn up by a committee, consisting of Messrs. Ephraim Wood, James Barrett, Samuel Bartlett, Jonas Lee, and Asa Brooks, and were attributed to the pen of Mr. Bartlett.[1]

From this time to 1812, no events of great importance took place in town, excepting such as will hereafter be mentioned in the miscellaneous history. June 6, 1794, there were detached 41 persons, under command of Captain William Jones, and composed part of the " Oxford Army."

In the war, declared in 1812, Concord furnished several enlisted and several drafted soldiers. The Honorable John L. Tuttle, a Colonel till his death,[2] and Frederick Hildreth, a

---

[1] Samuel Bartlett, Esq. was son of Roger Bartlett and Anna Hurd, and born in Boston, November 17, 1752. He was bred a goldsmith, and soon after commencing business removed to Concord in 1775, and was married the next year. While resident here he was an influential and useful man. In 1795 he was chosen register of deeds, and removed to Cambridge, where he died, September 29, 1821, aged 69; having held that office till his death. Of three sons, all born in Concord, Samuel was bred a mechanic; John, born May 23, 1784, graduated at Harvard College, in 1805, and is now minister at Marblehead; and Benjamin Dixon, born September 12, 1789, graduated at Harvard College in 1810, and is now settled as a physician in Maine.

[2] He will be noticed among the professional men.

Lieutenant a short time, were the only commissioned officers in the regular service. Lieutenant Sullivan Burbank was stationed, as a recruiting officer, in the house now owned by the Honorable Samuel Hoar.

The militia were called upon several times. The town voted, in May, 1812, to allow $3 each, in addition to their wages, to all who should be detached under the United States law. Early in September, 1814, orders were issued for calling out the militia of the state for the defence of the sea-coast. The Light Infantry and Artillery companies of Concord, and the Acton Blues, marched September 10th. Nehemiah Flint was Captain, John Brown, Lieutenant, and Artemas Wheeler, Ensign, of the Concord Infantry; and Reuben Brown, Captain, Francis Wheeler, First Lieutenant, and Cyrus Wheeler, Second Lieutenant, of the Artillery. The Infantry were attached to the first regiment, under the command of Col. Joseph Valentine. Eliab W. Metcalf was Adjutant, and the Reverend Nathaniel How, Chaplain. These companies were stationed at South Boston, and returned home, October 31.

Military affairs then much engaged the attention of the people. A company of exempts was organized here, September 13, 1814, and Colonel Roger Brown was chosen Captain, Colonel John Buttrick, Lieutenant, and Major James Barrett, Ensign. At a parade, October 3d, a standard was presented by the ladies, with appropriate ceremonies.

In 1813 several British naval officers, prisoners of war, resided in Concord on parole, some of whom were taken in the Guerriere. A number left here, November 23d, but their places were supplied by others the next day. Some of them were of distinguished families, and scattered their wealth with liberal hands.

In regard to the political sentiments of the town at this period, it will be sufficient to remark generally, that they partook of the excitement of the times. For many years the vote of the two parties was nearly equal, and in one instance a sick man was carried to the poll, and turned the scale. Many of the political conventions of the county were held here; and some of them were distinguished for the high party zeal with which they were managed. The political history of those times is, however, marked with no peculiar feature in this town, and is therefore omitted.[1]

---

[1] For a list of votes for governor, from 1780 to 1829, see Appendix.

In 1814 efforts to establish Concord as the principal shire town, where the county records should be kept, were made for the last time. And it may not be amiss in this place to give a brief history of these efforts.[1]

The county of Worcester was incorporated April 2, 1731 ; and in the following winter a convention of delegates, from several towns in Middlesex, was held in Concord ; and, by adjournment, May 26, 1732, when it was agreed to petition the General Court to have the towns of Concord, Sudbury, Framingham, Marlbo-

[1] During the colony charter, the county courts were held alternately at Cambridge and Charlestown. After the second charter, a new organization of the courts took place. In 1692 the Inferior Court of Common Pleas, and the Court of General Sessions of the Peace, were established, and ordered to sit at Cambridge on the 2d Tuesday of September; at Charlestown, on the 2d Tuesday of December and March ; and at Concord on the 2d Tuesday of June. In 1742, at Cambridge, 3d Tuesday of May ; at Charlestown, 2d Tuesday of December and March ; and at Concord, last Tuesday of August. In 1751 the session at Concord was altered to the 1st Tuesday of September. In 1765, at Charlestown on the 1st Tuesday of March and last Tuesday of November; at Cambridge, 3d Tuesday of May ; and at Concord, 2d Tuesday of September. In 1770, at Cambridge, 3d Tuesday of May ; at Charlestown, 2d Tuesday of March and last Tuesday of November; and at Concord, 1st Tuesday of September. November 9, 1775, both the sessions, before held at Charlestown, were ordered to be held at Concord at the same time. In 1778, a session was ordered at Groton, 3d Tuesday of May, and at Cambridge last Tuesday of November. In 1790, at Concord 3d Tuesday of March and 2d Tuesday of September, and at Cambridge last Tuesday of November. In 1795, an additional session at Concord, 3d Tuesday of May. In 1796 all the sessions were altered from Tuesday to Monday. In 1797, at Cambridge, the Monday next preceding the last Tuesday of November, and at Concord the Monday next preceding the 3d Tuesday of March, 1st Tuesday of June, and 2d Tuesday of September, and at Cambridge 3d Tuesday of December. In 1812 and since, at Concord 2d Monday of March, 2d of June, and 2d of September, and at Cambridge 2d of December.

The Supreme Court was first held in Concord on the 2d Tuesday of April, 1776, having before been annually held in Charlestown at the same time. In 1783, at Concord 2d Tuesday of April, and at Cambridge last Tuesday of October. In 1800, at Cambridge 4th Tuesday of October, and, in 1805, 1st Tuesday of November. In 1816, at Concord 1st Tuesday of April. In 1820, the 2d after the 4th Tuesday of September at Cambridge, and at Concord the 4th Monday of March. In 1826, on the 2d Tuesday of April, and at Cambridge on the 3d after the 4th Tuesday in October.

rough, Groton, Chelmsford, Billerica, Stow, Littleton, Bedford, Dunstable, Westford, Dracut, and North Town [?], incorporated into a separate county, of which Concord was to be the shire town. Messrs. Benjamin Whittemore and John Fox were chosen, by Concord, to aid the object. It does not appear, however, that any definite measures were taken.

In 1763 petitions were again presented from several towns, and the agents had a hearing in January, 1764. Captain Abel Lawrence and several others, of Groton and the adjacent towns, renewed the petition, at the following June session, to have the western part of Middlesex, and the northern part of Worcester, erected into a separate county. These petitions were continued under agitation till 1766. Remonstrances were sent in by the town of Concord, and others more easterly; and also petitions for Concord to become the only shire town in the county. Several towns were very anxious that the last project should be carried into effect. The whole subject, however, was finally abandoned after several orders of notice had been issued, and several different committees of the General Court had had it under consideration.

In May, 1791, Duncan Ingraham of Concord, Aaron Brown of Groton, Zaccheus Wright of Westford, Charles Whitman of Stow, Jonas Brooks of Acton, and John Minott of Chelmsford, the representatives from those towns, petitioned the legislature to have Concord made the only shire town in the county; and that accommodations for the safe keeping of the public records be made in the new court-house proposed to be erected there by the county. An order of notice passed on this petition, May 9, 1792, but here ended the proceedings on this subject.

The county buildings at Cambridge had become so much out of repair, that the authorities began, in 1812, to consider the subject of erecting new ones. This was a favorable time to attempt again to have the county offices removed to Concord. January 16, 1812, the town chose Samuel Hoar, Jr., Joseph Barrett, and Jonas Lee, Esquires, to draft a petition to the legislature for this object. The following was reported and accepted; and the same committee, with the addition of Messrs. Tilly Merrick, Isaac Hurd, Jonas Buttrick, Francis Jarvis, and Benjamin Prescott, Jr., were chosen to sign and present it to the legislature.

"To the Honorable Senate and House of Representatives of the Commonwealth of Massachusetts.

"The inhabitants of the town of Concord, in the county of Middlesex, humbly show, that the existing laws, requiring some of the sessions of the courts for said county to be holden in said Concord, and others in Cambridge in said county, are in their execution attended with many inconveniences. The clerk of said courts is required to transport a large number of dockets and other papers from his office in Cambridge to Concord, when the courts are to hold a session in the latter place; delays are often produced in the trial of causes by the unforeseen demand of papers, in the public offices, at a distance from the place of trial; a large bill of costs is annually created to said county by the transportation of prisoners, from one of those towns to the other, for trial; parties, jurors, and witnesses, when the courts sit at Cambridge, are drawn to one extremity of the county to attend the trial of causes; much useless expense to said county is created, not only in building, but in the frequent repairing two court-houses and two jails. The court-house and jail in Cambridge are now old and decayed, and unfit to answer the purposes for which they were built; and others, if the courts are hereafter to be holden there, must soon be erected.

"Your memorialists further represent, that said Concord is nearly in the centre of said county, and that a court-house and jail in said town have recently been erected at a considerable expense, which are commodious and sufficient for the use of said county; that in the court-house in Concord, convenient rooms for all public offices for said county may be fitted up at a trifling expense, in which the public records may be deposited more safely than in their present situation.

"Wherefore your memorialists pray, that said Concord may be made the shire town of said county, and that all the courts for said county may in future be holden in said town of Concord. And as in duty bound will ever pray."

Orders of notice were passed on this petition, and sent to all the towns in the county. Twelve towns in the lower part of the county, containing 19,559 inhabitants, voted in favor of Cambridge; and thirty-two towns, containing 23,233 inhabitants, in favor of Concord; and petitioned the legislature accordingly.

All these efforts, however, were unavailing, and the Court of Sessions finally determined to build at Cambridge. It then became a question of great interest to each party, whether these buildings should be at Old Cambridge or Lechmere Point. The agents for each of those places appeared before the Court of Sessions, and made public offers of the encouragement they would afford, in case their wishes should be preferred; and several times bid upon each other. At length Messrs. Craigie, Otis, and Coolidge, agents for Lechmere Point, made a private, written proposition, which was not disclosed in open court, agreeing to give the land and $24,000 in money; and it was determined in their favor at an adjourned session, October 19, 1813. The agents for the town of Cambridge preferred a petition to the legislature, in which they state at length the arguments for preferring Old Cambridge to the Point, and praying the interference of the legislature in their favor. An order of notice passed January 18, 1814. They had offered the land and 5,000. At the same session, Messrs. Joseph Hosmer, Jonas Lee, and Tilly Merrick, agents for the town of Concord, petitioned again in favor of that town. But these petitions were in vain; the legislature did not interfere definitely and the decision of the Court of Sessions in favor of the Point was adhered to; subjecting the inhabitants to have the greater part of the business transacted at one extremity, instead of the centre of the county.

CHAPTER X.

ECCLESIASTICAL HISTORY.

Organization of the Church. — Installation of the Rev. Mr. Bulkeley and Mr. Jones. — Church Covenant. — Proceedings of the Church. — Notice of the Rev. Mr. Jones. — Letters of the Rev. Mr. Bulkeley, and Notice of his Life and Writings. — Rev. Edward Bulkeley. — Rev. Joseph Estabrook. — Rev. John Whiting.

EMBARRASSMENT attends any attempt to prepare the early history of the church in Concord. No records are preserved during the first hundred years of its existence; and such facts only can be given, during this long and interesting period, as can be gleaned from early historians, ancient manuscripts, and family records. By careful and laborious researches, I am fortunately enabled to supply some important information.

This church was organized at Cambridge, July 5, 1636; and was the thirteenth established in the colony.[1] The meeting was called by the Rev. Peter Bulkeley,[2] and the Rev. John Jones, who, with others, had previously begun the settlement at Concord. The governor and deputy-governor were invited to be present on the occasion, but, because they supposed there was an informality in the invitation, at variance with their over-precise notions of etiquette, they did not attend. " They sent word, three days before, to the governor and deputy, to desire their presence; but they took it in ill part, and thought not fit to go, because they had not come to them before, as they ought to have done and as others had done before, to acquaint them with their purpose."

On the 6th of April, 1637, the church " kept a day of humiliation " at Cambridge, preparatory to the ordination, or installation, of Mr. Bulkeley, whom they chose teacher, and of Mr. Jones, whom they chose pastor. Delegates were present from most of the churches in the colony to assist in this ordination; but, says Winthrop, " the governor, and Mr. Cotton, and Mr. Wheelwright, and the two ruling elders of Boston, and the rest of that church which were of any note, did none of them come to this meeting. The reason was conceived to be, because they counted these as

---

[1] Winthrop, vol. i. p. 95. See also pp. 189 and 217.

[2] This name is also spelt Bulkley, Bulkly, and Buckly. The Rev. Peter and his family wrote it Bulkeley, which orthography I have followed.

legal preachers, and therefore would not give approbation to their ordination." One of the delegates from Salem proposed a question which led to the adoption of the following opinions. Such as had been clergymen in England, and received ordination in the established church by the bishop, were to be respected as having there legally sustained the office of ministers by the call of the people; and such ordination was considered valid here. But for receiving this ordination by the bishop they ought to humble themselves, acknowledge their sin, and repent. Having come to this country, they should not consider themselves regular ministers until called by another church. When thus elected, they were to be considered as ministers even before ordination.[1]

No man had a greater aversion to Episcopacy than Mr. Bulkeley, as his writings most fully show. There was, however, some difference in opinion between him and some of the leading men in the colony. He was supposed to attach too much importance to good works, though from his letters and treatise on the Covenant the supposition appears to be without foundation. The ostensible reason assigned for not giving approbation to his ordination was, that he was considered a *legal* preacher, — one who was for a *covenant of works* instead of a *covenant of grace*, or one who held to the doctrines of the law in distinction from the doctrines of grace. The former were denominated Legalists, and the latter Antinomians. The discussion of this question produced great excitement

---

[1] Some historians, for whose opinion I have great respect, have asserted, that the first settlers of Massachusetts were Episcopalians. But this, as it seems to me, if true at all, can be so only in a very limited sense. The colonists regarded Episcopacy with abhorrence, and looked with jealousy on the least appearance of propagating it in this American wilderness. They came here to get rid of Episcopacy; and if they did not cease to be Episcopalians when they refused to conform to the ceremonies of the "mother church," when, it may be asked, did they cease to be Episcopalians? They lived Non-conformists in England, and were Congregationalists on their arrival in America. They acknowledged a respect to the church of England as *their mother*, but being *free children* they set up for themselves in ways of their own choosing,— pure Congregationalists. Their ministers even considered it a sin, to have received their ordination from such a mother. It might be equally proper to call a Congregationalist, who had chosen to adopt the peculiar ceremonies of the Baptist church, a Congregationalist after he was really a Baptist; and in the same manner of any other change from one denomination to another.

and alienation; and all classes of society joined in it.[1] It probably influenced the gentlemen invited to this ordination. I have a long letter before me, written by Mr. Bulkeley before his ordination, to the Rev. Mr. Cotton, of Boston, in which this subject is discussed in his usual logical style. Its great length prevents its insertion here. In a postscript he says, "I should have acquainted you yesterday, that the *ordination of the elders of the church of Concord* is to be on *Wednesday come sevenight*. It is to be *here at New-Town*. I pray take notice of it. If it be necessary to give any other notice to other persons, or in any other way, we would not be wanting therein for avoiding of offence. And I have spoken also to Mr. Wilson." The distinguished reputation of Mr. Bulkeley, of noble family, a man of wealth, a scholar and divine, might have excited the envy of his fellow clergymen. He however received their approbation; and, on the 30th of the following August, was chosen one of the moderators of the first great ecclesiastical council, or synod, of the colony, which was then held in Cambridge. Winthrop mentions the Rev. Mr. Hooker as also a moderator. This assembly was attended by nearly all the clergy and magistrates, and many other distinguished laymen of the colony. It continued in session twenty-four days, and examined and condemned eighty-two opinions which had crept into the churches, "some blasphemous, others erroneous, and all unsafe."

Among other old family papers, transmitted from an early member of the church, is the following, endorsed "Concord Church Covenant, which was adopted by them." Though without signatures or date, it has internal evidence of authenticity, and of being the first church covenant. The orthography only is altered.

"Considering the instability and inconstancy of our hearts in cleaving to the Lord in that which is good, we do bind ourselves one with another this day before the Lord, that we will endeavour, by the grace of God assisting us, henceforward to walk as becometh the people of God, according to the gospel of our Lord

---

[1] Neal, in his "History of New England," informs us, that this question was agitated even by the soldiers composing the army sent against the Pequots, in 1636; and that they had to stop in the wilderness and settle the question, whether they were in a *covenant of works*, or a *covenant of grace*, before they could proceed!

Jesus Christ. And more particularly we do promise and covenant before the Lord, that, whereas he hath of his great goodness brought us from under the yoke and burdening of men's traditions to the precious liberty of his ordinances, which we now do enjoy, we will, according to our places and callings, stand for the maintenance of this liberty to our utmost endeavour, and not return to any human ordinances from which we are escaped. And we further covenant to subject ourselves to every ordinance of Christ, which he shall please to make known to us to be his will. Also we do take him to be our only Priest to instruct us, our only High Priest to make peace with the Father for us; so we will set him up as our King and Sovereign to command us, to rule in us and reign over us by the help of his word and Spirit. And that we may the better be kept in an holy subjection to him and his will, we will watch over each other in the Lord, admonishing one another, both to prevent the evils into which we might fall, and to recover ourselves out of those that we have been overtaken with, not suffering any raging pollution or spiritual uncleanness amongst us, but labor to cast it forth by the power which Christ hath given to his church. And further, considering that we are members one of another, and have civil respect, and are liable to be oppressed and devoured one of another; and considering also the increase of this evil, daily getting strength through the abounding of self-love so mightily prevailing in us; we do therefore here solemnly promise before the Lord, that we will carefully avoid all oppression, griping, and hard dealing, and walk in peace, love, mercy, and equity, towards each other, doing to others as we would they should do to us. And in testimony of our willing assent to this covenant we have hereunto subscribed our names."

"Letchford's Plain Dealing" mentions the church in Concord as the first one in the colony which had adopted the practice of catechizing children. Mather says, this was one of the constant exercises of the Sabbath. All the unmarried people were required to answer questions, after which expositions and applications were made by Mr. Bulkeley to the whole congregation. This exercise was, however, soon after adopted in other churches.

The church was numerous soon after its organization, and continued some time in harmony.[1] But the unexpected pecuniary

---

[1] One case of discipline is mentioned by the Hon. James Savage, in his

difficulties of the town, occasioned by its peculiar local situation and its condition at that time, induced many to remove, which rendered it difficult for the remainder to support two ministers; Mr. Bulkeley's salary as teacher being £70 per annum. Some difficulties arose in the church on this account. The subject of a separation was often discussed; and on the 28th of July, 1642, " some of the elders went to Concord, being sent for by the church there to advise with them about the maintenance of their elders, &c. They found them wavering about removal, not finding their plan-

---

valuable notes on Winthrop (vol. i. p. 289), of Ambrose Martin, who was fined £10, " and counselled to go to Mr. Mather to be instructed by him," for calling the church covenant " a stinking carrion and a human invention," and uttering some other impudent expressions. The following petition, containing the original signatures of the first two pastors and several members of the church, relates to him.

"To the Honoured Court. The Petition of the church of Concord in behalfe of our brother Mr. Ambrose Martin.

" Your humble Petitioners do intreate, that whereas some years ago our said brother Mr. Martin was fined by the Court for some unadvised speeches uttered against the church-covenant, for which he was fined £10, and had to the value of £20 by distress taken from him, of which £20 there is one halfe remayning in the hands of the country to this day, which £10 he cannot be persuaded to accept of, unless he may have the whole restored to him (which we doe impute unto his infirmitye and weakness.) We now considering the great decay of his estate, and the necessityes (if not extremityes) which the familye is come unto, we entreat that this honored Court would please to pittye his necessitous condition, and remit unto him the whole fine which was layd upon him, without which he cannot be perswaded to receive that which is due to him. Wherein if this honoured Court shall please to grant this our petition, we shall be bound to prayse God for your tender compassion toward this our poor brother.

Peter Bulkeley,	Luke Potter,
John Jones,	Joseph Wheeler,
Richard Griffin,	Thomas Foxe,
Simon Willard,	William Busse,
Robert Merriam,	Henry Farwell,
Thomas Wheeler,	James Hosmer,
George Wheeler,	John Graves."
Robert Fletcher,	

" *The 5th of the 4th month,* 1644. The case appears to the magestreates to be now past help through his own obstinacye; but for the overplus upon sale of the distresse he or his wife may have it when they will call for it. Jo: ENDECOTT, Gov."

tation answerable to their expectation, and the maintenance of two elders too heavy a burden for them. The elders' advice was, that they should continue and wait upon God, and be helpful to their elders in labor and what they could, and all to be ordered by the deacons, (whose office had not formerly been improved this way amongst them,) and that the elders should be content with what means the church was able at present to afford them, and if either of them should be called to some other place, then to advise with other churches about their removal." [1]

The advice of this council was followed a short time; but about October, 1644, a separation took place, and Mr. Jones removed to Fairfield, Connecticut. Mather gives the following account of this affair in his own peculiar style. Upon Mr. Bulkeley " pressing a piece of charity, disagreeable to the will of the ruling elder, there was occasioned an unhappy *discord* in the church of *Concord*; which was at last healed by their calling in the help of a council, and the ruling elder's [Mr. Jones] abdication. Of the temptations which occurred on these occasions, Mr. Bulkeley would say, ' he thereby came, 1. To know more of God. 2. To know more of himself. 3. To know more of men.' Peace being thus restored, the small things in the church there increased in the hands of their faithful Bulkeley, until he was translated into the regions which afford nothing but *concord* and *glory*; leaving his well-fed flock in the wilderness under the pastoral scare of his worthy son Mr. Edward Bulkeley."

The Rev. JOHN JONES was born, educated, and regularly ordained as a preacher of the gospel, in England; but at what place is not known. He arrived in New England, October 2, 1635,[2] with the Rev. Mr. Shepard, afterwards of Cambridge, and the Rev. John Wilson of Boston. After remaining as the colleague pastor of the church in Concord about eight years, he removed with part of his society to Fairfield, and there undertook the charge of a newly organized church, where he spent the remainder of his life. He attained an age exceeding "three score and ten," and died about 1664. Few records are preserved concerning this early, devoted friend to the cause of Christian liberty, or concerning his family. Tradition gives him a highly respectable

---

[1] Winthrop, vol. ii. p. 73.   [2] Shepard's Journal.

character. He left six children. John was graduated at Harvard College in 1643; and Eliphalet, another son born in this town, January 9, 1640, studied divinity, and was the first minister of Huntington, L. I., where he died about 100 years old.

After the removal of Mr. Jones, the sole care of the church devolved on Mr. Bulkeley for the remaining fourteen years of his life. At this time, according to Johnson, it contained about seventy communicants; but none of its proceedings have been transmitted to us. The following letters of Mr. Bulkeley are deemed worthy of publication.

"To his dear and loving friend, Mr. Shepard, Pastor of the Church att Cambridge.

"DEAR SR. — I hear the Lord hath so far strengthened you, as that you were the last Lord's day at the assembly. The L. go on with the work of his goodness towards you. Being that now the Lord hath enabled you thus far, I desire a word or two from you, what you judge concerning the teacher in a congregation, whether the administration of discipline and sacraments doe equally belong unto him with the pastor, and whether he ought therein equally to interest himself. I would also desire you to add a word more concerning this, viz. what you mean by the execution of discipline, when you distinguish it from the power. We have had speech sometimes concerning the churches' power in matters of discipline, wherein you seemed to put the power itself into the hands of the church, but to reserve the execution to the eldership. Here also I would see what you comprehend under the word *execution.* I would gladly hear how the common affairs of the churches stand with you. I am here shut up, and do neither see nor hear.[1] Write me what you know. Let me alsoe understand which way Mr. Phillips doth incline, whether towards you or otherwise; and which way Mr. Rogers is like to turn, whether to stay in these parts or goe into Coniticote [Connecticut]. I wrote to you not long agoe advising you to consider *quid valent humeri.* I know not whether you received that let-

---

[1] Mr. Bulkeley often laments his situation. In a letter to the Rev. Mr. Cotton, dated December 17, 1640, he says "I lose much in this retired wilderness in which I live; but the Lord will at last lighten my candle. In the mean while, help us with some of that which God hath imparted unto you."

ter. The Lord in mercy bless all our labours to his churches' good. Remember my love to Mrs. Shepard with Mrs. Herlakenden. Grace be with you all.

"Yours in Christ Jesus, P. BULKELEY.
"*Febr.* 12, 1639."

"To his reverend and loving friend Mr. Cotton, Teacher of the Church at Boston.

"REVEREND IN THE L. — These are to desire you to convey this letter inclosed in one of your own to Boston. I do the rather send it to you, because I suppose those you commit your letters to, will be careful of the delivery, and this letter concerns matters of some moment, in regard whereof I desire you to take the more notice of it, and convey it by a safe hand. If the business concerning Virginia be finished, I desire to know how it stands ; or if not finished, what is intended or thought upon. My wife hath bin ill ever since our coming home, but now, I thank the Lord, begins to recover. This day she began to go down into the house. Remember her in your prayers, and us all. And so with both our loves to yourself and Mrs. Cotton, I leave you with all yours to the Lord's rich goodness and grace, resting yours ever in him.

"*Sept.* 26, 1642. PET : BULKELEY."

"To the Reverend his honoured friend Mr. Cotton, Teacher of the Church at Boston, give these.

"REVEREND IN THE LORD,

* * * * *

"Some other things I am full of, but will not write with paper and ink ; only in a word I bless God for what I hear, how the Lord doth fill your ministry with abundance of grace, life, and power, to the exceeding joy of those that are true-hearted towards the Lord. But withall I stand amazed and wonder att God's forbearance, considering what I hear in another kind ; which I doe also believe to be true in some parts ; true I mean, as done and spoken by some, though untrue, in respect of any cause given on your part. Truly, Sir, it is to me a wonder, that the earth swallows not up such wretches, or that fire comes not downe from heaven to consume them. The L. hath a number of holy and humble ones here amongst us [in the country generally], for whose sakes he doth spare, and will spare long; but were it not for such a remnant, we should see the L. would make quick work amongst us. Shall I tell you what I think to be the ground of all this insolency which discovers itself in the speach of men? Truly I cannot ascribe it so much to any outward thing, as to the putting of too much liberty and power into the hands of the multitude, which they are too weak to manage, many growing conceited, proud, arrogant, self-sufficient, as wanting nothing. And I am persuaded, that except there be some means used to change the course of things in this point, our churches will grow more corrupt day by day; and tumult will arise hardly to be stilled. Remember the former days which you had in old Boston, where though (through the Lord's blessing upon your labours) there was an increase daily added to your church, yet the number of professors is far more here, than it was there. But answer me, which place was better governed? Where matters were swayed there by your wisdom and counsel, matters went on with strength and power for good. But here, where the heady or headless multitude have gotten the power into their hands, there is insolency and confusion. And I know not how it can be avoided in this way, unless we should make the doors of the church narrower. This we have warrant for from the word; which course, if it should be taken, would bring its inconveniency also in another kind. But of these things no more. Only I pray the L. to heal the evils of the places and times we live in, and remove that woful contempt of his gospel which doth abound. O what mischief doth one proud, lofty spirit that is in reputation for understanding, amongst a number of others that are weak; and some of both such there are in every place. But our comfort is, God's end and work shall go forward. Some shall be converted, some hardened. The God of mercy carry on his work in our hearts and hands to the glorifying of his rich grace in Christ Jesus. I pray remember my harty love to good Mrs. Cotton, thanking her for her kind remembrance of my little ones. I pray God give us both to see his grace increasing in those that he hath continued towards us. Farewell, dearly beloved and honoured in the Lord, comfort yourself in him, who is most ready to be found in time of need. In him I rest. Yours ever,

"*April* 4, 1650. Pet: Bulkeley.

"I could wish you would write to Mr. Goodwin to deal with those that are in place of authority in England, to take care that the Scripture may be printed more truly. I have a bible, printed 1648, which hath (little and great) above an 100 faults in the printing of it. And I have an old Bible, printed 1581, which hath but one or two, and those very small ones. I intend to write to my nephew, St. John, about it. A word from yourself to Mr. Goodwin, who is a man of so much respect there, would do much good."

The Rev. PETER BULKELEY, B. D., was of honorable and noble descent. He was of the tenth generation from Robert Bulkeley, Esq., one of the English Barons, who, in the reign of king John (who died in 1216), was lord manor of Bulkeley in the county palatine of Chester.[1] He was born at Woodhill, in Bedfordshire, January 31, 1583. His father, the Rev. Edward Bulkeley, D. D., was a faithful minister of the gospel, under whose direction his son received a learned and religious education, suited to his distinguished rank. About the age of sixteen he was admitted a member of St. John's College at Cambridge, of which he was afterwards chosen fellow, and from which he received the degree of Bachelor of Divinity. He succeeded his father in the ministry in his native town, and enjoyed his rich benefice and estate; where he was a zealous preacher of evangelical truth about twenty years, and, for the most part of the time, lived an

---

[1] The names of the lineal descendants from Robert, furnished me by Charles Bulkeley, Esq., of New London, a great grandson of Gershom, were, 1. William; 2. Robert; 3. Peter, who married Nicholaus Bird, of Haughton; 4. John, who married Andryne, daughter and heir to John Colley, of Ward, and died 1450; 5. Hugh, who married Helleh Wilbriham, of Woodley; 6. Humphrey, who married Cyle, daughter and heir of John Mutten; 7. William, who married Beatryce, daughter and heir to William, of Bulausdale; 8. Thomas, who married Elizabeth, daughter of Randelle Grovenor; 9. Edward, D. D., of Woodhill, who married Olive Irlby, of Lincolnshire; 10. Peter, of Concord. He had two brothers, Nathaniel and Paul. The latter died fellow of Queen's College, Cambridge. From William, a brother of Peter, of the third generation, were also many ennobled descendants; among whom are recorded, in the Irish Peerage, seven Viscounts in succession. Other branches have been much distinguished. The motto adopted in the family coat of arms was, "*Nec temere, nec timide*," — "Neither rashly nor timidly"; and contains a beautiful sentiment, characteristic of the eminent father of the American family.

unmolested non-conformist. At length, his preaching meeting with distinguished success, and his church being very much increased, complaints were entered against him by Archbishop Laud, and he was silenced for his non-conformity to the requirements of the English church. This circumstance induced him to emigrate to New England, where he might enjoy liberty of conscience. He arrived in Cambridge in 1634 or 1635,[1] and was the leader of those resolute men and self-denying Christians, who soon after " went further up into the woods and settled on the plantation at Musketaquid." Here he expended most of his estate for the benefit of his people; and after a laborious and useful life, died March 9, 1659, in his 77th year.

Mr. Bulkeley was remarkable for his benevolence. He had many servants, on whom, after they had lived with him several years, he bestowed farms, and then received others to be treated in a like benevolent manner. By great familiarity of manners he drew around him persons of all ages; and his easy address, great learning, and eminent piety, rendered his society pleasing and profitable to all. Persons seldom separated from his company, without having heard some remark calculated to impress the mind with the importance of religion. Though sometimes suffering under bodily infirmities, he was distinguished for the holiness of his life, and a most scrupulous observance of the duties of the Christian ministry. He avoided all novelties in dress, and wore his hair short. Being strict in his own virtues, he was occasionally severe in censuring the follies of others. He was considered as the father of his people, and " addressed as father, prophet, or counsellor, by them and all the ministers of the country." Had the scene of Mr. Bulkeley's labors been in Boston, or its immediate vicinity, and not, as he expresses it, "shut up" in this remote spot, then of difficult access, his name would have appeared more conspicuously in the published annals of the country. He was a thorough scholar; an elevated, devotional Christian; laborious in his profession; and, as a preacher, evangelical, faithful, and of remarkably energetic, powerful, and persuasive eloquence.

---

[1] The Rev. Edward Bulkeley was admitted *freeman*, May 6, 1635; and from the Cambridge Records it seems probable that Mr. Bulkeley came to America in 1634.

He often wrote a series of sermons on a particular book or passage of Scripture. One of these series, on Zachariah ix. 11, was published as " the first-born of New England," and passed through several editions. The edition before me bears the following title. " The Gospel Covenant, or the Covenant of Grace opened; wherein are explained, 1. The difference between the covenant of grace and covenant of works. 2. The different administration of the covenant before and since Christ. 3. The benefits and blessings of it. 4. The conditions. 5. The properties of it. Preached at Concord, in New England, by Peter Bulkeley, sometime fellow of Saint John's College in Cambridge. [Here follow quotations, Genesis xvii. 1 – 7, and Isaiah lv. 3.] The second edition, much enlarged and corrected by the author. And the chiefe heads of things (which was omitted in the former) distinguished into chapters. London, printed by Mathew Simmins, dwelling in Aldersgate-street, next door to the Golden Lion, 1651." pp. xvi. and 442, quarto. It was dedicated " to the church and congregation at Concord"; and to his nephew, " the Rt. Hon. Oliver St. John, Lord Embassador extraordinary from the Parliament of the Commonwealth of England to the High and Mighty Lords, the States General of the United Provinces in the Netherlands; and Lord Chief Justice at the Common Pleas." It is a work of great merit for that age, and considering that it was " preached in the remote ends of the earth." " The church of God," says the Rev. Mr. Shepard, of Cambridge, " is bound to bless God for the holy, judicious, and learned labours of this aged, experienced, and precious servant of Christ." After reading this book, President Stiles observes, " He was a masterly reasoner in theology, and equal to the first characters in all Christendom and in all ages."

Two of Mr. Bulkeley's manuscripts are preserved in the library of the American Antiquarian Society. One contains answers to several theological questions, and is addressed to the Rev. Mr. Phillips of Watertown. The other is on the character and government of the church. The following analysis is given at the close of this work. Part I. " The visible church is, 1. For the efficient cause, called of God. 2. For the material cause, a number of visible saints and believers in the judgment of men. 3. For the formal cause, union by an explicate and implicate covenant together. 4. For the final cause, to set out God's praises." Part II. "The churches' government, 1. Is originally in the people's hands. 2. Which people are to elect their own officers, — teachers, elders, and deacons. 3. By which officers they are to rule and govern, — by admitting fit members, and by watching over, admonishing, and casting out those that be bad." This is a most able defence of Congregationalism in opposition to Episcopacy; and touches, with the author's peculiar power and clearness, the ecclesiastical questions in discussion at that period. I can scarcely resist an inclination to extract some passages. Its publication entire is recommended to the Society to whom it belongs.

Mr. Bulkeley married, for his first wife, Jane, daughter of Sir Thomas Allen, of Goldington, whose nephew was Lord Mayor of London. By her he had nine sons and two daughters. Edward, Thomas (who married a daughter of the Rev. John Jones, removed to Fairfield, and died about 1652), John, Joseph, William, and Richard, are all the names I have seen mentioned. He lived eight years a widower, and then married Grace, daughter of Sir Richard Chitwood, by whom he had three sons and one daughter, — Gershom, Eleazer, Peter, and Dorothy. His wife survived him, and removed to Connecticut a few years after his death.

His will, dated February 26, 1659, appears in the Middlesex Records, in which he specifies legacies in books to his sons, Edward, John, and Joseph, his cousin Samuel Hough, and his nephew Oliver St. John, " as a thankful acknowledgment of his kindness and bounty towards me; his liberality having been a great help and support unto me in these my lonely times and my struggles." Legacies are also made to the widow of his son Thomas, deceased, and to his three youngest children, Eleazer, Peter, and Dorothy; " and in case any of my children before named by me in this my will, to whom I have bequeathed the legacies named, shall prove disobedient to their mother, or otherwise vicious and wicked (which God in his mercy prevent), then I will that the legacy before bequeathed to any of them so proving disobedient and wicked, shall be wholly in the power of my said wife, their mother, to deal with them therein, as she herself in Christian wisdom shall think meet, either to give their legacy, or to keep it to herself." He alludes to his " wasted estate, which is now very little in comparison of what it was when I came first to these places," having made great sacrifices in "the beginning of these plantations," and "having little to leave to the children God hath given me, and to my precious wife, whose unfeigned piety and singular grace of God shining in her, doth deserve more than I can do for her." The inventory of his estate amounted to £1302, of which £123 was in books. He had previously given a part of his library, and some other donations, to Harvard College.

The Rev. Edward Bulkeley succeeded his father in the ministerial care of the church with an annual salary of £80. The duties of his office increasing with the growth of the town, assistance was judged necessary, and the Rev. Joseph Estabrook was ordained as his colleague in 1667. His salary was also £80, of which £40 was to be paid in money, and £40 in grain, — wheat to be estimated at 5s., rye at 4s., and corn at 3s. per bushel.

March 12, 1681, the town voted, "that every householder that hath a teame, greater or lesser, shall carry yearly one load of wood to the minister; and every other householder or votable person shall cut wood one day for the minister; and that the wood be equally divided to the ministers as the selectmen shall appoint." The arrangement, which the following vote specifies, was made March 5, 1694. "Whereas the Rev. pastor, Mr. Edward Bulkeley, is under such infirmities of body, by reason of great age, that he is not capable of attending the work of the ministry as in times past; being also sensible of the obligations the town is under to afford him a comfortable maintenance during the term of his natural life; that thereby the people may testifie their gratitude for his former services in the gospel, they do hereby oblige the town to pay Mr. Bulkeley yearly, during his natural life, the sum of £30 in lieu of his former salary." This proposition was assented to by Mr. Bulkeley, on condition that he should have liberty to preach or not as he should choose.

The Rev. EDWARD BULKELEY was the eldest son of the Rev. Peter Bulkeley, and born and chiefly educated in England. He emigrated to this country, and was admitted a member of the First Church in Boston in 1634. Having acquired a professional education under the instruction of his father, he was licensed to preach the gospel, and ordained at Marshfield in 1642 or 1643. On the death of his father in 1659, he was dismissed and installed over the church in Concord. He died at a great age, in the 53d year of his ministry, at Chelmsford, January 2, 1696, probably on a visit to his grandson, and was buried in Concord. Few records are preserved concerning his ministry or himself. He is represented by tradition to have been lame, and of a feeble constitution. He was, however, greatly respected for his talents, acquirements, irreproachable character, and piety. He preached an Election Sermon in 1680, from 1 Sam. ii. 30; and one before the Ancient and Honorable Artillery Company in 1679, from 1 Peter ii. 11. His only printed work, that I have seen, is that noticed in our general history, under date of 1676, preached in commemoration of the safe return of Captain Thomas Wheeler and his associates, after the battle at Brookfield.

I have not learned whom Mr. Bulkeley married. His children were John, Peter, Jane (who married Ephraim Flint), and Elizabeth, who married, in 1665, the Rev. Joseph Emerson, great grandfather of the Rev. William Emerson, hereafter to be noticed, and after Mr. Emerson's death (which took place in Concord, January 3, 1680), for a second husband, John Brown, Esq., of Reading. She was the only child of Mr. Bulkeley, it is supposed, who had issue.

The Rev. JOSEPH ESTABROOK died September 16, 1711,[1] aged 71. He was born in Enfield, England, and, after receiving a preparatory education, emigrated to this country, entered Harvard College, and was graduated in 1664. The following obituary notice, dated September 18th, appeared in the "Boston News Letter." "This day was interred in Concord the Rev. Mr. Joseph Estabrook, minister of the gospel in said town for about forty-four years (and for many of them was colleage with the famous Mr. Bulkeley.) He was eminent for his skill in the Hebrew language; and a most orthodox, learned, and worthy divine, of excellent principles in religion, indefatigably laborious in the ministry, and of holy life and conversation." He was a man of great worth, and eminently fitted for his office. In his preaching he was plain, practical, and persuasive; and in his intercourse with his people, grave, affectionate, communicative, and conciliatory, earnestly desiring their happiness and religious welfare. His appearance carried with it so

---

[1] The Rev. Dr. Ripley [Half Century Sermon, p. 28.] says, 23d *May*. But all other authorities concur in the 16th of September.

much patriarchal dignity, that people were induced to love him as a friend, and reverence him as a father. These distinguished traits in his character obtained for him, in the latter part of his life, the name of *The Apostle.* His judgment was much respected, and his advice sought for in all the neighbouring churches. He was much admired wherever he preached; and was invited to remove from Concord; for, said his admirers, " He was too bright a star to be muffled up in the woods amongst the Indians, and ought to come to Boston where he could do more good." [1] His only printed work, which has come down to us, is an Election Sermon preached in 1705.[2]

Mr. Estabrook married Mary, daughter of Captain Hugh Mason, of Watertown, May 20, 1668; and had 6 children. 1. Joseph, born 1669, lived several years in Hingham, but settled in Lexington, where he died September 24, 1733, aged 65, having been a deacon 17 years (he was grandfather to the Rev. Joseph Estabrook, late of Athol); 2. Benjamin; 3. Mary, married Jonathan Green of Newton; 4. Samuel; 5. Daniel, born 1676, married Abigail Flint of Concord, and settled first in Cambridge, but removed to Sudbury, where he died; and 6. Ann, married Joshua Haynes of Sudbury. Benjamin and Samuel will be noticed among the college graduates.[3]

After the death of Mr. Estabrook, a committee of the town, consisting of Deacon John Heywood, Mr. Benjamin Whittemore, and Lieutenant William Wilson, was chosen to " procure preaching." The Rev. Edward Holyoke, afterwards president of Harvard College, the Rev. Benjamin Prescott, one of our native graduates, and the Rev. John Whiting, were employed as candidates for

---

[1] MSS. of the late Rev. Joseph Estabrook of Athol, and Dr. Joseph Lee.
[2] It is entitled, " Abraham, the Passenger, his Privilege and Duty, described in an Election Sermon at Boston, N. E., May 30, 1705. By Joseph Estabrooks, A. M. and Pastor of the Church at Concord. [Here follow quotations from John viii. 39, and Gal. iii. 29; and also a Latin one from Calvin.] Boston. Printed by Bartholomew Green; sold by Benjamin Eliot, at his shop under the west end of the Town House, 1705." pp. 24. quarto. Text, Gen. xii. 2.
[3] Thomas Estabrook, a brother of the Rev. Joseph, married Sarah Temple, May 3, 1683, and had a son Thomas, born 1685, who had sons,— Samuel, Thomas, and Abraham, born 1710, '13, and '17; and from whom most of the name in Concord were descended.

six Sabbaths. A liberal settlement was offered the town by Mr. Prescott's father, should he be chosen, but the proposition was not accepted. The church gave Mr. Whiting a *call*, in which the town concurred by 110 votes in his favor, November 19, 1711. December 7th following, it was agreed by 84 to 37 "paper votes," to give him £100 as a settlement, and £100 as an annual salary, and pay the expenses of his ordination, which took place May 14, 1712.

Judge Sewall, one of the delegates, makes the following entry in his journal on that day. "I go to Concord in Austin's calash; set out from home at 5 *a. m.*, got to Mr. Whiting's at 10. Exercises began about half an hour past eleven, ended about a quarter past one. Great assembly. Mr. Whiting prayed, and preached from 1 Tim. iii. 1. Mr. Nehemiah Hobart asked if any had to object, 1. Of the church; 2. Of the congregation; 3. Of all the present assembly. Declared that the elders and messengers of churches had appointed him to give the charge; Mr. Angier, Brattle, and Hancock, to join in laying on hands. Mr. Hobart prayed excellently, and so gave the charge. One word in it was diligence or labour, or to that purpose; prayed again. Declared that Mr. Angier was to give the right hand of fellowship, which he did. Sung the 47th psalm. Mr. Whiting blessed the people. Went and dined at young Mr. Prescott's. Set out to come down about half an hour after three."

Fifteen pounds were subsequently granted to provide Mr. Whiting with fire-wood; and, in addition to his stated salary, special contributions and grants were frequently made. From 1728, he received £150; in 1734, £180; and in 1735, £190. These grants were probably owing to the depreciation in value of the public currency. During this period Mr. Timothy Minott occasionally assisted Mr. Whiting, and was compensated by contributions or town assessments. In 1732 the town raised £20 for this purpose.[1]

Some objections were brought against Mr. Whiting in the latter part of his ministry; and several councils were called to inves-

---

[1] I have in my possession "A Sermon, preached at Concord, Dec. 29, 1737 [by the Rev. Israel Loring of Sudbury], at the request of two religious societies of young men there," who used to "meet for the exercises of religion on the evenings of the Lord's day and at other times."

tigate them. In March, 1737, the deacons were chosen a committee " to treat with the Rev. Mr. Whiting, to see whether he would join with the town in calling another minister." He approved of this proposition. On presenting their report, on the 16th of May following, the town voted, 41 to 33, " to call and settle another minister with Mr. Whiting." On the 18th of October, an ecclesiastical council was convened here, of which the Rev. John Hancock, of Lexington, was moderator, which, after a public examination of the charges, advised the church to dismiss Mr. Whiting.[1] The result was read on the 21st, and the church accepted it, 83 yeas, and 11 nays; and voted, that the pastoral relation it held to Mr. Whiting, should be dissolved. The town concurred on the 6th of March following, " nemine contradicente."

The Rev. JOHN WHITING died May 4, 1752, aged 71. He was the son of the Rev. Joseph Whiting, who was graduated at Harvard College in 1661, and was afterwards minister of Southampton, Long Island. His mother, I suppose, was daughter of the Hon. Thomas Danforth of Cambridge, deputy governor of Massachusetts colony; and as he died without issue, perhaps a good portion of his estate descended to Mr. Whiting. His grandfather was the Rev. Samuel Whiting of Lynn, whose last wife was Elizabeth St. John, daughter of the Right Honorable Oliver St. John, nephew to the Rev. Peter Bulkeley, and mentioned in the history of England. The father of the Rev. Samuel was John Whiting, mayor of the city of Boston, Lincolnshire. The Rev. John, of Concord, was the sixth son of the Rev. Joseph Whiting, the five preceding him having died in infancy. He was born at Lynn, June 20, 1681.[2] He was graduated at Harvard College in 1700, and was subsequently chosen a tutor and fellow of that institution. He was pastor of the church in Concord about twenty-six years. After his dismission he resided in this town principally as a private citizen. He was a man of wealth, learning, influence, and talents; and, as his modest epitaph informs us, " a gentleman of singular hospitality and generosity, who never detracted from the character of any man, and was a universal lover of mankind."

He married Mary, daughter of the Rev. John Cotton, of Hampton, N. H., granddaughter of the Rev. Seaborn Cotton, great

---

[1] The Rev. Joseph Sewall's MS. Journal. He was one of the delegates.
[2] MS. Biographical and Genealogical Dictionary, by John Farmer, Esq.

granddaughter of the Rev. John Cotton, of Boston, and Governor Simon Bradstreet, and great great granddaughter of Governor Thomas Dudley ; and had four sons and four daughters ; — Mary, who married the Rev. Daniel Rogers, of Littleton ; John, of Royalston ; Thomas, Esq., of Concord ; Stephen, of Boston ; Elizabeth, who married the Rev. Samuel Webster, of Salisbury ; and three others, who died in infancy or unmarried. She died May 29, 1731. He married for a second wife the widow of Dr. Jonathan Prescott.

CHAPTER XI.

Ordination of Mr. Bliss. — State of the Church. — Revivals. — Proceedings of different Ecclesiastical Councils and of the Church. — Divisions in the Parish and Church. — Death of Mr. Bliss. — Ordination of Mr. Emerson. — Proceedings of the Church. — Notice of the Rev. Mr. Emerson, — Ordination of Mr. Ripley. — Proceedings of the Church. — Covenants. — Funds. — Ordination of Mr. Goodwin. — Succession of Deacons. — Trinitarian Church.

The dismission of Mr. Whiting left the church again destitute of a minister. It did not, however, long remain so. The Rev. Daniel Bliss was chosen by the church, August 22, 1738, in which act the town concurred, 14th September, 70 to 32. October 19, it was voted, 63 to 12, to give him £500 as a settlement, and £200 as a salary, in the old-tenor province bills of credit. The settlement was subsequently paid by the sale of town lands. February 14, 1739, was appointed for his ordination, when a council of seven churches, of which the Rev. John Hancock was moderator, convened for the purpose ; but some difficulties having arisen, it adjourned, and met again on the 6th of March, with two additional churches, called by the church, and three by the dissatisfied members. By the decision of this council it was agreed to abide. The charges brought against Mr. Bliss were principally personal. But the council, after a full examination, came to a result in his favor on the 7th of March, when his ordination took place.

On this occasion, the Rev. John Barnard, of Marblehead, made the introductory prayer ; the Rev. William Williams, of Weston, preached from Acts xxvi. 17, 18; the Rev. Ebenezer Hancock, Sen., of Lexington, gave the charge; and the Rev. John Gardner, of Stow, the right hand of fellowship. The church, at this time, consisted of 85 members, 35 males and 50 females.

This was an important era in the ecclesiastical history of New England. Much of the zeal which had characterized the churches at an early period had subsided; the sermons from the desk had become cold and formal; and spiritual lethargy and indifference ensued. About this time a powerful revival of religion commenced in many churches in the colony. These remarks will be true, whether applied to the general history of the country, or the particular history of Concord.

Mr. Bliss was one of the most distinguished of the clergy, who, at that day, were denominated by their opposers *new lights*. He introduced a new style of preaching, — bold, zealous, impassioned, and enthusiastic, forming a striking contrast to that the church had previously enjoyed. The truths of divine revelation, which people from infancy had been taught to regard with reverence, were now exhibited in a manner new and surprising. And it had a powerful effect. The attention of the people generally was soon greatly awakened, and their feelings were excited on the subject of religion.

On the 13th of October, 1741, the celebrated Whitfield first visited Concord. "About noon," says his Journal, " I reached Concord. Here I preached to some thousands in the open air; and comfortable preaching it was. The hearers were sweetly melted down. About £45 was collected for the orphans. The minister of the town being, I believe, a true child of God, I chose to stay all night at his house, that we might rejoice together. The Lord was with us. The Spirit of the Lord came upon me, and God gave me to wrestle with him for my friends, especially those then with me. They felt his power. Brother B**s, the minister, broke into floods of tears, and we had reason to cry out it was good for us to be here. O blessed be thy name, O God, for the sweet refreshing in our way towards the heavenly Canaan."

The preaching of Whitfield, though somewhat resembling that of Mr. Bliss, tended to keep alive and increase these powerful religious feelings. The number of those who publicly professed religion, and joined the church in full communion, was unusually large. *Fifty* joined in 1741, and *sixty-five* in 1742. *Eighteen* in one day. The feeling pervading society was such, that religious meetings were held every day in the week; hundreds sought advice from their pastor; and persons might often be seen, apparently suffering under extreme agony from a sense of their guilt, or in an extasy of joy under the consolations of religion. This revival, though attended with much enthusiasm in feelings and action, and extravagant pretensions to religious influences, produced the most salutary effects on many individuals. As is ever the case when the attention of the people is called to think seriously on the subject, the number of those who were reformed and became really pious, is stated to have been very great.

But though productive of much good, many evils resulted from the proceedings of those times. Much controversy and division in towns took place, which hardly find a parallel in modern times, and in which most of the leading clergymen of the colony were engaged as partisans or counsellors. Concord partook largely in these troubles. An unhappy controversy was here generated, which continued many years, and produced some important revolutions in the town. This controversy involved so many principles of importance to the church generally, and to this town in particular, that I trust I shall be excused for minuteness of detail.

The dismission of Mr. Whiting was not approved by every inhabitant; and, as has been shown, there was not entire unanimity in settling Mr. Bliss. Under these circumstances, his character and preaching were likely to be carefully examined, and all his errors exposed. As early as July, 1740, several brethren "made application to the church for redress"; and Messrs. Timothy Minott, James Minott, Samuel Heywood, Samuel Merriam, and Nathaniel Whittemore, were chosen a committee " to hold a Christian conference with them, and to receive and report their particular grievances to the church." At the same time, Messrs. Timothy Wheeler, Jonathan Ball, and John Jones, were chosen a committee to obtain from others the reason for absenting themselves from the communion. It does not appear that reports were made till the following year. Not being satisfied, the aggrieved brethren requested the church to join with them in calling in a council, but it was refused.

At length an *ex parte* council was convened, before whom fifteen articles of complaint were examined. This council, consisting of the Rev. Messrs. John Barnard of Marblehead, moderator, John Prentice of Lancaster, Samuel Ruggles of Billerica, William Cook of East Sudbury, Thomas Parker of Dracut, Oliver Peabody of Natick, Willard Hall of Westford, and delegates from their respective churches, met here first in June, 1742, and during the following year, by several adjournments.

The charges submitted to this council were referred to the church, before whom they were examined; and the vindication of the accused was made, and voted to be satisfactory. After this examination (August 26, 1742), four of the brethren were suspended from the privileges of the church.

In consequence of the dissatisfaction that prevailed, the church had also called in the aid of a council, of which the Rev. Samuel Moody, of York, was moderator, and which met here, June 21, 1743, " to hear and consider these proceedings, and inform them, if in any thing they have deviated from the rules of the gospel." Messrs. Deacon Dakin, Nathaniel Billings, John Dakin, Daniel Adams, David Whitaker, Nathaniel Ball, David Melvin, Nathaniel Whittemore, and Timothy Wheeler, were chosen on various committees to confer with the council on different subjects.

Both of these councils were in session in Concord at the same time. That called by the disaffected brethren had requested Mr. Bliss to appear before it, to refute any charges which might be brought against him; but he refused to recognise them as the proper tribunal, before whom he or his church ought to appear. The church's council were then invited to unite, and both to sit together as a mutual council. This was also refused. And they came to a result, June 24, 1743, in which they state that the complaints of the aggrieved brethren were well founded, and advise them to secede from the ministry of Mr. Bliss, and support public worship among themselves, unless proper acknowledgments and reformation, agreeably to their views, took place.

The other council, after examining all the proceedings of the church, from December, 1741, to that day, and the charges of the aggrieved brethren, adjourned without coming to a result, only advising the church to consult with the aggrieved brethren, and invite an additional number of churches to join them at their adjourned meeting, and then to sit as a mutual council. This was consented to by both parties ; and a council, consisting of ministers and delegates from fourteen churches, met here September 13, 1743. The ministers were the Rev. Nathaniel Rogers and Samuel Wigglesworth, of the first and third churches in Ipswich ; Samuel Moody, of the first church in York ; Israel Loring, of Sudbury ; William Williams, of Weston ; Peter Thatcher, of Middleborough ; John Cotton, of Newton ; Nathaniel Appleton, of Cambridge ; Joshua Gee, of Boston ; Wareham Williams, of Waltham ; Joseph Parsons, of Bradford ; Ebenezer Turell, of Medford ; David Hall, of Sutton ; and Solomon Prentice, of Grafton. John Cotton was moderator, and Joshua Gee and Nathaniel Rogers, scribes. It continued in session six days. Ten of these fourteen ministers, with the Rev. Mr. Bliss, were part of the hundred and sixteen who had fully approved the existing revivals, " as the glorious work of God," and given in their attestation at the meeting in Boston on the 7th of the preceding July.[1]

Twenty-two articles of grievance, containing "exceptions against the doctrines, discipline, and conduct of the reverend pastor of the church," obtained a full and impartial examination. These charges involved some of the points of theology most disputed at that time. The following extracts from the complaints, Mr. Bliss's defence, and the result of council, are given as examples.

COMPLAINT 5th. — " His asserting that every person that was converted must know it ; and afterwards denied the same."

Defence. — " That all persons converted, when adult, must receive a change so great that they will necessarily be acquainted therewith, is what I believe ; but at the same time, that they shall as certainly know this to be true and real conversion to God, is what I deny."

Result of Council. — " We judge that many who are converted do know it, and that it is the duty of Christians to give all diligence to make their calling and election sure ; yet the doctrine that Mr. Bliss hath taught, namely, that every person that is converted must know it, is what we apprehend to be unsound ; but

---

[1] Christian History, Emerson's History of the First Church, page 190, Trumbull's Connecticut, Chauncy's Seasonable Thoughts, and Edwards's and Whitfield's Works, may be consulted for a history of those times.

in what he offered to the council he expressed himself more cautiously to our satisfaction."

Complaint 6th. — "Mr. Bliss hath asserted that the main reason any man cannot enter in at the strait gate, is because they are not elected."

Defence. — "The truth of what you object against, I think clear from the word of God in many places, particularly Romans xi. 5 – 8. The originating cause of the salvation of any of the children of men, I believe to be the electing goodness and grace of God ; and of consequence the main cause why others are not saved as much as those that be, is because they were not elected ; but with the same breath desire to have it well remembered, this is no excuse for us continuing in unbelief."

Result. — The charge "was fully proved. We judge Mr. Bliss's expressions very improper, tending to make an ill improvement of the important Scriptural doctrine of election."

Complaint 8th. — "In mentioning that text, 'He that believeth not is condemned already,' he said, 'But I say he is damned already ; every person that hath not a true saving faith is in a state of damnation ; you believe, and so doth the devil ; but your faith is a cursed, damned faith.'"

Defence. — "I hold that every man that believeth not is damned according to the sense and meaning of John iii. 18 ; that he is kept out of hell by mere unpromised, uncovenanted mercy and goodness ; that all faith which produceth not good fruits working by love, &c., is accursed and soul-destroying, I have said, and purpose still to say it, though some may be offended."

Result. — "Voted that the expressions are very unsuitable and improper."

Complaint 10th. — "Mr. Bliss said in a sermon that it was as great a sin for a man to get an estate by honest labor, if he had not a single aim at the glory of God, as to get it by gaming at cards or dice."

Defence. — "I am suspicious whether you have done me justice ; because I can find no such expressions in my written sermon on 1 Cor. x. 31. The nearest thereto is this : 'If husbandmen plow and sow that they may be rich, and live in the pleasures of this world, and appear grand among men, they are as far from true religion in their plowing, sowing, &c., as men are, that game for the same purpose.' If I had the same expression which you mention, I suppose it to be true in this sense only; that they are both enemies to God, self-lovers, self-seekers, and idolaters. That the one doth not take more sinful ways in carrying on his designs against God, I never thought of affirming."

Result. — " Voted, that the expressions are unwarrantable and of dangerous tendency; and therefore ought to be carefully guarded against. But Mr. Bliss, in his vindication, declared he was not apprehensive of his ever having delivered himself as testified by the witnesses."

COMPLAINT 12th. — " In preaching from that text, 'He that came down from heaven is above all,' he said a person might go on in sins, in drunkenness, in Sabbath-breaking even to rioting; but I must tell you for your comfort, if you belong to the election of grace, Christ will bring you home."

Defence. — " I did not encourage sin, in preaching upon John iii. 31, in saying that persons might go on in sin, &c. By the word *might*, I had not the intention to give them liberty. But if they were so perverse, that they would for some time longer continue in sin and increase iniquity; yet if they belonged to the election of grace they should be brought home by faith and repentance; which affords comfortable thoughts, but such, I think, as must most certainly reprove and reproach such as yield themselves to sin with hopes of after repentance."

Result. — " We judge these words are a very ill and unwarrantable use of the doctrine of election, and of very dangerous tendency."

COMPLAINT 14th. — " We are uneasy with his wandering from town to town to the disturbance of towns and churches, and neglecting his own church at home."

Defence. — " I have never preached in other churches without the consent of their pastors, nor in other towns without invitation, which I suppose a privilege granted in the gospel to the ministers of Christ, that I propose by the grace of God never to part with. If you will instance to me any criminal neglect of my own church, I shall endeavour to be suitably thankful to you, and, by the Lord's help, amend for the future."

Result. — " Voted, that we, having reason to fear that Mr. Bliss hath been incautious in his compliance with invitations to preach in some other ministers' parishes, exhort him for the future carefully to observe the testimony and advice of the late convention which he hath signed. But we do not find he hath neglected his own charge, but on the contrary his faithfulness and diligence were testified by many."

Mr. Bliss had been almost incessantly occupied in attending religious meetings, and also, says the result, in attending "the multitude of souls that have flocked to him for his advice and direction." His sermons, generally extemporaneous, had been produced without much previous study, and contained many hasty expressions and mistakes, which more mature reflection would have prevented. This was one of the main causes of difficulty on his part. The council also state, that "principles contrary to the doctrines of grace have been espoused by some persons in this place, which hath occasioned their stumbling at some truths which had been delivered to them."[1] This, and the spirit of opposition and prejudice on the part of the people, caused them to "overlook," in the language of the council, "the zeal, faithfulness, and love of souls, with which, we are persuaded, he hath ministered to his people." While the council disapproved of the incautious and improper manner in which Mr. Bliss had treated some of the doctrines of the Bible, it bore testimony to his usefulness as "the instrument of God in carrying on his remarkable gracious work in this town." Both parties were admonished, and advised to mutual confession and reconciliation. Mr. Bliss made a confession in presence of the council, satisfactory to them and the church, a large majority of which was always in his favor.[2]

---

[1] Christopher C. Baldwin, Esq., the Librarian of the American Antiquarian Society, has furnished me with extracts from the Rev. David Hall's MS. Journal. Under March 7, 1742, he says, "Was at Concord last week. Discoursed with some of Mr. Bliss's opposers. I find they are rank Arminians. Was at several houses. Mr. Beaton made me a present of Shepard's 'Sound Believer'; and it is indeed a valuable present." Mr. Hall was an admirer of Mr. Bliss and Mr. Whitfield. In several places in his journal he speaks of the affairs of Concord, and generally in favor of Mr. Bliss.

[2] In the Boston Evening Post, of March 14, 1743, is published a letter from a "gentleman of unquestionable veracity in Hopkinton," giving an account of a sermon preached there by Mr. Bliss, in which it is said, "He began in a low, moderate strain, and went on for some time in the same manner; but towards the close of his sermon, he began to raise his voice,

The proceedings of this council, like many other similar attempts to settle difficulties, did not allay public excitement, nor heal the divisions in the town. New instances of withdrawal took place, notwithstanding the efforts of different committees, chosen by the church, to treat with the disaffected.

September 4, 1744, the town voted, not to hear "the result of the last venerable council that sat"; not to free those persons who had separated from Mr. Bliss from their proportion of the ministerial tax; and not to allow them the privilege of holding public worship in the town-house. But a petition of 47 inhabitants, "who have, by the advice of two councils, separated from the ministry of Mr. Bliss," was presented to the General Court, October 17; and they were exempted, by an act passed January 19, 1745, from all ministerial charges since (June, 1743,) they had maintained or shall maintain public worship among themselves. They petitioned the town several times afterwards for assistance to build a meeting-house, but were unsuccessful.

On the 12th of December, 1745, *twenty* male communicants subscribed a covenant, and organized the West Church. Among them were some of the most wealthy, respectable, influential, and pious men in town. Others soon after united with them, and, in conjunction with some who were not communicants, they were accustomed to hold public worship regularly in a house which stood near the present residence of the Hon. Nathan Brooks.[1]

From this time there were two incorporated religious societies in Concord. Individuals living in the easterly part of the town had also several times petitioned to be set off into a separate precinct or parish; and they were successful in 1746. In that year, what is now Concord was incorporated as the first precinct or parish, and what is now Lincoln, as the second. In the latter precinct, many of the aggrieved brethren united with others, and formed the third church in the town.

---

and to use many extravagant gestures, and then began a considerable groaning amongst the auditors, which as soon as he perceived, he raised his voice still higher, and then the congregation were in the utmost confusion. Some crying out in the most doleful accents, some howling, some laughing, and others singing, and Mr. Bliss still roaring to them to come to Christ,—they answering,—'*I will, I will, I'm coming, I'm coming.*'"

[1] This was a public house. The sign had a black horse painted on it. Hence this church was called, by way of derision, the *black-horse church.*

The first meeting of the first parish was held September 19, 1746, at which the parish officers were chosen. The two societies in this parish continued to hold separate meetings. Another council was called by the disaffected brethren, whose proceedings I have not been able to find. Additional charges were also laid before the church, February 20, 1746, and at eight subsequent meetings examined. Mr. Bliss's defence, June 6th, appears at length on the church records, but the charges are not found there. As far as appears from the defence, they related principally to his preaching in the parishes of other ministers, or encouraging lay preachers in his own, or to alleged personal indiscretions. Mr. Bliss had preached to the separatists in Boston, at Springfield, and at Worcester, where he had been " earnestly requested by a multitude of souls." Mr. Cotton, of Newton, excluded him from his pulpit.

At length, the difficulties continuing to increase, a parish committee was chosen, May, 1747, to consider what measures should be taken to promote peace and unanimity between the two societies. This committee recommended that five persons, not inhabitants, be chosen to give their advice. Three of these being selected, the parish could not agree on the others, and the project failed. After several unsuccessful attempts, however, to adjust the difficulties, it was voted, at a meeting of the parish, March 1, 1748, "That a committee of seven ministers be chosen, and be desired to hear and examine into the difficulty the parish labors under; particularly to take into their consideration the result of the venerable council called by the church; and also the result of the last council called by those who lately separated and formed into a church state; and also to hear and examine into any matters of grievance which have arisen since the result of said councils; and to give their advice, in order to be laid before the churches in this parish for their consideration, for an accommodation and union of both churches, if it can be found practicable."

This council was composed of the Rev. Dr. Joseph Sewall, moderator, and John Webb of Boston; Hull Abbot of Charlestown; William Hobby of Reading; and Nathan Stone of Southborough. Two others were invited, but did not attend. They met the 16th of May at Mr. Ebenezer Hubbard's, and came to a result on the 20th. The charges brought against Mr. Bliss, before this council, related to his encouraging Elisha Payne and the Rev. Mr. Dutton in preaching and selling books in his parish; to his hasty suspension of several brethren of the church; to his preaching in other ministers' parishes without their consent, and contrary to advice of former councils and his own promise, &c., and were generally supported, as appears from the result. This was laid before the church and accepted; and the pastor made such acknowledgments as the council had pointed out, which were voted to be satisfactory. At the same time the vote by which the church suspended several members was reconsidered.

The West Congregation had voted, May 27th, "to adhere to the results of the venerable councils called by them, and the indulgence obtained from the Great and General Court." [1] The proceedings of the above council were laid before it, August 15; but for reasons ably drawn up, the advice they contained was not complied with. They were advised to unite with the other church, and settle a colleague with Mr. Bliss. This they could not do; for, being a minority, they had no hopes of obtaining a person of their choice. "We came out from Mr. Bliss and his church," say they, "not on account of any sudden transport of passion, but with mature consideration, with true principles of Christianity, and with the best of advice." They also stated,

---

[1] On the 18th of February, 1748, the Hon. James Minott and several others, a committee of the West Congregation in Concord, petitioned the General Court, praying that they may be enabled to settle an orthodox minister among themselves at the joint charge of the inhabitants of the first precinct in said town, and to erect a suitable house for public worship. A similar one had been presented to the town, May 15, 1745, but not granted. Orders of notice passed on this petition. Committees were appointed to take it into consideration at several successive meetings of the Legislature, before whom the remonstrances of the precinct, the first church, and Mr. Bliss, were made. The Legislative Journal says, April 12, 1749, "Whereas the petition of the West Society in Concord has been continued over to this time, that the parties therein concerned might agree their differences among themselves, but there being no prospect of such agreement," voted, that a committee be appointed "to take said petition, and answers thereto, and all other papers in the case, under their consideration, hear the parties now attending, and report what they judge proper for the Court to do thereon." Reported April 21, and again referred to the next session, and "the parties recommended to compromise their difficulties in the mean time." How it was finally disposed of, I have not learned.

that Mr. Bliss was not on terms of fellowship with many neighbouring churches; and, should a reunion be effected, they were desirous of having this restored. The following documents relate to this subject. The first appears on the church records; and the second was among the papers laid before the General Court.

The following vote of the church was passed February 9, 1749.

"1. We have not any certain intelligence given, that any churches are not in charity with us, as is thought and supposed by our brethren that have withdrawn from us.

"2. The ground mentioned by them of this their surmise is, 'that this church hath passed many votes in vindication of Mr. Bliss, before and since the sitting of the church's council, which have been reversed by the said council, and the committee of reverend ministers lately with us.' This we look upon to be insufficient to give dissatisfaction to any church whatsoever, if it be remembered that this church accepted and complied with the advice given by both the councils and committees aforesaid.

"3. Whereas our brethren point us to the churches whereof the council was formed, that advised to their withdrawal from Mr. Bliss, which they conceive to be among the dissatisfied; let it be observed, that as this church had nothing to do in calling or laying any matters before that council, so we apprehend that for this church to make application to those churches to give them satisfaction, would be a contradiction to that which we have said before the late venerable committee was with us, and hath not been reversed by complying with the result, which hath this passage, viz.; 'Yet we cannot think that this will justify your withdrawal, or that of any others from the church, and embodying in a new church state without asking a dismission from the church;' which passage, if our brethren would own to be just, we apprehend they would no more say any thing concerning our making satisfaction to the churches whereof that council consisted, which advised to their withdrawal from us. And indeed we apprehend it to be sufficient to give satisfaction to any church or churches, when we shall be properly informed by them of their uneasiness together with the reason thereof. Further we think it needless to reply; but on the whole would say, that, this church having accepted the result of the late venerable committee of reverend ministers, viz. Messrs. Joseph Sewall, moderator, John Webb,

Hull Abbot, William Hobby, and Nathan Stone, which was chosen by the first parish in Concord, it must not be expected by any that this church will go into any measures contradictory to said result. **Daniel Bliss,** *Pastor.*"

"This may certify all whom it may concern, that we have seen and heard so much proved (as we apprehend) against Mr. Bliss of Concord, especially with respect to his notorious prevarications and wronging the truth; and the meanness and mistakes in his public performances, and what has passed thereupon in councils; that we cannot comfortably hold communion with him, nor those that abet him. The confessions drawn by him, or for him, are far from being satisfactory. The withdrawal of the West Church will therefore be justified by knowing, impartial judges. The proposals for union offered last year by the reverend ministers seem to them impracticable, until Mr. Bliss and church have sought to obtain the charity of neighbouring churches, which they have neglected or refused, under pretence they knew of none that are not in charity with them, as they have represented. Whereupon it don't appear to us practicable for the West Church in Concord to return to the First Church; nor can it serve any interest of religion till the outstanding difficulties above mentioned be removed, with their other apparent aversions to all our Christian proposals. Nor can we look upon ourselves bound by the laws of Christ, and the order of these churches, to hold further communion with them. Upon which we humbly offer on their behalf, that their distressed condition may find relief by this honorable Court, that their hands may be strengthened to build upon that foundation this Court hath laid for them. All which we humbly submit and pray.

   John Hancock, Oliver Peabody, Thomas Parker,
   John Barnard, John Gardner, William Cook.

"The First Church in Lancaster as having received no satisfaction.

        Timothy Harrington, *Pastor.*
        Daniel Rogers, [of Littleton.]

"*May* 8, 1749."

In the mean time several meetings of the parish were held, at which measures were taken to reconcile the two societies, and effect a union; but being unsuccessful, the following proceedings were had, February 13, 1750.

"The votes of both churches having been read; and it appearing that the First Church has agreed to accept of and comply with the advice of the late venerable committee of ministers, called by the parish to give their Christian advice; and are very unwilling to come into any measures contradictory to, or inconsistent with, the said advice; and the Second Church, having refused to comply with said advice, have made other proposals, which have been considered and answered by the First Church in the parish as being not satisfactory to them; and inasmuch as a reconciliation and union seem at present difficult and almost impracticable; therefore voted, that nothing further be done at this time towards calling and settling a colleague with Mr. Bliss."

Another council, consisting of the Rev. Messrs. Israel Loring of Sudbury, John Gardner of Stow, and William Cook, invited by the West Church, met here, October 8, 1750, to consult on the propriety of their proceedings, and advised the members not to unite with the other church. From this time, however, the controversy principally ceased. Many, disaffected with the First Church, found an asylum in the church at Lincoln, after the incorporation of that town in 1754; others had become reconciled by mutual concessions. A few only remained separate till the death of Mr. Bliss.

The West Church existed about fourteen years, and supported public worship the most part of the time, though no minister was settled. The Rev. Messrs. John Whiting, John Gardner, Ebenezer Winchester, Benjamin Stevens, and —— Marsh, and probably others, were preachers; Samuel Miles and Jonathan Buttrick, deacons; and Josiah Hosmer and Ezekiel Miles, "choristers to set the tune for the congregation."[1] The Rev. Mr. Loring administered the sacrament, March 25, 1750, and at several other times.

---

[1] The prudential affairs of the society were managed by a clerk, treasurer, or committee of three, and two collectors. Captain Stephen Hosmer was clerk (whose papers have furnished me with many facts), and Nathaniel Colburn and Charles Prescott, Esq., at different times, treasurers. The Hon. James Minott was a leading member. Three hundred pounds currency were raised to support preaching, in the same

The secession from Mr. Bliss was not made, like most others in New England,[1] because the pastor was not zealous enough in promoting the religious excitement of the times, but on account of his supposed or real errors in his preaching and pastoral conduct. Some thought he was too zealous and too enthusiastic; and, though wishing the spread of true religion, they thought Mr. Bliss took improper measures to promote a revival. It cannot be denied that the influence of the clergy was very great in promoting and confirming the unhappy divisions in this town, though acting conscientiously in opposition to Mr. Bliss. The troubles in Concord were the cause of great disturbance in the neighbouring churches; some individuals espousing the cause of Mr. Bliss, and some that of his opponents. A division took place in the Rev. Mr. Loring's society; and several councils were called to settle them. Similar effects were produced elsewhere.

These facts give but an imperfect idea of the condition of the town in this important period of its history. Did the limits of this work permit, a more full account of the ecclesiastical documents, which have accidentally fallen into my hands (a part only of which are in the church records), would be given; but the details already made lead us to view this controversy too important to be passed over without a particular notice. Though mingled with much personal feeling and altercation, producing division among ministers, in societies and families, between husbands and wives, parents and children, which scarcely finds a parallel even in modern sectarianism, and the details of which it might be well to bury in oblivion; yet it involved many important principles in theology and church discipline, and teaches the inefficiency of ecclesiastical councils to settle personal difficulties. To its results may be traced the introduction of those more liberal feelings and sentiments, which lead people to think and judge for themselves, and not to depend too exclusively on the opinions of the clergy.

In April, 1741, Timothy Minott, Deacons Dakin and Heywood, and Timothy Wheeler, were appointed a committee to assist the pastor in preparing a new covenant. One was reported, and pub-

---

proportion as other taxes, in 1747; £500 in 1748; and £800 in 1749. The collectors were vested with the same authority as in towns.

[1] See Trumbull's History of Connecticut, Vol. II.

licly signed, May 11, 1749, by ninety-two male members of the church. The Rev. Thomas Prince, of Boston, preached on this solemn and interesting occasion.

The genuine principles of religion obtained little influence during the progress of the controversies in town. Great apathy prevailed. In 1748 one person only united with the First Church; and for some years before and after that period a comparatively small number. After these troubles subsided, special attention to the subject again prevailed. In 1763 *thirty* individuals united with the church. Less enthusiasm and more lasting benefit, it is said, attended this revival than that of 1741 and 1742.

Mr. Whitfield visited Concord again, March 10, 1764. The next day being Sabbath, Mr. Bliss, at the special request of Mr. Whitfield, preached in the morning, and Mr. Whitfield in the afternoon. This was one of Mr. Bliss's most powerful efforts, and made such an impression on Mr. Whitfield as led him to remark, " If I had studied my whole life, I could not have produced such a sermon." But it was the last time Mr. Bliss ever appeared in the pulpit. He was soon after taken sick with a consumption, in which he languished till his death. A special fast, on his account, was held in Concord, May 4. The Rev. Daniel Emerson, of Hollis, prayed; and the Rev. William Lawrence preached, from Psalm ciii. 3, in the morning; and the Rev. Mr. Clark prayed, and the Rev. Jonathan Loring preached from Psalm lxv. 2, in the afternoon. All difficulties between Mr. Bliss and the neighbouring ministers were happily settled at this meeting. He died about 12 o'clock at noon, just a week after. He was buried on the 16th. His bearers were the Rev. Messrs. Martin, Stone, Swift, Bridge, Lawrence, Emerson, Clark, and Loring.

During the ministry of Mr. Bliss, 290 persons were admitted to the church in full communion, 328 owned the covenant, and 1424 were baptized.

The Rev. DANIEL BLISS was son of Mr. Thomas Bliss, and born at Springfield, in January, 1715. His grandfather, Samuel, one of ten children, five sons and five daughters, who removed with his mother, Mrs. Margaret Bliss, to that town in 1646 (her husband's name not being known), married Mary, daughter of John Leonard, in 1664, and died in 1720. Thomas was born in 1667, and died in 1733. The Rev. Daniel was graduated at Yale College in 1732. While at College he imbibed those principles of thought and action for which he was distinguished in after life. Some time after he left College he received an invitation to settle at Guilford in Connecticut, but was not ordained. The following long epitaph appears on his monument in the Hill Burying-Ground.

"Here lies Interred the Remains of the Rev. Mr. Daniel Bliss, Pastor of the Church of Christ in Concord, who Deceased the 11th day of May, Anno Dom : 1764, Ætatis suæ 50.

"Of this beloved Disciple and Minister of Jesus Christ 't is justly observable, that, in addition to his natural and acquired abilities, he was distinguishedly favoured with those eminent Graces of the Holy Spirit (Meakness, Humility, and Zeal), which rendered him peculiarly fit for and enabled him to go thro' the great and arduous work of the Gospel Ministry, upon which he entered in the 25th year of his age. The Duties of the various Characters he sustained in Life, were performed with great stricteness and fidelity. As a private Christian he was a bright Example of Holiness in Life and Purity in Conversation. But in the execution of ye ministerial office he shone with Peculiar Lustre, — a spirit of Devotion animated all his performances : — his Doctrine drop'd as ye Rain and his lips distilled like the Dew : — his Preaching was powerful and Searching ; — and he who blessed him with an uncommon Talent in a particular Application to ye Consciences of men, crowned his skilful Endeavours wth great success. As ye work of the Ministry was his great Delight, so he continued fervent and diligent in ye Performance of it, till his Divine Lord called him from his Service on Earth to the Glorious Recompense of Reward in Heaven ; where as one who has turned many unto Righteousness he shines as a star for ever and ever.

> "'His soul was of ye Angelic Frame,
> The Same Ingredients, and the mould ye same,
> Whom ye Creator makes a Minister of Fame.'
> WATTS."

Mr. Bliss married Phebe Walker, of Strafford, Connecticut, in 1738. She died July 2, 1797, aged 84, having had 9 children.
1. Daniel, who will be noticed among the college graduates ;

2. Phebe, who married the two ministers who were successors of her father; 3. John, who died young; 4. Thomas Theodore, who lived at Brimfield, held a commission in the army of the American Revolution, and was a brave, but unfortunate officer. He was taken prisoner at the first campaign in Canada, at the Three Rivers, with all his company, and retained as a hostage during the war. He died at Cambridge in 1802. 5. Hannah, who was drowned at Springfield; 6. John; 7. Samuel, who was an officer in the British army, during the revolution, in New York and New Jersey. He had an island in the Bay of Fundy granted to him. 8. Martha, who married Isaac Hoar. 9. Joseph, who died at Plymouth, New Hampshire. It is somewhat remarkable, that two of Mr. Bliss's sons should have been ardent tories, and two ardent whigs.[1]

May 23, 1764, Deacon Samuel Minott was chosen standing moderator, the Rev. Daniel Emerson, of Hollis, New Hampshire, "moderator extraordinary," and Messrs. Simon Hunt, John Cuming, Jonathan Puffer, Ephraim Brown, and James Barrett, a committee "to assist the moderator in hearing and preparing any matters to be laid before the church." Early in June a day of fasting and prayer was kept in the church; and the Rev. Messrs. Hall of Sutton, Hutchinson of Grafton, Searls of Stoneham, and Bridge of Framingham, assisted in the public religious exercises on the occasion. On the 11th of October, 1765, the church voted, though not unanimously, to receive into its communion members of the late West Church, who chose to offer themselves. Some had already united; and some others were disposed to do so. That all difficulties might be settled before the ordination of

---

[1] Mr. Loring preached on the next Sabbath two funeral sermons; in the morning, from Zach. i. 5, and, in the afternoon, from Job xix. 25, 26, 27.

Ebenezer Hartshorn made Mr. Bliss's coffin. "Five hundred broadheaded coffin-nails and five hundred small white tacks were put on the cover." "White ones used to be used, but lately they use them that are japanned black." Gloves and rings were given at the funeral. The late Thomas Clark, Esq., of Boston, had in his possession a ring, given to his grandfather the Rev. Jonas Clark, as one of the pall-holders. His funeral expenses, paid by the town, were £66 13s. 4d.

Mr. Bliss published the following work: "The Gospel hidden to them that are lost. Being the substance of two sermons preached. Published at the repeated request, and free cost, of some who heard them. 1755."

another minister, a council was called, consisting of the Second church in Cambridge, and the churches in Grafton, Wilmington, Framingham, and Marlborough; and met here, November 26, 1765. Their proceedings are not recorded.

On the 18th of February, 1765, the church chose William Emerson to be their pastor; and in this vote the town concurred, in March, 128 to 62. The only other candidate mentioned was Mr. Samuel Williams. It was agreed to give him £200 as a settlement, and £100 as an annual salary. He was ordained January 1, 1766. The council, on the occasion, was composed of ministers and delegates from the First and Second churches in Sudbury, the Second in Cambridge, the Second in Wells, the Second in Reading, and the churches in Malden, Stow, Littleton, Acton, Chelmsford, Topsfield, Lexington, Hollis, Pepperell, Lincoln, Bedford, and Billerica. The Rev. John Gardner, of Stow, was moderator. The Rev. Daniel Rogers, of Littleton, made the introductory prayer; the Rev. Joseph Emerson, of Malden, preached from 1 Chron. xxix. 1; the Rev. John Gardner gave the charge; the Rev. William Cook, of East Sudbury, made the last prayer; and the Rev. John Swift, of Acton, gave the right hand of fellowship.

When Mr. Emerson began his ministry, some of those feelings, which had been fostered in the previous controversies, were still existing. But though he came into office under these disadvantageous circumstances, his piety, talents, and popular manner, as a preacher, secured the affection and support of a great majority of the church and town. The subsequent difficulties in his church arose principally from the rejection of an individual who offered himself as a candidate for admission. When the church was called upon to act on his admission, it was well known that objections existed in the minds of some of the communicants against him; and Deacon Simon Hunt arose, after the question was put, and before the vote was declared, and requested it to be made certain. Considering this as an unjustifiable act, the candidate immediately withdrew. This happened in 1767; and *nine* of the members of the church, uniting with some who were not professors of religion, and considering its proceedings improper and arbitrary, and Mr. Emerson as partial for approving them, espoused the cause of the rejected individual, and composed the principal opposition, and were known as the *aggrieved brethren.*

In the progress of the controversy, many frivolous complaints were brought forward, and much personal feeling was excited; but few important principles in doctrine or discipline were discussed or settled. The records concerning these transactions are very imperfect.

A mutual council sat here, April 11, 1769, whose result was favorable to the church, but was not accepted by the aggrieved brethren. After repeated "hearings," the candidate was still excluded; and notwithstanding frequent efforts of the church to promote peace and harmony, the difficulties remained unsettled. Under these circumstances, an *ex parte* council met at Mr. Ebenezer Hubbard's, August 28, 1770, consisting of the Rev. Messrs. Gad Hitchcock of Pembroke, moderator, Jacob Cushing of Waltham, Samuel Woodward of Weston, Jonas Clark of Lexington, Jonas Merriam of Newton, Elias Smith of Middleton, Phineas Whitney of Shirley, Zabdiel Adams of Lunenburg, and delegates from their respective churches. On the second day of their session they addressed a letter to the church, requesting the members to adjust the difficulties among themselves, or join in calling a mutual council. To effect the first object, five members of each party were chosen to agree, but they were unsuccessful. The church not complying with the other request, the council met again, October 23, with five additional churches, — those of the Rev. Messrs. John Mellen of Lancaster, Daniel Shute of Hingham, Joseph Jackson of Brookline, Phillips Payson of Chelsea, and Jason Haven of Dedham. It again adjourned, and met November 13. Eleven articles of grievance against the church, five against the pastor, and eight against particular members, were examined. The result was unfavorable to the church, and in favor of the aggrieved, as might have been anticipated. This being published in the Boston Gazette, and industriously circulated, tended by no means to allay public excitement. At length, after several more unsuccessful attempts towards an accommodation, another mutual council was called, June, 1772, consisting of the First and Second churches in Rowley, the First in Hingham, the First in Newbury, the First in Stoughton, the First in Portsmouth, the Second in Shrewsbury, and the churches in Weymouth, Byfield, Groton, Milton, Upton, Haverhill, Newbury, and Newton. The pastor, Deacon Hunt, John Flint, James Barrett, Jr., Deacon Brown, and Amos Wood were chosen a committee to lay matters before the council. A public examination was had in the meeting-house. The result was generally acceptable. After this period little was said on the subject; and, the more immediate author of these difficulties having become unpopular with the friends of liberty, all was settled, on July 1, 1774, when the following vote was passed by the church:

"That inasmuch as our aggrieved brethren, Benjamin Wheeler and others, have for some considerable time withdrawn from our communion, on account chiefly of the non-admission of Mr. Joseph Lee into full communion, a draft of a confession was made, and several times read in church meeting, which, if the said Joseph Lee consented to by signing his name to the said confession, the church voted that it should be satisfactory to them, so as that they could receive him into their communion and fellowship. The aggrieved brethren, being informed that the church had passed the above mentioned vote, signified in church meeting that the difficulty in their minds was hereby removed, as to the church's former refusal of Mr. Joseph Lee's admission into full communion, so as that they could return to their duty, if there was no objection in the minds of the brethren on any other account. Upon which it was agreed on all sides, that, as it had been a day of temptation, there should be a mutual confession of our faults one to another, and that the brethren aggrieved should return to the communion and fellowship of the church, without any thing further being said or done."

The 11th of July, 1776, was set apart as a day of fasting and prayer, when the covenant was renewed and signed by 62 male communicants. On this occasion the Rev. Mr. Bridge preached in the forenoon, and the Rev. Mr. Penniman of Bedford in the afternoon. This covenant, somewhat resembling the one entered into in 1749, proposed to take the Assembly's Catechism as "an excellent compendium" of the Bible. During Mr. Emerson's ministry 66 persons were admitted to full communion, 135 owned the covenant, and 506 were baptized.

The Rev. WILLIAM EMERSON, son of the Rev. Joseph Emerson, of Malden, was born May 21, 1743, and graduated at Harvard College in 1761. His father was the son of Edward Emerson of Chelmsford, and grandson of the Rev. Joseph Emerson of

Mendon, who married a daughter of the Rev. Edward Bulkeley, and died in Concord, January 3, 1680. His mother was a daughter of the Rev. Samuel Moody of York. The Rev. Joseph Emerson of Pepperell, and John Emerson of Conway, were his brothers. The Rev. William Emerson was pastor of the church in Concord about ten years. His ardent love for his country, as a "high son of liberty," prevailed on him to contribute, by his intellectual and personal services at home and abroad, in the great conflict of the American revolution. On the 16th of August, 1776, he left his people with their consent, his church, his friends, and all the endearments of domestic life, to join the army at Ticonderoga as chaplain. He continued in office till advised by his physicians to resign on account of ill health, and was discharged by General Gates, September 18. He commenced his return home, but, his disease increasing, he could not proceed. He stopped at the Rev. Benajah Roots's, of Rutland, on Otter Creek, where he remained, suffering under a severe bilious fever, till his death, which took place at 5 o'clock on Sunday morning, October 20, at the age of 33. He was interred there with the honors of war by a detachment from Colonel Vandyke's regiment, commanded by Major Shepard. His last sickness was borne with great composure, resignation, and Christian fortitude. He often spoke of the endearing kindness of his people toward him, and the pleasure he should enjoy, if it were the will of God to give him opportunity, to show his gratitude by exerting himself more vigorously for their good. When the hour of dissolution seemed to be near, he appeared like one waiting "to depart and be with Christ." The regret, apparent in all existing records, that he should be prematurely cut off in his promising career of usefulness, evinces the esteem of the society of which he was pastor. Mr. Emerson's personal appearance was pleasing and prepossessing; his manners familiar and gentlemanly; his conversation communicative and facetious, though not inconsistent with his ministerial character; in his preaching he was popular, eloquent, persuasive, and devotional, adapting himself, with remarkable ease, to all circumstances and occasions; and his doctrine was evangelical. "Fervency of spirit," ardent zeal, love of his profession and his people, characterized all his performances. A monument was erected by the town to his memory in 1826, on which his character is delineated as "enthusiastic, eloquent, affectionate, and pious; he loved his family, his people, his God, and his country. And to this last he yielded the cheerful sacrifice of his life."

Mr. Emerson married Phebe, daughter of the Rev. Daniel Bliss, August 21, 1766, by whom he had William (noticed among the college graduates), Hannah Bliss, Phebe, Mary Moody, and Rebecca. His widow married the Rev. Ezra Ripley, November 16, 1780, and died, February 16, 1825, aged 83, having had by him two sons and a daughter.[1]

Deacon Simon Hunt was moderator of the church, from the death of Mr. Emerson to the ordination of his successor. Committees of the church and town were chosen to supply the pulpit, as had been the case at similar times before; and a day of fasting and prayer was kept, September 14, 1777, in commemoration of the death of their late pastor, and preparatory to the choice of another. On the 11th of May, 1778, Mr. Ezra Ripley was unanimously chosen pastor on the part of the church, in which the town concurred on the 1st of June following, 94 to 1. He was ordained, November 11, 1778. In the religious services on the occasion, the Rev. Josiah Bridge of E. Sudbury made the first prayer; the Rev. Jason Haven of Dedham preached from 2 Timothy ii. 2; the Rev. Josiah Dana of Barre "prayed after sermon"; the Rev. Ebenezer Bridge of Chelmsford "prayed before and gave the charge"; and the Rev. Jonas Clark of Lexington gave the right hand of fellowship. The council was composed of these gentlemen, and delegates from their respective churches; and also the churches of the Rev. Eli Forbes of Gloucester, the Rev. Peter Thacher of Malden, the Rev. Jonathan Newell of Stow, and the Rev. Moses Adams of Acton.

The town agreed to give Mr. Ripley £550 currency as a settlement, and £100 as an annual salary, founded on the prices

---

[1] The Rev. Ralph Waldo Emerson of Boston kindly loaned me a concise private journal, kept by his grandfather, from January, 1775, to August, 1776; and several letters to his wife written at Cambridge and at the Northward; which, beside detailing some important historical facts, are remarkable for their easy, sprightly style. The Rev. Mr. Roots addressed a letter to the church, giving an account of his last sickness. A notice of his character appeared in the Boston Gazette, November 4, 1776.

of articles of produce, — rye at 4s. per bushel, corn at 3s., beef at 2½d. per pound, and pork at 4d.; the salary to rise and fall according to the variation in the prices of these articles. He was also to enjoy all the ministerial perquisites, and to be provided with 30 cords of firewood. A salary thus established was found to be attended with much uncertainty; and some years to fall short of £100. This was the occasion of much embarrassment. The town ascertained that the real value of the £550, when paid, was but £40, and the first year's salary £41; and in 1785, £200 were specially granted to make up the deficiency. In 1793, £100 were also granted. In 1812 the contract was very properly altered; and instead of this uncertain income it was agreed to give him $750 as his permanent salary, which, with his firewood, estimated at $100, and the perquisites $15, gave him the annual salary of $865. At the ordination of his colleague, in 1830, he relinquished $250 of his salary and 10 cords of wood.

From time immemorial it has been the custom of the church to administer the ordinance of baptism to such adults and their children, as "owned the covenant," without joining the church in full communion. This covenant was the same as that which admitted to full communion, with the exception of the clause which referred to the communion, and was used for both cases till 1795, when the following was adopted to be subscribed by the individuals who "own it." Three hundred and two have signed it since 1795.

"I do now seriously profess my belief in one God, who is over all and blessed for ever more.

"I believe the Holy Scriptures were given by inspiration of God, and are able to make wise unto salvation, through faith, which is in Christ Jesus; and I will endeavour to observe them as the rule of my life in faith and practice.

"I believe that Jesus Christ is the Son of God; and that God so loved the world as to give his only Son to die, the just for the unjust, that whosoever believeth in him might not perish, but have everlasting life.

"I believe that repentance towards God and faith in Jesus Christ are the gospel conditions of salvation, and therefore, penitently confessing all my sins to God, I look for salvation through Christ alone.

"I believe that baptism is a Christian ordinance, a sign of visible discipleship to Christ, and an act of dedication to God, and that the proper subjects of it are believers in the Christian religion, and their offspring and charge. And I now promise that I will endeavour, by the grace of God assisting, to educate my children and charge according to the Christian religion.

"In testimony of this my belief and promise I hereunto subscribe my name."

The covenant for admission into full communion, used by Mr. Emerson, was taken with him into the army and lost, no copy being in the records. In 1779 a new one was prepared, and used till 1795, when the following, now in use, was substituted.

"Professing a firm belief of revealed religion, and that the Holy Scriptures, which contain it, are given by inspiration of God, and resolving to take them for your rule of faith and practice, you do now, as far as you know your own heart, sincerely avouch and choose the one only living and true God to be your God and portion; the Lord Jesus Christ to be your Mediator and Saviour; the Holy Ghost to be your sanctifier and guide; giving up yourself unto God, the Father, Son, and Holy Ghost, to be his and his only for ever.[1]

"Sensible that in many things you have offended, and that your sufficiency is of God, you do now, with penitence for your sins, humbly implore the divine aid to enable you henceforth to walk before God in love, and in all holy conversation and godliness.

"Convinced of the importance of early instruction in virtue and piety, you now promise, that you will conscientiously endeavour to educate all such as are, or may be, committed to your care, agreeably to the prescriptions of God's holy word.

"You do also covenant with this church of Christ and promise, that you will walk with us as a member of our body; that you will attend on the administration of the word and ordinances among us, and submit to the Christian watch, discipline, and regulations of this church, so long as God shall continue your life and abode with us.

---

[1] The expression, "the Father, Son, and Holy Ghost," was stricken out in 1826.

"All this you profess and promise in the presence of the all-seeing God, and by the help of his spirit and grace will live agreeably to the same.

"I do, therefore, as a minister of Jesus Christ, and as pastor of this church, acknowledge you a member, and receive you into fellowship; and we declare, that we do and will look upon you as a member of the same body with ourselves, and will treat you with that affection and watchfulness which your relation to us now calls for; watching over you not for your halting, but for your edification; praying God, now and ever, to build up you, and us, and all his saints, a spiritual building, an holy house, a living temple unto himself the Lord our God. Amen."

At the adoption of this covenant, some alterations in the customs of the church were made. The practice of giving relations of religious exercises of mind before admission to the communion, of "making public confession of particular crimes committed previously to any voluntary engagement and profession of religion," and of calling for a vote on the admission of members, was discontinued. Members are now admitted before the church on examination of the pastor only, after having been publicly propounded, and no objection appearing. Since 1828, they have remained in their pews when the covenant is read to them.

During the ministry of the Rev. Dr. Ripley, to the ordination of his colleague, 383 persons were admitted to the church in full communion, 449 owned the covenant, 1541 were baptized, 101 were regularly dismissed, and one was excommunicated. At the death of Mr. Emerson the number of communicants was estimated at 150. January 1, 1815, the church contained 156,— 54 males and 102 females. The number now is about 138.

The funds of the church amount to $350. John Cuming, Esq. gave $111 for the benefit of poor communicants. The "Minott Fund," of $132, was begun in 1778, by Mrs. Bulah Minott and other members of the church, for the purchase of the elements and other purposes, at the discretion of the minister and deacons. Miss Abigail Dudley, in 1813, bequeathed a legacy to the church, which was set apart for a singing fund. One of the communion vessels was given by Margaret Bridges, of Ireland, April 6, 1676; another by Thomas Brown, Sen. (the town clerk several years from 1689); another by the wife of

Duncan Ingraham, Esq.; four were purchased by the treasurer of the church in 1714; eight with a donation from John Cuming, Esq. of $222·22 for that purpose; and the baptismal basin from a part of the Minott fund.

The version of Psalms and Hymns, by Sternhold and Hopkins, was used in the church prior to 1766, each line of which was read separately by the deacons when sung. On the 18th of February of that year, it was voted "to sing Tate and Brady's version three months on trial." In June following, Watts's version was introduced, and used till June 1, 1828, when the Cambridge collection was substituted. Singers were first seated about 1774, when the custom of giving out the line by the deacons was discontinued; and the church then voted, that Deacon Wheeler should lead in singing one half of the time, and the singers in the congregation the other half. In 1779 it took into consideration "the melancholy decay of singing in public worship, and chose 20 persons, who should sit together in the body seats below, and take the lead in singing." The women to sit separate from the men. They removed into the gallery soon after the repair of the house in 1792. Under various leaders the church music has improved conformably to the spirit of the times.

The Rev. EZRA RIPLEY, D. D., was born at Woodstock, Connecticut, May 1, 1751. He was graduated at Harvard College in 1776, and has received the honorary degree of Doctor of Divinity from the same institution. He was invited early in the spring to Concord, and was ordained November 7, 1778. During a long and useful ministry few things have occurred to interrupt the uncommon harmony which prevailed in the church and town at his ordination. In one instance only has the advice of neighbouring ministers been called to settle difficulties, and this did not relate to the pastor. It was in 1784, and terminated happily. It is a remarkable fact, that, for 40 years of his ministry, not a single individual paid a ministerial tax to any other society, and that for 190 years, till 1825, excepting in Mr. Bliss's day as already noticed, the whole town were united in one society. The 11th of November, 1828, was the 50th anniversary of his ordination, and on that occasion he delivered his half-century sermon, which was published. In this he informs us he had written more than 2500 sermons. By perseverance in a constant and systematic exercise of his corporeal and mental powers, his great natural energy of character has been preserved, his life and usefulness lengthened, and he is now (June, 1833) able to perform with remarkable ease the duties of the ministerial office.

In August, 1829, the Rev. Dr. Ripley made a formal request to his people for assistance in his ministerial labors. A committee was chosen, a town meeting was called, and other preliminary measures were taken to effect this object. Mr. Goodwin, after having preached several Sabbaths, was invited by the town, January 3, 1830, (the church having voted not to act on the subject in a separate capacity,) to settle as his colleague, with an annual salary of $700 during the life of Dr. Ripley, and $900 afterwards, and 25 cords of wood. He accepted the invitation, and was ordained February 17, 1830. The introductory prayer, on the occasion, was made by the Rev. Convers Francis of Watertown; reading of the Scriptures by the Rev. Jonathan Cole of Kingston; sermon by the Rev. James Kendall, D. D., of Plymouth, (which was printed); consecrating prayer by the Rev. Samuel Ripley of Waltham; charge by the Rev. Joseph Field of Weston; fellowship of the churches by the Rev. Ralph Waldo Emerson of Boston; address to the people by the Rev. John White of Dedham; and concluding prayer by the Rev. Nathaniel Whitman of Billerica. These and the Rev. Messrs. George Ripley of Boston, John B. Wight of East Sudbury, William H. White of Littleton, Thomas B. Gannet of Cambridge Port, Caleb Stetson of Medford, Frederick H. Hedge of West Cambridge, Daniel Austin of Brighton, Wilkes Allen of Chelmsford, and delegates from their respective churches, composed the council, of which the Rev. Dr. Kendall was moderator, and Thomas B. Gannett scribe. The church in Harvard College, the Twelfth church in Boston, the Second in Waltham, the First in Cambridge, and the churches in Stow and Sudbury, were also represented in the council by a delegate, the pastors being engaged at the same time in an ordination at Natick.

The Rev. HERSEY BRADFORD GOODWIN was born at Plymouth, August 18, 1805, graduated at Harvard College in 1826, and at the Theological School in Cambridge in 1829. The first child he baptized bears his name. He married Lucretia, daughter of Benjamin M. Watson, Esq. of Plymouth, June 1, 1830. She died greatly lamented, November 11, 1831, aged 23, leaving one son.

SUCCESSSION OF THE DEACONS.

Names.	Time of Birth.	Election.	Decease.	Age.
1. Richard Griffin.	——————	About 1636.	April 5, 1661.	—
2. Robert Merriam.	——————	——————	Feb. 15, 1681.	72
3. Luke Potter.	——————	——————	Oct. 13, 1697.	—
4. James Blood.	——————	——————	Nov. 26, 1692.	—
5. Humphrey Barrett.	——————	——————	Jan. 3, 1716.	—
6. John Heywood.	April 8, 1662.	——————	Jan. 2, 1719.	57
7. John Wheeler.	——————	About 1717.	Dec. 1, 1736.	—
8. Edward Wheeler.	July 17, 1669.	——————	Feb. 17, 1734.	65
9. Joseph Dakin.	——————	About 1717.	March 13, 1744.	75
10. Samuel Heywood.	——————	About 1719.	Oct. 28, 1750.	63
11. Samuel Merriam.	July 25, 1681.	About 1736.	June 1, 1764.	83
12. Samuel Miles.[1]	March 14, 1681.	About 1734.	Oct. 11, 1758.	77
13. Samuel Minott.	March 25, 1706.	May 30, 1744.	March 17, 1766.	60
14. Ephraim Brown.	Nov. 7, 1710.	May 30, 1744.	Oct. 9, 1788.	78
15. Amos Heald.[2]	May 23, 1708.	Oct. 24, 1751.	Jan. 4, 1775.	67
16. Thomas Barrett.	Oct. 2, 1707.	Feb. 18, 1666.	June 20, 1779.	72
17. David Wheeler.	Dec. 27, 1707.	June 16, 1766.	March 24, 1784.	77
18. Simon Hunt.	Sept. 3, 1704.	June 16, 1766.	Dec. 13, 1790.	87
19. George Minott.	Oct. 22, 1741.	Aug. 3, 1779.	April 13, 1808.	65
20. John White.[3]	Aug. 23, 1749.	Dec. 6, 1784.	Jan. 9, 1830.	80
21. William Parkman.[4]	——————	Dec. 20, 1788.	Feb. 5, 1832.	91
22. Joseph Chandler.[5]	May 5, 1748.	June 30, 1791.	Jan. 19, 1813.	64
23. Thomas Hubbard.	——————	April 30, 1812.	——————	—
24. Francis Jarvis.	——————	April 30, 1812.	——————	—
25. Reuben Brown, Jr.	——————	May 3, 1827.	——————	—
26. Cyrus Hosmer.	——————	May 3, 1827.	——————	—

The TRINITARIAN CHURCH, then consisting of 16 members,— 5 male and 11 female, was organized, June 5, 1826, by a council, consisting of the Rev. Dr. Beecher, moderator, Messrs. Samuel Green and Asa Rand of Boston, Paul Litchfield of Carlisle, Samuel Stearns of Bedford, Warren Fay of Charlestown,

---

[1] He seceded from the church under Mr. Bliss, and was deacon of the West Church.

[2] He was dismissed from the church in Lincoln, September 27, 1772, and removed to Townsend, wnere he died. He is said to have been a deacon in three churches, — Concord, Lincoln, and Townsend.

[3] He was dismissed at his request, January 7, 1827, and united with the Trinitarian Church.

[4] He was excused from active services on account of age and infirmities, January 1, 1826.

[5] He resigned on account of ill health, December 4, 1811.

Sewall Harding of Waltham, George Fisher of Harvard, and delegates from their respective churches. Mr. Green made the first prayer, and gave the fellowship of the churches; Dr. Beecher preached; Mr. Fay read the confession of faith and covenant (which has since been published with collateral references to Scripture for proof); and Mr. Fisher made the concluding prayer. A corner-stone of a meeting-house had been laid on the 22d of May previous, which was completed and dedicated on the 6th of December following. On this occasion, the Rev. Samuel Green preached a sermon, which was printed. During this time the pulpit was principally supplied by the Rev. Mr. Rand. Mr. Southmayd preached his first sermon here January 21, 1827, and on the 19th of February received the unanimous invitation of the church to become their pastor, with an annual salary of $600, to which he gave an affirmative answer on the 30th of March. He was ordained April 25th. The Rev. Edward Beecher of Boston made the first prayer; James Murdock, D. D., of Andover preached; the Rev. Samuel Stearns made the consecrating prayer; the Rev. Lyman Beecher gave the charge; the Rev. John Todd of Groton presented the right hand of fellowship; the Rev. Benjamin B. Wisner of Boston addressed the church and people; and the Rev. George Fisher made the concluding prayer. These gentlemen and the Rev. Messrs. Paul Litchfield, Sewall Harding, and Asa Rand were members of the council, of which the Rev. Dr. Murdock was moderator.

The Rev. DANIEL S. SOUTHMAYD was born at Castleton, Vermont, February 11, 1802, graduated at Middlebury College in 1822, and at the Theological Seminary at Andover in 1826. After sustaining the pastoral office a little over five years, he asked for a dismission, June 8, 1832, which was granted by the church, and confirmed by a council on the 15th, consisting of the Rev. Samuel Stearns of Bedford, moderator, the Rev. Elijah Demond of Lincoln, scribe, the Rev. Sewall Harding of Waltham, the Rev. Leonard Luce of Westford, and delegates from their respective churches. From the time the church was organized to Mr. Southmayd's ordination, 6 members were added to the church, and during his ministry 77, (53 by original profession, and 30 by letter from other churches,) and 30 were males and 53 females; 4 have been dismissed, 2 excommunicated, and 5 have died; present number of members 88, of whom 30 are males. Several, however, have removed from town. Mr. Southmayd administered 46 baptisms, and married 26 couples. He now lives at Lowell.

John Vose, chosen Deacon June 1, 1827; excused from active duty, March, 1832, and died in 1833.

Moses Davis, chosen June 1, 1827; removed to Lowell, September, 1831.

Francis Hunt and Samuel A. Thurston, chosen March 30, 1832.

Deacon John White bequeathed to this church $700, and Miss Sarah Thoreau $50, which has been vested as a fund for its use.

CHAPTER XII.

NATURAL HISTORY.

Climate. — Geology. — Botany. — Ponds.. — Rivers. — Brooks. — Fish. — Quadrupeds. — Birds.

IN several of its divisions the *Natural History* of Concord does not essentially differ from that of the surrounding county and state. Situated but sixteen miles from Boston, and nearly in the same latitude, in its climate it does not vary essentially from that city. It was said by Mr. John Josselyn, who visited this country in 1673, that " this place [Concord] is subject to bitter storms." [1] Though it is not easy to see how the remark is particularly applicable to Concord, yet local circumstances have been supposed to have some influence in the changes of its atmosphere. The evaporation from a sluggish river and extensive meadows sometimes produces here, at night, a damp atmosphere; but the waters are pure; and the sun's rays, reflected from a loose soil, soon dry and purify it. Few places are more healthy, or exhibit a higher average term of human life. The extremes of heat and cold are, however, probably greater than in many places, though the average temperature may not be so low. Two instances are recorded, one in 1755,[2] and the other in July, 1825, when the heat was so great

---

[1] Voyages, p. 170.   [2] Minott's Continuation, Vol. I. p. 107.

that fish died in the river. Probably others have occurred. At the latter period the thermometer rose to 105 degrees of Fahrenheit in the shade, and continued nearly as high for several days. Snow does not usually fall quite so deep here as in the adjoining towns, and frequently goes off earlier. The cold is, however, sometimes felt in great intensity; and the thermometer often sinks to 8, 10, and sometimes 12 degrees below zero. It stood at this last point on Tuesday, February 1, 1814, noted as *the cold Tuesday.*

GEOLOGY. — The geology of Concord, though it has not been very thoroughly explored, exhibits considerable variety and some peculiarity. The situation is low and the surface generally level, not giving to the streams of water sufficient current to afford many sites for manufacturing purposes. A few small hills only appear to beautify the scene and relieve the eye from a uniform prospect. Among these may be mentioned Ponkawtassett, or Barrett's, in the northeast; Annursnuck, in the northwest; Nawshawtuct, or Lee's, near the centre; Fairhaven, in the south; and Rocky Hills, near Walden Pond, partly in Lincoln. There is also a sandy hill, apparently of secondary formation, extending about a mile in length, easterly of the village. The uneven soil at the north and northeastern, and the south and southwestern parts of the town, appears to be of primary formation, and is composed chiefly of a thin, gravelly loam, mixed with various combinations of sand, clay, decayed vegetable matter, and rocks. Though not uniformly well calculated for agricultural purposes, it contains some highly productive farms. A large section, lying on the borders of the rivers, and extending from the southwest to the northeastern parts of the town, and through the centre, appears to be principally either secondary formation or alluvial deposits, and free from stones. The meadows and some parts of the upland contain a dark, rich, fruitful soil; and others a loose, sandy one, easily affected by drought, and hardly worth cultivation.[1]

Clay is rare. It is sometimes found in its usual beds, and sometimes in peculiar strata between others of sand. It has been wrought into bricks in several places. Marl is found, though not abundantly. Peat, fibrous and compact, is found in great abundance, composing extensive meadows, and affording an inexhaust-

---

[1] The chapter on the Statistical History gives the number of acres of each kind.

ible supply of fuel and manure, for which purposes it is used by the inhabitants. It is formed of the vegetables which have grown or been deposited where it exists. In some instances it seems to rest on the surface of water, and when cut in sections for roads or other purposes, the included parts, if heavily loaded, have been known to sink.

Geologists divide all rocks into three classes, — primary, secondary, and trap. The rocks in Concord are principally of the primary class, and varieties of granite, sienite, and mica-slate. Granite, suitable for building material, is not very common in Concord, but is found in abundance in Acton, Carlisle, and Lincoln.

The following minerals, some of which are rare, are found in Concord: Several species of lime-stone in the north part of the town; formerly manufactured into lime. Calcareous Spar, a sub-species of the carbonate of lime, composed of lime and carbonic acid, is common. Garnet in beautiful crystals. Cinnamon-stone, a very rare mineral, is found in the north part of the town. Several varieties of quartz generally distributed. Mica, in large laminæ and in several varieties. The lamellar hornblende, actynolite, and pargasite, sub-species and varieties of hornblende, frequent. Feldspar is found in great variety; the cream-colored is the most beautiful. Also, argillite, or clay-slate, novaculite, and scapolite. Sahlite, a variety of augite, or pyroxene of a greenish grey, occurs massive and crystallized.[1] Sulphate of iron, or copperas, occurs with a vein of sulphuret of iron, or pyrites in green stone. Sulphate of iron is also disseminated in clay-slate. (*Robinson.*) Lead ore has been found in various places. Iron ore is found in several places disseminated in rocks and other minerals. Bog iron ore is found in abundance. As early as 1660, it was smelted and wrought in bars for the customary purposes of life, by a company at the present site of the cotton-factory. The works were, however, abandoned after about 50 years, the pro-

---

[1] Prof. John W. Webster informs me, that he found all the minerals mentioned above, in this town. The late Samuel Davis, Esq. of Plymouth conjectured, that Annursnak, the Indian name of one of our hills, has the same meaning as Quunosnuck, signifying *a pestle*, from the circumstance that rocks, out of which the natives made their mortars and pestles, were to be found there. Porphyry, of which the Indians used to make their arrow-heads, is also found there.

prietors having found that a better quality of iron could be imported at less expense. Several tons of this ore have recently been carried in boats from this town to the furnace in Chelmsford, and it is said to produce good castings. I have no doubt that other minerals might be found, if the town were more thoroughly explored.

BOTANY. — Wood grows here with great rapidity; and it is supposed there is as much now as there was twenty years ago. Walden woods at the south, and other lots towards the southwest parts of the town, are the most extensive, covering several hundred acres of light-soil land. Much of the fuel, which is consumed, is, however, brought from the neighbouring towns. The most common trees are the oak, pine, maple, elm, white birch, chestnut, walnut, &c. &c. Hemlock and spruce are very rare. The ornamental trees transplanted, in this as in most other towns, do not appear to have been placed with much regularity; but as they are, they contribute much to the comfort and beauty of the town. The elm, buttonwood, horse-chestnut, and fruit trees have very properly taken the place of sickly poplars, in ornamenting the dwellings. The large elm in front of the court-house, — the pride of the common, — is almost unrivalled in beauty. It is about " three score and ten," but is still growing with youthful vigor and uniform rapidity.

Dr. Jarvis, who is familiar with the botany of Concord, informs me, that " most of the plants found in the middle parts of the state grow here, excepting the alpine flowers. The extensive low lands produce abundantly the natural families of the aroideæ, typhæ, cyperoideæ, gramineæ, junci, corymbiferæ, and umbelliferæ. These genera especially abound. There are also found, the juncus militaris (bayonet rush), on the borders of Fairhaven pond; cornus florida; lobelia cardinalis (cardinal flower), abundant on the borders of the river; polygala cruciata, in the east parts of the town; nyssa villosa (swamp hornbeam), at the foot of Fairhaven hill." The cicuta Americana (hemlock) grows abundant on the intervals. Every person should know and shun it for its poisonous qualities.

There are many excellent and well cultivated farms in the town, which produce winter rye, corn, potatoes, and the usual productions of the vicinity. Garden seeds have been extensively raised.

Teasels and the culture of silk have recently been introduced. Considerable attention has of late been paid to the cultivation of fruit trees, grape vines, and other horticultural productions, and, though a too long neglected branch of agriculture in this town, there is no doubt that nature has done enough for the soil to ensure great success.

PONDS. — *White Pond* lies in the southwest part of the town, and receives its name from the purity of its waters. It has no visible outlet, and contains 43 acres.[1] *Fairhaven Pond* forms a kind of bay in Concord river which passes through it, containing about 73 acres. *Walden Pond* lies in the south part of the town easterly of Fairhaven, and contains 65 acres. This pond also has no visible outlet. It is said no fish were caught in it, till they were transplanted there from other waters. Pickerel and other fish are now plenty there. *Goose Pond*, lying easterly of Walden Pond, is one of a number of small ponds, in a tract of land peculiarly broken into ridges and vales, which in some seasons are nearly dry. *Bateman's Pond* lies east of Mr. Daniel Wood's, and contains 30 acres.

RIVERS. — *Concord River*[2] is the largest stream of water. One branch of it rises in the south part of Hopkinton; and another from a pond and a large cedar-swamp in Westborough, and running into Hopkinton forms the boundary line between that town and Southborough. Thence in a northerly direction it passes through Framingham, and forms the boundary line between Sudbury and East Sudbury (where it is sometimes called Sudbury River), and enters Concord at the south part of the town. After passing through it in a diagonal direction, it receives the North River, and, going out at the northeast part between Bedford and Carlisle and through Billerica, empties into the Merrimack at Lowell. It is remarkable for the gentleness of its current, which is scarcely perceptible by the eye. At low water mark it is from 4 to 15 feet deep, and from 100 to 300 feet wide. Where it enters Concord it is 200 feet, and where it leaves it 330. At

---

[1] The estimates of the number of acres in these ponds, and the width of the rivers, is from a survey made by Judge Wood in 1794, and returned to the Secretary's office in Boston, agreeably to an order of the General Court.

[2] Sometimes called *Great River* and *South River*.

the former place it is 114 feet above low-water mark in Boston.[1] In times when the river is highest, it overflows its banks, and is in many places more than a mile wide. Great inconvenience has resulted to the town from this circumstance. Commissioners were appointed at various times, for the first hundred years after its settlement, to clear it out and drain the water off; and contributions were made by this and some other towns on the river to pay the expense. At other times grants were made by government. In 1722, Jonas Bond, Francis Fullam, and Francis Bowman were the commissioners, and Samuel Heywood, receiver, who paid £18 13*s.* for work done by the inhabitants of Concord. As early as 1710, measures were taken to erect mills in Billerica, and remonstrances were sent to the General Court from this town against them; but though they delayed, they did not finally prevent, the accomplishment of the project. Boats frequently pass from Boston, through the Middlesex canal and this river, to this town and to Sudbury; and with little expense, it is thought, there might be a profitable inland navigation.

The *North* or *Assabeth River*[2] has its source in Grafton, and receiving most of the waters of that town, Westborough, Shrewsbury, Northborough, and Bolton, passes through Marlborough, Stow, and a corner of Acton, and unites with the Concord about half a mile northwest of the meeting-house. It is not so large as the Concord, being at the confluence about 130 feet wide. It falls 30 feet from Sherman's mill-pond to its confluence with Concord river, and has some sites for mill privileges, the principal of which is occupied by a cotton factory. In its course through this town it receives several tributary streams, among which are Fort Pond Brook and Spencer Brook.

Fort Pond Brook, or *Law's Brook*, takes its rise in Fort Pond and the vicinity in Littleton, and, after running in a southeasterly direction through Acton, flows into the North River, near Mr. Loring's. This brook receives the tributary stream of *Nashobah Brook*, one branch of which rises in Nagog Pond, and another called Wright's Brook, in Westford, and, passing through Acton in a southeasterly direction, unites with Fort Pond Brook soon

---

[1] Canal Report, p. 113.
[2] This river is sometimes called Elzebeth, Elzebett, Elizabeth, and Asabet. See Worcester Hist. Mag. Vol. II.

after it enters Concord. Near this place a saw-mill was erected soon after the town was first settled.

Spencer Brook, or *Fifty Acre Brook*, has its source in Carlisle, and, running southerly, flows into the North River, having Barrett's saw-mill and grist-mill near its mouth.

Mill Brook, arising in Lincoln, flows through the centre of this town, and empties into the Concord river north of the village. The waters of this brook were used, about 190 years since, to turn the first grist-mill ever built in the town; but since 1826 they have been very properly suffered to flow through their accustomed channel undisturbed.

Saw-Mill Brook, or *Ralph's Brook*, rises in Carlisle, and running a southerly course empties into the Concord river near Bedford line.

Nut-Meadow Brook rises in Nut-Meadow, and enters the Concord river below James Miles's.

ZOOLOGY. — The *fish* formerly most abundant in Concord were salmon, shad, alewives, pike or pickerel, dace *(cyprinus leuciscus*, a small fish resembling the roach), and some others. Beside affording to the inhabitants an important article of food, for several years after the town was settled they were used as manure for agricultural purposes. They produced a luxuriant growth for one season, but tended to impoverish the land. Some diminution of their numbers took place when the dams were erected across the river in Billerica in 1712; and unsuccessful petitions were presented to the General Court to have these obstructions removed, on account of the fisheries. They were notwithstanding the source of considerable revenue to the town from sales which were made to people living in other towns. At certain seasons of the year, the fish-officers of Concord went to the dams in Billerica to see that the sluice-ways were properly opened to permit the fish to pass. The exclusive right to the fisheries was sold by the town in 1732, for five years, at £5 per year; and the purchaser had the privilege of erecting a *wier* across the river to aid him in taking the fish, a plan which was practised by the Indians before the town was settled by the English. This right continued to be sold in that manner, and for nearly the same amount, till about 1800. There were six principal fishing-places, viz., south of Mr. Dennis's, west of Deacon Hubbard's, nearly opposite Lee's hill in Mr. Merrick's pasture, against the Brown farm, and down the river near Ball's hill. Since the interruption by the Middlesex canal, and the factories at Lowell, those once welcome visiters in our waters, salmon, shad, and alewives, have taken up their summer residence in waters more easily accessible, and have totally deserted these peaceful shores. The principal fish, which now inhabit these waters, are pike, perch, lamprey and common eel, pout, and several other smaller fish.

The principal *quadrupeds* found here, at the first settlement of the town, were the bear, moose, wolf, deer, fox, otter, beaver, muskrat or musquash *(mus zibethicus)*, marten, &c. &c. Wolves were many years very troublesome in killing calves and sheep, and rewards were offered for destroying them. The fur-trade here was once very important. As early as 1641, a company was formed in the colony, of which Major Willard of Concord was superintendent, and had the exclusive right to trade with the Indians in furs and other articles; and for this right they were obliged to pay into the public treasury one twentieth of all the furs they obtained.[1] The right to the fur-trade, in particular districts, was afterwards sold by commissioners of the General Court. Captain Thomas Brooks bought the right in Concord, in 1657, for £5. The solitary ponds, rivers, and meadows in Concord, were peculiarly the favorite resorts of the beaver and other amphibious animals, and now contain remarkable evidence of their former existence. The larger animals have long since emigrated to other regions beyond the extension of civilization, and few only of the smaller ones remain unattacked by the sportsman.

The *Birds* have no peculiar locality in this town. Those most troublesome to the inhabitants have been the black bird, which frequent the low meadows in great numbers, the crow, and the jay. Rewards were paid for the heads of the two latter kinds. As late as 1792, the town voted to give for destroying "those pests to cornfields, called crows," the following rates; "for each old crow 1*s.*, for each young crow 6*d.*, and for each crow's egg, that is found in said town and taken out of the nest, 3*d.*"

---

[1] Colony Records.

CHAPTER XIII.

TOPOGRAPHICAL HISTORY.

Boundaries. — Roads. — Bridges. — Stages. — Post-Office. — Public Buildings. — Printing-Office. — Burying-Grounds.

The Court-House in Concord lies, north $58\frac{1}{4}°$ west, distant 15 miles 285 rods in a straight line from the City Hall in Boston, 16*m*. 40*r*. by the turnpike, 17*m*. 212*r*. through Lexington, and 20*m*. 188*r*. through Waltham. Bedford bears from Concord north 62° east, distant 3*m*. 276*r*. in a straight line, and 5*m*. 32*r*. by the road; Lexington, south 78° east, 5*m*. 296*r*., and by the road 6*m*. 163*r*.; Lincoln, 4*m*. 77*r*. by the road; East Sudbury, south $12\frac{1}{2}°$ west, 6*m*. 201*r*., and by the road 8*m*. 201*r*.; Harvard College, south $56\frac{3}{4}°$ east, 12*m*. 207*r*., and East-Cambridge court-house, 14*m*. 250*r*.[1] Concord lies about 13 miles from Lowell, 18 from Groton, and 30 from Worcester.

Concord is bounded on the southwest by Sudbury, by a line running from "bound rock," near Concord river, north 55° west, 1178*r*. to Acton corner, near Joseph Hayward's; thence westerly on Acton by a straight line, running north 35° east, 1656*r*. to Carlisle corner, near Paul Dudley's; thence northerly on Carlisle by a line having 28 angles. Southerly it is bounded on Lincoln, by a line beginning at bound rock before mentioned, and running with the river to the mouth of Well Meadow Brook, and thence by a line having fourteen angles to Bedford line; thence on Bedford by a line having thirteen angles to Concord river, and by Concord river to Carlisle bounds. These lines, giving to the town an exceedingly irregular shape, were surveyed in 1829, and stone bounds put up at all the angles.

The principal road to Boston, before the Charlestown bridge was built, went south through Lincoln, Waltham, and Watertown. That now most travelled is the great county road from Boston, through Lexington and Concord, to Groton and to New Hampshire. The Concord and Union Turnpike from Bolton to Boston, laid out in 1802, passes through this town, but, being hilly, is not

---

[1] Hale's Survey of Boston and its Vicinity. pp. 69 – 71.

much travelled. It was made a free road in 1829. From $1000 to $1,500 is annually expended in repairing the high ways.

The first *bridge* was built across the Concord river, from the point of land below Joseph Barrett's, Esq., to Lee's hill. In 1665 it was washed away, and another built the next year, where the present south bridge stands. Six or seven new bridges have since been built on the same spot. In 1660 there were three new bridges in the town, the north bridge (which the events of the 19th of April, 1775, have made memorable), the great south bridge, and one where Darby's bridge now stands. A few years previous to that time, the town had been allowed £20 by the county towards maintaining these bridges. An effort was then made to have the whole expense borne by the county, but the town could obtain but £30 annually for that purpose. When they were first supported entirely by the town, is uncertain. They have been often swept away by the floods; and large sums of money are annually raised to keep them in repair, which has very much increased the expenses of the town. The bridge by Captain Hunt's was first built about 1792, that by the Rev. Dr. Ripley's in 1793, those on the turnpike in 1802, and that beyond Deacon Hubbard's in 1802. There are now eight bridges entirely supported by the town.

Public Stages were first run out of Boston into the country through Concord, in 1791, by Messrs. John Vose & Co. There are now (1833), on an average, 40 stages which arrive and depart weekly, employing 60 horses between Boston and Groton, and carrying about 350 passengers; 150 have passed in one day.

The *Post-Office* was first established in this town, February 20, 1795. Six mails then arrived and departed weekly. Sixteen now arrive and depart. Since 1813, the net proceeds of the office to government have been about $3,000, varying from $30 to $70 per quarter. The following account of the post-masters was furnished me by the Post-Master General.

1. William Parkman, Esq., P. M., from February 20, 1795, to December 31, 1810, resigned.

2. Hon. John L. Tuttle, P. M., from January 1, 1811, to February 14, 1813, resigned.

3. Hon. John Keyes, P. M., from February 15, 1813, at present in office.

Public Buildings. — Meeting-houses. — To provide suitable accommodations for public religious worship, was one of the first acts of the town after its incorporation. And hence we find it recorded in a fragment of the proceedings of the town in 1635 — " Ordered that the meeting-house stande on the hill near the brook on the easte of Goodman Judgson's lott." Tradition informs us, that this was on the hill some distance easterly from the common. This house served as a place of worship about 30 years.

In 1667, a new meeting-house was ordered to be built, to stand between the present house and Deacon Jarvis's. It was nearly square and had a gallery. The lower floor had a few pews on the out side ; and the remainder was filled with seats. The roof was square and ornamented with four projections on the sides, resembling luthern windows or gable ends, having a window in each. In the centre was a "turret," or cupola, in which the bell was hung.[1] On the spire was a vane in which was cut " 1673," the date of the completion of the house.

Arrangements were made in 1710, after several meetings and considerable discussion, for building another house. It was 60 feet long, 50 wide, and 28 " stud " ; had no pews till some time after it was built, and then only by special vote of the town, as a favor to distinguished individuals ; two galleries ; no porches nor turret ; and was completed in 1712 at an expense of £608. This house was several times repaired. In 1749 pews were built around the lower floor, and some in the lower gallery.

January 31, 1791, the town voted to enlarge and repair the house in its present form. It is 72 feet long, 50 wide, and 28 high ; and has three porches, a spire 90 feet high, and square pews on the lower floor, and by the walls in the gallery. Builders, Abner Wheeler and Reuben Bryant; expense, £924. It was dedicated January 24, 1792, when the Rev. Dr. Ripley preached a sermon, which was printed.

The Trinitarian meeting-house, built in 1826, is 60 feet long, 58 wide, and 22 high, with a spire of 68 feet. The entrance is at one end, and it has narrow pews facing and descending towards the pulpit, and a gallery at one end. Building committee, Moses Davis, John Vose, and Ebenezer Hubbard ; builder, Thomas Benjamin ; expense (including a bell weighing 1125 lbs.), be-

---
[1] Dr. Lee's MSS.

tween $5,000 and $6,000. It was dedicated December 6, 1826, when the Rev. Mr. Green of Boston preached a sermon, afterwards printed.

A town bell was procured very early, but at what time does not appear. At first it was hung on a tree, and its tones are said to have been terrible to the neighbouring Indians. About 1696 it was broken, and sent to England to be recast. In 1700 it was " hanged on the meeting house in the turret," where it remained till the court-house was built, on which it was placed till 1791, when it was removed to the meeting-house. A new bell was procured, in 1784, from Hanover, weighing 500 lbs., but being broken, another was ordered from England in 1789, which continued till 1826, when the present one, weighing 1572 lbs., was obtained. The clock in the front gallery of the meeting-house was given to the town in 1793, by Mr. John Minott; and that in the belfry was procured by subscription, in 1827, for $450.

No subject seems to have excited greater interest, or required the exercise of greater talents, than " seating the meeting-house." Large committees were accordingly chosen almost every year prior to the erection of pews, and as late as 1784, to tell the people where to sit when attending public worship. Few were able to perform such duties and escape censure. Singers were first seated in 1774.

Court-Houses. — The first house for the accommodation of the courts and town-meetings, was built in 1719, principally of materials in the old meeting-house, and stood near the present site of the county-house occupied by the jailor. It was 34 feet long, 26 wide, and 14 high, with a cupola in the centre, on which was placed the vane of the meeting-house, dated " 1673." The expense, excepting £30 was paid by the town. The new court-house is a commodious wooden building, 70 feet long, 50 wide, and 28 high. In the centre of the roof an octagon cupola rises 60 feet from the ground. It was built in 1794, by Daniel Davis of Acton. The whole expense was $4,583, of which the town paid £100, and gave the land on which it stands, and has the right to use it for public meetings.

The first *Jail* was built in 1754 in the rear of Dr. Heywood's old house. Prior to that time, prisoners were confined in Cambridge snd Charlestown. In 1770 it was removed to the west end of the burying-ground, near Mr. Bigelow's tavern. The present jail was built of stone in 1788, and received its first tenants in the April following. It is 65 feet long, 32 wide, 3 stories high, and has 18 apartments, 7 of which are for criminals. It cost £3,084.

The *Academy*, built in 1822, is 40 feet long, 30 wide, and 2 stories high. The grammar schoolhouse is of the same size, the lower story being occupied as a school-room, and the upper one as a masonic hall. It was built in place of one burnt December 31, 1819, and dedicated, with two other new ones, for primary schools, September 7, 1820. In 1799, seven new school-houses, one in each district, including the centre, were built at an expense to the town of about $4,000.

A *Printing-Office* was opened in this town by Nathaniel Coverly in 1794, but it was continued but a short time. April 20, 1816, Messrs. Bettes and Peters issued the first newspaper, entitled the *Middlesex Gazette*, and it has since been continued, under various names and proprietors, till the present time.

Burying-Grounds were laid out at an early period, but the date is unknown. The monument on the Hill Burying-Ground, containing the inscription, "JOSEPH MERRIAM, AGED 47 YEARS, DIED THE 20 OF APRIL, 1677," is the oldest in town. The oldest in the West Burying-Ground is that of Thomas Hartshorn, who died November 17, 1697. No other one appears there till 1713. The first person buried in the New Burying-Ground was Mrs. Anna Robbins, who died July 13, 1823, and the fact is properly noted on her monument. Beside these, tradition reports that the ground first used for interring the dead was on the hill easterly of the present one; but no traces of it can be discovered, if indeed one was ever there. Some of the epitaphs, which have marks of originality, are annexed. Others appear elsewhere in this work.

"In Memory of
Capt. JOHN STONE,
the Architect of that Modern
and justly Celebrated Piece of
Architecture, Charles River Bridge.
He was a man of good Natural abilities,
which seemed to be adorned with Moral
Virtues and Christian Graces.
He departed this life in the year of
our Lord, 1791, in the 63 year of his age."

There is much beauty in the following concise epitaph :
"Vivens,
Dilectissima
ORPAH BRYANT.

born December 24, 1797.
died October 1, 1798.

She was the joy of her father,
And the delight of her mother.

Mortua, Lachrymabillima."

On the only upright *white* stone, then in the Hill Burying-Ground, the subjoined appears, relating to the donor of the singing-fund.

"This stone is designed
by its durability
to perpetuate the memory,
and by its colour
to signify the moral character,
of
Miss ABIGAIL DUDLEY,
who died Jan. 4, 1812,
aged 73."

Few grave-yards within my knowledge have so many monuments, on which character is drawn, as ours. These inscriptions have considerable similarity, but discover the peculiar taste of the age in which they were written. The character in the subjoined is drawn with peculiar force.

"In Memory of
Mrs. REBECCA HUNT, consort of
Lieut. Reuben Hunt, who died
June 28, 1790, aged 47.
Her virtues,
social, conjugal, parental, and Christian,
commanded respect and rejoiced acquaintance,
sweetened life, consoled in sickness,
made a friend of death, and confirmed
the hope of celestial glory.
This stone
perpetuates her memory
and invites
imitation.

' Frail man give ear;
The dearest joys of earth resign,
Secure those joys that are divine.' "

The following, generally attributed to the pen of Daniel Bliss, Esq., has often been published and admired.

> " God wills us free ; — man wills us slaves.
> I will as God wills ; God's will be done.
> Here lies the body of
> JOHN JACK,
> A native of Africa, who died
> March, 1773, aged about sixty years.
> Though born in a land of slavery,
> He was born free.
> Though he lived in a land of liberty,
> He lived a slave ;
> Till by his honest, though stolen labours,
> He acquired the source of slavery,
> Which gave him his freedom :
> Though not long before
> Death, the grand tyrant,
> Gave him his final emancipation,
> And put him on a footing with kings.
> Though a slave to vice,
> He practised those virtues,
> Without which kings are but slaves."

CHAPTER XIV.

STATISTICAL HISTORY.

Population. — Valuation. — Finances. — Employment. — Maintenance of the Poor. — Education. — Bill of Mortality.

POPULATION. — Concord possesses few of those advantages of water-power, peculiar to many manufacturing towns, which favor a rapid growth. It is dependent on the industry of its inhabitants, its improvements in agriculture and the mechanic arts, and the general advancement of the surrounding county, for its increase in wealth and population. The incorporation of other towns, principally within its original limits, has, at various times, reduced its population and resources, and renders it difficult to estimate its growth with accuracy. In 1706 the polls were 230, nearly half as many as they now are ; but they were scattered throughout six now incorporated towns. In 1753, just before the incorporation of Lincoln, the polls were 442, greater than at any other period in our history prior to 1820; and it is probable the population and wealth of the town was proportionably great. The population in 1764, including part of Carlisle, then belonging to Concord, was 1584, of whom 736 were white males, 821 white females, and 27 negroes. There were 6 *slaves* in 1725; 21 in 1741; and 19 in 1754. September 1, 1783, three years after the town was reduced to its present territorial limits, it contained 1321 inhabitants, of whom 15 were blacks. In 1790, there were 1590. The following table gives the number at three different periods since.

	1800		1810		1820	
	Male.	Fem.	Male.	Fem.	Male.	Fem.
Under 10 years	202 +	195	207 +	195	210 +	207
From 10 to 16	121	126	115	101	117	138
From 16 to 26	142	189	153	168	184	165
From 26 to 45	159	172	162	175	186	205
45 and upwards	158	177	150	179	150	192
	782 +	859	787 +	818	847 +	907
Blacks	. .	38		28		34
	Total	1679		1633		1788

In 1820 there were 9 foreigners not naturalized, 262 engaged in agriculture, 16 in commerce, and 140 in manufactures.

From the above statement and a subsequent one on the valuation, it will appear that the town, from 1800 to the close of the war in 1815, remained nearly stationary. Since that time it has had a slow but gradual increase. The proportion of births to t' ᴖᴖths is estimated at about 3 to 1, producing a large redundant pop · tion, which is scattered in every state in the union. The associations with " Old Concord " are dear to many in distant l ιds, who owe their ancestral origin to its inhabitants.

The following is the census taken by authority of the United States, June 1, 1830.

	Male.	Fem.	Tot.		Male.	Fem.	Tot.
Under 5 years	151	126	277	Of 40 and under 50	80	82	162
Of 5 and under 10	119	116	235	Of 50 and under 60	48	63	111
Of 10 and under 15	104	115	219	Of 60 and under 70	30	46	76
Of 15 and under 20	116	89	205	Of 70 and under 80	26	27	53
Of 20 and under 30	192	195	387	Of 80 and under 90	11	11	22
Of 30 and under 40	124	120	244	Of 90 and under 100	0	2	2

1001 + 992 = 1993

Free persons of color, of whom 15 are males and 13 females, 28

Total 2021

VALUATION. — From the returns of the assessors in the offices of the secretary of the Commonwealth and the town clerk, I have compiled the following tables, which will afford interesting information, illustrative of the wealth of the town at different periods. The only articles mentioned in the valuations of personal property, taken under the province charter, were horses, oxen, cows, sheep, swine, slaves, and faculty. The total valuation of personal and real estate, in 1706, as reduced to our present currency nearly according to the received tables[1] of depreciation, was $9,898, and for several subsequent periods, was as follows.

Year.	Polls.	Horses.	Oxen.	Cows.	Sheep.	Swine.	Tot. Value.
1719	310	272	454	704	814	422	$12·695
1725	375	326	562	975	1371	551	12·071
1740	359	278	474	866	——	550	7·623
1753	442	298	542	1024	1166	510	50·002
1760	335	268	301	813	627	418	44·306
1771	371	216	422	951	706	375	44·940

Since the revolution new state-valuations have been taken, once in ten years, and that after the taking of the census. In

---

[1] The emissions of paper money were at par when first issued, but constantly depreciated in value from 1700 to 1750. The value of "old tenor," and the currency mentioned in this and other histories of those times, may be known from the following table. It was compiled by Captain Stephen Hosmer, one of the most accurate men of that day, and found among his papers; and is deemed worthy of publication. The first column contains the date, the four next the price of silver, in shillings, in the spring, summer, fall, and winter of that year; and the four last the rate of discount on Bills of Credit in the same seasons. In this table it is said, "the price of silver from 1706 to 1714 was 8s. 6d. per ounce," lawful money; and the Bills of Credit at 50 per cent. discount.

Date.	Sp.	Su.	F.	W.	Sp.	Su.	F.	W.	Date.	Sp.	Su.	F.	W.	Sp.	Su.	F.	W.
1714	—	8 1-2s. per ounce.	—	—	50 per cent.				1737	—	26 1-2	—	—	—	—	400	—
1715	—	9 2-12	—	—	—	70	—	—	1738	—	27	—	—	—	—	400	—
1717	—	12	—	—	—	125	—	—	1710	24 1-2	28	—	—	—	—	440	450
1721	—	13	—	—	—	130	—	—	1711	28	—	—	—	—	—	450	—
1722	—	14	—	—	—	160	—	—	1742	28	27 1-2	28	27 1-2	—	450	—	460
1725	—	16	—	—	—	180	—	—	1743	—	—	29 1-3	30	470	475	—	—
1726	—	15 1-2	—	—	—	210	—	—	1744	30	32	—	33	—	—	500	—
1730	—	18	—	—	—	—	—	—	1745	36	—	—	—	—	—	600	650
1731	—	19	—	—	—	250	—	—	1746	36	38	40	42	700	725	775	800
1733	—	21	—	—	275	—	300	325	1747	52	—	60	58	850	900	850	950
1734	24	25	27	27	350	—	—	430	1748	55	56	57 1-2	—	900	925	900	950

On the 31st of March, 1750, the bills of the "old tenor" were redeemed in specie at the rate of 6s. for 45 ; and of the "new tenor" and "middle tenor," at 6s. for 11s. 3d.; and from that time ceased to pass. (Colony Laws, pp. 768, 771.) The fluctuation in the value of this currency was the source of great general embarrassment; and this was an important era in the history of the province.

these valuations various articles of personal property are required to be enumerated and described, not however uniformly alike. In the following table some of the principal only are mentioned.

Articles of Property.	In 1781.	In 1791.	In 1801.	In 1811.	In 1821.	In 1831.
Polls	326	340	390	390	425	489
Dwelling Houses	193	188	227	224	235	253
Barns	174	142	184	183	203	225
Other Buildings	—	—	64	79	265	125
Acres of Tillage Land	1188	1063	1112	1156	1137	1098
" English Mowing	753	721	840	992	1205	1279
" Meadow	2089	1827	2236	2131	2153	2111
" Pasturing	3099	4308	3800	2982	3852	4059
" Woodland	3878	4436	3635	3386	3262	2048
" Unimproved	—	—	1282	1732	1392	2833
" Unimprovable	—	—	384	—	395	612
" Used for Roads	—	—	—	348	286	—
" Water	—	—	—	515	695	—
Barrels of Cider	882	799	1376	1767	1079	—
Tons of English Hay	—	—	731	848	880	836
" Meadow Hay	—	—	1434	1453	1270	1370
Bushels of Rye	—	—	4738	2942	3183	2327
" Corn	—	—	10505	10052	11375	11424
" Oats	—	—	1388	1463	2372	4129
Horses	137	146	182	179	145	177
Oxen	324	288	374	326	337	418
Cows	916	775	934	831	743	725
Swine	137	308	290	269	294	408

The total valuation, in 1801, was $20,322, in 1811, $24,554, in 1821, $25,860, and in 1831, $36,681·29.

FINANCES. — In the early ages of the town, several lots of land were reserved for the " public good," and donations were made by individuals for the same purpose. Most of them, however, were disposed of without producing much permanent benefit, or accomplishing the wishes of the donor. Captain Timothy Wheeler,[1] in 1687, bequeathed to the Rev. Edward Bulkeley and the

---

[1] Captain TIMOTHY WHEELER died July 10, 1687, aged 86. He came to Concord in 1638, and, as tradition says, from Wales. Besides holding, at different times, most of the important trusts in various town affairs, he was captain of a military company, and represented the town *eighteen* years in the General Court, between 1653 and 1672. In all stations he appears to have conducted himself with great propriety. At his death he was possessed of a very respectable estate. His will, which is recorded in the Suffolk Probate Records, was dated the 1st of March next before his death.

Rev. Joseph Estabrook, who were then the ministers of the town, 20s. apiece; and to the town about three acres of land, with a house standing on the same, to be improved, all but half an acre (which was "laid out to the training-place" at the northwesterly end of the public common), "for the furtherance of learning and the support of a school in the said town." This lot was that on which the grammar school-house now stands, and then embraced nearly all which would be included in a line drawn from the north side of the house recently built by Ephraim Merriam, to the brook, and by the brook round to the Middlesex Hotel and the common. These premises were several years leased and the rents applied according to the wishes of the donor; but piece after piece was unfortunately sold, till the school-house lot was contracted to its present highly inconvenient dimensions. Captain Wheeler also bequeathed to the town 40 acres of woodland, "to be improved from time to time for the use and benefit of the ministers of the said town." This was the present ministerial lot; and the people were long accustomed to hold a *bee*, when a sufficient quantity of wood for the minister's annual consumption was drawn from this lot to his door.

The town directed, April 1, 1811, that the wood on this lot, and on one in Carlisle, should be cut off and sold; and that pews should be erected on some vacant floor in the meeting-house, and also sold; and that the proceeds should be vested in the hands of trustees, as a ministerial fund. Their first report was made November 7, 1814, and shows the following results.

Proceeds of sales of wood on the ministerial wood-lot $2,566·13
Proceeds of sales of wood on a lot in Carlisle . 364·27
Proceeds of sales of pews in the meeting-house . 1,365·55

Total on interest from January 1st, 1814 $4,295·95

The first trustees were John White, Francis Jarvis, and John L. Tuttle; and they and their successors were incorporated by an act passed February 27, 1813, as "The Trustees of the Congregational Ministerial Fund in Concord." This fund has since

---

His second wife was Mary, daughter of Captain Thomas Brooks. They had no male issue. One of his daughters, Elizabeth, married Ebenezer Prout, some time clerk of the House of Representatives; and another, Rebecca, married James Minott, Esq., and was the ancestor of many distinguished individuals.

been accumulating; and it received the additional legacy of Humphrey Barrett,[1] in 1829, of $500. No appropriations were made from it till 1830; and on the first of January, 1831, it amounted to $11,431·45.

In 1732, a committee was appointed, consisting of the Rev. Mr. Whiting, James Minott, Jr., John Fox, and Samuel Heywood, to make sale of the common and ministerial land in the town, and vest the proceeds in other real estate. A "ministerial pasture and plow land" was accordingly bought west of the almshouse, and some time used as a "perquisite" lot. During the Rev. Mr. Emerson's ministry, it was sold for £75, or $250, and the annual interest, $15, applied for the benefit of the minister. In consequence of losses sustained during the revolution, it became reduced to $100 nearly. In 1819, the town voted that the minister should receive $15, the original perquisite; and the balance $9, has been annually raised by a tax.

Mr. Hugh Cargill[2] bequeathed to the town the "Stratton Farm," so called, which was valued, in 1800, at $1,360, "to be improved as a poor-house, and the land to be improved by, and for the benefit of the poor, and to be under the special direction of the town of Concord, for the time being, for the purpose afore-

[1] HUMPHREY BARRETT was son of Lieutenant Humphrey Barrett, and died without issue, March 13, 1827, aged 75. Abel B. Heywood inherited, and lives on, his real estate.

[2] Mr. CARGILL's history is better described in the subjoined epitaph on his grave-stone, than by any other source of information I possess. He came to this country in connexion with the British army; but acquired his estate as a trader in Boston.

"Here lyes interred the remains of Mr. Hugh Cargill, late of Boston, who died in Concord January 12, 1799, in the 60th year of his age. Mr. Cargill was born in Bellyshannon in Ireland, came to this country in the year 1774, destitute of the comforts of life; but by his industry and good economy he acquired a good estate; and, having no children, he at his death devised his estate to his wife, Mrs. Rebecca Cargill, and to a number of his friends and relations by marriage, and especially a large and generous donation to the town of Concord for benevolent and charitable purposes.

"How strange, O God, who reigns on high,
  That I should come so far to die;
  And leave my friends, where I was bred,
  To lay my bones with strangers dead.
  But I have hopes when I arise
  To dwell with thee in yonder skies."

said for ever." This is now used for the pauper establishment. He also gave several other parcels of real estate, valued at $372, the income of which " to be solely applied for the support of the poor."

Another class of donations has been made to the town for the relief of the *silent* poor, — those individuals who are needy, but do not wish to throw themselves on the town for support. They are as follows; from

Peter Wright [1]	$277·42	Abel Barrett [3]	$500·00
John Cuming [2]	833·33	Jonathan Wheeler [4]	500·00

The annual income of these donations is distributed by the minister and selectmen according to the direction of the donors. The town voted, December 5, 1759, that collections should be taken in the meeting-house on Thanksgiving and Fast days, annually, for the same object. The custom has since been continued; and from $50 to $100 is distributed, obtained in this manner.

The town has, also, a fund of $833·33, given by John Cuming, Esq., for the benefit of the " private schools," in the language of his will, which has been distributed in all the districts but the centre one. Another donation, now amounting to $744·92, was given by John Beaton, Esq.,[5] for the support of schools and

---

[1] PETER WRIGHT was a weaver, son of Captain Edward Wright, and died January 15, 1718, aged 53. He bequeathed all his real estate, after the death of his wife and Cousin Elizabeth Hartwell, to the poor of Concord, to be under the direction of the selectmen, and of the minister, who is "to have a double vote to any of the selectmen." What belonged to the town was sold, in 1731, for £500 currency.

[2] JOHN CUMING. See notice in the Biographical History in the sequel.

[3] ABEL BARRETT was brother to Humphrey just mentioned. He commenced the mercantile business in Concord, but afterwards removed to Boston. He died in Liverpool, England, January 12, 1803.

[4] JONATHAN WHEELER was son of Ephraim Wheeler, and was successively a merchant in Concord, Boston, Baltimore, and England. He died, September 4, 1811, in the city of New York, ten days after his arrival from Europe.

[5] JOHN BEATON, Esq. was a native of Scotland, and emigrated to this town, where he acquired a respectable estate as a merchant. He was remarkable for his honesty, integrity, and Christian virtues, and had the unlimited confidence of his fellow citizens. " As honest as John Beaton," was long a current saying, expressive of the character of a strictly honest man. He was town treasurer 17 years from 1754, and appointed justice of the peace, by the crown, June 6, 1765. He died without issue, June 9, 1776, aged 47.

the poor. The income of these donations for the silent poor and for schools, annually distributed, is about $221. They are managed by the trustees of the ministerial fund and are loaned to individuals in the town.

These donations, being for specific objects, do not essentially affect the general expenses of the town. In consequence of having to maintain *eight* bridges, and the liberal appropriations for schools and other objects, the taxes in Concord are supposed to be higher, in proportion to its wealth, than in many towns, amounting to about $3 on every inhabitant. In 1803, the roads and bridges, independent of a highway tax of $1000, cost $1,244; in 1805, $967; in 1807, $1,290; and on an average, for the last 40 years, about one eighth of all the town expenses. The following table will exhibit the appropriations for several periods since.

Year.	State Tax.	County Tax.	Minister.	Incidental.	Total.
1785	£711 6s. 4d.	£25 3s. 3d.	£100 10s. 9d.	£748 8s. 1d.	£1585 8s. 5d.
1790	128 9 4	32 16 6	113 19 6	596 12 11	871 18 3
1795	$613·33	$233·16	$646·66	$2,327·15	$3,820.31
1800	611·33	161·56	567·26	2,763·52	4,103·67
1810	662·14	398·92	633·05	3,010·47	4,704·58
1820	568·94	331·13	794·17	4,243·92	5,938·16
1830	222·00	417·17	709·00	4,072·01	4,781·01

The amount of debts due from the town, in 1825, was $3,284·04, and in 1831, $5,228·65.

EMPLOYMENT. — Agriculture is the greatest source of wealth to the town. Manufactures are next in rank. Three farmers in the town own about 1000 sheep, the value of whose wool was estimated, in 1831, at $1500. There were raised 884,000 teasles. The oldest cotton-mill now in this state was commenced in this town in 1805, and the manufacture of cotton soon after began by Messrs. Hartwell and Brown, and has since been carried on by Ephraim H. Bellows through the various fluctuations of the business. The proprietors were incorporated in 1832. The mill contains 1100 spindles, 20 looms, employs 9 men, 3 boys, and 30 girls, works 50,000 lbs. of cotton, and makes 188,000 yards of cloth annually, valued at $17,900. David Loring commenced the manufacture of lead pipes in 1819, and of sheet lead in 1831. He employs 6 men, and upwards of 300,000 lbs. of lead are annually wrought, valued, when ready for sale, at about 20,000. In the extensive establishments for the manufacture of chaises, harness, and carriages, owned by Colonel William Whiting and the Messrs. Robbins, the value of the articles manufactured last year was estimated at $14,000. The smithery, where the iron work is made, used upwards of 100,000 lbs. of iron, and 4,000 of steel, in 1831. Henry H. Merrill, the proprietor, erected, in 1832, a steam-engine, and has otherwise enlarged his works. Elijah Wood commenced the manufacture of boots and shoes in 1812, and makes, annually, about $6,000 worth. Nehemiah Ball began the same business in 1832. From 3000 to 6000 gross of black lead pencils and points are annually made in town. William Monroe commenced the manufacture of these in 1812; and his method of making them he regards as his own invention, having, he informs me, had no instruction from any one in relation to the subject. "The lead for the first pencil was ground with the head of a hammer, was mixed in a common spoon, and the pencil sold to Benjamin Andrews in Boston." In 1814 he made 1212 gross, which he sold for $5,946. He has since made about 35,000 gross; in some years 4,000 gross of pencils, and 1,000 of points. John Thoreau and others in the town have also carried on the business extensively, but the profits are now very much reduced. Mr. Thoreau also makes red lead pencils and glass paper. There were also made, in 1831, 50 brass time-pieces, 1,300 hats, 562 dozen bellows, 100 guns, 300,000 bricks, 500 barrels, 20,000 lbs. bar soap, 5,000 nail-kegs, and cabinet ware, the value of which was estimated at $14,860. This is what is generally termed wholesale business, and includes very little *custom work*; the articles manufactured being principally sold abroad. There are 6 warehouses and stores; 1 bookstore and bindery; two saw-mills; and two grist-mills, at which it was estimated that 12,000 bushels of grain were ground the last year. The manufacturing and mechanical business of the town is increasing, and promises to be a great source of wealth.

MAINTENANCE OF THE POOR. — This has long been an important item in the expenses of the town. From the earliest town records it appears that they were supported by subscription, or by several individuals voluntarily agreeing to keep them, in rotation. The first poor-rate, £10, was raised in 1721. About 1753, a small alms-house was built, principally by subscription where Dr. Bartlett now lives, and where part of the poor were kept for nearly 50 years. Five years prior to 1800 they were let out collectively by contract. They cost £185 in 1791, $936·50 in 1796, and $900 in 1801. In 1800, the selectmen were directed to put them out to the lowest bidder, " either altogether, in lots, or singly." This auction usually took place immediately after the town meeting in May. This practice continued till 1821, when a contract was made to keep the poor together for $1,450; in 1824, for $1,200; and in 1827 for $1,150. Since then they have been supported in the pauper establishment belonging to the town.

The rent of the Cargill farm, after it came into possession of the town, was vested as a fund for the erection of an alms-house. In 1816 this fund amounted to $2,359, and the town raised the additional sum of $650, and commenced the erection of the proposed building. Just before it was completed, October 28, 1817, it was burnt. In 1827, the buildings on the farm were enlarged and repaired in their present form.

For all genuine objects of charity, the people of Concord have ever been ready to bestow their aid with generosity. In 1819 the town gave $200, and individuals $110 more, to the Lunatic Asylum, in connexion with the Massachusetts General Hospital.[1] This is one of many similar acts of benevolence, which might be mentioned.

EDUCATION. — Many of the original inhabitants of Concord were well educated in their native country; and, "to the end that learning be not buried in the graves of the forefathers," schools were provided at an early period for the instruction of their children. In 1647, towns of 50 families were required to have

---

[1] After acknowledging, in very complimentary terms, the receipt of this donation, James Prince, Esq., the treasurer, remarks, in a letter dated June 29, 1819; — "This act of liberality and compassion, the *first* which has been displayed towards the Asylum from our citizens *in their corporate relation*, affords additional pleasure from the circumstance, that it emanated from a town, whose citizens were enrolled in the front ranks of patriotism and valor, at a most interesting period of our national history; and the trustees cannot but hope, that the influence of their bright example will now, as it did then, stimulate to wise imitation other towns within the state, and thus essentially subserve those principles of philanthropy and charity which led to the establishment, and which must be continued to secure the continuance, of this interesting institution."

a common school, and of 100 families, a grammar school. Concord had the latter before 1680. An order was sent to this town, requiring "a list of the names of those young persons within the bounds of the town, and adjacent farms, who live from under family government, who do not serve their parents or masters, as children, apprentices, hired servants, or journeymen ought to do, and usually did in our native country"; agreeably to a law, that "all children and youth, under family government, be taught to read perfectly the English tongue, have knowledge in the capital laws, and be taught some orthodox catechism, and that they be brought up to some honest employment." On the back of this order is this return: "I have made dillygent inquiry according to this warrant, and find no defects to return. Simon Davis, Constable. March 31, 1680." During the 30 years subsequent to this period, which I have denominated the *dark age* in Massachusetts, few towns escaped a fine for neglecting the wholesome laws for the promotion of education. Though it does not appear that Concord was fined, a committee was appointed in 1692, to petition the General Court " to ease us in the law relating to the grammar school-master," or to procure one " with prudence for the benefit of learning, and saving the town from fine." From that time, however, this school was constantly maintained. For several years subsequent to 1700, no appropriations were made to any other school. In 1701, grammar scholars paid 4d. and reading scholars 2d. per week towards its support; and from that time to 1712, from £20 to £30 were annually raised. In 1715, it was kept one quarter, in different parts of the town, for £40. The next year £50 were raised for schools; £35 for the centre, and £5 for each of the other three divisions. In 1722, Timothy Minott agreed to keep the school, for 10 years, at £45 per year. In 1732, £50 were raised for the centre, and £30 for the "outschools"; and each schoolmaster was obliged to teach the scholars to read, write, and cipher, — all to be free. In 1740, £40 for the centre, and £80 for the others. These grants were in the currency of the times. In 1754, £40 lawful money were granted, £25 of which were for the centre. Teachers in the out-schools usually received 1s. per day for their services. The grammar-school was substituted for all others in 1767, and kept 12 weeks in the centre, and 6 weeks each, in 6 other parts, or

" school societies " of the town. There were then 6 school-houses, 2 of which were in the present limits of Carlisle, and the others near where Nos. 1, 2, 4, and 6, now stand. This system of a *moving school,* as it was termed, was not, however, continued many years. In 1774 the school-money was first divided in proportion to the polls and estates.

The districts were regulated, in 1781, nearly as they now are. The town raised £120, in 1784, for the support of schools, and voted, that " one sixteenth part of the money the several societies in the out-parts of the town pay towards this sum, should be taken and added to the pay of the middle society for the support of the grammar-school; and the out-parts to have the remainder to be spent in schools only." This method of dividing the school-money was continued till 1817, when the town voted, that it should be distributed to each district, including the centre, according to its proportion of the town taxes.

The appropriations for schools from 1781 to 1783, was £100 from 1784 to 1792, £125; 1793, £145; 1794 and 1795, £200 1796 to 1801, £250; 1802 to 1806, $1,000; 1807 to 1810 $1,300; 1811, $1,600; 1812 to 1816, $1,300; 1817 and since $1,400. There are 7 districts, among which the money, including the Cuming's donation, has been divided, at different periods, as follows. The last column contains the new division as permanently fixed in 1831. The town then determined the amount that should be annually paid to each district, in the following proportions. The whole school-money being divided into 100 parts, district, No. 1, is to have $52\frac{1}{2}$ of those parts, or $761·25 out of $1,550; district, No. 2, $7\frac{5}{8}$ parts; district, No. 3, $8\frac{1}{4}$ parts; district, No. 4, $8\frac{5}{8}$ parts; district, No. 5, $8\frac{1}{4}$ parts; district, No. 6, $7\frac{1}{8}$ parts; district, No. 7, $7\frac{1}{8}$ parts; and to individuals who pay their money in Lincoln and Acton, $\frac{1}{2}$ a part.

District. Old Names.	1801.	1811.	1821.	1830.	1832.
No. 1. Central	$382·92	$791·48	$646·15	$789·18	$761·25
" 2. East	95·28	155·45	160·26	109·69	110·56¼
" 3. Corner	68·49	135·48	142·48	117·00	119·62½
" 4. Darby	70·53	130·69	123·10	138·23	125·06¼
" 5. Barrett	107·29	163·51	145·89	125·11	119·62¼
" 6. Groton Road	64·63	105·41	93·55	79·16	103·31¼
" 7. Buttrick	67·64	126·68	114·16	84·77	103·31¼
Individuals	27·22	41·30	24·41	6·86	7·25
	$884·00	1,650·00	1,450·00	1,450·00	1,450·00

At the erection of new school-houses in 1799, the first school committee was chosen, consisting of the Rev. Ezra Ripley, Abiel Heywood, Esq., Deacon John White, Dr. Joseph Hunt, and Deacon George Minott. On their recommendation, the town adopted a uniform system of school regulations, which are distinguished for enlightened views of education, and which, by being generally followed since, under some modification, have rendered our schools among our greatest blessings.

The amount paid for private schools, including the Academy, was estimated, in 1830, at $600, making the annual expenditure for education $2,050. Few towns provide more ample means for acquiring a cheap and competent education. I have subjoined the names of the teachers of the grammar-school since the revolution, — the year usually beginning in September.

Nathaniel Bridge	1785,	9 mo.	Isaac Warren	1812,	1	yr.
JOSEPH HUNT [1]	1786,	2½ yr.	JOHN BROWN	1813,	1	"
William A. Barron	1788,	3 "	Oliver Patten	1814,	1	"
Amos Bancroft	1791,	1 "	Stevens Everett	1815,	9	mo.
Heber Chase	1792,	1 "	Silas Holman	1815,	3	"
WILLIAM JONES	1793,	1 "	George F. Farley	1816,	1	yr.
Samuel Thatcher	1794,	1 "	James Howe	1817,	1	"
JAMES TEMPLE	1795,	2 "	Samuel Barrett	1818,	1	"
Thomas O. Selfridge	1797,	1 "	BENJAMIN BARRETT	1819,	1	"
THOMAS WHITING	1798,	4 "	Abner Forbes	1820,	2	"
Levi Frisbie	1802,	1 "	Othniel Dinsmore	1822,	3	"
Silas Warren	1803,	4 "	James Furbish	1825,	1	"
Wyman Richardson	1807,	1 "	EDWARD JARVIS	1826,	1	"
Ralph Sanger	1808,	1 "	Horatio Wood	1827,	1	"
Benjamin Willard	1809,	1 "	David J. Merrill	1828,	1	"
Elijah F. Paige	1810,	1 "	John Graham	1829,	1	"
Simeon Putnam	1811,	1 "	John Brown	1831.		

The *Concord Academy* was established, in 1822, by several gentlemen, who were desirous of providing means for educating their own children and others more thoroughly than they could be at the grammar-school (attended, as it usually is, by a large number of scholars) or by sending them abroad. A neat, commodious building was erected, in a pleasant part of the town, by the proprietors, consisting of the Hon. Samuel Hoar, the Hon. Abiel Heywood, and Mr. Josiah Davis, who own a quarter each, and the Hon. Nathan Brooks and Colonel William Whiting, who own an eighth each. Their intention has always been to make the school equal to any other similar one. It was opened in September, 1823, under the instruction of Mr. George Folsom, who

---

[1] Those in SMALL CAPITALS were natives of Concord.

kept it two years. He was succeeded by Mr. Josiah Barnes and Mr. Richard Hildreth, each one year.

Mr. Phineas Allen, son of Mr. Phineas Allen of Medfield, who was born October 15, 1801, and graduated at Harvard College in 1825, has been the preceptor since September, 1827.

BILL OF MORTALITY. — Few subjects are more interesting than accurate bills of mortality. They are the most authentic evidence of the influence of climate and local circumstances on health and human life ; and teach a lesson, admonishing us of the destiny that awaits all mankind, and warning us " to live prepared to die." These considerations will be a sufficient reason for the minuteness of the following details.

The following table is compiled from a private record of the second town-clerk, and will afford some interesting statistical information, relative to the condition of the town at an early period.

Date.	Marriages.	Births.	Deaths.	Date.	Marriages.	Births.	Deaths.
1656	3	11	—	1667	8	15	6
1657	3	11	3	1668	4	21	5
1658	3	6	3	1669	4	24	5
1659	2	10	4	1670	2	21	2
1660	6	11	3	1671	6	22	7
1661	2	12	6	1672	5	20	3
1662	4	14	4	1673	6	29	6
1663	5	14	4	1674	3	20	5
1664	4	11	2	1675	5	21	11
1665	7	13	6	1676	4	13	13
1666	2	22	6	1677	11	22	6

This table gives 99 marriages, 110 deaths, and 363 births. Several died in 1675, and 6 in consequence of the Indian wars.

The town has seldom been specially visited with disease. Thomas Brown, then a town-clerk, however, recorded, January 20, 1718, that " the hand of God has of late come forth against the inhabitants of Concord in a very awful manner, in sending a very malignant and mortal distemper amongst us, whereby there hath been a considerable number of persons of men, women, and children, of all qualities, ages, and sects, attacked, and hath been removed from amongst us by death, most of whom has been very sudden and unexpected, so that from the last of November last past unto the day of the date above written, hath been removed not less than 27 persons." A catalogue of their names is annexed to this record. What this disease was, I cannot learn.

The small-pox prevailed in the town in 1703; but it does not appear that any died of the disease. In 1792 it was introduced by inoculation. A hospital was fitted up where Mr. Augustus Tuttle now lives; and 130 persons went there, at several times, to be inoculated under the care of the three physicians of the town. From some cause the disease spread. It appeared at Amos Wright's (Deacon Jarvis's), at Cyrus Hosmer's, at Deacon Chandler's, and at Ephraim Potter's. At the last place a new hospital was fitted up where the sick were taken, and near which a small burying-ground and grave-stone now mark the melancholy ravages of this disease. Ten persons were its victims, — 2 by inoculation and 8 by contagion, — and were buried by themselves; it being considered improper to inter them in the usual ground. Happily for mankind, the terrors which the appearance of this disease once inspired, are much mitigated by kine-pock inoculation.

The following table, exhibiting the number of deaths between several specified ages, the number each year, the aggregate amount of their ages, average age, &c. &c. during the 50 years commencing January 1, 1779, and ending December 31, 1828, was compiled from records carefully kept by the Rev. Dr. Ripley. Great labor has been expended to make it correct and intelligible.

Year.	Under 1	to 5	to 10	to 20	to 30	to 40	to 50	to 60	to 70	to 80	to 90	to 100	Total.	Aggre. Am. Age.	Average Age.
1779	2	0	0	1	2	0	0	0	2	4	1	0	12	578	48
1780	1	2	1	1	0	0	1	1	3	0	0	0	10	307	30
1781	3	1	0	1	0	2	0	1	1	2	1	3	15	721	48
1782	1	2	1	0	1	2	0	1	1	5	3	1	18	933	52
1783	5	2	1	0	4	2	3	1	2	3	1	0	24	811	34
1784	4	1	1	2	2	0	0	1	1	2	1	2	17	607	35
1785	2	0	1	0	3	2	2	3	2	2	0	0	17	672	39
1786	4	1	0	4	3	1	1	0	1	2	1	1	19	590	31
1787	2	2	0	0	1	2	1	1	2	0	1	0	12	416	35
1788	2	0	2	0	2	2	2	1	2	3	3	0	19	877	46
1789	3	1	0	1	2	3	0	1	1	4	1	0	17	694	41
1790	2	5	2	2	2	0	3	0	3	4	3	0	26	970	37
1791	3	1	0	0	0	1	2	1	3	3	3	0	17	841	49
1792	5	0	0	1	4	3	1	6	2	2	1	1	26	1021	39
1793	1	0	3	0	1	2	2	4	1	3	0	2	19	894	47
1794	1	1	1	0	4	3	0	1	5	1	3	1	21	1018	49
1795	0	2	0	4	3	4	1	1	2	2	2	0	21	824	39
1796	1	8	2	0	2	2	2	2	1	6	1	0	27	926	34

STATISTICAL HISTORY.

Year.	Under 1	to 5	to 10	to 20	to 30	to 40	to 50	to 60	to 70	to 80	to 90	to 100	Total.	Aggre. Am. Age.	Average Age.
1797	3	1	1	1	2	1	4	1	1	3	3	0	21	893	43
1798	4	3	0	2	2	0	1	0	1	5	2	1	21	831	39
1799	0	1	0	1	4	0	2	3	4	4	1	0	20	1006	50
1800	3	7	0	0	0	4	1	2	1	4	2	1	25	926	37
1801	3	3	2	6	3	0	2	2	3	4	4	0	32	1197	37
1802	2	4	1	3	2	2	1	3	1	6	2	0	27	1067	39
1803	2	7	2	3	4	9	3	0	3	2	2	1	38	1194	31
1804	4	4	0	3	3	1	3	3	1	4	2	1	29	1037	39
1805	12	1	0	3	6	2	0	2	2	2	5	0	35	1132	32
1806	5	4	0	1	6	2	1	3	4	1	4	1	32	1201	39
1807	7	1	0	2	6	2	3	1	3	4	2	1	32	1182	37
1808	1	5	1	0	0	1	3	2	4	0	2	0	19	722	38
1809	2	3	0	0	2	1	3	1	2	2	2	1	19	821	43
1810	5	1	1	3	3	4	4	3	6	4	3	1	38	1626	45
1811	1	2	2	0	4	1	1	2	4	2	2	0	21	881	42
1812	3	6	2	1	1	5	2	2	3	3	3	1	32	1131	36
1813	3	2	1	2	4	2	3	3	1	4	2	0	27	1094	40
1814	2	0	0	0	4	4	4	1	3	0	2	2	22	1012	46
1815	4	2	4	5	4	5	3	4	5	4	6	1	47	1910	41
1816	6	1	0	1	2	0	1	3	2	4	1	0	21	802	38
1817	2	4	2	2	4	0	5	1	1	0	0	0	21	495	28
1818	2	1	0	2	1	4	1	3	3	2	1	0	20	825	41
1819	2	2	1	4	0	3	3	4	2	4	1	1	27	1006	37
1820	2	3	0	0	2	3	2	5	0	5	6	0	28	1374	49
1821	3	5	0	2	0	1	3	3	2	10	4	0	33	1582	48
1822	2	10	1	3	5	2	2	3	2	4	2	2	38	1285	34
1823	5	3	1	1	2	1	3	3	2	1	3	1	26	970	37
1824	4	3	0	1	1	2	4	4	3	5	2	0	29	1244	43
1825	3	7	1	1	2	2	5	6	4	6	3	0	40	1645	41
1826	8	6	4	0	3	2	8	4	1	5	2	0	43	1387	32
1827	2	2	0	0	1	3	1	2	1	4	3	0	19	893	44
1828	4	4	0	0	0	1	3	1	2	5	1	2	23	1020	48

It is impossible to specify the diseases by which the several persons died. As far as they can be ascertained from the Rev. Dr. Ripley's records, it appears that about one seventh of the whole number died of consumption, one fifth of fevers of various kinds, one twelfth of old age, one sixteenth of canker-rash, one nineteenth of the dropsy, one twenty-fifth of paralytic affections, and nearly the same number each of dysentery and casualties.

By adding the columns in the above table, we shall find that the whole number, who died during the 50 years, was 1242; of whom 153 died under 1 year of age; 137 of 1 and under 5; 42 of 5 and under 10; 70 of 10 and under 20; 119 of 20 and under 30; 101 of 30 and under 40; 106 of 40 and under 50; 106 of 50 and under 60; 112 of 60 and under 70; 161 of 70 and under 80; 106 of 80 and under 90; 28 of 90 and under 100; and a native black of 105. Of these 107 died in January, 111 in February, 118 in March, 103 in April, 88 in May, 81 in June, 88 in July, 95 in August, 115 in September, 121 in October, 121 in November, and 94 in December. These proportions generally hold good in particular years, more deaths occurring in the spring and autumn than at other seasons of the year. Of those who lived 80 years and over, 54 were males and 81 females; 90 and over, 8 were males and 21 females; 95 and over, 3 were males and 4 females. The year when the least number of deaths occurred was 1780, and when the greatest, 1815. The yearly average is 25 nearly. The least average age was in 1817, the greatest average in 1812. The aggregate amount of all the ages for 50 years, is 49,192, and the mean average age nearly 40. Estimating our population, during this period, at an average of 1665, which is nearly correct, as will appear on reference to our account of the population, we shall find that 1 in 66 dies annually.

153 or 1 in 8 1-8 died under 1 year.	620 or 1 in 2	lived 40 and upwards.
218 or 1 in 5 2-3 " under 2 years.	570 or 1 in 2 1-3 "	45 and upwards.
255 or 1 in 4 8-9 " under 3 years.	514 or 1 in 2 2-5 "	50 and upwards.
270 or 1 in 4 3-5 " under 4 years.	463 or 1 in 2 3-5 "	55 and upwards.
290 or 1 in 4 1-3 " under 5 years.	408 or 1 in 3 1-11 "	60 and upwards.
304 or 1 in 4 1-11 " under 6 years.	354 or 1 in 3 1-2 "	65 and upwards.
332 or 1 in 3 3-4 " under 10 years.	296 or 1 in 4 1-5 "	70 and upwards.
358 or 1 in 3 1-2 " under 15 years.	209 or 1 in 5 1-17 "	75 and upwards.
402 or 1 in 3 1-11 " under 20 years.	135 or 1 in 9 1-5 "	80 and upwards.
472 or 1 in 2 3-5 " under 25 years.	69 or 1 in 18 "	85 and upwards.
521 or 1 in 2 2-5 " under 30 years.	29 or 1 in 42 5-6 "	90 and upwards.
571 or 1 in 2 1-3 " under 35 years.	7 or 1 in 177 3-7 "	95 and upwards.
622 or 1 in 2 " under 40 years.	2 lived to 99, and 1 to 105.	

In these calculations minute fractions are omitted. They exhibit results highly favorable to the health of the town. Few towns are so healthy.[1]

---

[1] In France, 1 in 31 arrives to the age of 70; in London 1 in 10; in Philadelphia, 1 in 15; and in Connecticut 1 in 8. In Salem, 1 in 48 dies annually; in Philadelphia, 1 in 45; in Boston, 1 in 41; in London, 1 in 40; in Paris, 1 in 32; and in Vienna, 1 in 22. — See *History of Dedham* and *American Quarterly Review*, Vol. VIII. p. 396.

CHAPTER XV.

SOCIAL AND OFFICIAL HISTORY.

Military Companies. — Various Associations. — Concord Bank. — Agricultural Society. — Insurance Company. — Official History. — Town-Officers. — Representatives. — Senators. — County Officers. — Attorneys and Counsellors at Law. — Physicians.

GREAT respect appears to have been paid to military titles in the early history of the town. *Captain* was a greater mark of distinction than deacon, doctor, and many other offices. A vote of the town in 1700 is thus recorded: " Propounded whether Lieutenant Prescott, Sergeant French, Corporal Fox, Corporal Wood, and Samuel Jones be a committee to examine " &c. Such a record of titles is not uncommon. Officers also held their commissions much longer than in these days of degenerate military honors. Colonel James Minott and some others did duty under a commission more than *thirty* years. All between the ages of 16 and 60 were required by law to do military duty, and were afterwards requested to enroll themselves in *alarm lists.* Instances are not uncommon, where men of 80 and even 90 years of age have borne arms. There are now three military companies in the town, the Infantry, Artillery, and Standing Company; in all of which, in 1827, there were 238 enrolled.

The *Concord Light Infantry* is believed to be the oldest company in the Commonwealth, excepting the Ancient and Honorable Artillery. It was incorporated October 13, 1669, as " the Second Troop of Horse in Middlesex." Twenty-two of the original petitioners belonged to Concord, and 14 others to Billerica, Chelmsford, Groton, Lancaster, and Sudbury. April 30, 1777, the charter was altered, and it was incorporated as the Concord Light Infantry, and consisted of 39 members with liberty to increase the number to 45. In 1822 liberty was granted to enlist 64. The Captains, since 1777, have successively been, Joseph Hosmer, Samuel Jones, Roger Brown, James Colburn, Issac Hoar, John Buttrick, Jonas Buttrick, Nathan Wood, John Hayward, Jonathan Buttrick, William Brown, Nehemiah Flint, John Brown, Artemas Wheeler, Cyrus Hubbard, Edward Flint, Nehemiah Hunt, Francis Jarvis, Jr., Nathan Barrett, and Asa Brooks. Of these, James Colburn was promoted to the office of General in the Brigade, Roger Brown, John Buttrick, and Jonas Buttrick to Colonel, and John Hayward to Major.

The *Concord Artillery* was incorporated, on the petition of Charles Hammond and others, February 28, 1804; and held its first public parade on the 4th of July following. The charter says, " Whereas Major John Buttrick and Captain Isaac Davis, with a party of the armed yeomanry, did, on the birth-day of our revolution, attack and defeat a superior number of the invaders of our country, who were most advantageously posted at the north bridge of Concord," it is ordered that the prayer of the petition be granted, and that two brass field-pieces, with proper apparatus, be provided for said company, with suitable engravings, " to commemorate and render honor to the action which led to the victory of the day, and to perpetuate the names of the gallant Buttrick and Davis, and also to animate in future the ardour and bravery of the defenders of our country." The inscription is as follows : " The Legislature of Massachusetts consecrate the names of Major John Buttrick and Captain Isaac Davis, whose valour and example excited their fellow-citizens to a successful resistance of a superior number of British troops at Concord Bridge, the 19th of April, 1775, which was the beginning of a contest in arms that ended in American Independence." The Captains have successively been, Thomas Heald, Jesse Churchill, Henry Saunderson, Reuben Brown, Jr., Francis Wheeler, Cyrus Wheeler, Elisha Wheeler, Eli Brown, William Whiting, John Stacy, Joshua Buttrick, and Abel B. Heywood. Cyrus Wheeler and William Whiting were promoted to the office of Colonel.

The *Social Circle*, probably originating in the Committee of Safety, was formed about 1778, for free discussion and familiar conversation on such subjects as are connected with the interest and improvements of the town. Twenty-five members only can belong to the society at once ; and the meetings are held every Tuesday evening, from October to March, at the members' houses in rotation ; and these meetings, as the constitution expresses, tend " to strengthen the social affections, and disseminate useful communications among its members." Many improvements in the town originated in this useful society.

The *Corinthian Lodge* of Free Masons was organized July 5, 1797, and publicly installed June 25, 1798. The Discourse, delivered on the occasion by the Rev. Dr. Morse, was printed.

The *Concord Chapter* of Royal Arch Masons was formed in the spring of 1826, and its officers were publicly installed on the 6th of September following.

A *Library Company* was formed February 23, 1786. Whether there had previously been a library in town, and if any, how long it continued, and its number of volumes, is not known. A "Charitable Library Society" was formed May 25, 1795, depending chiefly on the voluntary donations of its members for support. Jonathan Fay, Esq., Jonas Minott, Esq., and the Rev. Ezra Ripley were successively presidents of this society. Its members united with others and composed the "Proprietors of the Concord Social Library," and were incorporated in 1821. The presiding officers since have been the Rev. Ezra Ripley, the Hon. Samuel Hoar, the Hon. John Keyes, and the Hon. Abiel Heywood. The library, divided into 50 shares, contains about 900 volumes, and constantly increases by the addition of new publications.

The Middlesex Bar commenced the formation of a law library in 1815, which now contains a very valuable collection of professional works. It is kept by the County Treasurer.

The *Concord Lyceum* was formed December 31, 1828, and the Debating Society, which had existed from 1822, was united with it. The officers of this useful association, for several years, have been the Rev. Ezra Ripley, D. D., President, the Rev. Daniel S. Southmayd and the Rev. Hersey B. Goodwin, Vice-Presidents, Lemuel Shattuck, Recording Secretary, Mr. Phineas Allen, Corresponding Secretary, Mr. Phineas How, Treasurer, and Dr. Josiah Bartlett, Mr. Nehemiah Ball, and Colonel William Whiting, Curators.

Juvenile Libraries were established, in 1827, in each of the religious societies, in connexion with the Sabbath schools.

Provision against Fire. — The Fire Society was organized May 5, 1794, and holds its annual meetings on the 2d Monday in January. The Presidents have been, Jonathan Fay, Esq., Dr. Joseph Hunt, Tilly Merrick, Esq., Dr. Isaac Hurd, Deacon Francis Jarvis, the Hon. Samuel Hoar, and Joseph Barrett, Esq. The Engine Company was formed, and the first engine procured, in 1794. A new engine was obtained in 1818.

A Volunteer Engine Company was organized in 1827, who procured by subscription a new engine in 1831.[1]

The *Concord Harmonic Society* was formed about 1800, for the purpose of improvement in sacred music. For several years past it has not been under regular organization. May 17, 1832, the *Concord Mozart Society* was formed, and takes place of the other. Ephraim Willey was chosen President, Elijah Wood and Francis Hunt, Vice-Presidents, and Phineas Allen, Secretary.

The *Concord Female Charitable Society* was formed in 1814 for "relieving distress, encouraging industry, and promoting virtue and happiness among the female part of the community." Two meetings are held annually for transacting the public business, and others monthly to prepare clothing, and to devise other means to relieve distress.

A society for the suppression of intemperance was organized January 6, 1814. Nathan Brooks, Esq. delivered the first address before it the following December.

Auxiliary Missionary, Tract, and Temperance Societies exist in the town, besides many other less public associations.

The *Concord Bank* was incorporated March 3, 1832, with a capital of $100,000. Daniel Shattuck, Esq., President, John M. Cheney, Esq., Cashier, and the President, Abiel Heywood, John Keyes, Nathan Brooks, Abel Moore, and Phineas How, of Concord, Rufus Hosmer of Stow, George F. Farley of Groton, John Merriam of Bedford, Benjamin Muzzy of Lexington, and Timothy Prescott of Littleton, Directors. A neat and appropriate

---

[1] The losses by fire in Concord have not been very great. Some memorandums of a few of them have been preserved. April 17, 1784, Samuel Heald's house was burnt, in which himself, son, and grandson perished. November 3, 1797, Mrs. Hartshorn's house and Richard Barber's shop were burnt. June, 1808, Widow Colburn's house was consumed by fire. October 24, 1810, Gaius Proctor's house was burnt; loss, $800. October 28, 1817, the alms-house was burnt; loss estimated at $3,500. May 28, 1818, Deacon White's house took fire, but was extinguished. December 11, 1818, Mrs. Woodward's store took fire, and was extinguished with great difficulty. December 12, 1819, the jail took fire, but was extinguished. December 31, 1819, the centre school-house was burnt. March 10, 1823, William Whiting's shop and part of his dwelling-house were burnt; loss estimated at $3,000. March, 1829, Samuel Burr's new house was burnt; loss $1,500.

building was erected for its own accommodation and that of the Middlesex Mutual Fire Insurance Company, in 1832.

Agricultural Society. — This, though properly a county society, is so connected with Concord, as to deserve to be noticed in its history. The members of the Massachusetts Agricultural Society, living in the westerly parts of the county, met at Chelmsford, January 6, 1794, and formed a society for the " promotion of useful improvements in agriculture," and were incorporated, February 28, 1803, as " The Western Society of Middlesex Husbandmen." It did not include Concord, nor the other towns in the easterly part of the county. Meetings were held semi-annually, alternately at Westford and Littleton, but no public exhibitions took place. The following gentlemen were successively elected Presidents ; the Rev. Jonathan Newell of Stow, the Rev. Phineas Whitney of Shirley, the Rev. Edmund Foster of Littleton, Ebenezer Bridge of Chelmsford, Dr. Oliver Prescott of Groton, Colonel Benjamin Osgood of Westford, Wallis Tuttle, Esq., of Littleton, and the Hon. Samuel Dana of Groton.

An act was passed, February 20, 1819, authorizing any agricultural society, possessing $1,000 in funds, to draw $200 from the state treasury, and in the same proportion for a larger sum. This society accordingly voted, in the following September, to extend its operation throughout the county, and to raise funds that it might avail itself of the grant of the state. An act passed, January 24, 1824, incorporating it as " The Society of Middlesex Husbandmen and Manufacturers " ; and it was agreed to have annual shows in Concord. The first was held here October 11, 1820 ; and they have since been annually repeated. The subjoined table exhibits the names of the presidents, orators, and amount of premiums awarded. The names of those orators, whose addresses have been published, are printed in *italics.*

Date.	Presidents.	Orators.	Premiums.
1820	Cyrus Baldwin, Esq.	No Address.	$244
1821	Cyrus Baldwin, Esq.	Rufus Hosmer, Esq.	277
1822	David Lawrence, Esq.	*Thomas G. Fessenden, Esq.*	245
1823	Colonel Joseph Valentine.	*Josiah Adams, Esq.*	259
1824	Colonel Joseph Valentine.	Hon. Luke Fiske.	359
1825	Rufus Hosmer, Esq.	*Rev. Charles Briggs.*	540
1826	Benjamin Dix, Esq.	Rev. Ezekiel L. Bascom.	491
1827	Josiah Adams, Esq.	Hon. Edward Everett.	492

1828	Hon. Luke Fiske.	Rev. Bernard Whitman.	496
1829	Hon. Luke Fiske.	John P. Robinson, Esq.	521
1830	Joseph Barrett, Esq.	*Elias Phinney, Esq.*	541
1831	Elias Phinney, Esq.	*John M. Cheney.*	510

The *Middlesex Mutual Fire Insurance Company* was incorporated March 3, and organized March 29, 1826. The Hon. Abiel Heywood was chosen President, and the Hon. Nathan Brooks, Secretary and Treasurer, who, with John Keyes, Daniel Shattuck, Elias Phinney of Lexington, and Daniel Richardson of Tyngsborough, have since been Directors. The other directors have been Samuel Burr, 1826 to 1830; Josiah Davis from 1830; Micah M. Rutter of East Sudbury, 1826 to 1828; Joshua Page of Bedford, 1826 to 1829; Rufus Hosmer of Stow, from 1829; and Charles Merriam of Weston, from 1830. The first policy was issued May 17, 1826; and the following table will show the amount of business in this excellent institution since that time.

Year End.	Policies.	Am't Insured.	Premium Notes.	Losses.
1827	440	$801,247	$41,276·41	$ 650·00
1828	226	387,871	22,177·47	100·00
1829	406	645,673	37,774·13	857·74
1830	590	857,700	53,173·80	2,924·50
1831	499	646,279	39,954·01	1,452·53
1832	508	708,064	45,184·85	3,150·75

OFFICIAL HISTORY.—*Municipal Officers.*—The Town Clerk, in addition to his ordinary duties, in early times, was generally authorized to issue summonses and writs of attachment, triable before a justice of the peace. There were also three officers, sometimes chosen by the town, and sometimes appointed by the County Court, called " *Commissioners* for the ending of small matters," whose powers were similar to those of justices of the peace. This Court somewhat resembled a city Police Court. At first 7 men were chosen " to manage the prudential affairs of the town," subsequently called *Selectmen.* About 1680 the number was reduced to 5, and in 1770 to 3. They have acted as *Overseers of the Poor* and as *Assessors,* excepting from 1714 to 1725, when 5 overseers of the poor were chosen. Assessors were chosen separately in 1822, and 1825 to 1831. The office of *Constable* was considered very important in early times. Distinguished men in the town were chosen, and then obliged to serve or pay heavy penalties; and they received a regular salary from the town. Prior to 1720, two were annually chosen, and three since then, with the exception of a few years. It was the custom till 1789, for them to perform the duty of *collectors*, which, at that time was made a separate office, and which, since 1792, has been filled by one person only, and that one generally, who agrees to collect the assessments at the lowest rate. The *Treasurer's* was a distinct office till 1824, when it was united with the collector's. *Fence-Viewers*, or *Surveyors of Fences* have been chosen from before the commencement of the last century; the number varying from 3 to 7. In 1697, seven *Surveyors of Highways and Bridges* were chosen; in 1733, nine; in 1750, twelve; in 1755, five; recently eleven till 1831, when one only was chosen. The number of *Tythingmen*, considered, particularly in early times, an important office, has varied from 9 to 3; of *Field-Drivers*, or *Haywards*, from 2 to 6. One *Sealer of Weights and Measures* has always been chosen; and from 1 to 3 *Sealers of Leather* till 1793, when the office ceased. From 2 to 3 *Horse-Officers*, or " persons to look after horses going at large on the common during Concord Court," were chosen from 1710 to 1802. From 1715 every man married in town during the year was chosen " to observe the law relating to swine," or to be *Hog-reeves*, as they were first called in 1721. Two to five *Clerks of the Market* were chosen from 1732 to 1800; two *Surveyors of Flax* from 1735 to 1737; two *Deer-reeves*, or deer-officers, from 1740 to 1797. *Cullers of Staves and Shingles*, or *Surveyors of Lumber*, were first chosen in 1752. *Wardens*, officers similar to *Tythingmen*, were chosen from 1761 to 1791. One *Surveyor of Wheat and Flour* from 1763 to 1767; four *Fish-Officers* since 1784; three or four *Measurers of Wood* since 1793; from 3 to 8 *Firewards* since 1797; one *Pound-Keeper* since 1800; a *Cow-Pock Committee* since 1812; and a *School-Committee* since 1800.

Town Clerks from the First Settlement of the Town.

Simon Willard	1635 — 1653	Thomas Brown	1704 — 1709
Robert Merriam	1654 — 1667	William Wilson	1710 — 1718
John Scotchford	1668 — 1679	John Flint	1719 — 1730
John Flint	1680 — 1688	Samuel Heywood	1731 — 1748
Thomas Brown	1689 — 1700	Ephraim Jones	1749 — 1754
Abraham Wood	1701 — 1703	Jonas Heywood	1755 — 1759

Benjamin Brown	1760, 1761	Ephraim Wood	1771 — 1795
Jonas Heywood	1762 — 1770	Abiel Heywood	1796 —

Town Treasurers since 1700.

Jonathan Hubbard	1700 — 1708	John Beaton	1754 — 1770
John Heywood	1709 — 1714	Abijah Bond	1771 — 1781
Samuel Jones	1715 — 1722	Timothy Minott	1782 — 1785
Samuel Chandler	1723 — 1727	Elnathan Jones	1786 — 1791
Samuel Merriam	1728 — 1733	Humphrey Barrett	1792 — 1795
Joseph Barrett	1734 — 1739	Samuel Jones	1796 — 1810
Ebenezer Hubbard	1740 — 1753	John Buttrick	1811 — 1824

Selectmen chosen since 1700.

Thomas Brown	1696 — 1709	Samuel Merriam	1727, 29, 35, 36, 59
Abraham Wood	1700 — 1704	John Jones	1730 — 33, 35, 36, 39 —
Joseph French	1700 — 1703		[55, 60, 61, 65, 66
Stephen Hosmer	1700, 3, 29	Hugh Brooks	1730 — 1733
William Wilson	1700 — 17, 22	Ephraim Brown	1730 — 1733
John Jones	1702, 4 — 6	Ephraim Jones	1734, 43 — 54
Samuel Buttrick	1702	Nathaniel Ball	1734, 37, 38
Noah Brooks	1702, 4, 9	Joshua Brooks	1734, 49, 50
John Wheeler	1703, 1704	Joseph Wright	1736 — 1746
Jonathan Hubbard	1703	David Melvin	1736 — 38, 40, 43
John Heywood	1705 — 1708	Daniel Adams	1736 — 1738
Samuel Fletcher	1705 — 7, 9 — 13	Chambers Russell	1739
Benj. Whittemore	1707 — 24, [27 — 29	Nathaniel Whittemore	1743 — 46, [49, 50, 54
Thomas Wheeler	1708	Joshua Hubbard	1741
Jonathan Prescott	1709	Samuel Minott	1747 — 1749
Wm. Wheeler	1710 — 13, 15, 18, [19, 25, 26	Ephraim Wood	1749, 1750
		Simon Hunt	1749, 50, 54, 55, [63 — 66
Joseph Dakin	1710, 15 — 17		
John Heald	1711 — 1715	Abishai Brown	1752, 1753
Richard Parks	1714	Ephraim Hartwell	1752, 1753
Simon Dakin	1714	Thomas Brooks	1752, 1753
John Fassett	1714, 20 — 24	Stephen Hosmer, Jr.	1752 — 1759
John Flint	1716 — 29, 41, 42, 59	Samuel Farrar	1754
Daniel Brooks	1716 — 19, 25 — 29	James Barrett	1754, 55, 60, 61, 66
Samuel Chandler	1718 — 24, 30 — [36, 39	Thomas Jones	1756 — 1758
		Charles Prescott	1756 — 58, 62, [65, 66
Samuel Heywood,	1720 — 23, 27, [28, 30 — 48	Thomas Barrett	1756 — 58, 62
George Farrar	1723 — 1726	Jonas Heywood	1755 — 59, 62, 70
John Barker	1725, 1726	Samuel Minott	1756 — 58, 62
James Minott, Jr.	1727, 28, 35, 36, [40, 47 — 49	James Chandler	1759 — 61, 67 — 70
		Benjamin Brown	1760, 1761

SOCIAL AND OFFICIAL HISTORY. 235

Andrew Conant	1760, 1761	Jacob Brown	1788 — 1795
Thomas Davis	1762	Abiel Heywood	1796 —
John Cuming	1763 — 1766	Roger Brown	1796 — 1800
Jonas Minott	1767 — 1770	Reuben Hunt	1797 — 1801
David Brown	1767 — 1770	Thomas Hubbard	1801 — 1803
Humphrey Barrett	1767 — 1770	Stephen Barrett	1802 — 1807
Ephraim Wood	1771 — 1795	Nathan Wood	1804 — 1810
John Flint	1771 — 1774	James Barrett	1808 — 1810
Timothy Wheeler	1771 — 1773	Nathan Barrett	1811 — 1821
Nathan Merriam	1774 — 1778	Thomas Wheeler	1811 — 1815
Nehemiah Hunt	1775 — 1778	Isaac Lee	1816 — 1821
John Buttrick	1779 — 1784	Jonathan Hildreth	1822 — 1829
George Minott	1779 — 1784	Cyrus Hubbard	1822 —
Asa Brooks	1785 — 1795	Cyrus Stow	1830,
James Barrett	1785, 1786	Daniel Clark	1830 —
Joseph Chandler	1787, 1796	Elisha Wheeler	1830,

Deputies and Representatives from the first Settlement of the Town.

	7th December.	1659 — 1662	Thomas Brooks.
1636	Simon Willard.	1663 — 1666	Timothy Wheeler.
April, 17th May, 26th Sept., 2d Nov.		1667	John Smeadly.
1637	Simon Willard.	1668, 1669	Timothy Wheeler.
2d May, 6th Sept., 22d May.		1670	John Smeadly.
1638, 1639	{ Thomas Flint, Simon Willard.	1671, 1672	Timothy Wheeler.
		1673 — 1676	Peter Bulkeley.
4th Sept., 13th May.		1677	Thomas Brattle.
1639, 1640	{ Thomas Flint, Richard Griffin.	1678 — 1680	{ John Flint, Thomas Brattle.
7th Oct., 2d June, 7th Oct.		1681	Thomas Brattle.
1640, 1641	{ Thomas Flint, Simon Willard.	1682	John Flint.
		1683, 1684	Edward Oakes.
8th Sept., 10th May.		1685	Henry Woodhouse.
1642, 1643	Thomas Brooks.	1686	Edward Oakes.
7th March.		1687, 1688	(Andross' usurpation.)
1644	Simon Willard.	*9th May, 5th June, 5th Nov., 3d Dec., 12th Feb.*	
29th May.			
1644	Thomas Brooks.	1689	{ Simon Davis, Ebenezer Prout.
1645, 1646	Simon Willard.		
1647, 1648	Richard Griffin.	*28th May.*	
1649, 1650	Simon Willard.	1690	Simon Davis.
1651	{ Richard Griffin, Simon Willard.	*8th Oct., 10th Dec., 3d Feb., 14th April.*	
		1690, 1691	Henry Woodhouse.
1652, 1653	Simon Willard.	*20th May.*	
1654	{ Simon Willard, Thomas Brooks.	1691	James Blood.
		14th Oct., 8th Dec.	
1655 — 1658	Robert Merriam.	1691	Humphrey Barrett.

	4th May.	1776	{ Joseph Hosmer, John Cuming.
1692	Simon Davis.		
8th June, under the new charter.		1777 — 1780	Joseph Hosmer.
1692	{ Jonathan Prescott, Henry Woodhouse.	1781	David Brown.
		1782	James Barrett.
1693 — 1695	Jonathan Prescott.	1783 — 1785	Joseph Barrett.
1696	Ephraim Flint.	1786	James Barrett.
1697 — 1699	Jonathan Prescott.	1787	Isaac Hubbard.
1700, 1701	James Minott.	1788 — 1791	Duncan Ingraham.
1702	William Wilson.	1792 — 1796	Jonathan Fay.
1703, 1704	John Wheeler.	1797, 1798	Ephraim Wood.
1705	Simon Davis.	1799 — 1805	Joseph Chandler.
1706 — 1708	William Wilson.	1806	{ Jonas Lee, Joseph Chandler.
1709 — 1711	Benj. Whittemore.		
1712, 1713	Jonathan Prescott.	1807	Joseph Chandler.
1714	Benj. Whittemore.	1808	{ Joseph Chandler, Jonas Lee.
1715 — 1718	William Wilson.		
1719, 1720	Benj. Whittemore.	1809, 1810	Tilly Merrick.
1721	William Wilson.	1811	{ Joseph Chandler, Stephen Barrett.
1722 — 1724	Benj. Whittemore.		
1725	William Wilson.	1812	{ John White, Benjamin Prescott.
1726 — 1728	John Flint.		
1729 — 1736	Samuel Chandler.	1813	Tilly Merrick.
1737, 1738	James Minott.	1814	Jonas Lee.
1739	Samuel Chandler.	1815	Tilly Merrrick.
1740	Chambers Russell.	1816	Not represented.
1741 — 1744	James Minott.	1817	Francis Jarvis.
1745 — 1749	Ephraim Jones.	1818 — 1820	Thomas Wheeler.
1750	{ Ephraim Jones, Chambers Russell.	1821, 1822	John Keyes.
		1823 — 1825	Nathan Brooks.
1751, 1752	Chambers Russell.	1826	Not represented.
1753	Ephraim Jones.	1827 — 1829	{ Reuben Brown, Jr., Samuel Burr.
1754, 1755	Simon Hunt.		
1756, 1757	James Barrett.	1830	{ Reuben Brown, Jr., Daniel Shattuck.
1758 — 1763	Charles Prescott.		
1764	James Barrett.	1831	Joseph Barrett.
1765 — 1767	Charles Prescott.	1832	{ Joseph Barrett, John Keyes.
1768 — 1775	James Barrett.		

Assistants and Counsellors.

1642 — 1655	Thomas Flint.	1677 — 1685	Peter Bulkeley.
1654 — 1676	Simon Willard.	1746 — 1759	James Minott.

Senators.

1785 — 1793	Joseph Hosmer.	1823 — 1828	John Keyes.
1808 — 1812	John L. Tuttle.	1825 — 1832	Samuel Hoar, Jr.

Nathan Brooks was of the Council in 1829 and 1830, and of the Senate in 1831.

SOCIAL AND OFFICIAL HISTORY. 237

County Officers.

The Hon. Joseph Hosmer was sheriff from March, 1794, to 1808.

Gen. William Hildreth was sheriff from May 10, 1808, to 1813. He died September 5, 1813.

Samuel Bartlett, Esq. was chosen Register of Deeds in 1794, and removed to Cambridge.

The Hon. John L. Tuttle was chosen County Treasurer from 1808 to 1813 inclusive; and the Hon. John Keyes since that time.

The Hon. Chambers Russell was judge of the Court of Common Pleas and of the Court of Vice-Admiralty, from 1747 to 1752.

Ephraim Wood, Esq., was appointed special judge of the Court of Common Pleas, March 12, 1785, and judge of the same court in 1797; and held the office till the new organization of that court in 1811.

The Hon. Abiel Heywood sustained the office of justice of the Court of Sessions, under its different modifications, from 1801 till the law organizing the Court of County Commissioners was passed.

The Hon. Nathan Brooks was appointed Master in Chancery for Middlesex June 29, 1827.

Attorneys and Counsellors at Law.

John Hoar, from 1660 to 1670. See notices of early families.

Peter Bulkeley. See Biographical Notices of Native Graduates.

Daniel Bliss, son of the Rev. Daniel Bliss, noticed among the college graduates.

Jonathan Fay, son of Captain Jonathan Fay of Westborough, who was graduated at Harvard College in 1773, settled in Concord soon after, married Lucy Prescott, and died June 1, 1811, aged 59.

William Jones, from 1798 to 1801. See Native Graduates.

John Merrick, from 1789 to 1794. See Native Graduates.

Thomas Heald was born in New Ipswich, New Hampshire, March 31, 1768, and graduated at Dartmouth College in 1797. He read law with Jonathan Fay, Esq., was admitted to practice in Concord in 1800, and removed from Concord in 1813. He died at Blakeley, Alabama, in the summer of 1821, while holding the office of judge of one of the courts there.

John Leighton Tuttle was born in Littleton, graduated at Harvard College in 1796, and commenced practice in Concord after the usual term of professional reading. While resident here he was Post-Master, County Treasurer, and Senator. He was appointed, in 1812, Lieutenant-Colonel Commandant of the 9th regiment of Continental Infantry, and died at Watertown, near Sacket's Harbour, New York, July 23, 1813.

Samuel Hoar, Jr., has practised with distinguished success in the town since 1807. See College Graduates of Lincoln.

John Keyes was born in Westford, graduated at Dartmouth College in 1809, and admitted to the bar, in this county, in September, 1812. He has been Post-Master and County Treasurer since 1813, was a delegate to the convention for amending the Constitution in 1820, and since a representative and senator in the General Court.

Nathan Brooks, since 1813. See College Graduates of Lincoln.

Elisha Fuller, son of the Rev. Timothy Fuller of Princeton, was graduated at Harvard College in 1815, admitted to the bar in 1823, and immediately after commenced practice in Concord. He removed to Lowell in June, 1831.

John M. Cheney opened an office in Concord in June, 1831. See Native Graduates.

Physicians.

Philip Reed died May 10, 1696. Little is known of him but his title.

Simon Davis, son of Lieutenant Simon Davis, born October 12, 1661, married Elizabeth Woodhouse, 1689, and lived where Mr. Hutchinson now lives in Carlisle. His practice was principally in surgery. His son John, who died November 16, 1762, aged 73, practised in the same profession.

James Minott came to Concord about 1680, and died September 20, 1735, aged 83. See Genealogy.

Jonathan Prescott, born April 5, 1677, died October 28, 1729, aged 54. See Genealogy.

Joseph Lee, son of Joseph Lee, born in Concord October 16, 1680, died October 5, 1736, aged 56. He lived where Joseph Barrett, Esq., now lives. His son Joseph, who was born June 6, 1716, and died April 10, 1797, practised physic in the early part of his life, though his attention seems not to have been exclusively devoted to it.

SOCIAL AND OFFICIAL HISTORY. 239

Alexander Cuming came to Concord about 1726.

Edward Carrington. The records say, he was "born at Barbadoes, came to Virginia, thence to Boston and Concord," where he died July 22, 1737, aged 24.

Ebenezer Hartshorn, probably son of Thomas Hartshorn, who was here before 1690, died January 29, 1781, aged 92.

John Prescott, went to Cuba. See Native Graduates and General History.

Abel Prescott, son of Dr. Jonathan Prescott, and brother of the preceding, was born April 7, 1718, and died October 24, 1805, aged 88. During a long period he enjoyed a most extensive professional patronage. His practice extended to nearly all the towns in the county. He lived in the house now owned by Captain Moore, just below the village. His son Benjamin studied physic, and commenced practice in Carlisle, but soon relinquished the profession.

John Cuming, died July 3, 1788, aged 60. See separate Biographical Notices.

Timothy Minott, died July 25, 1804, aged 78. See Native Graduates.

Joseph Hunt, died May 27, 1812, aged 63. See Native Graduates.

Isaac Hurd, son of Benjamin Hurd of Charlestown, born July 27, 1756, and graduated at Harvard College in 1776. He commenced practice in Billerica in 1778, and came from thence to this town in 1789. His Address before the Humane Society, June 11, 1799, was published.

Abishai Brown, having acquired some skill while in the revolutionary army, had considerable practice as a surgeon after his return.

Abiel Heywood commenced practice in Concord in 1790. See Native Graduates.

Benjamin D. Bartlett, son of Samuel Bartlett, Esq., born in Concord, graduated at Harvard College in 1810, came to Concord in 1813, and removed to Bath, Maine, in 1816.

Josiah Bartlett, son of Dr. Josiah Bartlett, of Charlestown, born November 20, 1796, and graduated at Harvard College in 1816, and at the Medical School in 1819; came to Concord June 1, 1820.

Dudley Smith, son of Dudley Smith, born at Gilsum, New Hampshire, September 15, 1799. He studied with Dr. Charles G. Adams of Keene, and Dr. Warren of Boston, was graduated at the Medical School, Dartmouth College, in 1825, and commenced practice in Concord the same year. He removed to Lowell in 1832.

CHAPTER XVI.

BIOGRAPHICAL NOTICES OF COLLEGE GRADUATES AND OTHER INDIVIDUALS BELONGING TO CONCORD.

[Considerable labor has been expended in compiling the following notes. It was intended that the list should be complete; but it is presumed that the College Catalogue contains other names of persons who were natives of Concord, but for want of authentic information they are not here given. Where no College is named, Harvard College is to be understood.]

1. JOHN BULKELEY, son of the Rev. Peter Bulkeley, was in the first class of graduates in 1642. He returned to England, and settled in the ministry at Fordham, but was ejected in 1662. He afterwards lived at Wapping in London, where he practised physic with good success. He died in 1689, aged 70.

2. JOHN JONES, son of the Rev. John Jones, was graduated in 1643, and admitted freeman in 1645. By an erroneous punctuation of Johnson [History of New England, p. 165], this person has been considered as having returned to England; but from the same author it appears, that he was "employed in the *western* parts of Nevis, one of the Summer Islands." This appears from the verses on his father, in which the author says,

> "Leading thy son to land, yet more remote,
> To feed his flock upon this *Western* wast:
> Exhort him then Christ's kingdom to promote;
> That he with thee of lasting joyes may tast."[1]

3. SAMUEL STOW was son of Thomas Stow, one of the early settlers of Concord, and was graduated in 1645. He emigrated to Middleton, Connecticut, with two of his brothers, about 1650,

---
[1] MS. Letter of John Farmer, Esq.

where he was a preacher about 10 years, though it does not appear that he was ever ordained. He subsequently relinquished the profession, and lived a private but highly respected citizen there till his death. He gave a lot of land to the town for the benefit of education, which still bears his name.

4. GERSHOM BULKELEY, son of the Rev. Peter Bulkeley, was born in Concord in 1636, and graduated in 1655. He was ordained at New London about 1660, from whence he removed, and was installed at Weathersfield in 1668. In 1676 he was dismissed on account of ill health, and afterwards became one of the most distinguished physicians and surgeons of his time. He was wounded in a battle with the Indians near Wachusett, while in the army as a surgeon, in 1676. To him the epithet *great* was applied on account of his eminent character. He died at Weathersfield, December 2, 1713, aged 77. On his monument is inscribed, — "He was honorable in his descent, of rare abilities, extraordinary industry, excellent in learning, master of many languages; exquisite in his skill in divinity, physic, and law, and of a most exemplary and Christian life.

In certam spem beatæ resurrectionis repositus."

He married Sarah, daughter of the Rev. Dr. Chauncy, President of Harvard College, October 26, 1659, and had 4 sons. 1. Peter, lost at sea; 2. Charles of New London; 3. Edward, who married Dorothy Prescott of Concord, and died at Weathersfield; and 4. John, who was graduated at Harvard College in 1699, and was the first minister of Colchester, Connecticut, father of the Hon. John Bulkeley, a physician and judge of the Supreme Court. The numerous and respectable families, bearing the name in Connecticut and New York, have all descended from Edward and John. Stephen Bulkeley, Esq., one of the grandsons of Edward, acquired a fortune in Charleston, South Carolina, and has recently purchased the estate in Hartford, on which the celebrated " charter oak " is situated.

5. SAMUEL WILLARD, one of the most eminent ministers in New England, was son of Major Simon Willard, and was born in Concord January 31, 1640. He was graduated in 1659, and ordained at Groton in 1662, from whence he removed to Boston when that town was destroyed by the Indians in March 1676, and was installed, as colleague pastor with the Rev. Mr. Thacher,

over the Old South Church, April 10, 1678. He officiated as Vice-President of Harvard College, from September 6, 1701, till his death. He died September 12, 1707, aged 67. His son was Secretary of the province 39 years, and his grandson, Joseph Willard, D. D., LL. D., was President of Harvard College. The notices in Farmer's "Register," Allen's "Biog. Dict." Wisner's "History of the Old South Church," and other works, are so copious, that any further account here is unnecessary.

6. PETER BULKELEY, the youngest son of the Rev. Peter Bulkeley, was born August 12, 1643, and graduated in 1660. He settled in Concord, and, in 1673 and the four subsequent years, represented the town in the General Court. In February, 1676, he was chosen Speaker of the House of Deputies; and in August of the same year was appointed, with the Hon. William Stoughton, agent to England on the complaints of Gorges and Mason, and reappointed in 1682. They sailed on the first mission October 30, 1676. On the 27th of February, 1679, he was reappointed, by King Charles the Second, with Stoughton, as agent to England respecting the Narraganset country. They returned December 23, 1679. In 1677 he was chosen one of the Judges, or Court of Assistants, and re-elected eight years. He was also one of the Commissioners of the United Colonies the greater part of that time. On the 8th of October, 1685, he was appointed by King James the Second one of the Council, of which Joseph Dudley, Esq., was President, which constituted the government of the colonies after the charter was forfeited. In 1680 the militia in the county was divided into two regiments, and Major Peter Bulkeley appointed to command one of them. This was an office in those days of great distinction. In all these and other important offices, he acquitted himself with honor and general acceptance. He was one of 20 who, in 1683, made the "million purchase" in New Hampshire, and had several special grants of land for public services. He died May 24, 1688, aged 44; and "was buried," says Judge Sewall, "the 27th, because he could not be kept, word of which was sent to Boston the same day to prevent any going in vain to his funeral."

He married Rebecca, only daughter of Lieutenant Joseph Wheeler, April 16, 1667, and had Edward, Joseph, John, and Rebecca; the 1st and 3d died young. His widow married Jonathan Prescott, and his daughter Jonathan Prescott, Jr. Joseph, born September 7, 1670, held a captain's commission, and was engaged in the public service. He married widow Rebecca Minott, daughter of John Jones, 1696. She died July 17, 1712; leaving by him Rebecca, who married Joseph Hubbard, grandfather to Deacon Thomas Hubbard; 2. Dorothy, who married Samuel Hunt; 3. John, who held a Colonel's commission, and died in Groton, in December, 1772, aged 69, father to John, who was graduated at Harvard College in 1769, who was a lawyer, and died in Groton December 16, 1774, aged 26. Captain Joseph Bulkeley married for a second wife Silence Jeffrey, in 1713, and had Joseph, Peter, Charles (whose descendants live in Littleton), and perhaps other children.

7. BENJAMIN ESTABROOK, son of the Rev. Joseph Estabrook, was born February 24, 1671, and graduated in 1690. He was invited, in 1692, to preach at Lexington, and was ordained first minister of that town October 21, 1696. He died July 22, 1697, aged 26. He married Abigail, daughter of the Rev. Samuel Willard.

8. JOSEPH SMITH was graduated in 1695, ordained in Middletown, Connecticut, first minister of the "Upper Houses," January 5, 1715, and died September 8, 1736, aged 62. His father's name was Thomas.

9. SAMUEL ESTABROOK, 3d son of the Rev. Joseph Estabrook, was born January 7, 1674, and graduated in 1696. He taught the grammar-school in Concord from 1706 to 1710, and assisted his father in the ministry. He was ordained at Canterbury, Connecticut, June 13, 1711, where he died June 26, 1727, aged 53.

10. BENJAMIN PRESCOTT, son of Captain Jonathan Prescott, was born September 16, 1687, and graduated in 1709. He was ordained at Salem Village (Danvers), September 23, 1713. "In this office," says a biographical notice in the Boston Gazette of 1777, "he continued about 45 years, discharging its duties with such capacity and fidelity as gave him an extensive reputation. When he thought himself called in Providence to resign his pastoral charge, he was introduced into the magistracy, which he supported with honor to himself and usefulness to the public; always appearing the same man, and exhibiting an uniform piety and virtue in every station. He had great political as well as theological knowledge. He well understood the laws, the rights,

and the interest of his country; and defended them with great strength of reason as well as generous warmth of heart. In this service his pen was frequently and largely employed, more especially at the commencement of the important controversy of the revolution, though his name was concealed; and the clearness, the consistency, the force and vivacity with which he would support a long train of argument, even when he had entered his 90th year, was truly surprising. Few, very few attained so great an age as he did with so much comfort to themselves and their friends, and so much usefulness. Besides employing himself in some writings which he left unfinished, but enough to show the remaining vigor of his mind, he transacted considerable business as a magistrate till within a week of his death. After he was seized with the violent fever that soon put an end to his life, he could speak but little; but he satisfactorily evinced, that he had those inward consolations and supports, which are the genuine result of that blessed religion which he had so long professed, preached, and practised." He died May 28, 1777, in his 90th year.

He married three times. 1. Elizabeth Higginson of Salem, by whom he had 2 sons and 3 daughters. Benjamin, the eldest, was graduated at Harvard College in 1736, married Rebecca, daughter of the Hon. James Minott in 1741, lived in Salem, and had 8 children. Rebecca, the eldest, married the Hon. Roger Sherman of New Haven. Her brothers, James and Benjamin, also lived there; the former married Rebecca Barrett of Concord. The Rev. Benjamin married, the second time, Mercy, daughter of the Rev. Henry Gibbs of Watertown, by whom he had Henry, who died at New Castle September 10, 1816, father to Benjamin, Henry, and William Pepperell of that town, and George Washington. His 3d wife was Mary, widow of the Rev. Benjamin Coleman, daughter of Sir William Pepperell.

11. TIMOTHY MINOTT was born June 18, 1692, a son of James Minott, Esq., and graduated in 1718. He studied divinity, and was licensed to preach the gospel, and in that capacity was accustomed to officiate for the Rev. Messrs. Whiting, Bliss, and Emerson, in Concord, and in many neighbouring churches. He was never ordained, but spent most of his long life in the more humble, but not less important office of a teacher of youth. His

first introduction to this employment was in 1712, before he left college, in the public grammar-school in Concord. He was then engaged at the rate of £20 per year, on condition, say the town records, " if any thing should exceed his abilities his father should assist him." He taught occasionally till 1721, and from that time constantly for above 40 years. According to the town records, for many years, it appears as a condition on which money should be raised to support the grammar-school, that " Mr. Timothy Minott undertake the work." This vote of the town shows that his services were held in high estimation, an opinion which is fully confirmed by tradition. His occupation gave him the title of *Master* Minott, and enabled him to be a very useful man. He was more distinguished, however, for the excellence of his principles and character as a man, and for his faculties as a schoolmaster, than for any peculiar force or elegance as a preacher. He died November 30, 1778, aged 86.

12. JONATHAN MILES, son of John Miles, was born February 13, 1701, and graduated in 1727. He died in Concord in February, 1775, aged 74.

13. JOHN PRESCOTT, son of Dr. Jonathan Prescott, was born May 8, 1707, and graduated in 1727. He was a physician in Concord, and highly esteemed for his professional skill and excellent character. When the unfortunate expedition to Cuba was proposed, he entered readily into the views of the government, and enlisted a company of 100 men from this neighbourhood. He sailed from Boston, as commander of this company, September 23, 1740, and was off " Don Maria Bay " in the following February. After the melancholy failure of the expedition, he returned to this country in 1743, and not long after went to England, at the request of the government, where he was treated with great respect. He died in London, of the small-pox, December 30, 1743, aged 35.

He married Ann, the 8th child of Nathaniel Lynde, Esq. She died May 12, 1795, aged 88. Her sister married Joseph Willard of Rutland, who was killed by the Indians in 1723. Her mother was Susannah Willoughby, and her father son of Simon and Hannah Newdigate, who came from London. In testimony of the esteem in which Captain Prescott's services were held, his widow received a pension from the British government during her life. She had 5 children, Ann, Rebecca, 2 sons, who died young, and Willoughby, who died in Concord April 15, 1808, aged 65.

14. PETER PRESCOTT, a brother of the foregoing, was born April 17, 1709, and graduated in 1730. He studied law, and resided here and in Boston. He dealt largely in wild lands. Peterborough, in New Hampshire, derived its name from him. He was out several times in the French war, and commanded a company at Crown Point in 1758. Some time before the revolution, he removed to Nova Scotia, where he was appointed clerk of one of the courts, and died in 1784.[1]

15. NATHANIEL WHITAKER, son of David Whitaker, was graduated in 1730. After being some time employed as a minister at Norwich in Connecticut, he went to England in 1765 or 1766, accompanied by Sampson Occum, the first Indian educated by the Rev. Mr. Wheelock, afterwards President of Dartmouth College, to solicit donations for the support of Mr. Wheelock's school "for the education of Indian youth, to be missionaries and schoolmasters for the natives of America." He was installed July 28, 1769, over the 3d church in Salem. In 1774 his meeting-house was burnt, and a division in his society took place. He and his friends erected a new house, and called it the Tabernacle Church in 1776; but, difficulties having arisen, he was dismissed in 1783, and installed at Canaan, Maine, September 10, 1784. He was again dismissed in 1789, and removed to Virginia, where he died.

16. EPHRAIM FLINT, son of Colonel John Flint, was born March 4, 1714, and graduated in 1733. He settled in Lincoln, and inherited the valuable estate of his uncle Edward, and great uncle Ephraim, who had successively owned and lived on the " Flint Farm "; both having died without issue. He was the first town clerk of Lincoln, and died December 26, 1762, aged 48.

17. AARON WHITTEMORE, son of Benjamin Whittemore, was born December 13, 1711, and graduated in 1734. He was ordained at Pembroke, New Hampshire, March 1, 1737, and died November 16, 1767, aged 55.

---

[1] Benjamin Prescott, a brother probably of Peter, entered College in 1744, but was not graduated. He was killed by the Indians.

18. JONATHAN HOAR, son of Lieutenant Daniel Hoar, was graduated in 1740. He was an officer in the provincial service during the war from 1744 to 1763. In 1755 he went as Major to Fort Edward, and the next year was a Lieutenant-Colonel in Nova Scotia, and aid to Major General Winslow at Crown Point. After the peace of 1763, he went to England, and was appointed Governor of Newfoundland and the neighbouring provinces, but died on his passage thither in 1771, aged 52.[1]

19. TIMOTHY MINOTT, son of Timothy Minott, teacher of the grammar-school, was born April 8, 1726, and graduated in 1747. He was a physician in Concord, where he died, July 25, 1804, aged 78.

20. ISRAEL CHEEVER, son of Daniel Cheever, was born September 22, 1722, and graduated in 1749. He was ordained at New Bedford, but was dismissed in 1759, and installed at Liverpool, Nova Scotia, where he died, in June, 1812, aged 90.

21. OLIVER MERRIAM was born June 5, 1722, son of Ebenezer Merriam, and graduated in 1749. He died in Concord, while a student in divinity, on the 29th of May, 1751, aged 29.

22. SAMUEL BROOKS, son of John Brooks, was born March 16, 1729, and graduated in 1749. He lived at Exeter, New Hampshire, was a Register of deeds, justice of the peace, and a worthy man. He died in March, 1807, aged 78.

23. STEPHEN MINOTT, a brother of Dr. Timothy Minott, was born June 30, 1732, and graduated in 1751. After obtaining a theological education, he was invited to the care of a church in Portland, Maine, but died before ordination, September 3, 1759, aged 27. "The gentleman, scholar, and the Christian," says his epitaph, "were so conspicuous in his life, that he was greatly respected while living, and at his death generally and sincerely lamented."

24. GEORGE FARRAR, son of George Farrar, was born November 23, 1730, graduated in 1751, and ordained at Easton, March 26, 1755. He died September 17th, 1756, aged 25, and was interred at Lincoln.

25. JOHN MONROE, son of Thomas Monroe, was born March 4, 1733, and graduated in 1751. He studied divinity, but was

---

[1] Daniel Hoar, a brother of Jonathan Hoar, entered College in 1730, but was not graduated.

never ordained. He taught a school several years in Concord and Harvard, whither he removed in 1772. He died there about 1796. His sister is now living, aged 97.

26. WILLIAM WILLARD WHEELER, son of William Wheeler, was born December 24, 1734, and graduated in 1755. He was the Episcopalian minister of St. Andrew's Church in Scituate, and succeeded the Rev. Mr. Thompson, whose daughter he married. He died January 14, 1810, aged 75.

27. JOSEPH WHEELER was graduated in 1757, ordained at Harvard, December 12, 1759, and dismissed on account of ill health, July 28, 1768. He subsequently relinquished the profession, and resided at Worcester, where he was representative, justice of the peace, and register of probate, from 1775 to his death, February 10, 1793, at the age of 58.

28. DANIEL BLISS, son of the Rev. Daniel Bliss, was born March 18, 1740, and graduated in 1760. He read law with Abel Willard, Esq., of Lancaster, and was admitted to the bar in Worcester county in May, 1765, and soon after commenced practice in Rutland. He removed to Concord in 1772. He married a daughter of Colonel Murray of Rutland, and, in imitation of his father-in-law, embraced principles opposed by the "sons of liberty." In March, 1775, he left Concord, and was afterwards commissary in the British army at Quebec. He subsequently settled in Fredericktown, New Brunswick, where he was a counsellor at law, and afterwards chief justice of the Court of Common Pleas. He died in 1806, aged 66. His was the only estate in Concord confiscated by government. He was a man of great talents, popular manners, and energy of character.

29. JOSEPH LEE, son of Joseph Lee, was born May 12, 1742, and graduated in 1765. He was ordained at Royalston October 19, 1768, and died February 16, 1819, aged 77.

30. JOSEPH HUNT, youngest son of Deacon Simon Hunt, was born March 1, 1749, and graduated in 1770. He was a physician at Dracut and Concord, and several years Secretary of the Massachusetts Medical Society. He died May 27, 1812, aged 63.

31. NATHAN BOND, son of Abijah Bond, was born March 31, 1752, and graduated in 1772. He was a merchant in Boston, and died there January 5, 1816, aged 64. His remains were interred, at his request, by the side of his mother in Concord.

COLLEGE GRADUATES. 249

32. TILLY MERRICK, son of Tilly Merrick, was born January 29, 1752, graduated in 1773, and now resides in Concord, the oldest native living graduate.

33. THOMAS WHITING, grandson of the Rev. John Whiting by his son Thomas Whiting, Esq., was born October 3, 1748, and graduated in 1775. He taught the grammar-school in Concord several years, and was afterwards a merchant here. He died September 28, 1820, aged 72.

34. SAMUEL LEE, brother of the Rev. Joseph Lee, was born March 28, 1756, and graduated in 1776. During the revolution he was a merchant at Castine, and after the peace at Tracadache in Canada, and Ristigouche in New Brunswick on Bay Chaleur. He held various offices, civil and military, under the government of that province, and died March 3, 1805, aged 56, at Shediac, on his return from Halifax to Ristigouche.

35. PETER CLARK, son of Benjamin Clark, was graduated in 1777, was a lawyer in Southborough, and died in July, 1792, aged 36.

36. EBENEZER HUBBARD, son of Ebenezer Hubbard, was graduated in 1777, ordained at Marblehead, January 1, 1783, and died December 15, 1800, aged 43.

37. ABIEL HEYWOOD, son of Jonathan Heywood, was born December 9, 1759, and graduated in 1781. He studied physic with Dr. Spring of Watertown, and commenced practice in Concord in 1790. In 1796 he was chosen town clerk and first selectman, and has since been reelected. He was appointed justice of the peace October 24, 1797, special judge of the Court of Common Pleas February 25, 1802, and an associate justice of the Court of Sessions from 1802 to the organization of the County Commissioners' Court, and has also held other important offices.

38. TIMOTHY SWAN, son of Samuel Swan, was graduated in 1781, was a physician, and died at Washington, North Carolina.

39. EZRA CONANT, son of Ezra Conant, was born September 18, 1763, graduated in 1784, ordained at Winchester, New Hampshire, February 19, 1788, and dismissed October 13, 1806.

40. SILAS LEE, brother to Joseph and Samuel before mentioned, was born July 3, 1760, and graduated in 1784. He settled as an attorney at Pownalborough, now Wiscasset, Maine, and in 1800 and 1801 represented the district of Lincoln and Ken-

nebec in the 6th Congress of the United States. In January, 1802, he was appointed United States Attorney for Maine, and in 1807, Judge of Probate for the county of Lincoln, and held these offices till his death, March 1, 1814, aged 54.

41. JOHN MERRICK, brother of Tilly Merrick, was born February 7, 1761, and graduated in 1784. He read law and practised in Concord, where he died. The following epitaph, at his request, was inscribed on his grave-stone.

" John Merrick
died 15 August, 1797, aged 36,
and here, here he lies!"

42. WILLIAM EMERSON, only son of the Rev. William Emerson, was born May 6, 1769, and graduated in 1789. He was ordained at Harvard May 23, 1792, but was dismissed on being called to a greater field of usefulness, and was installed over the First church in Boston October 16, 1799, where he obtained a distinguished reputation for talents, literary acquirements, and piety. He died May 11, 1811, aged 42. His History of his Church, a posthumous publication, and the Massachusetts Historical Collections, Vol. I. p. 256, (Second Series) contain full notices of his character, to which the reader is referred. *Four* of his sons, William, Ralph Waldo, Edward Bliss, and Charles Chauncy, were graduated at Harvard College with distinguished rank.

43. WILLIAM JONES, only son of Samuel Jones, was born September 15, 1772, and graduated in 1793. He read law with Jonathan Fay, Esq., and commenced practice in this town, but removed to Norridgewock, Maine, about 1801. He was appointed, June 29, 1809, clerk of the Court of Common Pleas for the county of Somerset, and on the 23d of April, 1812, clerk of all the courts in that county, and June 22, 1809, Judge of Probate. While resident in Concord he delivered an oration on the 4th of July, 1795, which was published. May 12th of that year he was appointed Captain of a company of cavalry, and April 17, 1799, Major in the 15th regiment of the United States' army stationed at Oxford. On the 27th of March, 1806, after his removal to Maine, he received a commission of Lieutenant-Colonel, and February 21, 1810, of Brigadier-General, in the militia of that state. He died at Norridgewock January 10, 1813, aged 40. His remains were removed, and interred in Concord.

COLLEGE GRADUATES. 251

44. JAMES TEMPLE, son of Benjamin Temple, was born September 20, 1766, and graduated at Dartmouth College in 1794. He taught the grammar-school in Concord in 1795 and 1796, and read law with Jonathan Fay, Esq. He commenced professional business in Cambridge, but died March 10, 1802, aged 35.

45. SAMUEL PHILLIPS' PRESCOTT FAY, son of Jonathan Fay, Esq., was born January 10, 1778, graduated in 1798, was admitted to the bar in 1803, and settled at Cambridge Port. He was appointed Judge of Probate May 1, 1821, and has since filled the office with distinguished ability.

46. RUFUS HOSMER, son of the Hon. Joseph Hosmer, was born March 18, 1778, and graduated in 1800. He was admitted to the bar in Essex in 1803, and soon after removed to Stow, where he has since resided as a counsellor at law.

47. STEPHEN MINOTT, son of Captain Jonas Minott, was born September 28, 1776, graduated in 1801, and settled as a lawyer in Haverhill. He was appointed a judge of the Circuit Court of Common Pleas, and held the office till 1820, when the law which created that Court was repealed. In 1824 he was appointed County Attorney for Essex, which office he resigned in 1830.

48. SAMUEL RIPLEY, son of the Rev. Ezra Ripley, D. D., was born March 11, 1783, graduated in 1804, and was ordained over the first religious society in Waltham November 22, 1809, where he still resides.

49. DANIEL BLISS RIPLEY, brother of the preceding, was graduated in 1805. He was an attorney, and died at St. Stephens, Alabama; April 30, 1825, aged 37.

50. BENJAMIN WARREN HILDRETH, son of Jonathan Hildreth, was born March 29, 1784, graduated in 1805, and settled as a physician in Marlborough.

51. JOHN WHITE, son of Deacon John White, was born December 2, 1787, graduated in 1805, and was ordained over the third parish in Dedham April 20, 1814.

52. JONAS WHEELER, son of Jotham Wheeler, was born February 9, 1789, and graduated in 1810. He read law with Erastus Root, Esq., of Camden, Maine, and settled in the profession in that town. He was justice of the peace, Colonel in the militia, delegate to form the constitution, a representative and a member of the Senate of Maine, of which he was President the two last years of his life. He died May 1, 1826, aged 37.

53. JOHN BARRETT, son of John Barrett, Jr., was born September 30, 1781, and graduated at Williams College in 1810. After obtaining a theological education he was employed by the Evangelical Society, and went to Ohio. He was ordained at Mesopotamia, Trumbull county, Ohio, February 22, 1827.

54. JOSHUA BARRETT, brother to the preceding, was graduated at Dartmouth College in 1810. He studied divinity, and was employed as a preacher and missionary till he was ordained, January 11, 1826, over the Second church in Plymouth near the Manomet Ponds.

55. JOHN BROWN, son of Samuel Brown, was graduated in 1813. He studied physic, but relinquished the profession, and is now a merchant near Buffalo, New York.

56. EPHRAIM BUTTRICK, son of Samuel Buttrick, was graduated in 1819, admitted to the bar in September, 1823, and settled at East Cambridge.

57. BENJAMIN BARRETT, son of Peter Barrett, was born February 2, 1796, graduated in 1819 and at the Cambridge Medical School in course, and settled in Northampton.

58. CHARLES JARVIS, son of Deacon Francis Jarvis, was born November 27, 1800, and graduated in 1821. He studied medicine with Doctors Hurd and Bartlett of Concord, and Shattuck of Boston, and received his medical degree in 1825. He settled in South Bridgwater, where he soon obtained a respectable practice. But in the following July he was attacked with a fatal disease, removed to his father's house, and died February 23, 1826, aged 25.

59. JOHN MILTON CHENEY, son of Hezekiah Cheney, was graduated in 1821. He settled as a lawyer in Concord, and was appointed Cashier of the Concord Bank in April, 1832.

60. GEORGE WASHINGTON HOSMER, son of Cyrus Hosmer, was graduated in 1826, and at the Cambridge Theological School in 1829. He was ordained at Northfield June 9, 1830.

61. EDWARD JARVIS, son of Deacon Francis Jarvis, was graduated in 1826. He studied physic and practised at Northfield, but removed to Concord in 1832.

62. REUBEN BATES, son of Captain John Bates, was born March 20, 1808, graduated in 1829, and at the Theological School in 1832.

63. JONATHAN THOMAS DAVIS, son of Jonathan H. Davis, was graduated in 1829.

64. HORATIO COOK MERRIAM, was graduated in 1829, and is now in the practice of law at Lowell.

65. WILLIAM MACKAY PRICHARD, son of Moses Prichard, was graduated in 1833.

66. WILLIAM WHITING, son of Colonel William Whiting, was graduated in 1833.

Undergraduates. — George Moore, son of Captain Abel Moore; Hiram Barrett Dennis, son of Samuel Dennis; Ebenezer Rockwood Hoar, son of the Hon. Samuel Hoar, members of Harvard University; Marshall Merriam, and Gardner Davis, son of Josiah Davis, of Yale, and Josiah Dudley, of Union College, New York.

JOHN CUMING, was born March 1, 1728. His father, Mr. Robert Cuming, was a distinguished Scotchman who emigrated to this country during the rebellion, about 1715, and, after residing a short time in Boston, removed to this town about 1722, where he spent the remainder of his life in agricultural pursuits. John inherited a large part of his father's estate. After acquiring a good academical education, and going through a regular course of medical studies, he embarked for Europe, where he completed his professional education, and afterwards returned to his native town. He received the honorary degree of Master of Arts at Harvard College in 1749. During the wars which prevailed in America from 1745 to 1763, he was several times called to take an active part. In one of these engagements he was wounded by a ball that lodged in his hip (where it remained till his death), captured by the Indians, and carried into Canada. The Indians at first treated him with severity; but after his remaining with them some time they became friendly, and by the influence of a French gentleman he obtained his liberty. He was out in 1758 and 1759, as Lieutenant-Colonel under Colonel Nichols, and was distinguished for the ability with which he discharged his duty. After the close of the war he acquired an extensive professional practice, in which he continued during life. He was early entrusted with important town affairs, and was often chosen representative in the General Court. At *ninety* of the town-meetings, from 1763 to 1788, he presided as moderator. When the great work of the American revolution commenced, he was one of its firmest advocates. He was chairman of the committee of correspondence, inspection, and safety, almost every year during the war. He received the commission of justice of the peace from the crown, and was one of the first appointed by the Provincial Congress, and was president of the county Court of Sessions about twenty years. By his extensive professional business in this and the neighbouring towns, he acquired a considerable estate which enabled him to make liberal donations to this church and town, Harvard College, and other objects. To the poor he was remarkably benevolent. He regulated his whole life by the precepts of religion, of which he was an exemplary professor about forty-five years, and, it is said, never charged for professional services rendered on the Sabbath. He died suddenly, while on a visit in Chelmsford, July 3, 1788, aged 60.

His benevolent and liberal disposition was manifest in the judicious disposition of his estate. Beside many other legacies, he bequeathed " for the use of the town of Concord *three hundred pounds sterling*, one moiety thereof to be equally distributed for the benefit of the private schools in the town of Concord, and to be especially under the direction of the selectmen for the time being; the other moiety thereof to be annually disposed of among the poor of said town, at the discretion of the minister and selectmen of the town of Concord for the time being, — the use of the above sum of money to be for the above purposes and for no other under any pretence whatever." He also made it the residuary legatee of one quarter of his real estate undisposed of at the death of his wife. The whole amounted to £500 lawful money, or $1,666·66. He gave " to the church in Concord *fifty pounds sterling*, to be laid out in silver vessels to furnish the communion-table "; and also " *twenty-five pounds sterling*, to be for ever kept as a fund " to be disposed of by the minister and deacons for the benefit " of the poor communicants "; and also £20 to the Rev. Dr. Ripley. He bequeathed " to the University in Cambridge *three hundred pounds sterling*, the income of the same to be appropriated for a professor of physic," and also made it a residuary legatee in the same manner as he did the town of Concord.

CHAPTER XVII.

HISTORY OF BEDFORD.

General History. — Ecclesiastical History. — Description. — Miscellaneous Notices.

BEDFORD lies northeasterly from Concord, and, as has already been stated, belonged originally in part to that town. The inhabitants of the Winthrop Farms, which were included in this territory, with others in Billerica, petitioned the General Court, in 1725, to be erected into a separate parish or town. An order of notice passed on this petition, but being opposed by Billerica it was unsuccessful. The following petition fully explains the motives which originated it, and met with more success.

" To the gentlemen the selectmen, and other inhabitants, of Concord in lawful meeting assembled; the petition of sundry of the inhabitants of the northeasterly part of the town of Concord humbly sheweth.

" That we your humble petitioners, having, in conjunction with the southerly part of Billerica, not without good advice, and we hope upon religious principles, assembled in the winter past, and supported the preaching of the gospel among us, cheerfully paying in the mean time our proportion to the ministry in our towns, have very unanimously agreed to address our respective towns to dismiss us, and set us off to be a distinct township or district, if the Great and General Court or Assembly shall favor such our constitution.

" We therefore the subscribers hereunto, and your humble petitioners, do first apply to you to lead us and set us forward in so good a work, which we trust may be much for the glory of Christ and the spiritual benefit of ourselves and our posterity. Our distance from your place of public worship is so great, that we labor under insupportable difficulties in attending constantly there as we desired to do. In the extreme difficult seasons of heat and cold we were ready to say of the Sabbath, Behold what a weariness is it. The extraordinary expenses we are at in transporting and refreshing ourselves and families on the Sabbath has added to our burdens. This we have endured from year to year with as much patience as the nature of the case would bear; but our increasing numbers now seem to plead an exemption; and as it is in your power, so we hope it will be in your grace to relieve us.

"Gentlemen, if our seeking to draw off proceed from any disaffection to our present Rev. Pastor, or the Christian Society with whom we have taken such sweet counsel together, and walked unto the house of God in company, then hear us not this day. But we greatly desire, if God please, to be eased of our burdens on the Sabbath, the travel and fatigue thereof, that the word of God may be nigh to us, near to our houses, and in our hearts, that we and our little ones may serve the Lord. We hope that God, who stirred up the spirit of Cyrus to set forward temple work, has stirred us up to ask, and will stir you up to grant, the prayer of our petition; so shall your humble petitioners ever pray, as in duty bound, &c.

"We humbly desire our limits may be extended from Mr. Stephen Davis's to Mr. Richard Wheeler's and to the river, the line to extend so as to include those two families."

This petition was dated Concord, May 1, 1728, and signed by Joseph French, Joseph Dean, John Fassett, Samuel Merriam, Stephen Davis, Daniel Cheever, Thomas Woolley, Joseph Bacon, Benjamin Colburn, Nathaniel Merriam, Zachariah Stearns, Andrew Wadkins, Jonathan French, David Taylor, Daniel Davis, Richard Wheeler, and James Wheeler; all belonging to Concord.

Concord gave them liberty to be set off; and the General Court passed an act, September 23, 1729, incorporating them as a town by the name of Bedford. The boundaries of the town, as described in this act, were nearly the same as they are at present, excepting the farm of Edward Stearns, which was set off from Billerica and annexed to Bedford by a special act, passed in 1766.

The first town-meeting took place October 6, 1729. The first town officers were, Samuel Fitch, Town Clerk; Jonathan Bacon, Samuel Fitch, Nathaniel Merriam, Nathaniel Page, and Daniel Davis, Selectmen; Israel Putnam and Stephen Davis, Constables; John Fassett, Town Treasurer; Job Lane and Samuel Merriam, Surveyors; Daniel Cheever and Josiah Fassett, Tithingmen; Obed Abbot and Benjamin Colburn, Fence-viewers; James Wheeler and Jonathan Bacon, Hog-reeves; John Lane, Sealer of Weights; and Thomas Woolly and John Whipple, Field-drivers.[1]

After the first organization of the town, there is nothing of peculiar interest to distinguish its civil history anterior to the revolution. It furnished its share of men and money in the intervening French and Indian wars; but the particulars I am unable to obtain. Several of its inhabitants held commissions.

Many facts in relation to the part Bedford acted in the revolution have already been detailed in the history of Concord. Such others as more immediately relate to the proceedings of the town, will now be given.

In March, 1768, the town voted " to encourage the produce and manufactures of this province, and to lessen the use of superfluities." A town meeting was held March 1, 1773, to take " into our most serious consideration the melancholy state of the British colonies in North America in general, and this province in particular," when, " after solemn prayer to God for direction," the subject was referred to a committee, consisting of Deacon Stephen Davis, John Reed, Esq., John Webber, Doctor Joseph Ballard, Mr. John Moore, Mr. Joseph Hartwell, and Mr. Hugh Maxwell. At an adjourned meeting, 23d May, they made a long report, which was unanimously accepted, expressing sentiments similar to those given in the History of Concord.

---

[1] The following were the taxable inhabitants in Bedford in 1748. *South List.* — Samuel Bacon, Stephen Davis, James Dodson, Joseph Fitch, Zachariah Fitch, Peter Fasset, John Fasset, Benjamin Fasset, Stephen Hartwell, Joseph Hartwell, Henry Harrington, William Hastings, James Housten, John Merriam, Amos Merriam, Samuel Merriam, Nathaniel Merriam, John Moore, Joseph Meeds, Walter Powers, Paul Raymond, William Raymond, Edward Stearns, James Rankin, David Taylor, Thomas Woolly, Jonathan Woolly, Thomas Woolly, Jr., Richard Wheeler, Samuel Whitaker.

North List. — Obed Abbot, Josiah Bacon, Josiah Bacon, Jr., Benjamin Bacon, Michael Bacon, John Bacon, Thomas Bacon, Jonas Bowman, James Chambers, John Corbet, Samuel Dutton, Benjamin Danforth, Cornelius Dandley, Benjamin Fitch, Jeremiah Fitch, Josiah Fasset, Jonathan Grimes, Benjamin Hutchinson, Timothy Hartwell, Benjamin Kidder, Deacon Job Lane, Colonel John Lane, Captain James Lane, John Lane, Jr., Job Lane, Jr., John Lane, 3d, Timothy Lane.

In March, 1774, it was voted not to use any tea till the duty was taken off; and on the 30th of June following the inhabitants of the town entered into a solemn covenant " to suspend all commercial intercourse with Great Britain till the said act should be repealed," — not to " buy, purchase, or consume, or suffer any person by, for, or under us, to purchase or consume, in any manner whatever, any goods, wares, or merchandise, which shall arrive in America from Great Britain," and to break off all " trade, commerce, or dealings " with those who do it, and to consider them as enemies to their country. This covenant was offered to all the inhabitants of the town for their signatures. Those who did not sign it were to be treated as enemies. At this meeting the first committee of correspondence was chosen, consisting of Deacon Stephen Davis, John Reed, Esq., Mr. Joseph Hartwell, John Webber, and John Moore.

A minute-company being formed, the town voted, 6th March, 1775, to allow 25 men " *one shilling* per week till the first of May, they exercising four hours in a week, and *two shillings* to be allowed to officers, they to equip themselves according to the advice of Congress." Jonathan Wilson was Captain of this company, and was killed on the retreat of the British from Concord on the 19th of April, in the 41st year of his age. He was a brave and meritorious officer.

The town voted, June 17, 1776, that " we will solemnly engage with our lives and fortunes to support the colonies in declaring themselves independent of Great Britain."

Bedford, like the neighbouring towns, contributed " her lives and fortunes " to obtain the independence of America. Though I cannot give a full view of what was actually done, a few facts taken from the town records, in addition to what has already been given in the History of Concord, will present the most favorable view of her patriotism.

November 24, 1777, the town raised £377 3s. 3d. to pay the following bounties to soldiers for services performed that year, as reported by a committee.

For the Continental soldiers' hire . . £236 10s. 0d.
For the bounty to the Rhode Island men   22 10 0
For the bounty to the men who went to Bennington 48 0 0
For one man to guard the Continental stores   6 0 0

GENERAL HISTORY. 259

For three 30 day men to join the Continental army	24 0 0
For allowance for hiring the Continental men	4 11 0
For fire-arms, lead, and flints for a town stock	35 12 3
	£377 3 3

November 16, 1778, the town allowed the accounts of the military officers and committee for hiring soldiers, amounting to £1746 16s. 3d. The following bounties for services the year previous were also allowed.

3 men, 2 months to Rhode Island, May 1, 1777,	no bounty
8 men, 3½ months to Bennington, August 21, 1777, each £15	£120 0s. 0d.
8 men, 30 days, "to take and guard the troops," September, 1777, £2	16 0 0
5 men, 3 months, "to Boston with Captain Farmer," February 1778, £12	60 0 0
8 men, 3 months, "to Cambridge with Captain Moore," April 1, 1778, £11	88 0 0
John Reed, to Rhode Island	9 0 0

The next year, in November, 1779, the following bounties were allowed.

1st tour of duty to Rhode Island, 2 men, £39 each	£78 0s. 0d.
2d to Rhode Island, 2 men, 48 bushels of corn, £9 per bushel each	864 0 0
3d to North River, 3 men, 2 of whom to have £300 each	600 0 0
The other to have £138 in cash, and 51 bushels of corn at £9 per bushel	587 0 0
4th to Boston, 2 men, £22, 10 each	45 0 0
5th to Claverick, 6 men 1⅓ month, £80 per month	640 0 0

In September, 1780, the town raised £550 to pay for hiring soldiers in the United States' service for the two last campaigns. In June previous, seven men, John Johnson, Rufus Johnson, Nathan Merrill, Jonas Bacon, Cambridge Moore, Jonas Duren, Cesar Prescott, had been hired to go to the North River 6 months for a bounty of 120 bushels of corn each; and 8 men, Joshua Holt, John Webber, Ebenezer Hardy, Amos Bemis, Jonathan Wilson, Andrew Hall, Isaac Simonds, and Israel Mead Blood, were hired for 3 months to Rhode Island for 90 bushels of corn each.

By the resolve of December 2, 1780, Bedford was required to furnish 8 men. One was hired by the town for $200 in silver; and the town was divided into 7 classes to procure the others. Captain John Moore was chairman of the first class, Moses Abbot of the second, Thaddeus Dean of the third, Christopher Page of the fourth, John Reed of the fifth, William Page of the sixth, and Stephen Davis of the seventh. The first five classes paid "20 head of horned cattle at 3 years old each," as a bounty; the 6th paid $250, and the 7th $220, in silver!

Daniel Hartwell Blood went to Rhode Island in June, 1781, and received £19 10s. in silver; and Nehemiah Wyman, Moses Abbot, Stephen Syms, Timothy Crosby, Joseph Merriam, and Israel Mead Blood went to join General Washington's army at West Point, and received £19 16s. each. The town was divided again in March, 1782, into three classes to hire 3 men for the war.

When it is recollected that the town then contained only about 470 inhabitants, it is truly wonderful that they could submit to so frequent and so heavy burdens of pecuniary and personal service.

In September, 1776, the town voted, that the General Court might form a constitution, but they must furnish a copy to the town before it was enacted. In May, 1779, voted, 34 to 1, not to have a new constitution formed at this time. The constitution formed that year was approved by the town, after considering it at three successive meetings, by 25 to 1. In 1820, the town unanimously voted to instruct their representative to vote in favor of calling a state convention to revise the constitution. On the question of adopting the new constitution, articles 2d, 3d, 6th, 7th, 8th, 11th, 13th, and 14th, had no votes against them; the 1st had 3; the 4th, 5; the 5th, 30; the 9th, 14; the 10th, 55 (all that were cast); and the 12th, 13.

ECCLESIASTICAL HISTORY.

The people began to erect a meeting-house before the town was incorporated; but it was not completed till 1730. In October, 1729, £460 was raised to pay the expense. Committees were chosen the next and many subsequent years " to seat the meeting-house," and were instructed, among other things, " to have respect to them that are 50 years of age and upward " ; those under this age " to be seated according to their pay," — " the front seat in the gallery to be equal to the third seat in the body-seats below." Thirteen pews were built in 1733, and eight more in 1754. A bell was procured in 1753, weighing about 600 lbs. and the town " voted (by polling the assembly) to hang the bell about two rods and a half northward of the school-house, and as near to Mr. Benjamin Kidder's wall as can be with conveniency ; and to build a house, not less than 12 feet nor more than 16 feet square, and so high as to hang the mouth of the bell 16 feet high."

A new meeting-house was erected in 1817. It is 58 feet long, 53 wide, and 30 feet posts, with a projection of 34 by 8 feet, and a spire. David Reed, Michael Crosby, John Merriam, Joshua Page, and Simeon Blodget, were the building committee ; and Joshua Page and Levi Wilson, the builders. Cost estimated at $6,101. The lower floor has 56 pews, and the gallery 16, which were sold for $7,110·50, after reserving one for the minister. It was dedicated July 8, 1817 ; and the sermon, preached by the Rev. Mr. Stearns on the occasion, was printed. A time-piece was presented to the town by Mr. Jeremiah Fitch of Boston, and placed in the front gallery ; and a new bell was procured from England, weighing 993 lbs.

Measures were taken soon after the incorporation of the town to obtain the regular enjoyment of public religious worship and ordinances, and William Hartwell and Job Lane chosen to carry these measures into effect. A candidate was employed ; and January 22, 1730, was observed as a day of solemn fasting and prayer to God for direction in the choice of a minister, when the Rev. Messrs. John Hancock of Lexington, Samuel Ruggles of Billerica, and John Whiting of Concord were present to conduct the religious services. Feb. 11th, the town chose Mr. Nicholas Bowes, by 43 votes, to be their minister ; and at the subsequent March meeting agreed to give him £90 the first year, and £100 and 25 cords of wood annually afterwards as a salary, so long as he should sustain the pastoral office ; the money to be paid semi-annually, and always to be in proportion to the then value of silver, which was 18 shillings per ounce. He was subsequently presented with 16 acres of land. These propositions were accepted, and he was ordained, July 15, 1730, when the church was organized. The churches in Lexington, Concord, Billerica, and Cambridge, by "their elders and messengers," composed the council, of which the Rev. John Hancock was moderator. In the public religious exercises, the Rev. Mr. Appleton of Cambridge made the introductory prayer; the Rev. John Hancock preached from 2 Cor. xi. 28, and gave the charge; the Rev. John Whiting gave the right hand of fellowship; and the Rev. Samuel Ruggles made the last prayer.

While the church was making arrangements preliminary to its organization, it was agreed by a vote of 14 to 9, that "every person admitted to the church should give in a confession of their faith to be read in public"; and, by a vote of 15 to 7, not to call for a "handy vote" on their admission. The original covenant which follows, was adopted and signed by 24 individuals, — all the male members of the church at its formation.

"We, whose names are underwritten, sensibly acknowledging our unworthiness of such a favor and unfitness for such a business, yet apprehending ourselves to be called of God in a way of church communion, and to seek the settlement of all the gospel institutions among us, do therefore, in order thereto and for the better promotion thereof as much as in us lies, knowing how prone we are to backslide, abjuring all confidence in ourselves, and relying on the Lord Jesus Christ alone for help, covenant as follows.

"We believe the Scriptures of the Old and New Testament to be given by inspiration of God, and promise by the help of the Divine Spirit, to govern ourselves both as to faith and practice according to that perfect rule; and we also engage to walk together as a church of Christ, according to all those holy rules of the gospel respecting a particular church of Christ, so far as God hath or shall reveal his mind to us in that respect.

"We do accordingly recognise the covenant of grace, in which we professedly acknowledge ourselves devoted to the fear and service of the only true God, our Supreme Lord, and the Lord Jesus Christ, the High Priest, Prophet, and King of his church, unto whose conduct we submit ourselves, on whom alone we wait and hope for grace and glory, to whom we bind ourselves in an everlasting covenant never to be broken.

"We likewise give ourselves up one to another in the Lord, resolving by his help to treat each the other as fellow members of one body in brotherly love and holy watchfulness over one another for mutual edification; and to subject ourselves to all the holy administrations, appointed by him who is the Head of his church, dispensed according to the rules of the gospel, and to give our constant attendance on all the public ordinances of Christ's institution, walking orderly as becomes saints.

"We do likewise acknowledge our posterity to be included with us in the gospel covenant; and, blessing God for such a favor, do promise to bring them up in the nurture and admonition of the Lord with the greatest care, and to acknowledge them in the covenant relation, according to the rules of the gospel.

"Furthermore we promise to be careful to our uttermost to procure the settlement and continuance of all the offices and officers appointed by Christ, the chief Shepherd for his church's edification, and accordingly do our duty faithfully for their maintenance and encouragement, and to carry it towards them as becometh us.

"Finally we acknowledge and do promise to preserve communion with the faithful churches of Christ for the giving and receiving mutual council and assistance in all cases wherein it shall be needful.

"Now the good Lord be merciful unto us, and, as he hath put it into our hearts thus to devote ourselves to him, let him pity and pardon our frailties, humble us out of all carnal confidence, and keep it for ever upon our hearts to himself and to one another for his praise, and our eternal comfort, for Christ's sake, to whom be glory for ever. Amen. — Nicholas Bowes, *Joseph French, *William Hartwell, Jonathan Bacon, *John Hartwell, *Nathaniel Merriam, Israel Putnam, Benjamin Kidder, *Daniel Davis, Samuel Fitch, Job Lane, *Josiah Fassett, John Lane, *Stephen Davis, *Richard Wheeler, Jacob Kendall, Christopher Page, *Daniel Cheever, Obed Abbot, Nathaniel Page, *David Taylor, *James Wheeler, *Eleazer Davis, Thomas Dinsmore."[1]

---

[1] Those marked with an asterisk were from Concord, the others probably mostly from Billerica. The church and town records of those towns give their genealogy.

The sacrament was first administered September 6, 1730, and every two months afterwards, at which times collections were taken for the use of the church. November 12, 1730, being public thanksgiving, £7 were contributed. " A short time after, the good people of Concord contributed for the use of the church in Bedford £6." Mr. Isaac Stearns, widows Sarah Bateman, and Eunice Taylor gave 10 shillings each. The last left a legacy of £5 more, and Deacon Merriam one of £6.

Among the peculiar customs which prevailed in the church from its first formation to the ordination of Mr. Stearns, was that of making public confession of particular offences committed by the members. These were drawn up in writing and read by the minister before the congregation. Frequent notices under different dates are specified in the church records, such as " the confession of ——— for the sin of intemperance," " for the breach of the seventh commandment," or other sins as the case might be, " was read before the congregation." This custom, though particularly revolting at the present day, was not peculiar to the church in Bedford. It prevailed to some extent in most of the colonial churches. But that a detail of one's own crimes, given in minute particulars before the public, even if publicly known, tends to reform the heart of the confessor, or promote the good morals of the people, is a proposition to which few will now assent.

It does not appear that any special attention to religion prevailed during the ministry of Mr. Bowes, as was then the case in Concord and some other places ; though the church received considerable yearly additions, and was in a flourishing state. Anterior to 1754, 161 individuals had belonged to the church ; and allowing the orignal members to have been 50, the admissions would be 111. To this time there had been 83 marriages, 350 baptisms, and 173 deaths.

The Rev. Nicholas Bowes is said to have been born in England. He was graduated at Harvard College in 1725. After sustaining the pastoral office about 24 years, some circumstances occurred which induced him to consider his usefulness at an end, and to ask a dismission. This was granted by the church August 22, 1754, and by the town, September 2d. In 1755 he went as a chaplain in the Northern army at Fort Edward ; but died at

Brookfield on his return home. He is represented to have been "a man respectable for his abilities and learning, and of sound evangelical sentiments." Mr. Bowes married Lucy, sister of the Rev. Jonas Clark of Lexington, and aunt of Governor Hancock, and had William, Lucy, Nicholas, Elizabeth, Dorcas, Thomas, and Mary, one of whom married the Rev. Samuel Cook of West Cambridge.

The town voted, September 29, 1755, "that the church should proceed to the choice of a gospel minister"; and on the 17th of November, "to concur in the choice of Mr. Nathaniel Sherman by 38 yeas," and agreed to give him £113 6s. 8d. as a settlement, and £53 6s. 8d. and 20 cords of wood as an annual salary. He was ordained February 18, 1756.

Some years after the settlement of the Rev. Mr. Sherman, a controversy arose concerning admitting persons to the privileges of baptism only, without admission to the communion, by assenting to the "half-way covenant." November 6, 1765, the regulations for the admission of members were revised, and a vote was passed, "that there should be but one church covenant." Candidates for admission to the communion were to be examined before the pastor only, who propounded them several days before admission, when he informed the church of "their knowledge, experience, and belief of religion." Faith in Christ, repentance for sin, holiness, and a belief in the Assembly's Catechism, were required of all candidates. If no objections were made, they were to be admitted without the vote of the church. The covenant was revised and adopted in a different form, principally effected by the influence of the pastor. Some of the alterations were unpopular with a majority of the church. In consequence of this controversy the affections of his people were alienated from Mr. Sherman. An ecclesiastical council was called December 5, 1766, who advised his dismission, which was accepted by the church, and concurred in by the town December 17th.

The Rev. Nathaniel Sherman was born at Newton, March 5, 1724. His father, William Sherman, was son of Joseph, and grandson of Captain John Sherman, who came from Dedham, England, to Watertown, in 1634 or 1635. His brothers were William Sherman, Esq. of New Milford, the Hon. Roger Sherman of New Haven, Connecticut, and the Rev. Josiah Sherman of Woburn. He was graduated at Nassau Hall in 1753. During his ministry of about twelve years, 46 were admitted to the church. In the unhappy controversy, which resulted in Mr. Sherman's dismission, nothing occurred that affected his religious character. After leaving Bedford he was installed at Mount Carmel, New Haven, Connecticut, where he preached many years, and then took a dismission, and removed to East Windsor, where he died July 18, 1797, aged 73 years. He married Lydia, daughter of Deacon Merriam of Bedford, March 1, 1759.

After Mr. Sherman's dismission several meetings were held to agree on the terms of communion. April 4, 1768, it was voted, "that this church will have but one covenant, and therefore require the same qualifications in all; yet if any person can desire to enter into covenant and receive baptism for himself or children, and yet fears to approach the Lord's table at present, he shall be received, he promising, (though he come not immediately to the Lord's table) that he will submit himself to the watch and discipline of this church." The other regulations of the church, though revised, were not materially varied from those already noticed. During the interval till the ordination of Mr. Sherman's successor, 28 persons were baptized, and 7 joined the church in full communion.

On the 7th of September, 1767, the church chose the Rev. Josiah Thacher, a graduate of Nassau Hall in 1760, to be their minister, and the town agreed to give him £120 settlement, and £60 as his annual salary. But before the application could be regularly made to him, he received and accepted a call at Gorham.

February 18, 1768, the church made a second attempt to settle a minister, and chose unanimously (by 22 votes) the Rev. Joseph Willard. The town concurred, and voted the same salary as to Mr. Thacher, excepting that when he should be unable to supply the pulpit, he was to receive but £30. Before the terms of his settlement were finally agreed upon, he declined being considered a candidate.[1]

In the next attempt the church did not proceed with much harmony. A majority were in favor of Mr. John Emerson of

---

[1] The Rev. Joseph Willard was a native of Grafton, was graduated at Harvard College in 1765, ordained at Mendon, April 19, 1769, dismissed December 14, 1782, and installed at Boxborough, November 2, 1785. He died in September, 1828, aged 86.

Malden, but "for peace sake," Mr. Asa Dunbar, "a young candidate newly begun to preach," was employed for a month. At length, August 22, 1769, the church chose Mr. Emerson by 18 votes, and the town concurred, and voted him £133 settlement, and £66 13*s.* 4*d.* salary. "But there was such an opposition in the town against Mr. Emerson settling here (though without any charge against his character either in doctrine or morals), that he was constrained to give the church and town a denial."

The next trial succeeded. Mr. Joseph Penniman was chosen, January 15, 1771, by 29 out of 31 votes, and the choice concurred in by the town. His salary was the same as was voted to Mr. Emerson. He was ordained May 22, 1771. The 'council consisted of the second church in Braintree, the second in Cambridge, the first in Woburn, and the churches in Billerica, Lincoln, Lexington, and Concord. The Rev. Mr. Sherman of Woburn made the first prayer; the Rev. Mr. Weld of Braintree preached from 2 Tim. ii. 2; the Rev. Mr. Cook of West Cambridge gave the charge; the Rev. Mr. Clark of Lexington made the last prayer; and the Rev. Mr. Lawrence gave the right hand of fellowship. The town voted, "that the day should be religiously observed agreeably to the solemnity of the occasion, that they were determined, as much as in them lay, to prevent all levity, profaneness, music, dancing, frolicking, and all other disorders."

After about twenty years, during which 42 persons were admitted to full communion, and 190 baptized, objections were brought against Mr. Penniman, and referred to a council, consisting of the churches in Waltham, Chelsea, East Sudbury, Billerica, Weston, and Charlestown. It met October 29, 1793, and, after three days' session, advised a separation. This was complied with by the church and town; and he was dismissed November 1, 1793.

The Rev. Joseph Penniman was born in Braintree, and graduated at Harvard College in 1765. After his dismission he removed to Harvard, where he died. Though possessed of respectable talents, he was very eccentric in his manners and public performances. His prayers were more like a familiar conversation with a fellow being than an address to Deity. Many of his expressions, more marked than the following, are still recollected by his people. On a certain occasion, when a plentiful rain had come after a drought, he said, "We prayed, O Lord, for rain, but we do not wish thou shouldest leave the bottles of heaven unstopped." Soon after the 19th of April, 1775, he is said to have used the expression, — "We pray thee to send the British soldiers where they will do some good; for thou knowest, O Lord, that we have no use for them about here!"

December 5, 1793, was kept as a fast by the church and town. The Rev. Messrs. Litchfield, Cummings, Ripley, Marrett, and Clark assisted in the public religious services on the occasion. The Rev. Samuel Stearns was chosen December 17, 1795, by the church, and December 28th by the town; having preached his first sermon in Bedford the 13th of the previous September. He was ordained April 27, 1796. The churches in Lexington, Billerica, second in Woburn, Concord, Lincoln, Carlisle, second in Andover, Epping, Chelmsford, and the Rev. Drs. Willard and Tappan of Cambridge, composed the council. The Rev. Mr. Stearns of Lincoln made the first prayer; the Rev. Mr. French of Andover preached from Isaiah xlix. 5; the Rev. Mr. Marrett of Woburn made the ordaining prayer; the Rev. Mr. Clark of Lexington gave the charge; the Rev. Mr. Cummings of Billerica gave the right hand of fellowship; and the Rev. Dr. Tappan made the closing prayer. The town agreed to give the Rev. Mr. Stearns $850 settlement, and $333·33 salary to be stated on the following articles: — corn 666 mills, and rye 833 mills per bushel; beef $4·166 per hundred weight, and pork 55 mills per pound; one quarter of the salary in each of the above articles. In 1811 a new contract was made, and the salary fixed at $560 and 20 cords of wood annually.

The confession of faith and the covenant were revised in 1798, and printed in 1821. The church then contained 105 members, of whom 40 were males and 65 females. In 1829 there were 140.

The Rev. Samuel Stearns, son of the Rev. Josiah Stearns, was born at Epping, New Hampshire, April 8, 1770, and graduated at Harvard College in 1794. His ministry has generally been remarkably peaceful and happy. It is only within the last two years that the town gave any decided indications towards a division of the religious society, after the example of many of her neighbours. In 1832 this division was made, and a new meeting house erected for Mr. Stearns.

SUCCESSION OF THE DEACONS.

Names.	Time of Birth.	Election.	Death.	Age.
Israel Putnam,	—— ——	Aug. 4, 1730.	Nov. 12, 1760.	62
Nathaniel Merriam,	Dec. 10, 1672.	Aug. 4, 1730.	Dec. 11, 1738.	66
Job Lane,	June 20, 1689.	Feb. 11, 1739.	Aug. 9, 1762.	74
Benjamin Bacon,	Dec. 6. 1713.	Feb. 19, 1759.	Oct. 1, 1791.	78
Stephen Davis,	Nov. 6, 1715.	Dec. 29, 1760.	July 22, 1787.	72
James Wright,	born in Woburn.	Sept. 1, 1785.	Dec. 24, 1818.	73
William Merriam,	—— ——	May 16, 1796.	removed from office.	
Moses Fitch,	March 3, 1775.	June 10, 1805.	Oct. 12, 1825.	71
Michael Crosby,	born in Billerica.	July 15, 1817.	—— ——	
Zebedee Simonds,	born in Woburn.	Jan. 1826.	Sept. 20, 1826.	40
Amos Hartwell,	—— ——	Nov. 21, 1826.	—— ——	

MISCELLANEOUS NOTICES.

Bedford is not very well situated for an agricultural town. About half of it is meadow land, unimproved and partly incapable of improvement. It contains, however, several very good farms, and nearly all the varieties of soil. Among the peculiarities of its geology is found a substance which has been used for painting, resembling yellow ochre, and commonly known as Bedford Yellow. It has not, however, been much used of late years. Lead has been found here.

The *Shawsheen* is the only considerable stream of water. It rises in Lincoln, and runs through Bedford in a northerly direction, receiving *Elm Brook*, which arises in Concord, *Farley Brook*, which arises in Lexington, and another which arises in Burlington. On the Shawsheen is a mill which was built before Philip's war in 1676, and was then owned by Michael Bacon, who was allowed to have two garrison soldiers stationed there for his safety.

Bedford is bounded westerly by Concord River, which separates it from Concord and Carlisle; southerly by Lincoln and Lexington; easterly by Lexington and Burlington; and northerly by Billerica. The lines are very irregular, and contain many angles.

In 1765 it contained 67 houses, 72 families, and 457 inhabitants, of whom 201 were males, 240 females, and 16 negroes. In 1800 it contained 538 inhabitants; in 1810, 592; in 1820, 648; and in 1830, 685.

The town contained in 1831, according to the return of the assessors, 8,593 acres of land. There were then 194 polls, 20 of whom were not taxed, 101 dwelling-houses, 3 shops adjoining, 16 other shops, 101 barns, 51 out-buildings, 295 acres of tillage land, 374 English mowing, 1405 fresh meadow, 2228 pasture, 784 wood land, 2,375 unimproved. There were raised 5,025 bushels of corn, 308 of rye, 50 of oats, 20 of barley, 364 tons of English hay, 689 of meadow; 486 cows.

Appropriations made by the Town at different Periods.

	1740	1750	1760	1770	1780	1790	1800	1810	1820	1830
Schools	£10	£20	—	£20	—	£40	$300	$400	$400	$300
Incidental		65	12	31	100	1000	—	300	300	500	900
Highways		60	15	30	20	1000	50	467	800	500	652
Price of Labor	6s.	2s. 4d.	2s.	2s.	£4 10s.	3s.	1	1	1	1

The *Page Fund*, for the support of the gospel ministry and sacred music, was constituted as follows: Anna Page, widow of Thomas Page, gave $663·93, William Page, $500, and Samuel Hartwell, $300. It is to be increased by adding one sixth of the income to the principal annually, and now amounts to upwards of $1,700.

Schools. — The first school was opened in 1733, and £5, equal to about 3 dollars, granted for its support. A committee was chosen the next year to hire a master to "settle a moving school." For several years one school only was kept, sometimes in the centre and sometimes in different parts of the town. A school-house was first built in 1743. In 1744 a part of the money was divided into four quarters, to be expended for the use of schools by "school dames." In 1758 a writing-school was kept four months in the centre of the town, and "a woman's teaching school six months in the quarters of the town;" in 1781 three months' writing-school in the middle of the town, and six weeks' women's school in each of the quarters. In 1790 the town voted to hire a master four months, and should "he have a very full school, he shall principally attend to those who write and cypher." In 1792 the town was divided into *five* districts,

Centre, East, West, North, and South, and in 1799 a school-house was erected in each district. In 1818 the town voted, that the money raised for the support of schools should be divided as follows. In proportion to $7,307, the Centre district shall draw $1,640, the East $1,550, the North $1,420, the South $1,400, and the West $1,297. This method has since been continued.

A building for a town-house and Centre school-house was erected in 1828 at an expense of $2,216·43. A fire-engine, which cost $482·32, was procured about that time.

Employment. — Agriculture is the employment of a large portion of the people. The manufacture of shoes for the Boston market was begun here in 1805 by John Hosmer and Jonathan Bacon, and has been increasing since under their management and that of others. The principal establishments in 1832 were owned by Reuben Bacon, Esq. and Mr. Chamberlain, in which were employed 60 men and 80 women. About 90,000 pairs of shoes, estimated to be worth $50,000, are made annually. This business has been the source of considerable wealth to the town. No shoes are in better credit than those made in Bedford. About 4,000 sets of "Bacon's Patent Lever Blind Fasteners" were made in Bedford in 1832, and it is the most approved article of the kind with which I am acquainted.

Individuals who have received a Public Education.

1. DAVID LANE, son of James Lane, was graduated in 1753, and went into the French war, in which he died.

2. JOB LANE, son of Job Lane, Jr., was graduated at Yale College in 1764. The following epitaph appears on the stone over his remains in New Haven.

"Siste Viator.
Hic juxta situs est
D. JOB LANE, A. M. Col. Yal. Tutor,
Vir ingenio, modestia, literis, atque pietate
præclarus.
Illum Bedfordi natum Massachus^m. An. 1741
Literarum a puero avidissimum fuisse ;
Studiis academicis præ cæteris eminuisse ;
Evangelium studiose triennium prædicasse,
Tutorisque officio biennium fideliter functum ;
Parentibus vixisse charissimum,
Amicis, omnibusque pietatis fautoribus dilectum,

> Discipulisque vero honoratum ;
> Et omnibus maxime defletum ;
> e vita migrasse Sept^s. 16. An^o. 1768 ;
> Hic tumulus brevi interiturus
> tibi declarat."

3. OLIVER WELLINGTON LANE, son of Captain James Lane, was graduated in 1772, and was a distinguished schoolmaster in Boston where he died.

4. JAMES CONVERS, son of Josiah Convers, was graduated in 1799, and is now a minister at Weathersfield, Vermont.

5. SAMUEL HORATIO STEARNS, son of the Rev. Samuel Stearns, was born September 12, 1801, and graduated in 1823, and at the Theological Seminary at Andover in 1828.

6. WILLIAM AUGUSTUS STEARNS, brother of the preceding, was born March 17, 1805, graduated in 1827, and at the Theological Seminary in Andover in 1831, and was ordained at Cambridge Port December 13, 1831.

7. JONATHAN FRENCH STEARNS, brother of the two preceding, was born September 4, 1808, and graduated in 1830. He is now a student in Theology.

8. EDWARD JOSIAH STEARNS, son of Elijah Stearns, Esq., was born February 24, 1810, and graduated in 1833.

Physicians.

Dr. JOHN FASSETT, who came from Harvard, was the first physician. He died January 30, 1737, aged 66.

Dr. JOSEPH BALLARD came from Lancaster to Bedford in 1767, and died there January 29, 1777. He was a delegate to the Provincial Congress in Concord in 1774, and was a distinguished man.

Dr. AMARIAH PRESTON from Uxbridge came to Bedford about 1790, and is now living there.

Among other physicians who have practised for short periods in Bedford, the names of Dr. Stephen Massy, Dr. Kendall, Dr. Gardner, and Dr. Kittredge, may be mentioned.

Justices of the Peace.

John Reed, Elijah Stearns, Amariah Preston, Thompson Bacon, William Webber, John Merriam, and Reuben Bacon.

Representatives.

When the year is not specified, the town was not represented.

John Reed, 1776, 1783; John Moore, 1780; John Webber, 1787; David Reed, 1805, 1806, 1808; William Webber, 1809–1811, 1821, 1823, 1824, 1827–1829; Thompson Bacon, 1812; John Merriam, 1813, 1814, 1816, 1818, 1830, 1831; Amos Heartwell, 1832.

Dr. Joseph Ballard and John Reed, Esq., were delegates to the Provincial Congress at Concord in October, 1774.

John Reed was delegate to Cambridge in February, 1775, and to the Convention to form the Constitution in 1779.

Town Clerks.

Samuel Fitch, 1729–1731, 1733–1737; John Fassett, 1732; Israel Putnam, 1738–1745; John Whitmore, 1746–1748; Stephen Davis, 1748–1760, 1766–1772, 1775; John Reed, 1761–1765, 1773–1775; John Webber, 1776–1779, 1783–1793; William Merriam, 1780–1782, 1794–1804; William Webber, 1805–1829; Reuben Bacon, 1830.

CHAPTER XVIII.

HISTORY OF ACTON.

General History. — Ecclesiastical History. — Description. — Miscellaneous Notices.

THE town of Acton lies wholly within the ancient limits of Concord. It does not, however, include any part of the six miles square first purchased of the Indians, but in subsequent grants and purchases, adjoining and lying westerly of the "old town." These lands were granted to the town of Concord " for feeding"; excepting the Iron-Work Farm, Major Simon Willard's farm in the north part of the tract, and two grants near Nagog Pond, one to the Indians, and the other to Joseph Wheeler and others. An account of these grants has already been given in the History of Concord. Their bounds, as renewed in 1706, began where the present southeast corner of Acton meets with Concord and Sudbury, and ran nearly on the present line separating Acton and Stow, Boxborough and Littleton, till it comes to the "westerly end of Nagog Pond," and from thence "up to the line of Chelmsford towards Tagnack," (near the Heartwell tavern now in Westford); from thence the line ran easterly to the north part of "Virginia Meadow," or "Blood's Dam," so called in Carlisle; and thence by Billerica to "Berry Corner," and by Concord old bounds to the place first mentioned. Though the bounds or extent of the several grants which make up this extensive tract of land, are not very particularly defined, the description is sufficiently accurate to enable us to form a tolerably correct idea of each. When actually surveyed, they were found to contain a greater number of acres than nominally specified in the grants. The section lying in the southeast part of the "Village," as it was then called, nominally containing 1,000 acres, but actually containing more than that number, was granted to Major Willard for the benefit of the Iron Works, and known as the Iron-Work Farm. This was conveyed to James Russell, Esq. of Charlestown, when Mr. Joseph Sherman was employed as an assistant in the business, and by him 600 acres of it were sold in 1701 to Samuel and Ephraim Jones, and Jonathan Knight, together with all his right in the Village, for £150. This tract and another northerly, conveyed by deeds from the Indians in 1684 already given,[1] the grants to Joseph Wheeler in 1660, to Major Willard in 1655 in the north part, and the half of Nashoba purchased by the Hon. Peter Bulkeley and the Hon. Thomas Henchman in 1686, covered much more land than is now included in Acton. Littleton took a part near Nagog Pond, and Westford and Carlisle a large tract in the north and northeasterly sections. Considerable difficulty arose between the proprietors of the Village and the proprietors of individual grants, included in the above described lands, concerning their boundary lines. The heirs of Robert Blood inherited the Willard farm. Their title was however doubted, and, after perplexing controversies and lawsuits, it was finally adjusted about 1710.

A settlement was commenced in these grants as early as 1656, and perhaps a few years earlier. The Shepherd and Law families were among the first. Captain Thomas Wheeler commenced an extensive improvement here in 1668, as noticed in the History of Concord.[2] Several others also had particular lots granted or sold to them by special vote of the town.

Many of the meadows were open prairies, and afforded, with little or no labor, grass in abundance. Some of the uplands had been cleared by the Indians, and were favorite places for feeding. The meadows were leased, and the rents either paid into the town treasury, or reserved for the proprietors. In 1706 the meadows were leased to Jonathan Knight and Ephraim Jones for £5 6s., and about the same sum was annually received for them for some years afterwards.

These lands were granted to the proprietors of the town of Concord at the time the grants were made. And, though the selectmen, under direction of the town, managed them as they did other common property, they were considered distinct from the whole town from about 1690. New emigrants into Concord were not considered as proprietors. In 1697 a committee was chosen to obtain a list of the proprietors, who, after several con-

---

[1] See pages 41, 42.   [2] See page 43.

sultations concerning the best method of admitting them, proposed, June 29, 1702, "that every freeholder that was possessed of house and land in the year 1684, and makes it so appear, shall be added to the former proprietors." The proprietors, as admitted by the committee according to the above regulation, were generally accustomed to hold their meetings immediately after the town meetings, and on the same day, from 1698 to 1710; and their proceedings were recorded by the town clerk with the proceedings of Concord. A Village clerk was first chosen in 1710.

The disposal of these lands, and the manner in which they should be divided, occupied the attention of the proprietors for many years. Meetings were held on the 16th of June, 1719, legally summoned by James Minott, Esq., on the 9th, 22d, and 29th of March, and on the 8th of July, 1720, at which several votes were passed, one of which was to admit persons who were freeholders in town in 1684 to rights in proportion to 1 to 3 of the freeholders in 1661; and committees were chosen to obtain lists of the proprietors agreeably to this vote; and to divide the meadows into 120 thirty-acre lots. As these committees proceeded in their business, so many obstacles presented themselves, that the plan was finally relinquished. Another vote was passed to divide it in proportion as 1 to 2 for the times abovementioned, but this was also unsuccessful.

At length a petition was preferred to the town of Concord, which resulted in the following proceedings.

"We the subscribers being chosen a committee by the town of Concord at a general meeting on May the 25th, 1722, continued by adjournment from the 15th of said month, to consider and make report what we think is proper for the said town to do about their Village or New Grant, report as follows.

"1. We find the grant from the General Court, as also the Indian deeds of conveyance from the Indians were made to the inhabitants and proprietors of the town of Concord.

"2. We find no act of the said town of Concord, in any town meeting legally warned for that purpose, that has fully settled the proprietors or altered the constitution thereof, but considerable to the contrary.

"We are therefore humbly of opinion as followeth.

"1. That the town pass an order to forbid all persons cutting wood, timber, &c., on the Village without order, and that the town do forthwith proceed and choose a committee, and fully empower them to prosecute at the law all persons that do any ways trespass on their said New Grants by cutting wood or timber contrary to order.

"2. That the town choose a committee to enquire into the matter of a farm-grant made out of the premises to Mr. Joseph Wheeler, whether the present proprietors thereof have not incroached and come beyond their bounds, and to make report.

"3. That the town, as soon as may be, settle the proprietors of the premises, and in order thereunto do choose a committee to consider of and report under their hands unto the town, what they think is the most just, honest, and safe rule, for stating the proprietors and dividing thereof, and present it to the town for their further consideration."

This document is dated November 12, 1722, and signed by Richard Parks, John Wheeler, Nathaniel Stow, Samuel Wright, Samuel Chandler, John Fassett, and David Whitaker.

The committee proposed in this report were chosen, and reported the next February, "that each freehold of house and lands, that was such in the year 1666 or in the year 1684, to have a five-acre right in said Village or Town's New Grant; and each freehold of house and lands, that was ratable in the year 1694, to have a four-acre right in the premises; and each free hold of house and land, that was ratable in the year 1704, to have a three-acre right; and each freehold of house and land, ratable in the year 1714, to have a two-acre right; and each freehold of house and land, ratable in 1722, to have a one-acre right, but none to draw in more than one order for one freehold abovementioned. And we think it very proper, that a committee be chosen to take a list of the proprietors in each order as abovesaid, that each proprietor may know his right, that when the Village is divided, it may be divided as abovesaid.

"Noah Brooks, Samuel Wright, Joseph Fletcher, Richard Parks, John Fassett, George Farrar, Samuel Chandler, John Fox, and Samuel Heywood."

This report was accepted by a ballot of 60 to 2; but after it was declared, 14 others came in and requested to have their dissent recorded. A committee, to make a list of proprietors agreeably to this vote, were chosen, who reported at length at a subsequent meeting; and other preliminary arrangements were made for dividing the Village. But 25 freeholders dissented; and there appeared so much want of harmony on the subject, that the plan was finally relinquished. Meantime some of the common land had been taken up and improved, and some of the occupants were prosecuted and tried before the court.

At length, after several more meetings, the proprietors voted, June 16, 1725, "That all such as are possessed of a freehold, consisting of a dwelling-house and improved land in Concord, which was such a freehold in the year of our Lord 1661, shall have or draw 3 acres; and all such as are possessed of a freehold, which consisted of a dwelling-house and improved lands in said Concord in the year 1684, shall have or draw 2 acres; and all such as are possessed of a freehold, which consisted of a dwelling-house and improved lands in said Concord in 1715, shall have or draw 1 acre; or agreeable to that proportion, except when the right of said Village or New Grant is sold or reserved from said freehold." And "Ensign William Wheeler, Mr. Samuel Jones, and Mr. Ebenezer Wheeler were chosen a committee to draw a list of all the proprietors of said Village or New Grant according to the votes of the proprietors."

This, though afterwards remodelled, formed the basis of the principle by which the division was made, and settled this difficult subject. It was rendered more explicit by a vote passed June 30, 1727, which was, "That the committee chosen for the laying out of said lands in said Village, be hereby directed to lay out so much of the best of the land as to lay to every acre right 10 acres, so that every '61 right (so called) being 3 acres, be laid into 30-acre lots; and every '84 right (so called) into 20-acre lots; and every late allowed right (so called) into 10-acre lots. And all the meadows be divided to each lot according to the several rights as aforesaid proportionably; and all said lots and the meadows to be laid so as to be made equally good as possible may be, either enlarging or abating of the number of acres in each lot, as said committee may think best to proportion the same."

And another vote passed May 17, 1728. — "Whereas it has been voted and agreed, that all the rights in the Village should be laid out into 10-acre lots, 20-acre lots, and 30-acre lots, so that every freehold, that consisted of a dwelling-house and improved land in '61, should draw 30 acres, and every freehold, that was so in '84, have 20 acres, and that every freehold, that was so in '15, have 10 acres; but since thought better to lay it out into bigger lots, viz. 100-acre lots; so that every 10 single rights may draw one of the 100-acre lots. And where it so happens that those that have but 10-acre lots, or those that have not 10 of those single rights to draw, and they can't agree to join 10 of them together to draw one of those 100-acre lots, it shall be in the power of the committee to join them and draw for them, or appoint somebody to draw; and if they can't agree to subdivide, the committee shall subdivide it at the charge of the propriety."

The committee for ascertaining the proprietors, and for dividing the Village according to the foregoing principles, were a long time in accomplishing the business. A list was finally reported, which was referred to the committee constituted by the following proceedings, had June 26, 1730.

" Voted, that Messrs. Samuel Chandler, Benjamin Whittemore, and William Wheeler be a committee to correct the list of proprietors (more especially the first order), and present the same to the proprietors for their approbation; as also to take an account of the proprietors that do agree to join in the same hundred-acre lot, and to join or couple such as cannot agree to do it themselves, and see that no two be joined upon the same right, and also to subdivide the hundred-acre lots where the proprietors cannot agree to divide themselves."

The common land was laid out into lots nominally, but not uniformly, of 100 acres, and numbered in the lists and on the plan. Several of the proprietors had their rights coupled or joined together, and their lots were then drawn according to this coupling-list, and subdivided according to each one's particular right. When lots happened to be poor, or of unequal value, some parts of other lots were taken and added to them. These were called *qualification* lots. This method of division, though it might have been equitable, destroyed the uniform size and shape of the lots, and rendered the farms disconnected and irregular.

Three divisions took place. At the first, September 9, 1730, were drawn 53 coupling lots, or 310 rights. At the second,

July 7, 1732, 60 coupling lots; and 37 at the third and last, December 4, 1745. The proceedings during these intermediate dates relate principally to the grants and division of the lands. At the last period, 1745, a vote was passed to sell all the common land then remaining. The proprietors' clerks were as follows: Thomas Brown, 1710 to 1715; Jonathan Prescott, 1715 to 1728; John Flint, 1728 to 1745; Stephen Hosmer, 1745 to ———; and John Robbins from 1786.

A plan of Concord Village was taken in 1730 by Captain Stephen Hosmer; and it then contained, exclusive of Major Willard's farm, 12,986 acres. A petition was presented to the town of Concord in 1731, for leave to be set off into a separate precinct, but it did not prevail. Three others, subsequently presented, met with the same fate. It seems that the petitioners were desirous of being incorporated as a precinct rather than a town. And though they were unsuccessful at first, the town voted, March 4, 1734, "to set off the Village or town's New Grant a separate town, together with Major Willard's Farm, and that the inhabitants and proprietors petition the General Court for a sanction." Samuel Hunt and others presented a petition accordingly; and the following act of incorporation was obtained just *one hundred years* from the first incorporation of Concord.

" Whereas the inhabitants and proprietors of the northwesterly part of Concord, in the county of Middlesex, called the Village, or New Grant, have represented to this Court, that they labor under great difficulties by reason of their remoteness from the place of public worship, and therefore desire that they and their estates, together with the farms, called Willard's Farms, may be set off a distinct and separate township, for which they have also obtained the consent of the town of Concord.

" Be it therefore enacted by his Excellency the Governor, Council, and Representatives, in General Court assembled, and by the authority of the same, that the said northwesterly part of Concord, together with the said farms, be and hereby are set off, constituted, and erected into a distinct and separate township by the name of Acton, and agreeably to the following boundaries, namely; beginning at the southwest corner of Concord old bounds, then southwesterly on Sudbury and Stow lines till it comes to the southwest corner of Concord Village, then northwesterly by Stow line till it comes to Littleton line, then bounded northerly by Littleton, Westford, and Chelmsford, then easterly by Billerica till it comes to the northwest corner of Concord old bounds, and by said bounds to the place first mentioned. And that the inhabitants of the lands before described and bounded, be and hereby are vested with all the town privileges and immunities that the inhabitants of the other towns within this province are, or by law ought to be, vested with.

"Provided that the inhabitants of the said town of Acton do, within three years from the publication of this act erect and finish a suitable house for the public worship of God, and procure and settle a learned, orthodox minister of good conversation, and make provision for his comfortable and honorable support." This act was passed July 3, 1735.

The history of the town from this time to the commencement of the revolution, contains no features worthy of particular notice. It had a slow but gradual increase in population and improvement. The proceedings for instituting schools, the preaching of the gospel, &c., were carried forward in harmony. During the wars which prevailed from 1740 to 1762, Acton contributed its share of men. But few particulars are preserved, either by tradition or records, concerning their services.

As early as the 21st of December, 1767, the town voted to "comply with the proposals, by the town of Boston, relating to the encouraging of manufactures among ourselves, and not purchasing of superfluities from abroad." On the 5th of March, 1770, the town entered into a covenant not to purchase nor use foreign merchandise, nor tea.

The state of public affairs was again brought before the town on the 21st of December, 1772, and referred to a committee, consisting of Captain Daniel Fletcher, Francis Faulkner, Deacon Jonathan Hosmer, Deacon John Brooks, Josiah Hayward, Ephraim Hapgood, Captain Samuel Hayward, Simon Tuttle, and Daniel Brooks. Their report was made on the 18th of the following month, and expresses the general sentiments of the people in this vicinity.

At this time the town had no representative in the General Court, and a vote was passed recommending to the representatives of the people, that they use every constitutional measure in their power to obtain a redress of all their grievances.

A minute company was raised and commanded by Captain Isaac Davis; and the town voted, on the 18th of January, 1775, to pay 30 men 8*d*. per day to drill twice a week, 3 hours each day, until the first day of May. The important services rendered by this company in the Battle of Concord, on the 19th of April, and the unfortunate death of Captain Davis and Mr. Hayward, have already been noticed in the History of Concord. This and the standing company were distinguished for their prompt and energetic action on that and other occasions.

In June, 1776, Deacon Mark White was chosen representative to the General Court, and received the following instructions from the town.

" To Mr. MARK WHITE.[1] — Sir, Our not being favored with the resolution of the Hon. House of Representatives, calling upon the several towns in this colony to express their minds with respect to the important question of American Independence, is the occasion of our not expressing our minds sooner; but we now cheerfully embrace this opportunity to instruct you on this important question. The subverting our constitution, the many injuries and unheard-of barbarities which these colonies have received from Great Britain, confirm us in the opinion, that the present age will be deficient in their duty to God, their posterity, and themselves, should they not form an American Republic. This is the only form of government we wish to see established. But we mean not to dictate. We freely submit this interesting affair to the wisdom of the honorable Continental Congress, who, we trust, are guided and directed in this important affair by the Supreme Governor of the world. And we instruct you, Sir, to give them the strongest assurance, that if they should declare America to be a free and independent republic, your constituents will support and defend the measure with their lives and fortunes."

The following average of services, rendered by Acton for the year ending on the 25th of May, 1778, was made by a committee of the town.

---

[1] Mark White died on the 24th of January, 1792, aged 82. He was deacon in the Baptist church.

4 men,	Rhode Island,	2¼ months,		May and June,	at £6	=£24
4 "	Northern Army,	4	do.	Aug. to Dec.	" 24 "	96
4 "	do.	1½	do.	Oct. and Nov.	" 9 "	36
4 "	Cambridge,	5	do.	Nov. to April,	" 12 "	48
6 "	do.	3	do.	April to July,	" 7¼ "	43½

A full estimate of the services cannot be made. This town had the honor of furnishing several officers during the revolutionary war. Lieutenant Colonel Francis Faulkner and Captain Simon Hunt were in the battle at White Plains, and at other times were also engaged in actual service.

The constitution was adopted by more than two thirds of the votes of the town.

The history of the town since the revolution is of little general interest. Like most towns in the vicinity, it has a gradual, but very slow growth.

ECCLESIASTICAL HISTORY. A Meeting-house, 46 feet long, 36 broad, and 21 high, was built in 1736, which served as a place of public worship till the present one was erected in 1808. Considerable difficulty having arisen on the question, where it should be situated, as often occurs in similar cases, Col. Holman of Bolton was employed to survey the town and find its centre. The report of this survey was not satisfactory; and after several other trials to fix upon a spot, it was agreed to refer the subject to Gen. Joseph Varnum of Dracut, Gen. John Whiting of Lancaster, and Mr. Walter McFarlane of Hopkinton. These gentlemen made a report which was amicably accepted, Oct. 6, 1806.

Public worship was first held in the meeting-house in January, 1738, and that year the town raised the first money — 50 pounds, for its support. In March a day of public fasting and prayer to Almighty God was kept, preparatory to establishing the preaching of the gospel; and the Rev. Messrs. Israel Loring, William Cook, John Gardner, Oliver Peabody, and Daniel Rogers, assisted in the exercises on the occasion.[1]

---

[1] The church records during Mr. Swift's ministry are so imperfect, that it will be impossible to give an account of its proceedings. They do not

In May, 1738, the town gave the Rev. John Swift a unanimous invitation to become its minister; and he was ordained the 8th of November following. He first received £250 as a settlement, and £150 as an annual salary, to be made of equal value, should the currency depreciate. The sum was altered several times, and permanently fixed at £70 lawful money. In 1741, the powerful revival of religion which prevailed in Concord and other places was experienced here. It is recorded that 28 persons made a public profession of religion, and 15 were baptized on the 28th of November, of that year.

The Rev. JOHN SWIFT was born in Framingham, and graduated at Harvard College in 1733. During the prevalence of the small-pox in Acton, in 1775, he was severely attacked, and never able to preach afterwards. He died 7th Nov. 1775, in the 62d year of his age, and the 37th of his ministry. He was a gentleman of talents, learning, and piety, though occasionally facetious, witty, and eccentric. His only printed publication which I have seen is a sermon preached at the ordination of the Rev. Joseph Lee at Royalston. Mr. Swift married Abigail Adams of Medway, and had one child, who graduated at Harvard College.

The 14th May, 1776, the town voted to invite four candidates to preach four sabbaths each on probation. And a committee consisting of Messrs. Samuel Hayward, Francis Faulkner, Nathaniel Edwards, Josiah Hayward, and John Heald were chosen "to take advice of the President of the College and the neighbouring ministers, who said candidates shall be." Mr. Moses Adams was subsequently engaged eight sabbaths on trial. The 20th of December was observed as a day of solemn fasting and prayer to Almighty God for direction and assistance in re-settling the gospel. Mr. Adams was invited to be their pastor 8th of January, 1777; and was ordained 25th of June, 1778. The first and fourth church in Dedham, second in Sudbury, second in Reading, and the churches in Concord, Stow, and Fitchburgh, composed the counsel. He received £200 as a settlement, and £180 salary, according to the value of silver at 6s. 8d. per ounce, and his fire-wood.

---

even mention the date of its organization, nor all the admissions of members.

In 1785, the singers were directed for the first time to sit together in the gallery. In 1793, the practice of performing sacred music by reading the line of the hymn as sung, was discontinued. A church bible was presented in 1806, by Dea. John White of Concord.

The Rev. MOSES ADAMS was a native of Framingham, and a graduate of Harvard College in 1771. He died 13th of October, 1819, aged 70. During his long and peaceful ministry, 147 were admitted to the church in full communion, 137 owned the covenant to receive baptism, 833 were baptized, and 246 marriages were solemnized. In his intercourse with his people he was conciliatory but independent. He had talents without ostentation, and piety without hypocrisy; all his public performances and private acts were distinguished for their superior good sense. He was emphatically a good, a worthy, and a useful man. Few have died and left a character more deservedly worthy of imitation than his.

On the 25th of February, 1820, the Rev. Marshall Shed, a native of Newton and graduate of Dartmouth College, 1817, was unanimously elected to be their pastor. The town agreed to give him $500 as a settlement, to which $200 were added by subscription, and $600 and 15 cords of wood, as his annual salary, so long as he shall supply the pulpit. He was ordained on the 10th of the following May. The introductory prayer on the occasion was by the Rev. John Pierce of Brookline; sermon by Rev. William Greenough of Newton; consecrating prayer by Rev. Jonathan Newell of Stow; charge by Rev. Jonathan Homer of Newton; fellowship of the churches by Rev. Rufus Hurlburt of Sudbury; address to the church and people by Rev. Thomas Noyes; and concluding prayer by Rev. Ezra Ripley. He was dismissed at his request, May 14, 1831, and has since removed to New-York.

SUCCESSION OF THE DEACONS.

NAMES.	CHOSEN.	DIED.	AGE.
Joseph Fletcher	Dec. 15, 1738.	Sept. 11, 1746.	61
John Heald	Dec. 15, 1738.	May 16, 1775.	82
Jonathan Hosmer		——— 1775.	64
John Brooks		March 6, 1777.	76
Samuel Hayward	Sept. 29, 1775.	March 6, 1795.	78

Francis Faulkner	Sept. 29, 1775.	Aug. 5, 1805.	78
Joseph Brabrook	Sept. 29, 1775.	April 28, 1812.	73
Simon Hunt	April 19, 1792.	April 27, 1820.	86
Josiah Noyes	March 27, 1806.	Dismissed and removed to Westmoreland, N. H., Oct. 16, 1808.	
Benjamin Hayward	March 27, 1806.	Excused, June 15, 1821.	
John Wheeler	April 18, 1811.	Dec. 17, 1824.	64
John White	April 18, 1811.	April 3, 1824.	54
Phineas Wheeler	June 15, 1821.		
Daniel F. Barker	June 15, 1821.		
Silas Hosmer	June 15, 1821.		

There are now three religious societies in the town. 1. The Orthodox, which seceded from the town and formed a separate parish during the latter part of the Rev. Mr. Shed's ministry. The Rev. James T. Woodbury, brother of the Hon. Levi Woodbury, and formerly a member of the bar in Grafton County, New-Hampshire, was ordained over the parish, August 29, 1832, when the Rev. Mr. Cleaveland, of Salem, preached. 2. The Unitarian, which worships in the meeting-house erected by the town; and 3. The Universalist, which was organized 19th of January, 1816, and incorporated 27th of January, 1825. At the former period it contained 11 members, at the latter 49, and in 1827, 61, twenty of whom resided in other towns. The two last have no settled minister.

DESCRIPTION. — MISCELLANEOUS NOTICES. The surface of the town is rough and uneven, though there are no considerable hills; and with some exceptions the soil is rocky, hard to cultivate, and not well calculated for a flourishing agricultural town. It contains, however, many good, well-cultivated farms, on which are grown grain, grass, and other usual productions of the region.

A gentleman, who is familiar with the natural history of Acton, informs me, "that the geology of this town is decidedly primitive; stones are mostly granite of every degree of fineness and variety of appearance. Rocks are gneiss, passing into mica and hornblende slate. The strata are perpendicular which abundantly explains the stubbornness of the soil. Lime rock is found in the south part of the town, and has been wrought, but not recently. Iron is found in various combinations in different places; none, however, of much value. Tradition tells us, that lead used to be found in abundance in the southwest part of the town. Tremolite, actynolite, radiated quartz, pudding-stone, and some other minerals are found here.

"The botany of this place is not peculiarly interesting. The forests are composed chiefly of oak, of all the common varieties, together with some pine, maple, birch, hickory, elm, locust, and chesnut. Among the forest trees, or shrubs, perhaps, ought to be noticed several varieties of the box or cornel, especially the cornus florida and sericea, the barks of which have been used with success as substitutes for the Peruvian."

Nagog Pond lying partly in Littleton is a beautiful collection of water. It is about a mile long, and is the source of *Nashoba Brook*. *Grass Pond*, lying south of Nagog, contains 133 acres. *Nashoba* and *Fort Pond Brooks* have been noticed in the history of Concord. On a branch of the former, which heads in Westford and unites with the main stream near Mr. Stearns's, are Wheeler's and Foster's Mills, and Robins's after their junction. On the latter are Jones's and Faulkner's Mills. *Assabet* river runs across the southwest corner of the town, where Sherman's Mills are situate.

The Population in 1764 was 611, in 1790, including Carlisle, 853; in 1800, 901; in 1810, 885; in 1820, 1047; and in 1830, 1128.

In 1821, there were 140 dwelling-houses; 230 other buildings; 513 acres of tillage land, on which was raised 705 bushels of rye, 932 of oats, 5833 of corn, 75 of barley, and 140 of beans; 1527 acres of mowing land, producing 956 tons of hay; 2026 acres of pasturing, keeping 939 cows, 196 oxen, 69 horses, and 181 swine; 2055 acres of wood; 3633 acres unimproved; and 1311 unimproveable; 240 used as roads and 500 covered with water. It then had 3 grist-mills, 2 carding-machines, 2 fulling-mills, and 4 saw-mills. In 1825, there were 236 polls. Valuation, $8629·28.

The principal employment of the inhabitants is agriculture. Barrels may be considered the *staple production* of the town.

From 15,000 to 20,000 of this article, it is estimated, are annually manufactured here, and this business is the source of considerable income.

During 20 years subsequent to 1800, there were published 208 intentions of marriages, and there occurred 161 marriages, 344 births (as recorded) ; 302 deaths, of whom 72 died under one year old, 32 were 80 and upwards, 8 were 90 and upwards, and 1 lived $99\frac{1}{2}$. The average number annually was 15, about one in 70 of the whole population. The mean average age was 35.

A Post Office was established here some time since and Mr. Perham appointed Post-Master; but it was not long continued. It was reëstablished in 1828, and Silas Jones, Esq. is the Post-Master.

The following table exhibits the appropriations made for several objects at different periods in the town.

Object.	1750.	1760.	1770.	1780.	1790.	1800.	1810.	1820.	1830.
Minister	£50	£52	£70	£3,562	80	$353	353	630	—
Schools	13	12	24	2,000	49	333	450	450	450
Roads	26	70	60	800	120	400	500	600	800
Incidental	20	12	80	10,000	100	500	1,000	1,400	600

The first town *School* was kept in 1741, when it was voted to have "a reading, writing, and moving school for six months." In 1743 a similar one was established and £18 old tenor, equal to about £3 lawful money, was raised for its support. Whether this afforded the only means of education does not appear. It is probable some schools might have been supported by private subscription. Several youth, as was then customary, resorted to the clergyman, for their education. People, however, enjoyed few other opportunities than were afforded in their own families. In 1760 the town was divided into six school districts, and in 1771 into seven. In 1797 the town was divided into four districts, East, West, South, and Middle, and several new houses were built. This division has since been continued. The money is divided among the districts in proportion to the taxes. From the return made to the state in 1826, it appears, that the aggregate time of keeping the schools was 28 months, and that they were attended by 412 pupils, of whom 227 were males, and 185 females. 139 were under 7 years of age, 160 from 7 to 14, and 113 from 14 upwards.

The *Acton Light Infantry* was organized in 1805, and then consisted of 41 members including officers. The following gentlemen have since successively commanded this company. Paul Brooks, Simon Hosmer, Abijah Hayward, Silas Jones, James Jones, Aaron Hayward, Jonathan Hosmer, John Fletcher, John Handley, Jr., Simon Davis, Abel Furbish, George W. Tuttle, and Thomas Brown. This and a standing company compose the militia of the town.

The municipal officers of the town have not essentially varied from those of other towns. The Selectmen have uniformly been assessors and overseers of the poor, of whom the town clerk has been chairman.

TOWN CLERKS.

Thomas Wheeler	1735, 1736.	John Robbins	1808 — 1817.
Simon Hunt	1737 — 1743.	Joseph Noyes	1818.
Jonathan Hosmer	1744 — 1755.	John Robbins	1819, 1820.
John Davis, Jr.	1756, 1757.	Joseph Noyes	1821.
Jonathan Hosmer	1758 — 1761.	Abraham Conant	1822.
Francis Faulkner	1762 — 1796.	Francis Tuttle	1823 — 1827.
Aaron Jones	1797.	Silas Jones	1828.
John Edwards	1798, 1799.	Stevens Hayward	1829.
David Barnard	1800 — 1807.	Francis Tuttle	1830.

REPRESENTATIVES.

Daniel Fletcher	1768.	Jonas Brooks	1804.
Josiah Hayward	1774, 1775.	Samuel Jones	1805, 1806.
Mark White	1776.	Jonas Brooks	1807 — 1811.
Simon Hunt	1780.	Stevens Hayward	1812.
Francis Faulkner	1782 — 1785.	Joseph Noyes	1813 — 1818.
Thomas Noyes	1787 — 1789.	Joseph Noyes	1821.
Ephraim Robbins	1790.	Francis Tuttle	1823 — 1827.
Jonas Brooks	1791 — 1802.	Stevens Hayward	1828, 1829.
Asa Parlin	1803.	Francis Tuttle	1830, 1831.

In 44 years, since the town was incorporated, it has not been represented. Dea. Ephraim Robbins and Asa Parlin, Esq. were of Carlisle, when it was a district of Acton. Capt. Daniel Fletcher was chosen a delegate to the convention in Boston, 22d of September, 1768; Francis Faulkner and Ephraim Hapgood, to the Provincial Congress in Concord, October, 1774; Josiah Hayward, to Cambridge, February, 1775, and again in May; Francis Faulkner, to the Convention in Cambridge, for forming the Constitution, September, 1779; Capt. Joseph Robbins to the Convention, in Concord, to regulate the prices of articles of produce, &c. October, 1779; Simon Tuttle and Thomas Noyes, to Concord, 23d of May, 1786; and Asa Parlin, to the Convention in Boston, in 1788, to ratify the Constitution of the United States.

Samuel Jones, Esq. resided here, as an Attorney, in 1805 and 1806, but left the town, and died at the south.

Dr. John Swift, noticed among the native graduates, was the first physician.

Dr. Abraham Skinner, was from Woodstock, Conn., and commenced practice in Acton, in 1781, where he died April 16, 1810, aged 53. He married Sarah, daughter of Francis Faulkner, Esq. 1788.

Dr. Peter Goodnow was from Bolton, commenced practice in Acton, 12th of October, 1812, left 18th of February, 1827, and is now a merchant in Boston.

Dr. Bela Gardner resided here from 1823 to 1828, removed to Vermont.

Dr. Harris Cowdry, born at South Reading, graduated at the Berkshire Medical Institution, 1824, commenced practice in October, 1826.

Dr. Paul C. Kittridge, from Littleton, commenced practice in Acton, August 30th, 1830.

JUSTICES OF THE PEACE.

Francis Faulkner	Stevens Hayward	John Edwards
Jonas Brooks	David Barnard	Francis Tuttle
Winthrop Faulkner	John Robbins	Simon Hosmer.
Joseph Noyes	Abraham Conant	

GRADUATES AT COLLEGE.

NATHAN DAVIS, son of Samuel Davis, born 30th of November, 1737, graduated at Harvard College, 1759, ordained minister at Dracut, 20th of November, 1765, dismissed about 1785, removed to Boston, and was appointed chaplain at Fort Independence, and a review officer. Died 4th of March, 1803, aged 65.

JOHN SWIFT, only child of the Rev. John Swift, born 18th of November, 1741, graduated 1762, and settled as a physician in Acton, where he died of the small-pox about 1775.

MISCELLANEOUS NOTICES.

Asa Piper, son of Josiah Piper, graduated 1778, and was ordained at Wakefield, New-Hampshire, 1785. He still resides in that town, retaining his relation to the church, though dismissed from his pastoral charge.

Solomon Adams, son of Lt. John Adams, born 18th of March, 1761, graduated 1788, ordained pastor at Middleton, 23d of October, 1793, and died September, 1813, aged 53.

Daniel Brooks graduated 1794, and settled as a trader in Westmoreland, where he held the office of Justice of the Peace. Died, several years since, at Springfield, Vermont.

Thomas Noyes, son of Thomas Noyes, born 5th of February, 1769, graduated 1795, and ordained pastor of the 2d Church in Needham, 10th of July, 1799, dissmissed in 1833 by mutual consent.

Luther Wright was born 19th of April, 1770, graduated 1796, ordained pastor of the first parish in Medway, 13th of June, 1798, dismissed September, 1815, installed at Barrington, Rhode-Island, 29th of January, 1817, and dismissed, 5th of July, 1821. In both instances he was dismissed at his own request by a council who recommended him to the employment of other churches. He now resides at Holliston.

Moses Adams, son of the Rev. Moses Adams, was born, 28th of November, 1777, graduated 1797, settled as a physician in Ellsworth, Maine, and was sheriff of the county of Lincoln.

William Emerson Faulkner, son of Francis Faulkner, Esq. was born 23d of October, 1776, and graduated 1797. He read law with his brother-in-law, the Hon. Jabez Upham, of Brookfield, with whom he formed a partnership in business. He died October 1, 1804, aged 28, and left a most worthy character.

Josiah Adams, son of the Rev. Moses Adams, was born 3d of November, 1781, graduated, 1801, read law with Thomas Heald, Esq., was admitted to the bar, June, 1807, and settled in Framingham, where he now resides.

Luther Faulkner, son of Francis Faulkner, Esq. was born 7th of May, 1779, graduated 1802, and has since been a merchant in Boston.

Jonathan Edwards Scott was a native of Nova Scotia, but a resident in Acton for some time before he entered College. He graduated 1802, and has since commanded a vessel at sea.

JOSEPH ADAMS, son of the Rev. Moses Adams, was born 25th of September, 1783, graduated 1803, and settled as an Attorney in West Cambridge, where he died, 10th of June, 1814.

JOHN RUGGLES CUTTING, son of Mr. William Cutting, graduated at Dartmouth College 1802, ordained at Waldoborough, Maine, August, 1807, dismissed, March, 1812, and has since been a teacher of youth.

HENRY DURANT graduated at Yale College, 1828, and is a tutor in that College, and pursuing theological studies.

All these excepting the two first and the last were prepared for College under the instruction of the Rev. Mr. Adams.

BIOGRAPHICAL NOTICE.

Col. Francis Faulkner was born in Andover, 29th of September, 1728, and died, 5th of August, 1805, aged 78. His great-grandfather, Edmund Faulkner, who emigrated from England, was one of the founders of the church in Andover, in 1645, had his house burnt by the Indians, in 1676, and died in January, 1687. His wife was Dorothy Robinson; and his sons, Francis and John. The former was born 1651, and died 1732, aged 81, leaving sons, Edmund, Ammiruhammah, and Paul, of whom the second, father to Col. Francis, removed to Acton, in 1735, and erected the mills, which have since been owned by his descendants, where he died, 4th of August, 1756. Col. Francis was early employed in public business, and was 35 years, from 1762, successively chosen town clerk. He was a member of the Provincial Congress in 1774, and a representative in the General Court, in 1783, '84, and '85; and also a member of the committee of safety, and of several important conventions, held during the revolution. He held a military commission under George III.; but the oppressive and arbitrary acts of Great Britain induced him to renounce his allegiance to the crown, and step forward as one of the foremost opposers to the measures of the government. Accordingly, in February or March, 1775, he was elected major of a regiment organized at that time to oppose any anticipated invasion. On the morning of the 19th of April, Doct. Prescott was sent on express to him with information that the

British troops were on their way to Concord. He immediately fired three guns in quick succession, which was the pre-concerted signal for an alarm. The express arrived at day-light, and at the rising of the sun he marched with a considerable number of men, who constituted a part of the troops collected at the North Bridge, in Concord. He was in the engagement there that morning, and with his men pursued the British troops to Charlestown. He was afterwards several times engaged in actual service during the war; was Lieut.-Colonel in the regiment of Middlesex militia, called in to reinforce the continental army, when they took possession of Dorchester Heights, in March, 1776; was in service when Burgoyne was taken; and commanded the regiment which guarded the prisoners, taken on that occasion, to Cambridge. He was appointed Justice of the Peace in 1781, and on the 29th of September, 1775, was chosen one of the deacons of the church. In all places he exhibited the character of a gentleman of sound judgment, of a cultivated mind, and of good, practical common sense. He was a courageous military officer, an able legislator, an impartial justice, and an exemplary Christian.

He married, first, Elizabeth Muzzy of Lexington, in 1755, with whom he lived 2 weeks only before her death; and, secondly, in 1759, Rebecca, daughter of Capt. Keyes of Brookfield, who was killed in Lovell's fight, by whom he had 11 children. 1. Francis, Esq., Billerica; 2. Rebecca, married to the Hon. Dwight Foster of Brookfield; 3. Sarah, married to Dr. Skinner of Acton; 4. Elizabeth; 5. Mary; 6. Ammi; 7. Lucy, married to the Hon. Jabez Upham of Brookfield; 8. Susanna, married to Hannibal Hamlen, Esq., sheriff of the county of Oxford, Maine; 9. Winthrop, Esq. died in Acton, very much lamented, 17th of March, 1813, aged 39; 10. William Emerson, H. C. 1797; and 11. Luther, H. C. 1802.

CHAPTER XIX.

HISTORY OF LINCOLN.

General History. — Ecclesiastical History. — Description. — Statistics. — Biographical Notices.

THE inhabitants in the southeasterly part of Concord, petitioned that town several times, between 1734 and 1743, to be set off into a separate precinct or town; but, being unsuccessful, a petition was preferred to the General Court, August 10th, 1744, which obtained favor, though opposed by a committee of the town ; and the following individuals, living in the easterly part of Concord, westerly part of Lexington, and northerly part of Weston, were incorporated as the Second Precinct of Concord, April 24, 1746, viz. Joshua Brooks, Thomas Garfield, Benjamin Brown, James Brooks, Robert Gage, Ephraim Segard, John Whitney, Benjamin Allen, Ebenezer Hunt, Thomas Baker, Samuel Dakin, Joseph Parks, John Wright, Ambrose Tower, Daniel Reed, Mary Conant, Jeremiah Clark, Thomas Garfield, Jr., Benjamin Brown, Jr., Hannah Corey, Jonathan Wellington, Jonathan Gove, George Pierce, Joseph Brooks, Jordan Clark, Amos Merriam, Joseph Pierce, James Pierce, Zebediah Smith, Ebenezer Lampson, John Headley, Timothy Wesson, Benjamin Monroe, John Gove, Samuel Bond, Thomas Wheeler, Ephraim Flynt, Joseph Pierce, Jr., Joshua Brooks, Jr., John Garfield, Ebenezer Cutler, Nathan Brown, Edward Flynt, Stephen Wesson, John Adams, John White.

The following individuals, living within the limits of the proposed precinct, did not sign the petition ; and were exempt in the act of incorporation, unless they should choose voluntarily to comply with its provisions : Daniel Brown, Thomas Nelson, Nehemiah Abbott, Jabez Stratten, Nathaniel Billings, Daniel Billings, John Billings, Timothy Billings, Joseph Billings, Daniel Parks, Zaccheus Parks, Amos Heald, Samuel Farrar, Joseph Wheat, Joseph Wheat, Jr., John Wheat, Jonas Wheeler, Benjamin Wheeler, Nathaniel Whittemore, Samuel Billings, George

Farrar, George Farrar, Jr., Job Brooks, Daniel Brooks, Samuel Brooks, Hugh Brooks, Joseph Brooks, Jr., Timothy Lampson, Ephraim Hartwell, Josiah Brown, John Jackson, William Hager, Joseph Underwood.

Several attempts were made to procure an incorporation as a town, and in 1753 the exempted persons were consulted on the subject, and Chambers Russell, Esq., Capt. Samuel Bond, and Deacon Joshua Brooks, were chosen to present a petition to the General Court. The town of *Lincoln*, named by Chambers Russell, Esq. after Lincolnshire, England, the residence of his ancestors, was incorporated, April 19, 1754. The bounds were then the same as they now are.

The estates in Concord in 1753 were £15,007 9*s.*; and the polls, 442. That part set off to Lincoln contained £3372 15*s.*; and of the polls, 88 ; about one-fifth.

The proceedings of the town appear to have been conducted with harmony, and no occurrence worthy of notice marks its history till the great question of opposition to England was agitated. In this controversy, it became early enlisted, and uniformly on the popular side ; and was distinguished for its ardent, decided, and independent patriotism, and for its intelligence and originality.

March 15, 1770, the town voted, "that they will not purchase any one article of any person that imports goods contrary to the agreement of the merchants of Boston"; and in a long answer to a circular sent to the town, they say, February, 1773, "We will not be wanting in our assistance according to our ability, in the prosecuting of all such lawful and constitutional measures, as shall be thought proper for the continuance of all our rights, privileges, and liberties, both civil and religious ; being of opinion that a steady, united, persevering conduct in a constitutional way, is the best means, under God, for obtaining the redress of all our grievances."

The first committee of correspondence was chosen November 2, 1773, — Deacon Samuel Farrar, Capt. Eleazer Brooks, and Capt. Abijah Pierce ; a similar one was elected annually till 1784. The sentiments of the town, on several questions then agitating the province, being requested by the citizens of Boston, were communicated in the subjoined very interesting letter, on the 20th of December.

"Gentlemen,— We have read your letter, enclosing the proceedings of the town of Boston at their late meeting; as also another letter enclosing the proceedings of a collective body of people, not only of Boston, but the adjacent towns; in which, after some very pertinent observations on the alarming situation of our public affairs, you desire our advice and to be acquainted with the sense of this town respecting the present gloomy situation of our public affairs. We rejoice at every appearance of public virtue, and resolution in the cause of liberty; inasmuch as, upon our own virtue and resolution, under Divine Providence, depends the preservation of all our rights and privileges.

"We apprehend, that we, in America, have rights, privileges, and property, of our own, as well as the rest of mankind; and that we have the right of self-preservation, as well as all other beings. And we are constrained to say, that after the most careful and mature deliberation, according to our capacities, weighing the arguments on both sides, we apprehend our rights and privileges have been infringed in many glaring instances, which we mean not to enumerate, among which the late ministerial plan, mentioned in your letter, is not the least.

"The Act imposing a duty on tea is alarming, because, in procuring the same, our enemies are dealing by us, like the great enemy of mankind, viz. endeavouring to enslave us by those things to which we are not necessitated, but by our own contracted ill habits; although, if tea were properly used, it might be of some advantage. When we speak of our enemies, as above, we mean those persons on either side of the water, who by many ways, either secret or open, are sowing the seeds of strife and discord between Britain and her colonies; or are in any way the active instruments of our distress.

"Now since it must be granted, that our rights and privileges are infringed, and that we have the right of self-defence; the important question is, by what means to make such defence. Doubtless the means of defence in all cases ought to quadrate with the nature of the attack; and since the present plan seems to be to enslave us, we need only (had we virtue enough for that) to shun the bait, as we would shun the most deadly poison. Notwithstanding, considering so many are so habituated to the use of tea, as perhaps inadvertently to ruin themselves and their country thereby; and others so abandoned to vice, expecting to share in the profits arising from the ruin of their country, as to use all means in their power to encourage the use of tea; we cannot, therefore, but commend the spirited behaviour of the town of Boston, in endeavouring to prevent the sale of the East India Company's teas, by endeavouring to persuade the consignees to resign their office, or any other lawful means; and we judge the consignees, by refusing to comply with the just desire of their fellow-citizens, have betrayed a greater regard to their private interest than the public good and safety of their country, and ought to be treated accordingly.

"The situation of our public affairs growing more alarming, and having heretofore tried the force of petitions and remonstrances and finding no redress; we, the inhabitants of this town, have now come into a full determination and settled resolution, not to purchase, nor use any tea, nor suffer it to be purchased or used in our families, so long as there is any duty laid on such tea by an act of the British Parliament. And we will hold and esteem such, as do use such tea, enemies to their country; and we will treat them with the greatest neglect. And we beg leave to recommend it to the several towns within this province, who have not done it, to go and do likewise.

"How easy the means! How sure the event! But be the event what it may, suppose this method should not obtain a repeal of the act, which we judge to be unrighteous, but the event should be a total disuse of that destructive article, we might then (if we may so express ourselves) bless God, that ever he permitted that act to pass the British Parliament.

"We trust we have courage and resolution sufficient to encounter all the horrors of war in the defence of those rights and privileges, civil and religious, which we esteem more valuable than our lives. And we do hereby assure, not only the town of Boston, but the world, that whenever we shall have a clear call from Heaven, we are ready to join with our brethren to face the formidable forces, rather than tamely to surrender up our rights and privileges into the hands of any of our own species, not distinguished from ourselves, except it be in disposition to enslave us. At the same time, we have the highest esteem for all lawful authority ; and rejoice in our connexion with Great Britain, so long as we can enjoy our charter rights and privileges."

This able paper is attributed to the pen of the Hon. Eleazer Brooks. The original agreements of the town about the disuse of tea and non-consumption of imported articles of merchandise have been found among his papers, and are now deemed worthy of preservation.

"Whereas, the town of Lincoln did, on the 27th day of December current, by a full vote, come into a full determination and settled resolution, not to purchase nor use any tea, nor suffer it to be purchased or used in their families, so long as there is any duty laid on such tea by act of the British Parliament; and that they would hold and esteem all such as do use such tea, as enemies to their country ; and that they will treat them with the greatest neglect ; — We, the subscribers, inhabitants of said town, pursuant to the same design, do hereby promise and agree to and with each other, that we will strictly conform to the tenor of the abovesaid vote. In witness whereof we have hereunto subscribed our names.

"Lincoln, Dec. 27th, 1773."

This was signed by 52 of the principal inhabitants. The following by 82.

"We, the subscribers, inhabitants of the town of Lincoln, do sincerely and truly covenant and agree to and with each other, that we will not for ourselves, or any for or under us, purchase or consume any goods, wares, or manufactures, which shall be imported from Great Britain, after the thirty-first day of August, seventeen hundred and seventy-four, until the Congress of Deputies from the several colonies shall determine what articles, if any, to except ; and that we will thereafter, respecting the use and consumption of such British articles, as may not be excepted, religiously abide by the determination of said Congress."

This was a time when it was impossible to stand on neutral ground and escape censure. Those who were not decided in opposition to the measures of Great Britain, were supposed to favor them. Of the suspected was the minister of the town ;

and, though the suspicion was groundless, and of short duration, the people in September assembled around the meeting-house on a Sabbath, and prevented him from entering to preach. Two or three individuals were subsequently obliged to leave the town for not conforming to the prevailing sentiments of the people. One of the largest estates in the town was for some time in the hands of government.

March 6, 1775, "voted, that £52 4s. be granted to provide for those persons, who have enlisted as minute-men, each one a bayonet, belt, cartridge-box, steel rammer, gun-stock, and knapsack; and that they attend military exercises four hours in a day twice a week, till the first day of May next. In case any one refuse to attend, 2s. for each four hours, and in proportion for a smaller time, shall be deducted from their wages."

The part performed by Lincoln in the county conventions at Concord, and by her minute-men and militia on the 19th of April, has been noticed in the History of Concord, and was highly honorable to her patriotism and valor.

At length, on the 24th of June, 1776, the town passed this important vote: "That, should the Honourable Congress, for the safety of the United American Colonies, declare themselves independent of Great Britain, we, the inhabitants of this town will solemnly engage, with our lives and fortunes to support them in the measure."

About this time the town was requested to instruct their representative, according to the general custom at that period; but it was thought more proper to "empower him to act according to his best judgment and discretion."

The following table, compiled from a report, made May 8, 1778, to the town, by its committee to estimate the services rendered by the citizens in the war, furnishes important information.

Date.	Men.	Places.	Service.	£.	s.	d.	£.	s.	d.
1775	32	at Cambridge	8 months, hired at	8	0	0 =	256	0	0.
1776	7	" ditto.	2 "	2	0	0	14	0	0.
1776	7	" Canada	12 "	18	0	0	126	0	0.
1776	6	" the Southward	12 "	12	0	0	72	0	0.
1776 and 1777	6	" Boston	12 "	4	0	0	24	0	0.
1776	19	" Ticonderoga	5 "	12	10	0	237	10	0.
1776	4	" ditto.	4 "	15	0	0	60	0	0.
1776	5	" Roxbury	4 "	6	0	0	30	0	0.

HISTORY OF LINCOLN.

1776 and 1777	17	at Dorchester	3 months,	hired at 1	0	0	= 17	0	0.
1776	12	" New-York	2 "		6	0	0	72	0	0.
1776 and 1777	8	" ditto.	3 "		9	0	0	72	0	0.
1777	4	" Providence	2 "		4	10	0	18	0	0.
1777	10	" Saratoga	3 "		11	5	0	112	10	0.
1777	12	" ditto.	1 "		3	0	0	36	0	0.
1777 and 1778	9	" Cambridge	5 "		7	10	0	67	10	0.
1777		26 Continental Army	3 years		30	0	0	780	0	0.
1777		8 at Worthington			1	10	0	12	0	0.

£ 2006 10 0.

These bounties were paid by the town, beside many other charges for the public service. When it is recollected, that the town did not then contain more than 187 male inhabitants over 16 years of age, and that several enlisted into the army not included in the above estimate, it will appear that Lincoln contributed a large proportion of men to promote the great revolution. I have no means of ascertaining the precise number furnished subsequently to the above dates, but the town always contributed promptly all required; though it was supposed at the time the burden was not justly proportionate to other towns. A petition was presented to the council early in 1778, to obtain some relief. In this petition it is said, " The large farm of Dr. Charles Russell, now in the hands of the public, greatly augments the tax on the town, and consequently the number of men required." Several officers were furnished for the army from this town. The Hon. Eleazer Brooks was at Ticonderoga, in 1776, as a Colonel, and the Hon. Samuel Hoar, as a Lieutenant, and both were at the taking of Burgoyne. The former was at Dorchester Heights in 1777. On the 4th of September, of that year, Brig.-General Prescott sent an order to Col. Brooks to have his enlisted men formed into companies and to meet in Concord the following Saturday, to appoint his field-officers. He wrote in this order, that " he never received one of greater importance," and entreated him " not to fail paying attention to it, as he valued his own reputation or the salvation of his country." These orders, like all others, were promptly obeyed. Col. Pierce, Capt. Samuel Farrar, and others, were also distinguished in the service.

March, 1778, £3880 were granted to pay soldiers; and in 1780 it was voted, " that each person that furnishes one cotton shirt for the continental soldiers, shall receive out of the town treasury, £4½ ; and each person that furnishes a pair of shoes for the same purpose shall have £3½ ; and each person that furnishes one pair of socks shall receive £2." On the 2d of June, £18,000 were granted to hire men for the war; and in September, £15,840 for the same object, and £8,500 to purchase beef for the army. On the following January, £16,240 more were granted for the same object. During 1781, large sums were raised to hire men, buy clothing, and for other public objects, till this town, like many others, became exceedingly embarrassed.

Such are a few items selected from the proceedings of the town in relation to the revolution. They are sufficient to show the undeviating and devoted patriotism of the town ; a patriotism not consisting in resolves only, but in a series of noble sacrifices of self-interest for the general good, alike honorable to it as a town and to the individuals composing it, and worthy of being remembered and imitated.

The town guarded their rights with careful jealousy. When the constitution, formed by the State Convention, February 28th, 1778, was submitted to the town, it voted, 39 to 38, to disapprove of it. In May, 1779, it was voted, "that the town will not choose at this time to have a new constitution or form of government made"; but on July 28th, the Hon. Eleazer Brooks was chosen a delegate to the convention in Cambridge, "for the sole purpose of framing a new constitution, and the delegate was instructed to cause a printed copy of the form of a constitution, they may agree upon in said convention, to be transmitted to the selectmen of each town." This constitution was submitted to the town, 22d of May, 1780.

"On the 2d Article in the 1st Section of the 1st Chapter in the form of government, voted, that this town disapprove of the said article ; 1. Because we think the legislative, executive, and judicial powers ought to be in separate departments, and not exercised by the same body or bodies of men, either in whole or in part. 2. Because we judge this article to be repugnant to the 17th and 30th articles in the bill of rights ; as also to the 1st article in the frame of government, which we think to be founded in reason.

"On the 2d Article in the 3d Section of the 1st Chapter, voted, that the town disapprove of this article; because we think the mode of representation pointed out in this article is not founded upon the principles of equality as provided by the preceding article. We apprehend that all circumstances ought to be taken into consideration to determine a representation founded in equality, and that neither the number of rateable polls nor any other circumstance, singly considered, determines such a representation. This state is constituted of a great number of distinct and very unequal corporations, which are the immediate constituent parts of the state; and the individuals are only the remote parts in many respects. In all acts of the legislature which respect particular corporations, each corporation has a distinct and separate interest, clashing with the interests of all the rest. And, so long as human nature remains the same it now is, each representative will be under an undue bias in favor of the corporation he represents; therefore any large corporation, having a large number of representatives, will have a large and undue influence in determining any question in their own favor. Should the number of rateable polls in any particular corporation increase till they overbalance all the others, they could completely tyrannize over all the rest, and every degree of inequality gives power for the same degree of tyranny. Another circumstance which renders the mode of representation pointed out in this article unequal is, that the small corporations can have no voice in government without being at the whole expense of a full representation; whereas, the large corporations, by dividing the attendance of their representatives, can vastly lessen their expense, and yet, in such cases as respect their particular and separate interests, have a full representation."

The 3d Article in the Declaration of Rights was accepted 46 to 2; the last clause of the 10th Article, 3d Section, and 1st Chapter was rejected 30 to 11. Voted unanimously to revise the constitution in 7 years by 40 votes, and to accept it with the foregoing exceptions.

The first meeting under the new constitution was held on the first Monday of September, when there were 41 votes cast, all of which but one were for the Hon. John Hancock.

ECCLESIASTICAL HISTORY. The ostensible object of those who obtained the act of incorporation for the town of Lincoln, was to enjoy the preaching of the gospel. Measures were taken, even before the precinct was formed, to effect this object by private individuals in their houses. Mr. Edward Flint gave a lot of land on which a meeting-house was erected and nearly completed by the following individuals by whom it was given to the precinct, — viz.

Benjamin Brown	Benjamin Monroe	Jon. Wellington
Edward Flint	John Hadley	Ephraim Flint
Judah Clark	Samuel Dakin	Thomas Wheeler
Joseph Brooks	Ebenezer Cutler	Joseph Pierce
Joshua Brooks	Jeremiah Clark	Nathan Brown
Samuel Bond	Amos Merriam	Jonas Pierce
Jonathan Gove	John Gove	Timothy Wesson.
George Pierce		

Money was raised to complete this house, by the precinct and a vote passed in 1747, that pews should be built and allotted to the inhabitants according to their valuation, — the highest to take the first choice. A steeple was built in 1755 and furnished with a bell, the gift of Mr. Joseph Brooks. This house has been several times repaired and its appearance is still respectable.

On the 18th of August, 1747, twenty-five male members of the churches in Concord, Lexington, and the second precinct in Weston, met together and agreed to embody themselves into a distinct church. The public organization took place on the 20th of the some month, when Mr. Benjamin Brown was chosen permanent moderator till the ordination of a minister ; and the Rev. Messrs. John Hancock, Israel Loring, William Williams, and Wareham Williams, assisted in the public religious exercises on the occasion. A covenant was adopted and signed by the following persons.

Jonathan Gove	Woodis Lee	George Pierce
John Hadley	Thomas Wheeler	Ephraim Flint
Joshua Brooks	Benjamin Brown	Jonas Pierce
Josiah Parks	Thomas Garfield	Joseph Brown
Joseph Pierce	Edward Flint	John Garfield
Samuel Bond	Joseph Brooks	Nathan Brown
John Gove	Timothy Wesson	Judah Clark
Stephen Wesson	Benjamin Monroe	William Lawrence.
Thomas Garfield, Jr.	Benjamin Brown, Jr.	

The persons employed as preachers in 1746, '47, and '48, were John Brown, Benjamin Stevens, Jonathan Winchester, Cotton Brown, Samuel Pemberton, and Samuel Turrell. Mr. William Lawrence was first employed in April, 1748, on trial. On the 18th of May, the church and precinct, being together, voted, 22 to 7, to invite him to become their minister. It was agreed to give him £800 currency as a settlement, and £400 and 10 cords of wood, as an annual salary. This salary was finally fixed according to the prices of corn at 15s. and rye at 20s. per bushel, and pork at 1s. 8d., and beef at 1s. per pound. The estimate to be made near the close of the year.

He was ordained the 7th of December following; and £100 were granted to pay the expenses. The council on the occasion consisted of the Rev. John Hancock, of Lexington, moderator, who prayed and gave the charge; Rev. William Williams, of Weston; Rev. Nathaniel Appleton, of Cambridge, who made the introductory prayer; Rev. Caleb Trowbridge, of Groton, who preached from 1 Tim. iii. 15; Rev. Wareham Williams, of Waltham, who gave the right hand of fellowship; Rev. Daniel Rogers, of Littleton, who prayed after the charge; Rev. Samuel Cook of West Cambridge; and delegates from their respective churches.

Few important occurrences took place worthy of notice for several years. The church voted, in May, 1751, to receive any member of the church in Concord who should be dissmissed. In 1763, the reading of the Scriptures was first introduced as a part of the exercises of public worship; and in 1768, a short prayer was made before this reading. A vote was passed, 27th of April, 1767, " that in future Dr. Brady's and Mr. Tate's version of David's Psalms, and some Hymns of Dr. Watts, which are now bound up and published with this version, shall be made use of and sung in carrying on the public worship of God in this place." In 1771, forty-two persons, " who had attained a good degree of understanding in the rules of singing," were seated together by vote of the town on the lower floor.

The Rev. WILLIAM LAWRENCE, son of the Hon. William Lawrence, and grand-son of Jonas Prescott, Esq., of Groton, was born, 7th of May, 1728, and graduated at Harvard College, 1743.

During his ministry, his church, unlike many in the neighbourhood, enjoyed great peace. 122 persons were admitted into full communion, 31 of whom were from other churches, the remainder by original profession ; 120 owned the covenant ; 605 were baptized ; 122 marriages were solemnized ; and 294 died. His epitaph appears in the Lincoln burying-ground thus :

"In memory of the Rev. William Lawrence, A. M. Pastor of the Church of Christ in Lincoln, who died April 11, 1780, in the 57th year of his age, and 32d of his ministry. He was a gentleman of good abilities both natural and acquired, a judicious divine, a faithful minister, and firm supporter of the order of the churches. In his last sickness, which was long and distressing, he exhibited a temper characteristic of the minister and Christian. ' Be thou faithful unto death, and I will give thee a crown of life.'

His funeral expenses, amounting to £366 currency, and £300 to purchase mourning for the surviving widow, were paid by the town. He married Love, daughter of John Adams, who died January 3, 1820, at the advanced age of 95, and had the following children, William, Love (married to Dr. Joseph Adams,) John P. (died 1808,) Susanna, Sarah, Phebe (married to the Rev. E. Foster of Littleton, 1783,) Ann, and Abel.

Dea. Samuel Farrar was moderator of the church from the death of Mr. Lawrence to the ordination of his successor. A day of fasting and prayer was held, according to the usual custom in such cases, on the last Thursday in August, 1780, and the Rev. Messrs. Cushing, Woodward, and Clark were present on the occasion.

Mr. Charles Stearns was first employed to preach in Lincoln in October, 1780, and on the 15th of January, 1781, the church voted unanimously (29 votes) to invite him to be their pastor ; and in this vote the town concurred on February 5th, 65 to 5 ; and agreed to give him " £220 in hard money, or its equivalent," (to which £70 were subsequently added,) as a settlement, and £80 and 15 cords of wood, as an annual salary. His ordination took place November 7, 1781. The church then consisted of 96 members. The churches in Waltham, Weston, Lexington, Lunenburgh, Leominster, East Sudbury, Sudbury, 1st in Reading, Stow, and Concord, were represented in the council, of which the Rev. Mr. Cushing was moderator. The Rev. Zabdiel Adams preached on the occasion from 1 Timothy iii. 3, and his sermon was printed.

In consequence of the fluctuating relative value of money, the town voted, in 1797, "that the Rev. Mr. Stearns's salary should be £80 per year, at all times when the current price of Indian corn is 3s. and rye 4s. per bushel, and beef 20s. and pork 33s. per hundred; and to be increased or diminished according as the prices of those articles vary."

In 1789, the church voted, that the reading of the psalm by line, after it has been once distinctly read, be discontinued.

The church has never had a confession of faith. The covenant into which the communicants enter does not differ materially from that in the Concord church. The principles of the first organization of the church appear to have been somewhat more liberal than those of the Rev. Mr. Bliss. As early as 1749, it was voted not to "require public relations of religious exercises, as a condition of admission into the church," but it was left optional with the candidates to do it or not. Public confessions before the whole church and congregation for crimes, were not uncommon until late in Dr. Stearns's ministry.

The Rev. CHARLES STEARNS, D. D. was son of Thomas, and grandson of Charles Stearns, whose ancestors first settled in Lynn. He was born in Leominster, graduated at Harvard College in 1773, and died July 26, 1826, in the 75th year of his age, and 45th of his ministry. At the time of his ordination the church consisted of 96 members, and during his ministry 155 persons were admitted to full communion, 78 owned the covenant, 536 were baptized, 201 marriages were solemnized, and up to 1818, 387 died. The town erected a monument to his memory, on which the distinguishing traits of his character are drawn with force and accuracy.

"He was distinguished for his high attainments in various branches of science; for strength and soundness of mind; for method and accuracy in reasoning, and facility in communicating knowledge. By his piety, benevolence, and learning, he gained the affection and respect of his beloved people, the esteem and confidence of his numerous friends, and the well-deserved honors of literary societies. His life was full of practical goodness, the genuine fruit of deep-felt piety, and his death of religious hope and peace. By the habitual exercise of faith, humility, patience, and charity, he exhibited Christianity in a strong and prominent light ; and is gone, it is believed, to enjoy the rewards of a good and faithful servant of Jesus Christ."

The Rev. Dr. Stearns [1] married Miss Susanna Cowdry, of Reading, 1781, and had the following children, Susanna, Charles, Thomas, Julia, Sarah, Elizabeth Francis, William Lawrence, Daniel Mansfield, Rebecca, Samuel, and Edwin.

During the ministry of Mr. Lawrence and Mr. Stearns, the church and town were in great harmony. No council was at any time called to settle difficulties. After the death of the latter, Dea. Thomas Wheeler was chosen moderator, and Dea. Eleazer Brooks, clerk, to serve till the ordination of another minister.

On the 13th of August, 1827, the church gave the Rev. Elijah Demond a unanimous call to be their pastor. He was born at Barre, November 1, 1790 ; graduated at Dartmouth College, 1816 ; and had been minister of West Newbury. In this vote the town concurred, and voted him $600, as an annual salary. He was installed November 7, 1827. The public exercises were performed as follows : Introductory prayer, by the Rev. Rufus Hurlbut, of Sudbury ; sermon by the Rev. John Codman, D. D., of the 2d church in Dorchester ; installing prayer by the Rev. Gardner B. Perry, of Bradford ; charge by the Rev. Samuel Stearns, of Bedford ; right hand of fellowship by the Rev. Sewall Harding, of Waltham ; address to the

---

[1] The following works were published by Dr. Stearns : —

The Ladies' Philosophy of Love ; a Poem in four Cantos. Written in 1774, while a student in College, and published in 1797.

A Sermon at the Exhibition of Sacred Music in Lincoln.

Dramatic Dialogues, for the use of Schools. Published in 1798.

A Sermon, preached Nov. 11, 1806, at the Interment of the Hon. Eleazer Brooks.

A Sermon, delivered at Concord before the Bible Society, April 26, 1815.

A Sermon, delivered before the Convention of Congregational Ministers in Massachusetts, in Boston, June 1, 1815.

Principles of Religion and Morality. First edition in 1798, 2d in 1807.

A Sermon at the Interment of Mrs. Foster of Littleton.

people, by the Rev. Rodney G. Dennis, of Topsfield; and the concluding prayer by the Rev. Marshall Shed, of Acton. These and the churches in East Sudbury and Weston composed the council, of which the Rev. Mr. Stearns was moderator. He was dismissed in 1832, and installed at Holliston, October 31, 1833.

On the 16th of January, 1833, the Rev. Ebenezer Newhall, a native of New Ipswich, New-Hampshire, and recently a minister at Oxford, was installed over this society. The introductory prayer on the occasion was by the Rev. Mr. Gilbert, of Newton; sermon by the Rev. Mr. Nelson, of Leicester; installing prayer by the Rev. Mr. Hurlbut, of Sudbury; charge by the Rev. Mr. Allen, of Shrewsbury; right hand of fellowship by the Rev. Mr. Demond, the late pastor; and the address to the people by the Rev. Mr. Harding, of Waltham.

SUCCESSION OF THE DEACONS.

NAMES.	CHOSEN.	DIED.	AGE.
Benjamin Brown	Aug. 20, 1747.	April —, 1753.	—.
Joshua Brooks	April 18, 1749.	June 26, 1768.	80.
John Gove	April 18, 1749, was in office about 40 years.		
Samuel Farrar	Dec. 28, 1763.	April 18, 1783.	75.
Joshua Brooks, Jr.	Dec. 28, 1763.	March 8, 1790.	70.
Edmund Wheeler	May 6, 1784.	June 1, 1805.	74.
Samuel Farrar	May 6, 1784.	Sept. 19, 1829.	93.
Eleazer Brooks	Nov. 6, 1794.	Nov. 9, 1806.	80.
John Hartwell	April 9, 1804.	Nov. 2, 1820.	73.
Thomas Wheeler	Sept. 2, 1805.		
James Farrar	April 27, 1812.		
Eleazer Brooks	April 27, 1812.		

DESCRIPTION. Lincoln lies about three miles and a half southeasterly from Concord, and is bounded southwesterly by East Sudbury, southerly by Weston, southeasterly by Waltham, easterly by Lexington, northerly by Bedford, and northwesterly by Concord. Its greatest length is about five miles, and greatest breadth three and a half, nearly; and it contains about 7000 acres. It has all the varieties of soil from the richest to the poorest. Though rough and uneven, it contains some of the best farms in the county. The most celebrated is that known at different times as the Russell, Codman, and Percival farm.

Farming constitutes the principal employment of the inhabitants. The hill on which the meeting-house stands is 470 feet above high water mark in Boston. Two other hills, one 370 and the other 328 feet high, lie near the Lexington bounds.

Flint's or *Sandy Pond*, the only considerable collection of water, contains, according to the estimate of the Hon. Samuel Hoar,[1] 197 acres. It derives its name from the first owner, being situated in the farm of Ephraim Flint, one of the principal original owners of Lincoln. This pond is a favorite resort for pickerel; and its fisheries have been considered of sufficient importance to require the interference of the Legislature to regulate them. An Act was passed February 16, 1824, prohibiting any person, under penalty of $2, from fishing with "*more than one hook*"! between the first of December and April; providing, however, that the town may repeal its operation for one year at a time. This pond is the source of Stony Brook, and receives Lilly Brook, the outlet of *Beaver Pond*, lying near the south line, and containing about 50 acres; and it flows into Charles River at the northwest corner of Waltham. Its waters also have flowed by an artificial channel, made, as is supposed, for the benefit of the Mill which once stood in the centre of Concord, by Mill Brook into Concord River.

A Post-office was established in the southwest part of the town, in 1825, in which the Post-masters have been, David S. Jones, from January 24, 1825, to September 18, 1826, resigned; Luke Gates, from September 19, 1826, present Post-master.

A county road and the Cambridge and Concord Turnpike (which was also made a county road in May, 1829,) run through the north part of the town. Another similar road runs through the south part. These add greatly to the expense, and very little to the convenience of the inhabitants.

According to a valuation taken in 1784, it appears that there were then 143 polls, 26 of whom were not rateable; 88 dwelling-houses, 84 barns, 1 tan-yard, 1 grist-mill, and 21 other buildings;

---

[1] Hon. Samuel Hoar, Lt. William Lawrence, and Mr. Nathan Weston, were chosen a Committee August 21, 1794, to take a plan of the town agreeably to a resolve of the General Court the previous June, to be deposited in the Secretary's office.

454 acres of tillage land, 429 of English mowing, 800 meadow, 1502 pasturing, 2057 wood land, 2128 'other land,' and 137 unimproveable ; 840 barrels of cider were made, 105 horses, 155 oxen, 266 neat cattle, 378 cows, 155 sheep, and 136 swine were held. Probably, if an estimate was made now, it would not essentially vary from the above. The polls in 1790, were 156 ; the houses in 1801, 104. The population in 1764 was 639, including 28 negroes, and in 1790, 740 ; in 1800, 756 ; in 1810, 713 ; in 1820, 786 ; and in 1830, 709.

In 1820, there were 3 foreigners not naturalized, 81 engaged in agriculture, 5 in commerce, and 34 in manufactures. The militia is comprised in one company of about 50. An estimate, made by Dr. Stearns in 1820, appears in the church records in which the following " averages from the beginning of the town are determined, (the nearest being taken when there is a fraction :) births, 22 in a year; baptisms, 19 ; admissions into church, 4 ; marriages, 4 ; and deaths, 10." These average annual estimates, will hold good now, excepting in the baptisms, the number of which has diminished.

Appropriations made by the Town at different Periods.

Date.	1755.	1765.	1775.	1785.	1795.	1805.	1815.	1825.
Minister	£56	£69¾	£70¾	£85	£105	$ —	$600	$460.
Schools	13½	20	13½	50	85	—	480	520.
Highways	25	50	40	80	80	450	600	400.
Incidental charges	24½	19	37	250	125	830	1450	500.

The existing records are not sufficiently particular to enable us to compile the annual bill of mortality. A summary of several years is sometimes placed together. The subjoined statement may be considered as nearly correct.

	From 1760 to 1770,	to 1780,	to 1790,	to 1800,	to 1810,	to 1820.	— Total.
Intentions of Marriage	56	79	65	69	73	59	= 401.
Marriages	38	40	35	48	87	56	= 274.
Births	185	196	186	192	168	164	=1091.
Deaths	83	122	104	86	118	94	= 607.

It appears from this table that the excess of births over the deaths is 484, more than two to one ; and, according to the census, that, from 1790 to 1800, one in 86 died annually ; from 1800 to 1810, one in 64 ; and from 1810 to 1820, one in 78 ; a result which is highly favorable to the healthiness of the town.

Schools. Lincoln has always given liberal support to her common schools, and has been rewarded in the distinguished character of her educated sons. At its incorporation in 1754, it was divided into three districts; and a 'moving school' was kept in each. A school-house was built in the middle of the town in 1762; and in 1763, £5 were granted to build one in the southwest district, £5 for the southeast, and £10 for the north. In 1768, the schools were kept in three instead of four places; and in 1770, and some other years, the grammar school was substituted for all the others. In 1780, the town was again divided into four districts, which have been continued, excepting a few years since. In 1791, a committee was appointed to make a general regulation for dividing the school money, who reported, that the east district have 21 weeks, the south 17 weeks, and the north 14 weeks, in proportion to the 12 months' schooling. This regulation was accepted by the town, which was divided into three districts; but continued a few years only. It was so altered in 1791, as to give 17 weeks to the south, 14 to the north, 11 to the east, and 10 to the middle district. Since 1812, the south has drawn $\frac{11}{36}$ and the three others $\frac{15}{36}$ each of the money. Among the teachers of the grammar school, I find the names of Jacob Bigelow, Timothy Farrar, Fisher Ames, and others who have been distinguished in public life. Mr. Joseph Brooks, among other liberal donations, made one for the support of schools, which has been of great service to the town. It amounted in 1761, to £388, and now to more than $1,000, the annual interest of which is divided among the districts in the same proportion as other school money. An institution called the "liberal school," similar to an academy, was established by the Rev. Dr. Stearns, and several other gentlemen in 1793, and was successfully continued about 10 years. From the annual return made to the State in 1829, it appears that the aggregate time, for which the four public schools were kept, was 32 months, 17 by males, and 15 by females; and that they were attended by 220 scholars. $576·70 were paid for their support. There were two private schools, and 8 pupils attending academies. The estimated amount of tuition was $70. None are unable to read in the town. The north district contains 40 scholars, the south 86, the east 42, and the middle 44.

The poor were supported previous to 1785 in such families as undertook it at the lowest rates. £8 were granted for this purpose in 1760, £35 in 1762, and £18 in 1783. A committee was chosen in 1785, consisting of the Hon. James Russell, Edmund Wheeler, and Eleazer Melvin, by whom a poor-house was built; principally from the liberal donation of the chairman. The land on which it stood was presented by Mr. John Adams. The poor were supported here till about 1800, when the house was abandoned, and the old system of letting them out to the lowest bidder was again adopted. The annual expense now is between $400 and $500.

There are two burying-grounds in town, one the gift of Mr. Ephraim Flint, and the other of Dea. Samuel Farrar.

TOWN CLERKS.

Ephraim Flint	1746 – '62, '54, '56, '57.	Grosvener Tarbell 1799 – 1803.
Ebenezer Cutler	1753, 1755, 1759.	Thomas Wheeler 1804 – 1806.
Samuel Farrar	1758, 1760 – 1766.	Elijah Fiske 1810 – 1821.
John Adams	1767 – 1777.	Stephen Patch 1822 – 1827.
Abijah Pierce	1778, 1779, 1781.	Charles Wheeler 1828 – 1830.
Samuel Hoar	'80, '82,'87–'98, 1807–'9.	Elijah Fiske 1831.
Richard Russell	1783 – 1786.	

REPRESENTATIVES.

Chambers Russell	'54–57,'59,'61,63,'5.	Joshua Brooks 1809 – 1811.
Samuel Farrar	1766 – 1768.	Leonard Hoar 1812 – 1814.
Eleazer Brooks	'74–'78, '80,'5,'7,'90–'2.	William Hayden 1815, 1816.
Chambers Russell	1788.	Elijah Fiske 1820 – 1822.
Samuel Hoar	'94,'95,'97,'98,1801,'3–'8.	Joel Smith 1824.
Samuel Farrar, Jr.	1800.	Silas P. Tarbell 1827, 1828.

Not represented 1758, '60, '62, '69–'73, '79, '81, '82, '86, '89, '93, '96, '99, 1802, '17, '23, '25, '26.

SENATORS.

Hon. Eleazer Brooks   1780 – '86, '88 – '95.
Hon. Samuel Hoar   1813 – 1816.

COUNSELLORS.

Hon. Chambers Russell   1759 – 1766.
Hon. Eleazer Brooks   1788, '92 – 1800.

JUSTICES OF THE PEACE.

Chambers Russell	Chambers Russell	William Hayden
James Russell	Samuel Hoar	Charles Wheeler
Charles Russell	Eleazer Brooks, Jr.	Elijah Fiske
Eleazer Brooks	Joshua Brooks	Stephen Patch
Joseph Adams	Grosvener Tarbell	Joel Smith.

Clergymen and Physicians are the only professional men who have resided in town. The former have already been noticed in the Ecclesiastical History; the physicians are the following:

Dr. Charles Russell, son of the Hon. James Russell, born in Charlestown, graduated at Harvard College, 1757, and inherited his uncle Chambers's estate in Lincoln, where he resided as a physician. He married Miss Elizabeth Vassall of Cambridge, and from his father-in-law he contracted opinions opposed to the measures of the people in the revolution, and left Lincoln on the 19th of April, 1775, and went to Martinique, in the West-Indies, where he died.

Dr. John Binney died August 14th, 1760, aged 55. His widow married Capt. Daniel Adams.

Dr. Joseph Adams was also unfriendly to the revolution, and went to England, where he died.

Dr. Mann practised in Lincoln between 1780 and 1790. He afterwards removed to Castine, Maine, and married a daughter of Mr. John Adams.

Dr. Richard Russell was son of Mr. Richard, a brother of the Hon. Chambers Russell, born in Charlestown, settled in Lincoln in 1778, drowned in Beaver Pond August 12th, 1796, aged 46.

Dr. Grosvener Tarbell was from Sturbridge, settled in Lincoln in 1796, and died in 1822.

Dr. George Russell, son of Dr. Richard Russell, born September 23d, 1795, graduated at the Medical Institution at Cambridge, in 1820, and has since practised in Lincoln.

GRADUATES AT COLLEGE.

STEPHEN FARRAR, son of Dea. Samuel Farrar, was born September 8th, 1738, and graduated 1755. He studied divinity, and was ordained as the first minister of New Ipswich, New Hampshire, October 22d, 1760, and performed the duties of his office with distinguished ability till his death, June 23d, 1809.

TIMOTHY FARRAR, brother of the foregoing, was born June 28, 1747, and graduated 1767. He studied law and settled in New Ipswich, New Hampshire, was elected Judge of the Court of Common Pleas, under the temporary constitution of N. H. in January, 1776; was a Counsellor in the year 1780, 1782, and 1783; appointed Judge of the Superior Court in 1790; resigned that office 1803; appointed Judge of the Court of Common Pleas in 1803 or 1804; and was afterwards Chief Justice of the Circuit Court of Common Pleas. Besides these offices, he was an elector of President and Vice-President of the United States in 1792, 1796, 1800, and 1808 [1]; and in 1804, and since, one of the trustees of Dartmouth College.

CHARLES RUSSELL of Lincoln. He received a Medical degree at Aberdeen, died at Antigua, May 27th, 1780, aged 42.

JOSEPH FARRAR, son of George Farrar, was born June 30th, 1744, and graduated 1767; was ordained at Dublin, New-Hampshire, June 10th, 1772, when the church was organized; dismissed, January 7th, 1776; installed at Dummerston, Vermont, in 1779; dismissed 1784; and is probably the same who afterwards settled in Eden, Vermont. He died at Petersham.[2]

JONATHAN GOVE, son of Dea. John Gove, born August 22d, 1746, and graduated 1768. He studied medicine and lived many years in New Boston, New Hampshire; was Representative at the General Court, a popular physician, and one of the oldest in practice, at the time of his death, in the county of Hillsborough. He was also a Justice of the Peace. One of his sons, Charles F. Gove, is an Attorney at Law in Goffstown.[3]

---

[1] MS. Letter of John Farmer, Esq. [2] Ibid.
[3] Farmer & Moore, Gazetteer of New-Hampshire, p. 143.

Moses Brown, graduated in 1768, and settled as a merchant at Beverly ; Justice of the Peace and of the Quorum ; died June 15th, 1820, aged 72.

Jonas Hartwell, son of Ephraim Hartwell, was born June 26th, 1754, and graduated 1779. After he graduated he engaged in mercantile pursuits, went to Bilboa in Spain, and while innocently engaged in his vocation, was arrested and confined in the Inquisition, where he died, March 2d, 1784.

Nathaniel Pierce, was born September 27th, 1754, and graduated 1775. He was a merchant in Boston. Died in Watertown, December 3d, 1783, aged 30.

Abel Flint, son of Mr. Ephraim Flint, was born June 22d, 1758, and graduated 1780. He taught a school several years in Haverhill and elsewhere, and died in Lincoln of consumption January 25th, 1789, aged 32.

William Brooks, son of Dea. Joshua Brooks, was born March 13th, 1757, and graduated 1780. He settled as a merchant in Augusta, Maine, and has held several civil and military offices in that State.

Daniel Stone, graduated 1791, and was ordained at Augusta, Maine, October 21st, 1795, and dismissed by mutual consent, May, 1809. He has since lived a respectable private citizen in that town.

Daniel Adams, son of Joseph Adams, graduated at Dartmouth College 1797, and received a medical degree at Harvard College ; settled in Keene, New Hampshire, and obtained an extensive professional business.

Samuel Farrar, son of Dea. Samuel Farrar, born December 13th, 1773, graduated 1797, was tutor one year, studied law and settled in Andover, is the President of the Bank in that place, and Treasurer of the Theological Seminary.

Samuel Hoar, son of the Hon. Samuel Hoar, born May 18th, 1778, graduated 1802. He studied law and was admitted to the bar September, 1805, and immediately after settled in Concord. He was a member of the Convention for revising the Constitution of the State in 1821, and of the Senate in 1825 and 1832.

John Farrar, son of Dea. Samuel Farrar, born July 1st, 1779, graduated 1803, was tutor from 1805 to 1807 ; and appointed that year Hollis Professor of Mathematics and Natural Philosophy in Harvard University, and yet continues in that office.

NATHAN BROOKS, son of Joshua Brooks, Esq. born October 18th, 1785, graduated in 1809, established himself in the profession of law in Concord, represented the town in 1823, 1824, and 1825, and was Counsellor in 1829, and Senator in 1831.

NATHANIEL PIERCE HOAR, son of the Hon. Samuel Hoar, born September 2d, 1784, and graduated 1810. He read law with his brother in Concord, and commenced practice in his profession at Portsmouth, New Hampshire, in 1813, where he soon obtained an extensive business. Being attacked by a fatal disease, he removed to his native town, and died deeply lamented, May 24th, 1820, aged 35.

THOMAS FISKE, son of Elijah Fiske, Esq., graduated 1819, read law, and began his professional business in Charleston, South Carolina, in 1826.

WILLIAM LAWRENCE STEARNS, son of the Rev. Dr. Stearns, born October 13th, 1793, graduated in 1820, studied divinity and was ordained at Stoughton, November 21st, 1827.

DANIEL MANSFIELD STEARNS, a twin-brother of the preceding, graduated at Brown University, 1822, and was ordained minister at Dennis, May 21st, 1828.

JOSEPH GREEN COLE, son of Capt. Abraham Cole, graduated 1822, read law with Gov. Lincoln in Maine, and is now settled in his profession at Paris in that state.

GEORGE FISKE, son of Elijah Fiske, Esq., born August 22d, 1804, graduated at Brown University in 1825, and is now Episcopal minister in New-York.

HUMPHREY FARRAR, son of Humphrey Farrar, was born September, 15th, 1773, and graduated at Dartmouth College, 1794.

JOSEPH FARRAR, born February 14th, 1775, brother to the above, graduated as his classmate, and studied law.

GEORGE FARRAR, graduated at Dartmouth College, 1800, brother to the two abovementioned, and is an eminent physician in Derry, New Hampshire, and Fellow of the New Hampshire Medical Society.

WILLIAM FARRAR, another brother, born October 2d, 1780, graduated at Dartmouth College in 1801.

BIOGRAPHICAL NOTICES.

Mr. Joseph Brooks died September 17th, 1759, aged 78. He was son of Joshua, and grandson of Thomas Brooks, the first American ancestor of the Brooks family. He acquired a respectable estate, as a farmer, and while living was distinguished for his liberality. From him the church in Lincoln received a part of its communion plate; and the town, the meeting-house bell, and the school fund. These, and several other acts of liberality, render his name deserving of lasting remembrance.

Hon. Chambers Russell, was son of the Hon. Daniel Russell, of Charlestown, who died December 6th, 1763, aged 78, a member of the Council, commissioner of imposts, and treasurer of the County of Middlesex upwards of fifty years. His grandfather was the Hon. James, and great-grandfather the Hon. Richard Russell, who, in 1640, at the age of 29, came from Herefordshire, England, and settled in Charlestown, was a most eminent merchant, a member of the Council, and otherwise distinguished. His mother was daughter of the Hon. Charles Chambers. He graduated at Harvard College in 1731, and soon settled in that part of Concord which is now Lincoln, on the estate of his father-in-law, which has since been known as the Russell, Codman, and Percival estate. He represented the town of Concord several years in the General Court; and was the chief instrument in obtaining the act of incorporation for the town of Lincoln. After this town was set off, he was eight times elected its representative. In 1759 he was chosen a Counsellor, just a century from the time when his great-grandfather was chosen to the same office. He was appointed, September, 1747, Judge of the Court of Admiralty, and at his death sustained that office, and also that of Judge of the Superior Court. He died without issue, according to the Lincoln records, at Guilford, in Surry, England, 24th of November, 1767. He married Mary Atkins, who died in Lincoln, 13th of August, 1762.

Hon. James Russell, brother of the foregoing, was born in Charlestown, 5th of August, 1715, and succeeded to all the public honors of his respected ancestors, as a Representative,

Counsellor, and Judge. He represented the town of Charlestown 13 years from 1746, was a Counsellor many years, and 16th of May, 1771, was appointed one of the Judges of the Court of Common Pleas. When Charlestown was invaded by the British in 1775, he removed to Dunstable; and after his son Charles, who inherited his brother Chambers's estate, left the country, he removed to Lincoln, where he lived fifteen or twenty years. This town is indebted to him for several valuable donations. The expense of the poor-house, erected in 1786, was principally borne by him. He married Katharine, daughter of the Hon. Thomas Graves, a descendant, of the third generation, from the Hon. Thomas Graves, who arrived in Salem in 1629, and soon after settled in Charlestown. She died in Lincoln 17th of September, 1778, aged 61. He died in Charlestown. His children were Hon. Thomas, a most eminent and opulent merchant of Boston; James, who went to England; Dr. Charles, Harvard College, 1757; Chambers, who died in S. Carolina; Katharine, who married Mr. Henly of Charlestown; Rebecca, who married, first, Judge Tyng, and secondly, Judge Sewall; Margaret, who married John Codman; and Sarah and Mary, who died single.

Hon. Eleazer Brooks, was the son of Mr. Job Brooks, and a descendant of the fourth generation from Capt. Thomas Brooks, one of the first settlers of Concord, was born 10th of September, 1727, and died 19th of November, 1806, aged 79. His grandfather was Daniel, and great-grandfather Joshua Brooks. His father was a respectable farmer, and intended his son for the same employment. The circumstances of the times, when he lived, were such, that his education did not equal that of many of his contemporary young farmers, which at best was very ordinary. Considering that he was self-instructed, his future intellectual improvements were truly remarkable. He early discovered indications of talents; and, before the great work of the Revolution commenced, he was called into office. He was appointed, by Governor Barnard, a Lieutenant of a foot company in Lincoln, 11th of May, 1768, and a Captain by Hutchinson, 13th of July, 1773; by the Council, a Colonel of the 3d regiment, 14th of February, 1776, and a Brigadier-General, 15th of October, 1778, and to the same office under the new constitution, 22d of August, 1781. He commanded a regiment of the Middlesex militia at the battle of White Plains, in 1776, and at several other times appeared in the camp, where he distinguished himself for his cool and determined bravery. The laborious duties, which his military office imposed during the revolutionary war, were performed with great ability and decision. He was often chosen a member of the town's committee of safety, and the state's committee of secrecy, was a member of the Provincial Congress in 1774, and was afterwards annually a member of the General Court or executive Council till 1800. He was appointed Justice of the Peace in 1777; and on the 27th of March, 1786, a special Judge of the Court of Common Pleas. He was delegate to the convention at Cambridge in July, 1779, to form the constitution, and at Boston, in 1788, to ratify the Constitution of the United States; and in various other places, during his public life, his services were put in requisition. After being 27 years a public man, he declined, in 1800, being a candidate for the suffrages of his fellow-citizens, and retired to private life. As a military man, he was brave, patriotic, and considerate in designing, but expeditious in executing his plans. His habits of thought and action were systematic and correct; his industry untiring. By a judicious improvement of his faculties, by reading, conversation, and reflection, he compensated for the neglect of his early education. Possessing the confidence of his associates in public life, he acquired great influence, and his opinions were much respected. But for nothing was he more respected than for his strict probity, real goodness of heart, and exemplary piety. He united with the church early in life, and was chosen one of its deacons in 1794. In all his important trusts he set a noble example of what may be accomplished by a judicious application of one's own powers of mind, and left a character worthy of remembrance and imitation.

CHAPTER XX.

HISTORY OF CARLISLE.

General History. — Miscellaneous Notices. — Ecclesiastical History.

The internal party divisions in Concord, occasioned principally by the religious controversies from 1740 to 1750, originated several projects for separate societies and districts. From this cause Lincoln was incorporated; and an unsuccessful attempt was made by the inhabitants of the Nine Acre Corner to be set off. The northerly part of Concord also had several times petitioned the town for a separation; and though liberty was not granted, a petition was presented to the General Court, and *Carlisle* was incorporated as a district of Concord, April 19th, 1754. The ostensible reason for this petition was "being remote from the public worship of God." The bounds began at the mouth of Ralph's or Sawmill Brook, on Concord River, southeasterly of Capt. Jonathan Buttrick's house, and run westerly over Gravel Hill, by Daniel Cole's (now Mr. Clark's,) to Acton line, including the Temple farm; from thence on the old bounds of Concord, between Acton and Billerica, till it came to Concord River, including Blood's farms, and by the river to the place first mentioned. These bounds included about one quarter of the present limits of Concord.

The first meeting was held at Joseph Adams's, May 3d, 1754, when John Hartwell was chosen District Clerk, and he and Messrs. John Green, Joseph Adams, Jonathan Puffer, and William Fletcher, Selectmen, and Dea. Ephraim Brown, Treasurer.

The first object of the inhabitants was the selection of a site on which to erect a meeting-house. This was a peculiarly fruitful source of difficulty. The discordant materials, which could not agree while connected with the town of Concord, were found equally fond of disunion here. Their proceedings are, perhaps, more a subject of curiosity, than utility; yet, as they caused the dissolution of the district, and throw light on the history of those times, they are worthy of being transmitted and remembered.

The selection of a site for the meeting-house was first brought before the district 2d of May, 1754, considered, and referred to the next meeting. July 17th, it was agreed to select a convenient place on Lt. Jonathan Buttrick's plain. October 9th, a committee was chosen to take a plan of the district and find its centre. This survey was made by Capt. Stephen Hosmer. On the 13th of the same month, Messrs. John Varnum of Dracut, Jonas Prescott of Westford, and Samuel Dakin of Sudbury, were chosen a committee to view the district, and select a place where to build a house. Five men in the east and five in the west part were a committee to wait on those gentlemen. They reported January 1st, 1755; but not agreeably to the wishes of the district. January 22d, voted to build on Capt. J. Buttrick's land. March 3d, Messrs. Jonathan Puffer, Thomas Davis, and Samuel Heald, were chosen a committee to petition the General Court for an increase of territory on the south line as far as Concord river. April 30th, voted to build on "Poplar Hill." June 3d, four places proposed to the meeting were rejected. July 9th, a committee was chosen to petition the General Court for a committee to select a spot. January 27th, 1756, voted to build, but to refer the selection of a place to the next meeting. February 3d, voted to build on Capt. Buttrick's plain. March 1st, a committee was chosen to purchase two acres of land of Capt. Buttrick, and £50 was ordered to be raised towards the payment. April 6th, "chose Maj. John Jones, Esq., Col. William Lawrence, Esq., of Groton, and Maj. Ephraim Curtis, Esq., of Sudbury, to view all the circumstances of the district and prefix a place." It was surveyed by Maj. Jones, and a new plan taken. The committee reported that the most convenient place "is south 41 degrees west, 26 poles from the centre of the angles," which is on Poplar Hill. This report was accepted June 16th, and a committee chosen to purchase two acres of land there for the purposes contemplated. This however was not generally satisfactory, and another unsuccessful attempt was made to fix the spot on Dea. Brown's land.

In consequence of these unharmonious proceedings, the following petition was presented to the selectmen : —

"We, the subscribers, being sensible of the great difficulties we labor under, and the great hardships we are unavoidably exposed to, if we are obliged, under such circumstances, as we are in at present, to build a meeting-house and settle a minister, and pay for highways, that will be necessary to accommodate the inhabitants, if we proceed according to the design of being set off; the situation of the district being such that but a small part of the inhabitants can be much better accommodated with the public worship in any place that has been proposed, than they are in the town of Concord ; — desire that you would call a meeting of the district, as soon as can or may be, to see if the district will not agree by their vote to petition the General Court, that said district may be set back to the town of Concord, with all our former privileges ; and choose a committee for that purpose. — Carlisle, June 24th, 1756. — Ephraim Stow, Samuel Laughton, Jonathan Puffer, Samuel Buttrick, Jr., Ephraim Melvin, David Whittaker, Phineas Blood, Abraham Temple, Ephraim Whittaker, Jonathan Harris, John Laughton."

A committee was chosen July 14, 1756, to petition the General Court agreeably to the views above expressed. The following persons, however, remonstrated against it. Jonathan Blood, David Blood, Zaccheus Green, Nathaniel Taylor, Nathaniel Taylor, Jr., Joseph Taylor, John Hartwell, David Parlin, Joseph Parlin, James Russell, Leonard Spaulding, Timothy Wilkins, John Green, Jr., James Russell, Jr.

An act was passed, January 11th, 1757, setting the district back to Concord, with all its former privileges. The necessary measures being taken for closing the concerns of the district, a vote was passed, "that none of the inhabitants be set off again into a separate town, district, or precinct, excepting such as shall hereafter sign a petition to the General Court to be set off."

During the existence of "Old Carlisle," as this incorporation is called, religious worship was generally maintained either at Dea. Brown's, Mr. Ephraim Smith's, or elsewhere. Money was raised to pay the expenses for schools and other usual municipal purposes.

After the occurrence of those unpleasant circumstances which led to the dissolution of Old Carlisle, no more definite attempts were made to obtain a separation, till about fifteen years afterwards. During this time, however, the occasional preaching of the gospel had been supported, and a meeting-house was begun as early as 1760, though not completed before 1783. Several petitions were presented to the adjoining towns to obtain their consent, and one to the General Court by the inhabitants of Blood's farms and the extreme parts of Concord, Acton, Chelmsford, and Billerica ; and an act was passed April 28th, 1780, incorporating them as a district of *Acton*, by the name of *Carlisle*.[1] This act provided that one sixth part of the expense of maintaining the north bridge in Concord, should be paid till another be built by themselves; and that all the poor within the district should be supported there. It also provided, that the farms of Thomas Brown, Nathan Buttrick, Oliver Barron, Samuel Kibby, John Blood, and Willard Blood, of Concord, living within the limits prescribed by the act, should be exempted, and continue to belong to Concord, unless they should within one year " insert their names in the Secretary's office, that they choose to belong to Carlisle." These families had not petitioned for the act; and, agreeably to the vote passed at the dissolution of Old Carlisle, they were exempted from its operation. They never left their names with the Secretary, and still belong to Concord. Hence arises that zigzag, crooked line, which runs round these farms, and now separates Concord from Carlisle. An act passed March 1st, 1783, to annex David Parker to Chelmsford, and another September 12th, 1780, to annex Josiah Blood to Concord.

The first meeting took place May 8th, 1780, when Phinehas Blood presided as moderator, and the customary officers were chosen.

After the incorporation of the district, the inhabitants bore with cheerfulness their proportional part of the burdens of fur-

---

[1] The line run, beginning on land belonging to Issachar Andrews on Concord River ; thence, north 60° west, 36 rods ; n 9° w., 62 rods ; n. 58° w., 40 rods ; n. 32° w., 245 rods ; n. 27° e., 150 ; n. 36° w., 115 rods ; n. 50° w., 90 rods : n. 52° w., 162 rods ; north 22° east, 18 ; n. 68° w. 382 rods ; south 6.° west, 368 rods ; south 3° east, 235 rods ; south 75° west, 160 rods ; s. 1° w., 172 rods ; south 7° east, 435 rods ; s. 58° e 107 rods ; . 79° e., 515 rods ; s. 64° e., 600 rods, to Concord, and by the river to the bounds first mentioned.

nishing men, money, and provisions to prosecute the revolutionary war to its close. On the 30th of May, 1780, *seven* men were raised for the continental army, and six more on the following February. When the subject was brought before the district, a committee was chosen to procure the men, and Capt. Samuel Heald embodied the men then present, to see if any would enlist, but none volunteered. The district was then divided into six classes to procure one in each class. One man was sent to Rhode Island in 1781, and three more to the Continental army. Committtees of safety were regularly chosen.

On the 6th of June, 1804, the district voted, that "it is expedient to be disconnected from the town of Acton." Jonathan Heald, Esq. was chosen to present the subject to the General Court, and an act was passed, February 18th, 1805, conferring on the district all the privileges of a town.

Since this period the general history of the town, is doubtless familiar to the inhabitants ; and no event of importance has taken place to render it expedient to pursue it further.

MISCELLANEOUS NOTICES. The surface of the town is generally uneven and rocky, though there are no considerable elevations ; and the soil is unfavorable to agriculture. Concord River washes its eastern bounds ; and a brook arising in *Heat Pond* in Chelmsford, runs easterly through the north part, which affords sites for two or three small mills. The principal employment of the inhabitants is agriculture. There is one physician, one store, two taverns, and a few mechanics' shops to accommodate the immediate wants of the inhabitants.

The population in 1800 was 634 ; in 1810, 675 ; in 1820, 681 ; in 1830, 566. In 1820, 119 persons were engaged in agriculture, 1 in commerce, and 34 in manufactures.

The valuation in 1831 gives the following results : 138 rateable polls, 17 not rateable, 83 dwelling-houses, 88 barns, 4 grist and saw mills ; 314 acres of tillage land, 524 acres of upland mowing, 661 acres of meadow, 294 acres of pasturing, 882 acres of woodland, 3607 acres unimproved, 884 unimprovable, 213 acres used for roads, and 109 acres covered with water ; 46

horses, 200 oxen, 474 cows and steers; 3668 bushels of corn, 541 bushels of rye, 490 of oats, 362 tons of English hay, and 468 tons of meadow hay. By comparing the valuations for several periods since the incorporation, it will appear that the town has made little or no progress, but in many things has retrograded.

Appropriations by the Town for various Purposes.

Object.	1785.	1790.	1795.	1800.	1805.	1810.	1815.	1820.	1825.	1830.
Minister	£91	90	85	$285	290	280	320	275	320	500.
Schools	36	30	60	300	300	360	360	450	360	360.
Roads	60	45	60	300	480	350	400	400	350	400.
Town Charges	74	60	50	300	500	550	550	700	600	600.
County Tax	—	11¾	22	58	—	117	72	99	56	22.
State Tax	484	48	64	227	—	210	130	180	—	65.

SCHOOLS. The town from its first incorporation has been divided into *six* school districts; and the money raised by the town has been divided equally among them. There is a school fund amounting to $500 given by Mr. Simon Blood, the annual interest of which is appropriated in the same manner as other moneys.

The following individuals have been educated at college.

AMOS SPAULDING, son of Zebulon Spaulding, graduated at Dartmouth College 1805, and settled as a lawyer in Andover. He has been member of the House of Representatives and the Senate of Massachusetts several years.

JOEL ADAMS, son of Capt. Timothy Adams, graduated at Harvard College 1805, admitted to the bar September, 1808, and settled as a lawyer in Chelmsford, where he has since resided.

ASA GREEN, son of Zaccheus Green, graduated at Williams College 1807, and is a lawyer and post-master at Brattleborough.

FRANKLIN LITCHFIELD, son of the Rev. Paul Litchfield, was born August 18th, 1790, and graduated at Harvard College 1810. He went to Charleston, S. Carolina, and studied physic under Dr. Ramsay, but left there in June 1812, for Carthagena, South America, where he resided till 1815, having, during this time, made a tour to the city Quibdo or Zetara by the river Atrato, near 500 miles from Carthagena. This tour has been mentioned by Baptiste Irvine. At the last mentioned date he emigrated with other distinguished citizens to the Island of Jamaica, where he remained till 1819, when he removed to St. Thomas, and resided there till 1821. At this time the city of Caraccas was occupied by the Patriots, under the command of the distinguished Bolivar; and he now proceeded to that city, and remained there till 1824, when he removed to Puerto Cabello, having been appointed Consul of the United States for that city, by President Monroe in December, 1823. Here he has since resided, and been extensively engaged as a commission merchant. From the time of his departure from Charleston, he devoted much time in giving statements of the progress of the war in South America, which eventuated in the final overthrow of the Spanish authority in that region and the acknowledgment of its independence. He married Garcia de Sena, a lady of the city of Caraccas, at Jamaica in 1826. Her eldest brother, *Ramon*, was Secretary at War of the government under General Bolivar, and was killed at the battle of La Puerta, as Adjutant-General of the Army. Another brother, *Manuel*, was Secretary at War of the government of Carthagena. Mr. Litchfield's life has been most eventful. In the various revolutions he has witnessed, he has experienced in an eminent degree, the enjoyments and trials, resulting from the ups and downs of life, and the acquisition and loss of fortune.

WILLIAM L. RUSSELL, son of James Russell, graduated at Harvard College 1826, and is a physician at Barre.

ALBERT NELSON, son of Dr. John Nelson, born March 12th, 1812, graduated at Harvard College 1832, and is now a student at law at that institution.

FREDERICK PARKER, son of Maj. James Parker, graduated 1833.

With the exception of the clergy, the physicians have been the only professional men. Thomas Jewett, now of Rindge, New Hampshire, practised physic here several years.

Dr. JOHN NELSON, son of Josiah Nelson of Milford, was born Sept. 8th, 1790. After being two years at Brown University, he left it, and afterwards studied his profession with Dr. Thurber of Mendon. He came to Carlisle in 1816, and is a member of the Massachusetts Medical Society.

TOWN CLERKS.

Zebulon Spaulding	1780 – 1784.	Jonathan Heald, Jr.	'13, '14, '18 – '20.
Asa Parlin	1785 – 1802, 1806 – '8.	John Heald	'15 – '17, '21 –'25, '27 –'29.
John Jacobs	1803, 1809 – '12, 1-26.	Cyrus Heald	1829 – ——.
Jonathan Heald	1804, 1805.		

TREASURERS.

Samuel Heald	1780 – 1785.	Nathan Green	1804 – 1819.
Simon Blood, Jr.	1786 – 178?.	Nathan Green	1820 – 1828.
Samuel Green	1789 – 1803.	John Nelson	1829 – ——.

Selectmen. The town clerk has always been the first selectman; and the board have acted as assessors and overseers of the poor. The following persons have been selectmen, arranged in order as they were first chosen: Zebulon Spaulding, Phinehas Blood, John Heald, Samuel Green, Issachar Andrews, Asa Parlin, Zaccheus Green, Nathaniel Hutchinson, Nathan Parlin, Jonathan Heald, Simon Blood, Jr., Ephraim Robbins, Leonard Green, John Jacobs, Nathan Green, Jr., John Green, Thomas Spaulding, Frederick Blood, Ezekiel Nichols, Nehemiah Andrews, Timothy Heald, Thomas Heald, Jonathan Heald, Jr., Benjamin Robbins, Jonas Parker, John Heald, Eliakim Hutchins, Aaron Robbins, Aaron Fletcher, Paul Furbush, Isaiah Green, Cyrus Heald, James Green, Cyrus Green, Thomas Heald, Jr.

Representatives. While Carlisle was a district of Acton, Dea. Ephraim Robbins, in 1790, and Asa Parlin, Esq., in 1803, were chosen jointly by both places. Since its incorporation, as a town, the following individuals have been its representatives. (Except in the years specified, it was not represented.)

Dea. Ephraim Robbins	1807, 1808.	Jonathan Heald, Jr., Esq.	1816.
Rev. Paul Litchfield	1808 – 1811.	John Heald, Esq.	1818, 1821, 1823.
Capt. Timothy Heald	1812, 1813.	Dr. John Nelson	1824.
Capt. Thomas Heald	1815.	John Heald, Esq.	1826, 1827, 1830.

JUSTICES OF THE PEACE.

Name.	Died.	Age.	Name.	Died.	Age.
Asa Parlin,	Oct. 8, 1822.	68.	Nath'l Hutchinson,	July 30, 1820.	34.
Jonathan Heald,	Dec. 28, 1816.	60.	John Heald.		
Jonathan Heald, Jr.			John Nelson.		

Bill of Mortality. No records were kept, by which to form a bill of mortality, before 1800. From that date to 1826, the Rev.

Mr. Litchfield regularly recorded the deaths as they took place. From these records the following facts are obtained. The total number of deaths in these 27 years is 334, about 13, or one in 50 of the inhabitants annually; the aggregate amount of ages is 11600, and the mean average 34¾ nearly. The least average age was 15, in 1808; and the greatest 58, in 1826. Of these 334 deaths, 58 died under the age of 1 year, 44 between 1 and 5; 17 between 5 and 10; 18 between 10 and 20; 29 between 20 and 30; 23 between 30 and 40; 20 between 40 and 50; 36 between 50 and 60; 20 between 60 and 70; 30 between 70 and 80; 26 between 80 and 90; and 13 between 90 and 100. The proportion of males to females, who died from 90 and upwards was as 6 to 7; and 80 to 90, as 11 to 15. By this it appears that 1 in 20 nearly arrive to the age of 90; 1 in 9 to 80; 1 in 5 to 70; 1 in 4 to 60; and 1 in 3 to 50. One fifth nearly, die under 1 year, and one third under 2 years. It appears from a careful examination of the records that the month in which the least number of deaths occurred was May, and the greatest, in October. 23 died in January, 23 in February, 22 in March, 37 in April, 19 in May, 22 in June, 22 in July, 32 in August, 35 in September, 41 in October, 33 in November, and 25 in December. In 1817, fourteen died of the disentery, 10 of whom were under 5 years. In 1819, of those under 1 year, 8 died. In 1821, the canker rash prevailed and was fatal to many. I subjoin a few remarkable instances of longevity, which may interest some readers.

Date.	Name.	Age.	Date.	Name.	Age.
1800, April 19,	Jon. Spaulding,	95.	1817, April 28,	Wid. M. Parker,	93.
1803, June 28,	Wid. S. Fletcher,	94.	1819, Sept. 23,	Amos Kidder,	90.
1807, Sept. 11,	Wid. R. Heald,	90.	1821, Dec. 5,	Wid. R. Monroe,	99.
1808, April 4,	Wid. E. Nichols,	94.	1815, Jan. 21,	William Wilson,	94.
1810, Feb. 5,	Wid. L Spaulding,	93.	1816, Jan. 10,	Isaac Wilkins,	92.
1812, Dec. 22,	Joseph Barrett,	91.	1826, Nov. 17,	Wid. L. Russell,	95.
1816, Nov. 30,	John Waters,	98.			

ECCLESIASTICAL HISTORY. The first house for public religious worship was commenced about 1760, and completed in 1781, when 24 pews on the lower floor were sold for $950·50;

and in 1793, nineteen in the gallery for £58. This house was struck by lightning in May, 1810, and entirely consumed. The present house was dedicated the second Sabbath in December, 1811, and contains 44 pews on the lower floor and 16 in the gallery, which were sold that year for $2746·50. The builders were Joseph Wyman and John Sawyer; and the whole expense of the house, including the preparation of the spot, was $4866·81. A bell was procured in 1812 at an expense of $350. In consequence of the unfortunate loss of the old house the state tax for 1811 was remitted.

The church was organized February 28th, 1781, and then consisted of 10 male and 24 female members. Nathaniel Taylor, John Green, Phinehas Blood, and their wives, Joseph Monroe, Ebenezer Chase, Agnes Foster, Mercy Monroe, Ruth Monroe, Abigail Parlin, and Rebecca Heald had been members of the church in Concord. The other male members were Joshua Monroe, Jonathan Spaulding, Thomas Spaulding, Job Spaulding, John Robbins, and David Dickinson.

On the 17th of May, 1781, the church voted unanimously to invite Mr. Paul Litchfield to become their first pastor. In this vote the town concurred the 25th of the same month by a vote of 43 to 3. It was agreed to give him £150 as a settlement; and £80 in silver money, and 20 cords of wood annually, as a salary, so long as he should supply the pulpit. He was ordained November the 7th, 1781, on the same day as Mr. Stearns at Lincoln. The council on the occasion was composed of pastors and delegates from the churches in Billerica, Bedford, Concord, Acton, Westford, Ashby, 2d in Scituate, Abington, 2d in Medway, Franklin, North in Newburyport, and 2d in Salem; and were invited by Jonathan Spaulding, Thomas Spaulding, and John Green, a committee of the church. In the public religious exercises, the Rev. Samuel Spring, of Newburyport, made the introductory prayer; the Rev. Samuel Niles, of Abington, preached the sermon from 1 Cor. iv. 2; the Rev. Nathaniel Emmons of Franklin, made "the prayer during the imposition of hands"; the Rev. David Sanford of Medway, gave the charge, the Rev. Samuel Spring the right hand of fellowship, and the Rev. Samuel Whitman of Ashby made the concluding prayer.

The first communion was held December 31st, 1781, when it was voted to require a written or verbal relation by candidates, before the church and congregation, of the religious exercises of their minds before admission into the church. This embarrassing regulation was so modified two years afterwards, as to permit them to do it before a committee of the church. The doctrines contained in the confession of faith, and preached by Mr. Litchfield were strictly Calvinistic, coinciding in many points with that system of theology known by the name of Hopkinsianism.

No records are preserved to show the number of admissions into the church during Mr. Litchfield's long and peaceful ministry. In 1798, an interesting revival of religion prevailed, in which considerable additions were made to the church. The number of communicants in 1829, were 3 males and 24 females.

Deacons of the Church. Dea. John Robbins, chosen November 29th, 1781, excused from active duty, on account of infirmities October 5th, 1815, and died March 28th, 1826, aged 82 years; Dea. Ephraim Robbins, a brother of the preceding, admitted to the church May 9th, 1784, chosen into office soon after, and died July 29th, 1820, aged 63; Dea. John Green, chosen October 5th, 1815, and Dea. John Jacobs, chosen in 1812, are at present in office; the former in the Rev. Mr. Hull's, and the latter in the other church.

The REV. PAUL LITCHFIELD, died November 7th, 1827, in the 76th year of his age; and on the 46th anniversary of his ordination. He was the eldest of twelve children, and born of respectable parents in Scituate, March 12th, 1752. His youth was marked for sober and exemplary deportment, and for warm attachment to the friends of evangelical truth. With an intention to qualify himself for the gospel ministry, he entered Harvard College, and graduated in 1775. After he left college, he studied theology with the Rev. Dr. West, of Stockbridge; and was subsequently employed at several places till his engagement in Carlisle. Here he performed the ministerial duties with general acceptance. His views of evangelical truth were formed in the school of Hopkins, Emmons, and their associates; and were agreeable to the views of orthodoxy which were maintained by the rigid Calvinists at the time of his ordination. Of doctrinal theology, he was particularly fond, and was often accustomed to present its peculiar traits to his hearers. In his intercourse with his people he was kind, familiar, charitable, and peaceful. He rejoiced at the prosperity of the church, and aided by his personal services, and his wealth, many of the great religious charities of the age. To the Massachusetts Domestic Missionary Society he bequeathed, at his death, a generous legacy. He died in the full belief of that Christian faith, which he had inculcated, and of that hope which the Christian religion inspires.

The funeral sermon preached at his interment by the Rev. John H. Church, D. D., was printed, to which the reader is referred for a more particular notice of his character. Mr. Litchfield married, for his first wife, Miss Mary Bailey of Scituate, who died July 12th, 1809, aged 59, by whom he had 6 children, — 5 sons, Paul, Roland, Philo, Benjamin, and Franklin (who was graduated at Harvard College), and a daughter, who died in childhood. He married, for his second wife, Mrs. Sarah Capen of Braintree, October 12th, 1811, who still survives.

The Rev. STEPHEN HULL, the successor of the Rev. Mr. Litchfield, was born at Stonington, Connecticut, February 17th, 1779, and installed at Carlisle, December 29th, 1830, having previously been minister at Amesbury and Raynham, and dismissed at his own request. On this occasion, the Rev. Mr. Whitman made the introductory prayer; the Rev. Mr. Barry read selections from Scripture; the Rev. Peter Eaton, D. D., of Boxford, preached the sermon; the Rev. Dr. Ripley made the consecrating prayer; the Rev. Mr. Allen gave the charge; the Rev. Ephraim Randall gave the right hand of fellowship; the Rev. Charles Briggs addressed the people; and the Rev. John Goldsberry, of North Bridgewater, made the concluding prayer. These gentlemen, and the Rev. Mr. White of Littleton, and the Rev. Dr. Packard of Chelmsford, with delegates from their respective churches, composed the council. The Rev. Messrs. Samuel Stearns, Marshall Shed, and William Lawrence were invited to the council, but did not attend. Mr. Hull's church then consisted of *one* male, and *ten* female members, and worship in the meetinghouse erected by the town. *Three* male and *eight* female members had before seceded, and, with several others not members, erected a separate house, where they worship.

APPENDIX.

No. I. (SEE PAGE 103.)

HISTORICAL VIEW OF THE EVIDENCE RELATING TO THE EVENTS OF THE 19TH OF APRIL, 1775.

FIFTY years after the events of the 19th of April, 1775, occurred, some statements relating to the history of those events became the subject of controversy. The following questions embrace the most material points in discussion.

1. Did the Lexington company disperse as directed by the British officers? and were they *first* fired upon *while dispersing*?

2. Was the *first forcible resistance* to the British armed soldiers made by the provincials at Lexington in the morning; and did they *then* return the fire of the enemy?

Some individuals are satisfied with a history which describes the whole of the events of that day under the local name of Lexington Battle, whether reference be had to the affair at Lexington in the morning, or to the fight at Concord, or to that in the afternoon, continued during the whole course of the retreat from Concord to Charlestown; and they will consider it of little importance how these questions are answered. But those who regard truth as important in historical matters, even in minute particulars, will look at the subject in a different light. Without any intention of reviving the controversy, or of stating at length the reasons for the opinions I entertain, or of casting a comparative shade over the honor acquired by the brave " sons of liberty" in either town for the part they acted, I deem it due to historical truth to make the following detail of facts, that the subject may be fairly understood; and that those who entertain or promulgate opinions relating to these historical events, may have the means of doing it accurately.

The origin of this controversy will appear from the following statements. On the 2d of September, 1824, Lafayette passed through Lexington and Concord; and in an address to him in

Concord the Hon. Samuel Hoar said, "You now behold the *spot on which the first forcible resistance* was made" to British oppression. The same idea had often been given before by Morse, Worcester, and others, who had in their Gazetteers, described the geography of the town. In the following October the Bunker Hill Monument Association published an address to the public, soliciting subscriptions in aid of its objects, in which it is said, "At Concord the first [British] blood was shed between the British and armed Americans." — "It is also intended to erect a suitable monument at Concord, where the first conflict was had, bearing proper inscriptions to commemorate the glorious spirit of independence which manifested itself there." This produced two illiberal newspaper articles in "The Boston Patriot," and a reply from the Hon. William Sullivan, chairman of the committee. During the approaching winter the citizens of Concord made arrangements to celebrate by public performances the fiftieth anniversary of the 19th of April, 1775. The Hon. Edward Everett was engaged as the orator, and Lexington and the neighbouring towns were invited to unite in the ceremony. The Bunker Hill Monument Association appropriated $500, — which was somewhat less than the amount of the subscriptions to that Association in Concord, — towards the erection of a monument in that town, and sent to the committee of arrangements a plan of the monument, and proposed that the cornerstone should be laid on the day of the celebration.[1]

In the mean time the inhabitants of Lexington had taken measures to collect and publish a statement, intended, as we are informed in the preface to the publication, to counteract the influence of the two statements above mentioned; and also the testimony given under oath in 1775; and the narrative of the Rev. Mr. Clark published in 1776. The result of these measures was, "The History of the Battle at Lexington," written by Elias Phinney, Esq., a member of the committee chosen by the town for that purpose. This pamphlet was placed in the hands of the honorable and accomplished orator, and he states in a note to the historical Oration, pronounced at the celebration, that his "aim has been not to pronounce on questions in con-

---

[1] This money has been vested on interest by the town for this object. The Directors of the Bunker Hill Monument Association have also more recently pledged themselves to pay the additional sum of $1000; and when received, the whole will be appropriated to building a monument, probably on the very spot where the first British blood was shed, — where the first British life was taken, in the cause of American liberty, and **where are the graves of the slain.**

troversy," — "reference being had to the testimony contained" in Mr. Phinney's pamphlet. These two publications (the Oration and History) appeared in print about the same time; and, so far as relates to the particular facts in question, stand equally on controversial ground. In 1827, "the Rev. Ezra Ripley, D. D., and other citizens of Concord, published a "History of the Fight at Concord," intended to invalidate some of the statements contained in the two pamphlets just mentioned. All three of these publications, though they contain much valuable historical matter, must be considered in regard to the points at issue, controversial.

About the time these publications were made, several highly controversial articles appeared in the newspapers; but they cannot be regarded by candid minds in the serious light of historical truth. A new lithographic edition of Doolittle's Historical Engraving, first published in 1775, also appeared. In the original no one is represented as firing at the British soldiers at Lexington, but several as dispersing and some as slain. As this would be rather an awkward representation of a *battle*, the editors, as is sometimes the practice of historians, thought fit to improve the original to suit their views of what the engagement should have been. From this picture wood cuts have been prepared, which appear in some school-books to perpetuate error.

The original evidence, which was for the first time obtained and printed in the above pamphlets, was taken *ex parte*, and designed, so far as relates to the question at issue, to establish some particular facts in controversy, and cannot therefore be considered strictly impartial. If there was an influence which produced defective evidence in 1775, as has been stated, is it not more reasonable to suppose that some other influence, operating fifty years afterwards, when the facts could not be so distinctly remembered, and the points then in controversy were a subject of frequent conversation, might produce evidence so stated and expressed as to give erroneous impressions? Whatever weight might be attached to either of these publications, no accurate historian will be satisfied with their statements merely, or pronounce on questions in controversy, without a reference to the whole original evidence. In this case, as well as in many others, where historians copy the errors of other writers, it will be found to differ materially from the modern version. And what are the original sources of the evidence? What is its purport? And how was it understood?

Some account of those events was published in the "Essex Gazette" of April 21st and 25th, and May 5th, 1775, which, including an introduction, a list of the killed and wounded, and a "Funeral elegy to the immortal memory of those worthies which were slain in the Battle of Concord, April 19, 1775," soon after appeared in a hand-bill 20 inches long and 15 wide, entitled "Bloody Butchery by the British Troops, or the Runaway Fight of the Regulars"; — "being the Particulars of the Victorious Battle fought at and near Concord." Just above the title were pictured 40 coffins over which were printed the names of the slain.

On the 22d of April a committee of the Provincial Congress, consisting of Col. Elbridge Gerry of Marblehead, Hon. Thomas Cushing of Cohasset, Col. James Barrett of Concord, Capt. Josiah Stone of Dracut, Dr. John Taylor of Lunenburgh, Mr. Samuel Freeman of Falmouth, Abraham Watson, Esq. of Cambridge, and Jonas Dix, Esq. of Waltham, was chosen to take the depositions relating to the conduct of the British on the 19th; another was appointed to draw up a narrative, and another to make an additional copy of the depositions. After it was collected, the evidence was transmitted to the Continental Congress, and to England;[1] *part* of it was published in the "Pennsylvania Ledger," and copied into other American and English newspapers. The whole was published by Isaiah Thomas, by an order of the Provincial Congress passed May 28th, in a pamphlet of 22 pages, 8vo., entitled, "A Narrative of the Incursions and Ravages of the King's Troops under command of General Gage on the Nineteenth of April, 1775, together with the Depositions taken by order of Congress to support the truth of it." The pamphlet was ordered to be sent to every town in the province, though I have seen but one copy, which is owned by William Lincoln, Esq., of Worcester. These depositions were all taken the next week after the battle; and it is a fact worthy of notice, that those

---

[1] Capt. John Derby of Salem was despatched with these papers to England, where he arrived the 29th of May. He was the bearer of the "Essex Gazette," containing the first published account of these events, which was printed and circulated in London on the day of his arrival, and gave the first notice of the affair in England. It produced great commotion. General Gage's official account, although despatched four days before Capt. Derby sailed, did not arrive until the 10th of June, eleven days after Capt. Derby's arrival, subjecting the ministry to no small embarrassment and chagrin. The depositions taken out by Capt. Derby were the originals first taken, and contain the real signatures of the deponents. They were intended for the British government, but for some causes not known were never communicated. They have been returned to this country, and are now in the Library of Harvard College. See Washington's Writings, Vol. III. p. 35. The depositions and the letters sent by Capt. Derby may be found in the printed Journals of Congress for 1775.

relating to Concord were dated the 23d, and those relating to Lexington the 25th of April.

" A Narrative of the Concord Fight, with 104 Depositions to support the truth of it," was written by the Rev. Mr. Gordon of Roxbury, and published in George's Almanac for 1776, "by particular desire and for the use of the gentlemen officers and soldiers of the American Army." Lowe's Almanac for that year contains another account by the same gentleman, describing " what he saw, or collected from unquestionable authority on the spot," relating to the same events.

The Rev. Jonas Clark published his Narrative, referred to in our General History, in connexion with his Anniversary Sermon in 1776. He informs us that he was an eye-witness; and that it is " a plain and faithful narrative of facts, as they appeared unto us in this place."

A " circumstantial account" of this affair was transmitted by Gov. Gage to Gov. Trumbull;[1] and an official account was sent to England, which was not published by the ministry till June 10th, and which drew forth some severe but well deserved criticisms in the " Remembrancer " and other English papers. Gordon says it "had little truth in it;" and all who had even an imperfect knowledge of the facts will say the same. This statement of the material facts is contradicted by the original depositions, by Mr. Clark's Narrative, and by all the recent publications above noticed. It was so drawn up as *especially* to answer a particular purpose, and as a lame apology of Gage to England for murdering innocent citizens. It was probably compiled from letters of Smith and Percy, or from a narrative of the occurrences written by Ensign D. Bernicre, which was left in Boston, when the British evacuated it, and published in 1779, says the title, " for the information and amusement of the curious."[2] This remark in some measure shows the estimation in which its statements were then held. It was not believed by most of the English historians of those times, who have been considered accurate and impartial; though some, who appear willing to adopt the errors of others from prejudice or without careful investigation, have believed and sent it forth as truth.

These were all the material printed original sources of evidence.[3] Most other writers anterior to 1825 have described the

---

[1] 2 Massachusetts Historical Collections, ii, p. 224.
[2] 2 Massachusetts Historical Collections, iv, p. 215.
[3] The letter of Paul Revere relates to other occurrences of the day not in controversy. 1 Hist. Coll., Vol. v. p. 106.

events without being eye-witnesses, — without thorough examination, or have been mere copyists from some one of these authorities with comments to suit their own peculiar views.

And what is the purport of this evidence? In these depositions, Capt. Parker, commander of the Lexington company, testifies under oath, that on the approach of the British troops he "immediately ordered the militia to disperse, and not to fire; immediately said troops made their appearance." John Robbins, that when commanded by the British troops to disperse, they did disperse before any firing took place. 34 others, that "the company began to disperse, and, when their backs were turned upon the troops, they were fired upon." Timothy Smith, that "the troops marched up to the company then dispersing" before the firing. Thomas Fessenden, that "as soon as ever the officer cried 'Disperse, you rebels,' the said company dispersed as fast as they could; and, while they were dispersing, the regulars kept firing at them." Edward T. Gould, a British officer, that "on our approach they dispersed, and, soon after, firing began." The Rev. Mr. Clark fully confirms these depositions. The British account says, "when the troops came within one hundred yards of them they began to file off towards some stone walls."

How was this testimony understood? Isaiah Thomas, in the *Massachusetts Spy* of May 3d, 1775, published an account of this affair, "collected from those whose veracity is unquestioned," in which he says, "it is to be noticed they fired upon our people as they were dispersing agreeably to their command, and *that they did not even return the fire*." — "Thus did the troops of the British king fire first at two several times [at Lexington and Concord] upon his loyal American subjects, and put a period to ten lives *before a gun was fired upon them*. Our people THEN returned the fire and obliged them to retreat." The London "Remembrancer" (Vol. I, p. 56) says, "The positive oaths and veracity of witnesses render it unquestionable that the King's troops began the fire, and that too upon a very small body of provincials *who were dispersing*." Gordon, in the Narrative to which I have referred, says, "Upon seeing the regulars they dispersed." — "The Lexington company upon seeing these troops, and being of themselves so unequal a match for them, were deliberating for a few moments what they should do, when several dispersing of their own heads, the Captain soon ordered the rest to disperse for their own safety." This was before the firing of the British. "They killed 3 or 4 on the common, the rest on the other side of the walls, and while dispersing." This is confirmed by the British account. The Rev. Mr. Pemberton says, "They were fired upon *while dispersing;* "[1] and repeats the same idea in his manuscript history.

It has been said that this evidence was " *ex parte* and made for particular purposes," — to decide the question " whether the Americans fired first, and not whether they fired at all." It has also been said, that those " who gave in their evidence would not disclose any " facts which might in all probability expose themselves or their friends to the British halter." These objections, to be of force, must, as seems to me, apply equally to all the testimony, to that which relates to Concord as well as to Lexington; and even to the Narrative of Mr. Clark. The Concord deponents testified *before* " Gen. Gage and other apologists of British outrage," (in the language of Mr. Phinney's preface,) " had asserted that the people of Lexington commenced the attack on the king's troops," that they returned the fire and killed some of the British troops; and they testified *two days before* the Lexington deponents gave in their testimony to the same committee. If the Lexington company returned the fire, why, it has been asked, should they not have testified to it *after* the Concord deponents had done it? Why should one fear the halter more than the other? And why should it be more criminal in one to tell the whole truth than in the other? And it is especially difficult to perceive how Mr. Clark should be influenced by such or any other improper motives. His Narrative was drawn up after being a year on the spot, and after daily conversations on the subject. It is not easy to perceive how any motive could have influenced him to make an imperfect statement, or " color it for a particular purpose." He could not have suppressed the truth, because he feared " the halter"; nor was it necessary at that time to rouse the indignation of the Americans towards the British by erroneous statements, nor to refute their assertions, nor to show that they had committed " the most deliberate murder" at Lexington. Bunker Hill battle had been fought, Washington for some time had had the command of the army; and, among other great events, the enemy had removed from our neighbourhood, and evacuated Boston. Why should his Narrative not be believed and received as he says it is, — as " a plain and faithful Narrative of facts as they appeared to us in this place" [Lexington]? And with far more authority than any foreign historian?

None of the original authorities to which I have referred, states that the fire was returned, though it is inferred from what is testified that some guns were fired. But these could not have

---

[1] 1 Massachusetts Historical Collections, ii, p. 48.

been fired till after Capt. Parker had "ordered the militia to disperse and not to fire." — "Very few of our people," says Mr. Clark, "fired at all; and even *they* did not fire till, after being fired upon by the troops, they were wounded themselves, or saw others killed, or wounded by them, and looked upon it next to impossible to escape." But does not the expression *returning the fire*, as usually understood, convey some other meaning than that implied by Mr. Clark? Would two or three guns from behind the walls or from neighbouring houses or even on the common, on each one's own responsibility, after orders had been given by the commanding officer " to disperse and not to fire," be considered, in military affairs, or in the ordinary use of language, as returning the fire, and making a regular, forcible resistance? Whether any British blood was shed or not at Lexington in the morning, so far as regards the sources of evidence to which we have adverted, rests entirely on the assertion in the British account, that a single man was wounded in the leg. Whether this be true is problematical, since this account is not now relied on by any one as authority. It is not pretended by any one, that a single individual of the enemy was killed at Lexington in the morning.

Notwithstanding the distinguished part Concord acted on that occasion, her citizens never took the trouble to have the particulars published to the world. This is partly to be ascribed to the premature death of that devoted patriot, the Rev. William Emerson. He and several others left matter in manuscript which has aided me in this work. Lexington, on the other hand, celebrated the day by military parades and religious services on eight successive anniversaries; and the sermons preached on the occasion were printed. The legislature also granted on the 28th of February, 1797, on the petition of Joseph Simonds, then a representative from Lexington, $200 to erect a monument in that town. Mr. Thomas Park of Harvard built the monument. After some progress had been made in its erection it was found that a further sum would be necessary to complete it, and the selectmen petitioned for more aid. $200 more were granted on the 13th of January, 1798.[1] It was proper that such a monument should be placed there; and the inscription it bears is happily designed for its object. This monument, however, and the celebrations above noticed, combined with various other circumstances, have tended to take off the public mind from an examination of the whole history of the events of the 19th of April, 1775, and to mark this spot for other purposes than the monument

---

[1] **Resolves of the General Court.**

was intended, — the spot where the *first American blood was shed;* where *the first American life was taken.*

The inhabitants of Lexington deserve great credit for the stand they took in the morning, and the part they acted during the day. That her militia were slain with arms in their hands is an important fact, and highly honorable to their patriotism and valor. As to resistance there, it is not contended by any one that any was made or attempted, which could have impeded the progress of the troops. Mr. Clark speaks of the place, as "the field, not of battle, but of murder and bloodshed." This was undoubtedly true. It would have been rash and inconsiderate for 70 militia men to have placed themselves in the attitude of opposition to 800 chosen troops; and much more so to have engaged in a battle. It would have been folly, and not bravery. It was much more honorable to disperse. It was not so at Concord. There the circumstances were different, and the numbers of both opposing parties more nearly equal. All testimony concurs in saying that *there* was cool, deliberate, and effectual opposition, by order of the commanding officer. There was the first forcible resistance, — there the enemy were *first compelled to retreat:* and *there the first British life was taken.*

I annex all the depositions taken by authority of the Provincial Congress, and published officially in the pamphlet of which we have given the title on page 336. The signatures of the deponents, and the certificates of the Justices of the Peace and Notaries Public, only, are omitted.

"We, SOLOMON BROWN, JONATHAN LORING, and ELIJAH SANDERSON, all of lawful age and of Lexington, in the County of Middlesex, and colony of the Massachusetts-Bay, in New England, do testify and declare, That on the evening of the eighteenth of April instant, being on the road between Lexington and Concord, and all of us mounted on horses, we were, about ten of the clock, suddenly surprised by nine persons whom we took to be regular officers, who rode up to us, mounted and armed, each holding a pistol in his hand, and after putting pistols to our breasts, and seizing the bridles of our horses, they swore that if we stirred another step we should be all dead men, upon which we surrendered ourselves, they detained us until two o'clock the next morning, in which time they searched and greatly abused us, having first enquired about the magazine at Concord, whether any guards were posted there and whether the bridges were up, and said four or five regiments of regulars would be in possession of the stores soon, they then brought us back to Lexington, cut the horses bridles and girts, turned them loose, and then left us.

"*Lexington, April 25th,* 1775."

"I, ELIJAH SANDERSON above-named, do further testify and declare that I was in Lexington Common the morning of the nineteenth of April aforesaid, having been dismissed by the officers above-mentioned, and saw a large body of regular troops advancing towards Lexington Company, many of whom were then dispersing, I heard one of the regulars, whom I took to be an officer, say, 'Damn them we will have them,' and immediately the regulars shouted aloud, run, and fired on the Lexington Company, which did not fire a gun before the regulars discharged on them, eight of the Lexington company were killed, while they were dispersing and at considerable distance from each other, and many wounded, and, although a spectator, I narrowly escaped with my life.

"*Lexington, April 25th, 1775.*"

"I, THOMAS RICE WILLARD, of lawful age, do testify and declare, that being in the house of Daniel Harrington, of Lexington, on the nineteenth instant, in the morning, about half an hour before sun-rise, looked out at the window of said house and saw (as I suppose) about four hundred of regulars in one body coming up the road and marched toward the north part of the Common back of the meeting-house, of said Lexington, and as soon as said regulars were against the East-End of the meeting-house, the commanding officer said something, what I know not, but upon that the regulars ran till they came within about eight or nine rods of about an hundred of the militia of Lexington who were collected on said common, at which time the militia of Lexington dispersed, then the officers made an huzza, and the private soldiers succeeded them, directly after this, an officer rode before the regulars, to the other side of the body, and hollowed after the Militia of said Lexington, and said 'Lay down your arms, damn you, why don't you lay down your arms,' and that there was not a gun fired till the militia of Lexington were dispersed, and further saith not.

"*April 23d, 1775.*"

"*Lexington, 25th of April, 1775.*

"SIMON WINSHIP of Lexington, in the county of Middlesex, and province of the Massachusetts-Bay, in New England, being of lawful age testifieth and saith, that on the nineteenth of April instant, about four o'clock in the morning, as he was passing the public road in said Lexington, peaceably and unarmed, about two miles and an half distant from the meeting-house in said Lexington, he was met by a body of the King's regular troops, and being stopped by some officers of said troops was commanded to dismount, upon asking why he must dismount, he was obliged by force to quit his horse, and ordered to march in the midst of the body, and being examined whether he had been warning the minute-men he answered no, but had been out and was then returning to his father's. Said Winship further testifies, that he marched with said troops until he came within about half a quarter of a mile of said meeting-house, where an officer commanded the troops to halt, and then to prime and load ; this being done, the said troops marched on till they came within a few rods of Capt. Parker, and company, who were partly collected on the place of parade, when said Winship observed an officer at the head of said troops, flourishing his sword and with a loud voice giving the word ' Fire,' which was instantly followed by a discharge of arms from said regular troops, and said Winship is positive, and in the most solemn manner declares, that there was no discharge of arms on either side, till the word fire was given by said officer as above."

"*Lexington, April* 25*th*, 1775.

" I, JOHN PARKER, of lawful age, and commander of the militia in Lexington, do testify and declare, that, on the 19th instant, in the morning about one of the clock, being informed that there were a number of the regular officers riding up and down the road, stopping and insulting people as they passed the road, and also was informed that a number of the regular troops were on their march from Boston, in order to take the province stores at Concord, ordered our militia to meet on the common in said Lexington, to consult what to do, and concluded not to be discovered nor meddle or make with said regular troops (if they should approach) unless they should insult or molest us, and upon their sudden approach, I immediately ordered our militia to disperse and not to fire. Immediately said troops made their appearance and rushing furiously, fired upon and killed eight of our party, without receiving any provocation therefor from us."

"*Lexington, April* 24*th*, 1775.

" I, JOHN ROBBINS, being of lawful age, do testify and say, that on the 19th instant, the company under the command of Captain John Parker, being drawn up sometime before sunrise, on the green or common, and I being in the front rank, there suddenly appeared a number of the King's troops, about a thousand, as I thought, at the distance of about sixty or seventy yards from us, huzzaing, and on a quick pace towards us, with three officers in their front on horseback, and on full gallop towards us, the foremost of which cried, ' Throw down your arms, ye villains, ye rebels,' upon which said company dispersing, the foremost of the three officers ordered their men, saying, ' Fire, by God, fire,' at which moment we received a very heavy and close fire from them, at which instant, being wounded, I fell, and several of our men were shot dead by me. Capt. Parker's men, I believe, had not then fired a gun, and further the deponent saith not."

" We, BENJAMIN TIDD, of Lexington, and JOSEPH ABBOT, of Lincoln, in the county of Middlesex, and colony of the Massachusetts-Bay, in New England, of lawful age, do testify and declare, that, on the morning of the nineteenth of April instant, about five o'clock, being on Lexington common and mounted on horses, we saw a body of Regular Troops marching up to the Lexington company which was then dispersing; soon after, the regulars fired, first a few guns, which we took to be pistols, from some of the regulars who were mounted on horses, and then the said regulars fired a volley or two before any guns were fired by the Lexington company. Our horses immediately started and we rode off and further say not.

"*Lexington, April 25th, 1775.*"

"WE, NATHANIEL MULLIKEN, PHILIP RUSSELL, MOSES HARRINGTON, Jun., THOMAS and DANIEL HARRINGTON, WILLIAM GRIMER, WILLIAM TIDD, ISAAC HASTINGS, JONAS STONE, Jun., JAMES WYMAN, THADDEUS HARRINGTON, JOHN CHANDLER, JOSHUA REED, Jun., JOSEPH SIMONDS, PHINEAS SMITH, JOHN CHANDLER, Jun., RUEBEN LOCK, JOEL VILES, NATHAN REED, SAMUEL TIDD, BENJAMIN LOCK, THOMAS WINSHIP, SIMEON SNOW, JOHN SMITH, MOSES HARRINGTON, 3d., JOSHUA REED, EBENEZER PARKER, JOHN HARRINGTON, ENOCH WILLINGTON, JOHN HOSMER, ISAAC GREEN, PHINEAS STEARNS, ISAAC DURANT, and THOMAS HEADLY, Jun., all of lawful age, and inhabitants of Lexington, in the county of Middlesex, and Colony of the Massachusetts-Bay, in New England, do testify and declare, that on the nineteenth of April instant, about one or two o'clock in the morning, being informed that several officers of the regulars had, the evening before, been riding up and down the road, and had detained and insulted the inhabitants passing the same, and also understanding that a body of regulars were marching from Boston, towards Concord, with intent (as it was supposed) to take the stores belonging to the colony in that town, we were alarmed and having met at the place of our Company's parade, were dismissed by our Captain, John Parker, for the present, with orders to be ready to attend at the beat of the drum, we further testify and declare, that about five o'clock in the morning, hearing our drum beat, we proceeded towards the parade, and soon found that a large body of troops were marching towards us, some of our company were coming up to the parade and others had reached it, at which time the company began to disperse, whilst our backs were turned on the troops, we were fired on by them, and a number of our men were instantly killed and wounded, not a gun was fired by any person in our company on the regulars, to our knowledge, before they fired on us, and they continued firing until we had all made our escape.

"*Lexington, April 25th, 1775.*"

"We, NATHANIEL PARKHURST, JONAS PARKER, JOHN MUNROE, Jun., JOHN WINDSHIP, SOLOMON PEIRCE, JOHN MUZZY, ABNER MEADS, JOHN BRIDGE, Jun., EBENEZER BOWMAN, WILLIAM MUN-

APPENDIX. 345

roe, 3d., MICAH HAGAR, SAMUEL SANDERSON, SAMUEL HASTINGS, and JAMES BROWN, of Lexington in the county of Middlesex and colony of the Massachusetts-Bay, in New England, and all of lawful age, do testify and say, that on the morning of the nineteenth of April, instant, about one or two o'clock, being informed that a number of regular officers had been riding up and down the road the evening and night preceding, and that some of the inhabitants as they were passing had been insulted by the officers and stopped by them, and being also informed that the regular troops were on their march from Boston, in order (as it was said) to take the colony stores then deposited in Concord, we met on the parade of our company in this town; after the company had collected, we were ordered by Capt. John Parker (who commanded us) to disperse for the present, and to be ready to attend the beat of the drum, and accordingly the company went into houses near the place of parade. We further testify and say, that about five o'clock in the morning, we attended the beat of our drum, and were formed on the parade; we were faced towards the regulars then marching up to us, and some of our company were coming to the parade, with their backs towards the troops, and others on the parade began to disperse, when the regulars fired on the company, before a gun was fired by any of our company on them; they killed eight of our company and wounded several, and continued their fire until we had all made our escape.

"*Lexington, 25th April,* 1775."

"I, TIMOTHY SMITH of Lexington, in the county of Middlesex and colony of Massachusetts-Bay, in New England, being of lawful age, do testify and declare, that on the morning of the nineteenth of April instant, being at Lexington common, as a spectator, I saw a large body of regular troops, marching up towards the Lexington company, then dispersing, and likewise saw the regular troops fire on the Lexington company, before the latter fired a gun. I immediately ran, and a volley was discharged at me, which put me in imminent danger of losing my life: I soon returned to the Common, and saw eight of the Lexington men, who were killed, and lay bleeding at a considerable distance from each other, and several were wounded; and further saith not.

"*Lexington, April 25th,* 1775."

"We, LEVI MEAD and LEVI HARRINGTON, both of Lexington, in the county of Middlesex, and colony of the Massachusetts-Bay, in New England, and of lawful age, do testify and declare, that on the morning of the nineteenth of April, being on Lexington Common, as spectators, we saw a large body of regular troops marching up towards the Lexington company, and some of the regulars on horses, whom we took to be officers, fired a pistol or two on the Lexington company, which was then dispersing. These were the first guns that were fired, and they were immedi-

ately followed by several volleys from the regulars, by which eight men belonging to said company were killed, and several wounded.
"*Lexington, April 25th,* 1775."

"*Lexington, April 25th,* 1775.

"I, WILLIAM DRAPER, of lawful age, and an inhabitant of Colrain, in the county of Hampshire, and colony of the Massachusetts-Bay, in New England, do testify and declare, that being on the parade of said Lexington, April 19th, instant, about half an hour before sunrise, the King's regular troops appeared at the meeting-house of Lexington; Captain Parker's company, who were drawn up back of said meeting-house on the parade, turned from said troops, making their escape by dispersing, in the mean time the regular troops made an huzza, and ran towards Captain Parker's company who were dispersing, and, immediately after the huzza was made, the commanding officer of said troops (as I took him) gave the command to the troops, ' Fire, fire, damn you, fire,' and immediately they fired, before any of Captain Parker's company fired, I then being within three or four rods of said regular troops; and further saith not."

"*Lexington, April 23d,* 1775.

"I, THOMAS FESSENDEN, of lawful age, testify and declare, that being in a pasture near the meeting-house, at said Lexington, on Wednesday last, at about half an hour before sunrise, I saw a number of regular troops pass speedily by said meeting-house, on their way towards a company of militia of said Lexington, who were assembled to the number of about an hundred in a company, at the distance of eighteen or twenty rods from said meeting-house, and, after they had passed by said meeting-house, I saw three officers on horseback advance to the front of said regulars, when one of them, being within six rods of said militia, cried out, ' Disperse, you rebels, immediately,' on which he brandished his sword over his head three times ; meanwhile the second officer, who was about two rods behind him, fired a pistol, pointed at said militia, and the regulars kept huzzaing till he had finished brandishing his sword, and when he had thus finished brandishing his sword, he pointed it down towards said militia, and immediately on which, the said regulars fired a volley at said militia, and then I ran off as fast as I could, while they continued firing till I got out of their reach. I further testify, that as soon as ever the officer cried, ' Disperse, you rebels,' the said company of militia dispersed every way as fast as they could, and while they were dispersing, the regulars kept firing at them incessantly; and further saith not."

"*Lincoln, April 23d,* 1775.

"I, JOHN BATEMAN, belonging to the fifty-second regiment, commanded by Colonel Jones, on Wednesday morning, on the nineteenth day of April instant, was in the party marching to Concord, being at Lexington in the county of Middlesex, being nigh the meeting-house in said Lexington, there was a small party of men gathered together in that place, when our said troops marched by, and I testify and declare, that I heard the word of command given to the troops to fire, and some of said troops did fire, and I saw one of said small party lie dead on the ground nigh said meeting-house, and I testify, that I never heard any of the inhabitants so much as fire one gun on said troops."

"*Lexington, April* 23*d,* 1775.

"We, JOHN HOAR, JOHN WHITEHEAD, ABRAHAM GARFIELD, BENJAMIN MUNROE, ISAAC PARKS, WILLIAM HOSMER, JOHN ADAMS, and GREGORY STONE, all of Lincoln, in the county of Middlesex, Massachusetts-Bay, all of lawful age, do testify and say, that, on Wednesday last, we were assembled at Concord, in the morning of said day, in consequence of information received, that a brigade of regular troops were on their march to the said town of Concord, who had killed six men at the town of Lexington : about an hour afterwards we saw them approaching, to the number, as we apprehended, of about twelve hundred, on which we retreated to a hill about eighty rods back, and the said troops then took possession of the hill where we were first posted ; presently after this, we saw the troops moving towards the North Bridge about one mile from the said Concord meeting-house, we then immediately went before them and passed the bridge, just before a party of them, to the number of about two hundred, arrived : They there left about one half of their two hundred at the bridge, and proceeded with the rest towards Colonel Barret's, about two miles from the said bridge ; we then, seeing several fires in the town, thought the houses in Concord were in danger, and marched towards the said bridge, and the troops who were stationed there, observing our approach, marched back over the bridge, and then took up some of the plank ; we then hastened our march towards the bridge, and when we had got near the bridge, they fired on our men, first, three guns one after the other, and then a considerable number more, and then, and not before, (having orders from our commanding officers not to fire till we were fired upon,) we fired upon the regulars, and they retreated ; on their retreat through this town and Lexington, to Charlestown, they ravaged and destroyed private property and burned three houses, one barn, and one shop."

"*Lexington, April* 23*d,* 1775.

"We, NATHAN BARRET, Captain ; JONATHAN FARRER, JOSEPH BUTLER, and FRANCIS WHEELER, Lieutenants ; JOHN BARRET, Ensign ; JOHN BROWN, SILAS WALKER, EPHRAIM MELVIN, NATHAN BUTTERICK, STEPHEN HOSMER, Jun., SAMUEL BARRETT, THOMAS JONES, JOSEPH CHANDLER, PETER WHEELER, NATHAN PIERCE, and

Edward Richardson, all of Concord, in the county of Middlesex, in the province of the Massachusetts-Bay, of lawful age, testify and declare, that on Wednesday, the 19th instant, about an hour after sunrise, we assembled on a hill near the meeting-house in Concord aforesaid, in consequence of an information that a number of regular troops had killed six of our countrymen at Lexington, and were on their march to said Concord, and about an hour after we saw them approaching, to the number, as we imagine, of about twelve hundred, on which we retreated to a hill about eighty rods back, and the aforesaid troops then took possession of the hill where we were first posted. Presently after this, we saw them moving towards the North Bridge, about one mile from said meeting-house; we then immediately went before them, and passed the bridge just before a party of them, to the number of about two hundred, arrived; they there left about one half of those two hundred at the bridge, and proceeded with the rest towards Colonel Barrett's, about two miles from the said bridge; we then, seeing several fires in the town, thought our houses were in danger, and immediately marched back towards said bridge and the troops who were stationed there, observing our approach, marched back over the bridge, and then took up some of the planks; we then hastened our steps towards the bridge, and when we had got near the bridge, they fired on our men, first, three guns, one after the other, and then a considerable number more, upon which, and not before, (having orders from our commanding officers not to fire till we were fired upon,) we fired upon the regulars, and they retreated. At Concord, and on their retreat through Lexington, they plundered many houses, burnt three at Lexington, together with a shop and a barn, and committed damage, more or less, to almost every house from Concord to Charlestown."

"*Lexington, April* 23*d*, 1775.

"We, Joseph Butler and Ephraim Melvin, do testify and declare, that when the regular troops fired upon our people at the North Bridge, in Concord, as related in the foregoing depositions, they shot one, and, we believe, two of our people, before we fired a single gun at them."

"*Concord, April* 23*d*, 1775.

"I, Timothy Minot, Jun., of Concord, on the nineteenth day of this instant April, after that I had heard of the regular troops firing upon the Lexington men, and fearing that hostilities might be committed at Concord, thought it my incumbent duty to secure my family: After I had secured my family, some time after that, returning towards my own dwelling, and finding that the bridge on the northern part of said Concord, was guarded by regular troops, being a spectator of what had happened at said bridge, declare that the regular troops stationed on the bridge, after they saw the men that were collected on the westerly side of said bridge, marched towards said bridge, then the troops returned towards the easterly side of said bridge, and formed themselves, as I thought, for a regular fight, after that, they fired one gun, then two or three more, before the men that were stationed on the westerly part of said bridge fired upon them."

"*Lexington, April 23d*, 1775.

"I, JAMES BARRETT, of Concord, Colonel of a regiment of militia in the county of Middlesex, do testify and say, that on Wednesday morning last, about day-break, I was informed of the approach of a number of the regular troops to the town of Concord, where were some magazines belonging to this province, when there was assembled some of the militia of this and the neighbouring towns, when I ordered them to march to the North Bridge, so called, which they had passed and were taking up ; I ordered said militia to march to said bridge and pass the same, but not to fire on the King's troops unless they were first fired upon ; we advanced near said bridge, when the said troops fired upon our militia, and killed two men dead on the spot, and wounded several others, which was the first firing of guns in the town of Concord ; my detachment then returned the fire, which killed and wounded several of the King's troops."

"*Lexington, April 23d*, 1775.

"We, BRADBURY ROBINSON, SAMUEL SPRING, THADDEUS BANCROFT, all of Concord, and JAMES ADAMS, of Lincoln, all in the County of Middlesex, all of lawful age, do testify and say, that on Wednesday morning last, near ten of the clock, we saw near one hundred of regular troops, being in the town of Concord, at the North Bridge in said town (so called), and, having passed the same, they were taking up said bridge, when about three hundred of our militia were advancing toward said bridge, in order to pass said bridge, when, without saying any thing to us, they discharged a number of guns on us, which killed two men dead on the spot, and wounded several others, when we returned the fire on them, which killed two of them, and wounded several, which was the beginning of hostilities in the town of Concord."

"*Concord, April 23d*, 1775.

"I, JAMES MARR, of lawful age, testify and say, that in the evening of the 18th instant, I received orders from George Hutchinson, Adjutant of the fourth regiment of the regular troops stationed in Boston, to prepare and march, to which order I attended, and marched to Concord, where I was ordered by an officer, with about one hundred men, to guard a certain bridge there ; while attending that service, a number of people came along, in order as I supposed, to cross said bridge, at which time a number of regular troops first fired upon them."

"I, Edward Thornton Gould, of his Majesty's own regiment of foot, being of lawful age, do testify and declare, that on the evening of the 18th instant, under the order of General Gage, I embarked with the light infantry and grenadiers of the line, commanded by Colonel Smith, and landed on the marshes of Cambridge, from whence we proceeded to Lexington; on our arrival at that place, we saw a body of provincial troops armed, to the number of about sixty or seventy men; on our approach they dispersed, and soon after firing began, but which party fired first I cannot exactly say, as our troops rushed on, shouting, hazzaing, previous to the firing, which was continued by our troops so long as any of the provincials were to be seen. From thence we marched to Concord; on a hill near the entrance of the town, we saw another body of provincials assembled, the light infantry companies were ordered up the hill to disperse them; on our approach they retreated towards Concord, the grenadiers continued the road under the hill towards the town, six companies of light infantry were ordered down to take possession of the bridge which the provincials retreated over; the company I commanded was one of the three companies of the above detachment, went forward about two miles; in the mean time the provincial troops returned, to the number of about three or four hundred; we drew up on the Concord side of the bridge, the provincials came down upon us, upon which we engaged, and gave the first fire: this was the first engagement after the one at Lexington; a continued firing from both parties lasted through the whole day: I myself was wounded at the attack of the bridge, and am now treated with the greatest humanity and taken all possible care of, by the provincials at Medford.

"*Medford, April 20th, 1775.*"

"A paper having been printed in Boston, representing that one of the British troops killed at the bridge at Concord, was scalped and the ears cut off from the head, supposed to be done in order to dishonor the Massachusetts people, and to make them appear to be savage and barbarous, the following deposition was taken, that the truth may be known.

"'We, the subscribers, of lawful age, testify and say, that we buried the dead bodies of the King's troops that were killed at the North Bridge in Concord, on the nineteenth day of April, 1775, where the action first began, and that neither of those persons were scalped, nor their ears cut off, as has been represented.

"'Zechariah Brown,
"'Thomas Davis, Jun.

"'*Concord, May 11th, 1775.*'"

"Hannah Adams, wife of Deacon Joseph Adams, of the second precinct in Cambridge, testifieth and saith, that on the nineteenth day of April last past, upon the return of the King's troops from Concord, divers of them entered our house, by bursting open the doors, and three of the soldiers broke into the room in which I then was, laid on my bed, being scarcely able to walk from my bed to the fire, not having been to my chamber door from my being delivered in child-birth to that time. One of said soldiers immediately opened my curtains with his bayonet fixed, pointing the same to my breast. I immediately cried out 'For the Lord's sake do not kill me;' he replied, 'Damn you;' one that stood near said, 'We will not hurt the woman, if she will go out of the house, but we will surely burn it.' I immediately arose, threw a blanket over me, went out, and crawled into a corn-house near the door, with my infant in my arms, where I remained until they were gone; they immediately set the house on fire, in which I had left five children and no other person, but the fire was happily extinguished, when the house was in the utmost danger of being utterly consumed.

"*Cambridge, Second Precinct*, 17th *May*, 1775."

"*Cambridge, May* 19th, 1775.

"We, BENJAMIN COOPER and RACHEL COOPER, both of Cambridge aforesaid, of lawful age, testify and say, that in the afternoon of the 19th day of April last, the King's regular troops, under the command of General Gage, upon their return from blood and slaughter, which they had made at Lexington and Concord, fired more than an hundred bullets into the house where we dwell, through doors, windows, &c.; then a number of them entered the house, where we and two aged gentlemen were, all unarmed; we escaped for our lives into the cellar, the two aged gentlemen were immediately most barbarously and inhumanly murdered by them, being stabbed through in many places, their heads mauled, skulls broke, and their brains out on the floor, and walls of the house; and further saith not."*

---

* In March, 1834, while these sheets were passing through the press, the Rev. Dr. Ripley, with his characteristic patriotism and liberality, presented to the town of Concord, a lot of land of convenient size with a passage-way to it, where the Battle at the North Bridge took place, and where the first British soldier was killed and buried, on condition that the town erect a suitable monument there to commemorate those events, within three years from the 4th of July next. The town accepted this generous donation, and chose Daniel Shattuck, Ephraim Merriam, and Josiah Davis, a Committee to accomplish the wishes of the donor.

No. II. (SEE PAGE 124.)

NOTICES OF MILITARY SERVICES PERFORMED BY THE PEOPLE OF CONCORD IN THE REVOLUTION.

The numbers and dates refer to the Table of Campaigns, on pages 124 and 125 of the text.

2. April 20, 1775. The officers in the regiment, to which these men were attached, were, John Nixon, Colonel; Thomas Nixon, Lieutenant-Colonel; John Buttrick, Major. The officers of two companies, of 84 and 103 men, belonged to Concord. Joseph Butler was Captain; Silas Walker, Lieutenant; Edward Richardson, Ensign; Moses Richardson, Wareham Wheeler, Joseph Chesley, and Edward Heywood, Sergeants of one: and Abishai Brown was Captain; Daniel Taylor, Lieutenant; Silas Mann, Ensign; and Nathan Stow, Ephraim Minott, John Cobs, and Bradbury Robinson, were Sergeants of the other. Rev. William Emerson was Chaplain a part of the time; and Dr. Joseph Hunt was mate to Dr. Foster in Cambridge hospital. The men enlisted the last week in April, and the officers were commissioned June 5th. At the battle of Bunker Hill, Captain Butler's company, under command of Lieutenant Walker, were engaged at the northern declivity of the hill by the "rail fence"; and a part of the other company were on guard, and not ordered on in season to take part in the battle. Benjamin Ball received a mortal wound, of which he died in Boston. John Meers was killed. Amos Wheeler, Ephraim Minot, and some others, were wounded; the first died of his wounds at Cambridge, a short time after. As soon as the news of the battle arrived, the whole of the militia marched to Cambridge, but returned after a few days. A chest of clothing, and other articles necessary for the wounded, were contributed by the "patriotic ladies" in Concord, and sent to the hospital in Cambridge, for which they received public thanks. "This instance of their humanity and public spirit," says a public notice, " does honor to the town, and will, we hope, induce others to imitate so good an example." During this campaign, Danforth Hayward and William Buttrick died.

4. Jan. 20, 1776. Middlesex was ordered to raise a regiment of 571 men; Concord 26, Bedford 6, Acton 13, Lincoln 8. Concord, however, furnished 36. John Robinson was Colonel; John Buttrick,

APPENDIX. 353

Lieutenant-Colonel; Samuel McCobb, Major; Joseph Thaxter, Chaplain; Nathan Stow, Quarter-master; Jabez Brown, Adjutant. The Captains' names were, John Ford, Simon Edgel, Josiah Warren, Asahel Wheeler, Benjamin Edgel, Job Shattuck, and John Lamont. Silas Mann was a Lieutenant there under Wheeler.

A new organization of the militia was made in February, 1776, and Concord, Lexington, Weston, Acton, and Lincoln were assigned to the 3d Regiment. Oliver Prescott was then chosen Brigadier-General, Eleazer Brooks, Colonel of this regiment, Francis Faulkner, Lieutenant-Colonel; Nathan Barrett, 1st Major; Samuel Lamson, 2d Major; and Joseph Adams, Surgeon.

The following were the officers of the several companies:

CO.	LOCATION.	CAPTAIN.	1ST LIEUT.	2d LIEUT.
1.	Concord.	George Minott,	Edward Wright,	Emerson Cogswell.
2.	Weston.	Jonathan Fiske,	Matthew Hobbs,	Josiah Severns.
3.	Lexington.	John Bridge,	William Munroe,	Ebenezer White.
4.	Concord.	Thomas Hubbard,	Ephraim Wheeler,	Amos Hosmer.
5.	Acton.	Simon Hunt,	John Heald, Jr.	Benj. Brabrook.
6.	Lincoln.	Samuel Farrar,	Samuel Hoar,	James Parks.
7.	Concord.	Thomas Barrett,	Samuel Heald,	Asa Green.

Col. James Barrett was appointed to raise men in this county December 2d, 1775; and was muster-master from December 28th, 1776, till his death. Capt. Joseph Hosmer succeeded him in 1780.

The Concord Light Infantry was organized soon after, (of which Joseph Hosmer was Captain; Samuel Jones, Lieutenant; and Samuel Hosmer, 2d Lieutenant); and attached to this regiment.

5. March 1, 1776. This was a detachment of nearly all the militia, to take possession of Dorchester Heights just before the British evacuated Boston. The officers of the 3d Regiment abovementioned were generally there. An attack on Boston was anticipated, and a considerable quantity of lint and bandages was sent from Concord to the hospital.

6. April 9, 1776. This was an enlisted company for the purpose of fortifying and defending Boston and its vicinity. Officers; — Josiah Whitney, of Harvard, Colonel; Ephraim Jackson, of Newton, Lieutenant-Colonel; John Miller, Major. For the Middlesex company, — Abishai Brown, Captain; Abraham Andrews, 1st Lieutenant; Silas Proctor, 2d Lieutenant; Jeremiah Williams and Edward Heywood, all of Concord, were Sergeants. They were stationed at Hull. This company assisted in taking Col. Campbell, about three hundred Highlanders, and several

45

provision ships. They left Concord June 1st, and were discharged December 1st. Thaddeus Blood, Esq., is the only person now living in Concord who belonged to this company.

8. June 25, 1776. Dr. John Cuming was appointed Commander in this expedition, but declined. The whole consisted of five thousand men. One company, consisting of ninety-four men, was commanded by Capt. Charles Miles, of Concord. Edmond Munroe, was Lieutenant; Matthew Hobbs, 2d Lieutenant; and Jonas Brown, Ensign. They were attached to Col. Jonathan Reed's regiment. His muster-roll gives sixty-one from Concord, (differing from the report from which the above is compiled); Weston, twenty-seven; Lexington, four; and two from Tyconterage. Being ready to march, they were paraded on the common in Concord, with several other companies from the adjoining towns, and attended religious services in the meeting-house. Rev. William Emerson preached from Job v. 20, and afterwards went as Chaplain, sacrificed his life to his patriotism, and never returned. Another Company, commanded by Capt. Asahel Wheeler, whose Lieutenant was Samuel Hoar, of Lincoln. Samuel Osburn was 2d Lieutenant, and Daniel Hosmer, Ensign.

9. Sept. 12, 1776. This embraced one fifth of the Militia under fifty years of age, not in actual service. The drafts from this county formed one regiment, which was commanded by Eleazer Brooks, of Lincoln. Rev. Moses Adams, of Acton, was Chaplain; Dr. Joseph Hunt, Surgeon; and Samuel Hartwell, of Lincoln, Quarter-master. Concord furnished twenty-three men; Lexington, sixteen; Acton, fifteen; and Lincoln, twelve, which formed one company, whose officers were Simon Hunt, of Acton, Captain; Samuel Heald, of Concord, Lieutenant; Ebenezer White, 2d Lieutenant. They were in the battle of White Plains. A return after the battle gives forty-two fit for duty, seven sick, four wounded, two of whom, David Wheeler and Amos Buttrick, belonged to Concord. Thomas Darby, of Acton was killed. Col. Brooks's Regiment behaved bravely on that occasion.

10. These were part of a company of eighty-nine men, taken from nearly every town in this county, commanded by John Minott, of Chelmsford, and attached to Col. Dykes's Regiment. John Hartwell, of Lincoln, was Lieutenant. Acton furnished five; Lincoln, four; and Bedford, three.

11. Nov. 21, 1776. This was one fourth of the Militia in Middlesex County, and formed one Regiment of six hundred and seventy men, commanded by Col. Samuel Thatcher, of Cambridge. Cyprian How, of Marlborough, was Lieutenant-Colonel;

APPENDIX. 355

Joseph Bryant, of Stoneham, Major. Concord furnished thirty-four ; Weston, eighteen ; Lexington, fourteen ; Acton, thirteen ; Lincoln, thirteen, which composed one company. John Bridge, of Lexington, was Captain ; Jacob Brown, of Concord, Lieutenant ; and Josiah Stearns, of Weston, 2d Lieutenant; William Burrows, Orderly Sergeant. They marched to New-York and New-Jersey before they returned, and were stationed at Woodbridge. Dissolved March 6th.

12. Dec. 1, 1776. It appears from a roll of this company in the Secretary's office, that Capt. John Hartwell was commander of it. Thirteen in this and six in other companies were from Lincoln. They were attached to Col. Dykes's Regiment.

13. Dec., 1786. These were attached to the Artillery.

14. Jan. 20, 1777. These were the first three-years men enlisted. Col. James Barrett mustered all the men from this county. Ephraim Wood paid the bounty of those enlisted in Concord. Nathan Wheeler, Ephraim Wheeler, Ephraim Minott, and Wareham Wheeler, were Lieutenants in the three years' service. The forty-four names follow.

Thomas Wood, Matthew Jameson, Amos Nutting, Job Spaulding, John Hodgman, William Wilson, Josiah Blood, Patrick Neiff, David Jenners, Abraham Davis, Thomas B. Ball, Pomp Cady, James Bray, Daniel Brown, James Barrett, Edward Butt, Edward Wilkins, John Sherwin, Samuel Dutton, John Corneil, Samson Yammon, Daniel Stearns, Amos Darby, William Wheeler, Charles Prescott, John Darling, Charles Lloyd, Lemuel Wheeler, Nathaniel Draper, Oliver Rice, Stephen Stearns, James Melvin, James Allen, Richard Anthony, Oliver Barnes, John McGath, Thomas Fay, Cesar Minott, Samuel Butler, Francis Legross, Charles Swan, James Marr, Nathaniel Taylor, Tilly Holden (died), Samuel Blood, Daniel Cole.

15. April 12, 1777. This was a detachment to reinforce General Spencer. Amos Hosmer and Thaddeus Hunt were Lieutenants.

17. July, 1777. Abishai Brown was Captain ; Daniel Davis, of Acton, 1st Lieutenant ; James Brown, of Lexington, 2d Lieutenant ; Thaddeus Blood, Orderly Sergeant ; Abel Davis, Drummer. They left about the 1st of June. Dr. Isaac Hurd was Surgeon of the regiment, which was commanded by John Jacobs and Lieut.-Col. Robinson, and was under Gen. Spencer. Abishai Brown was appointed Major in this campaign. The town estimate gives fourteen only in this campaign, but is probably incorrect. Dea. White's MS. says, " July 23, 1777, an alarm, — draughted the following persons to go to R. Island," and gives the names of twenty-nine.

18. Aug. 9, 1777. These constituted one sixth of the militia. George Minott was Captain. They were at the battle of Saratoga, and at the taking of Burgoyne. They subsequently marched to New Jersey.

19. Sept. 22, 1777. This was a volunteer company of sixty-three men from Concord and Acton, commanded by John Buttrick. John Heald and Silas Mann, were Lieutenants; John White, Samuel Piper, Reuben Hunt, and Peter Wheeler, Sergeants. They were under Col. Reed. They left Concord, October 4th, passed through Rutland, Northampton, &c., and arrived at Saratoga on the 10th, where they encamped two days. The 13th they went to Fort Edward. The 14th and 15th, went out on a scout, and the 16th brought in fifty-three Indians, several Tories (one of whom had 100 guineas), and some women. The 17th "we had an express," says Dea. White's Journal, "to return to Saratoga, and had the pleasure to see the whole of Burgoyne's army parade their arms, and march out of their lines; a wonderful sight indeed; it was the Lord's doing, and it was marvellous in our eyes." They guarded the prisoners to Cambridge. $206 were subscribed to encourage these men, beside the bounty specified in the table. Samuel Farrar commanded a company from Lincoln and Lexington in this campaign.

20. Nov. 28, 1777. Capt. Simon Hunt, of Acton, commanded the company to which most of the Concord men were attached, under Col. Eleazer Brooks and Gen. Heath. Nine companies guarded Burgoyne's troops down, five marching before and four behind.

21. March 3, 1778. Resolutions were passed February 7th, for four hundred men, and March 11th and 13th, each for five hundred more to guard the stores at Boston. These men were called out for that purpose, and were under the command of Gen. Heath. Thomas Barrett was Captain a part of the time; Daniel Harrington, the other part; Elisha Jones and Asa Green, Lieutenants. They were under Col. Jonathan Reed.

22. April 12, 1778. These men were raised for the defence of Rhode Island under Gen. Spencer. The officers of the regiment were John Jacobs, Colonel; Frederick Pope, Lieutenant-Colonel; Abishai Brown, Major. They were chosen February 27th. Thaddeus Blood, of Concord, was Ensign in this campaign. The committee chosen by the town to hire them, were Col. James Barrett, Col. John Buttrick, Mr. Ephraim Wood, Jr., Jonas Heywood, Esq., and John Cuming, Esq.

23. April 20, 1778. These men were Oliver Buttrick, Benjamin Gould, Jason Bemis, William Diggs, Joseph Plummer,

Cesar Kettle, David White, Benjamin Perkins, Jeremiah Hunt, Jr., and John Stratten. These were hired by the town, as in the last, and all subsequent campaigns. These were part of two hundred men. Acton and Lincoln furnished five each, and Bedford three. They marched first to Rhode Island, and afterwards to New York. They were to serve nine months from the time they arrived at Fishkill.

24. April 20, 1778. Their names were William Burrows (a Lieutenant), Reuben Parks, Timothy Merriam, Jeremiah Williams, Jonathan Curtis, Jacob Ames, Timothy Hoar, Wareham Wheeler, Joseph Cleisby.

25. June 23, 1778. These men guarded the prisoners to the new barracks built at Rutland. Ephraim Wood was appointed to superintend their removal.

26. June 27, 1778. These men were sent to reinforce General Sullivan. John Buttrick was Lieutenant-Colonel, and was wounded at Sullivan's retreat. Samuel Jones and Emerson Cogswell were Lieutenants under Capt. Francis Brown, of Lexington. Thaddeus Blood was Ensign in the State troops at the same time. Benjamin Prescott was Surgeon. One Sergeant and three Corporals were from Concord.

27. Sept. 6, 1778. The town received the order, September 10th, and held a meeting the next day, when a committee was chosen to hire them. They were paid £23 per month, including the public wages. The men were, Timothy Killock, Charles Shepherd, Daniel Wheat, Timothy Wetherbee, Jesse Parkins, Thomas Hodgman, and Silas Parlin.

28. Sept. 19, 1778. This constituted one third-of the militia, required to march to Boston at a minute's warning. They volunteered under Col. Cuming, and were to receive $5 bounty, and $15 per month, including the pay allowed by the public. The orders were countermanded and they did not march. This is the only instance in all the campaigns of the men not marching when called.

29 and 30. April and June, 1778. The town chose a committee June 16th, to hire the men for these two campaigns, consisting of Col. Nathan Barrett, the four commanding officers of the militia companies, the Selectmen, Col. John Cuming, Mr. Jonas Heywood, Capt. David Brown, Capt. Joseph Butler, and James Barrett, Esq. Acton furnished four; Bedford, three; Lincoln, five; and the whole county, two hundred and forty-five in the nine months' campaign. The detachment to Rhode Island took one hundred men more from this county, who were under Col. Jacobs. The 3d Regiment was required to furnish one Ser-

geant and eleven privates. Thaddeus Blood was a Lieutenant in the United States' service; Jonas Wright was Sergeant.

31. June, 1779. The town received orders for these men September 1st, and chose the Selectmen, Col. Nathan Barrett, Jonas Heywood, Esq., and the four militia Captains, a committee to procure these and all others "when small drafts are called," without calling the town together.

33. Sept., 1779. These belonged to a company of thirty-eight men from this and the adjoining towns, under Samuel Heald, Captain; Enoch Kingsbury, Lieutenant; Stephen Hosmer, 2d Lieutenant; and John Jacobs, Colonel. Henry Flint was Sergeant Major. They were discharged in November, and the whole amount of their wages was 10*s*. 6*d*. in silver each!

OFFICERS OF THE 3D REGIMENT OF MILITIA MARCH 7TH, 1780.

CO.	LOCATION.	CAPTAIN.	1st LIEUT.	2d LIEUT.
1.	Concord.	Jacob Brown,	John White,	Asa Brooks.
2.	Weston.	Matthew Hobbs,	Josiah Livermore,	Daniel Livermore,
3.	Lexington.	John Bridge,	William Munroe,	
4.	Concord.	Thomas Hubbard,	Ephraim Wheeler,	Amos Hosmer.
5.	Acton.		John Heald,	Benj. Brabrook.
6.	Lincoln.	Samuel Farrar,	Samuel Hoar,	James Parks.
7.	Concord.	Samuel Heald,	Issachar Andrews,	Stephen Barrett.
8.		Francis Brown,	Isaac Addington,	Thos. Fessenden.
9.	Concord.	Samuel Jones	Elisha Jones,	Stephen Hosmer.

34. Sept. 1, 1779. The names of these men were, Charles Shepherd, Lot Lamson, Francis Baker, Timothy Wesson, Nathan Page, Asa Piper, Timothy Sprague, Nathaniel Breed, Charles Hanley, John Stratten, Ezekiel Hager, Jeremiah Shepherd, Nathaniel French, Josiah Melvin, Jr., Joshua Stevens, Phillip Barrett, Lemuel Wheeler, Chandler Bryant, Daniel Cole. Acton furnished eleven; Bedford, seven; Lincoln, nine; Carlisle, seven. These men were procured by a committee chosen by the town, June 12th, in addition to that chosen in September previous, consisting of John Cuming, Esq., Capt. David Brown, Capt. Andrew Conant, Capt. David Wheeler, and Lieut. Stephen Barrett. They were also to procure others, " if the draught does not exceed sixteen; if it does, the town to be called together."

35. June 5, 1780. These men were hired by the same committee. They were intended to march to Albany to prevent the incursions of the Indians, but counter orders were issued and they went to Rhode Island. Cyprian How was Colonel; —— Bancroft, of Dunstable, Lieutenant-Colonel; —— Stone, of Ashby, Major; Abraham Andrews, Captain; Silas Walker and Eli

Conant, Lieutenants. Bedford furnished eight ; Acton, eleven ; Lincoln, twelve ; and Carlisle, nine.

37. Dec. 2, 1780. These men were to serve three years or during the war. The town decided, after considerable debate, by a vote of 53 to 42, to hire them in classes. The Selectmen, James Barrett, Esq., Jonas Heywood, Esq., Mr. Isaac Hubbard, Mr. Samuel Hosmer, Col. Nathan Barrett, and Mr. Job Brooks were chosen to divide the town into as many classes as there were men to hire, according to wealth. The town voted to " proceed against " any who should neglect to pay their proportion in the several classes ; each one of which hired a man at as low a rate as possible. The men's names were Charles Adams, Richard Hayden, Jonathan Wright, Joseph Dudley, Isaac Hall, Lot Lamson, Francis Barker, Joseph Adams, Benjamin Barron, William Tenneclef, Richard Hobby, Leonard Whitney, Samuel Farrar, John Stratten, Daniel McGregor, and Jonathan Fiske. Bedford furnished eight; Acton, ten ; Lincoln, ten ; Carlisle, six. They were mustered by Capt. Joseph Hosmer.

39. June 15, 1781. Bedford furnished seven ; Acton, eight ; Lincoln, eight ; Carlisle, four, for this campaign. The whole State furnished two thousand seven hundred.

40. June 30, 1780. These men were hired by classes. Dea. John White was Chairman of the 3d class, which was assessed £180 to hire Joseph Cleisby. The 5th class, of which Reuben Hunt was Chairman, hired Jacob Laughton, for £90 lawful money as a bounty. Sometimes $100 were given by a single individual. All property seemed to be at the disposal of government, if required. The soldiers were paid off in government sureties which were sold for 2s. 6d. on the pound. Nathaniel French received ninety bushels of rye.

NO. III.

NOTICES OF EARLY FAMILIES AND DISTINGUISHED MEN.

Genealogical history is necessary in Europe to show the titles to honor and estate; but in this country, where wealth and distinction depend almost exclusively on each one's own merits and exertions, it is a subject of curiosity rather than absolute importance. As a subject of useful curiosity, however, it has recently attracted considerable attention. The student of human nature looks to the rise and fall of families as an important subject of investigation. And it cannot but afford satisfaction to trace our ancestors back through the different generations to the first one who emigrated from England, and to know that some of their blood flows in our veins. That we were descended from individuals, distinguished for their good character, should excite us to imitate their excellencies, if otherwise, to avoid their errors. It has often been remarked, that, when families continue on their own native soil and intermarry with their neighbours, they are apt to degenerate; and observation often teaches us the truth of this remark. Like the productions of the vegetable world, man seems to be designed to flourish better when transplanted, and mingling his own with different natures. In reviewing the biographical history of Concord, it will be perceived that many families who were once distinguished in its annals have become extinct; and others have arisen, in many instances from comparative obscurity, to take their places in conducting the affairs of the town.

Happily for our country, its foundation was not laid in a fabulous age, but the precise date of its origin is known, and very many of the names of its intrepid founders are registered for the admiration of their posterity. It has occurred to me that a brief notice of the families in Concord, whose names are found on record prior to 1700, would be an acceptable article in the appendix to this work. When I first instituted the inquiry in relation to the first American ancestors of the Concord families, I found a tradition prevailing that *three brothers* came over from England, and the tradition went so far as to designate particularly the place where each first settled. When I found this same tradition in many different families I became incredulous, and on

APPENDIX. 361

examination found it incorrect. It is not difficult to trace our ancestors back to the commencement of the last century, — to what I have styled the dark age of New England; but to go three generations farther back to the first settlers in 1635, and through seven successive generations from them to us, is attended with great difficulty. The following notes are compiled from a large mass of facts collected with great labor from existing public and private records and papers; and, though containing but a small portion only of what might be given, it is hoped they will be satisfactory and not considered the least valuable part of this work.

N. B. In the following pages *b.* stands for born, *m.* for married, *d.* for died, *da.* for daughter and *a.* for aged.

ADAMS. Three of the sons of Henry Adams (who came from Devonshire, England, and settled in Quincy, ancestor of John Quincy Adams), came to Concord about 1646, of whom two, Samuel and Thomas, removed to Chelmsford in 1654, and were leading men in that town; and the other, John, removed to Cambridge, or Charlestown. John's children were John, Mary, Daniel, b. in Concord; and John and Daniel his grandsons settled here. John m. Love Minott 1722, and d. Oct. 25, 1725, a. 28, leaving John, who m. Lucy Hubbard 1749, and Love, who m. Rev. Wm. Lawrence of Lincoln. Daniel m. Elizabeth Minott 1715, settled where the tavern in the south part of Lincoln stands, and d. Feb. 9, 1780, a. 90. She d. 1766, a. 68. They had Daniel, Elizabeth, Joseph, Rebecca, Mary, James, Lydia, and Martha, whose descendants live in Lincoln, Boston, Townsend, and Keene, many of whom have been eminent physicians.

JAMES ADAMS, of another family, said to have been banished from Scotland by Oliver Cromwell, m. Priscilla Ramsden of Concord 1662, and d. Dec. 2, 1707. Had Priscilla, Elizabeth, James, Hannah, John, Nathaniel, and Dorcas, whose descendants are found in Carlisle and Acton.

ANDREWS. *John Andrews* was here before 1640, and might have been the ancestor of the families who afterwards lived in Carlisle, but his family is traced with much difficulty.

ATKINSON. *Thomas Atkinson* was here in 1638, and d. 1646; had daughters Susannah, m. Caleb Brooks ancestor of the Hon. Peter C. Brooks and Gov. John Brooks, and Hannah. The name soon after disappears.

BAKER. *William Baker* owned land here before **1665.** He, or a son of the same name, came from Charlestown, m. and had several children between 1680 and 1696. James, Amos, and Nathaniel of this town and Lincoln in 1828, were grandsons of Jacob, who according to tradition came from Killingsly, Conn.

BALL. *John Ball* d. Oct. 1, 1655, said to have been from Wiltshire, Eng. His son, Nathaniel, settled within the present limits of Bedford, and had Ebenezer, Eleazer, John, and Nathaniel. — The last was father to Caleb, (grandfather to Reuben), who m. Experience Flagg, 1713, and had eight children, three of whom lived to be over 90 years old. Other sons of the first John settled in Watertown and Lancaster.

BAGNLEY. Thomas Bagnley d. March 18, 1643.

BARKER. *Francis Barker* was here in 1646, and was probably the father of John, who m. Judah Simonds in 1668, bought a large tract of land in Concord, and had several descendants, some of whom were remarkable for their longevity.

BARNES. *John Barnes* was here in 1661, m. Elizabeth Hunt 1664, and was killed in Sudbury fight 1676. He has descendants still living here.

BARRETT. *Humphrey Barrett* came to Concord from England about 1640, and settled where Abel B. Heywood now lives; d. Nov. 7, 1662, a. 70; his wife in 1663, a. 73. They left Thomas, Humphrey, John of Marlborough, James of Charlestown, and probably other children. Thomas was drowned in Concord river; his widow m. Edward Wright; his son Oliver d. 1671, a. 23; and his da. Mary m. Samuel Smeadly. His brother Dea. Humphrey, m. (1) Elizabeth Payne 1661, and had Mary, who m. Josiah Blood; and (2) Mary Potter, 1675. He d. Jan. 3, 1716, and she Nov. 17, 1713, leaving two sons, Joseph and Benjamin, ancestors of the numerous and respectable families which have borne the name in Concord.

I. JOSEPH m. Rebecca Minott 1701, lived with his father, was a captain, d. April 4, 1763, a. 85. She d. June 23, 1738. They had eight children. 1. Mary m. George Farrar; 2. Joseph of Grafton; 3. Rebecca, m. Elnathan Jones; 4. Oliver of Bolton; 5. Humphrey, m. Elizabeth Adams 1742, and d. March 24, 1783, leaving two sons, Humphrey and Abel, and six daughters; 6. Elizabeth, m. Charles Prescott; 7. John, m. Lois Brooks; and 8. Samuel.

II. BENJAMIN, m. Lydia Minott, sister of the above, 1705, d. Oct. 25, 1728, a. 47. They had eight children; 1. Benjamin, d. in Concord Oct. 23, 1738, and had Benjamin, Jonas, and Rebecca; 2. Dea. Thomas, m. Mary Jones, and had Thomas, Charles of New Ipswich, Samuel, Amos, Ruth, and Mary ; 3. Col. James (see below), m. Rebecca Hubbard, and had James, Nathan, Lydia, Rebecca, Perses, Stephen, Peter, and Lucy ; 4. Lydia, m. Samuel Farrar ; 5. Timothy of Paxton ; 6. Mary ; 7. Stephen of Paxton ; 8. Rebecca.

Col. JAMES BARRETT, son of Benjamin Barrett, was born July 29, 1710. Having early embraced those principles of religion, which are calculated to make men respected, useful, and happy, and having arrived to mature age in an important period of our history, he received from his townsmen frequent marks of their confidence in civil and military life. In 1768 he was chosen representative to the General Court, and was re-elected each year till 1777. He was also member of many of the county and state conventions held during that important period ; and a member of each of the Provincial Congresses. When it was decided to collect and deposit military stores at Concord, Col. Barrett was appointed to superintend them, and aid in their collection and manufacture. He accepted the office of Colonel of the regiment of militia, organized in March, 1775, and was in command on the 19th of April, though then 64 years old. How he conducted himself on that great day, has already been related. Of the various committees chosen by the state, county, or town, for raising men, procuring provisions, &c., he was usually a member. He died suddenly, April 11, 1779, in his 69th year.

BARRON. *John Barron* was here early, but removed. Some of the name have, however, since lived in town.

BATEMAN. Two brothers of this name were among the earliest settlers. William removed to Chelmsford, where his descendants have since lived. Thomas settled easterly of Humphrey Hunt's, d. Feb. 6, 1669, a. 55, left estate £348 ; and sons Thomas, Peter, John, and Ebenezer, b. prior to 1659. Thomas m. Abigail ——, and from him most of the name in this town derived their descent. He was known as *Sergeant* Bateman, an office he held with honor about thirty years.

BLISS. See pages 166 and onward.

BELLOWS. *John Bellows*, m. Mary, da. of John Wood of Marlborough, 1655, and had Mary, Samuel, Abigail, Daniel, and Benjamin, b. between 1655 and 1676. Removed to Marlborough, and some of his descendants to Walpole, N. H.

BENNETT. James Bennett here before 1637 ; had children b. in this town ; removed to Fairfield with Rev. Mr. Jones, in 1644.

BEATON. John Beaton. (See p. 216.)

BILLINGS. *Nathaniel Billings* here before 1640, freeman 1641, d. 1673; left two sons, Nathaniel and John. John m. Elizabeth Hastings 1661, d. March 31, 1704, and had John, Nathaniel, Samuel, John, Elizabeth, Mary, Sarah, and Joseph. Nathaniel, the second son, was father of Daniel (who lived where William Hayden, Esq. now lives), whose only child m. Dea. Amos Heald. The family originally settled in the south parts of the town, now Lincoln, where, and in Acton, the sixth and seventh generations now reside.

BLOOD. *James Blood* came to Concord in 1639, said to have been a brother of Col. John Blood, known in English history for his designs on Charles II. He had a great estate; d. Nov. 17, 1683. His wife Ellen, 1674. They left Mary, m. Lt. Simon Davis, and four sons.

1. *Richard,* one of the first settlers and largest proprietors of Groton; left several children, whose descendants have been numerous in that town and vicinity.

2. *John,* unmarried, found dead in the woods with his gun in his hand, Oct. 30, 1692. He and his brother Robert sold a cottage in Puddington, Nottingham Co. Eng., 1649, when they were in Concord. They owned over two thousand acres of land, including *Bloods' Farms,* which fell to Robert's children.

3. *James,* m. Hannah, da. of Oliver Purchis of Lynn, 1657; lived where Rev. Dr. Ripley lives; deacon in the church; d. Nov. 26, 1692; she d. 1677; left an only child, Sarah, m. William Wilson.

4. *Robert,* lived on his "farm"; m. Elizabeth, da. of Major Willard, 1653; he d. Oct. 27, 1701; she Aug. 29, 1690; had twelve children, — Mary, Elizabeth, Sarah, Robert, Simon, Josiah, John, Ellen, Samuel, James (grandfather to Thaddeus Blood, Esq.), Ebenezer, and Jonathan.

BOWSTREE. William Bowstree d. Nov. 31, 1642.

BRABROOK. Two of this name, probably brothers, were here as early as 1669; Thomas, m. Abigail Temple 1669, d. 1692. Joseph, from whom those who have borne the name, descended, m. Sarah Greaves 1672, and had 1. Joseph, m. Sarah Temple, and d. 1719, father to Benjamin, and grandfather to Dea. Joseph, late of Acton; 2. John, d. " a soldier at Lancaster " 1705; and several daughters. Of the descendants, James d. at Fort Lawrence in Nova Scotia, and Samuel at Rainsford Island in 1756.

BROOKS. Capt. *Thomas Brooks*, freeman 1636, and in

Concord about that time, said to have come from London, representative seven years, d. May 21, 1667. Grace, his wife, d. May 12, 1664. They had Joshua, Caleb, Gershom, Mary, m. Capt. Timothy Wheeler of Concord, and probably Thomas, who went to Haddam, Conn., Hugh, and John of Woburn, and probably other children.

Caleb m. (1) Susannah Atkinson 1660, and had Susannah, Mary, Rebecca, and Sarah; and (2) Ann ———, by whom he had Ebenezer, ancestor of Governor John Brooks, and Samuel, ancestor of Hon. Peter C. Brooks. He sold his estate in Concord in 1670, and removed to Medford.

Gershom m. Hannah Eckels 1667, and had Mary, Hannah, Tabathy, Daniel, and Elizabeth, but their descendants are unknown.

Joshua, m. Hannah, da. of Capt. Hugh Mason of Watertown, was a tanner in Lincoln, where his descendants have lived, three of whom, in succession, have held the office of deacon. He was the ancestor of nearly all of the name since in Concord and Lincoln. His children were, 1. *Noah*, d. Feb. 1, 1739, a. 83, having had by his wife Dorothy,— Dorothy, Joshua, Ebenezer, Benjamin, Mary, Thomas, and Elizabeth. 2. *Grace*, m. Judah Potter 1686. 3. *Daniel*, m. Ann Merriam, d. Oct. 18, 1733, a. 69, and had Daniel, Samuel, Ann, Job (father of John, and grandfather of Hon. Eleazer Brooks), Mary, and John (father to Samuel, who graduated H. C.). 4. *Thomas*. 5. *Esther*, m. Benjamin Whittemore 1692. 6. *Joseph*, m. Rebecca Blodget 1706, d. Sept. 17, 1759, a. 78, (see p. 317), had Mary, Rebecca, Joseph, Nathan, Amos, Jonas, Isaac, and James. 7. *Elizabeth*, m. Ebenezer Merriam 1705. 8. *Job*, d. 1697, a. 22. 9. *Hugh*, m. Abigail Barker 1702, d. Jan. 18, 1746, a. 70, and had Abigail, Jonathan, Sarah, and Mary.

BROWN. *Thomas Brown* here in 1640, removed to Cambridge, where he lived some time. His son Thomas was town clerk in Concord, and d. 1717, a. 67; he married Ruth Jones 1677, and had several children. Boaz, another son of Thomas sen. m. Mary Winship 1664; d. April 7, 1724, a. 85, having had Boaz, who removed to Stow, Thomas, Mary, and Edward. This name has been very common, but it is difficult to trace the connection of the descendants.

BUTTRICK. *William Buttrick*, probably the ancestor of all the name in New-England, came here in 1635; gave his deposition in relation to the purchase of the town from the Indians; lived where his great-great-grandson, Col. Jonas B., now lives. "Having served the town for many years, honorably, as a sergeant," says the record, a post then of distinction, he petitioned, at the age of 65, to be excused from the office. He d. June 30, 1698, a. 82; Sarah Bateman, his first wife, d. 1664; his second wife was Jane Goodnow of Sudbury. Children, all by his first wife, Mary, William, John, m. Sarah Blood and removed to Stow, Samuel, Edward, Joseph, killed in Sudbury fight, Sarah, married a Barrett, and Mary.

Samuel, the fourth child, m. Elizabeth Blood 1677, and had Elizabeth, Samuel, who removed to Charlestown, William, Sarah, Abigail, and Dea. Jonathan, who m. Elizabeth Wooley 1717, and d. March 23, 1767, a. 77; and " was followed to the grave," says his monument, " by his widow, and thirteen well-instructed children." Their names were Samuel, Joseph, Daniel, Jonathan, Nathan, John (see below), Ephraim, Willard, Mary, Abigail, Elizabeth, Rachel, Lois, and Sarah, who died young.

Major JOHN BUTTRICK was one of the officers in command on the 19th of April, 1775, and his name will be handed down to posterity with distinguished honor for the noble stand he took, and the bravery he manifested, in leading a gallant band of militiamen on to meet the invading enemy at the North Bridge, and for beginning the first forcible resistance to British arms. He then returned the fire by commanding his own company to fire, saying, " Fire, fellow-soldiers, for God's sake, fire!" and discharged his own gun the same instant. (See page 100 and onward). — He was buried with military honors. The following epitaph is engraved on his monument:

In memory of
COLONEL JOHN BUTTRICK,
who commanded the militia companies
which made the first attack upon
The British Troops,
at Concord North Bridge,
on 19th of April, 1775.
Having, with patriotic firmness,
shared in the dangers which led to
American Independence,
He lived to enjoy the blessings of it,
and died May 16, 1791, aged 60 years.
Having laid down the sword
with honor,
he resumed the plough
with industry;
by the latter to maintain
what the former had won.
The virtues of the parent, citizen, and Christian
adorned his life,
and his worth was acknowledged by
the grief and respect of all ranks
at his death.

BULKELEY. See notices of this family in pages 157 – 162, and 240 – 242.

APPENDIX.

BURGESS. *Thomas Burgess* was in Concord in 1666, but removed to Groton.

BUSS. *William Buss* came here before 1639; lived where Elijah Wood now lives; was a lieutenant; bought the mill on Mill-brook 1668. His brother lived in Tunbridge, Eng. He d. Jan. 31, 1698; first wife, Ann, d. 1674; second wife (widow Dorcas Jones), 1709. Children, Hannah, m. William Wheeler; Richard, Ann, Nathaniel, and Joseph, who m. Elizabeth Jones 1671, and had several children.

CHANDLER. *John Chandler* here in 1640, at which time he had a daughter born and was admitted freeman. Roger Chandler, and twenty others of Plymouth Colony, had a grant of four hundred acres of land in Concord in 1658; was employed by Dolor Davis to build a house; m. Mary Simonds 1671; d. 1717; she 1728; left several children, of whom Samuel m. Dorcas Buss 1695; d. 1745; and had Joseph, Samuel, John, Huldah, Rebecca, Elizabeth, and James, who was father of Dea. Joseph C.

CHEEVER. *Daniel Cheever*, probably descended from Daniel of Cambridge, was here from about 1710.

CLARK. *Samuel Clark* came here before 1686, probably the son of Jonas C. of Cambridge. He d. Jan. 30, 1730; his wife Ruth 1722: children, John, William, Susannah, Hannah, Benjamin, and Arthur; of whom Benjamin was father of Benjamin, who d. Feb. 11, 1809, a. 91, whose wife (Rebecca Flagg), d. Oct. 4, 1805, a. 83.

CONANT. *Lot Conant*, probably a great-grandson of the celebrated Roger C. of Salem, came into this town in the early part of last century; d. Sept. 20, 1767, a. 90. His son Andrew had by his wife Elizabeth, Elizabeth, Andrew, Lydia, Nathan, and Ezra, who was drowned 1806; his wife d. May 23, 1828, a. 95. Andrew was father to Andrew, Eli, Silas, Abel, and Nathan, and two daughters.

COMY. *Daniel Comy* here in 1664, d. March 31, 1676.

COOKSEY. *William Cooksey* was here in 1666; and in 1700 was the only poor person then maintained by the town.

COSLIN. *William Coslin* was here in 1642, removed with Rev. Mr. Jones.

COTTON. *John Cotton* had Deliverance and Thankful, twin children, b. here in 1679. Little else is on record concerning him.

DAKIN. *Thomas Dakin*, the common ancestor, was here before 1650; d. Oct. 21, 1708. His first wife d. 1659; second wife (widow Susan Stratton), 1698; had John, m. Sarah Woodhouse, Sarah, Simon, d. Jan. 11, 1739, a. 76; and Joseph, who was deacon, lived by Flint's Pond, where Mr. Smith now lives, and whose son Samuel m. Mercy Minott 1722; was a Captain in the French war, and killed at Halfway Brook in 1758. There were several collateral families, and the name is yet preserved in the town.

DAVIS. *Dolor Davis* was of Cambridge in 1634, a petitioner for Groton in 1656, having before resided in Barnstable, where he died 1673. He was one of twenty who had lands granted in Concord in 1659, and was employed as a carpenter. He m. Margery, sister of Major Simon Willard, and had a daughter Ruth m. Stephen Hall, and two sons, Simon and Samuel, who settled in this town, and were the fruitful vines whose numerous branches extend over this and Worcester counties, and part of New Hampshire, and are constantly sending forth new and flourishing shoots.

Simon was a Lieutenant, representative, and otherwise distinguished, m. Mary, da. of James Blood, 1660, d. June 14, 1713, a. 77; and had Simon, Mary, Sarah, James, Ellen, Ebenezer, and Hannah. Of whom Dr. *Simon* m. Elizabeth Woodhouse, 1689; she d. Nov. 12, 1711; and had John, Simon, Henry, Elizabeth, Mary, Samuel, Ebenezer, and Peter. Simon, the second son, b. 1692, m. Dorothy ―― 1713, and had Simon, Israel, and Joseph b. in Concord, removed to Rutland about 1720, and had there Eleazer, Oliver of Princeton, and two daughters. The eldest son Simon, b. May 17, 1714, was father to David of Paxton, Dea. Isaac of Northborough, father to Hon. John Davis of Worcester, Samuel of Oakham, John of Paxton, and several daughters. Joseph, brother of Simon, b. in Concord July 16, 1720, was minister of Holden; d. March 4, 1799, a. 79. *James*, second son of the first Simon, m. Ann Smeadly 1701, d. Sept. 16, 1727, a. 59, having had James, Ruth, Thomas, (who died Nov. 18, 1786, a. 81, father to James of Holden, Jonathan and Josiah of New Ipswich, Nathan of Westford, Thomas of Chelmsford, Amos of Groton, Abel of this town, and three other sons), Joseph, Zachariah, and Benjamin. *Ebenezer*, the sixth child of Simon sen., had by his wife Dinah, Ebenezer, Josiah (killed in Lovewell's fight), and several others.

Samuel, the other son of Dolor, m. Mary Meads 1665, settled in the present limits of Bedford, where his descendants yet live. Had Mary, Samuel, Daniel, Martha, Simon, and perhaps others. *Samuel*, the eldest son, m. Abigail Reed 1698; and had Abigail, Mary, Samuel, Jacob, Eleazer, and Stephen. Daniel, the third child, was one of the first members of the church in Bedford, m. Mary Hubbard 1698, and had Jonathan, Daniel, Mary, Ephraim,

Nathan, Amos of Grafton, Josiah, and Nathaniel. Their father d. Feb. 11, 1741, and their mother Feb. 2, 1769, a. 87.

DEAN. *Thomas Dean* was here 1645, d. Feb. 5, 1676; his wife Elizabeth d. 1673. His son Joseph m. Elizabeth Fuller 1662, d. 1718, a. 80, and had Thomas, Joseph, Daniel, Elizabeth, Sarah, and Deborah. Lieut. Daniel Dean, probably the son of Thomas, first mentioned, held a large estate, which was principally inherited by his son-in-law, Capt. Daniel Adams.

DILL. *Peter Dill* was here 1670; and by his wife, Thanks, had several children.

DOWDY. *George Dowdy* was admitted freeman in Concord 1645.

DOGGET. The wife of *Thomas Dogget* d. 1642; he removed from town.

DRAPER. *Roger Draper* was here as early as 1639; his da. Lydia m. John Luce 1660; his son Adam m. Rebecca Brabrook 1666, and had Samuel, Joseph, Elisha, and Adam. They removed to Marlborough about 1680.

DUDLEY. *Francis Dudley*, a supposed connexion of Gov. Thomas D., came to this town about 1663; m. Sarah Wheeler 1665, and was father to Mary who m. Joseph Fletcher, Joseph, Samuel, Sarah, John, and perhaps other children. *Joseph* m. Abigail Gobble 1691; d. 1702; she d. 1705, having had Abigail, James, Joseph, Benjamin, Mary, and Sibbella. *Samuel* m. Abigail King 1704; removed to Littleton, where his wife, as mentioned by Hutchinson (vol. ii. p. 26), was affected with witchcraft; about 1728 he removed to Sutton, where he died 1775, aged 109! having had twenty children; of whom Samuel, Francis, David, Abigail, and Jonathan, (the three last at one birth,) were born in Concord. *John*, the other son of the first Francis, m. Hannah Poultier of Medford 1697, and had John, Hannah, and Sarah. Paul D., a descendant of the sixth generation, lives in the town.

EDMONDS. *Walter, Samuel*, and *Joshua Edmonds*, were here before 1640; but their names disappear from our annals after about twenty years. The name was early in Lynn.

EDWARDS. The children of *Robert Edwards*, a freeman 1642, and d. about 1650, owned land in 1660. Col. John, who d. in Acton, and Col. Abraham of Ashby, are probably descendants.

EMERSON. See pages 183 and onward.

47

ESTABROOK. See page 162.

EVARTS. *John Evarts* was one of the earliest settlers; had sons John, and Judah, b. 1639 and 1642. Removed to Connecticut with Rev. Mr. Jones, and was probably the ancestor of the late Jeremiah Evarts, Esq.

FARRAR. This family derive their origin from John and Jacob Farrar, who were proprietors of Lancaster in 1653. John d. there Nov. 3, 1669. Jacob, either a son of John or Jacob, m. Hannah, da. of John Houghton, Esq. 1668; he was killed by the Indians August 22, 1675. His sons Jacob, George, Joseph, and John, sold their property in 1697 to their uncle Houghton, and removed to Concord. Henry Farrar was killed in Lancaster Feb. 1676, and John d. Aug. 1707.

JACOB, above mentioned, m. Susannah Reddit of Concord, 1692; lived in the north part of the town; d. 1722; and had ten children; Jacob, the eldest, was killed in Lovell's fight, where his cousin Joseph was wounded. Jacob, son of Jacob last mentioned, d. Dec. 20, 1787, a. 65.

GEORGE m. Mary How 1692, settled where Dea. James, his great-grandson, now lives, and d. May 15, 1760, a. 89; his wife d. April 12, 1761; they had Joseph, Daniel, George, Mary, and Samuel. George m. Mary Barrett, and had nine children, including Rev. George, and Humphrey, father to Rev. Joseph. (See page 314). Deacon Samuel, his youngest brother, m. Lydia Barrett 1732, d. April 18, 1783, a. 75; and had Lydia, Dea. Samuel (father to Samuel and John, noticed among the college graduates), Rev. Stephen of New Ipswich, James, Rebecca, Lucy, and Timothy of New Ipswich.

FARWELL. *Henry Farwell*, freeman in 1638, resided in this town from its first settlement till the incorporation of Chelmsford; removed there, and d. Aug. 1, 1670; probably the common ancestor of the name in New England. His sons Joseph, John, and James, lived in this town, where the name has been preserved; the latter m. Sarah Wheeler 1658.

FASSETT. *Nathaniel Fassett* was taxed in 1666.

FLETCHER. *Robert Fletcher* was here in 1635; d. April 3, 1677, a. 85. Children — 1. *Francis*, m. Elizabeth Wheeler 1656, and had Samuel, Joseph, John, Elizabeth, Sarah, Hannah, and Benjamin, who lived in Concord. 2. *Luke*, d. 1665; 3. *William*, m. Lydia Bates 1645, removed to Chelmsford, 1656, d. Nov. 6, 1677; 4. *Samuel*, removed to Chelmsford. The name is extinct in Concord, but descendants are found in the adjoining towns, in Worcester county, and in New Hampshire.

APPENDIX.

FLINT. Hon. *Thomas Flint* came from Matlock in Derbyshire to Concord, in 1638, and brought with him, says a family genealogy, £4000 sterling. He possessed wealth, talents, and a Christian character; represented the town four years, and was an Assistant eleven. He d. Oct. 8, 1653. Johnson (Hist. Coll. iii. p. 161), calls him " a sincere servant of Christ, who had a fair yearly revenue in England, but having improved it for Christ by casting it into the common treasury, he waits on the Lord for doubling his talent, if it shall seem good unto him so to do, and the mean time spending his person for the good of his people in the office of magistrate."

" At Christ's commands, thou leav'st thy lands, and native habitation:
His folke to aid, in desert straid, for gospel's exaltation,
Flint, hardy thou, wilt not allow, the undermining fox,
With subtill skill, Christ's vines to spoil, thy sword shall give them knocks.
Yet thou base dust, and all thou hast is Christ's, and by him thou
Art made to be, such as we see ; hold fast for ever now."

This is what Johnson calls " remembering in short metre."

His will is the first recorded in the Middlesex Probate Records. His brother, Rev. Henry Flint of Braintree, and his uncle, William Wood, were executors. He had John and Ephraim, who lived in Concord, and perhaps Edward, Thomas, and William of Salem.

EPHRAIM m. Jane, daughter of Rev. Edward Bulkeley, and d. without issue 1722. About one thousand acres of land, including Flint's Pond, were owned by him.

JOHN m. Mary, da. of Urian Oakes, President of H. C., 1667; d. 1687; she d. 1690; had Abigail, m. Capt. Daniel Estabrook, John, Mary, Thomas, and Edward. *John* m. Abigail Buttrick; d. Oct. 26, 1746, a. 69, and was father to Ephraim (H. C. 1733), Abigail, Mary, John (who d. 1792, a. 70), Hannah, and Jane. *Thomas* m. Mary Brown, and had Dorothy, Mary, Thomas of Rutland, Lucy, Henry of Carlisle, Josiah, Charles, John, and Dr. Edward of Shrewsbury. *Edward* d. Nov. 15, 1754, a. 70, in Lincoln, without issue.

FOWLE. *George Fowle*, one of the early settlers, had four children born here; removed to Charlestown. The name does not again appear.

FOX. *Thomas Fox* a member of the church 1640. His first wife d. 1647; and he m. second time, Hannah Brooks, the same year. He d. 1658. Eliphalet, the only son who had issue, m. Mary Wheeler 1665; d. Aug. 15, 1711; she d. Feb. 24, 1679; children, Thomas, Eliphalet, Samuel, Joshua, Benoni, and Joshua. Descendants of this family are found in New Hampshire, but the name has been long extinct in Concord.

FRENCH. *Joseph French* was here as early as 1674; and by Elizabeth, his wife, had Samuel, Joseph, Elizabeth, Mary, Margaret, and Jonathan, b. between 1676 and 1690; was a lieutenant; lived in the present limits of Bedford.

FRISSIL. *William Frissil* m. Hannah Clark 1667, and was here till about 1680.

FULLER. William Fuller was a miller. His wife d. 1642; daughter Ruth m. Timothy Wheeler 1670; and Elizabeth m. Joseph Dean 1669.

GAMLIN. *Robert Gamlin* d. Oct. 7, 1642.

GOBBLE. *Thomas* here before 1640; d. 1657; left three sons and three daughters, and several grandchildren. Thomas and Daniel lived south of Walden woods.

GRAVES. *John Graves* was one of the first members of the church, and had several sons. Benjamin m. Mary Hoar; John, Mary Chamberlain; and Abraham, Ann Hayward; and had families; but the name soon disappears.

GREEN. There was a *John Green* who lived in town in 1690; but tradition does not make him the ancestor of the Concord families. John, a hatter from Malden, m. Martha, sister of Deacon Simon Hunt, and lived in the centre of the town; but sold out and removed to Carlisle, and was ancestor of the families there. He was father to *John*, who had Leonard, Jesse, Reuben, John, Amos, and Calvin; *Zaccheus*, who had Thomas, Zaccheus, Josiah, Samuel, Eli, Asa, and four daughters; *Nathan*, who had Nathan, Asa, William, Silas, Timothy, and Tilly; and *Samuel*, whose children died without issue.

GRIFFIN. *Richard Griffin* here 1635, elder in the church; representative, town commissioner; m. Mary Hayward 1660; d. April 5, 1661; gave his property to Christopher Woolley. His mother lived in Charlestown.

HADLOCK. *John Hadlock* was here in 1675, and onwards.

HALL. *William Hall* m. Sarah Merriam 1658; d. 1667. Stephen m. Ruth Davis 1663; sold one hundred and ten acres of land at the "old hogpen walk" to John Barker, 1684, and removed to Stow.

HALSTED. *William Halsted* d. July 5, 1645; gave to the town of Concord £5, to be laid out in a cow for the poor of the town. His brother, whose wife Isabel d. 1641, and a sister, inherited the property.

HAMILTON. *John Hamilton* was here a few years, before 1670, but removed to Marlborough.

HARRIS. *George Harris* here in 1669, and the name has since been frequent.

HARWOOD. *Nathaniel Harwood* was here in 1667, and had Nathaniel, Peter, John, and Mary, whose descendants still live in the adjoining towns.

HARDY. *Richard Hardy* had twins born, who d. 1639; his wife d. two days after.

HARTWELL. All of this name in New England are supposed to have originated from *William*, who was among the first settlers in 1636 ; and in subsequent life was distinguished by the title of *Quartermaster*, at that time honorable in military life ; d. March 12, 1690 ; his wife d. 1695. Children, William, John, Samuel, Jonathan, Nathaniel, and Martha. Of these, Samuel m. Ruth Wheeler 1665, and had Samuel, Mary, Ruth, William, John, and Hannah. The oldest, Samuel, m. Abigail Stearns 1692, whose son Ephraim m. Elizabeth Heywood 1732. He d. 1793, a. 87 ; she 1808 a. 94. They had fifteen children, five of whom died of the throat-distemper in October, 1740. This has been a prevalent name.

HASSELL. *Joseph Hassell*, son of Richard of Cambridge, came here in 1672.

HAYWARD. This name has been written Heaward, Heywood, and Howard, and although several now bear the last name, they originated from a common ancestor. Heywood is a distinct name. *George Hayward* came here in 1635 ; d. March 29, 1671 ; his wife d. 1693 ; estate £506 ; children, Mary, m. Richard Griffin, John, Joseph, Sarah, Hannah, Simeon, George, and perhaps others.

John m. Anna White 1671, and had Mary, George, Martha, John, Judith, and two others.

Joseph m. (1) Hannah Hosmer 1665, and had Joseph, Mary, John, Hannah, George, and Dorothy ; his wife d. 1675 ; he m. (2) Elizabeth Treadwell 1677, and had Ebenezer, James, and Simeon. The father d. Oct. 13, 1714, a. 71. Simeon, the last mentioned, was the ancestor of most of the name in this vicinity ; m. Rebecca Hartwell 1705 ; d. May 18, 1719, a. 36 ; she, after his death, m. a Temple, and d. 1776, a. 94. They had seven children,— 1. *Josiah*, m. Mary Hosmer, and settled in Acton, and had Josiah, John, Daniel, Simeon, and seven daughters ; 2. *Mary*, m. Ephraim Jones ; 3. *Abigail*, m. Merriam of Bedford ; 4. *Samuel*, m. Mary Stevens of Marlborough, and had Samuel, Paul, James (killed 19th April, 1775), Benjamin, Stevens, and three daughters; 5. *Joseph*, m. Abigail Hosmer, and had Simeon, Stephen, Joseph, Asa, John, James, and six daughters; 6. *Simeon*, m. Sarah Hosmer, settled in Sutton and had eight children; 7. *Ebenezer*, of Killingly, Conn.

HEALD. This name is sometimes erroneously spelled Hale or Held. *John* here in 1635, came from Berwick, Eng.; d. May 24, 1662; had John, Timothy, Dorcas, Gershom, Dorothy, Israel, and perhaps other children. Gershom m. Ann Vinton 1673, and removed to Stow.

John, jr., above mentioned, m. Sarah Dean 1661, and had Elizabeth, John, Gershom, Sarah, and perhaps others; of whom, John m. Mary Chandler 1690; d. Nov. 25, 1721, a. 55; had Mary, m. John Parling; John, deacon in Acton; Timothy, great-grandfather of John, Esq. of Carlisle; Josiah, Elizabeth, Samuel, Amos, deacon in Concord, in Lincoln, and in Townsend; Ephraim, and Dorcas.

HEYWOOD. *John* here before 1650; m. Rebecca Atkinson 1656; and had John and Benoni; his wife d. 1665; and he m. again, Sarah Simonds, 1665. He d. Jan. 11, 1707. Dea. John, jr. d. Jan. 2, 1718, who, by his wife Sarah, had ten sons and three daughters. Sarah, Thomas, Samuel, Edmond, Josiah, Daniel, Eleazer, Nathan, Sarah, John of Lunenburg, Mary, Phineas of Sterling, and Benjamin. Of these, Samuel m. Elizabeth Hubbard 1710, was deacon, town-clerk, and otherwise distinguished; d. Oct. 28, 1750, a. 63. He had thirteen children; Samuel, Amos, Elizabeth, Samuel, Jonathan (father to Hon. Abiel), Amos, Jonas, Charles, Rebecca, Aaron, John, Sarah, and Mary. Some collateral branches of this family have been distinguished in public life in Worcester county.

HOAR. The ancestor of this family, according to tradition, was a wealthy banker from London, and died soon after his arrival in Boston. Mrs. Joanna, probably his wife, died in Braintree 1661. Her children were as follows: 1. Joanna, wife of Col. Edmond Quincy; 2. Margery, wife of Rev. H. Flint; 3. Daniel, went to England 1653; 4. Leonard, President of H. C.; and 5. John of Concord, who lived in Scituate from 1643 to 1655, came to Concord about 1660; was a lawyer, distinguished for bold, independent mind and action; d. April 2, 1704; his wife Alice d. June 5, 1697. His daughter Elizabeth m. Jonathan Prescott, and Mary m. Benjamin Graves; and his only son Daniel m. Mary Stratton 1677, and had John, Leonard, Daniel, Joseph, Jonathan, Mary, Samuel, Isaac, David, and Elizabeth. Of these, Lieut. Daniel, third son, m. Sarah Jones 1705, and d. Feb. 8, 1773, a. 93, having had four sons, John, Daniel, Jonathan, and Timothy, and seve-

APPENDIX. 375

ral daughters. John m. Elizabeth Coolidge of Watertown, and was father to Hon. Samuel and Leonard H. of Lincoln, and grandfather to Hon. Samuel of Concord.

HOSMER. Two of this name, *Thomas* and *James*, supposed to be brothers, from Hockhurst, county of Kent, came to America. Thomas was of Cambridge 1632, and probably removed to Connecticut, and was ancestor of Rev. Stephen, H. C. 1699, the Hon. Titus, and Hon. Stephen Titus Hosmer, all distinguished men in that State. James came to Concord among the first settlers; d. Feb. 7, 1685; his first wife d. 1641, and second wife, Ellen, 1665. They had James, John (a petitioner for Chelmsford, who died, according to tradition, in Ireland), Hannah, m. Joseph Hayward, Mary, m. Thomas Smith, and Stephen, b. 1642.

James, the eldest son, m. Sarah White 1658, and was killed at Sudbury fight; his widow m. Samuel Rice. He had James of Woodstock, Mary, m. Samuel Wight, Dorothy, Hannah, m. Col. How of Marlborough, and Thomas, who m. Hannah Hartwell 1696, and was father to Hannah, Sarah, Thomas, Mary, and James, of whom Thomas, the third child, m. Prudence Hosmer 1731, and had Lucy, Hon. Joseph, Perses, Dinah, Lydia, and Benjamin, whose united ages were 465, or 78 each, nearly. James, the brother of Thomas last mentioned, m. Elizabeth Davis of Bedford, and had Samuel, James, Elizabeth, Bulah, Ruth, and Elijah.

Stephen, youngest child of the first James, m. Abigail Wood 1667, and had Mary, Abigail, m. George Wheeler, John, Bridget, Dorothy, Stephen, and James. Of whom Stephen m. Prudence Billings 1707, and had children, Prudence, m. Thomas Hosmer, above mentioned; Captain Stephen, the distinguished surveyor; Jonathan, grandfather to Simon, Esq. of Acton; Josiah, father to John and Jesse, Abel and Josiah of Templeton; Jane, and Ephraim of Acton, father to Samuel.

Hon. JOSEPH HOSMER, above mentioned, was born Dec. 25, 1735, and died Jan. 31, 1821, a. 85. His father's name was Thomas, and his mother's Prudence Hosmer, second cousins, and great-grandchildren of James Hosmer, the first American ancestor. Possessing popular talents, he was early called to share the public duties of society. In the great events of the revolution he acted a conspicuous part, always in favor of liberty. Whilst the preliminary measures were under discussion, one of his townsmen made a powerful speech in which he attempted to ridicule the doings of the "sons of liberty." Mr. Hosmer immediately replied in a strain of natural, unaffected, but energetic eloquence (for which he was afterwards distinguished), which particularly attracted public attention and introduced him to public favor. He was a militia officer on the 19th of April, 1775, and the first captain of the

Concord Light Infantry company, and was afterwards promoted to major. He was a representative five years, and a senator twelve, and was an active, influential member. He was appointed sheriff of the county in 1792, and sustained the office fifteen years. Major Hosmer was endowed by nature with strong, active powers of mind, and the character he formed enabled him to meet all events with that fortitude which is an earnest of success. He early made a public profession of religion. Ardent without rashness, bold without presumption, and religious without fanaticism, he was eminently a useful man.

HOW. *William How* had several children b. 1657 – 1665; removed to Chelmsford or Marlborough.

HUNT. *William Hunt* was here before 1640; d. in Marlborough Oct. 1667; his wife Elizabeth 1661; estate £596; left sons Nehemiah, Isaac, William, and Samuel, who m. and had families. Nehemiah m. Mary Tool 1663, whose son John m. Mary Brown 1703; d. May 3, 1765, a. 92; father to Dea. Simon Hunt, who was father to Dr. Joseph, and grandfather to Capt. Humphrey. — Nehemiah, a brother of John, m. Eleanor Hunt 1705, and wa great-grandfather of Nehemiah Hunt, sen., now living. Collatere descendants now live in this and the adjoining towns.

HUBBARD. *Jonathan* was here as early as 1680, probably from Connecticut, m. Hannah Merriam. He d. July 17, 1728, a. 70; she d. April 9, 1747, a. 89; inherited part of the property of his uncle, Dea. Robert Merriam, on whose place, near the new meeting-house, he lived. Had Jonathan, Samuel, Joseph, Elizabeth, John, Daniel, Thomas, Abigail, and Ebenezer, b. between 1684 and 1700. Capt. Joseph, the third child, m. Rebecca, da. of Capt. Joseph Bulkeley, 1713, and d. April 10, 1768, a. 80; she d. 1772, a. 76; having had Rebecca, Elizabeth, Lucy, Abigail, Thomas and Lucy (twins), of whom Capt. Thomas d. Oct. 12, 1810, a. 80, father of Dea. Thomas H.

Ebenezer, ninth child of the first Jonathan, m. Mary Conant, and d. May 21, 1755, a. 54. Of his sons, four died young, and Ebenezer, another one, d. Oct. 1, 1807, a. 82; whose wife d. 1807, a. 77; being parents of Rev. Ebenezer, and grandparents of others living on the paternal spot.

Samuel d. Dec. 12, 1753, a. 66. Isaac, his son by second wife, d. Aug. 15, 1803, a. 75, whose son lives in Holden.

HUTCHINSON. *Francis*, probably son of William of Boston, d. Nov. 17, 1661.

JONES. Rev. *John Jones* has been noticed in pages 5 and

153. *John*, whether connected with him or not, is uncertain, came from Cambridge to Concord about 1650; d. 1673; his widow m. William Buss; had Samuel, Ephraim, Elizabeth, m. Joseph Buss, Joseph, John, Dorcas, and Rebecca, m. James Minott, a cousin of James Minott, Esq., and, after his death, Capt. Joseph Bulkeley.

Samuel, m. Elizabeth Potter 1672, and had Samuel, Nathaniel, Ephraim, Joseph, and perhaps others. Of whom *Samuel* m. Ruth Brown 1698, d. Nov. 5, 1755, a. 82; she d. 1764, a. 86, whose children were 1. Elizabeth; 2. Thomas (m. Mary Miles 1727; he d. Aug. 3, 1774, a. 72; she d. Oct. 26, 1782, a. 73); 3. Ruth, m. a Foot; 4. Samuel; 5. Rebecca, m. first, Benjamin Barrett, and second, Jonas Prescott of Westford; 6. Joseph; 7. Mary, m. Dea. Thomas Barrett; 8. Lucy, m. Dr. Joseph Lee. Nathaniel, second son of Samuel, m. Mary Reddit 1696, and had Elnathan, Josiah, Ebenezer, Ann, Mary, Dorcas, Susannah, and Sarah. *Ephraim*, third son of Samuel, above mentioned, m. Hepsibah Chandler 1701, and was killed by the fall of a timber 1710; whose son Ephraim m. Mary Hayward 1728, and d. Nov. 29, 1756, a. 51; having been captain, town-clerk, and otherwise distinguished, and having had Ephraim, Mary, Jonas, and Rebecca.

Ephraim, the second son of the first John, m. Ruth Wheeler, 1673. He d. 1676; she m. again, Thomas Brown, having had John and Mary Jones.

John, the fourth son, m. Sarah Temple 1684; d. 1726, a. 68; had 1. Sarah, m. Daniel Hoar; 2. John, m. Anna Brooks 1716; he d. March 12, 1762, a. 72; she d. 1753, leaving John, Olive, Ebenezer, Daniel, and Farwell; 3. Timothy; 4. Bartholomew, m. Ruth Stow, d. Sept. 16, 1738, a. 42.

JUDSON. *William Judson*, from whom all of the name in the country are supposed to have originated, with his sons Joseph, Jeremiah, and Joshua, came to New England in 1634, and lived in Concord till their removal to Hartford about 1640, where his descendants now live. A connexion was early formed between this and the Bulkeley family.

LAW. *John Law*, m. Lydia Draper 1660; lived where Joel Conant now lives in Acton; his wife d. Jan. 6, 1733, a. 94; had John, Thomas, Stevens, and Samuel, who was a physician, and d. in Groton, Conn., April 29, 1727, a 47.

LEE. *Joseph Lee*, son of John, who came from London to Ipswich in 1635, and d. 1671, came to Concord; m. three times. 1. Mary Woodhouse; 2. widow Mary Wigley; and 3. Mary Fox. He d. Nov. 4, 1716, a. 73, having had by his first wife, whose father's estate he inherited, and on which he lived, Joseph, Mary, m. John Wood, Ann, Henry, John, Woodis, and Hannah.

Of whom, *Joseph* was a physician, m. Ruth Goodnow 1713; he d. Oct. 5, 1736, a. 56, having had twelve children; Joseph, Ruth, Joseph, (m. Ruth Jones 1739, father to Joseph, Jonas, Lucy, John, Ruth, Samuel, Silas, three of whom graduated at Harvard College) John, Ruth, m. Samuel Edwards, Mary, Elenor, Jonathan, and three others, who died young.

Henry, m. three times. 1. Rebecca Heywood, 1713; 2. Caty Payson; 3. Catharine ——, by whom he had twenty-one children, among whom were John, Abner, Benjamin, Henry, Samuel, Charles, Ezekiel, William, and Joshua, who have a very numerous posterity. He lived in Worcester, but d. in Concord, Feb. 25, 1745, a. 60.

Woodis, m. Elizabeth Wood 1715, lived in Concord, and had Woodis, Bathsheba, Seth, and Elizabeth, and have descendants here.

LETTIN. *Richard* was here from 1638 – 1644; removed.

MASON. *John Mason*, supposed to be a son of Capt. Hugh Mason of Watertown, m. Hannah Ramsden in Concord 1662; d. 1667, leaving one son, who has descendants in the town.

MARBLE. *Samuel Marble* was here from 1666 and onwards.

MARTIN. *Ambrose Martin* was among the first settlers; fined £10 for calling the church-covenant a " stinking carrion " (see p. 152, and Winthrop, i. 289); removed.

MELVIN. *John Melvin* was here about 1700; and had, by his wife Margaret, Eleazer, and David, noted in the French war; the latter m. Mary Farrar 1716.

MERRIAM. There were three brothers of this name among the first settlers, *Robert, George*, and *Joseph*. *Robert* was a trader, lived where the Trinitarian meeting-house stands; was town-clerk, commissioner, representative, and deacon; m. Mary Sheafe; d. without issue Feb. 15, 1681, a. 72; she d. 1693, a. 72.

George, d. Dec. 29, 1675; had by his wife Susannah, Susannah, m. John Scotchford; Elizabeth, m. Henry West of Salem; Samuel, m. Elizabeth Thompson, and had four daughters; Hannah, m. William Taylor; Abigail, m. Thomas Bateman; and Sarah.

Joseph, ancestor of the Concord families, d. Jan. 1, 1641. His son Joseph m. Sarah Stow 1653, and d. April 20, 1677, a. 47, leaving one daughter. His grave-stone is the oldest in the town. Another son, John, m. Mary Cooper 1663; she d. March 5, 1731,

a. 85, and had John, Nathaniel, Joseph, Dea. Samuel, and some daughters. Of whom, Joseph m. Dorothy Brooks 1705; d. Dec. 10, 1750, a. 74, having had Dorothy, Mary, Joseph, Samuel, and Josiah. This last m. Lydia Wheeler 1746; d. April 23, 1809, a. 83, father to Josiah and Joseph of Concord, and Dr. Timothy of Framingham.

MILES. *John Miles* was here in 1640; his first wife Sarah, d. 1678, leaving one daughter, who m. first, Edmond Wigley, and second, Joseph Lee; he m. again, in his old age, Susannah Redit, April 10, 1679; d. Aug. 28, 1693; his widow m. Lt. William Wilson of Billerica; he left John, Samuel, and Mary, who m. Edmond Putnam of Salem.

John, m. Mary Prescott 1702; d. Oct. 23, 1725; estate £1,708; and had John, Jonathan, H. C., Mary, m. Thomas Jones, Elizabeth, James, and Benjamin; of whom John m. Elizabeth Brooks, and was father to John, Noah, and Abner, all of Westminster; Abel of New Ipswich, Elizabeth, Oliver, James of Winchendon, and Dorothy.

Samuel, son of the first John, m. Sarah Foster 1706; was a deacon; d. March 13, 1756, and had Samuel, Joseph, Sarah, Ezekiel, Esther, Martha, Nathan, Reuben of Westminster, and Charles, a captain in the revolution.

MIDDLEBROOK. *Joseph Middlebrook* removed from town in 1644.

MINOTT. This distinguished family is traced to Thomas Minott, Esq., Secretary to the Abbot of Walden, by whom he was advanced to great possessions. His son George was born Aug. 4, 1594, in Safron Walden, Essex, Eng.; came to New England among the first settlers of Dorchester, where he was a ruling elder in the church thirty years; d. Dec. 24, 1671, a. 78. His sons were John, James, Stephen, and Samuel; of whom John was father to James, John, Stephen, and Samuel.

James, the eldest son of John, b. Sept. 14, 1653, graduated H. C. 1675, and came to Concord about 1680. While resident here, he was employed as a preacher in Stow in 1685, for "12s. 6d. per day, one half cash, and one half Indian corn"; and in 1686 " for what older towns had given their ministers — £13 for thirteen Sabbaths." He was again invited there in 1695, but declined. He practised physic, was a captain, justice of the peace, representative, and eminently a useful man. Tradition accords to him a character worthy the following epitaph, which is engraven on his grave-stone:

> "Here is interred the remains of
> JAMES MINOTT Esq A M an
> Excelling Grammarian, Enriched
> with the Gift of Prayer and Preaching,
> a Commanding Officer, a Physician of
> Great Value, a Great Lover of Peace
> as well as of Justice, and which was
> His greatest Glory, a Gent'n of distinguished
> Virtue and Goodness, happy in a Virtuous
> Posterity, and living Religiously Died
> Comfortably, Sept. 20. 1735 Æt. 83."

He m. Rebecca, da. of Capt. Timothy Wheeler, and lived on the estate left by his father-in-law, near Capt. Stacy's. She d. 1734, a. 68. They had 1. Rebecca, m. Joseph Barrett; 2. Lydia, m. Benjamin Barrett; 3. Mary, m. Ebenezer Wheeler; 4. Timothy, H. C. 1718; 5. James; 6. Elizabeth; 7. Martha, m. James Lane of Billerica; 8 and 9. Love and Mercy, twins; the former was m. to John Adams, the latter, to Samuel Dakin, on the same day, by their father; and 10. Samuel.

Hon. JAMES MINOTT, the fifth child, was one of the most distinguished men of his times. He was a military officer about thirty years, and advanced to colonel, justice of the peace, representative, and a member of the King's Council; m. 1. Martha Lane 1716; had John, Rebecca (who m. Benjamin Prescott of Danvers), and James. His wife d. 1735; and he m. again, Elizabeth Merrick; and had Martha, m. Rev. Josiah Sherman of Woburn; Ephraim, and Elizabeth, m. Rev. Daniel Rogers of Littleton 1763. Col. Minott d. Feb. 6, 1759, a. 64.

Samuel, the tenth child of James, Jr., was a deacon; d. March 17, 1766, a. 60. He m. 1. Sarah, da. of Jonas Prescott of Westford, and had Samuel, Jonas, and Thankful Sarah, m. Dea. Amos Dakin of Mason, N. H. His wife d. 1737; and he m. again, Dorcas, sister of his wife; she d. 1803, a. 91; had Dorcas, m. Thomas Barrett, George, Rebecca, m. Charles Barrett of New Ipswich, Daniel, and Mary, m. Elnathan Jones. Of these, Jonas had a grant in 1775, of the greatest part of Wilmot, N. H.; d. March 20, 1813, a. 78; and George m. Rebecca Barrett 1765; was a captain in the revolution, deacon in the church, and otherwise distingushed.

MITCHEL. *Jonathan Mitchel*, from Halifax, Yorkshire, came to Concord in 1635, and two years after, "his beginnings were consumed by fire." He removed shortly after to Connecticut; was father to Rev. Jonathan M. of Cambridge.

ODELL. *William Odell*, one of the first settlers, removed to Fairfield 1644.

OAKES. *Edward Oakes*, father to Urian Oakes, President of Harvard College, came to Concord about 1682; was representative 1684; d. Oct. 13, 1689.

APPENDIX. 381

PARKS. *Richard Parks*, a lieutenant, representative, &c., was son of Richard P. of Cambridge; m. Elizabeth Billings of Concord, 1690; d. June 19, 1725, a 58. Children, Joseph, Elizabeth, Sarah, Josiah, Abigail, Jonathan, Hannah, David (d. 1701, " being scalded in wort," a. 2), Isaac, and Rebecca. Of whom Joseph m. and had eight children, born between 1719 and 1736; Benjamin, Stephen, David, Louis, Sarah, Elizabeth, Benjamin, and George.

PARLIN. *John Parlin* was here about 1680. He d. Feb. 24, 1750, a. 84; having had John, Joseph, Jonathan, and Esther; of whom John m. Mary Heald, May 12, 1718, and was father to Jonathan, who had Jonathan, Nathan, Samuel, Asa, and five daughters. Jonathan d. at Lake George in the army, 1758. Asa was town-clerk, representative, &c., in Carlisle, and d. Oct. 8, 1822, a. 68.

PASMORE. *James* was here in 1644.

PELLET. *Thomas Pellet* m. Mary Dean 1660; d. Dec. 1, 1694; said to have given the burying-ground near Dr. Hurd's, to the town. Children, Mary, Jonathan, Thomas, Elizabeth, Daniel, Samuel, Richard, and John. Name now extinct.

POTTER. *Luke Potter* was one of the first settlers of the town, and deacon of the church. He m. a second wife, Mary Edmonds, 1644; she d. 1710. Eunice, Remembrance, Luke, Samuel, Dorothy, Mary, m. Humphrey Barrett, and Bethia, were his children by his first wife. Of whom Samuel m. Sarah Wright 1673, and was killed in Sudbury fight in 1676; Judah m. Grace Brooks 1686, and was burnt to death in his dwelling-house, June 20, 1731. She d. 1753, a. 93. " In Judah alone was the name preserved," and his descendants have been remarkable for their longevity. His children were Mary, Hannah, Eunice, Luke, who d. Sept. 25, 1784, a. 92, and whose son Samuel d. June 14, 1814, a. 96. Another Samuel d. Feb. 15, 1800, a. 95.

POWERS. *Walter Powers* was probably the son of John of Charlestown; m. a daughter of Ralph Shepherd, and lived near Nagog Pond, and his descendants were among the first incorporators of Littleton.

PRESCOTT. *Jonathan Prescott* was the common ancestor of the Concord branch of this distinguished family. His father, John P., from Lancashire, Eng., m. Mary Platts of Yorkshire, and came to this country about 1640; and, after living a short time at Watertown, was a leading settler of Lancaster, where he d. 1683. His children were Mary, m. Thomas Sawyer, Sarah, m. Richard

Wheeler, Lydia, m. Jonas Fairbank, Martha, John, Jonathan, Joseph, and Jonas.

Of these, *Jonathan* came to Concord; m. Elizabeth Hoar 1675; she d. 1687; he m., second time, Peter Bulkeley's widow, and third time, Ruth Brown. He d. Dec. 5, 1721; had Jonathan, Elizabeth, m. John Fowle, Dorothy, m. Edward Bulkeley, John, Benjamin, H. C. 1709, and Mary, m. John Miles. Of whom, Jonathan has the following epitaph on his monumental slab:

" Here lyes the remains of
Major JONATHAN PRESCOTT, Esq.,
a gentleman of virtue and merit, an accomplisht physitian,
but excelling in chirurgery.
Of uncommon sagacity, penetration, and success in his practice,
and so of very extensive service.
But his life was much valued, and his death very generally lamented.
He married the amiable and only daughter of the
Honorable Colonel PETER BULKLEY, Esq.,
by whom he had ten children.
He was removed from ministring to men's bodies, to the world of spirits,
October 28th, 1829, Ætatis suæ 54."

His widow Rebecca m. Rev. John Whiting. The children were 1. Jonathan, settled in Littleton, and he has descendants there and in Nova Scotia; 2. Rebecca; 3. John, and 4. Peter, noticed among the college graduates; 5. Charles, m. Elizabeth Barrett, representative, colonel, &c., d. Feb. 2, 1779, a. 68; she d. 1799, a. 82; 6. Elizabeth, m. Rev. David Hall of Sutton; 7. Dorothy; 8. Abel, an eminent physician, m. Abigail Bugbee; d. Oct. 24, 1805, a. 88; father to Abel and Samuel, noticed in the events of 19th April, 1775, John, Benjamin, Abigail, Dorothy, and Lucy, m. Jonathan Fay, Esq.; 9. Mary; 10. Benjamin, killed by the Indians 1744.

The descendants of John, Joseph, and Jonas, children of the first Jonathan, were numerous and respectable. John continued at Lancaster, where his sons lived. Joseph lived at Sudbury; Jonas settled at Groton, was a captain, justice of the peace, and had a large estate; m. Mary Loker 1672; d. Dec. 31, 1723, a. 75; she d. Oct. 28, 1735, a. 81, having lived to see 176 descendants. She had twelve children. Mary m. Benjamin Farnsworth; Elizabeth m. Eleazer Green; Jonas m. Thankful Wheeler of Concord; Nathaniel; Dorothy m. John Varnum; James; Sarah m. John Longley; Abigail m. James Parker; Martha m. Shebuel Hobart; Susanna m. William Lawrence; Deborah m. Samuel Parker; and Benjamin, who m. Abigail Oliver of Cambridge, 1718, d. Aug. 3, 1738, a. 58, (she d. Sept. 13, 1765, a. 68,) and was father to Hon. James and Hon. Oliver, M. D. of Groton, and Col. William, a distingushed officer at Bunker Hill in 1775.

Samuel P., supposed to have been a son of Jonathan by a wife had before Elizabeth Hoar, m. Esther Wheeler 1698, and had Amos and six daughters, who lived principally in Acton.

The Prescott family, once so numerous and influential, has no one now bearing its name in Concord.

PROCTOR. *Robert Proctor* m. Jane Hildreth 1645; d. April 28, 1697; had Sarah, Gershom, Mary, Peter, Elizabeth, James, Lydia, Thomas, John, Samuel, and Israel. The first four were born in Concord, and the remainder in Chelmsford, whither he removed in 1654.

PROUT. *Ebenezer Prout*, son of Timothy of Boston, m. Elizabeth, da. of Capt. Timothy Wheeler, 1678; was captain, representative 1689 – 90, and afterwards Clerk of the House of Representatives; d. in Watertown. His father and brother lived some time in Concord.

PURCHIS. *Oliver Purchis*, whose da. m. Dea. James Blood, came from Lynn to this town 1691, and was styled, on the records, "the worthy gentleman"; d. Nov. 20, 1701.

REED. *Philip Reed* was here from 1670; had several children, one of whom was styled Dr. Philip R., presumed to be a practising physician.

RICE. *Richard Rice*, d. June 9, 1709, "being accounted," says the record, "more than one hundred years old." Samuel R., whether a connexion is uncertain, m. Sarah Hosmer 1676. The name is not a prevalent one in Concord, though it is in Sudbury.

ROBBINS. *Robert Robbins* was here before 1670; m. Mary (Maxwell, according to tradition), and had George, John, Robert, James, Eleazer, and perhaps other children. The name is still prevalent here, though the connexion is not easily traced.

ROBINSON. *William Robinson* had children born here 1670 – 1675.

RUGG. *John Rugg* had Daniel and Jonathan, b. 1679 and 1680.

ROSS. *George Ross*, d. June 20, 1649.

SCOTCHFORD. *John Scotchford* was among the first settlers; m. Susanna Merriam; was town-clerk; d. without issue, June 10, 1696; she d. 1707.

SHEPHERD. *John Shepherd* was here about 1648. In 1661 he had thirty acres of land granted him by the town "in consideration of the hand of God upon him in the loss of one of his arms." This land lay near Mr. Silas Holden's. He subsequently had a tract granted at Nagog Pond. He had a son John, b. 1661, and a da. Mary, 1662 (taken captive in 1676). Isaac Shepherd m. Mary Smeadly 1667; killed with his brother Jacob in 1676. Abraham Shepherd m. Judith Till 1672. All had families.

SMEADLY. Two brothers came to Concord before 1639. *Baptiste* d. Aug. 16, 1675; his son Samuel m. Hannah Wheeler 1667, and was killed at Brookfield, Aug. 2, 1675. Mary, and James, who m. Mary Barrett 1671, were also his children.

John S., brother to Baptiste, had a son born 1646, who m. Sarah ——, and d. Oct. 1675. This name has long since been extinct.

SMITH. *Thomas Smith*, m. Mary Hosmer 1663, and had Thomas, James, and John born here, after which he is supposed to have removed to Connecticut.

SPENCER. A "Mr. Spencer" is said to have been present at the purchase of the town, but I have not been able to identify any one of the name as a proprietor or inhabitant till 1666; and the John here at the latter period was probably a different person from the one here in 1635.

SQUIRE. *George Squire* was here in 1640, but his name does not again appear.

STANIFORTH. *Thomas Staniforth* was here 1644, but removed.

STOW. *Thomas Stow* came to Concord before 1640; was father to Samuel, H. C. 1644, Thomas, Nathaniel, and perhaps other children. Thomas and Samuel owned jointly six hundred acres of land between Fairhaven pond and Sudbury line. Thomas sold his to Thomas Gobble and Daniel Dean 1660; Samuel sold his to Mr Woodhouse, with the other two mentioned; both removed to Connecticut. Nathaniel lived here; m. second wife Martha Brignell, 1662; d. 1683; she d. 1717, a. 90. He had Thankful, Nathaniel, Ebenezer, beside several who d. young; of whom Nathaniel m. Ruth Merriam 1690, and had John, Joseph, Samuel, Nathaniel, Thomas, Benjamin, Jonathan, and perhaps others.

STRATTEN. *Samuel Stratten* d. Oct. 27, 1674, having had by his wife Mary, Mary, m. Daniel Hoar, Samuel, John, and several who died young. Samuel m. Hannah Wheat 1675, and had children, whose posterity lived on the alms-house farm, which once bore the name of the family. Elizabeth Stratten d. April 19, 1762, a. 100.

APPENDIX. 385

SYMONDS. *William Symonds* was one of the first settlers; his wife d. 1641; da. Judith m. John Barker, and Sarah m. John Heywood.

TAYLOR. There appear to have been two by this name as early as 1650. *William* m. Mary Merriam; d. Dec. 6, 1696; having had John, Samuel, Abraham, Isaac, Joseph, and Mary. *James* m. Isabel Tompkins; d. Jan. 22, 1690, having had several children. They lived within the present limits of Bedford. S muel m. in 1686, and had a large family.

TEMPLE. *Richard Temple*, probably from Charlestown, was here before 1650; d. March 15, 1689. Among the names of his children, all of which are not preserved, I find Richard, d. 1698, father to Richard, Isaac, John, and Abraham; Abraham, m. Deborah Hadlock 1673; she d. 1743, a. 94; Abigail, m. Thomas Brabrook. Rebecca Temple d. March 14, 1776, a. 94.

THWING. *Benjamin Thwing* was here in 1642, and probably removed to Boston.

TOMPKINS. *John Tompkins* had Ruth and John b. here, 1640 and 1642. Removed to Fairfield.

TURNEY. *Benjamin* was here in 1638, but removed.

UNDERWOOD. *William Underwood* was here as early as 1638, where his children, Remembrance, m. Josiah Richardson, Sarah, m. Daniel Blodget, Priscilla, m. Edward Spaulding, Aquilla, and Rebecca were born. Removed to Chelmsford in 1654.

WHEAT. Two brothers, *Joshua* and *Moses Wheat*, came from England. In 1640 Joshua sold his lands in Concord to his brother Moses, and returned to his father, then living in England, on condition that he would relinquish his right to any legacy from his father. Moses d. May 6, 1700; his wife Tameson d. 1689; having had Moses, Samuel, Joshua, Hannah, who m. Samuel Stratten, Remembrance, John, and Sarah, whose descendants are yet found in Carlisle.

WHEELER. This name was originally and has ever been borne by more persons than any other in the town. George, Joseph, and Obadiah were among the first settlers; and Ephraim, Thomas, and Timothy came in 1639, and were all heads of families. Tradition says they came from Wales, but it is uncertain. Their descendants have been so numerous, and so many have borne the same Christian name, that their genealogy is traced with great difficulty. Among the births recorded by the town-clerk between 1650 and 1670, *six* bore the name of *John* Wheeler.

49

George d. 1684, having had by his wife Katharine, Elizabeth, who m. Francis Fletcher; Mary, who m. Eliphalet Fox; Ruth, who m. Samuel Hartwell; John, and perhaps other children. Of whom, John m. Sarah Larkin 1663, and d. Sept. 27, 1713, a. 70; she d. Aug. 12, 1725; they were parents of Samuel, John, Edward, Ebenezer, and perhaps others. Edward was deacon, and father to Dea. David, whose son Ephraim was father to Ephraim now living. Children of the eighth generation, including the first George, now live on the spot where their first ancestor settled.

Joseph was a lieutenant in the militia, and otherwise distinguished; was twice married, and had several children, all of whom died young, excepting Rebecca, who m. Hon. Peter Bulkeley, and, after his death, Capt. Jonathan Prescott. Her mother, Sarah, d. 1671. He traded with the Indians, and had a tract of land granted him in 1660, "especially for satisfying the Indians in their right," extending from Nashoba line at the north end of the great pond to Chelmsford.

Obadiah d. Oct. 27, 1671, a. 63; his wife Susannah d. 1650. They had Joshua, Obadiah, John, Josiah, Samuel, and several daughters; of whom, Obadiah m. Elizabeth White 1672, and was father to Obadiah, Josiah, Samuel, Joseph, and other children, whose descendants I cannot trace.

Ephraim had a son Ephraim 21 years of age in 1650, and a son Isaac b. in 1642; but his history I cannot determine satisfactorily.

Thomas. Capt. Thomas Wheeler, commanded the company at Brookfield, August, 1675; he bought eight hundred acres of land north of Groton in 1674, granted to the Flints of Concord; m. Ruth Wood; d. Dec. 10, 1676; his sons Thomas and Nathaniel died the January following. Serjeant Thomas Wheeler had several children born between 1649 and 1664; and Thomas Wheeler, Jr., several between 1658 and 1673. These numerous families were connected, but how, is uncertain. Thomas, a grandson, settled in Lincoln, and was father to Dea. Edmond, and ancestor of others of the name there.

Timothy m. for his second wife, Mary Brooks; he d. June 7, 1687; she d. 1693; leaving no male issue. He gave the ministerial lot to the town, and is noticed in another place.

Joshua m. and had several children born 1660 – 1670.

William m. Hannah Buss 1659; he d. Dec. 31, 1683, having had Hannah, Rebecca, Elizabeth, William, John, and Richard; of whom William d. May 29, 1752, a. 86, having had by Sarah, his wife, William, Joseph, Francis, Hezekiah, Nathaniel, and Elizabeth. Of these, Francis d. Nov. 1774, a. 76; m. (1.) Mary, who d. 1737, by whom he had Mary, Francis, Rhoda, Nathaniel,

Merriam, Solomon, and others, who d. young ; and second wife, Sarah Blood, 1741, and had Sarah, Samuel, Phineas, Hannah, and Noah, now living. This line includes all the families of the name in " Nine acre corner."

WHITAKER. *Jonathan Whitaker* was here before 1690 ; son of John of Watertown, b. 1664. Nathaniel and David m. about 1700, and had large families in the town. David d. Aug. 1791, a. 84 ; his wife d. 1798, a. 90. Elizabeth d. Jan. 1708, " an aged woman."

WHITING. See Ecclesiastical History, p. 165.

WHITTEMORE. *Benjamin Whittemore* m. Esther Brooks, 1692, and afterwards resided in the town ; d. Sept. 8, 1734, a. 65 ; she d. 1742, a. 73. He was representative several years ; left Benjamin and Nathaniel, who had families in the town.

WIGLEY. *Edmond Wigley* m. Mary, da. of John Miles, about 1667, but left no issue.

WILLARD. Major *Simon Willard* was one of the most distinguished leaders in the first settlement of this town. He came from the county of Kent, and resided in Cambridge in 1634, when he became acquainted with the situation of Musketaquid by trading with the Indians. He accompanied Rev. Peter Bulkeley, assisted in making the first purchase from the natives, resided in Concord with the first company, one of the leading men of the town, being town-clerk till 1654, and representative fourteen years. In 1660 he removed to Lancaster, and was at Groton in 1672. He had a large tract of land granted him at Nonascoicus, between Lancaster and Groton. He d. at Charlestown, April 24, 1676. He was the first military commander in the town, was promoted to the rank of major in 1654, and commanded the forces in Ninigret's and Philip's war. He was chosen an Assistant twenty-two years, from 1654 to his death, and was very much employed in the public business of the country. When Philip's war broke out, he gave directions to the several towns in Middlesex county, in relation to their garrison-houses. His first wife was Mary Sharp ; second, Elizabeth Dunster, sister of President Dunster of Harvard College ; and third, her sister Mary. By them he had seventeen children ; of whom, John m. Mary Hayward of Concord, 1698, and had David, Jonathan, Mercy, and Simon; of whom, Jonathan only m. and lived here. From Simon Willard have descended all or nearly of all the name in New England, many of whom have been much distinguished in public life.

WILSON. *William Wilson* m. Sarah Blood 1686; he d. 1745, a. 76; she d. 1717, a. 56. His second wife, Hannah Price. He was town-clerk, representative, captain, and otherwise distintinguished. His children were Samuel, Sarah, and Hannah.

WOOD. *William Wood* was the distinguished ancestor of this family, and came here in 1638, with his nephew, the Hon. Thomas Flint. From his connexions, and other circumstances, he is supposed to have been the acute author of a book entitled " New England's Prospect." That author was the first one who mentions the original name of Musketaquid, either applied to the place or the river in Concord. He d. May 14, 1671, a. 89, leaving an only son Michael, and a daughter Ruth, the wife of Capt. Thomas Wheeler. Michael d. May 13, 1674, having had Abraham, Isaac, Thomson, Jacob, John, and Abigail, who m. Stephen Hosmer. Of whom, Jacob m. Mary Wheeler 1697; he d. Oct. 6, 1723, a. 40, having had Jacob, Mary, Ephraim, Dorcas, Hannah, Milicent. Of these, Ephraim m. Mary Buss; d. March 20, 1789, a. 88, and was father to Ephraim, town-clerk, judge of the court of common pleas, &c., and grandfather to Daniel Wood, now living. The collateral branches of this family have been numerous.

Hon. EPHRAIM WOOD was born Aug. 1, 1733, and d. April 8, 1814, in his 81st year. He was son of Ephraim, and grandson of Jacob Wood. He was bred a shoemaker, and had no other advantages of education than what were afforded by the very imperfect common schools of that day. Though he did not possess what are popularly called brilliant talents, or ardent feelings, he had a calm, considerate mind and sound judgment, which peculiarly fitted him to act an important part in the times in which it was his lot to live. As early as 1771, he was chosen town-clerk, selectman, assessor, and overseer of the poor, and re-elected twenty-seven years, and for much of the spirit of those times which has come down to us as matter of record, we are indebted to him, as this History will fully show. He was one of the first justices appointed by the Council after the secession from British authority, and held the office during the remainder of his life. He was also one of the judges of the Court of Common Pleas. "In him," says a notice published soon after his death, "were united those qualities and virtues, which formed a character at once amiable, useful, respectable, and religious. Early in life he engaged in civil and public business, and by a judicious and faithful discharge of duty acquired confidence and reputation with his fellow-citizens and the public. The American revolution called into exercise his active and vigorous powers; and as a magistrate and in various departments he rendered important services to the community. The rights and liberties of his country were near his heart, and he was a warm and zealous defender of them against all encroachments. He was a true disciple of the great Washington, a friend to "liberty with order," and firmly attached to the union of the States and the constitutional independence of the individual States. In domestic life, his disposition and example were highly amiable and worthy. As a Christian, he was devout and humble, sincere and ardent. Having lived the life, he died the death of the righteous."

WOODHOUSE. *Henry Woodhouse,* or Woodis, as his name was sometimes written, came to Concord from London, about 1650, freeman 1656. His farm, estimated at three hundred and fifty acres, lay between the two rivers, and descended to his son-in-law, Joseph Lee, whose posterity successively held it for more than one hundred years. Joseph Barrett, Esq. now occupies it. He d. June 16, 1701; his first wife, Ellen, 1693; second wife in 1717; had one son, who d. young, and four daughters, b. between 1650 and 1662. Mary m. Joseph Lee; Hannah m. Cheney; Milicent m. Joseph Estabrook; Sarah m. John Daken; Elizabeth m. Simon Davis.

WOOLLEY. *Christopher Woolley* m. Priscilla Woodell 1646, and had several children. He d. Jan. 28, 1701; she 1674; second wife, Mary How, d. Dec. 26, 1695. His son Thomas d. Nov. 18, 1726. Jonathan Woolley, says the Bedford records, d. July 25, 1766, a. 61, " by a fall from a stone-wall, which killed him in a minute."

WRIGHT. *Edward Wright* came to Concord about 1650; d. Aug. 28, 1691; his wife Elizabeth d. Feb. 15, 1690. Children, Nathan, Martha, Sarah, Edward, Hannah, Peter, and Samuel. Of whom, Peter, "a weaver," d. Jan. 15, 1717, a. 53, and left a legacy for the benefit of the poor of the town. Samuel d. Oct. 1, 1741, a. 80; his wife Sarah, 1758, a. 92; their son Joseph d. Oct. 16, 1815, a. 94, grandfather to Anthony and Nathan M., now living.

NO. IV.

OLD AND NEW STYLE.

It is proper to explain what is meant by *old* and *new* style. — The new style was adopted by Great Britain in 1751, when a law was passed enacting that the year 1752 should begin on the 1st day of January; that the 3d of September should be reckoned the 14th, and that the intermediate eleven days should be omitted in the calendar. In the old, or Julian style, the year began the 25th of March, and contained 365d. 6h.; in the new, or Gregorian style, the year began the 1st of January, and contained 365d. 5h. 49m. 12s.; differing from the true tropical year twenty-two seconds only; and making a difference in the two styles of one day in 129 years. One is made nearly conformable to the other by dropping one day from the old, and adding one to the new style in each century, excepting every fourth, whose centennial year is considered leap-year. The new style was first adopted by Catholics in 1582; and not generally by Protestants till some time afterwards, and not yet by Russia. To meet the wishes of both, it was generally customary from the first settlement of this country till 1752, though not uniformly, to give a double date from January 1st to March 25. Thus, January 9, 1725, was written January 9, 1724 – 5, or 172$\frac{4}{5}$. March was also reckoned the first month, April the second, May the third, &c., and dates were sometimes made accordingly. Thus, 18th 4mo. 1667, or "18. 4. 67," was 18th June, 1667. In the preceding history, the dates are given as if the year began on the first of January, in all cases where it could be ascertained, and the latter of all double dates between that time and the 25th March is used. Thus, January 9, 172$\frac{4}{5}$, is given January 9, 1725. In other respects the dates anterior to 1752 are in old style. To ascertain the day in new style at the present time, corresponding to any date in the old style, it is necessary to add ten days from 1500 to 1700 (1600 being a leap-year), and eleven days from 1700 to 1752. Thus, the 2d of September, 1635, the date of the incorporation of Concord, will correspond with the 12th September, 1835; and July 3, 1735, the date of the incorporation of Acton, with the 14th of July, 1835. Want of careful attention to double dates, and difference in style, has occasioned many mistakes; and among others, the anniversary of the landing of the Pilgrim fathers at Plymouth has been erroneously celebrated on the 22d, instead of the 21st of December, the latter being the true date corresponding with the old style.

NO. V.

[After the History of Bedford was printed, the Rev. Mr. Stearns died. The following biographical notice is extracted from a sermon preached by the Rev. Samuel Sewall at his interment.]

"Rev. Samuel Stearns, of Bedford, was a son of Rev. Josiah Stearns of Epping, N. H., by his second wife, a daughter of Rev. Samuel Ruggles of Billerica. He was born at Epping, April 8, 1770; fitted for college after his father's death, at Exeter Academy, under the patronage of Hon. John Phillips, its founder; and graduated at Harvard College in 1794. His theological studies he pursued under the direction of Rev. Jonathan French of Andover, (whose daughter, Miss Abigail French, he afterwards married,) and was ordained over the Church and Society in Bedford, April 27, 1795. A new religious society having been legally formed, Nov. 9, 1832, by the name of the "Trinitarian Congregational Society"; and the Church having voted, at a meeting, May 9, 1833, to dissolve its connexion with the First Parish, and to accept an invitation given it to unite itself with the new society, for the purpose of maintaining public worship and the institutions of the Gospel, Rev. Mr. Stearns was solemnly constituted the Minister, or Religious Teacher of that society, June 5, 1833. He died Dec. 26, 1834, of a decline, the result, probably, of a scrofulous affection, with which he had been many years more or less afflicted. It is worthy of remark, that during the whole of his protracted ministry, almost thirty-nine years, he was never absent from his people at any communion season but one, viz. that which occurred about a fortnight before his death. Previously to the communion before, viz. that on the second Sabbath in October, he had cherished an earnest desire that he might be able, if it were God's will, to officiate once more on the interesting occasion, and then bid his church farewell; though he was apprehensive that the weather, or the state of his health, would be such, as to prevent him. But in this particular, divine Providence was propitious to his wishes. The weather on that day was remarkably fine; and (to use his own words) "his spirits were enlivened, and strength seemed to be given him for the occasion." Having obtained his son, Rev. William A. Stearns of Cambridgeport, to perform the previous services, the venerable man about the close of the sermon, with thankful heart, yet with emaciated countenance and feeble step, entered the house of God; and there, having once more, according to his desire, ministered the memorials of Christ's dying love, and united with the church in singing a hymn, he took his final leave of them in the solemn, affecting address, alluded to in the foregoing discourse. From that day he went no more abroad, being confined to his house, and most of the time to the room in which he died, till his death."

No. VI.

VOTES FOR GOVERNOR.

Date.	Candidates.	Con.	Bed.	Act.	Lin.	Car	Candidates.	Con.	Bed.	Act.	Lin.	Car.	Scat.
1780.	Hancock	121	25	54	42	28	Bowdoin	—	2	—	1	—	—
1781.	Hancock	83	30	38	20	31		1	—	—	—	—	—
1782.	Hancock	76	19	34	11	6	Bowdoin	2	—	—	4	—	31
1783.	Hancock	86	22	48	38	8		1	—	—	—	—	—
1784.	Hancock	80	27	22	17	4		—	—	—	—	—	12
1785.	Bowdoin	26	30	2	29	—	Cushing	34	—	16	—	—	50
1786.	Bowdoin	75	29	35	33	17		1	—	—	—	—	—
1787.	Hancock	113	42	62	25	38	Bowdoin	43	3	17	35	5	7
1788.	Hancock	114	43	55	48	35	Gerry	9	—	—	—	3	1
1789.	Hancock	95	35	45	26	—	Bowdoin	24	—	10	12	—	24
1790.	Hancock	72	39	47	30	34	Bowdoin	20	—	—	8	2	—
1791.	Hancock	76	40	26	39	31	Gerry	5	—	—	—	—	11
1792.	Hancock	80	32	32	35	32	Dana	16	—	—	—	—	27
1793.	Hancock	78	26	33	42	31	Gerry	5	—	—	—	—	25
1794.	Adams	105	41	50	33	31	Cushing	17	—	1	—	2	35
1795.	Adams	118	36	50	46	44	Cushing	4	—	—	—	—	37
1796.	Adams	76	50	57	52	58	Sumner	51	—	5	2	—	2
1797.	Sumner	47	6	11	18	—	Sullivan	63	41	43	38	60	11
1798.	Sumner	88	31	14	41	2	Sullivan	35	3	22	3	52	2
1799.	Sumner	83	28	15	27	1	Heath	79	27	68	45	64	6
1800.	Strong	64	17	12	11	—	Gerry	71	40	67	66	63	7
1801.	Strong	82	26	12	15	11	Gerry	90	36	77	53	70	—
1802.	Strong	92	26	15	20	4	Gerry	91	31	77	55	63	—
1803.	Strong	91	30	13	23	15	Gerry	62	13	76	39	51	—
1804.	Strong	84	33	16	23	3	Sullivan	94	27	86	60	83	1
1805.	Strong	107	28	52	21	10	Sullivan	118	54	108	62	93	1
1806.	Strong	116	31	32	23	1	Sullivan	113	51	103	61	102	11
1807.	Sullivan	122	55	191	64	99	Strong	122	29	22	20	7	5
1808.	Sullivan	124	51	108	73	97	Gore	104	26	24	25	3	2
1809.	Gore	119	27	25	37	7	Lincoln	124	60	122	75	107	3
1810.	Gerry	127	68	120	92	106	Gore	129	28	19	26	7	2
1811.	Gerry	146	69	112	80	102	Gore	113	25	15	28	4	—
1812.	Strong	148	34	26	26	7	Gerry	140	71	113	95	92	—
1813.	Strong	148	37	36	32	14	Varnum	139	61	114	82	94	—
1814.	Strong	140	33	42	36	8	Dexter	151	62	110	85	101	3
1815.	Strong	145	30	46	36	8	Dexter	145	56	116	82	97	1
1816.	Brooks	139	26	35	22	6	Dexter	148	50	127	25	104	1
1817.	Brooks	142	29	35	23	4	Dearborn	134	58	97	90	97	—
1818.	Brooks	108	26	31	23	7	Crowninshield	104	58	101	66	91	—
1819.	Brooks	108	32	33	25	6	Crowninshield	76	56	90	84	102	—
1820.	Brooks	89	30	28	23	3	Eustis	94	57	87	70	92	—
1821.	Brooks	82	31	37	25	4	Eustis	94	50	95	72	81	—
1822.	Brooks	82	30	31	21	1	Eustis	88	58	98	80	78	—
1823.	Eustis	151	77	123	125	127	Otis	99	23	28	19	—	—
1824.	Eustis	152	83	127	112	128	Lathrop	115	35	30	26	—	—
1825.	Lincoln	142	95	117	106	67		—	—	—	—	—	—
1826.	Lincoln	126	88	123	72	80		—	—	—	—	4	2
1827.	Lincoln	128	25	86	72	32	Jarvis	12	67	81	3	34	—
1828.	Lincoln	170	76	124	68	56	Morton	2	2	—	—	—	2
1829.	Lincoln	127	74	114	72	77	Morton	—	—	1	—	—	2
1830.	Lincoln	151	90	82	69	74	Morton	15	13	29	6	13	2

END.

INDEX OF HISTORY OF CONCORD

-A-

Abbot, Hull 175, 178
Abbot, Joseph 343,
Abbot, Obed 263, 257
Abbott, Moses, 110, 260,
Abbott, Nehemiah 294,
Adames, John 34,
Adams, Abigail 284,
Adams, Charles G., 240, 359,
Adams, Daniel 51, 75, 169, 234, 315, 369,
Adams, Elizabeth 362,
Adams, Hannah 350,
Adams, Henry 361,
Adams, James 38, 349, 361,
Adams, Joel 325,
Adams, John 291, 294, 312, 313, 347, 361, 380,
Adams, John Quincy 361,
Adams, Joseph 292, 305, 313, 315, 320, 350, 353, 359,
Adams, Josiah, 231, 291,
Adams, Love 305,
Adams, Moses 188, 284, 285, 291, 354,
Adams, Samuel 361,
Adams, Solomon 291,
Adams, Thomas 361,
Adams, Timothy 325,
Adams, Zabdiel 185, 306
Addington, Isaac 358,
Ahattawance, John 27,
Allen, Benjamin 294,
Allen, James 355,
Allen, Phineas, 223, 229, 230,
Allen Thomas 14,
Allen, Wilkes 193,
Ames, Fisher 311,
Ames, Jacob 357,
Andrews, Abraham 353, 358,
Andrews, Benjamin 218,
Andrews, Issachar 323, 327, 358,
Andrews, John 361,
Andrews, Nehemiah 327,
Andros, Edmund 66,
Annursnuck 197,
Anthony, Richard 355,
Appleton, Nathaniel 170, 304
Appleton, Rev. Mr. 262,
Asten, Abiel 67,
Asten, Obadiah 67,
Atkins, Mary 317,
Atkinson, Rebecca 374,
Atkinson, Susannah 361, 365
Atkinson, Thomas 361,
Austin, Daniel 193,

Austin, John 95,
Avery, John 134,
Ayer, Ebenezer 67,
Ayer, William 67,

-B-

Bacon, Benjamin 257, 269
Bacon, John 257,
Bacon, Jonas 259,
Bacon, Jonathan 256, 257, 263, 271
Bacon, Joseph 256,
Bacon, Josiah 257,
Bacon, Michael 257, 269
Bacon, Reuben 271, 272, 273
Bacon, Samuel 257,
Bacon, Thomas 257, 362
Bacon, Thompson 272, 273
Bailey, Mary 331,
Baker, Amos 38,
Baker, Francis 358,
Baker, Thomas 294,
Baker, William 37, 361
Baldwin, Christopher C. 75, 171
Baldwin, Cyrus 231,
Ball, Benjamin 352,
Ball, Caleb 362,
Ball, John 362,
Ball, Jonathan 168,
Ball, Nathaniel 37, 169, 234, 362
Ball, Nehemiah 218, 229
Ball, Thomas B. 355,
Ballard, Joseph 91, 257, 272, 273
Bancroft, Amos 222,
Bancroft, Samuel 88,
Bancroft, Thaddeus 349,
Barber, Richard 230,
Barker, Abigail 365,
Barker, Daniel F. 286,
Barker, Francis 359, 362
Barker, John 72, 73, 234, 362, 372, 385
Barker, Wm. 72,
Barnard, David 289, 290
Barnard, John 166, 169, 178
Barnes, John 58, 73, 362
Barnes, Josiah 223,
Barnes, Oliver 355,
Barnes, Thomas 70,
Barns, Hannah 108,
Barret, Humphrey 37, 45
Barret, John 347,
Barret, Joseph 120,
Barrett, Abel 215, 216
Barrett, Amos 140,
Barrett, Benjamin 75, 222, 252, 377
Barrett, Charles 380,

- 393 -

Barrett, Colonel James 104, 105, 106, 109, 111, 113
Barrett, Elizabeth 382,
Barrett, Humphrey 98, 194, 215, 234, 235, 362, 381
Barrett, James 77, 91, 92, 93, 97, 98, 110, 119, 121, 127, 142, 143, 183, 185, 234, 235, 236, 336, 349, 353, 355, 356, 357, 359, 363
Barrett, John 252
Barrett, Joseph 38, 75, 145, 205, 229, 232, 234, 238, 328
Barrett, Joshua 252,
Barrett, Mary 370,
Barrett, Captain Nathan 110, 116, 228, 235, 347, 353, 357, 358, 359
Barrett, Peter 252,
Barrett, Philip 358,
Barrett, Rebecca 244, 380
Barrett, Samuel 222, 347
Barrett, Stephen 103, 109, 235, 358
Barrett, Thomas 77, 194, 234, 353, 356, 377, 380
Barrett, Timothy 73,
Barron, Benjamin 359,
Barron, Elias 67,
Barron, John 363,
Barron, Oliver 323,
Barron, William A., 222
Bartlett, Benjamin Dixon 142, 239
Bartlett, Dr. 219,
Bartlett, John 142,
Bartlett, Josiah 229, 239
Bartlett, Roger 142,
Bartlett, Samuel 131, 134, 142, 237, 239
Bascom, Ezekiel L. 231,
Bateman, John 117, 346
Bateman, Richard 46,
Bateman, Sarah 264, 366
Bateman, Thomas 17, 37, 363, 378
Bateman, William 363,
Batemen's Pond 200,
Bates, John 252,
Bates, Lydia 370,
Bates, Reuben 252,
Batman, Thomas 34, 35
Beaton, John 114, 216, 234, 364
Beecher, Rev. Dr. 194, 195
Beecher, Rev. Edward 195,
Beecher, Rev. Lyman 195,
Beeman, Captain 107,
Beers, Richard 40,
Bellows, Ephraim H. 217,
Bellows, John 363,
Bemis, Amos 259,
Bemis, Jason 356,
Benjamin, Thomas 206,
Bennett, James 363,

Bernard, Lieutenant Colonel Benjamin 116,
Bernicre, Ensign D. 337,
Bigelow, Hartwell 108,
Bigelow, Jacob 311,
Bigelow, Mr. 208,
Billings, Daniel 294, 364
Billings, Elizabeth 381,
Billings, John 38, 45, 294, 364
Billings, Jonathan 71,
Billings, Joseph 294,
Billings, Nathaniel 38, 169, 294, 364
Billings, Prudence 375,
Billings, Samuel 294,
Billings, Thomas 73,
Billings, Timothy 294,
Binney, John 313,
Blakeley, Wm. 69,
Blanchard, Joseph 72,
Blanchard, Luther 112, 116
Bliss, Daniel 88, 96, 120, 178, 181, 188, 210
Bliss, Mr. 179, 180, 181, 192
Bliss, Phebe 188,
Bliss, Rev. Daniel 74, 77, 166, 244
Bliss, Samuel 181,
Bliss, Thomas 181,
Bliss, Thomas Theodore 96,
Blodget, Rebecca 365,
Blodget, Simeon 261,
Blodgett, Daniel 385,
Blood, Daniel Hartwell 260,
Blood, David 322,
Blood, Elizabeth 366,
Blood, Frederick 327,
Blood, Israel Mead 259, 260
Blood, James 17, 35, 37, 41, 194, 235, 364, 383
Blood, John 14, 37, 323, 364
Blood, Jonathan 322,
Blood, Josiah 323, 355, 362
Blood, Mary 364, 368
Blood, Phineas 322, 323, 327, 329
Blood, Richard 364,
Blood, Robert 14, 37, 65, 275, 364
Blood, Samuel 355,
Blood, Sarah 388,
Blood, Stephen 98,
Blood, Simon 65, 325, 327
Blood, Thaddeus 354, 355, 356, 357, 358
Blood, Willard 323,
Blood, Zachariah 70,
Bohow, Benjamin 42,
Bohow, Sarah 42,
Bond, Abijah 92, 234, 248
Bond, Jonas 201,
Bond, Joshua 97, 116
Bond, Nathan 127, 248

Bond, Samuel 294, 295, 303
Boon, Mr. 57,
Bosworth, Benj. 44,
Botany 199,
Bowes, Nicholas 261, 263, 264
Bowes, Rev. Mr. 72,
Bowman, Ebenezer 344,
Bowman, Francis 201,
Bowman, Jonas 257,
Bowstree, William 364,
Brabrook, Benj. 353, 358
Brabrook, Joseph 364,
Brabrook, Rebecca 369,
Brabrook, Thomas 364,
Bradstreet, Simon 166,
Brattle, Thomas 235,
Bray, James 355,
Breed, Josiah 116,
Breed, Nathaniel 358,
Brewer, Daniel 73,
Brewer, Samuel 72,
Bridge, Ebenezer 82, 188, 231
Bridge, John 344, 353, 355, 358
Bridge, Josiah 188,
Bridge, Nathaniel, 222
Bridge, Rev. Mr. 186,
Bridges, Margaret 189,
Briggs, Charles 231, 331
Brignell, Martha 384,
Brobrook, Joseph 286,
Broclebank, Capt. 58,
Brook, Isaac 37,
Brooke, Thomas 18, 34, 35, 36, 39, 45, 203, 214, 234, 235, 317, 318, 364, 365
Brooks, Asa 142, 228, 235, 358
Brooks, Caleb 37, 361, 365
Brooks, Daniel 72, 234, 281, 291, 295, 318, 365
Brooks, Dorothy 379,
Brooks, Ebenezer 295, 365
Brooks, Eleazer 82, 91, 106, 300, 307, 308, 312, 318, 353, 354, 356
Brooks, Ephraim 73,
Brooks, Esther 387,
Brooks, Gershom 45, 365
Brooks, Governor, 114
Brooks, Grace 381,
Brooks, Hannah 371,
Brooks, Hugh 234, 295
Brooks, James 294,
Brooks, Job 295, 318, 359
Brooks, John 247, 281, 285, 365
Brooks, Jonas 145, 289, 290
Brooks, Jonathan 72,
Brooks, Joseph 294, 303, 311, 317
Brooks, Joshua, 37, 45, 71, 234, 294, 295, 303, 308, 312, 313, 315, 316, 317, 318, 365,

Brooks, Mary 214,
Brooks, Nathan 174, 222, 230, 232, 236, 237, 238, 316
Brooks, Noah 42, 234, 277, 365
Brooks, Paul 289,
Brooks, Peter C. 365,
Brooks, Samuel 247, 295
Brooks, Seth 122,
Brooks, William 315,
Brown, Aaron 145,
Brown, Abishai 98, 121, 234, 239, 352, 353, 355, 356
Brown, Benjamin, 234, 294, 303, 308
Brown, Boaz 38, 44, 73, 365
Brown, Cotton 304,
Brown, Daniel 72, 294, 355
Brown, David 92, 105, 110, 121, 123, 131, 235, 357, 358
Brown, Deacon 185,
Brown, Eli 228,
Brown, Ephraim 37, 183, 194, 234, 320
Brown, Ezekiel 72,
Brown, Jabez 45, 353
Brown, Jacob 235, 355, 357, 358
Brown, James 345, 355
Brown, John 143, 162, 222, 227, 252, 304, 347
Brown, Jonas 112, 116, 354
Brown, Joseph 303,
Brown, Josiah 295,
Brown, Mary 371, 376
Brown, Moses 315,
Brown, Nathan 294, 303
Brown, Nicholas 72,
Brown, Reuben 99, 103, 104, 114, 117, 143
Brown, Reuben, Jr. 194, 228
Brown, Roger 140, 143, 227, 228, 235
Brown, Ruth 377, 382
Brown, Samuel 72, 252
Brown, Solomon 102, 341
Brown, Thomas 38, 72, 73, 189, 223, 233, 234, 280, 289, 323, 365, 377
Brown, William 227,
Brown, Zachariah 112,
Brown, Zechariah 350,
Bryant, Chandler 358,
Bryant, Joseph 355,
Bryant, Orpah 209,
Bryant, Reuben 206,
Buckly, Mr. 18,
Buckminster, Capt. 70,
Bugbee, Abigail 382,
Bulkeley, Charles 72, 241
Bulkeley, Dorothy 243,
Bulkeley, Edward 36, 38, 50, 59, 153, 157, 161, 211, 241, 242, 382
Bulkeley, Gershom 241,

- 395 -

Bulkeley, Grace 37,
Bulkeley, Jane Allen 160, 371
Bulkeley, John 19, 240, 241, 242
Bulkeley, Joseph 66, 242
Bulkeley, Peter 5, 7, 8, 9, 14, 22, 31, 43, 50, 65, 148, 152, 157, 165, 235, 237, 240, 241. 275. 387.
Bulkeley, Rebecca 342, 376
Bulkeley, Robert 157,
Bulkeley, Stephen 241,
Burbank, Sullivan 143,
Burgess, Thomas 367,
Burke, Richard 44,
Burr, Samuel 230, 232
Burrows, William 89, 355, 357
Burying-Grounds 208,
Buss, Hannah 386,
Buss, Joseph 377,
Buss, Sargent 35,
Buss, William 36, 37, 46, 367, 377
Busse, William 152,
Butler, Joseph 347, 348, 352, 357
Butler, Samuel 355,
Butt, Edward 355,
Buttrick, Abigail 371,
Buttrick, Amos 354,
Buttrick, Ephraim 252,
Buttrick, John 44, 103, 110, 121, 127, 143, 227, 228, 234, 235, 352, 356, 357, 366
Buttrick, Colonel Jonas, 105, 106, 111, 145, 228, 365
Buttrick, Jonathan 72, 179, 320, 321
Buttrick, Joseph 58, 71
Buttrick, Joshua 37, 228
Buttrick, Major 111,
Buttrick, Nathan 323, 347
Buttrick, Oliver 356,
Buttrick, Samuel 44, 72, 234, 322, 366
Buttrick, William 7, 33, 37, 44, 352, 365

-C-

Cady, Pomp 355,
Capen, Sarah 331,
Cargill, Hugh 215,
Carrington, Edward 239,
Carter, Left. 60,
Carter, Nathaniel 72,
Chafin, Robert 89,
Chamberlain 372,
Chamberlain, John 67,
Chamberlain, Mr. 271,
Chambers, Chas. 317,
Chambers, James 257,
Chandler, Deacon 224,
Chandler, James 91, 98, 234

Chandler, John 344, 367
Chandler, Joseph 194, 235, 347
Chandler, Joseph C. 367,
Chandler, Samuel 72, 75, 234, 236, 277, 279
Charlestown Bridge 204,
Chase, Ebenezer 329,
Chase, Heber 222,
Chauncy, Rev. Dr. 241,
Chauncy, Sarah 241,
Cheaver, Wm. 58,
Cheever, Daniel 247, 256, 263, 367
Cheever, David 97,
Cheever, Israel 247,
Cheever, Mr. 95,
Cheney, Hezekiah 252,
Cheney, John M. 230, 232, 238
Cheney, John Milton 252,
Chesley, Joseph 352,
Choat, Mr. 66,
Church, John H. 331,
Churchill, Jesse 228,
Clark, Benjamin 249, 367
Clark, Daniel 235,
Clark, Hannah 372,
Clark, Jeremiah 294, 303
Clark, Jonas 103, 183, 185, 188, 265, 337
Clark, Jonas C. 367,
Clark, Jordan 294,
Clark, Judah 303,
Clark, Lucy 265,
Clark, Peter 249,
Clark, Rev. Mr. 101, 181
Clark, Samuel 367,
Clark, Thomas 61, 183
Cleaveland, Rev. Mr. 286,
Cleisby, Joseph 357, 359
Cobs, John 352,
Codman Farm 308,
Codman, John 307, 318
Cogswell, Emerson 353, 357
Colburn, Benj. 256, 257
Colburn, James 227, 228
Colburn, Nathaniel 71, 179
Colburn, Widow 230,
Cole, Abraham 316,
Cole, Daniel 320, 355, 358
Cole, Rev. Jonathan 193,
Cole, Joseph Green 316,
Coleman, Rev. Benj. 244,
Coleman, Mary 244,
Comy, Daniel 58, 367
Conant, Abraham 290,
Conant, Andrew 94, 235, 358, 367
Conant, Eli 359,
Conant, Ezra 249,
Conant, Joel 377,
Conant, Jonathan 72,

Conant, Lot 367,
Conant, Mary 294,
Conant, Roger C. 367,
Conaway, Peter 42, 52
Concord River 200,
Convers, James 272,
Convers, Josiah 272,
Cook, Joseph 44,
Cook, Samuel 265, 304
Cook, William 169, 178, 179, 184, 283, 367
Coolidge, Elizabeth 375,
Cooper, Benjamin 351,
Cooper, Mary 378,
Cooper, Rachel 351,
Cope, Henry 69,
Corbet, John 257,
Corey, Hannah 294,
Corey, William 72,
Corneil, John 355,
Coslin, William 367,
Cotton, Rev. John 165, 170, 367
Cotton, Mary 165,
Cotton, Mr. 148,
Cotton, Rev. Seaborn 165,
Court Houses 207,
Coverly, Nathaniel 208,
Cowdry, Harris 290,
Cowdry, Susanna 307,
Cragin, John 73,
Crane, Benj. 45,
Cray, Daniel 98,
Crosby, Michael 261, 269
Crosby, Timothy 260,
Cuming, Alexander 239,
Cuming, John 73, 75, 77, 121, 123, 128, 183, 192, 216, 235, 239, 253, 254, 356, 357, 358
Cuming, Robert 253,
Curtis, Ephraim 49, 321
Curtis, Jonathan 357,
Cushing, Jacob 185,
Cushing, Thomas 336,
Cutler, Ebenezer 294, 303, 312
Cutting, John Ruggles 292,
Cutting, William 292,

-D-

Daken, Thomas 34,
Dakin, Amos 380,
Dakin, Deacon 169, 180
Dakin, John 169, 368
Dakin, Joseph 194, 234
Dakin, Samuel 73, 294, 303, 380
Dakin, Simon 234, 321
Dakin, Thomas 38, 367
Dana, Josiah 188,
Dana Samuel 231,
Dandley, Cornelius 257,
Dane, Thomas 35,
Danforth, Benjamin 257,
Danforth, Jonathan 56,
Danforth, Samuel 20, 86
Danforth, Thomas 7, 8, 44, 165
Darby, Amos 355,
Darby, John 73,
Darby, Joseph 44,
Darby, Thomas 44, 354
Darling, John 355,
Davis, Abel 355,
Davis, Abraham 355,
Davis, Daniel 207, 256, 263, 355, 368
Davis, Deliverance 72,
Davis, Dolor 367, 368
Davis, Ebenezer 368,
Davis, Eleazer 67, 263
Davis, Elizabeth 375,
Davis, Gardner 253,
Davis, Gershom 72,
Davis, Isaac 110, 111, 112, 116, 228, 282
Davis, James 368,
Davis, John 253, 289
Davis, Josiah 38, 67, 222, 232, 258, 358
Davis, Moses 196, 206
Davis, Nathan 290,
Davis, Ruth 372,
Davis, Samuel 5, 198, 290, 368
Davis, Simon 49, 66, 220, 235, 236, 238, 289, 364, 368
Davis, Stephen 82, 256, 257, 258, 260, 263, 269, 273
Davis, Thomas 94, 98, 112, 235, 321, 350
Davis, Zachariah 73,
Dawes, William 101,
D'Bernicre, Ensign 96, 107
Dean, Daniel 38, 369, 384
Dean, Joseph 37, 256, 372
Dean, Mary 381
Dean, Thaddeus 260,
Dean, Thomas 369,
Demond, Rev. Elijah 195, 307
Denison, Daniel 61,
Dennis, Hiram 253,
Dennis, Mr. 202,
Dennis, Rodney G. 308,
Dennis, Samuel 3, 38, 253
Derby, John 336,
de Sena, Garcia 326,
Devens, Andrew 31,
Devens, Goodwife 60,
Dickinson, David 329,
Diggs, William 356,
Dill, Peter 369,
Dinsmore, Othniel 222,

Dinsmore, Thomas 263,
Dix, Benjamin 231,
Dix, Jonas 336,
Dix, Jonathan 88,
Dodd, John 71,
Dodson, James 257,
Dogget, Thomas 369,
Don Maria Bay 245,
Doublet, Sarah 32,
Doublet, Tom 52,
Dowdy, George 369,
Draper, Adam 369,
Draper, Lydia 377,
Draper, Nathaniel 355,
Draper, Roger 15, 369
Draper, William 346,
Dudley, Abigail 189, 209
Dudley, Francis 369,
Dudley, James 73,
Dudley, John 369,
Dudley, Joseph 50, 242, 359, 369
Dudley, Josiah 253,
Dudley, Paul 204,
Dudley, Samuel 369,
Dudley, Thomas 13, 166
Dudley, Thos. D. 369,
Dunbar, Asa 267,
Dunster, Elizabeth 387,
Durant, Henry 292,
Durant, Isaac 344,
Duren, Jonas 259,
Dutton, Samuel 257, 355

-E-

Eager, Zerubabel 75,
Eames, Thomas 51,
Eastabrook, Robert 72,
Eaton, Peter 331,
Eaton, William 73,
Eckels, Hannah 365,
Edgel, Benjamin 353,
Edgel, Simon 353,
Edmans, Joshua 33,
Edmonds, Joshua 369,
Edmonds, Mary 381,
Edmonds, Samuel 369,
Edmonds, Walter 17, 369
Edwards, Abraham 369,
Edwards, John 289, 290, 369
Edwards, Nathaniel 284,
Edwards, Robert 369,
Edwards, Samuel 378,
Eliot, Jacob 59,
Eliot, John 20, 24, 26
Eliot, Rev. Mr. 50,
Emerson 369,
Emerson, Chas. Chauncy 250,
Emerson, Daniel 181, 183

Emerson, Edward, 186,
Emerson, Edw. Bliss 250,
Emerson, John 187, 266
Emerson, Joseph 162, 184, 186, 187
Emerson, Ralph Waldo 188, 193, 250
Emerson, Rev. Mr. 94, 244
Emerson, William 91, 93, 105, 162, 184, 187, 250, 340, 352, 354
Emmons, Nathaniel 329,
Endecott, Gov. 152,
Engoldsbey, Ebenezer 43,
Estabrook 370,
Estabrook, Abraham 163,
Estabrook, Benjamin 243,
Estabrook, Daniel 371,
Estabrook, Joseph 161, 162, 163, 214, 243
Estabrook, Samuel 73, 163, 243
Estabrook, Thomas 163,
Evarts, Jeremiah 370,
Evarts, John 370,
Evarts, Judah 370,
Everett, Edward 231, 334
Everett, Stevens 222,
Eyre, John 43,

-F-

Fairbank, Jonas 382,
Fairhaven Hill 199,
Fairhaven Pond 200,
Farley, George F. 222, 230
Farmer, John 240, 314
Farnsworth, Benjamin 382,
Farrar, Abel 73,
Farrar, George 234, 247, 277, 295, 314, 316, 362, 370
Farrar, Henry 370,
Farrar, Humphrey 316,
Farrar, Jacob 67, 370
Farrar, James 308,
Farrar, John 315, 370
Farrar, Jonathan 105,
Farrar, Joseph 67, 314, 316, 370
Farrar, Mary 378,
Farrar, Samuel 82, 91, 110, 122, 130, 234, 294, 295, 300, 305, 308, 312, 314, 315, 353, 356, 358, 359
Farrar, Stephen 314,
Farrar, Timothy 311, 314
Farrar, William 316,
Farrer, Jonathan 347,
Farweles, Henry 34,
Farwell, Henry 152, 370
Farwell, John 37,
Farwell, Josiah 67,
Fasset, Benj. 257,
Fassett, John 234, 256, 257, 272, 273, 277

Fassett, Josiah 256, 257, 263
Fassett, Nathaniel 370,
Fassett, Peter 257,
Faulkner, Ammiruhammah 292,
Faulkner, Edmund 292,
Faulkner, Francis 82, 91, 281, 283, 284, 286, 289, 290, 291, 353
Faulkner, John 292,
Faulkner, Luther 291,
Faulkner, Paul 292,
Faulkner, Sarah 290,
Faulkner, William Emerson 291,
Faulkner, Winthrop 290,
Fay, Jonathan 229, 237, 251, 382
Fay, Mr. 195,
Fay, Samuel Phillips Prescott 251,
Fay, Thomas 355,
Fay, Warren 194,
Fessenden, Thomas 338, 346, 358
Fessenden, Thomas G. 231,
Field, Rev. Joseph 193,
Fifty Acre Brook 202,
First Academy 208,
First Jail 207,
Fisher, George 195,
Fiske, Elijah 312, 313, 316
Fiske, George 316,
Fiske, Jonathan 353, 359
Fiske, Luke 231, 232
Fiske, Thomas 316,
Fitch, Benjamin 257,
Fitch, Jeremiah 261,
Fitch, Joseph 257,
Fitch, Moses 269,
Fitch, Samuel 256, 263, 273
Fitch, Zach. 257,
Flagg, Eleazer 75,
Flagg, Experience 362,
Flagg, John 73,
Fletcher, Aaron 327,
Fletcher, Daniel 73, 281, 289
Fletcher, Francis 37, 370, 386
Fletcher, James 72,
Fletcher, John 289,
Fletcher, Joseph 277, 285, 369
Fletcher, Luke 370,
Fletcher, Robert 17, 18, 152, 370
Fletcher, Samuel 234, 370
Fletcher, Thomas 71,
Fletcher, Wid. S. 328,
Fletcher, William 370,
Fletcher, William 320,
Flint, Abel 315,
Flint, Abigail 163,
Flint, Edward 227, 303, 371
Flint, Ephraim 38, 162, 236, 246, 303, 309, 312, 315, 371
Flint Farm 246,
Flint, Henry 358, 371

Flint, John 37, 41, 45, 47, 59, 70, 75, 77, 79, 82, 185, 233, 234, 235, 246, 280, 371
Flint, Mr. 19,
Flint, Nehemiah 143, 227
Flint, Thomas 9, 15, 19, 24, 235, 236, 371, 388
Flynt, Edward 294,
Flynt, Ephraim 294,
Folsom George 222,
Forbes, Abner 222,
Forbes, Eli 188,
Ford, John 353,
Fort Pond Brook 201,
Foster, Agnes 329,
Foster, Dr. 352,
Foster, Dwight 293,
Foster, E. 305,
Foster, Edmund 231,
Fowle, George 19, 371
Fowle, John 382,
Fox, Corporal 227,
Fox, Eliphalet 37, 371, 386
Fox, John 145, 215, 277
Foxe, Thomas 152, 371
Francis, Rev. Convers 193,
Freeman, Joseph 44,
Freeman, Samuel 336,
French, Jonathan 256,
French, Joseph 234, 256, 263, 372
French, Nathaniel 358, 359
French, R. 37,
French, Reuben 38,
French, Sergeant 227,
Frisbie, Levi 222,
Frissil, William 372,
Frye, Jonathan 67,
Fullam, Francis 201,
Fullam, Jacob 67,
Fuller, Abraham 88,
Fuller, Elisha 238,
Fuller, Elizabeth 369,
Fuller, Timothy 238,
Fuller, William 19, 372
Furbish, Abel 289,
Furbish, James 222,
Furbish, Paul 327.

G

Gage, General 115, 116
Gage, Robert 294,
Gallap, Antil 89,
Gamlin, Robert 372,
Gannet, Thomas B. 193,
Gardner, Bela 290,
Gardner, Dr. 272,
Gardner, Henry 88, 92, 108
Gardner, Rev. John, 167, 178, 179, 184, 283

Gardner, Mr. 108,
Gardner, Samuel 58,
Garfield, Abraham 347,
Garfield, John 294, 303
Garfield, Thomas 294, 303
Gates, Luke 309,
Gates, Thomas 44,
Gee, Joshua 170,
Gerry, Elbridge 98, 336
Gibbs, Henry 244,
Gibbs, Mercy 244,
Gilbert, Col. 72,
Gill, Moses 98,
Gilson, Joseph 67,
Gobble, Abigail 369,
Gobble, Daniel 63, 372
Gobble, John 45,
Gobble, Stephen 62,
Gobble, Thomas 38, 372
Goffe, David 69,
Goffe, John 67,
Goldsberry, John 331,
Goodnow, Jane 366,
Goodnow, Peter 290,
Goodnow, Ruth 378,
Goodwin, Hersey Bradford 229,
Goodwin, Lucretia Watson 193,
Goodwin, Mr. 193,
Gookin, Daniel 8, 44, 61
Gookin, Major 50,
Goose Pond 200,
Gouch, William 69,
Gould, Benjamin 356,
Gould, Lieutenant Edward Thornton 107, 112, 116, 338, 350
Gould, Henry 71,
Gove, Charles F. 314,
Gove, John 294, 303, 308, 314
Gove, Jonathan 294, 303, 314
Graves, John 152,
Great River 200,
Greaves, Sarah 364,
Green, Asa 325, 353, 356
Green, Cyrus 327,
Green, Eleazer 382,
Green, Isaac 344
Green, Isaiah 327,
Green, James 327,
Green, John 93, 320, 322, 327, 329, 330, 372
Green, Jonathan 163,
Green, Leonard 327,
Green, Mr. 195,
Green, Nathan 327, 372
Green, Samuel 194, 195, 207, 327, 372
Green, Zaccheus 322, 325, 327, 372
Greene, John 94,
Greenough, William 285,

Griffin, Richard 17, 19, 152, 194, 235, 372
Grimer, William 344,
Grimes, Jonathan 257,

-H-

Hadley, John 303,
Hadlock, John 372,
Hagar, Micah 345,
Hager, Ezekiel 358,
Hager, William 295,
Hall, Andrew 259,
Hall, David 170, 171, 382
Hall, Lieutenant Edward 116,
Hall, Isaac 359,
Hall, Samuel 44,
Hall, Stephen 44, 368
Hall, Willard 169,
Hall, William 372,
Halsted, William 372,
Hamilton, John 373,
Hamlen, Hannibal 293,
Hammond, Charles 228,
Hancock, Ebenezer 167,
Hancock, John 91, 261, 262, 302, 303, 304
Hancock, John 129, 165, 166, 178
Handell, Stephen 45,
Handley, John 289,
Hanley, Charles 358,
Hapgood, Ephraim 82, 91, 281
Hapgood, Shadrach 44,
Hapwood, Sydrach 44,
Harding, Rev. Sewall 195, 307
Hardy, Ebenezer 259,
Hardy, Richard 373,
Harrington, Daniel 342, 344, 356
Harrington, Henry 257
Harrington, John 344,
Harrington, Levi 345,
Harrington, Moses 344,
Harrington, Thaddeus 344,
Harrington, Thomas 344,
Harrington, Timothy 178,
Harris, George 372,
Harris, Jonathan 72, 73, 322
Hartshorn, Ebenezer 183, 239
Hartshorn, Mrs. 230,
Hartshorn, Thomas 208, 239
Hartwell, Amos 269,
Hartwell, Elizabeth 216,
Hartwell, Ephraim 234, 295, 315, 373
Hartwell, Hannah 375,
Hartwell, John 37, 257, 263, 308, 320, 322, 354
Hartwell, Jonas 315,
Hartwell, Joseph 257, 258

Hartwell, Mr. 115,
Hartwell, Rebecca 373,
Hartwell, Samuel 270, 354, 373, 386
Hartwell, Stephen 257,
Hartwell, Timothy 257,
Hartwell, William 35, 37, 45, 261, 263, 273
Harvard Professors 120,
Harwood, John 67,
Harwood, Nathaniel 373,
Hassell, Joseph 373,
Hastings, Elizabeth 364,
Hastings, Isaac 344,
Hastings, Samuel 345,
Hastings, Wm. 257,
Haughthorn, Capt. 59,
Haven, Jason 188,
Haven, Jason 185,
Haven, Joseph 88,
Hawley, Thomas 58,
Hayden, Richard 359,
Hayden, William 312, 313, 364
Haynes, Aaron 110,
Haynes, John 44,
Haynes, Joshua 163,
Haynes, Walter 57,
Hayward, Abigail 373,
Hayward, Abijah 289,
Hayward, Ann 372,
Hayward, Benjamin 286,
Hayward, Danforth 352,
Hayward, Ebenezer 374,
Hayward, George 36, 38, 44, 373
Hayward, James 115, 116
Hayward, John 44, 71, 82, 110, 228, 373
Hayward, Joseph 75, 114, 121, 204, 373, 375
Hayward, Josiah 91, 281, 284, 289, 373
Hayward, Mary 372, 387
Hayward, Samuel 281, 284, 285
Haywood, Joseph 45, 290, 373
Headley John 294,
Headly, Thomas 344,
Heald, Alexander 71,
Heald, Amos 71, 194, 294, 364
Heald, Cyrus 327,
Heald, Daniel 89,
Heald, Gershom 44, 374
Heald, Isaac 44,
Heald, Israel 44,
Heald, John 37, 66, 110, 234, 284, 285, 353, 356, 358, 374
Heald, Jonas 140,
Heald, Jonathan 324, 327
Heald, Mary 381,
Heald, Rebecca 329,
Heald, Samuel 230, 321, 324, 327, 353, 354, 358

Heald, Thomas 228, 237, 291, 327
Heald, Timothy 73, 327
Heald, Wid. R. 37, 328
Heartwell, Amos 273,
Heaward, Georg 35,
Heaward, George 39,
Hedge, Frederick H. 193,
Henchman, D. 60,
Henchman, Thomas 31, 47, 275
Heyden, William 37,
Heywood, Abel B. 37, 215, 228, 362
Heywood, Abel B. 104,
Heywood, Abiel 222, 229, 230, 232, 234, 235, 237, 239, 249, 374
Heywood, Deacon 180,
Heywood, Dr. 105, 207
Heywood, Edward 352, 353
Heywood, Elizabeth 373,
Heywood, John 38, 163, 194, 234, 374, 385
Heywood, Jonas 71, 91, 92, 97, 98, 119, 121, 131, 233, 234, 356, 357, 358, 359
Heywood, Jonathan 70, 98
Heywood, Mrs. 114,
Heywood, Rebecca 378,
Heywood, Samuel 75, 168, 194, 201, 215, 233, 234, 277
Higginson, Elizabeth 244,
Hildreth, Benj. Warren 251,
Hildreth, Ephraim 44,
Hildreth, Frederick 142,
Hildreth, Jane 383,
Hildreth, Jonathan 235,
Hildreth, Richard 223,
Hildreth, William 237,
Hill Burying Grounds 208,
Hill, Samuel 75,
Hitchcock, Gad 185,
Hoar, Benjamin 71,
Hoar, Ebenezer Rockwood 253,
Hoar, Elizabeth 382,
Hoar, Daniel 247, 374, 384
Hoar, Isaac 183, 227
Hoar, John 51, 52, 71, 237, 347, 374
Hoar, Jonathan 72, 73, 247
Hoar, Leonard 312, 374
Hoar, Leonard H. 375,
Hoar, Mary 372,
Hoar, Nathaniel Pierce 316,
Hoar, Samuel 110, 130, 143, 145, 222, 229, 253, 300, 309, 312, 313, 315, 316, 334, 353, 354, 358, 375
Hoar, Samuel Jr. 238,
Hoar, Timothy 357,
Hobart, Nehemiah 164,
Hobart, Shebuel 382,
Hobbs, Humphrey 71,
Hobbs, Matthew 353, 354, 358

- 401 -

Hobby, Richard 359,
Hobby, William 175, 178
Hodgman, John 355,
Hodgman, Thomas 357,
Holbrook, Capt. 59,
Holden, Silas 43, 47, 384
Holden, Tilly 355,
Holdridge, Richard 44,
Holman, Colonel 283,
Holman, Silas 222,
Holmes, Rev. Dr. 21,
Holt, Joshua 259,
Holyoke, Edward 163,
Hooker, Rev. Mr. 150,
Hopkins, Thomas 58,
Hosmer, Abigail 373,
Hosmer, Abner 112, 116
Hosmer, Amos 73, 353, 355, 358
Hosmer, Daniel 354,
Hosmer, Deacon Cyrus 105, 194, 224, 252
Hosmer, Elijah 73,
Hosmer, George Washington 252,
Hosmer, Hannah 373,
Hosmer, James 35, 38, 58, 73, 152, 375
Hosmer, John 47, 271, 344, 375
Hosmer, Jonathan 281, 285, 289, 375
Hosmer, Joseph 91, 92, 98, 106, 110, 111, 119, 121, 126, 131, 132, 147, 227, 236, 237, 350, 359
Hosmer, Josiah 179,
Hosmer, Mary 373, 384
Hosmer, Prudence 375,
Hosmer, Reuben 73,
Hosmer, Rufus 230, 231, 251
Hosmer, Samuel 353, 359
Hosmer, Sarah 374,
Hosmer, Silas 286,
Hosmer, Simon 289, 290
Hosmer, Stephen 71, 72, 77, 179, 210, 234, 280, 321, 347, 358, 375
Hosmer, Stephen Jr. 234,
Hosmer, Thomas 98, 375
Hosmer, Titus 375,
Hosmer, William 347,
Hough, Atherton 14,
Hough, Samuel 160,
Houghton, Hannah 370,
Houghton, John 370,
Houston, James 257,
How, Cyprian 354, 358
How, Ezekiel 110,
How, James 370,
How, Mary 370,
How, Nathaniel 143,
How, Phineas 229, 230
How, William 89, 376
Howard, Danforth 73,

Howe, James 222,
Howe, Thomas 75,
Hubbard, Cyrus 227, 235
Hubbard, Deacon 3, 202, 205
Hubbard, Eb. 37,
Hubbard, Ebenezer 98, 175, 185, 206, 234, 249
Hubbard, Elizabeth 374,
Hubbard, Isaac 98, 121, 140, 359
Hubbard, Jonathan 234, 376
Hubbard, Joseph 71, 243, 376
Hubbard, Joshua 234,
Hubbard, Lucy 361,
Hubbard, Mary 368,
Hubbard, Thomas 98, 194, 235, 243, 353, 358, 376
Hull, Stephen 331,
Hunt, Captain 205,
Hunt, Ebenezer 294,
Hunt, Elizabeth 362,
Hunt, Francis 196, 230
Hunt, Humphrey 14, 363, 376
Hunt, Jeremiah 357,
Hunt, John 75,
Hunt, Joseph 222, 229, 239, 248, 352, 354, 376
Hunt, Nehemiah 45, 227, 235, 376
Hunt, Mrs. Rebecca 209,
Hunt, Reuben 209, 235, 356, 359
Hunt, Samuel 38, 243, 280
Hunt, Deacon Simeon 185, 248
Hunt, Simon 110, 183, 184, 188, 194, 234, 236, 283, 289, 353, 354, 356, 372, 376
Hunt, Thaddeus 355,
Hunt, William 17, 376
Hunter, John 61,
Hunting, Capt. 58,
Hurd, Ann 142,
Hurd, Benjamin 239,
Hurd, Dr. 47,
Hurd, Isaac 145, 229, 239, 355
Hurd, Thomas 110,
Hurlburt, Rufus 285,
Hurlbut, Rufus 307,
Hutchins, Eleakin 327,
Hutchins, Thomas 130,
Hutchinson, Benjamin 257,
Hutchinson, Capt. 63,
Hutchinson, Edward 48,
Hutchinson, Francis 376,
Hutchinson, John 238,
Hutchinson, Mr. 238,
Hutchinson, Nathaniel 327,

-I-

Ingraham, Duncan 132, 145, 192

-J-

Jack, John 210,
Jackson, John 295,
Jackson, Joseph 185,
Jacobs, John 327, 330, 355, 356, 358
Jameson, Matthew 355,
Jarvis, Chas. 252,
Jarvis, Deacon 105, 206, 224
Jarvis, Edward 252,
Jarvis, Edward 222,
Jarvis, Francis 145, 194, 214, 228, 229, 252
Javis, Dr. 199,
Jeffrey, Silence 243,
Jefts, John 67,
Jehojakin 7, 8, 9
Jenks, Joseph 43,
Jenners, David 355,
Jethro 8,
Jewett, Thomas 326,
Johnson, Ichabod 67,
Johnson, John 259,
Johnson, Josiah 67, 88
Johnson, Noah 67,
Johnson, Rufus 259,
Jones, Aaron 289,
Jones, Captain 108,
Jones, David S. 309,
Jones, Dorcas 367,
Jones, Eliphalet 154,
Jones, Elisha 98, 356, 358
Jones, Elizabeth 367,
Jones, Elnathan 32, 97, 234, 362, 380
Jones, Ephriam 72, 75, 108, 233, 234, 236, 275, 353, 373, 377
Jones, John 5, 7, 8, 16, 37, 39, 148, 152, 153, 168, 234, 240, 243, 321, 376, 377
Jones, Josiah 67,
Jones, Mr. 18,
Jones, Ruth 365,
Jones, Samuel 32, 98, 227, 234, 250, 275, 278, 353, 357, 358, 377
Jones, Sarah 374,
Jones, Silas 288,
Jones, Thomas 98, 234, 347
Jones, Timothy 130,
Jones, William 142, 222, 237, 250
Josselyn, Mr. John 196,
Judgson, Goodman 206,
Judson, William 377,

-K-

Kehonowsqua 30,
Kelley, Lieutenant 112,
Kendall, Jacob 263,
Kendall, James, D.D. 193, 272
Kerley, William 44,

Kether, Goodwife 60,
Kettenanet, Job 51,
Kettle, Cesar 357,
Keyes, John 205, 229, 230, 232, 237, 238
Keyes, Mr. 114,
Keyes, Rebecca 293,
Kibby, Samuel 323,
Kidder, Amos 328,
Kidder, Benjamin 67, 257, 261, 263
Kies, Solomon 67,
Killock, Timothy 357,
King, Abigail 369,
King, Charles 242,
King, James II 242,
Kingsbury, Enoch 358,
Kittredge, Dr. 272,
Kittridge, Jonathan 67,
Kittridge, Paul C. 290,
Knight, Jonathan 275,
Knowlton, John 72,

-L-

Lakin, Isaac 67,
Lamont, John 353,
Lampson, Eben. 70,
Lampson, Ebenezer 294,
Lampson, Timothy 295,
Lamson, Lot 358, 359
Lamson, Samuel 353,
Lane, David 271,
Lane, James 257, 271
Lane, Job 116, 256, 257, 261, 263, 269, 271
Lane, John 257, 263
Lane, Martha 380,
Lane, Oliver Wellington 272,
Lane, Timothy 257,
Langdon, Samuel 121,
Larkin, Sarah 386,
Laughton, Jacob 359,
Laughton, John 322,
Laughton, Samuel 322,
Law Family 275,
Law, John 377,
Lawrence, Abel 145,
Lawrence, David 231,
Lawrence, Peleg 32,
Lawrence, William 181, 303, 304, 309, 321, 331, 361, 382
Lawrie, Captain 107,
Law's Brook 201,
Lee, Henry 378,
Lee, Isaac 235,
Lee, Jeremiah 98,
Lee, Jonas 120, 142, 145, 147
Lee, Joseph 77, 86, 89, 90, 163, 186, 238, 248, 249, 284, 377, 378, 379

- 403 -

Lee, Samuel 117, 249
Lee, Silas 249,
Lee, Woodis 303, 378
Legross, Farancs 355,
Leonard, John 181,
Leonard, Mary 181,
Lester, Ensign 114,
Lettin, Richard 15, 378
Lincoln, Benjamin 91,
Lincoln, William 94, 336
Litchfield, Franklin 325,
Litchfield, Paul 194, 195, 325, 327, 329, 330
Livermore, Daniel 358,
Livermore, Josiah 358,
Lloyd, Charles 355,
Lock, Benjamin 344,
Lock, Rueben 344,
Loker, Mary 382,
Longley, John 382,
Loring, David 217,
Loring, Israel 170, 179, 283, 303
Loring, Jonathan 102, 181
Loring, Deacon Joseph 116,
Loring, Mr. 201,
Lovewell, Capt. 67,
Lovewell, John 67,
Lowdon, Richard 56,
Luce, John 369,
Luce, Rev. Leonard 195,
Lynde, Ann 245,
Lynde, Nathaniel 245,
Lynnfield, Edward 67,
Lyon, Aaron 70,

-MC-

McCobb, Samuel 353,
McFarlane, Walter 283,
McGath, John 355,
McGregor, Daniel 359,

-M-

Magus, John 62,
Mann, Daniel 71,
Mann, Dr. 313,
Mann, Silas 352, 356
Marble, Samuel 378,
Marr, James 349, 355
Marsh, 179,
Marsh, James Rumney 62,
Marshal, Abel 73,
Martin, Ambrose 152,
Martin, Ambrose 378,
Mason, Hannah 365,
Mason, Hugh 56, 365, 378
Mason, John 378,
Mason, Mary 163,

Mason, Robert 7,
Mason, Thaddeus 88,
Massy, Stephen 272,
Maxwell, Hugh 257,
Maxwell, Mary 383,
Mead, Levi 345,
Meads, Abner 344,
Meads, Mary 368,
Meeds, Joseph 257,
Meers, John 352,
Meeting houses 205,
Mellen, John 185,
Melsin, Eleazer 67,
Melsin, Josiah 99,
Melvin, David 67, 68, 70, 169, 234, 358
Melvin, Eleazer 71, 312
Melvin, Ephraim 322, 347, 348
Melvin, Jacob 72,
Melvin, James 355,
Melvin, John 71, 378
Melvin, Nathan 72,
Meriam, Ebenezer 71,
Meriam, Georg 34,
Meriam, George 37,
Meriam, John 37, 73
Meriam, Joseph 75,
Meriam, Nathan 82,
Meriam, Robert 34, 35, 37
Merriam, Amos 257, 294, 363
Merriam, Ann 365,
Merriam, Charles 232,
Merriam, Ebeneezer 247, 365
Merriam, Ephraim 214, 351
Merriam, George 378,
Merriam, Hannah 376,
Merriam, Horatio Cook 253,
Merriam, John 130, 230, 257, 261, 272, 273, 378
Merriam, Jonas 185,
Merriam, Joseph 121, 208, 260, 378, 379
Merriam, Josiah 94, 379
Merriam, Lydia 266,
Merriam, Marshall 253,
Merriam, Mary 385,
Merriam, Nathan 235,
Merriam, Nathaniel 256, 257, 263, 269
Merriam, Oliver 247,
Merriam, Robert 152, 193, 194, 233, 235, 376, 378
Merriam, Ruth 384,
Merriam, Samuel 168, 194, 234, 256, 257
Merriam, Sarah 372,
Merriam, Susanna 383,
Merriam, Timothy 357, 379
Merriam, William 269, 273

Merrick, John 237, 250
Merrick, Mr. 203,
Merrick, Tilly 145, 147, 229, 249, 250
Merrill, David J. 222,
Merrill, Henry H. 218,
Merrill, Nathan 259,
Metcalf, Eliab W. 143,
Middlebrook, Joseph 379,
Middlebrooke, Joseph 17,
Middlesex Gazette (first newspaper) 208,
Miles, Charles 110, 116, 354
Miles, Ezekiel 179,
Miles, James 202,
Miles, John 36, 38, 45, 71, 245, 379, 382
Miles, Jonathan 245,
Miles, Mary 377,
Miles, Nathan 71,
Miles, Oliver 72,
Miles, Samuel 179, 194, 379
Mill Brook 202,
Miller, Jacob 110,
Miller, John 353,
Mills, The 287,
Minerals 197,
Minot, Ephraim 352, 355
Minot, Timothy 348,
Minott, Benjamin 244,
Minott, Bulah 189,
Minott, Cesar 355,
Minott, Elizabeth 361,
Minott Fund 189,
Minott, George 98, 110, 121, 194, 222, 235, 353, 379
Minott, James 70, 72, 168, 176, 179, 214, 227, 234, 236, 238, 244, 276, 377, 380
Minott, John 145, 207, 354
Minott, Jonas 229, 235, 251
Minott, Love 361,
Minott, Lydia 362,
Minott, Mercy 368
Minott, Rebecca 243, 244, 362
Minott, Samuel 183, 194, 234, 247, 251, 380
Minott, Timothy 108, 113, 164, 168, 180, 220, 234, 239, 245, 247
Mitchel, Jonathan 380,
Monroe, Benjamin 294, 303
Monroe, John 247,
Monroe, Joseph 329,
Monroe, Joshua 329,
Monroe, Mercy 329,
Monroe, Nathaniel 70,
Monroe, Ruth 329,
Monroe, Wid. R. 328,
Monroe, William 140, 218, 345
Moody, Samuel 170, 187

Moore, Abel 230, 253
Moore, Cambridge 259,
Moore, David 110,
Moore, George 253,
Moore, John 44, 82, 110, 257, 258, 260, 273
Morse, John 60,
Morse, Rev. Dr. 229,
Moulton, Martha 108,
Muckquamuck, Peter 41,
Mulliken, Mr. 101,
Mulliken, Mrs. Lydia 116,
Mulliken, Nathaniel 344,
Munroe, Benjamin 347,
Munroe, Edmund 354,
Munroe, John 344,
Munroe, William 353, 358
Murdock, James, D.D. 195,
Murray, Col. 248,
Muzzy, Benjamin 230,
Muzzy, Elizabeth 293,
Muzzy, John 344,

-N-

Nagog Pond 201,
Nahshawtuck 7,
Nanepashemet 2,
Nas hoban Brook 201,
Natanquatick 6,
Natototos, James 39,
Nawshawtuct 197,
Neepanaum, Mary 41,
Neiff, Patrick 355,
Nelson, Albert 326,
Nelson, John 326, 327
Nelson, Josiah 326,
Nelson, Thomas 294,
New Burying Grounds 208,
Newdigate, Simon and Hannah 245,
Newell, Jonathan 188, 231, 285
Newhall, Ebenezer 308,
Newton, Joseph 44,
Nichols, Ezekiel 327,
Nichols, Wid. E. 328,
Niles, Samuel 329,
Nimrod 8,
Nixon, John 110, 352
Nixon, Thomas 110, 352
North or Assabeth River 201,
North River 200,
Notawquatuchquaw 8, 9
Nowell, Increase 14,
Noyes, Ensigne 40,
Noyes, Joseph 290,
Noyes, Josiah 286,
Noyes, Peter 15,
Noyes, Thomas 39, 40, 122, 130, 285, 289, 291

- 405 -

Nut-Meadow Brook 202,
Nutting, Amos 355,
Nuttunkurta 7,

-O-

Oakes, Edward 235, 380
Oakes, Edward 380,
Oakes, Mary 371,
Oakes, Urian 380,
Occum, Sampson 246,
Odell, William 380,
Oliver, Abigail 382,
Oliver, Nathaniel 43,
Orne, Azor 122,
Osburn, Samuel 354,
Osgood, Benjamin 231,
Osgood, Capt. 72,
Oxford Army 142,

-P-

Page, Anna 270,
Page, Christopher 260, 263
Page, Joshua 232, 261
Page, Nathan 358,
Page, Nathaniel 256, 263,
Page, Thomas 270,
Page, William 260, 270
Paige, Elijah F. 222,
Park, Thomas 340,
Parker, Captain 102,
Parker, David 323,
Parker, Ebenezer 344,
Parker, Frederick 326,
Parker, James 44, 49, 326, 382
Parker, John 343, 344
Parker, Jonas 327, 344
Parker, Joseph 55,
Parker, Moses 42,
Parker, Oliver 139,
Parker, Samuel 382,
Parker, Thomas 169, 178
Parker, Wid. M. 328,
Parker, Zachariah 67,
Parkhurst, Nathaniel 344,
Parkins, Jesse 357,
Parkman, William 94, 194, 205
Parks, Daniel 294,
Parks, Isaac 347,
Parks, James 353, 358,
Parks, Joseph 294, 381
Parks, Joshua 303,
Parks, Reuben 357,
Parks, Richard 234, 277, 381
Parks, Zaccheus 294,
Parlin, Abigail 329,
Parlin, Amos 72,
Parlin, Asa 130, 289, 327, 381

Parlin, David 322,
Parlin, John 381,
Parlin, Joseph 322,
Parlin, Nathan 327,
Parlin, Silas 357,
Parsons, Captain 113,
Parsons, Joseph 43, 170
Parsons, Capt. Lawrence 107,
Pasmore, James 381,
Patch, Stephen 312, 313
Patten, Oliver 222,
Paugus 67,
Payne, Elisha 176,
Payne, Elizabeth 362,
Payson, Phillips 185,
Peabody, Oliver 169, 178, 283
Peirce, George 294,
Peirce, Solomon 344,
Pelham, Herbert 15,
Pellet, Thomas 37, 381
Pemberton, Samuel 304,
Pennakennit 27,
Penniman, Joseph 267,
Penniman, Rev. Mr. 186,
Pepper, Joseph 58,
Pepperell, Benj. 244,
Pepperell, Henry 244,
Pepperell, William 244,
Percival Farm 308,
Percy, Right Honorable Hugh Earl, 115,
Perham, Postmaster 288,
Perkins, Benjamin 357,
Perkins, Mark 44, 71
Perry, Gardner B. 307,
Petty, Joseph 71,
Petuhanit, Robert 48,
Petuhanit, Sampson 48,
Philip, 47, 61, 63
Phillips, Thomas 69,
Phinney, Elias 232, 334
Phipps, David 89,
Pierce, Abijah 82, 91, 110, 122, 295, 312
Pierce, George 303,
Pierce, James 294,
Pierce, John 285,
Pierce, Jonas 303,
Pierce, Joseph 294, 303
Pierce, Nathan 347,
Pierce, Nathaniel 51, 315
Pierpont, R. 98,
Pigeon, John 95,
Piper, Asa 291, 358
Piper, Josiah 291,
Piper, Samuel 356,
Pitcairn, John 101,
Pitcairn, Major 103, 113
Pittemey, Andrew 43,

- 406 -

Pittimee, Andrew 62,
Plummer, Joseph 356,
Plympton, Thomas 57,
Pole, Captain Mundey 107,
Pollard, Benjamin 70,
Ponkawtassett 197,
Pool, William 73,
Pools, Capt. 61,
Pope, Frederick 356,
Post Office 205,
Potter, Elizabeth 377,
Potter, Ephraim 98, 121, 224
Potter, Isaac 117,
Potter, Judah 365,
Potter, Luke 35, 37, 152, 194, 381
Potter, Mary 362
Potter, Samuel 58,
Powers, John 73, 381
Powers, Walter 73, 257, 381
Prenter, James 62,
Prentice, John 169,
Prentice, Solomon 170,
Prescott, Abel 114, 239,
Prescott, Abel, Jr. 116,
Prescott, Ann and Rebecca 246,
Prescott, Benjamin 71, 145, 163, 239, 243, 244, 357, 380
Prescott, Ceasar 259,
Prescott, Charles 75, 77, 89, 179, 234, 236, 355
Prescott, Dorothy 241,
Prescott, James 82, 382
Prescott, John 69, 239, 245
Prescott, Jonas 304, 321, 377
Prescott, Jonathan 66, 71, 75, 105, 166, 234, 236, 238, 239, 243, 245, 280, 292, 374, 381,
Prescott, John P. 381,
Prescott, Lieutenant 227,
Prescott, Lucy 237,
Prescott, Oliver 231, 353, 382
Prescott, Peter 72, 73, 75, 246
Prescott, Samuel 101, 114
Prescott, Samuel P. 382,
Prescott, Sarah 380,
Prescott, Timothy 230,
Prescott, Colonel William 111,
Prescott, Willoughby 97, 98
Preston, Amariah 272,
Price, Hannah 388,
Prichard, Wm. Mackay 253,
Prince, James 219,
Prince, Thomas 181, 219
Printing Office 208,
Proctor, Gaius 230,
Proctor, Robert 382,
Proctor, Silas 353,
Prout, Ebenezer 214, 235, 383
Prout, Timothy 383,

Public Buildings 205,
Puffer, Jabez 110,
Puffer, Jonathan 183, 320, 321, 322
Purchis, Oliver 43, 383
Putnam, Edmond 379,
Putnam, Israel 256, 263, 269, 273
Putnam, Simeon 222,

-Q-

Quincy, Edmond 374,
Quunosnuck 198,

-R-

Ralph's Brook 202,
Ramsden, Hannah 378,
Ramsden, Priscilla 361,
Rand, Asa 194,
Rand, Henry 44,
Rand, Rev. Mr. 195,
Randall, Ephraim 331,
Rankin, James 257,
Rawson, Edward 39, 40
Raymond, Paul 257,
Raymond, William 257,
Reddit, Mary 377,
Reddit, Susannah 370,
Reed, Abigail 368,
Reed, Daniel 294,
Reed, David 261, 273
Reed, John 82, 91, 257, 258, 260, 272, 273
Reed, Jonathan 354, 356
Reed, Joshua 344,
Reed, Nathan 344,
Reed, Philip 238, 383
Reed, Philip R. 383,
Reed, Samuel 138,
Revere, Paul 101,
Rice, Gershom 75,
Rice, Jonathan 110,
Rice, Oliver 355,
Rice, Richard 7, 34, 37, 46, 383
Rice, Samuel 375,
Richardson, Daniel 232,
Richardson, Edward 98, 348, 352
Richardson, Josiah 385,
Richardson, Major 72,
Richardson, Moses 352,
Richardson, Thomas 67,
Richardson, Timothy 67,
Richardson, Wm. 72,
Richardson, Wyman 222,
Ripley, Daniel Bliss 251,
Ripley, Rev. Dr. 37, 105, 162, 189, 193, 205, 206, 224, 254, 351
Ripley, Erza 131, 134, 188, 192, 222, 229, 251, 285, 335

- 407 -

Ripley, George 193,
Ripley, Samuel 193, 251
Robbins, Aaron 327,
Robbins, Mrs. Anna 208,
Robbins, Ephraim 289, 327, 330
Robbins, Jonathan 67,
Robbins, Joseph 110, 122
Robbins, Robert 32, 383
Roberts, John 58,
Robinson, Bradbury 349, 352
Robinson, Col. 95,
Robinson, John 73, 111, 280, 290, 329, 330, 338, 343
Robinson, John 352,
Robinson, John P. 232,
Robinson, Lieutenant-Colonel 111,
Robinson, William 383,
Rocky Hills 197,
Rogers, Rev. Daniel 166, 178, 184, 283, 304, 380
Rogers, Major 73,
Rogers, Nathaniel 170,
Root, Erastus 251,
Roots, Benajah 187,
Roots, Rev. Mr. 188,
Ross, George 383,
Row, Amos 71,
Rowlandson, Mrs. 52,
Rugg, John 383,
Ruggles, Samuel 122, 169, 261
Russell, Chambers 234, 236, 237, 295, 312, 317
Russell, Charles 300, 313, 314, 318
Russell, Daniel 317,
Russell, David 73,
Russell Farm 308,
Russell, George 313,
Russell, James 43, 110, 274, 312, 313, 317, 322, 326
Russell, Philip 344,
Russell, Richard 312, 313, 317
Russell, Wid. L. 328,
Russell, Wm. L. 326,
Rutter, Jabez 44,
Rutter, Micah M. 232,

S

Safety Committee 94,
Sagamore 7,
Sanderson, Elijah 341, 342
Sanderson, Samuel 345,
Sanford, David 329,
Sanger, Ralph 222,
Saunderson, Elijah 102,
Saunderson, Henry 228,
Savage, James 151,
Savage, John 73,
Saw Mill Brook 202,

Sawyer, John 329,
Sawyer, Thomas 381,
Scotchford, John 38, 233, 378, 383
Scott, Jonathan Edwards 291,
Scott, Mr. 62,
Seaver, Nathaniel 58,
Segard, Ephraim 294,
Selfridge, Thomas O. 222,
Severance, Samuel 71,
Severns, Josiah 353,
Sewall, Joseph 175, 177
Sewall, Judge 164, 242
Shambery, Joseph 43,
Sharp, John 58,
Sharp, Mary 387,
Shattuck, Daniel 7, 99, 230, 232, 351
Shattuck, Job 134, 139, 353
Shattuck, Lemuel 229,
Shays, Daniel 140,
Shay's Insurrection 129,
Sheafe, Mary 378,
Shed, Marshall 285, 308, 331
Shepard, John 39,
Shepard, Major 187,
Shepard, Thomas 21,
Shepherd, Abraham 54, 384
Shepherd, Charles 357, 358
Shepherd Family 275,
Shepherd, Isaac 54,
Shepherd, Jeremiah 358,
Shepherd, John 383,
Shepherd, Mary 55,
Sherman, John 265,
Sherman, Joseph 274,
Sherman, Josiah 265, 380
Sherman, Nathaniel 265,
Sherman, Roger 244, 265
Sherman, William 265,
Sherwin, John 355,
Shute, Daniel 185,
Sill, Capt. 59,
Sill, Joseph 61,
Simonds, Isaac 259,
Simonds, Joseph 340, 344
Simonds, Judah 362,
Simonds, Mary 367,
Simonds, Sarah 374,
Simonds, Zebedee 269,
Skinner, Abraham 290,
Skinner, Dr. 293,
Smeadley, John 65,
Smeadly, Ann 368,
Smeadly, Baptiste 384,
Smeadly, John 235,
Smeadly, John S. 384,
Smeadly, Mary 384,
Smeadly, Samuel 49, 362
Smedley, Bapties 34, 37
Smedley, James 38,

Smedley, John 17, 35
Smedly, John 37,
Smith, Colonel 103, 107,
Smith, Dudley 240,
Smith, Elias 185,
Smith, Ephraim 322,
Smith, Francis 101, 115, 116
Smith, Joel 312, 313
Smith, John 344,
Smith, Joseph 243,
Smith, Nathan 134,
Smith, Phineas 344,
Smith, Sylvanus 134,
Smith, Thomas 100, 243, 375, 384
Smith, Timothy 345,
Smith, William 110,
Smith, Zebediah 294,
Snow, Simeon 344,
Soper, Consider 73,
Southmayd, Daniel S. 195, 229
South River 200,
Spaulding, Amos 325,
Spaulding, Edward 385,
Spaulding, Job 329, 355
Spaulding, Jon. 328, 329
Spaulding, Wid. L. 328,
Spaulding, Leonard 322,
Spaulding, Thomas 327, 329
Spaulding, Zebulon 325, 327
Speen, James 41, 62
Speen, John and Sarah 41,
Spencer Brook 202,
Spencer, Mr. 7, 8
Spencer, William 14,
Sprague, Timothy 358,
Spring, Samuel 329, 349
Squaw, Sachem 2, 8, 20,
Squire, George 384,
St. John, Elizabeth 165,
St. John, Oliver 160, 165
Stacy, John 7, 228
Staniforth, Thomas 384,
Stearns, Abigail 373,
Stearns, Charles 305, 306
Stearns, Daniel 355,
Stearns, Daniel Mansfield 316,
Stearns, Dr. 310,
Stearns, Edward 256, 257,
Stearns, Edward Josiah 272,
Stearns, Elijah 272,
Stearns, Isaac 134, 264
Stearns, Jonathan French 272,
Stearns, Josiah 268, 355
Stearns, Phineas 344,
Stearns, Rev. Mr. 261,
Stearns, Rev. Samuel 194, 195, 307, 311
Stearns, Samuel Horatio 272,
Stearns, Stephen 355,

Stearns, Thomas 306,
Stearns, William Augustus 272,
Stearns, Wm. Lawrence 316,
Stearns, Zach. 256,
Stephens, Wm. 72,
Sternhold and Hopkins 192,
Stetson, Caleb 193,
Stevens, Benjamin 179, 304
Stevens, Joshua 358,
Stevens, Mary 373,
Stevens, Thomas 44,
Stickney, William 88,
Stone, Daniel 315,
Stone, Gregory 347,
Stone, Capt. John 208,
Stone, Jonas 344,
Stone, Josiah 336,
Stone, Moses 110,
Stone, Nathan 175, 178
Stoughton, William 242,
Stow, Cyrus 38, 235
Stow, Ephraim 73, 322
Stow, Nathan 121, 352, 353
Stow, Nathaniel 277, 384
Stow, Samuel 240,
Stow, Sarah 378,
Stow, Thomas 33, 384
Stratten, Elizabeth 384,
Stratten, Hezekiah 71,
Stratten, Jabez, 294,
Stratten, John 357, 358, 359
Stratten, Samuel 38, 384
Stratton, Mary 374,
Stratton, Susan 368,
Stuart, George 69,
Sudbury River 200,
Sullivan, William 334,
Sunderland, Lieutenant 112,
Swan, Charles 355,
Swan, Samuel 249,
Swan, Timothy 249,
Swift, John 184, 283, 284, 290
Symonds, William 385,
Syms, Stephen 260,

-T-

Tahattawan 2, 7, 8, 28
Tantumous 8,
Tarbell, Grosvener 312, 313
Tarbell, Silas P. 312,
Taxable inhabitants of Bedford in 1748, 257,
Taylor, Daniel 352,
Taylor, David 256, 257, 263,
Taylor, Eunice 264,
Taylor, Isaac 71,
Taylor, Jacob 75,
Taylor, James 385,

Taylor, John 336,
Taylor, Joseph 75, 322
Taylor, Nathaniel 322, 329, 355
Taylor, William 37, 378, 385
Temple, Abigail 364,
Temple, Abraham 322,
Temple, Benj. 251,
Temple, James 222, 251
Temple, Richard 37, 45, 385
Temple, Sarah 163, 364
Tenneclef, William 359,
Tenney, Mr. 32,
Thacher, Josiah 266,
Thacher, Rev. Mr. 241,
Thatcher, Peter 170, 188
Thatcher, Samuel 222, 354
Thaxter, Joseph 353,
Thom 62,
Thomas 8, 9
Thomas, Isaiah 336, 338
Thomas, John 27, 30, 39, 42
Thomas, Solomon 42,
Thompson, Daniel 115,
Thompson, Elizabeth 378,
Thompson, Rev. Mr. 248,
Thoreau, John 218,
Thoreau, Miss Sarah 196,
Thurston, Samuel A. 196,
Thwing, Benjamin 385,
Tidd, Benjamin 343,
Tidd, Samuel 344,
Tidd, William 344,
Till, Judith 384,
Todd, Rev. John 195,
Tolman, Elisha 104,
Tompkins, Isabel 385,
Tompkins, John 385,
Tool, Mary 376,
Tower, Ambrose 294,
Treadwell, Elizabeth 373,
Trinitarian Church 194,
Trowbridge, Caleb 304,
Turell, Ebenezer 170,
Turney, Benjamin 385,
Turrell, Samuel 304,
Tuttle, Augustus 224,
Tuttle, Francis 290,
Tuttle, George W. 289,
Tuttle, John L. 142, 214, 236, 237
Tuttle, John Leighton 238,
Tuttle, Hon. John T. 205,
Tuttle, Simon 130, 281
Tuttle, Wallis 231,
Tyng, Major 66,

-U-

Uktuck, John 62,
Underwood, Joseph 295,

Underwood, William 385,
Upham, Jabez 291, 293
Usher, Robert 67,

-V-

Valentine, Joseph 143, 231
Vandyke, Colonel 187,
Varnum, John 321, 382
Varnum, Joseph 283,
Vassall, Elizabeth 313,
Vernon, Edward 69,
Viles, Joel 344,
Vinton, Ann 374,
Vose, John 38, 196, 206
Vose, Messrs. John & Co. 205,

-W-

Waban, Merchant 9,
Waban, Thomas 39, 42
Wadkins, Andrew 256,
Wadsworth, Capt. 52,
Wadsworth, Samuel 58,
Walden Pond 197, 200
Walker, Phebe 182,
Walker, Silas 347, 352, 358
Ward, Thomas 44,
Warren, Dr. 240,
Warren, Isaac 222,
Warren, Joseph 102,
Warren, Josiah 353,
Warren, Silas 222,
Waters, John 328,
Watson, Abraham 336,
Watson, Benjamin M. 193,
Watson, James 75,
Webb, John 175, 177
Webber, John 82, 257, 258, 259
Webber, William 272, 273
Webster, Prof. John 198,
Webster, Rev. Samuel 166,
Weld, Thomas 14,
Wellington, Jonathan 294, 303
Wentworth, Thomas 69,
Wesson, Stephen 71, 294, 303
Wesson, Timothy 294, 303, 358
West Burying Grounds 208,
West, Henry 378,
Weston, Nathan 309,
Wetherbee, Mr. 99,
Wetherbee, Timothy 357,
Wetherby, John 44,
Wheat, Daniel 357,
Wheat, Hannah 384,
Wheat, John 294,
Wheat, Joseph 294,
Wheat, Joshua 385,
Wheat, Moses 37, 385

Wheeler, Abner 206,
Wheeler, Artemas 143, 227, 352
Wheeler, Asahel 110, 353, 354
Wheeler, Benjamin 186, 294
Wheeler, Cyrus 143, 228, 312, 313
Wheeler, Darius 70, 110, 121, 194, 354, 358
Wheeler, Deacon 192,
Wheeler, Ebenezer 75, 278, 308
Wheeler, Edmund 312,
Wheeler, Elisha 228, 235
Wheeler, Elizabeth 214, 370, 383
Wheeler, Ensign 34, 35
Wheeler, Ephraim 15, 98, 216, 353, 355, 358, 385, 386
Wheeler, Francis 73, 110, 143, 228, 347
Wheeler, Georg 33, 34, 35
Wheeler, George 17, 38, 39, 152, 375, 385, 386
Wheeler, James 44, 257, 263
Wheeler, John 38, 194, 234, 277, 286, 385
Wheeler, Jonas 215, 216, 251
Wheeler, Jonas 294,
Wheeler, Joseph 17, 36, 37, 39, 40, 43, 44, 46, 72, 75, 152, 242, 248, 274, 275, 385, 386
Wheeler, Joshua 38, 386
Wheeler, Jotham 251,
Wheeler, Lemuel 355, 358
Wheeler, Lydia 379,
Wheeler, Mary 371,
Wheeler, Obadiah 34, 385
Wheeler, Peter 347, 356
Wheeler, Phineas 73, 286
Wheeler, Rebecca 242, 380
Wheeler, Richard 256, 257, 263, 382
Wheeler, Ruth 373,
Wheeler, Samuel 38, 42, 72, 73
Wheeler, Sarah 369, 370
Wheeler, Thankful 382,
Wheeler, Thomas 15, 37, 43, 44, 45, 48, 152, 162, 234, 235, 275, 289, 294, 303, 307, 308, 312, 385, 388,
Wheeler, Timothy 7, 8, 15, 17, 39, 41, 46, 50, 72, 79, 94, 98, 99, 104, 107, 168, 169, 180, 211, 235, 364, 372, 380
Wheeler, Wareham 352, 355, 357
Wheeler, William 234, 278, 279, 355, 367, 386
Wheeler, William Willard 248,
Wheelock school 246,
Wheelwright, Mr. 148,
Wheler, Georg 35,
Wheler, Joseph 35,
Whipple, John 257,
Whitaker, David 169, 246, 277, 387

Whitaker, Nathaniel 246,
Whitaker, Samuel 257,
White, Anna 373,
White, David 357,
White, Ebenezer 353, 354
White, John 193, 194, 196, 214, 222, 230, 251, 285, 286, 294, 356, 358, 359
White, Mark 282, 289
White Pond 200,
White, Sarah 375,
White, William H. 193,
Whitehead, John 347,
Whitfield, Rev. 181,
Whiting, Elizabeth 166,
Whiting, John 163, 165, 166, 179, 249, 261, 283, 382,
Whiting, Mary 166,
Whiting, Samuel 67, 165, 244
Whiting, Stephen 166,
Whiting, Thomas 166, 222, 249
Whiting, William 218, 222, 228, 229, 230, 253
Whitman, Bernard 232,
Whitman, Charles 145,
Whitman, Rev. Nathaniel 193,
Whitman, Samuel 329,
Whitmore, John 273,
Whitney, Isaac 67,
Whitney, John 294,
Whitney, Josiah 353, 359
Whitney, Moses 44,
Whitney, Phineas 185, 231
Whitney, Richard 44,
Whitney, Samuel 91, 93, 94, 98, 119
Whitney, Solomon 73,
Whittaker, David 322,
Whittaker, Ephraim 322,
Whittemore, Aaron 246,
Whittemore, Benjamin 145, 163, 234, 236, 246, 279, 365, 387
Whittemore, Nathaniel 168, 169, 234, 294, 387
Wibbacowitts 2, 8
Wigglesworth, Samuel 170,
Wight, John B. 193,
Wight, Samuel 375,
Wigley, Edmund 38, 44, 379, 387
Wilkins, Edward 355,
Wilkins, Isaac 328,
Wilkins, Timothy 322,
Willard, Abigail 243,
Willard, Benjamin 222, 241, 245, 266
Willard, Major 18, 39, 46, 61, 203, 241, 243,
Willard, Margery 368,
Willard, Simon 5, 7, 8, 9, 11, 15, 22, 24, 35, 49, 152, 233, 235, 236, 241, 274

Willard, Thomas Rice 342,
Willey, Ephraim 230,
Williams, Jeremiah 353, 357
Williams, Samuel 184,
Williams, Thomas 45,
Williams, Wareham 170, 303, 304
Williams, William 166, 170, 303, 304
Willington, Enoch 344,
Willis, Roger 44,
Willoughby, Susannah 245,
Wilson, John 153,
Wilson, Jonathan 110, 115, 116, 258, 259
Wilson, Levi 261,
Wilson, Samuel 388,
Wilson, Wm. 72, 163, 233, 234, 236, 328, 355, 379, 388
Winchester, Ebenezer 179,
Winchester, Jonathan 304,
Windship, John 344,
Winnetow, Dorothy 41,
Winship, Mary 365,
Winship, Simon 342,
Winship, Thomas 344,
Winslow, John 69,
Winslow, Maj-Gen. 72, 247
Winthrop 2, 13
Winthrop Farms 255,
Wisner, Rev. Benjamin B. 195,
Wood, Abraham 233, 234
Wood, Abigail 375,
Wood, Amos 109, 186
Wood, Mrs. Amos 109,
Wood, Corporal 227,
Wood, Daniel 200,
Wood, Elijah 37, 218, 230
Wood, Ephraim 77, 79, 82, 88, 91, 93, 94, 98, 108, 119, 121, 123, 127, 128, 139, 142, 234, 355, 356, 357
Wood, Horatio 222,
Wood, Judge 200, 363, 378
Wood, Mary 363,
Wood, Michael 38, 388
Wood, Michel 34,
Wood, Mihel 35,
Wood, Nathan 235,
Wood, Ruth 386,
Wood, Samuel 71,
Wood, Thomas 355,
Wood, William 4, 10, 17, 19, 36, 371, 388
Woodbury, James T. 286,
Woodhouse, Elizabeth 238,
Woodhouse, Henry 38, 47, 65, 235, 236
Woodhouse, Sarah 368,
Woodies, Henry 33,
Woodis, Henry 7, 41
Woods, Daniel 67,

Woods, Henry 140,
Woods, Nathaniel 67,
Woods, Thomas 67,
Woodward, Mrs. 230,
Woodward, Samuel 185,
Wooley, Elizabeth 366,
Wooley, Joseph 43,
Wooley, Thomas 256,
Woolley, Christopher 372,
Woolly, Jonathan 257,
Woolly, Thomas 257,
Woolly, Thos. Jr. 257,
Wright, Amos 224,
Wright, Anthony 3,
Wright, Edward 216, 353, 362
Wright, James 269,
Wright, John 294,
Wright, Jonas 358,
Wright, Jonathan 359,
Wright, Joseph 234,
Wright, Luther 291,
Wright, Peter 216,
Wright, Samuel 277,
Wright, Sarah 381,
Wright, Zaccheus 145,
Wright's Book 201,
Wyman, James 344,
Wyman, Joseph 329,
Wyman, Nathaniel 115,
Wyman, Nehemiah 260,
Wyman, Seth 67,

-Y-

Yammon, Samson 355,
Young, Henry 49, 70

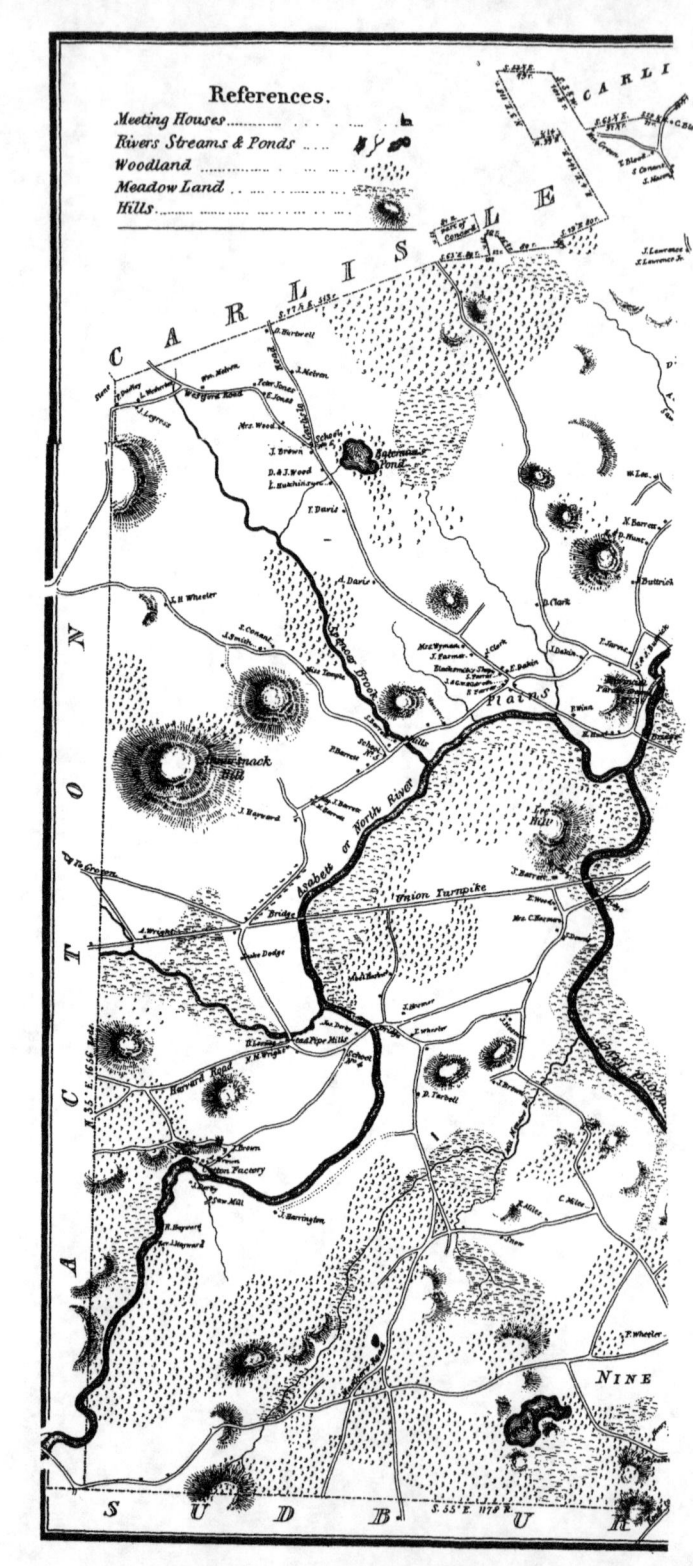

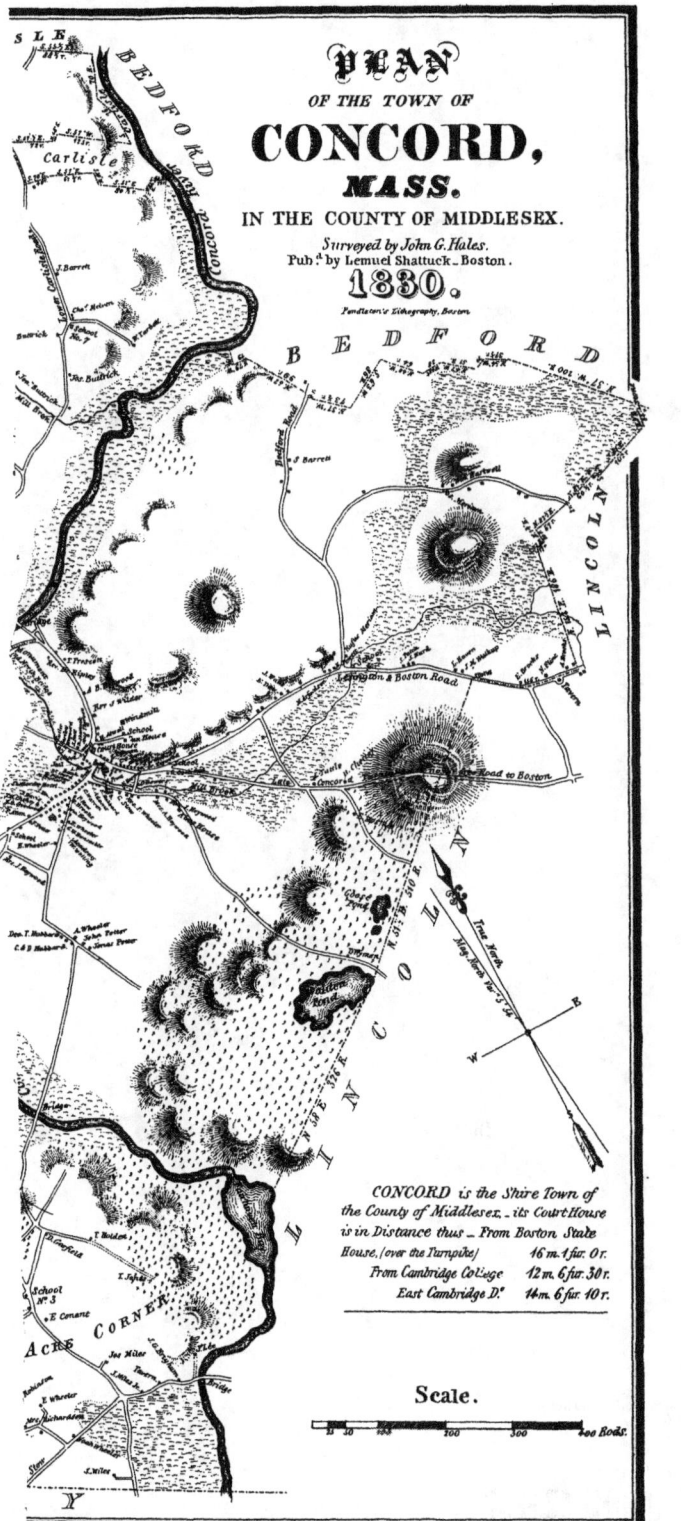

www.ingramcontent.com/pod-product-compliance
Lightning Source LLC
Chambersburg PA
CBHW071236300426
44116CB00008B/1055